Teaching Individuals with Developmental Delays

Teaching Individuals with Developmental Delays

Basic Intervention Techniques

O. Ivar Lovaas
with
Andrew Bondy
Greg Buch
Howard G. Cohen
Kathryn Dobel
Svein Eikeseth
Lori Frost
Ronald Huff
Eric V. Larsson
Nina W. Lovaas
Gary S. Mayerson
Tristram Smith
Valerie Vanaman
Jacqueline Wynn

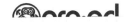

pro-ed

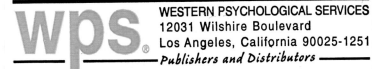

pro•ed
An International Publisher

8700 Shoal Creek Boulevard
Austin, Texas 78757-6897
800/897-3202 Fax 800/397-7633
www.proedinc.com

Library of Congress Cataloging-in-Publication Data

Lovaas, O. Ivar (Ole Ivar), 1927–
Teaching individuals with developmental delays : basic intervention techniques / O. Ivar Lovaas.
p. cm.
Includes bibliographical references.
ISBN 0-89079-889-3
1. Autistic children—Education. 2. Developmentally disabled children—Education. I. Title

LC4717.L68 2002
371.94—dc21

2001048762

This book is designed in Goudy, American Typewriter, and Frutiger.

Printed in the United States of America

1 2 3 4 5 6 7 8 9 10 06 05 04 03 02

This manual is dedicated to
all parents of children with developmental delays
in recognition of
the heavy burdens they carry
and the models they provide for all parents to follow.

Full many a gem of purest ray serene,
the dark unfathom'd caves of ocean bear.
Full many a flower is born to blush unseen,
and waste its sweetness on the desert air.

—Thomas Gray, "Elegy"

Contents

SECTION 1
Basic Concepts

SECTION 2
Transition into Treatment

SECTION 3
Early Learning Concepts

SECTION 4
Expressive Language

SECTION 5
Strategies for Visual Learners

SECTION 6
Programmatic Considerations

SECTION 7
Organizational and Legal Issues

Preface

Individuals are evaluated on many dimensions, including emotional development, social skills, educational achievements, and language skills. Within behavioral psychology, the branch of psychology that forms the foundation of this teaching manual, such dimensions are referred to as *behaviors*. Behavioral psychology thus assesses such observable aggregates as intellectual behaviors, emotional behaviors, social behaviors, educational behaviors, language behaviors, aggressive behaviors, occupational behaviors, and self-help behaviors.

Insofar as behaviors can be observed, they can also be separated and objectively measured. This factor is essential for assessing whether a client improves, stands still, or regresses. It will become apparent just how complex and rich the subject matter of behavior is when one attempts to teach or alter behaviors as described in this manual. Any one of the behaviors mentioned, such as language, may be broken down into a large number of separate behaviors, yielding more precise measurements and requiring different kinds of treatments. To the extent that we can accurately and objectively measure behaviors, we can use scientific methods to solve the problems of persons in need of help. Without scientific methodology, significant help may not be rendered.

It is generally recognized that human behavior is a product of biological makeup as well as exposure to a particular environment during development. No two persons' nervous systems are exactly alike, but each possesses enormous complexity. Likewise, no two persons' environments are exactly alike, although they are equally complex. Considering such intricate involvement, there is ample opportunity for behavioral development to go astray.

Almost all parents concern themselves with helping their children develop into happy and constructive adults. Even before a child is born, parents often wonder about genetic makeup. They may worry about whether there are familial instances of mental retardation, schizophrenia, or alcoholism that may be potentially problematic for the unborn child. During pregnancy, one may become concerned about maintaining a proper diet and avoiding stress, secondhand smoke, alcohol, vaccinations, and medications that may have deleterious effects upon the fetus. After the child is born, one may be concerned as to whether the child started to breathe soon enough after birth and received an adequate supply of oxygen.

The first few days after birth provide abundant opportunities for continued apprehension: Is the baby receiving adequate milk? Is it held correctly? Does the baby sleep too much or too little? Are defecation and urination on schedule? There are also fevers, colds, the flu, and bladder infections to be concerned about. When the child finally goes off to preschool, parents may wonder whether the teacher cares for their child or favors other children instead. What are the other children like? Is the teacher affectionate and warm or strict and angry?

Even if all goes well during the early years, the child in all probability changes upon entering middle school. Suddenly, Mom and Dad are accused of doing everything wrong: They don't look right, Mom's hair is weird, Dad dresses strangely, Mom can no longer cook or drive a car. When driven to school, the child may demand, "Don't get out when you let me off," in fear that the parent will be seen by classmates. During these years, parents often wonder what they have done to make their child become so alienated. Years of concern about drugs, violence, and teenage pregnancies are on the horizon. If the child survives all of these issues, parents may still show concern regarding whom their child marries and how their grandchildren are raised.

Most parents accept and learn to live with some less than optimal behavioral development. For example, one may become the parent of a youngster who fails to finish high school or a child who seems emotionally aloof and does not reciprocate the amount of affection parents feel they deserve. One may also parent a child who is very angry and rejects society or who becomes addicted to drugs and goes to jail. It is possible for a person to exhibit two or three behavioral deviations and still function adequately, contributing to the variability of human behavior within society.

Once in a while a child is born who fails to develop eye contact, who behaves as if he or she cannot see or hear, who resists being held and cuddled, and who does not seem to miss family members when they leave. Such behaviors may be noticeable within the first year of life. In the second year of life, the child may fail to talk or understand what parents say. The child is unlikely to play with toys as other children do and may seem completely oblivious to the company of others, spending his or her days in meaningless and repetitive motions such as rocking, gazing at lights, tapping objects, and pacing back and forth across the floor. The child may also develop excessive tantrums and severe self-injurious behaviors, fail to learn to sleep through the night, fail to learn to dress himself or herself, and fail to become toilet trained, remaining in diapers into adulthood. Some children develop normally up to the age of 18 to 24 months, only to suddenly lose all language and social behaviors within a period of 2 to 3 weeks for reasons no one as of yet understands.

Imagine yourself as a person whose child begins to show most or all of these difficulties. You may hope the child will "grow out of it," but after a year or two the problems intensify, and you finally turn to a professional for help. You may be told to continue to wait, to allow the child to outgrow the behaviors. After more time passes, and after many blind leads, new opinions are offered and a diagnosis is finally provided.

Depending on the number and type of behavioral delays displayed, the child may receive one (or sometimes more) of several different diagnoses, such as pervasive developmental disorder (PDD) autistic disorder, PDD not otherwise specified (PDD-NOS), Asperger's syndrome, mental retardation, and so on. Estimates of the frequency of autism have risen in recent years; reports place the prevalence as high as 1 in 500 births. The prevalence of PDD and Asperger's syndrome is higher still. Then comes the prognosis: Little or nothing can be done about the problem; only 5 out of every 100 children diagnosed with autism will be able to live outside of institutions or without custodial care.

Frequently, parents are advised to go home and try to live with their child while seeking help from school districts and professionals. Although there are exceptions, most parents face major battles, starting with the Individualized Education Program (IEP). It is usually not the teachers who provide the obstacles, but rather personnel in the school administration department where funding is a central issue. Parents soon discover that seeking effective treatment is a stress that adds to the weight of living with a child with autism. The full extent of the burden on parents is difficult for an outsider to grasp; the pattern of hopes and losses that occurs time and time again seems unique to parents of children with special needs. Many parents end up facing divorce, the stress being too disruptive on the marriage.

In all this darkness, there are some signs of hope. One centers on the reduction of certain misunderstandings about the cause of autism. In the past, some professionals implied that the child's parents caused the autism. The number of proposed causes was limitless because professionals found it easy to be inventive, considering their ignorance of the etiology of behavioral delays. These delays already tend to be amplified by the parents' guilt and anxiety over the possibility of having contributed to the problem (a characteristic of most parents regardless of the child's problem). A professional may have proposed that the trip to Paris taken when the child was 2 years old caused a traumatic separation from the security of the home environment, hence the autism. Or, after the parents admitted to anxiety about not being "good enough," the parents' compulsive need to be perfect may have been proposed as the cause of the problem. Other possibilities include claiming that the mother's returning to work too soon after the child's birth prevented "bonding" from taking place, or that the birth of another child too soon after the birth of the first child caused the behavior problems. Through this misattributed blame, it was not uncommon for a professional to imply that the child wanted to have nothing to do with his or her parents and therefore withdrew into an "autistic shell." In one such case, a parent who asked for professional advice about how to help prevent her child from poking himself around the eyes received the destructive answer, "He pokes his eyes because he does not want to see you." The professional then considered it necessary to isolate the parent from the child's treatment. It is difficult to understand how anyone, especially a professional, could make such heartless, unfounded remarks, adding to parents' already high levels of anxiety and depression. However, one can take some comfort in understanding that, as knowledge of a problem increases, a concomitant decrease is shown in misunderstandings and arbitrary opinions about causes and treatments.

The second major source of relief comes from parent organizations, which have multiplied and grown in size over the last 40 years. Aided by Internet communication and increased access, parents can now keep abreast of developments in effective treatments and help advise one another on where to turn and what to do in specific situations (see Chapter 36). Parents are becoming increasingly involved in and knowledgeable about their children's treatment and, in many cases, are the primary providers of services (see Chapters 37 and 38 for information on helping to secure funding for treatment).

There are other sources of help as well, such as religious institutions, to which parents may turn in times of stress. As a case in point, after enrolling his daughter Ellen in treatment for several years and observing very little progress (Ellen remained mute and noncommunicative), the father told me, "I know I will talk with Ellen in heaven." This is the sort of comfort persons who develop and provide treatment need in order to continue working.

This teaching manual should assist parents acting as treatment providers. There are other resources as well, referred to throughout this manual and in the reference section at the end of the manual. Our first teaching manual (subtitled *The ME Book*; Lovaas, 1981) was based on programs developed some 30 to 40 years ago. Since that time, several new teaching programs have been developed and older ones have been discarded or revised. This manual reflects those changes and includes extensive and detailed descriptions of how to teach each program. Because of this detail, parents and teachers are in a better position to provide more effective help. The combination of increased detail and new programs requires the publication of two manuals: one for basic programs (described in the present manual) and another for advanced programs (described in an upcoming manual). The programs are cumulative in the sense that the advanced programs build on the basic programs. This necessitates that both the adult (parent, other family member, teacher, or aide) and the individual with developmental delays (who is a student once treatment begins) work through the beginning programs before starting on the more advanced programs.

The development and analysis of many new behavioral treatment programs over the last 30 years have led to three major advances. First, the outcome has been found to be particularly favorable when intensive one-on-one behavioral treatment is started early in a student's development. Second, it has been possible to identify subgroups of students in terms of who gains the most and the least from the present programs, allowing for development and testing of new programs for those who do not receive optimal benefits. Factors relating to this issue are discussed throughout this manual. Third, advances in the teaching of socially appropriate forms of communication are associated with concomitant reductions in self-injurious and other destructive behaviors in the majority of students. Because of this concomitant reduction, the use of aversive interventions to reduce destructive behaviors may no longer be necessary.

This teaching manual places a major emphasis on describing treatment programs confirmed effective based on methods of scientific inquiry. The final goal of scientific inquiry is to make the treatment procedures and data on treatment outcome believable and replicable to the scientific community and to parents, teachers, and others who want to apply them. This in turn means that one's investigative efforts are subject to review, commonly referred to as peer review, by other scientists so as to establish the validity of these efforts. The validity and efficacy of behavioral treatment is based on thousands of scientifically sound studies of learning processes investigated for over 100 years and published in journals with competent peer review by a large number of researchers from across this country and abroad.

The knowledge of effective treatment has been built cumulatively, which is an ideal manner in which to proceed. Because such research is an ongoing process, this manual may be best viewed as preliminary; it will be improved upon when future research so dictates. Much more has to be investigated and learned for us to become truly successful teachers so as to help all individuals with developmental delays become functioning members of society.

We owe a great deal to the scientists working within the areas of Learning and Behavior and Applied Behavior Analysis who have contributed to the discovery of the learning mechanisms that form the empirical foundation for the programs presented in this manual. We are also indebted to the large number of students who have joined in the search for solutions to the many difficulties facing individuals with developmental delays. To illustrate, at any one time over the past 40 years, between 30 and 50 students from the University of California, Los Angeles (UCLA), have been enrolled in practicum courses lasting 6 to 12 months, searching for creative ways to apply learning principles to the domain of helping children with developmental delays grow emotionally, academically, and socially. Between 10 and 20 graduate students as well as full-time staff members have stayed on the project for several years and helped to generate scientific studies and supervise the treatment program. These are young people who have yet to develop strong biases against any one approach. Not only are they flexible and open-minded, they are also mature and creative. Most have worked several hours above and beyond what is required to meet course requirements or job descriptions. Through such dedication and with the support from the National Institute of Mental Health, a network of some 14 clinical sites has been established over this country and abroad, attempting to replicate, improve upon, and develop new and more effective teaching programs. How could one fail to make progress under such conditions?

We have also been fortunate to work with parents of children with developmental delays and learn of the love they have for their children, their courage, and the patience and intelligence with which they confront their problems and help search for solutions. These parents' behaviors collectively serve as a model for all persons who are parents and for those who will become parents in the future. We hope that society will reciprocate their contributions in recognition of the guidance they have offered society.

We apologize to parents for the complexity of the programs that many of them will have to learn about and supervise, as well as for the delay among professionals in helping develop and adopt effective treatment programs (see Chapter 32). It may comfort both parents and others who work with individuals with developmental delays to see themselves from a historical perspective. Doing so may help reduce some of the stress involved in feeling as though not enough is being done.

The first detailed and documented intervention designed to aid children with developmental delays was presented 200 years ago by a young French physician, Jean M. G. Itard. Itard worked with a mentally retarded boy, Victor, who had many of the behavioral delays shown by children who would now be diagnosed with autism. Itard, who worked shortly after the French Revolution, had as his goal not only the rehabilitation of Victor, but also the presentation of educational programs designed to raise the social competence of all citizens, enabling them to participate more meaningfully in democracy. It may be interesting to review Lane's (1976) brilliant critique of Itard's work and the context in which it appeared, as many programs in Itard's work with Victor bear striking similarity to those presented in this manual.

Itard's work was carried forth in the context of special education by persons such as Fernald, Kephart, and Montessori (Ball, 1971). Sadly, the only one of Itard's many programs that survived is sensory motor training, a program that has yet to demonstrate effectiveness. A most likely reason for this is that Itard did not know how to take data and gain objective scientific knowledge about which parts of his interventions worked and should be kept, and which parts did not work and should be abandoned.

When service providers in the fields of special education, clinical psychology, and psychiatry fail to document the effectiveness of their interventions, they have, like Itard, not been able to discard some programs while keeping others. Objectivity is replaced by subjectivity, and programs that seem good and appear to be helpful are often preferred. We have also been steered into blind alleys by grand and seductive theories of human behavior; the 20th century largely belonged to theoreticians such as Kraeplin, Freud, and Piaget. As a result, there appears to be more than a 20-year delay in the application of what is known about effective treatment for individuals with developmental delays to professions such as special education, psychiatry, and psychology. We are optimistic that those who offer help to individuals with developmental delays in the future will turn to science to help relieve parents of the uncertainties and heavy burdens they now carry from helping their children gain access to the most appropriate treatment.

In this context, we would like to express our thanks to Bernard Rimland, a father of a child with autism and a psychologist himself. Dr. Rimland was one of the first psychologists to address the importance of evaluating the treatment of autism by scientific criteria. In so doing, he helped lay to rest psychodynamic theories in the treatment of autism and became a spokesperson for behavioral and other data-based interventions. Maurice (1993) and Johnson and Crowder (1994) have presented detailed accounts of how parents can help evaluate treatments and take responsibility for their children's treatment.

We would also like to express our thanks to Lois Howard for putting up with the constant changing and rewriting of programs, creating a stack of typewritten drafts over 7 feet tall. Lois Howard faced it all with high spirits. Kristin O'Hanlon and Marie Bragais contributed to making the text better organized and more readable, working evenings and weekends to accomplish this task.

We would like to thank the National Institute of Mental Health (NIMH) for providing both peer review and financial support for our treatment–research on an almost continuous basis during the close to 40-year duration of our project. Preparation of this manual was facilitated by a grant from the NIMH (Multi-Site Young Autism Project NIMH 1 R01 MH48863-01A4).

Many thanks also to our colleagues and the administrative staff at UCLA for providing ideal facilities for treatment–research. Three colleagues deserve special mention: Ronald Huff, Howard Cohen, and Rick Rollens. All three persons worked many hours into the night and over weekends to help inform colleagues in special education, psychology, medicine, and the government about behavioral treatment. They did so by providing accurate and up-to-date information about treatment outcome data. Further, they facilitated parental access to information about effective treatments and helped parents organize support groups for which membership is in excess of 30 thousand families (as of Summer 2000), a number that is constantly growing in the United States and abroad.

Finally, we would like to thank the following staff members of the UCLA Project and acknowledge their significant contributions to this manual: Jason M. Bertellotti, Jodie Deming, Brigitte Elder, Sabrina Marasovich, Kristin O'Hanlon, Stacy Tomanik, and Janet Yi.

Contributors

Andy Bondy, PhD
Pyramid Educational Consultants, Inc.
226 West Park Place, Suite 1
Newark, DE 19711

Greg Buch, PhD
The Foundation for Autistic Childhood Education and Support
1150 West Hillsdale Blvd.
San Mateo, California 94403

Howard G. Cohen, PhD
Valley Mountain Regional Center
P. O. Box 692290
Stockton, CA 95269-2290

Kathryn Dobel, Esq.
2026 Delaware Street
Berkeley, CA 94709

Svein Eikeseth, PhD
Akershus College
P.O. Box 372
1301 Sandvika, Norway

Lori Frost, MS, CCC
Pyramid Educational Consultants, Inc.
226 West Park Place, Suite 1
Newark, DE 19711

Ronald Huff, PhD
Developmental Centers Division
Quality Assurance Section, Room 340
1600 Ninth Street
Sacramento, CA 95814

Eric V. Larsson, PhD
FEAT of Minnesota
15612 Highway 7 #D260
Minnetonka, MN 55345

Nina W. Lovaas, MA
Lovaas Institute for Early Intervention
11500 West Olympic Boulevard, Suite 460
Los Angeles, CA 90064

O. Ivar W. Lovaas, PhD
Lovaas Institute for Early Intervention
11500 West Olympic Boulevard, Suite 460
Los Angeles, CA 90064

Gary S. Mayerson, Esq.
250 West 57th Street #624
New York, NY 10107

Tristram Smith, PhD
Children's Hospital at Strong
Strong Center for Developmental Disabilities
601 Elmwood Avenue, Box 671
Rochester, NY 14642

Valerie Vanaman, Esq.
Newman, Aaronson, Vanaman
14001 Ventura Boulevard
Sherman Oaks, CA 91423

Jacqueline Wynn, PhD
Children's Hospital Autism Center
6421 East Main Street
Reynoldsburg, OH 43068

Introduction

Section 1: Basic Concepts

Section 1 of this manual consists of eight chapters. The first chapter in this section describes characteristic ranges of various behaviors demonstrated by individuals with developmental delays, focusing on behavioral delays as well as excesses and typical behaviors.

Chapter 2 describes the Continuity Model, an alternative to the placement of persons into discrete diagnostic categories. From the behavioral viewpoint, individuals with developmental delays are considered different from typical individuals in degree rather than kind. As such, persons with developmental delays can be seen as instances of the variability that both characterizes all living systems and is essential for survival. Chapter 2 also advocates the value of staying as close to the average environment as possible when treating individuals with developmental delays, providing for educational opportunities during most of the person's waking hours, conducting the treatment in the person's home and everyday community, and involving the person's parents and other significant adults. Through such treatment, persons with developmental delays have the opportunity to acquire many of the educational opportunities provided to typical individuals.

Chapter 3 provides a summary of outcome data from children having undergone behavioral intervention, and it evaluates intensive one-on-one behavioral treatment.

Chapter 4 describes the beginning steps involved in arranging for a person's treatment, including the importance of learning how to teach, how to set small and reachable goals for both the student and the teacher, how not to be frightened by the student's problem behaviors, and how to teach the student to become more responsible. This chapter also describes the need to form a teaching team to provide the many hours of one-on-one behavioral intervention necessary for effective treatment, and ways to recruit people to participate in such a team. Suggestions regarding how to best manage a treatment team are provided, including advice concerning how to work with parents and teachers.

Chapter 5 summarizes some of the main findings concerning excessive tantrums and self-injurious behaviors. Far from considering such behaviors as symptoms of autism and as indicators of irreversible central nervous system damage, the data show that tantrums and self-injurious behaviors follow the laws of learning that organize the behaviors of all living organisms. Both types of behaviors are seen as forms of communication. Various interventions, however well intended, may worsen these behaviors, whereas other interventions may help alleviate them.

Chapter 6 describes self-stimulatory behavior: the ritualistic, stereotyped, and obsessive behavior evidenced by many individuals with developmental delays. Like self-injurious behavior, self-stimulatory behavior appears lawful and rational and is seen as an effort by the organism to provide the nervous system with the sensory input necessary to avoid atrophy.

Motivational problems are discussed in Chapter 7, and important pointers are provided on how to help motivate individuals with developmental delays to learn the skills taught to them. The basic recommendations are to identify effective rewards (reinforcers) and simplify the teaching situation so the person's successes can be maximized and failures minimized. Chapter 8, on attentional problems, views such problems as secondary rather than primary to the development of behavioral delays. Attentional problems are seen as related to the success a student encounters in particular social and educational situations.

Section 2: Transition into Treatment

Section 2 presents various programs designed to facilitate the transition into treatment and includes those programs considered to be the most basic and thus the easiest for the student to learn as well as for the adult to teach. Chapter 9 describes events that are likely to happen in the first hours of treatment when the teacher attempts to build cooperation and deal with ensuing tantrums. The first hours are considered very important for both the student and the teacher. If some progress is made in the first hours of treatment, then the teacher and the student are provided with the reinforcement needed to motivate continuance. Most of the reinforcement teachers need is provided by evidence of the student's progress. The first hours are likely to be the most stressful ones in teaching students with developmental delays, and appropriately working through these first hours is essential.

Chapter 10 provides a summary of the basic treatment steps that are introduced in the first hours of treatment and repeated throughout the remaining programs presented in this manual. These steps concern such topics as providing proper use of instructions, prompts, and reinforcement.

Chapters 11, 12, and 13 provide information about how to help the student match and imitate. Both Chapters 12 and 13 describe programs that are relatively easy to teach and ones that most students find enjoyable. By learning to match stimuli based on relevant cues and imitate the behaviors of other persons, the student gains extremely important strategies for learning to acquire new and more complex behaviors.

Chapters 14 and 15 provide an introduction to teaching language by presenting the first steps toward teaching the student receptive language skills (i.e., responding nonverbally to the teacher's verbal instructions).

Section 3: Early Learning Concepts

Chapter 16 describes discrimination learning procedures. Discrimination learning teaches students to attend to their environment, what they see and what they hear. Delays in attention have been considered by many to be a significant reason for the delays in learning. These procedures are difficult for teachers to acquire, yet, without knowledge of them, a teacher will fail to provide the kind of help students need to maximize their potential. It is recommended that the chapter on discrimination learning be read more than once and that the teacher go back to this chapter intermittently while teaching the remaining programs in this manual.

The programs Receptive Identification of Objects and Receptive Identification of Behaviors (Chapters 17 and 18, respectively) provide the teacher with ample opportunity to apply the principles described in the discrimination learning chapter. Acquiring full working knowledge of discrimination learning is absolutely essential before presenting more advanced programs, such as Chapter 22 on teaching the student to imitate the speech of others.

Chapters 19, 20, and 21 deal with early play skills, arts and crafts, and self-help skills, respectively. These programs are introduced at this point to help break up the intensity required by the more difficult programs. At the same time, the acquisition of appropriate play (Chapter 19), getting an early start on arts and crafts (Chapter 20), and mastery of self-help skills (Chapter 21) will help the student prepare for group settings such as preschool and kindergarten.

Note that once the student reaches this point in the curriculum, the teacher will be able to choose from among several programs and distribute them optimally during the day. For example, in a 3-hour session of treatment, the student may match and sort objects, imitate the teacher's behaviors, gain increased mastery of receptive language, and increase his or her play and self-help skills. As one gains skill in administering these programs, one also learns how to pattern programs in such a fashion that one program facilitates the student's acquisition of another program and maximizes the student's overall motivation.

Section 4: Expressive Language

Through the programs introduced in Section 4, the student is taught to use expressive language to communicate and to use certain early abstract language as well as early grammar. This section begins with Chapter 22, which describes how to teach the student to imitate the speech of others. This program is by far the most difficult one to teach, as well as the most difficult program for the student to acquire. Keep in mind that it is counterproductive to set aside an entire day or several days in a row just to practice verbal imitation. Continuously working on a very difficult program is very likely to result in a student who resists further attempts to acquire the skills taught in that program. The more playful one can make a difficult program and the more one can intermix programs in which the student can experience success, the more likely it is the student will master a difficult program such as verbal imitation.

Although all students can learn most or all of the programs described in the previous sections, only half of the students receiving intensive and high-quality behavioral treatment learn to imitate words and strings of words with clear enunciation. Others evidence some verbal imitation but may have considerable problems pronouncing certain sound combinations despite months or even years of training. Should a student experience difficulty acquiring verbal imitation despite the teacher's best efforts, the programs in Section 5 may help the student increase his or her communicative skills because these programs rely on visual rather than vocal forms of communication.

Some students evidence the opposite problem, being echolalic (repeatedly duplicating the words spoken by another person) at intake or becoming echolalic after exposure to the Verbal Imitation Program. Excessive echolalia can interfere with the student's mastery of appropriate vocal language. Programs to reduce excessive echolalic speech are introduced at the end of Chapter 22.

Whereas Chapters 17 and 18 provide programs for teaching *receptive* identification of objects and behaviors, Chapters 23 and 24 contain programs for teaching *expressive* identification of objects and behaviors. Given that only half of the students treated are likely to master expressive language, many students will not be able to fully master the programs presented in Chapters 23 and 24. However, the same students who demonstrate difficulty with vocal language programs are likely to master comparable skills through visual means (e.g., expressive labels through writing rather than vocalizing answers, as taught in Chapter 29, Reading and Writing).

Typically, receptive language is taught before expressive language. However, some students experience considerable difficulty acquiring receptive language but acquire expressive language with relative ease (which, in turn, facilitates the acquisition of receptive language). This emphasizes the need for teachers to be flexible and able to shift among programs and formats within programs according to the needs of the particular student.

Chapters 25, 26, and 27 mark the most advanced abstract language programs in this manual. Most of the students who undergo behavioral treatment master the programs through at least the receptive phase of prepositions, such as placing an object or oneself next to, above, or beside an object or a person when so instructed. More advanced language programs involving such concepts as pronouns, as in the student's learning to discriminate between *you*, *me*, *him*, and *us*, will be introduced in an upcoming manual on advanced programs.

Chapter 28, the final chapter in Section 4, teaches the student about emotions. This chapter discusses how a student's emotional life becomes more varied and appropriate as a consequence of mastering the programs presented in this manual. Apparently, much of a person's emotional development is dictated by his or her experiences with success and failure. The emotional outbursts one often observes in students with developmental delays are most likely elicited by the students' failure to understand what parents and other adults attempt to teach, and these outbursts are exaggerated by the students' difficulty expressing themselves in a socially appropriate manner. Most of the programs presented in this manual, especially the language programs, will help decrease frustration and increase effective communication, which, in turn, will decrease angry emotional outbursts. On a broader scale, it should be noted that, through mastery of the programs presented in this manual, the student's emotional enrichment is something one gets "for free" in the sense that one does not have to work toward specifically achieving this improvement. Nevertheless, although the student may come to demonstrate many more emotions (e.g., pride, happiness, love for others) than he or she did before treatment, the appropriate expression and understanding of these emotions may have to be attended to, much as is done with typical persons. To aid in this, Chapter 28 contains information on how to help the student learn to recognize facial expressions of affect, label the affective states underlying these expressions, and identify the causes of affective states.

The reader may want to know whether behaviors other than varied emotional expression may also emerge "for free" after the teacher and student have worked intensively through this manual. The answer, however tentative, is yes. Attention to adults and other facets of the external environment increases; students no longer act as if they are blind and deaf. The increased attentiveness is most likely attributable to discrimination learning, which teaches the student to discriminate among, and thus attend to, various stimuli in the environment (see Chapter 16). In addition, there is a concomitant increase in cognitive growth, as evidenced in increased scores on IQ tests. IQ tests measure the knowledge and skills the student has learned up to the point of test administration. The more the student has learned, the higher the IQ score.

Section 5: Strategies for Visual Learners

Section 5 contains Chapters 29 and 30, which describe how to facilitate the communicative skills of students who encounter serious difficulties using vocal language. Chapter 29 introduces the Reading and Writing Program (by Nina W. Lovaas and Svein Eikeseth) and presents an outline on how to teach students to read and write and to use these skills in communication. Chapter 30 describes the Picture Exchange Communication System (PECS) developed by Andy Bondy. This chapter describes an efficient procedure for helping students use pictures and other visual stimuli to facilitate expressions of desires and other social communication. Both programs are relatively new and in need of more empirical research. Nevertheless, they are included here because they represent the best lead professionals have in helping visual learners at this time.

Section 6: Programmatic Considerations

Section 6 describes how to help students remember what they have learned (Chapter 31), the importance of parents' participation in treatment (Chapter 32), how to assess improvement (Chapter 33), how to locate and select consultants (Chapter 34), and how to identify and help solve problems in learning (Chapter 35).

Chapter 31 by Tristram Smith presents procedures for helping students retain what they learn in treatment. It is a well-known fact that treatment gains need to be practiced in order not to be lost. Chapter 3 presents some of the bitter disappointments of seeing how, in the early stages of our work, our clients regressed at follow-up assessment. The teacher's familiarity with Chapter 31 should help reduce such a problem. Difficulties in maintaining treatment gains are not unique to behavioral interventions. Rather, difficulties in maintaining and generalizing treatment gains are problems faced by all clinicians and teachers.

Chapter 32 by Eric V. Larsson describes the vitally important role of parents in extending and generalizing treatment gains. Information is also provided on how this role may be facilitated for optimal treatment. Now more than ever, parents are allowed considerable control over and responsibility for their children's treatment.

Chapter 33 by Greg Buch provides information on how a parent and teacher may be able to assess whether a student is improving, and in what specific areas progress is taking place. A scientist would want more detailed and comprehensive data than the kind gathered through the procedures detailed in this chapter; however, in day-to-day operations, the data collection methods presented in Chapter 33 are significant and essential to helping parents and teachers keep track of the students' progress or lack thereof. They are also important when seeking funding for services.

Chapter 34 by Tristram Smith and Jacqueline Wynn describes certain criteria that may be helpful for parents and professionals when selecting consultants to assist in formulating and supervising treatment.

Chapter 35 describes some of the common problems one encounters in teaching and ways in which these problems may be identified and overcome. Considering the enormous range of individual differences and the large number of decisions that have to be made at any given stage in teaching, it is likely that one will encounter problems. Being able to identify problems and solve them early are important attributes of a competent teacher.

Section 7: Organizational and Legal Issues

Section 7 deals with organizational and legal issues. In Chapter 36, Ronald Huff describes how parents can organize into functional and problem-solving groups to support each other's efforts. The value of such groups cannot be overestimated as they provide moral support, information about effective programs, and suggestions for approaching the community to increase understanding of the needs of children with developmental delays.

Chapter 37 is written by two attorneys, Kathryn Dobel and Valerie Vanaman. It concerns the rights of children to an appropriate education. Just as it is important to have parent organizations, it is also important to know what legal rights children with developmental delays have under the law. Many parents must turn to legal counsel in order to obtain funding for their children's treatment. Gary Mayerson provides additional legal information in Chapter 38.

In Chapter 39, Howard G. Cohen presents a series of recommendations to help parents, professionals, and administrators work together in a collaborative relationship so as to minimize conflict and legal battles and still arrange access to the most optimal educational programs.

Chapter 40 is provided in an attempt to reduce the misinformation and distortions that surround the teaching programs presented in this manual. Most of the misinformation is provided by professionals within the fields of psychiatry, psychology, and special education. Given the status of these professionals in their respective fields, parents may be led to place faith in their opinions. Chapter 40 should be helpful to legal counsel and to parents who must appear at fair hearings to seek funding for their children's treatment.

How To Use this Manual

Each program, especially in Section 3 of this manual, is laid out in considerable step-by-step detail. Such detail may seem redundant in some places, but we judge it better to be safe than presumptuous. Also to simplify the task for the teacher, considerable repetition of teaching steps pertaining to discrimination learning is introduced. We are aware that in college textbooks, a term or a process may be introduced only once or twice with the apparent intent to test students' recall of the material. Such exercises are less appropriate in a manual such as this one.

Teachers should keep in mind that the sequence of programs presented may not directly coincide with every student's abilities. A small minority of students may not have to be taught each step in the early programs to learn a given task. In such a case, the teacher may bypass those steps that are unnecessary for that particular student. On the other hand, success in the early programs is likely to behoove all students, given the students' failures at understanding what adults have tried to teach them in the past. Some students may have difficulty progressing from the early steps to the later steps within programs. In an attempt to help lessen these and similar difficulties, sections titled "Areas of Difficulty" are located in most chapters. You may also consult Chapter 35 if the student demonstrates problems progressing. Keep in mind that assistance from an experienced behavioral consultant (see Chapter 34) is likely to help rectify problems not discussed in this manual.

Although the programs in this manual are presented in order of complexity (from elementary to more advanced), many programs should be taught contemporaneously. For example, after 4 or 5 days of one-on-one teaching, students may work on programs such as Matching, Nonverbal Imitation, and Early Receptive Language (Chapters 12, 13, and 15, respectively) within a single teaching session. It is also possible that the student may be involved in some early play skills, as described in Chapter 19. The benefit of teaching parts of several programs in the same day is that the student may become less bored and inattentive, and hence learn more in a shorter period of time. However, the teacher must be careful not to overwhelm the student with too many new programs, especially during the first weeks or months of teaching. It may be helpful to focus on three or four fundamental programs during the first 2 or 3 weeks of teaching, and then slowly increase the number of programs. In the initial weeks of treatment, it is also helpful to begin with 20 hours of one-on-one treatment, and gradually increase to 40 hours after the first month. If the student is younger than 30 months old, the teacher should go slower and increase hours over several months of treatment (see Appendix A). With younger students, longer durations and more frequent intervals of play should be intermixed among the programs.

It is extremely important that all significant persons who interact with the student learn the basic teaching procedures introduced in this manual. For example, both parents (if there are two) should be involved from the first hour of treatment. Such involvement is essential for several reasons. First, teaching should be extended into all the student's waking hours, including weekends, holidays, and vacations, for the student to generalize (transfer) treatment gains from the teacher and the teaching environment to other locations and persons. The more hours of treatment provided to the student, even informally, the larger the student's gains. Second, one wants to avoid confronting the student with opposing consequences for the same behavior, as when one person accidentally reinforces tantrums (thus increasing them) while another person ignores tantrums (which helps to diminish them). Third, it will become increasingly difficult for a person to "catch up" as a teacher if one misses out on the early programs. The programs are cumulative in that the latter ones require increasingly sophisticated knowledge of behavioral treatment procedures. Finally, although it may be tempting to hire a professional to do the work and relieve parents of working as teachers, doing so is counterproductive. Chapter 32 (Involving Parents in Treatment) provides a substantial amount of advice on how to help parents take an active role in being teachers of their children.

As a general rule, most of the new programs should be reserved for the morning treatment sessions when individuals tend to learn most efficiently. The teacher should place a limit on the number of new programs "on acquisition" at one time to give the student the opportunity to both practice new programs and rehearse mastered programs during the daily teaching sessions. As can be observed from the timeline presented in Appendix B, several programs should be practiced concurrently, but not all programs should be introduced at the same time. It is inevitable that several programs will have to be practiced concurrently because many of the programs have no definite ending point. For example, there are thousands of receptive instructions a person must understand in order to function at some optimal level in life.

A mixture of technical and everyday language is used throughout this manual to refer to analogous processes. No technical language is introduced without illustrating it with examples from everyday life. Technical language is introduced because it carries more precision and is used in professional literature (numerous references to such literature are provided at the end of this manual). The reader may want to become familiar with this technical literature to facilitate the undertaking of more responsibility for the student's treatment.

While working through this manual, the reader may note that certain numbers do not remain the same across and within programs. For example, in describing numbers of trials to mastery, we may recommend that the student reach a mastery criterion of 9 correct out of 10 consecutive attempts, or, if the student fails that level, securing 19 correct out of 20 consecutive trials before advancing. At other times, we may recommend that the teacher consider 5 correct out of 5 trials or 9 correct out of 10 trials to be the criterion for mastery. Later on, the definition of mastery may be set at 2 out of 2, 3 out of 3, or 4 out of 5 correct trials. The reasons for changing the criteria for mastery are two-fold. First, as a student gains increasing competence within certain areas, less repetition may be necessary to solidify learning. At other times, certain discriminations are extremely difficult (e.g., the discriminations involved in verbal imitation), and it may be necessary to secure a higher level of mastery before introducing new steps. In short, the changing of criteria for mastery is not arbitrary but is made with the intent of facilitating the student's progress.

In writing this manual, we realize that we ask a large amount of work from parents and teachers of the student. We regret that we have found no shortcuts at this time. Human behavior is complex at all levels, and we know of no program that produces a "great step forward" in behavioral or psychological development. Perhaps nature favors small steps because big steps, if taken mistakenly, could be catastrophic. Mistakes far outnumber successes in the history of human development, or at least it seems that way to some historians.

Maybe someday the educational system will be changed so as to lessen the burden on parents to provide the kind of one-on-one treatment advocated in this manual. This will necessitate a major reorganization in the way the educational system is presently arranged. In the meantime, we advise that parents receive support and comfort from other parents who are faced with similar problems (see Chapter 36). Teachers or aides who intend to administer the programs in this manual should take comfort in the thought that they will bring much happiness and support to parents and children who are in very difficult positions.

Given the complexity involved in teaching students with developmental delays, it is important to know beforehand that teachers feel a great deal more confident 1 or 2 weeks into teaching as efforts begin to pay off. As one gains practice in administering these programs, one will learn to abstract certain essential steps in behavioral teaching and be better able to solve problems such as by adapting and revising programs to meet the needs of the specific student being taught. Nevertheless, there is no way that one person working alone can anticipate and constructively deal with all individual differences and solve all the problems one will encounter. Therefore, we strongly advise that one work within a group of other parents or teachers to take advantage of the contributions that many persons have to offer.

As mentioned earlier, the programs in this manual are arranged in order of difficulty so as to facilitate mastery both for the student and the teacher. Even so, it is likely that some sections will be hard to understand. We therefore advise that two or more people read the manual together to facilitate collaboration and discussion of problems that may arise. If either the teacher or the student fails to master the beginning steps, attempts at teaching and learning later steps will most likely fail because later steps are more complex than earlier steps. It is therefore of paramount importance that the basic programs in this manual be mastered before advanced programs in the subsequent manual are started. In all areas that require skill, such as sports, educational achievement, social interaction, dance, and music, one must build a foundation of basic skills before moving on to more complex skills. We have never been successful as teachers by starting the student on the more advanced programs, no matter how smart or high functioning the student may seem to be.

It has been difficult to settle on one particular label for the kind of intervention described in this manual, as well as a title for the persons who provide the treatment. Terms such as *behavioral intervention*, *teaching*, and *treatment* are used interchangeably, as are labels such as *teacher*, *parent*, *aide*, *adult*, and *tutor*. We also have alternated use of labels such as *student*, *client*, *child*, *he* and *she*, *persons*, and *individuals* across chapters. The label of *student* seems most appropriate when referring to persons undergoing intervention because it refers to both children and adults and is associated with programs that deal with teaching. The teaching programs presented in this manual should prove useful for both children and adults because the teaching steps outlined in these various programs are universal (i.e., the laws of learning apply equally well to persons of all ages).

The programs presented in this manual draw upon the contributions of hundreds of scientists. There are more than a thousand references in scientific literature to learning-based research studies and the application of such information to the treatment and education of humans. At the end of this manual is a list of references cited in the manual. We recognize that parents and teachers who read and use this manual are unlikely to have the time or opportunity to become familiar with all of these references; however, the reader should be able to identify certain references of particular interest, and these references should help the reader seek more familiarity with learning-based research in scientific journals. References to relevant publications are also provided for those chapters where legal and ethical issues are at stake for the protection of the parents and teachers seeking information about how to provide the best services for their students.

Our Teaching Philosophy

Behavioral psychologists have developed a special teaching environment for use with individuals with developmental delays that resembles the normal or average environment as much as possible. It may be helpful to briefly summarize the teaching principles that have emerged from such work.

1. Persons with autism and other behavioral delays are considered different in degree rather than kind when compared to typical individuals. Variability is built into nervous systems and is essential for the survival of all animals, including human beings. We need this variability because our environment is constantly changing and it is impossible to predict what the future will demand from any one of us. Democratic societies, which encourage variability among individuals, are more likely to be better prepared for the future. This is in contrast to totalitarian regimes, which restrict variability and therefore are likely to be at a disadvantage in a future that places quite different demands on its citizens. The future of civilized society may depend to a significant degree on those persons who are loners or who disagree with the majority. Van Gogh and Einstein are examples of such persons who helped prepare us for the future. Neither was likely to have obtained the highest scores on tests of social skills and conformity, and both may well have been considered to fall on the autistic continuum.

2. Although individuals with autism possess atypical nervous systems, it is not to our advantage to treat such individuals as ill or qualitatively different from others. Rather, the laws of learning apply, albeit to different degrees, to individuals with deviant organic structures. We shall present ample data to support this position.

3. The average (day-to-day) environment treats the average nervous system best, most likely because average nervous systems created that environment. Viewed from this position, the average environment does not provide a match with the deviant nervous system of individuals with autism and other developmental delays. Rather, most of the average environment passed the unusual nervous system by, leaving these individuals with little or no opportunity to learn and, consequently, with limited or no experience.

4. Special education and psychology may help those with deviant nervous systems by creating and constructing special teaching environments in which those who deviate may learn.

5. This special environment should differ as little as possible from the average (everyday) environment, largely because a primary goal of education for persons with developmental delays is to help them function more adequately when they return to the average environment. The smaller the difference is between the special therapeutic or educational environment and the average environment, the easier the transfer in skills will be from the special environment to the average environment. This is a primary reason for recommending that teaching take place in the student's natural community (in homes and neighborhood schools) and that parents, other family members, and friends become involved in the teaching process.

6. Note that typical (average) individuals learn all waking hours, every day, for their entire lives. To approximate that, an appropriate educational environment for persons with developmental delays should be in effect most hours of the day, weekends and holidays included. If needed, it should last for the lifetime of the persons involved. This is in apparent contrast to the current psychological and educational models, which may intervene 1 or 2 hours per week in a clinical setting (as in speech therapy, psychotherapy, and Sensory Integration) or 6 hours per day, 5 days per week (as in special education).

7. Should we intervene in the first place, given the emphasis on encouraging and retaining variability? Two points related to this question are worth noting. First, outcome data obtained after behavioral treatment document more rather than less variability, both across and within persons treated. Second, in most cases of autism, lifelong care in protective institutional settings is necessary. The resultant stress on the child and the parents is so enormous that one is left with no choice but to intervene. Ethics prescribe that treatment should first of all be in the interest of the individual, not society.

Basic Concepts

SECTION 1

Diagnoses, Behavioral Delays, Behavioral Excesses, and Typical Behaviors

CHAPTER 1

In this chapter we describe some of the behaviors that, when displayed in particular patterns, give rise to the diagnosis of autistic disorder, Asperger's syndrome, or pervasive developmental disorder–not otherwise specified (PDD-NOS). Through such categories, persons diagnosed with autism, Asperger's syndrome, or PDD-NOS have been viewed as being qualitatively different from each other and from typical persons, and thus as requiring unique forms of treatment. In Chapter 2 we present an alternative to placing individuals in distinct diagnostic categories by considering persons with developmental delays as differing in degrees from each other and varying on a continuum with typical (so-called average or normal) persons. It follows that a treatment developed for individuals diagnosed with autism would be appropriate for individuals who receive a different diagnosis, such as Asperger's syndrome or PDD-NOS. Furthermore, the knowledge that science has gained about the learning processes of typical individuals may provide some guidance in helping individuals with developmental delays to learn.

The diagnoses of autistic disorder, Asperger's syndrome, and PDD-NOS are based on a person's behaviors and are made in terms of a set of behavioral delays, a set of behavioral excesses, and a set of normally developing behaviors. Large individual differences exist among persons with developmental delays, including individuals within the same diagnostic category. Therefore, the description of the behavioral characteristics that follows does not characterize all individuals with developmental delays, but rather it is most characteristic of children diagnosed with autism, which is considered to be the most severe of the childhood delays. In describing these various delays and excesses, we recognize the seriousness of the problems, but we do not intend to communicate pessimism about what can be done to alter these behaviors. We have therefore refrained from using terms such as *disability*, *damage*, *pathology*, and *irreversibility*, because such labels are likely to communicate pessimism and delay development of effective treatments.

Behavioral Delays

▶ **1. Language.** Individuals with developmental delays are sometimes mute or echolalic (they echo what they hear). Receptive language is usually delayed in that many of these individuals, while capable of responding to simple instructions (e.g., "Sit down," "Eat," "Shut the door"), fail to understand more complex and abstract language. Individuals with developmental delays are also usually delayed in expressive language; that is, these individuals typically have difficulty vocalizing words and sentences as well as abstract relationships such as prepositions (e.g., *in*, *under*, *above*), pronouns (e.g., *yours*, *mine*, *his*, *hers*), and time (e.g., *first*, *last*, *later*).

This failure to understand or express language is the most common complaint of parents when they take their children to a service agency for help. Parents express sorrow and concern that they cannot talk with their children and that their children are unable to speak to them. Problems with language can be identified by the time the child has reached 2 years of age. Some children make progress in language but lose such gains between 15 and 24 months of age.

▶ **2. Attention.** Individuals with developmental delays often behave as if they cannot see or hear; however, closer examination typically reveals intact sensory modalities. Parents may describe their children as acting as if they are blind and deaf. Some report that their children have heightened pain thresholds because they do not cry like typical children when hurt. Parents may describe that their children do not look at them (fail to give eye-to-eye contact), reliably orient their heads to other people's speech, and fail to show startle responses to loud noises. On the other hand, these same children may show normal or unusual sensitivity to a limited range of stimuli, demonstrated through orientation to the sound of the unwrapping of a candy bar, concentrated attention to a barely audible siren, or prolonged visual attendance to a small piece of food or shiny object some considerable distance away. An apparent failure to develop typical sensory functions may be observed during the first year of life.

▶ **3. Range of emotions.** Children with developmental delays may not develop close, loving relationships with their parents. This can be evidenced during the first few months of life. Parents often complain that their children are not cuddly and may in fact resist physical contact by stiffening their backs and sliding away from their parents' embrace. Further, children with developmental delays may show little or no apparent fright when their parents leave them alone or when they are lost in a supermarket or other public place. These children may not acquire a fear of strangers and may fail to develop grief, sadness, guilt, sympathy, and shame the way typical children do.

▶ **4. Toy play.** Children with developmental delays do not develop toy play the way typical children develop such play. Instead of playing appropriately with toys, they often handle them in a peculiar and idiosyncratic fashion by, for example, turning a toy truck upside down and spinning its wheels, compulsively twirling a piece of string, or carrying a doll to smell or suck. The delay in developing toy play can be identified during the second year of life.

▶ **5. Peer play.** Play with friends is almost always missing in children diagnosed with autism. These children may stand by passively and observe other children without becoming involved in any sort of give-and-take play. Some may aggress at others and be prevented from attending preschool. Few, if any, children diagnosed with autism develop friendships. The delay in peer play becomes most noticeable during the second or third year of life.

▶ **6. Development of self-help skills.** Individuals with developmental delays often have problems learning to dress, use the toilet, and eat without assistance. Similarly, they may fail to recognize common dangers and may have to be closely guarded so they do not hurt themselves (e.g., by crossing a street in heavy traffic, playing with electrical equipment, or jumping into swimming pools or deep, swift-running rivers).

▶ **7. Delay in imitation.** Imitation of the behaviors of others is often delayed or missing in individuals with developmental delays. Typical persons begin to imitate before they are 6 months old. Given that imitation constitutes a major and effective learning mechanism, a person who does not imitate is likely to demonstrate serious delays in developing new behaviors.

▶ **8. Cognitive development.** The average IQ score earned by individuals with developmental delays falls within the retarded range. There are large individual differences, however, with some persons scoring within the profoundly retarded range (IQ scores below 35) and a few scoring within the average range (scores above 85). IQ scores vary depending on several factors, including the kind of IQ test employed and the context surrounding administration of the test. Children with developmental delays often obtain higher scores on nonverbal IQ scales, such as the *Merrill–Palmer Scale of Mental Tests* (Stutsman, 1984b) than on IQ scales that have several verbal items, such as the *Bayley Scales of Infant Development–Revised* (Bayley, 1993) and the Wechsler scales (e.g., Wechsler, 1991).

Behavioral Excesses

▶ **1. Tantrums and aggression.** Aggression may take the form of self-inflicted injury, as when individuals bite themselves, hit their heads with their fists, or bump their heads against the floor or sharp pieces of furniture. Persons may also direct their biting, scratching, or hitting toward others. Parents may complain that their children are very hard to manage, have a low frustration tolerance, and respond to even minor frustrations with a great deal of anger. These behaviors become significant problems by the second or third year of life. As the children grow older, they may have to be taken out of the home and placed in residential treatment settings because their parents become unable to cope with their severe aggression. Such individuals may need to be physically restrained or given tranquilizing drugs to prevent serious damage to themselves or others. Besides help in developing language, the request for help in managing tantrums is typically of foremost concern to parents.

▶ **2. Ritualistic and self-stimulatory behaviors.** Persons with developmental delays may show excessive amounts of certain behaviors that stimulate particular senses, such as rocking their bodies while in a standing or sitting position, flapping their hands at their wrists, spinning objects, gazing at lights, lining up objects into neat rows, jumping and spinning for prolonged periods of time, and preoccupying themselves with circular motions (e.g., observing rotating fans or water twirling in a toilet bowl). They may show obsessions with numbers, letters of the alphabet, toys with internal power sources, and objects with certain textures. We refer to all of these behaviors as self-stimulatory behaviors. Some of these behaviors may become noticeable during the first year of life.

Typical Behaviors

Many individuals with developmental delays show a set of typical or normal-like behaviors, some of which may be labeled *splinter skills* or *islets of intact intellectual functioning*. These normal-like behaviors congregate in the following categories.

▶ **1. Motor development.** Signs of adequate motor development are observed in terms of meeting normal developmental milestones, such as eating solid food, sitting up, and walking at the age typical children master such skills. Whereas some children show a delay in motor development, many others develop motor skills normally, being able to run, jump, and balance with a great deal of ease.

▶ **2. Memory.** Many individuals with developmental delays show signs of adequate or excellent memory in certain areas. Some individuals, for example, are able to echo or otherwise repeat entire commercials or other people's everyday speech, even after a considerable delay. Some persons with developmental delays have a good memory for visual details. For example, some individuals insist on "sameness," which means that they compulsively want to preserve a certain furniture arrangement, be served a particular food, or insist that their mothers wear a certain dress or a particular pair of glasses. Similarly, individuals with developmental delays may be able to trace their way to the homes of relatives through complex streets or remember exactly where a favorite food was hidden in a grandmother's house that was visited a year ago. This insistence on sameness implies that these individuals have good memories. When such routines are broken, however, persons with developmental delays often respond with self-injurious behaviors or aggression toward others.

▶ **3. Special and well-developed interests.** Some persons with developmental delays show certain special and well-developed interests, such as playing with mechanical objects (e.g., appliances, motorized toys, computers). They may also excel at taking objects apart. Some individuals demonstrate a great deal of interest and liking for music and dance. Others show considerable ability at putting together puzzles or demonstrate a liking for numbers, letters, calendars, or maps.

▶ **4. Special fears.** Some persons with developmental delays evidence a limited number of special fears that exist in more transient forms in typical persons. For example, some individuals with developmental delays fear the noises generated by vacuum cleaners or the sirens of passing ambulances.

Concluding Comments

The behavioral delays, behavioral excesses, and normal behaviors described in this chapter constitute descriptions that may apply in various degrees to all persons who fall behind in development. In contrast to the diagnoses of Down's syndrome and phenylketonuria (PKU), it has been difficult for diagnosticians to agree on when to apply a particular diagnosis to persons who display developmental delays. When the differential diagnosis of autism is given, it usually emphasizes limited or no peer play; limited emotional attachment or other social interaction with parents; language delays as evidenced by mutism, echolalia, or both; and self-stimulatory behaviors. This particular combination of behavioral deviations (a symptom cluster) has led to diagnoses that have varied over time and across diagnosticians, depending on the prevailing theory. Emotional detachment was once considered to be the critical variable in diagnosing autism. At other times it was a language delay, an apparent sensory deficit, or, more recently, an absence of peer play. At one time, children who would today be diagnosed with autism were diagnosed as having childhood schizophrenia.

Parents who seek a "definite and firm diagnosis" for their child and who visit a number of clinics to establish a diagnosis are likely to be provided with more than one diagnosis. Certain recent developments such as the *Autism Diagnostic Interview Revised* (Lord, Rutter, & LeCouteur, 1994) should help increase reliability in the use of labels such as *autism*. Invariably, the rendering of the diagnosis of autism constitutes a major shock to parents who are often counseled that the "condition" is irreversible and chronic, and to "go home and learn to live with it."

In the 1960s and 1970s, autism was widely considered reversible. In the 1980s and early 1990s, it was considered irreversible. In the near future, professionals may again consider the condition to be reversible. Despite these swaying opinions, there is universal agreement that the cause of autism has yet to be identified. There may, in fact, be many different causes, including different causes for different behaviors.

Given all these ambiguities, what usefulness could be derived from a diagnosis? In the case of autism, one advantage of the diagnosis pertains to knowledge of the future status of children so diagnosed. Data show that children diagnosed with autism do not improve with services available in the community (Freeman et al., 1991; Lord & Schopler, 1988). A reliable diagnosis also informs one of approximately the type of individual being treated. Furthermore, a change in the diagnosis from autism to normal functioning or some other diagnosis could function as one measure of treatment outcome. Finally, parents of children diagnosed with autism have been able to organize, support each other emotionally, and help build public awareness regarding the importance of improving the treatment and education of such children.

It is important for the reader to be aware of the very tentative and speculative nature of many psychiatric and psychological diagnoses such as autism and PDD-NOS. We raise reservations about diagnostic practices largely because of the premature inferences concerning chronicity and qualitative differences associated with various diagnoses. It is possible that the problems these individuals manifest have been conceptualized in a manner that delays the discovery of effective treatments. Suppose "autism" is a pseudo-problem, an unproductive hypothesis. Suppose the behavioral deviations do not cluster as a group and are not related to a common cause or treatment in the lawful manner as implied by the diagnosis of autism. If autism represents an arbitrary and chance collection of low-frequency behavioral deviations, then perhaps autism is a poor hypothesis, misleading inquiry into a blind alley.

The history of searching for a treatment for autism provides ample illustrations of such failures. Over the 50 years that have elapsed since Kanner (1943) proposed the diagnosis, announcements claiming a discovery of the cause of or treatment for autism have frequently been made. Therapies such as Facilitated Communication, Auditory Integration, Holding Therapy, the Option Method, Floor-Time, Sensory Integration, Gentle Teaching, and psychodynamic interpretations have all been offered as solutions but have failed to deliver on promises (see Chapter 3). Treatment–research of schizophrenia (another large hypothetical grouping of behaviors) has also failed to identify an effective intervention despite intensive research efforts over the past 25 years. Chapter 2 introduces a conceptualization of behavioral deviations that differs markedly from traditional clinical views but that has led to significant progress in treatment.

The Continuity Model: Alternatives to the Diagnoses[1]

CHAPTER 2

Traditional theories about persons with autism hypothesize that such persons have something in common that is unique to them, distinguishing them from other groups of persons. This view raises several problems. First, although persons with autism may initially appear to be a rather homogeneous group, closer inspection reveals a wide range of individual differences, casting doubt as to whether these persons really have much, if anything, in common. For example, prior to treatment, individuals with autism may range from showing some mastery of complex language and IQs within the normal range to being mute and scoring within the profoundly retarded range of intellectual functioning (American Psychiatric Association, 1987). They may also vary markedly in their response to treatment. For example, some persons with autism enter treatment with the ability to imitate the speech of others, some acquire speech very rapidly once treatment is begun, some acquire it very slowly, and a few fail to acquire verbal imitation and auditory communication even after extensive training. This final group must be taught visual forms of communication, such as reading and writing or the Picture Exchange Communication System (Chapters 29 and 30, respectively). Similar variability can be observed after treatment. Lovaas (1987) and McEachin, Smith, and Lovaas (1993) reported that three distinct outcome groups emerged when intensive behavioral treatment was given to preschool-aged autistic children: a group that reached normal functioning, an intermediate group that made some gains, and a small residual group that benefited little from the treatment.

The hypothesis that individuals with autism have unique and distinct problems may also be questioned because studies thus far have found that all of the behaviors shown by autistic individuals are also shown by other groups of persons, including normal infants (Rutter, 1978). For example, self-stimulatory behaviors such as rocking and hand flapping, which autistic persons often exhibit at high rates, are quite common in infants (Kravitz & Boehm, 1971). Echolalia, which was once considered a symptom of a psychotic disorder, can be observed in transient form in typical children. Typical children tantrum, and some bang their heads against hard surfaces just like children with autism, albeit to a lesser degree and for shorter periods of time. Indeed, if autistic individuals are matched by mental age to other individuals and their behaviors are compared, most differences disappear (DeMeyer, Hingtgen, & Jackson, 1981).

DeMeyer et al. (1981) and Rutter (1978) wrote excellent reviews of the difficulty posed by individual differences and behavioral overlap. In their reviews, they suggested that the diagnosis of autism may represent a multiplicity of behavior problems with a multiplicity of etiologies. Consequently, it is not surprising that efforts to identify causes or effective treatments with traditional approaches have thus far been largely unsuccessful. In essence, the problem is that the existence of an entity called autism is a hypothesis (Rutter, 1978). The tentativeness of this hypothesis is often overlooked. For example, stating that Leo Kanner was "the discoverer of autism" (e.g., Schopler, 1987) gives the misleading impression that autism is known to exist. It should be remembered that, like any other hypothesis, autism is a construct that may facilitate research or prematurely freeze or misdirect inquiry into the area of helping the persons to whom the term is applied (Lovaas, 1971b).

In an attempt to understand autistic individuals without pursuing the construct of autism, behaviorists have made three methodological decisions to increase the strength of their research designs and approach to treatment. In short, the large problem, autism, is broken down into smaller units, namely the separate behaviors shown

[1] The majority of this text has been presented in "A Comprehensive Behavioral Theory of Autistic Children: Paradigm for Research and Treatment," by O. I. Lovaas and T. Smith, 1989, *Behavior Therapy and Experimental Psychiatry*, *20*, pp. 17–29.

by autistic persons, which are reliably and precisely measured. This focus not only allows for precise measurement, it circumvents the problem of autistic persons' behavioral heterogeneity. Because behavior, rather than autism, is under investigation, a behavior may be studied even if not all autistic persons exhibit it, if different persons exhibit it to different degrees, or if persons without autism sometimes also exhibit it. In fact, such behavioral commonality may facilitate research and treatment of persons with autism because it makes it possible for these persons to be helped by findings from other groups of persons.

Finally, the possibility is left open that each behavioral deviation may have its own neurobiological etiology, and the delay in the development of a complex behavior such as language may be the product of many and diverse causes. This implies that remedying different language deviations may require separate and distinct interventions. For example, one kind of intervention may be implemented for a person who does not speak and another for a person with echolalia, and different interventions may be given to individuals who are at the level of acquiring grammar (syntax) in contrast to meaning (semantics).

Psychology and special education may help those with atypical nervous systems by creating and constructing teaching environments by which those with anomalous systems can learn. These special environments should differ as little as possible from the average (everyday) environment for several reasons. First, a primary goal of intervention designed for persons with developmental delays is to help them function more adequately in the typical, everyday environment. The smaller the difference between the special education environment and the average environment, the easier the transfer of skills gained from the special environment to the average environment. Second, the average environment has been developed and "shaped up" over centuries and contains much information despite its many limitations. Third, by treating individuals with developmental delays as different in degree rather than kind, one may be able to draw upon already acquired knowledge about how typical organisms learn and develop. Such knowledge includes laws of how people learn, a subject about which a great deal of scientific understanding has been acquired. Finally, by breaking down the complex category of autism into its behavioral components, professionals with experience in developing various behaviors, such as language, may be brought in to help with treatment. One need not necessarily be an expert on autism because that hypothetical entity is not addressed. Such was the strategy pursued by investigators who helped develop the treatment programs presented in this teaching manual.

Using the average environment as a model, note that a typical (average) individual learns from the beginning of life, all waking hours, every day, for the life of that individual. To approximate this, an appropriate educational environment for a person with developmental delays should be started as early as possible; be in effect most hours of the day, weekends and holidays included; and last for the lifetime of the person involved if so needed. This is in contrast to the current treatment–educational model which intervenes 1 or 2 hours per week (as in speech therapy, psychotherapy, and Sensory Integration) or 6 hours per day, 5 days per week (as in special education). The difference between the intensity of the appropriate intervention and that of the current one is likely to be based on differences in the assumptions underlying these two models of service delivery. If one assumes that there is a central deficit that can be corrected, then a limited intervention that focuses on this deficit may alleviate the problem and set the person free to learn. No empirical evidence exists as of yet, however, to support the beneficial effects of these short-term interventions (Smith, 1993).

Again using the average environment as a model, it should be clear that the intervention should be initiated in the home and involve the individual's parents, relatives, and neighbors. One would want to help the individual acquire a wide range of behaviors (e.g., language and appropriate play) and learning strategies (e.g., imitation) before placing him into a group learning situation such as preschool or kindergarten. Few 2-year-old typical children (with a mental age of 2 years) would be expected to cope with or learn much in a preschool or kindergarten setting.

The behavioral theory proposed in this manual has four tenets, which are outlined here and then described in more detail. First, the laws of learning help account for autistic persons' behaviors and provide the basis for treatment. Second, autistic persons have many separate behavioral deficits best described as developmental delays rather than a central deficit or disease which, if corrected, would lead to broad-based improvement. Consequently, teachers must give them knowledge piece by piece rather than focus on only one broad deficit at a time. Third, autistic persons give evidence of being able to learn like typical individuals if they are placed in special environments. Fourth, autistic persons' failure in normal environments and success in special environments indicate that their problems can be viewed as a mismatch between their nervous system and the environment. At present, given the limited knowledge available from neurobiological research, these persons' problems may be best solved by constructing functional treatment environments.

▶ Tenet 1.

Numerous findings indicate that the behaviors of autistic individuals can be accounted for by the laws of learning. When behaviors are reinforced, these individuals show acquisition curves similar to those obtained by other people and other organisms; when reinforcement is withdrawn, the behaviors show extinction curves similar to those gleaned from the behaviors of other organisms (Lovaas, Freitag, Gold, & Kassorla, 1965b). Behaviors that are not acquired in treatment are also related to identifiable reinforcement. For example, self-stimulatory behaviors such as rocking and hand flapping are maintained by the sensory feedback they provide for a person; if this feedback is removed, the behaviors extinguish (Rincover, Newsom, & Carr, 1979). Likewise, self-injurious behaviors and aggression against others (Carr & Durand, 1985) have been found to have one of three functions: They may be self-stimulatory, negatively reinforcing (allowing the individual to escape from aversive situations), or positively reinforcing (leading to attention from others). Prior to treatment, autistic individuals respond to a narrow range of reinforcers, but this range can be expanded through the use of principles derived from learning theory by pairing a stimulus that is neutral for autistic individuals (e.g., praise from others) with another stimulus (e.g., food) that is already reinforcing (Lovaas, Freitag, et al., 1966). Finally, in accordance with behavioral theory, discrimination training paradigms derived from learning theory have been found to be particularly useful in developing treatment programs for autistic individuals (Stoddard & McIlvane, 1986). Two kinds of discrimination learning provide the basis for teaching many behaviors: imitation and match-to-sample.

▶ Tenet 2.

Autistic individuals have many separate behavioral deficits rather than a central deficit that, if corrected, would lead to broad-based change. This tenet is derived from findings on limited response generalization and limited stimulus generalization, as well as the observation that an individual's various behaviors are controlled by different environmental variables.

Most traditional theories of child development hypothesize the existence of an "organizing construct" (e.g., a "self," a "capacity," or a "cognitive schema"), which emerges if a child reaches a certain maturational stage or experiences a particular event or situation. The emergence of this organizing construct creates changes in a wide range of behaviors, leading to what in behavioral terms is referred to as response generalization (changes in behaviors other than those that were specifically taught). In the 1960s, behavioral investigators devoted much effort to finding a pivotal aspect of behavior that would lead to response generalization in children with autism. However, these efforts were remarkably unsuccessful (Lindsay & Stoffelmayr, 1982). Rather than response generalization, a great deal of response specificity became evident. Changes in such behaviors as language did not result in obvious changes in other behaviors. Even within a seemingly basic or circumscribed unit of behavior such as the acquisition of abstract language terms, a striking amount of response specificity was shown to be evident. For example, mastery of one class of abstract terms (e.g., prepositions) did not necessarily facilitate understanding of other abstract terms (e.g., pronouns). Children were taught their names or the names of others, but this did not lead them to make a proclamation such as "different people have different names." Children were taught to make eye contact and to give and receive affection but, even with these skills, the children remained socially isolated in many ways (e.g., they did not begin to play with others unless explicitly taught to do so).

Like limits in response generalization, limits in stimulus generalization (Stokes & Baer, 1977) provide evidence against the presence of an internal, synthesizing, or organizing capacity. Individuals with autism do not show a capacity "to take their experiences with them" across environments unless they are directly taught to do so. To remedy this, the individuals must be taught to generalize. For example, Lovaas, Koegel, Simmons, and Long (1973) found that gains made in treatment during hospitalization did not transfer out of the hospital setting unless the children went home and their parents were trained to carry out the behavioral intervention. In more recent studies (Lovaas, 1987; McEachin et al., 1993), many autistic children were able to attain normal levels of functioning at home and school, giving every evidence of generalizing across behaviors and situations. In all likelihood, this came about because the children were taught to acquire information not only from aides working through a clinic, but also from parents at home as well as teachers and peers at school.

Many professionals have objected to behavioral treatment because of issues such as limited response and stimulus generalization, failing to note two important points. First, both kinds of generalization can be taught. Second, the failure to teach rapid generalization may not be characteristic only of behavioral treatment, and the failure to obtain such generalization may not be characteristic only of autistic persons. What is the survival value of rapid generalization considering that humankind may experience more failures than successes? A step in the wrong direction may be devastating if it quickly generalizes across other behaviors and environments.

The approach of a behavior-by-behavior treatment is the essence of the behavioral approach to the treatment and education of persons diagnosed with autism or mental retardation. This approach leaves open the possibility that the various behavioral delays and excesses associated with autism and mental retardation may be caused by several different kinds of underlying neurological deviations. The treatment, therefore, is not identical across all the individual's behaviors but rather addresses the idiosyncrasies of each behavior and the uniqueness of each individual.

Behavioral research has proceeded according to an inductive paradigm, and knowledge about treatment has been accumulated in a gradual and systematic manner. Progress in understanding persons diagnosed as having autism or pervasive developmental disorder (PDD) is considered to occur in small steps and gradually rather than suddenly as a result of the discovery of one pivotal problem or disease that controls all behaviors of all persons diagnosed. With behavioral treatment, many persons diagnosed as having autism or PDD achieve normal educational, emotional, social, and intellectual functioning if treatment is started early and given intensively. However, behavioral treatment does not provide a cure for such persons because a cure would have to rectify the root cause of the problem, which is likely to be various kinds of neurological deviations.

Another finding that counterindicates the presence of a central organizing and generalizing mechanism is that different behaviors have different kinds of lawful relationships with the environment, and even the same behavior may have different lawful relationships. For example, aggression is sometimes self-stimulatory, sometimes based on negative reinforcement, and sometimes based on positive reinforcement. It seems difficult to invoke some researchable central deficit that could be responsible for such heterogeneity.

Rather than a central deficit, persons with autism appear to have a number of separate behavioral difficulties. These difficulties are best described as developmental delays because, as noted by Rutter (1978), the behaviors are also evident in younger, normal children. Because autistic individuals have so many difficulties that need to be addressed separately, they need to be taught virtually everything, and the teaching needs to proceed in minute increments instead of major steps. Thus, at the beginning of treatment, the individuals may be regarded as being close to a tabula rasa. In this sense, they can be considered very young or recently born, as persons with little or no experience.

▶ Tenet 3.

Persons with autism can learn once a special environment is constructed for them (Simeonnson, Olley, & Rosenthal, 1987). This special environment should deviate from the normal environment only enough to make it functional. It should consist of regular community settings (as opposed to hospitals, clinics, etc.) and provide requests and consequences for behaviors just as the typical environment does, except that the requests and consequences should be more explicit and "meaningful" through the use of the learning theory principles discussed in Tenet 1. Preschool-aged children with autism appear to make substantial progress in such an environment (Simeonnson et al., 1987). For example, Lovaas (1987) provided an intensive behavioral intervention (approximately 40 hours of one-on-one treatment per week for many years) to young children with autism. It was found that almost half of the autistic children in Lovaas's sample attained normal levels of intellectual functioning (as measured by IQ tests) and performed satisfactorily in regular first-grade classes by the age of 7 years. These gains were shown to be maintained over time (McEachin et al., 1993).

Tenet 4.

Autistic persons' failure to learn in normal environments and success in special environments indicate that their problems can be viewed as a mismatch between their nervous systems and the normal environment rather than approached as a disease. Because of the dramatic nature of autistic individuals' problems, however, many investigators have been inclined toward dramatic explanations of the problems. From the 1940s to the early 1960s, the problems were attributed to the individuals' parents, who were regarded as extremely hostile. Later on the problems have been attributed to an incurable, organic disorder (DeMeyer et al., 1981). Viewing the individuals' problems as a mismatch between an atypical (though not necessarily diseased) nervous system and an average, day-to-day environment is less dramatic but is more consistent with the data (Lovaas, 1988).

Contrasting Behavioral and Traditional Theories

To clarify the behavioral position further, it may be useful to contrast it with traditional theories of autism. In traditional theories, some structure that is responsible for autistic persons' behavioral deviations is hypothesized to be present. It is this entity that is said to be sick, disordered, or diseased. The aim of treatment is to get inside the person and treat the diseased entity (the "autism"). If this is done, it is thought that the afflicted persons will begin to live life like others and develop normally. For medically oriented theoreticians, this entity is a neurobiological structure or process, and treatment involves pharmacotherapy, surgery, or other medical interventions. To psychodynamic clinicians, this entity is a self or an ego that must be normalized by refraining from placing demands on the sick individual, and by accepting her and relating through play and fantasy so that a small "crack in the autistic door" may be opened. This crack would then allow the self to emerge and enable others, such as parents and teachers, to relate to this healthy part of the individual so as to promote growth (Bettelheim, 1967).

Almost all currently available treatment approaches assume the existence of some such internal structure. For example, Holding Therapy (Tinbergen & Tinbergen, 1983) is based on the view that bonding has failed to occur between the mother and the autistic child. Treatment consists of having the mother forcibly hold the child to convey the message that she is available, to alleviate the child's rage and terror, and to cause the "autistic defense . . . to crumble" (Welch, 1987, p. 48). In contrast, a behavioral position suggests that there may be no intrapsychic conflicts or stress to resolve, no opposing forces, no rage, and no terror of abandonment because the individual never knew of another state. It follows that aides and parents should not feel disappointed when they "fail to reach the individual" because there was no nonautistic person to reach.

Sharing the psychodynamic emphasis on addressing internal states, cognitively oriented psychologists or speech therapists work to stimulate some hypothetical neurological structure to produce more language and other "higher mental processes" and in turn create and direct new behaviors. A psychomotor therapist also focuses on one aspect of a person's behavior (physical activities) and hypothesizes that neurological or motivational processes can thereby be activated or normalized. Facilitated Communication makes similar assumptions, as do Fast For Word, Sensory Integration, Option Method, Floor-Time, Play Therapy, Deep Pressure Therapy (e.g., use of squeeze machines), Auditory Integration, Music Therapy, Patterning, Drum Therapy, play with dolphins, horseback riding, "developmental" models of therapy, rotating chairs, and the many other treatments that have been proposed for individuals with autism.

However diverse these treatments and underlying theoretical systems might seem, they are all based on a belief in certain powerful theoretical variables. These variables, even with brief exposures to treatment in artificial environments, should substantially and permanently improve autistic persons' functioning in all settings. This position allows the therapist to involve only a limited number of professionals in treatment, locate treatment in a clinic or hospital away from the person's community, and set aside a limited number of hours for therapeutic contact. The interventions do not require the therapist or teacher to be familiar with the scientific research forming the basis of these interventions because such research does not exist. The practitioners may need only a few days of training to be qualified to deliver such treatments. Considering all of this, if the position could be supported, it would certainly have some practical advantages. However, data supporting the position have yet to be provided, and findings from behavioral research contradict it.

A related difference between behavioral and traditional theories can be expressed in technical terminology, terminology that will be further elaborated upon in this teaching manual. Behavioral treatment centers on *reinforcement control,* effecting behavior change by manipulating the consequences of behavior. The goal of treatment is to teach a large number of adaptive behaviors (cognitive, linguistic, social, etc.) by reinforcing increasingly closer approximations of the target behaviors and increasingly complex discriminations among situations. In contrast, traditional treatment centers on *stimulus control,* in which the major manipulations consist of changes in the variables preceding behavior. The showing of love and acceptance, holding, efforts to arrange a situation that will stimulate speech, and physical exercises are all examples of attempts at stimulus control. In short, behavioral treatments aim to build behavior while traditional treatments aim to cue and stimulate behaviors assumed to be present.

Certainly, cueing behavior is likely to be easier to administer and result in more rapid improvements than building behavior. From a behavioral standpoint, however, the main problem with cueing behaviors through stimulus control procedures is that doing so does not result in the acquisition of new behaviors. Stimulus control can only change already existing behaviors, and the behaviors targeted in the treatment of autism are largely in deficit or nonexistent in individuals with autism. Indeed, autistic individuals are identified on the basis of having little or no social behavior, language, or self-help skills. Thus, from a behavioral standpoint, stimulus control procedures are ineffective for most individuals with autism.

To illustrate the problems with stimulus control, consider a situation in which a teacher puts crayons and a coloring book on a table, seats himself or herself and an autistic child next to the table, and says with a friendly smile and eye contact, "Let's color." The teacher intends for these stimuli (the coloring book, crayons, eye contact, and request) to lead to behavioral changes from which he or she can infer emotional and intellectual growth, such as increased interest in the environment and expressions of creativity. In behavioral terminology, the teacher is attempting to signal, instruct, or otherwise communicate with the child through stimulus control procedures. The main basis for this teaching strategy is probably that it often works with average children. However, with autistic children, the strategy is likely to yield one of the following responses: (a) the child may simply remain seated at the table engaged in self-stimulatory behavior such as hand flapping; (b) the child may comply with the instruction; or (c) the child may knock over the table and try to bite the teacher, temporarily putting a stop to teaching efforts. In the first and probably most common case, stimulus control is absent (i.e., the stimuli are neutral or nonfunctional). In the second case, some stimulus control has been established, but it is unclear whether growth will occur. In the third case, stimulus control has also been established, but it yields behaviors that are the opposite of what the teacher intends, perhaps because these behaviors have previously been reinforced and shaped by negative reinforcement (termination of teaching sessions).

In this example, the teacher uses an easily understood, commonsense intervention that has the advantage of being supported by experience with other, more average individuals and by various traditional theories of development. However, the results of this intervention are likely to be disconcerting and disappointing, as there are no empirical data from controlled experiments to indicate that autistic individuals benefit from such interventions. By contrast, behavioral intervention requires more technical knowledge concerning stimulus and reinforcement control. Therefore, it is more complicated to understand and implement, but it comes closer to addressing the problems that autistic individuals present.

The parents and professionals who have to make decisions about a person's treatment are advised to raise the following questions: First, have outcome data been published in professional journals with peer review, and what other scientific research forms the basis for the intervention? Second, what kind of training has the provider received in administering the intervention, whether behavioral or not, and how long did this training last? If the answer is a workshop lasting a week or less with occasional consultations, remain highly skeptical of the adequacy of the services the individual will receive because the problems the individual is facing are likely to be more complex than the provider has training to handle.

One may wonder why it is difficult to give up the belief in a controlling and organizing entity that can be fixed and thus allow the individual freedom to develop. One argument for the existence of such organizing and facilitating brain mechanisms emphasizes the ease of application and efficiency of the intervention. With this argument, there is a more subtle and seductive promise involved: We human beings are born with all kinds of innate skills or capacities, such as prewired grammar (à la Chomsky), morality (à la Kohlberg), and maturational readiness for quick assimilation of cognitive skills (à la Piaget), once exposure has been achieved. The promise of these philosophical positions is that teachers and parents alike have to do less for our children; our nature of being human has a way of steering us on the right track. Such a promise may be false. The unfortunate consequence for individuals with autism and other developmental delays, and for typical children as well, is that less can be done to help them.

How may a behaviorist offer hope? First, consider the individual with autism to be a very young child. Young children do not give evidence of knowing much about the world around them. Second, consider the individual as having failed to develop in the average environment which has taught others, but capable of developing and growing in a special teaching environment as described in this manual. Whether the growth is small or large, satisfaction may be gained. As a parent once said, "My child's daily progress, however small, is my reinforcer."

If all of a person's behaviors become normalized, should the person still be considered autistic or retarded? A behaviorist would likely answer, "No." Many other professionals would likely consider such a situation as "autism in residual state," reflecting the pervasive hold that concepts such as autism and retardation exercise over treatment and research. A good illustration of this traditional position is provided by a teacher who observed a child she had first encountered shortly after the diagnosis of autism was rendered to that child. Two years of 40 hours per week of intensive behavioral treatment later, the teacher observed the same child in a typical class and exclaimed, "I looked and looked for the last couple of days and I want to know: Where is the autism?"

Ethical Considerations

Rather than the placement of atypical persons into discrete diagnostic categories such as autistic, schizophrenic, or mentally retarded, such persons can be viewed as differing in degree and as contributing to the variability of humankind. All living systems possess variability, and variability is essential for physical survival as well as for new directions in science and art. A society that restricts variability (e.g., regimes such as those proposed by Marx and Hitler) is at a disadvantage in facing the future because it does not possess the variability and flexibility necessary for coping with new environments that demand new behaviors in a future we cannot predict.

We came to view atypical persons as belonging to this continuum of variability, as different in degree rather than kind. One can accept such variability not only because of its potential contribution to survival in future environments, but also because it allows the rest of us to remain as we are. Those who differ are our protection in an uncertain future. For this we can admire and appreciate them.

Encouraging variability raises questions about whether to treat atypical persons. Consider Van Gogh, whose art influenced and helped define our culture. His lack of social skills is well known and pronounced; today he may have been diagnosed as having autistic features or having schizophrenia. What a sad fate for us all if we had successfully "treated" him. Successful treatment that centered on helping Van Gogh acquire social skills would have sensitized him to a large range of new rewards. Consequently, he may have left his socially isolated existence and spent time with friends and lovers, leaving little or no time to paint. The same fate may have been met by many other of our outstanding artists and scientists. Einstein, a social isolate, is a case in point. Why, then, treat socially isolated persons with autism? Because without a more varied behavioral repertoire, these persons could not survive on their own. A person with a varied behavioral repertoire has more options and is more likely to survive. In the case of autism, with its severe and multiple behavioral delays, nature may have overshot its mark.

Directions for Future Behavioral Work

Although we believe that the behavioral approach described in this manual addresses many of the questions posed through investigations into autism, we recognize that many other important questions remain unanswered and require further research. Answers to these questions will probably add to, rather than replace, the present approach because this approach is based on inductive, cumulative research instead of a specific hypothesis.

Some of the questions that remain are more practical than theoretical. For example, effective implementation of behavioral procedures requires a major reorganization of the way in which treatment is now delivered: Those who are best suited to deliver such treatment (e.g., special education teachers) need to receive instruction in the specialized skills required to do behavioral work with autistic persons, work in the home and community rather than in clinical settings or schools, change their curriculum, and collaborate closely with all significant individuals (including parents, teachers, siblings, and friends) who interact with the persons treated. Even though these changes might be very difficult to implement, they would result in substantial benefits for persons with autism and their families.

Although the improved functioning of persons with autism is clearly one benefit of intensive behavioral treatment, other practical benefits should not be overlooked.

Providing the treatment may require assigning one professional (e.g., a special education teacher) and several aides to work with one individual on a full-time basis for 2 years, which would currently cost approximately $120,000 and might enable about one half of young autistic children to attain normal levels of functioning. For each person who attains normal functioning, it is likely that more than $2 million in treatment costs alone would be saved by preventing lifelong supervision (special education classes, hospital admissions, residential placements, etc.).

Some problems that remain are both practical and theoretical, such as the development of instruments for identifying children with autism during the first or second year of life. Such identification would help investigators study the early history of autistic children's problems directly instead of having to rely on parents' recollections (cf. Rutter & Lockyer, 1967). Further, early identification may be the key to increasing the proportion of autistic children who attain normal functioning. For example, the group of children who did not reach normal functioning in Lovaas's (1987) Young Autism Project might have succeeded had treatment been started earlier.

Another treatment question is whether the interventions devised for individuals with autism are applicable to persons of other diagnostic groups. For example, persons with schizophrenia have been regarded as quite distinct from persons with autism (see, e.g., Rutter, 1978); however, from a behavioral standpoint, individuals diagnosed as having autistic disorder and individuals who develop schizophrenia, Asperger's syndrome, PDD not otherwise specified, and attention deficit disorder appear to have many similar behavior problems (e.g., poor social skills, attentional deficits, language and cognitive delays, stereotyped behaviors). Because the latter persons are less delayed in development than persons with autism, it seems that they may make progress with behavioral intervention. This would be important to determine because there has been very little progress in the treatment of persons from these other diagnoses.

Research that may offer new conceptual insights can be illustrated in the area of self-stimulatory (ritualistic and high-rate) behaviors. A wide variety of important behavioral phenomena appear to be self-stimulatory. For example, some instances of self-injurious behavior have been found to be self-stimulatory in nature (Favell et al., 1982). Echolalic speech also possesses characteristics of self-stimulatory behavior: It is repetitive, high rate, and shows resistance to extinction. Another conceptual insight provided by research into the area of self-stimulatory behavior is that many persons with autism who undergo intensive behavioral treatment begin to perseverate on spelling certain words, reciting numbers, memorizing calendars, and so on, when they are first exposed to these stimuli (Epstein, Taubman, & Lovaas, 1985). Why certain kinds of materials become part of some persons' self-stimulatory behavior remains a puzzle, but this phenomenon is important to research because it may facilitate treatment and because it is not well explained by learning theory as of yet.

As presented in our theory, individuals with autism generally develop slowly, and skills have to be taught explicitly. How does this development compare with the development of typical individuals? Most developmental theories such as that of Piaget (Flavell, 1963) posit stages during which children quickly and spontaneously transform in a number of ways as a result of a change in cognitive structure. Such theories describe a very different process from what behavioral studies have found in children with autism, but these theories have had considerable influence on the treatment of children with autism (e.g., Schopler & Reichler, 1976). Therefore, it is of interest to find out whether differences between these theories and behavioral data reflect actual differences in development or merely differences in theoretical orientation.

Another area of research that may lead to conceptual insights is further examination into links between behavioral treatment and neurology. Intensive behavioral intervention may act to reverse the neurological problems involved in autistic children's problems, especially considering that environmental interventions have been shown to bring about major changes in neurological structure under some circumstances, particularly in infants (Neville, 1985). Through investigation into this area, we may come close to providing a "cure" for the behavioral difficulties demonstrated by children with autism. The interventions applied through these studies may also prevent difficulties that have been found to emerge in autistic persons later in life, such as seizures and high serotonin levels (W. H. Green, 1988). Recent advances in brain imaging techniques (Sokoloff, 1985) may facilitate the study of brain–environment relationships in persons with autism. This in turn would open up new research areas and contribute to the understanding of the neurological deviations that underlie autism and the effects of environmental interventions on neurological activity.

Evaluation of Behavioral Treatment

CHAPTER 3

The small steps forward and the contributions made by hundreds of investigators have yielded the kind of outcome we have learned to anticipate in science. After some 40 years of behavioral treatment–research based on some 90 years of basic research in learning processes, thousands of scientific studies have been published, forming the many basic components of behavioral treatment. Cumulatively, enough data-based treatment procedures have been developed to yield a most favorable outcome: major improvements in intellectual, educational, social, and emotional functioning in children with developmental delays. This success includes average gains of approximately 10 to 20 IQ points on standardized tests of intelligence (e.g., Anderson, Avery, DiPietro, Edwards, & Christian, 1987; Harris, Handleman, Gordon, Kristoff, & Fuentes, 1991; Lovaas, 1987), similar gains on other standardized tests (e.g., Anderson et al., 1987; Hoyson, Jamieson, & Strain, 1984; McEachin, Smith, & Lovaas, 1993), and placement in less restrictive classrooms than those typically offered to children with developmental delays (e.g., Fenske, Zalenski, Krantz, & McClannahan, 1985; Lovaas, 1987). Smith (1999) provides a comprehensive review of these and similar studies.

In this chapter we illustrate how intensive and early behavioral treatment of individuals with developmental delays evolved, and we do so by focusing on data from treatment outcome studies. We also describe the criteria for appropriate treatment that resulted from the development of behavioral intervention. Note that in this discussion terms such as *we* and *our* are often used for editorial purposes. This should not be taken to imply that the major components of the treatment program were developed at the University of California, Los Angeles (UCLA). Rather, the design of the treatment was based on extensive research published in peer-reviewed journals by independent investigators. Most of the studies have been replicated. Also, note that none of these studies have reported a major breakthrough. Rather, progress in treatment developed in a gradual and stepwise fashion, such as that done in the building of a pyramid where a solid foundation (learning theory research) forms the basis for adding additional structure. Research projects at UCLA help to illustrate this development. Investigators have contended that the best way to know what aspects of a treatment make that treatment effective is by studying individual components of the treatment separately before performing an outcome study (Johnston, 1988).

The 1973 Treatment Study

The first comprehensive treatment study was started in 1964 and reflected many blind alleys in our own design (Lovaas, Koegel, Simmons, & Long, 1973). First, we worked with the hope that if we removed the children we treated from their natural environments and placed them in an institutional setting, they would be free from distracting stimuli and we would be in a better position to treat them. Second, we hoped that 1 year of intensive one-on-one treatment (2,000-plus hours) would be enough and that treatment gains would last. Finally, we focused our major efforts on developing language because we hoped that language would be pivotal in facilitating improvement in untreated behaviors. None of these hopes were realized. However, major gains in teaching complex behaviors such as language were observed. Many have questioned the efficacy of behavioral interventions in building language (Chomsky, 1965). Nonetheless, studies have indicated that effective procedures for teaching language to children with autism and other developmental delays can be derived from laboratory research on operant conditioning involving discrimination learning, discrete trials, prompting and prompt fading, shaping, and chaining (see Chapters 10 and 16).

To illustrate, beginning steps in language training involve teaching students to understand simple instructions (Lovaas, 1977). Subsequently, students are taught to imitate simple sounds, followed by combining these sounds into syllables and then words (Lovaas, Berberich, Perloff, & Schaeffer, 1966). Once students are able to imitate words, they are taught to label items and events and then to request favorite objects and activities (Risley & Wolf, 1967). Subsequently, students are taught to combine words into simple sentences such as "I want (item)" and "This is an (object)" (Risley, Hart, & Doke, 1972). Students who proceed at a rapid rate may then be instructed in how to use abstract concepts, including *yes–no* (Hung, 1980), plurals (Baer, Guess, & Sherman, 1972), adjectives (Risley et al., 1972), prepositions, pronouns, opposites such as *big–little* and *hot–cold*, and time relations such as *first–last* and *before–after* (Lovaas, 1977). Once these concepts are mastered, students are taught to ask questions (Hung, 1977; Lovaas, 1977) and engage in simple conversations (Gaylord-Ross, Haring, Breen, & Pitts-Conway, 1984; Lovaas, 1977).

Researchers have also described procedures for facilitating conversational speech between children with autism and normally developing peers (Charlop & Milstein, 1989; Gaylord-Ross et al., 1984; Haring, Roger, Lee, Breen, & Gaylord-Ross, 1986). Thus, experimentally validated procedures exist for helping students progress from being mute or echolalic to possessing some or all of the language skills displayed by typical children and adults. Children can also be helped to develop learning strategies such as nonverbal imitation and to reduce tantrums and self-injurious behaviors.

Despite all of our successes, we may have made the most progress by recognizing our mistakes. Our assumption that increases in language would be associated with concurrent improvements in other areas of functioning was not supported. This was a major disappointment because we had hoped that, once the children learned to talk, they would develop the kind of response generalization that would "push them over" into normalcy. Instead, the children revealed themselves to be without much prior knowledge. A "little child" did not seem to be hiding inside, waiting for the opportunity to come out from the autistic shell and talk with us, as many theoretical formulations had postulated (and still do). Nonetheless, the acquisition of language gave the clients access to future educational environments where additional appropriate behaviors could be built (a kind of "successive" response interaction).

The second lesson we learned during this time concerned the lack of generalization across environments, including posttreatment environments (see Stokes & Baer, 1977, for an instructive paper on ways to increase generalization across behaviors and environments). When we discharged the clients to the state hospital from which they came, they inevitably regressed. It was heartbreaking to observe Pam and Rick, children who had gained so much with us, slowly but surely lose the skills they had acquired. When we brought the children back for treatment a second time, they recovered many of the gains they had made during the first treatment period, only to lose them again after their second discharge. The data we secured before, during, and after treatment served as the most important guide for development of the project as it stands today. It may have been possible for us to fool ourselves without such data; others apparently had. By that time we knew there were no shortcuts. Instead, we realized there was a great deal of hard work ahead.

At about this same time, we learned another bitter lesson: Colleagues from other orientations considered it extremely difficult to adopt and test treatment programs developed from the behavioral perspective. Our pleas to continue working with the children placed in the hospital were met with immediate rejection by the hospital staff. It was their opinion that the children were to be regressed in order to recover the childhood experiences they had been deprived of. Only then, the hospital staff asserted, could the children develop into normal individuals. The staff could not imagine how this behavior modification program, the same one that trained dogs and pigeons into becoming robots, could ever actually facilitate the development of human beings.

Much in contrast to the children placed in the state hospital, the children who were discharged to parents eager to be informed about our treatment did much better at maintaining the skills gained through the intervention. The important role parents play as colleagues in treatment is discussed later in this manual.

The 1987 UCLA Young Autism Project

Six observations made during the 1973 treatment–research study played a major role in the design of our next effort (Lovaas, 1987). First, we made the serendipitous discovery that the youngest children in the 1973 study made the greatest progress. Second, we learned that treatment effects were situation specific. Thus, we moved treatment away from a hospital or clinic setting and into the children's homes and other everyday environments. Third, we found limited evidence for response generalization and therefore designed treatments for most or all of the children's behaviors. Fourth, we learned that parents could become skilled teachers, and they were the best allies one could ask for in accelerating and maintaining treatment gains. Fifth, we offered treatment for most of the children's waking hours for 2 or more years, and taught the children to develop friendships with typical peers in an attempt to continue treatment at that level. This arrangement more closely resembled that available to typical children who learn from their environment (parents, peers, etc.) from morning to night, vacations included. Finally, and most important, by the 1970s we possessed a large range of data-based procedures that could be amalgamated so as to enrich our treatment program. Through these procedures, our treatment expanded to consist of hundreds of separate teaching programs.

The 1987 UCLA Young Autism Project generated major and lasting increases in intellectual, educational, social, emotional, and other aspects of behavior (McEachin et al., 1993). The question is often raised as to why the younger children did so much better than the older ones. There could be several reasons for this. One reason may be that the intensive treatment (40 one-on-one hours per week) was started early enough so that a sizable minority (47%) could "catch up" and acquire an adequate amount of language, social, play, and self-help behaviors so as to be successfully mainstreamed among typical children in regular preschools. Once kindergarten was successfully passed, the children went on to successfully pass the first grade and subsequent classes in public schools. The development of friendships by these children with average children may have helped to build further prosocial behavior and protect against relapse.

There are other potential explanations for why younger children did better than older children. Laboratory studies on animals have shown that alterations in neurological structure are quite possible as a result of changes in the environment in the first years of life (Sirevaag & Greenough, 1988). There is reason to believe that alterations are also possible in young children. For example, children under 3 years of age overproduce neurons, dendrites, axons, and synapses. Huttenlocher (1984) hypothesized that, with appropriate stimulation from the environment, this overproduction might allow infants and preschoolers to compensate for neurological anomalies much more completely than older children. Caution is needed in generalizing these findings from studies on average children to early intervention with children with autism, particularly because the exact nature of the neurological anomalies in children with autism is unclear at present (e.g., Rutter & Schopler, 1987). Nevertheless, the findings suggest that intensive early intervention could help compensate for neurological anomalies in children with autism. Finding evidence for this type of compensation would help explain why the treatment in the UCLA study was effective. More generally, it might contribute to a better understanding of brain–behavior relationships in young children.

It is a compliment to the field of Applied Behavior Analysis that literally hundreds of investigators have been able to generate thousands of replicable studies that add in a cumulative manner to a vast array of useful knowledge. No other area within clinical psychology, special education, or other helping professions within the social sciences has accomplished this. Along the same lines, there is every reason to believe that progress in other fields (e.g., special education, psychotherapy) will not occur until such a strategy of replicable and cumulative findings is established.

Adversity

It was not always smooth sailing during our investigations. We would have been in a better position to protect ourselves from disappointments had we been forewarned of the adversity we would experience. Parents who have sought financial assistance from state agencies, such as school districts, to help pay for their children's treatment have too often been subjected to major distortions about the nature of behavioral treatment (see Chapter 40). Protection from disappointment for a service provider is also important when it appears that he or she must stay in it for the long run, as when trying to help severely disadvantaged children and their parents.

An area of disappointment we experienced pertains to dissemination. There is at least a 25-year delay between what is now known about how to teach children with developmental delays and what has been adopted. Paradoxically, special education teachers appear eager to receive training in behavioral treatment and are in a good position to deliver such treatment. It is difficult to know where the obstacles are. When treatment *is* adopted, it is often a watered-down version. Watering down of treatment is nothing new; it has occurred since the inception of attempts to treat individuals with developmental delays (cf. Lane's, 1976, description of Itard's work).

Another area of disappointment centers on pronouncements by colleagues representing other areas of investigation. These take on numerous forms. There has been an alarming tendency in psychological treatment–research to attribute failure to the client, as in invoking organic limitations when treatment fails. For example, in their review of research of autistic children, DeMeyer, Hingtgen, and Jackson (1981) concluded that "infantile autism is . . . accompanied by . . . permanent intellectual/behavioral deficits" (p. 432), adding that no one would even give lip service to changing such deficits. Zigler and Seitz (1980) suggested that one would fail in one's efforts to alter IQ scores to any substantial degree. Some also attribute failures to defects of the investigator. Spitz (1986) characterized those who have reported increases in intellectual functioning accompanying educational enrichments as "fools, frauds, and charlatans." Still other colleagues propose that behavioral treatment is harmful. Bettelheim (1967) attacked behavioral treatment as follows: "Perhaps we may say of the operant conditioning procedures what has been said of lobotomy: that lobotomy changes a functional disorder that is potentially recoverable into an organic one for which there is no treatment" (p. 411). More recently, Greenspan (1992) presented "behavioral schools of thought" as an example of a "common unhelpful approach" that "ignores the delayed child's many needs" and allows "disordered patterns to become more stereotyped and more perseverative as [the children] grow" (p. 5). These comments are obviously inconsistent with findings from scientifically sound research.

Implications of Data from Behavioral Treatment Research

Data from research that supports the need for persons with developmental delays to receive the comprehensive treatment described in this manual are summarized in this section. First, there is no evidence that the changing of one behavior changes any of the individual's other behaviors to a significant degree. There is no evidence for the existence of a "pivotal" or "critical" behavior which, when altered, suddenly brings about large-scale progress in overall functioning. For example, with increased language skills, there is little to no evidence that play behavior and self-help skills show a concurrent change. On the other hand, an increase in language skills should facilitate the teaching of later skills such as peer play and academic achievements. Similarly, helping an individual reduce tantrums and other interfering behaviors should facilitate the teacher's effectiveness and help the individual enter a less restrictive environment where alternate behaviors may further be taught. If scores on tests of intelligence represent what an individual has learned from his environment up to the time of testing, then one may reasonably expect such scores to increase with increased exposure to effective educational environments. Increased attention, higher IQs, and improvement in emotional functioning appear to represent the only areas that develop spontaneously (as side-effects) during treatment.

Second, little or no data exist to support the notion that the changes in behaviors learned in one environment or taught by one or two teachers transfer to other environments or to other persons. Rather, there is evidence for "situation specificity" in treatment effects. This implies that the individual must be treated in all significant environments (home, community, and school) and by all significant persons (family, teachers, and friends).

Third, there is strong evidence of relapse if treatment is discontinued. The only data-based exception to this can be observed in very young children with autism and developmental delays who are treated with intensive behavioral intervention through which a significant minority can be successfully mainstreamed and achieve normal functioning (McEachin et al., 1993). Other than such children, data from research implies that clients must be in special educational environments all their lives. In short, optimal treatment effects require a much more comprehensive intervention than previously considered.

Criteria for Appropriate Treatment

It has been possible to formulate a consensus among many scientific researchers and practitioners that appropriate treatment contains the following elements (Simeonnson, Olley, & Rosenthal, 1987).

▶ 1. **A behavioral emphasis.** This involves not only imposing structure and rewarding appropriate behaviors when they occur, but also applying some more technical interventions. These interventions include conducting discrete trials, shaping by successive approximations, producing shifts in stimulus control, establishing stimulus discriminations, and teaching imitation (R. L. Koegel & Koegel, 1988).

▶ 2. **Family participation.** Parents and other family members should participate actively in teaching the person who is developmentally delayed. Without such participation, gains made in professional settings such as special education programs, clinics, or hospitals rarely lead to improved functioning in the home or community (Bartak, 1978; Lovaas et al., 1973).

▶ 3. **One-to-one instruction.** For approximately the first 6 to 12 months of treatment, instruction should be individualized rather than in groups because persons with autism and other developmental delays learn more readily in one-on-one situations (R. L. Koegel, Rincover, & Egel, 1982). This training needs to be supervised by degreed professionals educated in Applied Behavior Analysis and trained in one-on-one treatment. Treatment may be administered by people who have been thoroughly trained in behavioral treatment, including undergraduate students and family members (O. I. Lovaas & Smith, 1988).

▶ 4. **Integration.** Prior to integration in a group setting, the individual should be taught as many socially appropriate behaviors as possible. When an individual is ready to enter a group situation, the group should be as typical (normal or average) as possible. Persons with autism perform better when integrated with typical persons than when placed with other autistic individuals (Strain, 1983). In the presence of other persons with autism, any social and language skills the individual may have developed usually disappear within minutes, presumably because these behaviors are not reciprocated (Smith, Lovaas, & Watthen-Lovaas, 2002). Mere exposure to typical persons, however, is not sufficient to facilitate appropriate behavior. Persons with autism require explicit instruction on how to interact with their peers (Strain, 1983).

▶ 5. **Comprehensiveness.** Persons with autism initially need to be taught virtually everything. They have few appropriate behaviors, and new behaviors have to be taught one by one. As mentioned earlier, this is because teaching one behavior rarely leads to the emergence of other behaviors not directly taught (Lovaas & Smith, 1988). For example, teaching language skills does not immediately lead to the emergence of social skills, and teaching one language skill, such as prepositions, does not lead directly to the emergence of other language skills, such as mastery of pronouns.

▶ 6. **Intensity.** Perhaps as a corollary for the need for comprehensiveness, an effective intervention requires a very large number of hours, about 40 hours per week (Lovaas & Smith, 1988). Ten hours per week is inadequate (Lovaas & Smith, 1988), as is 20 hours (Anderson et al., 1987). Although increases in cognitive function (as reflected in IQ scores) may be observed, this should be understood to mean not that the student will be successfully integrated among typical peers, but rather that the student may regress unless treatment is continued. The majority of the 40 hours, at least during the first 6 to 12 months of intervention, should place a major emphasis on remedying language deficits (Lovaas, 1977). Later, this time may be divided between promoting peer integration and continued remedying of language deficits.

▶ 7. **Individual differences.** Large individual differences exist in students' responses to behavioral treatment. Under optimal conditions, a sizable minority of children gain and maintain so-called normal functioning (McEachin et al., 1993). These are children who can be labeled auditory learners. The remaining children, visual learners, do not reach normal functioning with behavioral treatment at this time and are likely to require intensive one-on-one treatment for the remainder of their lives to maintain their existing skills and continue to develop new skills. Programs designed to facilitate communication for visual learners appear promising but are in need of further research and outcome data (see Chapters 29 and 30).

▶ 8. **Duration.** Treatment must last for the lifetime of the person with autism because termination of treatment is likely to lead to loss of treatment gains (Lovaas et al., 1973). As previously discussed, the only data-based exception to this is for that proportion of young children who reach normal functioning with intensive and early behavioral intervention by the time they are 7 years of age.

▶ 9. **Quality control.** Given the visibility of the UCLA data, it is important to specify as many dimensions of the treatment as possible so that it can be replicated by others. This becomes particularly important because almost anyone can falsely present oneself as qualified to deliver such treatment by, for example, having attended a 1-day or 1-week seminar and having read *The ME Book* (Lovaas, 1981) or the present manual. To help protect against potential misunderstandings, we strongly suggest that the reader refer to Chapter 34. To further protect against misunderstandings, a system of certifying aides needs to be created, helping to ensure that the quality of behavioral treatment remains high. The UCLA certification project may help guide such an effort. There are currently two levels of certification through the project: Level I (Staff Aide) and Level II (Supervising Aide).

Criteria for Certification at Level I, Staff Aide

1. Take the UCLA course Psychology 170A (Behavior Modification) or a similar course in learning theory that provides the theoretical and empirical bases for the experimental analysis of behavior and their application to autism and other developmental delays.

2. If Requirement 1 is passed with a grade of B or better, enter Psychology 170B (Fieldwork in Behavior Modification), which includes lectures and supervised practicum experience in one-on-one treatment for a minimum of 6 months (not less than 60 hours of one-on-one treatment) supervised by a Level II aide.

3. After completing Requirements 1 and 2, submit a 15-minute videotape of the applicant conducting one-on-one treatment with a client with whom the applicant has worked a minimum of 10 hours. The Level II aide who supervises the client selects one program that is currently on acquisition for the child in each of the following areas: (a) verbal imitation (if the child has not yet begun the Verbal Imitation Program, a component of the Nonverbal Imitation Program is selected; if the child has

mastered all components of the Verbal Imitation Program, a conversation-related program is selected); (b) receptive language; and (c) expressive language (if the child has not yet begun expressive language programs, a component of the Nonverbal Imitation Program is selected [if a Nonverbal Imitation Program component was used in {a}, this category should consist of a second component of the Nonverbal Imitation Program; for example, if {a} was imitation of facial expressions, this category may involve imitation of drawing or block building]). The applicant is videotaped as he or she conducts each program for 5 minutes. Only the applicant, the client, and the cameraperson are present during these sessions, and the cameraperson refrains from making any comments on the applicant's performance until after the completion of the videotaping. Scoring is based on a measure developed by R. L. Koegel, Russo, and Rincover (1977).

Criteria for Certification at Level II, Supervising Aide

1. Obtain Level I certification.
2. Complete an intensive 9-month, full-time internship or 1 year of full-time service as a staff member supervised by a Level II aide and a doctoral-level director of clinical services. For at least 3 of these months, the applicant must be engaged in training novice aides (i.e., aides who have not yet obtained Level II certification).
3. Complete assigned readings on the application of learning theory and obtain a satisfactory grade on a test based on these readings.
4. Obtain satisfactory ratings from the Level II supervisor and from the novice aides trained by the applicant.
5. After completing Requirements 1 through 4, submit a 20-minute videotape of the applicant conducting one-on-one treatment with a client with whom the aide has never worked. Based on a review of the client's records, the applicant teaches novel items to the client in each of the following areas: (a) verbal imitation (if the child has not yet begun the Verbal Imitation Program, a component of the Nonverbal Imitation Program is selected; if the child has mastered all components of the Verbal Imitation Program, a conversation-related program is selected); (b) receptive language; (c) expressive language (if the child has not yet begun expressive language programs, a component of the Nonverbal Imitation Program is selected [if a Nonverbal Imitation Program component was used in {a}, this category should consist of a second component of the Nonverbal Imitation Program; for example, if {a} was imitation of facial expressions, this category may involve imitation of drawing or block building]); and (d) interactive play. Only the applicant, the client, and the cameraperson are present during these sessions, and the cameraperson refrains from making any comments on the applicant's performance until after completion of the videotaping. The completed videotape is scored by a reviewer in the Multi-site Young Autism Project.
6. Obtain recertification every 2 years by submitting a videotape like the one in Requirement 5. Only Level II aides are authorized to supervise treatment or conduct workshops. All applications for Level I and Level II aides are reviewed by doctoral-level persons who are key personnel in the Multi-site Young Autism Project (NIMH 1 R01 MH48863-01A4).

Are Other Treatments Effective?

In deciding how to treat individuals with developmental delays, it is crucial to obtain information about the effectiveness of the various treatments that claim to be of help. A detailed review is not provided in this manual because there are several recent and comprehensive discussions and evaluations of the many treatments proposed to help persons with autism and other developmental delays. For example, G. Green (1996a) has provided certain guidelines by which one can evaluate whether a given treatment has proven to be effective. Facilitated Communication and Sensory Integration are used as examples to illustrate how such an evaluation may be conducted. G. Green (1996b) has also provided an assessment of early behavioral intervention for autism, describing the strengths and weaknesses of this particular treatment approach.

Smith (1996) wrote a critical review of a large number of alternative interventions, such as Project TEACCH; the Higashi School; sensory-motor therapies such as Sensory Integration, Auditory Integration, and Facilitated Communication; and psychotherapies such as Floor-Time, Holding Therapy, Option Method, and Gentle Teaching. It is distressing to note that, despite the wide use of these therapies, either outcome data are missing altogether or available data fail to support the effectiveness claimed by the originators of these programs. Likewise, many individuals with autism are provided with speech and language therapy, yet there appear to be no scientific studies demonstrating that speech and language therapy is effective with this population. The Natural Language Paradigm, Incidental Teaching, Pivotal Response Training, and Fast For Word have similarly not been supported by objective data pertaining to long-term and comprehensive treatment outcomes. While many treatments lack supporting scientific data, some treatments can actually cause harm.

Smith (1996) concluded his review of treatments by noting the large scientific support for behavioral treatment and advised parents that the best initial course of action may be to concentrate exclusively on carrying out behavioral treatment as well as possible rather than looking for ways to supplement it with other treatments. On the other hand, for individuals who are found to progress slowly in behavioral treatment, alternative interventions should be supplementary, although no guidelines exist at this time for deciding which ones.

When evaluating whether or not to apply a treatment, the cost of treatment should be considered. This issue relates to whether funds are distributed equally across those who need help or absorbed by a small group of individuals. Similar issues deal with whether the cost of treatment will eventually result in savings to the state. That consideration involves whether the client at some point will be able to seek employment, pay taxes to repay the state's expense, and no longer be in need of services.

A conservative estimate of the incidence of autism can be placed at 1 in 250, which means that in the United States approximately 800,000 people are diagnosed with autism. Autism is the third most common childhood disorder after cerebral palsy and mental retardation, and occurs at a higher rate than childhood cancer, cystic fibrosis, and Down syndrome. Autism has been estimated to cost the United States in excess of $10 billion per year. Intensive early behavioral intervention is estimated at $5,000 per month (slightly over $30 per hour), or $60,000 per year. The average length of treatment for the 47% of children who reach normal functioning is 2 years, resulting in a total expense of $120,000 per child. Such persons will in all likelihood be employed and pay taxes at some time after treatment. The estimated average cost per individual who needs lifelong protective and institutional care is $40,000 per year or $2.4 million for the 60 or more years that such services will be rendered. The savings accrued from intensive behavioral treatment for those who do not recover is also substantial (Jacobson, Mulick, & Green, 1996). A recent study by Smith, Groen, and Wynn (2000) compares the effectiveness of early and intensive behavioral intervention for two groups of children, one group diagnosed with autism and the other with pervasive developmental disorder–not otherwise specified (PDD-NOS). Data show that the children diagnosed with PDD-NOS may have gained even more from the treatment than the children diagnosed with autism. Besides showing support for the continuity model (see Chapter 2), these data support the inference that it is economically wise to invest in behavioral treatment.

Preparatory Steps

CHAPTER 4

Certain treatment guidelines transcend techniques specific to the individual programs discussed in this book. Those 11 guidelines are described in this chapter.

▶ **1. Learn how to teach.** Become an effective teacher and teach the student in his natural environment for as long as possible. A student's home is less restrictive than, for example, an institution, and it provides for more opportunities to acquire behaviors essential for increased independence. These behaviors range from basic self-help skills, such as going to the toilet, dressing and washing oneself, eating appropriately, and taking out the garbage, to more complex behaviors, such as crossing the street, forming attachments to parents and siblings, and meeting typical children in the neighborhood.

If you are the student's parent, make certain you are not excluded from learning how to teach. To become a competent teacher, you should be involved from the first hour on; do not make your start when programs become complex and difficult to teach. As a parent, you have the important task of extending treatment to most of the student's waking hours, including weekends, holidays, and vacations. Also, when you are adequately informed, you can make decisions about who can offer the best help to your child. There will likely be many professionals who will want to treat your child, but they may be unable to demonstrate effective treatment. Gaining your own knowledge about proper treatment is also important. Professional persons come and go; they may serve you now, but they may not be there in the future. If your child survives you, he will continue to need help. Therefore, begin to prepare for your child's future while both of you are young.

Another reason why parents should be actively involved in treatment is that most students do not reach normal functioning. If one-on-one intensive treatment is terminated for such students, data show that they may regress. For students who make moderate progress in treatment, there are indications that, as they become adolescents and adults, they may experience feelings of depression as they recognize they are different from typical individuals. However, if parents remain involved in treatment from early on, it is likely that they will be able to maintain and increase the gains the student has made because they can hire and train new teachers.

For students who do reach normal functioning, it is likely that they will not regress because they develop friendships with typical peers who help them continue to develop socially, emotionally, and intellectually. However, even for those who reach normal functioning, minor difficulties may persist after the intensive one-on-one treatment is terminated. An informed parent will be able to identify such problems and treat them. For example, a student may express reluctance to play with peers and a preference for playing alone on a computer. An informed parent will let the student have access to the computer provided the student plays with peers first. Increased skills in playing with peers may eventually make the social environment more reinforcing than the computer.

If for no other reason, parents should become involved in treatment because it may be demoralizing to be a passive observer and see relatively young persons with no parenting experience help the child make progress in reducing tantrums, increasing cooperation, and learning skills such as imitation, toy play, and language. To help avoid this scenario, it is best for parents to become involved at the outset of treatment. During the first hours of treatment, other persons will be present who are also beginners and receiving training for the first time.

▶ **2. Realize that improvement is slow.** Know that some students progress rapidly, whereas others learn at a slower rate. It is important not to overstress the student based on hopes of a sudden "breakthrough." Reports of such breakthroughs may provide entertaining reading, but they achieve very little else. Through the process of working with students with developmental delays, teachers often learn a very important lesson: not only to accept, but also to respect persons with autism even if they are not "perfect" or in possession of highly developed splinter skills. A student who works hard is likely to acquire dignity and equality with others, even if the student does not recover. A student's progress, however incremental and gradual, is likely to be a parent's best therapy.

▶ **3. Conquer guilt.** Parents of typical children often feel guilty about not having done enough for their children, or about having done something that will eventually lead to problems. Parents of children with developmental delays are particularly prone to guilt and depression no matter how much evidence demonstrates they did not cause their children's problems. Guilt and depression can be very handicapping states, forcing a parent or teacher to relinquish control. Do not let the student frighten you into quitting; doing so will only hurt the student in the long run. Think of it this way: All of her life the student has failed to understand what responsible parents and teachers have wanted her to understand. Naturally, then, the student does not want to enter learning situations which, she reasons, will introduce her to more failure. The student's angry emotional outbursts may lead you to give in to her and allow her to escape the teaching situation, inadvertently strengthening her tantrumous behavior.

▶ **4. Form a treatment team.** Typical persons learn all their waking hours; the student you work with should be equally provided with this opportunity. The difference between your student and a typical individual is that the latter picks up information in a more informal and incidental manner, whereas the person you work with needs a great deal more structure. The more hours of one-on-one treatment the student receives, the more progress he will make. We recommend that the student be provided with 40 hours per week of one-on-one behavioral treatment, and that gains made through this treatment be extended in a more informal way throughout the student's remaining waking hours. We also recommend that during the first 6 to 12 months of treatment, all teaching take place in the student's home environment, being extended into the community in gradual steps thereafter. If you are the student's parent, you may help provide some of the treatment hours, and you and other family members should help to generalize the skills acquired in the structured one-on-one learning sessions to the evenings and to different environments.

To take on such a large job, you need to form a treatment team. Forming a treatment team is an unusual task for most people, and it may initially seem daunting. However, once you start a system of recruitment, this task will likely become relatively simple and efficient. The three typical sources of prospective team members are local colleges or high schools, family members, and friends. Persons from high school or college may either work for course credit or for pay. If they work for pay, their hourly wage should be comparable to that of other paid positions advertised on campus. To recruit high school and college students, you may want to place ads in student newspapers and student employment offices, or post flyers near the departments of psychology, speech therapy, and education. A flyer might read as follows:

Position Available

Work with a team providing intensive behavioral intervention for a student with developmental delays. Experience in behavioral treatment helpful but not necessary. We will provide training.

Time commitment: 6–10 hours per week.
Call 555-5555.

A more efficient way to recruit team members may be to locate faculty members in psychology, education, and related departments and ask them if you may give a 5- or 10-minute presentation in their class describing what autism and other developmental delays are like and the kind of help you need. If your student does not display too many disruptive behaviors, introduce the student to the class. If the student has already made some progress in treatment, show the class what he has learned and how these skills were taught. There seems to have been a large change in the interests of college and high school students over the last 50 years. They seem to have become more mature, career oriented, and compassionate in their attitudes toward individuals with developmental delays.

When persons express interest in working as a part of your team, have them meet with you at home and ask them questions about their experience with individuals of the same age as your student. If you like the way a person presents himself or herself, and if he or she seems easy to instruct and not full of predetermined opinions about how to teach, then that applicant is likely to make a good teacher. Try to avoid persons who are "experts" in another area of treatment because they may be close-minded and thus very difficult to train.

Assemble a team of three to eight people to perform a total of 40 hours of treatment per week. To help avoid burnout, no one person should provide more than 4 to 6 hours of one-on-one treatment per day. Few persons are good at estimating when and if they will burn out; it typically occurs quite quickly, and the person who burns out may want to leave within a day or two. If a person works 6 hours in a row, then each hour should be interspersed with moving the student out of the one-on-one situation to more informal environments for the purpose of generalizing mastered gains. Generalizing treatment gains to the community is less intense than one-on-one treatment both for the teacher and the student, and it is less likely to result in burnout.

▶ **5. Learn how to manage your team.** Try to arrange the work so that each person stays with the team for at least 6 months. If you have hired only two or three people, ask them to advise you 2 or 3 weeks before leaving the team, giving you the opportunity to train a new member without losing treatment hours. During this sort of transition period, it is ideal to belong to an organization of parents who have had similar problems and who have employed other teachers. Through such an organization, you are likely to find replacement teachers because teachers are often able to work with more than one student. In addition, you may gain a larger pool of experienced teachers to draw from when recruiting new teachers than that provided by the sources mentioned earlier.

▶ **6. Learn how to train your team.** You will make some progress by having each member of the team read this manual. However, it is highly unlikely that you will maximize the student's gains without consultation from someone already experienced in providing behavioral treatment. Some suggestions on identifying an experienced consultant and what to expect from such a consultant are provided in Chapter 34.

When with your team, be sure to provide ample positive feedback and refrain from harsh criticism. Working analogously with the saying "One gets more bees with honey than with vinegar" is a good strategy. In addition, avoid singling out and praising one particular member of the team as the "wonder aide." Doing so may divide the team. Do not talk about a team member behind his or her back. Do not give lavish gifts, free dinners, and the like to the team; their salaries, course credit, and your appreciation should be enough. Do not become obligated to any one person beyond his or her work contract by accepting unusual favors such as babysitting or extra hours. By the same token, refrain from asking for such favors.

It is absolutely essential that the team meet together with the student weekly. During these team meetings, each member should work with the student in front of the team to get feedback regarding his or her performance. It is essential that this feedback be carried out in a constructive manner and that more positive than negative feedback is given. You want your treatment team to feel that they are important to your student's progress and that they are appreciated. Over time, the treatment team will become increasingly cohesive in that each member will strengthen the skills of the other members.

During weekly meetings, the student's gains and problems of the previous week are to be reviewed, difficulties demonstrated, and feedback sought on how to alleviate these difficulties. It is impossible for any one person to solve all the intricate problems the student will present. Rather, solutions to problems require a group effort in which each person receives some reinforcement for contributing potential solutions. Weekly meetings should be work oriented and last for 1 to 2 hours. Socializing should take place after the meeting.

If a team member does not attend weekly meetings, repeatedly arrives late to treatment sessions, introduces new programs without consulting the team, resists feedback regarding treatment procedures, or complains about pay or other team members, have this person leave your team before he or she does any damage. Such a person is not sufficiently equipped to conduct the important work of teaching individuals with developmental delays.

▶ **7. Be careful not to be misled about treatment outcome.** Parents of children with developmental delays love their children as much as other groups of parents love their children, but they are probably more anxious and vulnerable than other parents when seeking help for their children. Anyone familiar with the history of autism treatment has become aware of the misleading statements and promises that helping professionals have made over the last several years.

As mentioned earlier, Chapter 34 provides some guidelines concerning the selection of qualified behavioral treatment consultants. At present, almost anyone can claim to be competent at delivering behavioral treatment for young children with autism. The fact is, however, that early and intensive behavioral treatment of children with autism is a specialty within the field of Applied Behavior Analysis. To become proficient at delivering such treatment, a considerable amount of training is required. One does not reach proficiency by reading this or a similar teaching manual. Nor does one reach proficiency by taking a course in behavioral psychology, attending a workshop, or participating in a seminar. Before deciding on a consultant, carefully evaluate his or her credentials.

Most parents have gained some information about early and intensive behavioral intervention and may have been led to believe that 47% of all the children treated with this intervention reach normal educational, emotional, and social functioning. However, this statistic has been obtained only under the most optimal clinic-based treatment conditions. Workshop-based treatment is estimated to yield a recovery rate between 10% and 20% provided the workshop leader is qualified. The recovery outcome for workshops led by persons who are not qualified may not exceed 5% (see Chapter 34). Without a qualified workshop leader but with a team of involved teachers who work together and pool their resources, it is likely that the student will make steady progress, although it is not yet known to what degree. A student who works hard to get better and gain independence, however, is a joy to observe even if she does not reach normalcy.

▶ **8. Do not allow the inherent demands placed on parents through intensive behavioral treatment to jeopardize**

the marriage of the parents or their relationship with other children in the family. An intact family is a most important contribution to the student's development. Sometimes the mother, the father, or both parents become overly involved in their child's treatment; they think of nothing else and talk of nothing else. Other children, close family, and friends are neglected. Under these circumstances we have seen parents lose their personal relationship. The romance that brought them together and is essential throughout married life is suppressed. Such overinvolvement is dangerous because it may end in divorce.

Parents must take care of themselves and of each other. Take a vacation from autism every so often. We recommend arranging for respite care and leaving the house for 24 hours every 3 weeks or so. Check into a hotel some 60 miles away from home and forbid all talk about autism. The caretaker may call the parents' cell phone number *only* if absolutely necessary. No calls home should be made. Make no demands for intimacy; relax and let it happen naturally. If it does not, it may develop next time. Anticipate that the guilt about leaving home even for the short time of 24 hours will be strong. However, keep in mind that many or most children with autism are stronger than you might expect; coming home after 24 hours away and finding that all is well may be the best treatment for guilt.

Some persons may suggest that the student's father or mother move away to a treatment facility with his or her child while the other parent remains at home some hundreds of miles away. It is difficult to maintain a marriage if the husband and wife see each other only one or two weekends per month. By the same token, treatment should not be received from or provided to a family who has to sell or mortgage their home to pay for services. This is too risky an investment when one considers that a student may not reach normal functioning but rather may require lifelong care.

▶ **9. Enter the student in school after he masters the appropriate imitative, self-help, and language skills.** In selecting a class for the student, visit several classrooms. The following points are important to consider when choosing a teacher and a particular classroom: (a) Rather than choosing a teacher who is waiting for maturational stages to be activated with mere exposure to educational material (à la Piaget), select a teacher who is challenging and prefers structure. (b) Avoid classrooms with several students who have developmental delays because they will not aid your student's development of appropriate behaviors. (c) Do not disclose to the teacher the student's formal diagnosis. Many teachers have been informed that autism and other developmental delays are progressively deteriorating conditions that cannot be altered, and many have been told that parents caused the student's problems. State instead that the student has a delay in language and social skills and needs exposure to peers who can talk and interact. (d) Ask if the student can initially attend the class for a short period of time (e.g., 1 hour for 1 to 2 days per week) and if a person who helps tutor the student can be present at that time. (e) Ask if you can give the teacher some tips once in a while about how to handle some of the student's more unusual idiosyncrasies. (f) Ask if you can call the teacher, and if he or she can call you, when problems occur.

If the classroom provides all of these conditions, then that classroom environment will likely be beneficial for the student. Once you and the teacher establish a close and trusting relationship, inform the teacher of the student's diagnosis. At that time, the teacher may comment that he or she suspected the diagnosis. Apologize for not having revealed the information earlier and, after stating your rationale, nothing else may need to be said.

If your requirements are not met once the student is enrolled, change classrooms or, if necessary, schools. Be optimistic that you will be able to locate the right teacher and classroom. It is a credit to our society that we are now more likely to accept those who are not typical, and many teachers and principals go out of their way to help integrate a student who is likely to provide them with numerous challenges and learning opportunities.

▶ **10. Build confidence and self-esteem.** The programs outlined in this manual have been constructed so as to maximize success and minimize failure for the student, yourself, and your team members. With increased mastery of skills, it is not unusual to observe that a student prefers the teaching situation to wandering aimlessly.

Helping to solve a difficult problem and contributing something positive to future generations are basic motivations for most people working with individuals with developmental delays. This is likely to be true for you, your team members, and the student's classroom teacher. Anyone who comes to know the parents and teachers of students with developmental delays learns that these people have been given an enormous challenge to work with and meet. Their courage, compassion, and strength provide much hope for our future in a world so often beset by violence and intolerance.

▶ **11. Know the basic learning principles used throughout this manual.** Discovery of these learning principles date back almost 100 years to E. Thorndike's work at Columbia Teachers College and were initially encompassed under the term Trial and Error Learning, then the Law of Effect, then Instrumental Learning, and finally Operant Conditioning. The application of these principles has become known as Behavior Modification or Applied Behavior Analysis.

We observe and use operant learning principles every day because every day we modify the behaviors of others, and others in turn modify our behaviors. However, using operant learning principles effectively requires more than superficial knowledge, especially when trying to teach persons with developmental delays. This teaching manual describes the application of learning principles in considerable detail. The teaching steps are presented in everyday language whenever feasible, technical terms are described in detail, and parents and teachers learn to apply the procedures by carrying out the various programs. We recommend that the reader become familiar with certain introductory texts on learning theory and behavior modification.

There is a large range in the complexity of programs presented in this manual. Part of the complexity of a given program is dictated by the individual differences that exist among individuals of the same diagnostic label and even among those individuals who obtain similar scores on standardized tests of IQ, language skills, or overall adaptive functioning. After reading this manual, you should be able to apply many of the teaching procedures appropriately in order to begin meeting the individual needs of your student. However, even a so-called expert in these procedures will fall short of providing optimal help. No one person can solve all the problems that will arise, but there is strength in a team of collaborators who can help create solutions. Many parents and teachers of children with developmental delays have already begun behavioral treatment and are likely to provide significant help with solving many of the problems often encountered. Much of this is handled through the organization called FEAT (Families for Early Autism Treatment). We strongly recommend that the reader become familiar with Chapter 36, which includes important information on where to turn when seeking help.

The four chapters that follow introduce some of the difficult behaviors that students with developmental delays show when adapting to education, whether it occurs in the home or at school. Such behaviors include excessive tantrums and self-injurious behavior (Chapter 5), self-stimulatory behavior (Chapter 6), poor motivation (Chapter 7), and attentional difficulties (Chapter 8). Throughout this manual, numerous and detailed descriptions are provided concerning how to treat these difficult behaviors as they appear during the teaching of specific programs. Keep in mind, however, that not all students with developmental delays evidence all of the behaviors described in Chapters 5 through 8.

Excessive Tantrums and Self-Injurious Behavior

CHAPTER 5

In Chapter 1, tantrums and self-injurious behavior are introduced as examples of behavioral excesses often displayed by persons with autism. Such behaviors take several forms, such as screaming, biting, hair pulling, hitting, and throwing objects. Tantrums may be directed at others, toward oneself (as in self-injurious behavior), or both. Excessive tantrumous behavior may begin shortly after birth, but it is more likely to be observed in the second year of life and then, possibly, escalate over the next several years to life-threatening levels. As the child grows up, she may become dangerous to caregivers or herself, necessitating placement away from home, the use of physical restraints, or the use of sedative medication. It is important to remember that tantrums are common in childhood and that some typically developing individuals aggress off and on throughout their lives, sometimes to great magnitude, as when they kill others or themselves. Ways in which tantrums and self-injurious behavior may be managed are discussed in detail throughout this manual, but certain basic information is provided here:

1. Tantrums are triggered out of frustration. This frustration often occurs out of a loss of rewards, such as when the individual is denied access to a favorite food, television program, toy, or place to sit or sleep. Self-stimulatory and ritualistic behaviors appear to contain rewarding properties, and even momentary disruptions of such behaviors can spark tantrums. For example, an individual may want to eat only perfectly shaped Cheerios, and the sight of one that is not perfect may trigger screaming, which in turn may cause parents to spend hours sorting out the "imperfect" pieces of cereal from the cereal box. Being waited on by a male rather than a female food server may result in a tantrum, causing parents to leave a restaurant and in the future seek only restaurants with female servers. Being seated in a car while it backs up to get into or out of a garage may cause major tantrums, causing parents to build a circular driveway to avoid backing up the car. Changing one's route to a familiar place, such as a grandparent's home, may result in such an upheaval that parents have to return and stay home. A person with developmental delays may be reinforced by observing dust floating on a beam of sunlight in the living room and become upset on days with cloudy skies. Leaving a favorite activity, such as lining up objects, to come to a teacher is likely to cause disruptive behavior. Given the wide range of self-stimulatory rituals and the subtlety of the stimuli that are rewarding for individuals with autism, it is sometimes very difficult to ascertain the antecedents of tantrums.

Frustrating situations are also likely to occur when adults place demands on the individual with developmental delays. As described in Chapter 4, persons with developmental delays fail to understand what well-meaning adults succeed in communicating to typically developing persons. Thus, individuals with developmental delays often fail to correctly follow through when faced with demands, and such situations become frustrating. It follows that one may be able to reduce tantrums by not placing demands on the individual. On the other hand, by removing demands altogether, it is unlikely that the person will learn more effective ways of coping with frustration. Chapter 9 illustrates how one may go about teaching the individual with developmental delays to better deal with frustrating situations, and it outlines how to use differential reinforcement of other behaviors to achieve long-term suppression of tantrums.

Remember, the individual tantrums in order to achieve some control over his environment. Teaching the individual alternate behaviors for controlling his environment will reduce the tantrums or give him the means to replace the tantrums.

2. There is compelling evidence that, by giving an individual attention and love contingent upon tantrums or self-destructive behaviors, one can shape up and increase such behaviors (Lovaas & Simmons, 1969). In the technical literature, the expression of love and attention contingent upon behavior is referred to as *positive reinforcement*. The delivery of such reinforcement contingent upon tantrums and self-injurious behavior places these behaviors on acquisition.

3. Self-injurious behaviors and tantrums can be strengthened if such behaviors allow the person to escape demands (E. G. Carr, Newsom, & Binkoff, 1980). For example, most persons with developmental delays object to participating in teaching situations. If the teacher gives in to a student's objections and allows the student to get out of the situation while she is tantruming, the tantrumous behavior may be inadvertently strengthened. In this example, the tantrum serves as an escape–avoidance mechanism. In the technical literature, *negative reinforcement* is said to be operating in that the behavior is reinforced (i.e., strengthened) by the removal of a negative situation. Rather than allowing the student to leave the teaching situation contingent on tantruming, she should be allowed to leave contingent on some appropriate behavior such as *not* screaming. Through practice of this technique, appropriate behavior is strengthened while tantrums are reduced.

4. If tantrums are reinforced by the attention the person receives while tantruming, it is likely that the tantrums will decrease if the person tantruming is ignored. In the technical literature, acting as if you do not see or hear the tantrum if it is maintained by attention is known as *extinction*. Extinction is often hard on the teacher and the student because the student will continue to tantrum, often showing a peak (an extinction burst) before the behavior gradually decreases. While working through a tantrum by using extinction, protect yourself by wearing a long-sleeved shirt, heavy cotton jeans, a bathing cap (to prevent hair pulling), and a scarf (to protect your throat). Needless to say, working through a tantrum calls for support from members of your treatment team.

Keep in mind that there are numerous ways to inadvertently strengthen a tantrum. Even minor attention such as briefly looking at the student while he tantrums may be sufficient to maintain the tantrum. Data also show that if a child is physically restrained contingent on a tantrum, the intensity of the tantrum increases (Lovaas & Simmons, 1969). The common practice of holding the child while he tantrums may have similarly deleterious effects. Conversely, restraining or holding a child contingent on *not* throwing a tantrum can decrease the tantrumous behavior. This can be done by gradually shaping up "pauses" of nontantrumous behavior into increasingly longer intervals (see Chapter 9).

5. Time-out (turning away from the student or placing the student in isolation) is sometimes an effective way to handle tantrums if the tantrums are shaped or maintained by positive reinforcement, but not if the tantrums constitute an escape–avoidance mechanism for that student. In the latter situation, the use of time-out will worsen tantrumous behavior by the process of negative reinforcement. However, extinction (working through and ignoring the behavior) is effective in reducing tantrums that emerge from wanting a reward or attempting to avoid the situation.

The treatment of choice is to reduce tantrumous behavior while building alternative behaviors to replace the tantrums. Young typical children gradually replace their tantrums and fussing as they acquire socially appropriate behaviors, such as language, to control their environment. By the time they are 3 or 4 years old, the worst of the tantrums have subsided, at least in frequency and in most children. Individuals with developmental delays fail to learn appropriate behaviors unless they are explicitly taught. This manual is designed, in part, with the purpose of teaching these individuals better ways of communicating with and controlling their social environment.

6. Some forms of self-injury are not regulated by social consequences. Self-injury may be self-stimulatory in nature (see Chapter 6); that is, some forms of self-injury are strengthened by the sensory feedback generated by the behavior (Favell, McGimsey, & Schell, 1982). An example of self-injury that appears to be maintained by sensory feedback includes eye poking (this behavior is often observed in blind or partially blind individuals). Eye poking may be considered a substitute or replacement for the lack of sensory feedback provided by normal or intact vision. Other examples of self-injury that appear self-stimulatory include chewing on the inside of one's cheeks and repeatedly pulling out one's hair. Such behaviors are often observed in individuals who are mentally retarded or nonambulatory who are placed in restricted environments such as wheelchairs or institutions. These forms of self-injury, in contrast to social forms, are not confined to situations when others are present but rather may occur when the person is alone, as when a person pulls out hair at night. Extinction and time-out do not affect the strength of such behaviors, but the building of socially appropriate alternative behaviors that provide sensory input similar to self-injurious behavior should be attempted.

Note that it is possible for a person to exhibit more than one form of self-injury in different situations and at different times. Such an occurrence places increasing demands on treatment providers and emphasizes the need for outside consultation.

It is not easy to educate a person who scares parents and teachers or who has to be drugged and restrained to reduce self-injurious and assaultive behaviors. The very attempt to teach such a person often triggers tantrums or self-injury, causing the teacher to quit. This cycle inadvertently strengthens the tantrumous or self-injurious behavior. In such a situation, the individual's tantrums or self-injury can be seen as one of the causes of her behavioral delays. From the individual's perspective, she has typically failed in teaching situations, so why not put an end to any more failures that come her way? In the face of this, the teacher or other adult must take control of the situation. The individual must be taught in such a manner that she succeeds and builds confidence and trust in herself and others. The teaching programs presented in this manual are intended to help the student understand what others try to communicate, as well as facilitate the student's communication with others regarding what she wants.

It may help for you to think of tantrums as learned behavior. Like most people, individuals with developmental delays prefer to be in charge, have access to reinforcers, and in general be in control of the situation. Such goals are good signs. It is not in the students' favor, however, to be an expert at controlling you while you lose control over her. Do not let the student take control by tyrannizing you—you must take charge. At such times it helps to work in a group (a team) and to take strength from team members or other persons who have worked through or otherwise been able to reduce tantrums.

Some observations from the everyday lives of ordinary persons may help illustrate the universality of self-injurious and assaultive behaviors and their eventual treatment. Suppose you are in love, and the one you love helps provide you with access to your most significant reinforcers (acceptance, escape from loneliness, warmth, sex, etc.). Now suppose that one day your partner prefers someone other than you, and all the reinforcers you used to receive are no longer available to you. One or all of the following behaviors are likely to be elicited: (a) you try harder to please the person (you go through an extinction burst), (b) you become furious and contemplate hurting that person, and (c) you become depressed and consider hurting yourself. If you have received sufficient reinforcement for suicidal attempts in the past, been shaped up so to speak, you may well succeed if you attempt this option. The treatment of choice, however, is to accept the inevitable. First, you prepare for extinction (i.e., prepare for not receiving the rewards you received in the past for certain behaviors). The first few weeks of extinction are the hardest, but the intensity of the difficult feelings gradually diminishes over the next several weeks or months. It may help to keep an informal record of the amount and frequency of grief experienced, as well as the times when you feel happiness. Both can reassure you that you are headed in a positive direction, that life is getting better. You recover when alternate behaviors become established, such as dating someone else who possesses some of the reinforcement properties of the person you lost. Or, perhaps more important, you recover once you acquire access to a larger range of reinforcers that you yourself have better control over. Planting flowers, cooking, painting, bicycling, going back to school, and getting a job where you can meet new people are all examples of helpful strategies. In short, the strategy of choice is learning not to put all your eggs in one basket.

Self-injurious behavior maintained by sensory reinforcement, such as biting oneself, eye poking, and hair pulling, may seem unique to individuals with autism and other developmental delays unless it is considered that smoking and other forms of drug addiction all have the qualities of self-stimulatory and self-injurious behavior. Smoking tobacco is a repetitive, stereotyped, and high-rate behavior that occurs with amazing similarity across cultures. Alterations in the sensory–perceptual feedback from smoking, drinking, and drugs may well be the reinforcer that maintains these behaviors. As with eye poking in blind or partially blind persons, such self-stimulatory behavior can be fatal.

Summary

Tantrumous behaviors, like some self-injury and assaultive acts, appear to be instances of learned communicative behaviors. These behaviors are mostly under the control of social consequences, such as the delivery of attention or removal of demands (technically known as instances of positive reinforcement and negative reinforcement, respectively). Tantrumous behavior is usually instigated by frustration, as when a person fails to obtain a customary reward. These behaviors are rational and lawfully related to the environment, even though they may look bizarre.

There are four ways to reduce tantrumous and self-injurious behavior. One way is to work through and ignore the tantrum or self-injury, as when the adult behaves as if he or she does not notice the behavior. This is technically known as *extinction*. A second way to work through a tantrum or self-injury is by differentially rewarding or reinforcing alternate, socially acceptable behaviors. This is technically known as *DRO*, differential reinforcement of other behaviors. Third, time-out may reduce tantrums or self-injury in those instances in which the behaviors are maintained by the individual's gaining positive reinforcement. However, time-out will increase these behaviors if they are based on escaping–avoiding a difficult situation, as the tantrums or self-injury are in this situation strengthened through negative reinforcement. Finally, self-injury can be maintained by sensory feedback generated by the behavior performed. This is technically known as sensory–perceptual reinforcement. Manipulation of social consequences (extinction and time-out) is unlikely to affect this kind of self-injury. The treatment of choice for such forms of self-injury is to build alternate appropriate behaviors that provide stimulation similar to that provided by the self-injurious behavior (Favell, McGimsey, & Schell, 1982).

Self-Stimulatory Behavior

CHAPTER 6

Most individuals with developmental delays exhibit a wide range of repetitive, stereotyped behaviors, such as rocking their bodies, shaking their heads, spinning objects, running back and forth, flapping their arms, tapping objects, smelling and licking surfaces, gazing, rolling their eyes, squinting, lining up objects, moving their fingers across textured surfaces, vocalizing, echolalia, masturbation, and a host of other behaviors. These behaviors are collectively referred to as self-stimulatory behavior (or self-stimulation) because they provide stimulation to the person's afferent pathways. The stimulation can be olfactory, visual, auditory, kinesthetic, or tactile in nature. Usually these behaviors are repetitive and monotonous, and they may occur daily for years. The individuals are hardly ever still; they are always doing something. Self-stimulatory behavior and its high and repetitive rate occur with amazing similarity across persons with developmental delays and across individuals of different nationalities and ethnic compositions. My own observations of individuals with autism and pervasive developmental disorders (PDD) across Europe and the Far East reveal this similarity.

Young typical children and adults evidence similar behaviors, although to a lesser degree and in transient form. In behavioral theory, such behaviors are labeled *species specific*. In this instance, these characteristics are common to human beings; however, one can also observe a limited range of similar behaviors such as rocking, pacing, and self-injurious behavior in animals deprived of alternate behaviors, such as when they are held captive in a zoo. One rarely observes these behaviors in the wild where alternate behaviors are available.

Levels of Self-Stimulatory Behavior

Various forms of self-stimulatory behavior can be considered to fall into the following levels.

Level I: Self-stimulatory behaviors at Level I involve the body only; observation of the environment or actions upon objects in the environment result in no movement of the object or change in the object's position, size, or composition.

A. Self-stimulatory behaviors involving the eyes: Examples include repetitively blinking, squinting, rolling up one's eyes so only the whites are visible, opening one's eyes wide, staring at flickering lights or drifting dust, gazing with one's pupils positioned at the outer edges of the eyes, and gazing into space.

B. Large body movements: Examples include repetitively spinning one's body in circles, pacing, toe walking, bouncing or jumping up and down, walking repetitively around a pole, stereotyped nondirectional running, body posturing as in arching one's shoulders when standing or walking, shaking one's head side to side, and masturbation.

C. Self-stimulatory behaviors involving the hands: Examples include repetitively flapping or clapping one's hands, running one's fingers along surfaces, feeling textures, rubbing one's hands or fingers together, rubbing one's face with one's hands, feeling one's hair, opening and closing one's hands, flicking one's nose or ears with one's fingers, and sticking one's finger in one's nose.

D. Behaviors involving the mouth: Examples including putting one's own hand in one's mouth, repetitively opening and closing one's mouth, clicking one's tongue, swirling saliva, licking one's lips, manipulating one's breathing pattern, blowing on one's bangs and watching the hair fall, and sucking air through one's teeth.

E. Auditory and gustatory self-stimulation: Examples include smelling and licking objects and people, making nonsense sounds, repetitively screaming, babbling, echolalia, humming, and singing.

Level II: Behaviors at Level II involve an active arrangement of the environment to provide patterning of sensory–perceptual input.

A. Inappropriate manipulation or use of objects performed to provide sensory stimulation (the behavioral topography is not characteristic of correct object use): Examples include lining up objects into rows, spinning or twirling objects, tearing objects such as pages in a book, sifting sand in front of one's eyes, sucking or mouthing objects, splashing water against the wall of a pool, swirling ashes dumped out of an ashtray, throwing pieces of paper into the air and watching them fall, rubbing tissues on one's own body, throwing objects, and using objects to tap surfaces.

B. Apparent appropriate object manipulation performed solely to provide sensory stimulation (the behavioral topography is characteristic of correct object use): In this type of self-stimulatory behavior, the object is not used for its intended function or purpose. Examples include repeatedly switching lights on and off, opening and closing doors, turning a television on and off, pulling out and pushing in drawers, taking off and putting on shoes repetitively, swinging a tetherball around its pole and crouching to watch it go around, repetitively running up and down stairs, repetitively making dots on a piece of paper with a pencil, and collecting or hoarding objects.

C. Demand for sameness: In this type of self-stimulation, resistance is shown to the changing of object placement, interruption of behaviors, or interruption of ritual performances. Examples include insistence on using the same utensils at each meal, insistence on wearing the same clothes every day, insistence on taking the same route to school, and insistence on one's mother always wearing the same slippers.

Level III: In Level III, appropriate behavior occurs in inappropriate contexts or for inappropriate purposes.

A. Object use that is appropriate in topography, purpose, and context, but excessive: Examples include excessive use of signs (e.g., as words, letters, numbers, phrases) in a manner devoid of their symbolic content, recalling phone numbers or birthdays, lining up objects and counting them, repetitively singing or humming songs to oneself, and saying appropriate sentences in inappropriate contexts (e.g., during the day, walking outside and saying, "Is it dark outside?").

B. Appropriate but excessive use of objects relative to commonly accepted social norms: Examples include repetitive play requiring the appropriate use of objects, such as excessive bike riding, excessive rolling of a toy truck around the yard, excessive pretending to drive a car, and excessive assembling and reassembling of the same jigsaw puzzle.

Level IV: Behaviors at Level IV require considerable learning history. The behavior is excessive, used in an appropriate context, and involves a meaningful use of signs.

A. Behavior exhibited at a high intellectual level disparate with the current overall level of functioning: This type of self-stimulation is often referred to as a *splinter skill*. Examples include memory feats, ability to reproduce in totality a long list of credits following a movie or television show, ability to reproduce correctly on the piano songs previously heard (often on the first attempt), ability to sing any note asked for and tell what note and key is being played on an instrument, ability to perform near-instant calculations of calendar dates and knowledge of what day appears on what date and year into the past or future, and unusually advanced mathematical ability (e.g., an 11-year-old who can work out in his head all the prime numbers up to 1,000 and give prime factors for all odd numbers).

B. Appropriate but excessive use of an object or performance of an activity: To be considered representative of this level, this excessive use must be coupled with the performance of other behaviors (e.g., verbal or imaginative behaviors) related to that object or activity. Together, the performance of these related behaviors demonstrates a preoccupation with that object or activity. Note that behaviors in this category differ from those in Level III in that behaviors in this category are not only excessive but are coupled with the performance of related behaviors. An example is an obsession with clocks, as when a person constantly compares clocks in different locations and checks what time it is. Also, a persistent drawing of clocks and making of clock dials, excessive talking about days and dates and what days of the week certain dates fall on, and inquiring about the birthday of each person met would be considered self-stimulatory. Obsessions with buildings (counting floors of actual buildings and pictures of buildings and stacking of objects to represent buildings in order to count their floors), elevators (talking about elevators, drawing pictures of elevators, seeking out elevators, and using toys to play elevator), vacuum cleaners (constantly talking about and imitating the function and noise of vacuum cleaners and using other objects as if they were vacuum cleaners), stairs (going up and down stairs, repetitively talking about stairs, and constructing stairs with toys), and animals (talking about animals, drawing pictures of animals, and spending long periods of time acting like a particular animal) are all likely to be self-stimulatory in nature.

What Is Known About Self-Stimulatory Behavior

At first glance, lower levels of self-stimulatory behavior may look particularly bizarre, perhaps pathological. On closer examination, however, all self-stimulatory behavior shows itself to be rational and lawful just like tantrums and self-injurious behavior. The following is a summary of what is presently known about self-stimulatory behavior.

1. One method of reducing self-stimulatory behavior is to increase the strength of socially appropriate behavior. When other behaviors increase in frequency, self-stimulatory behaviors are likely to decrease. Similarly, the individual may alternate between different forms of self-stimulatory behaviors so that if one form of self-stimulatory behavior is suppressed, it is likely that another form of self-stimulation will increase. For example, the suppression of rocking may lead to an increase in hand flapping. An ideal treatment for low-level self-stimulatory behavior is to replace it with socially appropriate forms of self-stimulation (see Point 6).

2. It is likely that there is a biological need for sensory stimulation, that self-stimulation provides "food" for the nervous system. For example, if an afferent system such as the visual system is blocked from input by the surgical closure of one of an animal's eyes shortly after the animal's birth, then a reexamination of the optic nerve in that eye when the animal reaches adulthood will reveal structural deterioration. Similarly, the projection area of the brain that mediates the sensory input from that optic tract will also be less developed and the animal will be effectively blind in that eye. Conversely, there is evidence that animals raised in enriched environments with large amounts of sensory stimulation show an increase in brain cell growth. In other words, self-stimulatory behavior can be viewed as adaptive behavior. If you are unable to teach your student alternate behaviors, let the student self-stimulate so as to help avoid damage to the nervous system.

3. When observing certain high-level forms of self-stimulatory behavior, it may be helpful to distinguish between *sensory* and *perceptual* reinforcers. Gazing at lights (a Level I form of self-stimulation) may be controlled primarily by relatively unstructured sensory feedback from the light source. In contrast, the repetitive assembling and reassembling of jigsaw puzzles has as a consequence a specific arrangement or pattern of sensory stimuli: Circle goes with circle, square goes with square, and so on. The matching of stimuli seems to be the reinforcer that maintains the individual's behavior. Such matching represents a patterning of sensory feedback, hence the term *perceptual reinforcer*. Lining up objects into neat rows is another example of arranging separate stimuli into a perceptual whole. Matching of auditory inputs, exemplified by echolalia, also illustrates a perceptual reinforcer. In describing programs for teaching match-to-sample, nonverbal imitation, and verbal imitation (Chapters 12, 13, and 22, respectively), we provide examples of the power of sensory and perceptual reinforcers in building appropriate behaviors.

4. If self-stimulatory behavior is based on sensory perception, and if these reinforcers are primary and powerful, such as food and water rewards, then it may be difficult or impossible to reduce such behaviors. On the other hand, a teacher may use such stimulation as a reward for the student having behaved appropriately. The treatment of choice is to change lower levels of self-stimulatory behavior to higher levels (see Point 7 below). Numerous examples of this technique are provided throughout this manual.

5. The presence of self-stimulatory behavior decreases or blocks responsiveness to social reinforcers. This may come about because rewards derived from self-stimulation (a primary or biological reinforcer) may be stronger than social rewards the teacher can offer (secondary, symbolic, or acquired reinforcers). In an attempt to reduce the interference of competing reinforcers, the teacher may remove the objects used for self-stimulation. Or, if an individual uses her body only, the teacher may physically restrain her from doing so. As soon as the student responds correctly, the teacher may reward her by letting her self-stimulate for a brief period of time (5 to 10 seconds). If the student self-stimulates with toys, the teacher can provide access to such toys *after* the student engages in appropriate behavior. In short, the teacher may use self-stimulatory behaviors constructively by reducing them when the student is given an instruction and then letting the student self-stimulate as a reward after she responds correctly to the instruction.

6. Like tantrums and self-injurious behaviors, self-stimulatory behaviors are present in typical persons as well. For example, one can observe examples of body rocking and hand flapping in typical children and adults. Even casual observations can provide evidence of high levels of self-stimulatory behaviors in typical adults. Examples of such behaviors include repetitive and stereotyped motions such as smoking, lining up of objects such as glasses and silverware on a table, neatly folding and stacking towels, matching rows of figures as done when

playing slot machines, matching cards as done when playing solitaire, matching balls in holes as done in golf and basketball, marching in neat rows as done in parades, lining up and twirling as done in ballets or cheerleading performances, and clapping hands as done when applauding.

Note how society prescribes access to self-stimulatory behaviors as rewards, much as we recommend in teaching individuals with developmental delays. We self-stimulate after work, on weekends, and during vacations when we engage in playing golf, watching television, doing crossword puzzles, dancing, and a host of other high-level forms of recreational activities that involve self-stimulation. We jump up and down and repetitively clap our hands in a stereotyped manner at particularly good performances, actively reinforcing the performance with sensory reinforcers. Anyone who has watched children at school may note classic examples of the use of self-stimulatory behaviors during recess as rewards for having sat still and complied with the teacher during the hour preceding recess.

Typical persons also often engage in self-stimulatory behaviors when there is little or nothing else to do. Excellent places to observe typical adults engaging in self-stimulatory behaviors are congested streets and freeways. While traffic is stationary or moving slowly, one may observe drivers pick their noses in a stereotyped and repetitive manner, twirl their hair, finger-play with the steering wheel, look at themselves in mirrors, smack their lips, or smile and talk to themselves. As soon as traffic moves, or the driver notes that he or she is being observed, all or most forms of low-level self-stimulation decrease and are replaced by socially appropriate behavior. Adults rarely demonstrate low-level forms of self-stimulation when others are present, perhaps because society frowns upon engaging in such behaviors in public.

The point we are trying to make about self-stimulation is the same as the point we made in reference to tantrumous and self-injurious behaviors: Do not view such behavior as a sign of a distorted or damaged mind. Self-stimulation is rational and intelligent, obeying the laws that regulate the behaviors of all persons. To repeat, if you do not have more appropriate behaviors to offer the individual as a substitute for self-stimulation, consider letting the individual self-stimulate to keep his nervous system from deteriorating.

7. The treatment of choice is to help individuals with developmental delays transition from lower forms of self-stimulatory behavior to higher forms that are more socially appropriate. Socially appropriate forms of self-stimulatory behavior may be defined as behaviors that may be enjoyed through observation or participation by more than one person. A most desirable form of self-stimulation can be observed in instances in which a performer is *paid* for self-stimulating, as is the case with professional sports and other entertainment. Golf and basketball players may be paid millions of dollars for matching balls into holes, and the more difficult it is to achieve this match, the more we enjoy it. We clap our hands and jump up and down to add to our appreciation, reinforcing one form of self-stimulatory behavior (golf and basketball) with another form (clapping and jumping up and down). Many people work hard and pay to be present to watch twirling and toe-walking dancers in Tchaikovsky's *Nutcracker Suite*. Who is not fascinated by watching the first snowfall in the winter or the slight movements of leaves on an aspen or birch tree in the summer? A major therapeutic gain occurs when individuals with developmental delays become more like the rest of us through their transition from low-level forms of self-stimulation to higher and more socially acceptable forms of self-stimulation.

Motivational Problems

CHAPTER 7

Although motivation and attention appear to be closely related, we discuss them separately in an attempt to clearly describe the idiosyncrasies embedded in each. Most typical individuals seem motivated and eager to learn, but most individuals with developmental delays seem unmotivated when confronted with educational tasks. As described in Chapter 5, it is likely that the negativism shown by individuals with developmental delays is caused by the frustration they experience when failing to learn what well-meaning adults hope they would learn. To help reduce this continual failure, these individuals develop tantrums to ward off demands, isolate themselves by acting as if they cannot see or hear, and fail to develop eye contact. In turn, persons with developmental delays come to rely on their own reinforcers such as self-stimulatory rituals.

Early in treatment, social praise, the company of others, and most other subtle rewards that are important to typical individuals are unlikely to be effective reinforcers for most students with developmental delays. Similarly, being incorrect and receiving social feedback such as the teacher providing an informational "No" in the early stages of treatment often do not work to correct behavior. Technically speaking, these students show a delay in the acquisition of secondary (acquired, social, or symbolic) reinforcers.

We recommend that the teacher rely on primary or biological rewards, such as small bites of food, at the *beginning* of treatment. Food reinforcement has its limitations, as we shall describe later, but it constitutes a good reward in the early weeks of treatment. Food reinforcers may also signal a sense of security for the student. Anticipate, however, that the student may have difficulty accepting the teacher's food rewards in the first hours of teaching (see Chapter 9).

Allowing the student to escape from a stressful situation is also a powerful and primary reinforcer, as is giving the individual the opportunity to self-stimulate. Letting the student leave a stressful teaching situation, for a minute or so, contingent on a correct response may be the most effective reward in the early stages of treatment. As the teacher becomes more familiar with the student, the teacher will discover other types of reinforcers that are unique to and effective for that particular student.

Given the importance of social rewards to a typical individual's learning, it follows that an individual's functioning in society would be seriously curtailed if social rewards were not effective. On the other hand, if one could help the individual with developmental delays succeed, then one might concurrently "normalize" the individual's motivational structure. Over our years of working with individuals who have developmental delays, we have found that a much wider range of effective reinforcers are available than anticipated in the early days. Given access to this larger range of reinforcers, teachers have become more effective and the persons taught have become more motivated to learn. To illustrate our search for potentially rewarding consequences, the following story was provided by Gordon Hall, a grandfather of a child with autism.

Positive Reinforcement or What Would You Do for $1 Million

"Twenty-five reinforcers," our consultant said. "You need to come up with at least that many as Kendra is not working for just sips of Pepsi and pieces of a cookie." "You must be crazy," I thought. "There ain't 25 things I can think of that Kendra wants." Our consultant continued, "Kendra will teach you how to work with her, because if you don't do it right, she will punish you by not working. And the key to effective teaching is the use of proper reinforcers." Our consultant then asked, "Would you sit and stack blocks all day for $1 million?" My answer was, "Of course." The same principle, I learned, applies to working with what motivates the student.

I asked how I should start to discover effective reinforcers. Our consultant suggested I take Kendra to Toys "R" Us and buy whatever she became attracted to. I didn't go to Toys "R"

Us, but from working with Kendra, I have a good idea of the toys and activities she enjoys.

The hardest part for me was starting to make my 25-item list. Near the top of the list I placed the fallback items of food and drink: Mini M&M's, Fig Newtons (each Newton cut into 12 pieces), root beer (instead of other soda pop because root beer has no caffeine), and apple juice. We use small plastic containers for the food items and a 12 × 14-inch cake pan to place all the food, drinks, and other small items in so they are readily available. Next on the list are small tops that you can spin with your fingers. Kendra also loves trains, so we got some wind-up trains. The tops and wind-up trains go in the cake pan with the food and drink items so that they are easily accessible during the programs. Other items on the list include a bottle of soap bubbles, a small toy bug with bouncing beads inside, physical tickling, lightly pounding on the bottom of Kendra's feet, getting out of the chair to ring a bell across the room, getting out of the chair to put a block or beanbag in a bucket, and running across the room to push a key on the piano. Kendra especially loves out-of-the-chair activities.

As I started listing items, more and more came to mind: a Mexican rain stick that makes a pleasant sound, a Disney *Beauty and the Beast* talking book, an inflatable Yogi that Kendra likes to punch, a Farmer Says toy, a pop-up toy, and large beads to string. Also on the list are items that are used during Kendra's programs, such as Play-Doh. She likes to put her finger into it or pound on it. Kendra also enjoys stacking Lincoln Logs, so we hand her one at a time during the Verbal Imitation Program. In addition, we have a vibrating ball that she likes to hold or put on her back.

The way the programs are set up can make them reinforcing in and of themselves. For the Colors Program, we have felt swatches that are placed on the floor, and we make a game out of having one of the aides and Kendra alternate jumping onto the correct color. We often put an array of items in front of Kendra and let her pick her own toy or food item. She works better when she can decide what she is working for.

The list is of no good if it is not used, so I made two copies and tacked one on the wall above the table where we work. The other is kept with the list of daily programs. As it is so easy to revert to food and drink, we make a special effort to vary reinforcers among and within programs.

If you are having a problem discovering reinforcers, you might try the approach that was effective for me. Just sit down and start writing down the food, toys, and other items your student enjoys. Good luck!

One helpful way to deliver reinforcers is through the use of a prize board. A prize board provides a visual display of reinforcers, is economical, and is enjoyable to most students.

The Prize Board

A prize board is a visual display that clearly shows a prize the student may obtain once a preset number of tokens has been earned. Under a prize board system, a student can earn tokens by completing any of a number of different tasks and can later exchange these tokens for a valued prize, such as a favorite food, toy, or activity. In this sense, tokens are similar to money in that they can be traded in to obtain desired items.

When the student gives a correct response, the teacher gives the student a token to place on the board. Such tokens are similar to points typical children earn toward enjoying a favorite activity such as watching a certain television program or obtaining some other special treat such as ice cream. Tokens are also similar to grades in school where so many As can earn a special prize. Prize boards are commonly used with typical kindergarten and first-grade children who may need this type of visual display to compensate for the lack of skills needed to bridge the delay between a behavior and its eventual reinforcer. For students with developmental delays who tend to lack the verbal language necessary to make this bridge, the visual display appears to be helpful in maintaining the student's motivation. In addition, delaying reinforcement through the medium of a prize board may increase retention (memory) of learned material.

Another important reason for introducing a prize board is that it helps the student become accustomed to delays in obtaining primary reinforcement. During most of the early teaching performed from this manual, the student is exposed to instantaneous and powerful reinforcement: Each time the student responds correctly, she is immediately reinforced with a strong, often primary, reinforcer. To function in everyday life, however, the student must learn to work for delayed and "thinned-out" reinforcement schedules. For example, in a classroom setting, a student is not immediately rewarded by the teacher following each and every one of the teacher's instructions. The student may, however, be selected to go out first to recess because she followed the teacher's directions during the preceding hour. For displaying good behavior, the student may also be given some stars on a piece of paper, and later on grades, to show her parents at the end of the day or the week, a procedure very similar to that of the prize board.

Keep in mind that the prize board should not replace the one-on-one reinforcement the student already receives for correct responses in teaching sessions; rather, it should be used in addition to such reinforcement, particularly if the student's motivation seems to drift and decrease. The reinforcement the student gains through the prize board should be more valuable than reinforcers obtained after each correct response. For instance, a student may be given hugs or small bites of food for each correct response but receive an ice cream cone after earning five or more tokens.

Prize boards are easy to construct using the following common household materials: a large, durable poster board approximately 26 × 36 inches in size, paints or felt pens, and a variety of the student's favorite foods, drinks, toys, and activities (depicted in two-dimensional form). Tokens can be items as simple as coin-size plastic circles or as creative as three-dimensional toys such as Disney characters, Sesame Street figures, or finger puppets. Choose tokens that are interesting and enjoyable for the student, possessing some reinforcing properties of their own. Affix Velcro pieces to the back of each token and in one or two rows on the board, allowing the student to easily fasten the tokens to the board. A clear plastic bag can be affixed to the board to position the particular prize (or symbol of the prize) used in the teaching session.

An example of a prize board is displayed in Figure 7.1. Note that the number of Velcro pieces for placement of tokens should vary according to the student's familiarity with the prize board system (see the next section, Using the Prize Board). A transparent plastic bag for displaying various prizes one at a time is used for illustrative purposes. Other arrangements may be satisfactory.

Select the student's favorite foods as the initial prizes for the prize board. To maintain the reinforcing value of these foods, they should be available only through the prize board; that is, the student should not have any access to these reinforcers at other times. Once the student learns that the prize board can be used to gain preferred reinforcers, nonfood items, such as favorite toys, videotapes, or trips to a favorite restaurant or store, can be used as prizes. Regardless of the prize used, the student should be given a visual display of the prize she will obtain after earning a certain number of tokens. Prizes that are abstract or that do not fit inside the bag on the board, such as certain toys, videotapes, or trip destinations, are often best displayed through the use of photographs. For example, if the student's prize is a trip to Baskin-Robbins, a picture of Baskin-Robbins should be placed in the bag on the board.

As a general guideline, create a prize board that is visually appealing and fun for the student. Decorate the borders of the board, reserving the center space for token display. When the prize board is completed, it should be placed prominently near the student's table and chairs.

Using the Prize Board

For the most part, the student receives immediate reinforcement for responses through discrete trial procedures (see Chapter 10). It is difficult to assess the proper time

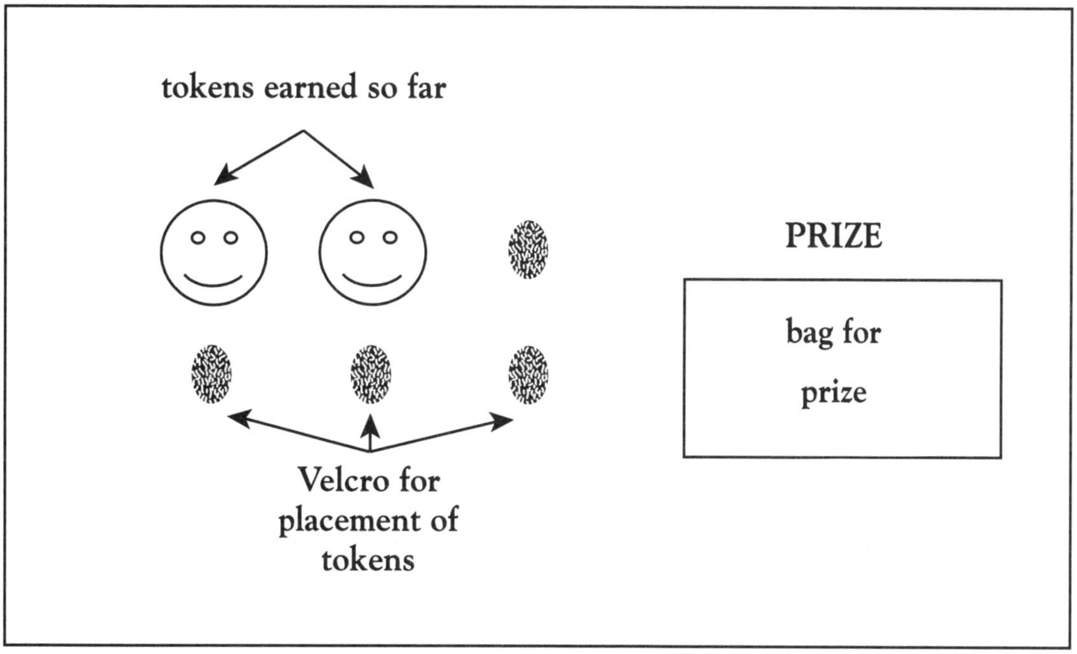

Figure 7.1. Example of a prize board.

to introduce a prize board system to a student, and it will not be known whether the student can learn this form of delayed reinforcement until one attempts to teach it. If, after the system is introduced, the student does not seem to be reinforced by the use of tokens, this may be an indication that she is not ready for delayed reinforcement and may need more immediate reinforcement for the time being. Before putting the prize board system on hold, however, make sure you implement the system properly and examine possible ways of clarifying the contingency for the student (e.g., by decreasing the number of tokens required to obtain the prize).

As previously mentioned, variations of the prize board system are often used with typical individuals. It is therefore not necessary to fade the use of this system altogether. You may, however, eventually want to naturalize the system so the student learns to mentally keep track of her "points" and earns more natural prizes, such as new toys. The following five steps are intended to help facilitate the use of the prize board.

▶ Step 1

Teach the association between responses, tokens, and prizes. Choose a program with which the student can be successful. Place the prize board near the table and in clear view of the student. Place several tokens on the board, leaving one slot open for the last token (e.g., if there are 10 slots, have 9 tokens already placed on the board). With the final token within your reach, call the student to the table and begin a trial as usual. Immediately after a correct response, praise the student, hand her a token, and say, "Put it on the board." Prompt the student to place the token in its correct position on the board, and then give her the prize in the bag. You may want to help the student associate the tokens with the reward by having the student count the tokens, after which you comment something to the effect, "Ten! You get a prize!" Through repeated practice of this procedure, it is likely that the student will learn the contingency between the tokens and the prize.

▶ Step 2

Increase the response requirement. After the student makes the connection between the tokens and the prize, increase the requirement by leaving the last two slots open on the board so that the student must earn two tokens to obtain the prize. After two to three times of giving two tokens for two correct responses (one token per correct response) within one program, give the student two tokens for two correct responses over two different programs.

It is important to vary the token requirement of the program and the schedule in which tokens are given so that the student does not learn a pattern of reinforcement delivery. Such a pattern would eventually need to be broken, leading to frustration when the teacher increases the token requirement or changes the schedule of token delivery. To illustrate, a student who is accustomed to earning a token for each correct response may become frustrated when the teacher begins giving tokens for every other correct response. The key to avoiding frustration is preventing the student from developing a pattern in the first place by randomizing the token schedule.

Increase the token requirement in gradual steps until the student must earn 10 tokens before the prize is delivered. As you increase the token requirement, be sure that the student can observe the board and that she acquires the required number of tokens within 30 minutes or less. This will help her tolerate the delay between earning the tokens and receiving the prize. Once this step is mastered, increase the time interval to 45 minutes. At this point, the student's prizes should have more value in order to keep her motivated for the duration of the longer time interval.

▶ Step 3

Lengthen the reinforcement delay. To approximate the reinforcement delay that typical first-grade students can tolerate (e.g., cashing in the tokens at the end of the day), start increasing the time interval in gradual steps between earning tokens and obtaining the prize. Students who have limited receptive or expressive language may need shorter time intervals (e.g., less than 30 minutes) between the last token delivery and the prize. Students who have mastered advanced receptive and expressive language, counting, and if–then reasoning (e.g., "If you get 10 tokens, then we'll go to McDonald's") may respond to a time interval of, for example, 3 hours between the time of receiving the last token and the prize.

▶ Step 4

Further increase motivation. Try giving the student a choice of prizes: At the beginning of the teaching session, have the student select her own prize from a display of two to three items. Be sure to hold the token requirement constant; if the student does not meet the requirement within the session (e.g., because her responding was not as good as usual for that session), then she does not earn her prize.

▶ Step 5

Use a prize board system to decrease *behavior*. Once a prize board system of reinforcement is established, it can also be used to decrease inappropriate behaviors. This can be accomplished through *response cost*, which involves the loss of a desired item contingent upon a behavior. Once the tokens have been established as valuable to the student, the removal of a token contingent upon an inappropriate behavior can decrease such behavior.

Begin this step by delineating which behaviors will result in the loss of a token. When the student engages in one of the predetermined behaviors, remove a token from the board while explaining the contingency to the student. For example, if the student has seven tokens on the board and needs three more to achieve a prize, and the student then engages in an inappropriate behavior (e.g., bites the teacher), the teacher should quickly bring the student to the board, remove a token from the board, and firmly state, "No biting. You lose a token." The student then would have only six tokens on the board and must earn the seventh token again.

Behaviors can also be decreased by creating a separate board system for inappropriate behaviors. In this system, the student is given a red card for engaging in a given behavior. If the student acquires a certain number of red cards (e.g., three) within a specific interval (e.g., a single 3-hour teaching session), the student receives an *undesirable* consequence. Sometimes a student's behavior is so extreme that one occurrence should earn a consequence. For example, if the student makes a threatening move toward a younger sibling, she may then be given a red card with the contingency explained during the delivery of the red card (e.g., "No hitting. You get a red card."). The student's parents can then determine an appropriate consequence to be used with this procedure.

Reinforcement and Success

The rewards described by Gordon Hall in the beginning of this chapter and those described here for use with the prize board are all extrinsic rewards; that is, they are rewards that are dispensed by persons other than the student. Such a reward system is undoubtedly essential to helping the student develop into a typical individual. There is another kind of reward discussed in Chapter 6 on self-stimulatory behavior. This type of reward consists of sensory–perceptual reinforcers, which seem less dependent on being provided by others, although many forms can be controlled by others. For example, a teacher may allow the student to self-stimulate (e.g., rock back and forth) for 5 to 10 seconds contingent on a correct response while blocking the self-stimulatory behavior at all other times.

The sensory–perceptual rewards described in Chapter 6 are inherent to self-stimulatory behaviors; that is, the behaviors themselves seem to provide rewarding consequences. One may refer to such rewards as *intrinsically motivating* in contrast to rewards that are *extrinsically motivating*. In many instances, the two forms of rewards become interrelated, such as when a teacher uses extrinsic rewards to teach a student a behavior that later becomes intrinsically rewarding. The following example is a good illustration of this process: When teaching nonverbal students to imitate the teacher's sounds or words, the use of extrinsic rewards, such as bites of food and then approval late in the program, result in about one half of the students becoming echolalic, perfectly matching the teacher's sounds or words (Lovaas, 1987). These students continue to echo *without* the adult having to reward them. The matching of the student's auditory output to that of the teacher becomes the student's reward, technically known as a *perceptual reinforcer*.

In Chapter 6 we describe how, in the course of teaching, one can change low-level forms of self-stimulatory behavior into higher, more socially acceptable forms of self-stimulation. The acquisition of higher level forms may depend on extrinsic (adult-mediated) reinforcement; however, once established, such behaviors do not appear to extinguish when social reinforcement is no longer available. The behaviors appear autonomous or self-perpetuated. This step is of considerable importance because it comprises one of the strategies that help prevent relapse once treatment is terminated.

For the student to be appropriately reinforced, the learning situation must be constructed in such a manner that the student is consistently successful. If one examines a student's continual failure, the opposite side of success, then one can construct a hypothesis as to why the student engages in tantrumous behavior and refrains from seeking the company of others. Why seek others when failure will ensue, in contrast to the steady supply of primary rewards engendered by the endless variety of self-generated self-stimulatory behavior? Why not avoid eye contact when engaging in eye contact has signaled failure in the past? The student may have the sort of view that "If I look at the adult, I will be asked to do something I don't understand; I will fail, so I won't look." These are the exact conditions under which giving eye contact can acquire negative or aversive consequences and reinforce gaze avoidance. In contrast, the student's success in the teaching environment may be the key element in helping to normalize the student's motivation so as to increase not only eye contact, but many forms of social interaction. Perhaps the most important observation one can make some time into treatment is seeing the student come to the teaching situation on his own, preferring the learning environment to staying by himself. Such a development helps to refute the many pessimistic predictions that have been made by so many people in their objections to behavioral treatment. Such pessimism includes the views that gains in treatment are short lived, that the students become robots, and that their emotional lives and intrinsic reinforcers are neglected. The longer one works with a student, the more uniqueness and richness one discovers both in terms of the increasingly large range of reinforcers effective for that student and the special skills or aptitudes possessed by the student.

Following are several methods by which motivation may be normalized so as to help the student succeed in acquiring new behaviors.

1. The basic rule is to maximize the student's success and minimize his failure. All professional persons and parents alike will agree with such a goal. Any differences in agreement rest in the methods by which this goal is achieved.

2. Simplify the learning situation such that the student and the teacher can succeed and gain confidence. Simplify instructions, prompt correct behaviors, and use powerful primary reinforces such as food or escape from stress. These reinforcers should be delivered *immediately* upon the display of correct behaviors. In an intensive one-on-one teaching session, the amount of time taken up by a reinforcer should not exceed 5 to 10 seconds so that the frequency of learning trials and the opportunities to learn new behaviors are maximized.

3. Exaggerate rewards in the beginning of treatment. Pretend you are an actor and show extreme enthusiasm when exclaiming, "Good!" "Fantastic!" "Far out!" "A winner!" and so forth while smiling, laughing, clapping, or gesturing as if you were attending a concert of great importance each time the student responds correctly. Merely saying, "Good," is often ineffective reinforcement in the beginning, but some other component of the consequence (e.g., clapping or laughing) may increase its effectiveness. You will need continuous reinforcement (one reward for each behavior, or a one-to-one reinforcement schedule) when shaping new behaviors. After the student masters a particular behavior, *gradually* move away from a one-to-one reinforcement schedule, shifting to intermittent reinforcement. "Thin" the reinforcement schedule by giving a reinforcer after two, three, or more correct responses. Such a schedule will help avoid satiation and help the student to maintain previously learned behaviors.

4. The reinforcement inherent in self-stimulatory behavior may compete with the reinforcement provided by the teacher, thereby interfering with the learning of new behaviors. Therefore, inhibit self-stimulatory behavior by, for example, holding the student's hands down (if he hand-flaps) as you instruct him. At a later stage, the student may be taught to respond to the instruction, "Hands quiet." If the student uses visual stimuli to self-stimulate (e.g., gazes at lights and patterns on wallpaper), use indirect lighting or remove distracting self-stimulatory objects from the student's sight. Some students seem hooked on certain cartoons and will continually rehearse lines or songs from the cartoons during teaching sessions. Help lessen these kinds of self-stimulatory behaviors by reducing or preventing the student's access to such stimuli.

The teacher may try to interrupt self-stimulatory behavior by instructing the student to perform a series of already acquired behaviors that are incompatible with the student's self-stimulatory behaviors. These behaviors may consist of clapping hands in imitation of the teacher if the student hand-flaps as self-stimulation or presenting three to five mastered tasks in quick succession such as "stand up," "turn around," "sit down," and "clap." These may be thought of as wake-up tasks. Once the teacher gains the student's attention, the instruction for the target response should be immediately presented.

As mentioned earlier, if the student is allowed to self-stimulate, it should be as a reward for following through with the teacher's instructions. Recess in a typical school is full of self-stimulatory behavior, and it is provided contingent on the student's attending to the teacher during class. Teachers who fail to differentiate between recess and class time are likely to be ineffective as teachers. Adults also allow themselves self-stimulatory behavior *after* work on evenings and weekends, as when they play golf, dance, read a novel, do crossword puzzles, listen to music, or just gaze at a pretty landscape.

5. A student who is anxious and angry about failure may be easier to motivate because you can help him reduce anxiety and anger by guaranteeing his success in the teaching situation. Aggressive behavior reflects that the student is bothered by failure and wants to control his environment. Anger is a good motivator and can be used constructively.

6. The artificial and exaggerated rewards used at the beginning of treatment should be gradually faded out and replaced by more typical rewards. Rewards such as the company of others, praise (e.g., saying, "Good"), success, mastery, grades in school, and money must eventually replace bites of food. Try to make the teaching situation look normal as soon as possible.

7. The use of artificial reinforcers, such as food rewards and tokens, is likely to lead to limited generalization (transfer) of treatment gains from one environment to another (as from the home to the community) or from teachers to novel persons. For example, if food rewards are used at home, the behaviors consequated with food reinforcers may not transfer to school, where food rewards are not ordinarily used. If the student sees that food is available, he will be teachable. If food is not available, the student may not cooperate. In our experience, most students with developmental delays are extremely skillful at discriminating whether or not effective rewards are available. To facilitate the generalization of skills, it is imperative that reinforcement delivery be gradually naturalized.

8. Reinforcers must be varied to help avoid satiation. In addition, the student's favorite reinforcers should be exclusive to the teaching environment and should not be provided excessively within that environment. If the student is provided with free access to reinforcers outside of the teaching environment, he will have little reason to be motivated within the teaching situation. Likewise, if the student is provided with large quantities of reinforcement for each response or is provided with only one type of reinforcer, the student is likely to rapidly satiate.

Concluding Comments

Normalizing the student's motivational structure is important for three reasons: It helps the student learn, it aids in the transfer of the student's new behaviors from the teaching situation to other environments, and it helps prevent relapse. The development of new behaviors and the all-important goal of preventing relapse are to a very large extent dependent on normalizing motivation, developing friendships with other persons, and learning from other persons. We will address the latter issues in an upcoming advanced manual in which programs geared toward integrating individuals with developmental delays with typical peers are described.

Attentional Problems

CHAPTER 8

Attentional deviations, like inadequate motivation, interfere with an individual's ability to learn. As described in Chapter 1, in the section on criteria for diagnoses, the presence of an apparent sensory deficit is one of the first indicators that a child's development is not proceeding normally. In fact, many consider attentional problems to be the main reason for the individual's failure to develop typically.

Itard, the first scientist–practitioner to study a child with severe developmental delays (Victor), considered deficits in sensory processes to be a main cause of Victor's delayed development. To help Victor develop more competent and appropriate behaviors, Itard placed a major emphasis on stimulating Victor's various sensory organs with the hope of opening them to normal receptions. He attempted to accomplish this by engaging Victor in bodily movements, stroking him, and exposing him to fearful situations, hot and cold sensations, electric stimulation of the skin, and a variety of other forms of stimulation. Many of Itard's interventions are still used some 200 years later, and a large range of similar interventions have been tried, all of them designed to alter sensory processing. Such interventions include Sensory-Motor Training, Auditory Integration, stroking with feathers, rubbing with sponges, squeeze machines, and placement in rotating chairs. Sadly, all of these interventions have failed to demonstrate effectiveness in increasing attention and learning (see Chapter 3).

One of the more recent developments postulates that a defect exists not in processing one sensory input but in processing two at a time (Mundy, 1995). For example, if a child can attend only to his mother's facial expressions or hand movements and not concurrently to her voice, then this would constitute a handicap in trying to understand the mother's verbalizations. The Joint Attention Hypothesis bears a strong similarity to what other researchers have earlier referred to as "stimulus overselectivity" or "overly narrow attention" (Lovaas, 1979), which is reviewed below.

The term *stimulus overselectivity* refers to findings showing that children with autism initially respond to only one element, or a restricted range of elements, in a stimulus compound. For example, when presented with a teacher's verbal request, a child may either read the teacher's lips or attend to the teacher's gaze instead of responding to the teacher's voice. When learning to tell the difference between a girl doll and a boy doll, a child may make the distinction based on the dolls' shoes rather than more pertinent characteristics. When the teacher removes the dolls' shoes, the child may no longer be able to tell the difference between the dolls. In learning the meaning of a word such as *mother,* the child may have to associate two or more concurrent stimulus inputs, such as the spoken word "mother" with the look, voice, feel, or other stimuli connected with her mother. Failure to associate these stimuli is likely to leave the word *mother* without meaning.

An alternate possibility is that restricted attention is not a causal variable per se, but rather the result of inadequate motivation and restricted learning opportunities. Over time, we have come to favor this possibility because overselective responding seems to diminish or, in the case of the best outcome children, vanish during intensive behavioral treatment without aides having to specifically address attentional problems. It seems reasonable to assume that if an individual was not reinforced in past learning situations for attending to his social environment because he did not understand what was happening around him, then he probably would not have any reason to attend to his social environment in the present or the future. For example, imagine a student (who could be any one of us) attending a boring class in school and drifting off into various subtle forms of reverie and other forms of self-stimulation. After an hour of lecture, the individual would likely be unable to recall any part of the lesson, either in terms of what the teacher said or what was written on the blackboard. Conversely, if the same student attended a class in which a teacher broke down the lesson into manageable parts, spoke clearly, and provided ample reinforcement for participation, then it is likely that most or all persons in the class would attend to the lecture and learn. Similarly, if individuals with developmental delays are provided with learning opportunities in which they are systematically reinforced for attending to what others say or show to them, then the individuals may not show attentional problems when exposed to such events in the future.

Two observations led us to favor a learning hypothesis as it applies to treating attentional problems. First, before treatment was started, the children we studied acted as if they could not see or hear unless they became confronted with a stimulus input that yielded a reward. For example, a particular child would not react to a loud siren and seemed completely oblivious to the people around her, only to spot a small piece of M&M candy some 30 feet away. Or, while appearing engrossed in a television show, a child would detect, out of the corner of his eye, that a parent went upstairs and left the front door unlocked. The child would then quickly go to the door, open it, and run away from the house, enjoying and being reinforced by the chase when discovered. Some children would always show up on time for their favorite television program and clearly identify the particular button that needed to be depressed to activate the system.

A pilot study done at the UCLA (University of California, Los Angeles) Autism Clinic provides a particularly vivid example of apparent sensory deficits in children with autism. In an attempt to ascertain where a nervous system sensory "block" may be located, the children's heart rates, galvanic skin response, pupillary dilations and constrictions, and orientation to stimuli were recorded. Clapping one's hands directly behind a child's back and observing a failure to startle is often used as a diagnostic indicator of autism. We failed to observe any response to hand clapping even though the clapping was loud. Subsequently, and without prior warning, we increased the loudness and fired a very loud noise (from a starting pistol) 2 feet behind each child's back. This sound was of sufficient strength to elicit a major startle in attending adults. In contrast, little or no change was detected in any of the children's behaviors, despite the sensitivity of the measurement instruments employed. However, there were major alterations in all recordings when, instead of firing the loud starting pistol, the children heard the slight sound of a candy bar being unwrapped out of sight. It seemed as if the children would attend to their environment if there was a payoff for doing so. In evaluating the outcome of this experiment, it is important to be reminded of the large differences among persons with autism. In regard to the experiment with the starting pistol, a child with a fear of unusual sounds, such as those from vacuum cleaners or ambulance sirens, may well have reacted differently from those children we observed in the study.

Other observations support the idea that learning is likely to be a major mechanism by which to establish attention. Discrimination learning provides such a mechanism by helping students attend to relevant stimuli such as the teacher's instructions. Teaching the student to discriminate among and attend to stimuli is reviewed in some detail in Chapter 16, and the steps involved are illustrated in considerable detail in almost all of programs presented in this manual. The teacher will discover that as students work through the programs in this manual, they gradually extend their attention to an increasingly larger range of stimuli if they are reinforced for doing so. Some of these stimuli are very subtle and require intact attentional mechanisms.

Whereas some young typical children show evidence of stimulus overselectivity, some children with autism or developmental delays do not. Such an observation leads us to believe that restricted attention may be an effect, rather than the cause, of failure to learn. Nevertheless, restricted attention is likely to be present at the beginning of treatment, before the individual learns to attend to the teacher's stimuli. It is likely that the student will sometimes respond to cues the teacher inadvertently provides while ignoring those that the teacher intends for the student to respond to. For example, if the teacher were to accidentally look toward an object while asking the student to point to it, the student might solve the task by following the teacher's gaze rather than attending to the teacher's vocal instructions. Reinforcement for a correct response in such an instance would only serve to strengthen the wrong association between the visual cue and the student's response. It is very easy to make such a mistake. It is our observation that persons with developmental delays often learn an association when reinforcement is contingent on a behavior; however, this association may not be the one the teacher intended. We discuss ways of avoiding such problems throughout the manual.

Concluding Comments

Applied Behavior Analysis has developed gradually and cumulatively, as discussed in Chapter 3. As findings emerge, older explanations are often revised or replaced by new explanations. A relatively recent observation sheds some new light on the attentional problems discussed in this chapter. It appears that the *mode* by which students are taught makes a difference. That is, some students learn to respond to an auditory mode such as speech. Others experience difficulty learning when the teacher uses auditory cues, but excel when the teacher uses visual cues. Such variations in receptor preferences have led us to distinguish between visual learners and auditory learners This finding may help people view attentional mechanisms from a new perspective. (See Chapters 12, 13, 29, and 30 for teaching procedures that accommodate visual learners.)

Transition into Treatment

SECTION 2

Establishing Cooperation and Tantrum Reduction

CHAPTER 9

A considerable amount of background material is covered in the preceding chapters. It may be helpful to start the first hours of treatment at this time to gain some practical experience, which will help make the abstract concepts presented earlier more understandable.

The concepts presented in this chapter (instructions, responses, response prompting, and reinforcement) are discussed more extensively in subsequent chapters. This chapter uses these concepts to help the teacher establish cooperation and reduce tantrums in the teaching situation. These initial steps are crucial to teaching the skills presented in the following chapters. Some members of the student's team should become familiar with the material presented later in this manual to be able to give constructive feedback during the first hours of treatment. Regardless, we advise all team members to read this entire chapter before beginning to teach.

The first hours are perhaps the most important hours and the most stressful hours in the student's treatment. These first hours are important because the student's success gives you the encouragement to continue teaching and gives the student confidence, trust in you, and a willingness to cooperate, all of which are critical to future educational efforts. These first hours are stressful in that most students tantrum and resist the situation, and you will most likely be scared for yourself and the student. Even 3- or 4-year-old children can be quite tantrumous and cause a large amount of fright in the adults who try to teach them.

Keep in mind two important observations we made earlier in this manual: First, the student's tantrum is a response to frustration over not understanding what you want to teach her. Second, through her tantrums, the student succeeds in resisting demands she does not understand. Her tantrums make you anxious and perhaps cause you to back down, removing your demands. You and the student have adapted to a very difficult situation: The student is reinforced for tantruming by the removal of your demands, and you are reinforced for withdrawing your demands because doing so leads to a reduction in your anxiety over the student's tantrums. After a year or more of such daily occurrences, there is reason to believe that this interaction becomes well established and difficult to change.

Remember, you can love the student and still place demands on her. Perhaps the love an adult gives to a student should be defined in terms of its effects on the student. If what you do helps the student live a fuller and more meaningful life, then that is love. Providing attention and love contingent on maladaptive behaviors worsens those behaviors. Such interventions should not be labeled love.

Because proper completion of the first hours of treatment is critical to getting off to a good start, it is important to plan them carefully. One piece of advice seems particularly important: View the student's displays of frustration as healthful. The student's past failures bother her, and you can use that motivation to help her succeed. You can say to yourself, "Look at all the energy she has that I can help her use for constructive purposes."

Organizing the Teaching Environment

In Chapter 4, guidance was given for locating persons who can help you provide the student with a large number of one-on-one teaching hours, managing a treatment team, and realizing the importance of a team in helping to solve teaching problems. In Chapter 36, Ronald Huff provides advice on how to organize a parent group so as to obtain emotional support and technical information for the efforts that lie ahead. Many of the parents and teachers in such a group may have already experienced the stress and success of the first hours; their advice to your team may be significant and should be sought.

Before beginning the first hours of treatment, arrange for a teaching room in your house. This could be any room that has a holding capacity of five to eight persons and contains a small table and two chairs (child sized, if appropriate). At weekly meetings, teachers should sit in a circle around the table so that each has a clear view of the student.

In the beginning of treatment, you do not need many materials; some wooden building blocks, a plastic bucket, and reinforcing items such as favorite toys and snacks should suffice. As the student progresses, the teaching materials become extensive, necessitating a large container full of stimulus cards and objects. There should be a log book in which to write down the programs that have been introduced and the extent to which items within the programs have been mastered (see Chapter 33). The log book will eventually contain hundreds of pages, becoming the student's record of progress through treatment.

If a behavioral consultant is hired to conduct a workshop, set aside 3 days for that consultation (see Chapter 34). It is important that you and *all* of your team members are present for the training. If you have to start the treatment without a consultant, it may be helpful to role-play the first hours before the student becomes involved. Choose one person from the team to play the student. This person should know the student well and have some familiarity with how the student is likely to behave when asked to comply.

Remember to give praise and reassurance to the team members who are being trained and let them express their apprehensions. Facing a common difficulty builds cohesiveness. Remember, each member should take turns practicing treatment and receive feedback on his or her performance. If you have hired a consultant, ask that person to begin the one-on-one treatment and demonstrate to you the actual and concrete steps involved. This will give you some impression of that person's competence (it is easy to talk and role-play, but it is much more difficult to actually treat the student). Such a demonstration is typically more productive and efficient than role playing.

Reinforcers

Chapter 7 provides detailed descriptions of the many reinforcers that can be used during treatment; thus, only a short recap of reinforcers is provided in this chapter. Of all the aspects involved in behavioral teaching, the types of reinforcers and use of reinforcers are the most important. Identify as many reinforcers as you can prior to beginning treatment. Have them readily available and within your reach, but not within the student's reach.

To help prevent satiation, make sure that all food reinforcement is given in small quantities. For example, reinforce by using pieces of toast the size of sugar cubes or one piece of cereal, such as Frosted Flakes, at a time. Although food is often a powerful reinforcer, some students may be too upset to take solid food during the first hours of treatment. However, the same students may accept sips of a favorite beverage. As with food, only small quantities of drink should be provided to the student. You may want to have beverages prepoured into small cups. Later, when you are more confident, you can provide sips from a full glass.

Do not feed the student a large breakfast or lunch prior to the teaching session. A person who is satiated by food will not find food to be reinforcing. Whenever possible, use healthful foods and stay away from candy and other sweets except as special treats. Choose food reinforcers that can be consumed quickly; avoid chewy snacks, which delay the interval between trials. Most reinforcer consumption should not last longer than 10 seconds; for the most part, 3 to 5 seconds make an ideal time limit. The more reinforced trials given, the more learning opportunities there are available to the student.

Some students may be rewarded by holding their favorite object for 5 seconds or placing a puzzle piece into a puzzle. Most students are rewarded by being allowed to leave the teaching situation and run over to their parents for comfort. Later, the student may also accept comfort from other adults. Additional reinforcers described in Chapter 7 include loud praise ("What a great kid!") and ample clapping by all adults present. Clapping is often a powerful reinforcer for students. Some reinforcers, such as playful jostling, can be used only after the student has settled down a few hours into treatment. Some students love to be tossed in the air, others thrive on having their feet rubbed. Some love to be mildly scared and surprised. Remember that the student must become comfortable with you to accept such play, and there are large individual differences in what each particular student finds rewarding. It is the discovery of new and often idiosyncratic reinforcers that makes you a better teacher and keeps the student motivated to learn.

Some students may not accept a favorite food or object when it is used as a reward. This may happen because they are too upset or because they may sense that you want to teach them and thereby change their routines. Changing a routine is often the last thing students will let you do during the early stages of treatment. They want to be in control. There are ways around such refusals, although you may need to be inventive in discovering them. We worked with one student who was resisting all commonly used rewards until we found that he was greatly reinforced by a 5-second playing of the Disney song "It's a Small World." With another student, we were at a complete loss in discovering effective reinforcers until we stumbled upon pouring water from one glass to another, one of his favorite self-stimulatory rituals. As reinforcement, we placed glasses and pitchers of water on the table and allowed the student to pour the water after he had done what the teacher wanted him to do. The reinforcing effects of pouring water lasted for hundreds of trials and, once the student worked for that reinforcer, other reinforcers were readily accepted and effectively used.

If you isolate an effective reward and use it correctly, you make the first step toward teaching the student. You achieve reinforcement control over the student's behaviors, which is the most important sign that you will aid in the student's development. In everyday language, you have been able to select rewards (reinforcers) and use these rewards in such a manner as to help the student learn. Before achieving such control, you are not very effective at helping the student. Consider the gaining of reinforcement control to be a major victory, no matter how trivial the student's achievements may appear to certain casual observers.

Once effective reinforcers are identified, place the reinforcers out of the student's reach; otherwise there will be a continual struggle to keep the student from getting to them without working for them. If the student is allowed free access to reinforcers, these reinforcers are likely to lose their effectiveness in the teaching environment. If possible, hold the reinforcers in your hand so you can deliver them immediately after the student performs correctly. As the student progresses through treatment, you may be able to place the reinforcers on the student's table within arm's reach because the student will, over time, learn to bridge the delay between her response and the desired reinforcement with your verbal reinforcer. Eventually, a verbalization such as "Good!" is likely to become a secondary, or learned, reinforcer after repeatedly being paired with a primary reinforcer such as food.

Sitting in the Chair

The main advantage of starting with an easy task such as sitting is that the student will likely be successful learning it and can thus be reinforced. Sitting in a chair is commonly taught first because sitting is a relatively simple behavior that is easy to prompt. Sitting in a chair is also discriminable to the student (as it involves gross motor behaviors) and a clear response, making it easy for the teacher to decide whether to reinforce it. In addition, sitting is a behavior that the student must eventually learn to do.

Most students are able to learn sitting as the first response taught. For other students, however, this task elicits so much emotional upheaval and is resisted with so much tantrumous behavior that it interferes with reinforcement delivery. We shall address potential solutions to this problem later in this chapter, noting for now that any reinforceable socially appropriate behavior is adequate as a first behavior. Examples of such behaviors also are provided later in this chapter. Given individual differences, it is best to keep three or four alternate behaviors in mind.

To teach sitting, arrange two chairs (child sized, if appropriate) such that they face each other and are 1 to 2 feet apart. The student should be placed in a standing position between your legs and facing you with her chair directly behind her so that sitting down (the correct response) is easy to perform. Place your legs behind the legs of the student's chair so the student cannot tip the chair back, get hurt, or run away. If the student is allowed to run away, she will have to be chased, which is likely to be a reinforcing event. If such a chase occurs, the behavior of running away may be reinforced and strengthened.

Instructions, Prompts, and Reinforcers for Teaching Sitting

It is important to practice the following steps with another adult playing the role of the student before you begin the actual treatment. After seating yourself and placing the student in front of her chair facing you, say, "Sit," in a clear and loud voice. It is important to present instructions in a succinct, definite, and audible manner. Do not show hesitation and do not use elaborate speech; the word "Sit" will suffice. Ideally, the student will sit and you can reinforce her for sitting. Most likely, however, the student will not sit when asked to do so and you will have to prompt her.

Prompt sitting by placing your hands on the student's shoulders and moving her backward into a sitting position onto the chair. Remember to place your legs behind the legs of the student's chair so that the chair does not move backward. Ideally, prompting should occur concurrently with the instruction. Different degrees in intensity of the prompt will be necessary depending on the student. Some students sit down just by being tapped on the shoulders, whereas others need to be more firmly placed in the chair.

As soon as the student is seated (and *before* the student gets up), she should be provided with all the reinforcement you can give her. When you reinforce the student, act as if she accomplished a most difficult task. What you want to do is build the student's trust and confidence in you as well as in herself. This may be done by providing the student with a rich schedule of reinforcement and a favorite drink, food, object to hold, or anything the student will accept and be comforted by at that time. In addition, everyone present should clap, smile, and provide a large amount of verbal praise.

As further reinforcement, the teacher should let the student go to her mother or father for comfort after she sits correctly. You may have to prompt the student to go to her parents. This may be done by placing the student in such a fashion that she can see her mother or father who, with outstretched arms, says, "Come here." Gently guide the student over to a parent's lap, where she is comforted. Even if the student did not seek her parent's company before this time, she will likely do so now that she is apprehensive.

This procedure, starting with the instruction and ending with the reinforcement, is one *trial*. Once the student is reinforced by sitting on her parent's lap for half a minute or so, repeat the process by again placing the student near the chair and present the second trial, following the exact steps used in the first trial; that is, give the instruction ("Sit"), prompt, and reinforce as done previously.

When first teaching the student to sit upon your request, you may be able to conduct one to two trials per minute. To maximize the student's learning, however, the length of time the student spends with her parent should, over time, be shortened to 10 to 15 seconds so that the task of sitting can be more frequently reinforced and strengthened. At the same time, the length of time the student spends sitting in the chair should be gradually increased from 3 or 4 seconds to 10 seconds or more.

No student can get more love than that provided in a well-run behavioral program. Once a student catches on to the task you are trying to teach (demonstrated by less fussing, needing fewer prompts, or both), it is not surprising to see the student glance at the aides in the room, anticipating and recognizing approval. Such an occurrence provides ample evidence that you are on the right track. At such a time your own anxiety level may also reduce, leaving room for relief and happiness. When this point is reached, treatment becomes a mutually reinforcing affair.

Prompt Fading

The main advantage of prompts is that they help the student correctly perform target behaviors. If you do not prompt, the student may never respond correctly to your instructions. The main disadvantage of prompts is that the student does not perform the behavior on her own when prompts are used; thus, she is not reinforced for responding to your request but rather for responding to the prompt. Because of this, the student may become prompt dependent. To avoid prompt dependency, you must fade the prompt. Prompt fading is accomplished by gradually using weaker and weaker prompts while keeping the instructions at full strength. To fade the prompt for the task of sitting, present the instruction ("Sit") while simultaneously lessening the physical prompt, providing just enough strength to occasion the correct response. For example, shift from fully placing the student into the chair to only placing your hands on the student's shoulders, then to touching her lightly with one finger, then to just gesturing to her with your hands while nodding your head, then to just nodding your head while looking at and pointing to the seat, and then to just looking at the seat. The instruction "Sit" should eventually be presented without any prompt.

If the student fails to respond correctly after the prompt is reduced or removed, reinstate the least amount of prompt necessary to reestablish correct responding. Remember that the verbal instructions should be expressed at full strength while the prompt is faded. Shifting control over the response from the prompt to the verbal instruction should be considered a major achievement; it is a sign that the student is learning.

In technical terms, fading out a prompt stimulus while fading in a verbal stimulus (in this case, the instruction "Sit") is known as a *shift in stimulus control*. Control over the student's behavior is shifted from the prompt stimulus to your verbal stimulus. As your verbal instruction gains strength as a reliable predictor of reinforcement, the prompt becomes increasingly less reliable. If you are very skillful at teaching, this transition is accomplished smoothly with the student making minimal or no errors. That is, the student receives almost continuous reinforcement and is less likely to respond to the loss of a reinforcer with a tantrum. Technically this is known as *errorless learning*. For those of us who made many errors in our past educational history, it may seem a dream to consider a teaching situation in which one almost always succeeds (and thus rarely fails). In an ideal teaching environment, successes should outnumber failures by a ratio of 4:1 to keep the student involved and learning. For your sake and for the student's sake, be sure to start simple so both of you can learn the basic steps and be reinforced.

Occasionally you may probe for mastery of a response by suddenly removing the prompt, thus testing whether the student correctly responds to your request to sit down without further prompt fading. If the student does not, reinstate the minimal amount of prompt needed to occasion the correct response, then fade the prompt gradually.

The rate of fading must be determined on an individual basis for each student. The guiding principle is to use the least amount of prompt necessary to help the correct response occur.

Shaping

Shaping is a term used to describe reinforcing progressively closer approximations to the desired behavior. As with all other technical terms, shaping is discussed in greater detail throughout this manual. In the first hours of teaching, this procedure may be carried out as follows: As soon as the student reliably sits when asked to do so, reinforce. Then gradually increase the amount of time the student sits from 1 or 2 seconds to 5 seconds and then to 10 to 15 seconds or more before providing reinforcement. Through this procedure, the amount of time the student sits in the chair is shaped by delivering reinforcement contingent on increasing lengths of time spent in the chair. One helpful way for you to monitor the time interval for sitting is to count silently to yourself, keeping track of the number of seconds required before delivery of reinforcement. A student who learns to sit in a chair for 15 seconds is likely to be more productive in future teaching sessions than one who learns to sit for only 2 seconds. Further increases in the length of time follow naturally as new programs are introduced.

Acquiring the Skill of Sitting

Learning to sit down as a first lesson may take anywhere from 1 to 10 hours to accomplish. There should be a gradual increase in the ease and rate with which the student sits as the session progresses. This increase in the rate of sitting achieved through reinforcement is referred to as *acquisition*. The concept of acquisition was first introduced in Chapter 5 on tantrumous and self-injurious behaviors. Self-injury, just like sitting in a chair, is a behavior; hence, it responds to reinforcement. Socially appropriate behaviors, such as sitting in a chair, gradually replace socially inappropriate behaviors, such as tantrums and self-injury, when appropriate behaviors are reinforced and inappropriate behaviors are not reinforced. In behavioral treatment, socially appropriate behaviors gain access to the same or similar reinforcers that tantrums and self-injury achieve, lessening the need for the student to engage in the latter.

Some students sit with minimal guidance and do not demonstrate any major disruptive behaviors from the very beginning of teaching. Other students tantrum a great deal, but as long as they remain seated for the required period of time, they should be rewarded by, for example, being allowed to briefly leave the teaching situation. Our experience has been that the repeated success sitting down and being reinforced for doing so is sufficient to reduce tantrums when first learning to sit given the instruction to do so. However, if tantruming does not subside at least somewhat within the first 2 hours of teaching, then go on to the next section on teaching the student not to tantrum.

Teaching the Student Not To Tantrum

For a student who continues to tantrum while sitting, it may be helpful to select not tantruming as the second response taught. Begin by having the student sit in the chair long enough to be quiet for 1 or 2 seconds. As soon as the tantrums and screams subside, the student should be amply reinforced (e.g., by getting out of the chair, receiving a favorite snack and verbal praises, or going to a parent). Gradually increase (shape) the length of time the student is to remain quiet.

As the student tantrums, nobody should look at him. Instead, all persons present should look down at the floor while the tantrum occurs. Even a short glance from a parent or team member can serve to reinforce the student's tantrums, even if a glance has never been effective in reinforcing any other of the student's behaviors. Perhaps an anxious glance is a sign to the student that someone will compromise and let him leave the situation. To avoid such glances, it may be helpful to have the student sit with his back to his parents in the early stages, because the parents are likely to be the most important persons to the student and the ones who are most anxious and uncertain about what to do. It is perhaps also the parents, being the ones who are most vulnerable, who are the most likely to give in and attend to the student during the tantrum.

Once a student learns to sit without tantruming, alternate teachers (including the parents) are introduced. This is referred to as *generalizing treatment gains*. Usually the student starts tantruming again when the second teacher is introduced, testing the new teacher. Testing occurs again and again, not only when new teachers are introduced, but also when teaching is introduced in new situations, as when the teaching sessions are moved from the original teaching room to other rooms of the house or outside environments (e.g., stores, restaurants, schools). The student must learn with each new adult and in each new situation that he cannot get away with tantrums. The student's tantrums and uncooperative behaviors will decrease over time with new teachers and across new environments providing that consequences of the student's actions remain constant and interfering behaviors are not reinforced but instead are placed on extinction (i.e., the inappropriate behaviors are not provided with the reinforcement that previously maintained the behavior).

Completing a Puzzle

Although most students learn to sit in a chair and reduce their tantrums during the first hours of treatment, some students experience this task as too upsetting or difficult. Not tantruming may also be difficult for some students to learn. Given the large individual differences among students, it is important to be flexible and change tasks if no progress is noted during the first hours (see Chapter 33, which deals with methods for recording progress).

The task of completing a puzzle can be taught on the floor or at the table. Begin by placing a puzzle with three pieces (e.g., square, circle, triangle) on the floor or table. Remove one of the pieces (e.g., the circle). Next, bring the student over to the puzzle and hand her the circle while instructing, "Put in." Prompt the correct placement and reinforce the behavior with food and praise. Note that matching the shapes, such as the circle to the circle, may constitute its own reinforcer. Repeat the trial while gradually fading the prompt. Over successive trials, gradually increase the number of pieces removed from the puzzle and given to the student from one piece to three pieces at a time. What the student learns in this situation is to complete a task when you ask her to do so. (Technically speaking, you bring her behavior under instructional control.)

Note that even if the student cooperates and gives signs of enjoying herself during this session, it is quite likely that tantrums will occur when she returns for the second session of learning to sit in a chair. Giving up control is not easy for most persons, whether or not they are developmentally delayed. The goal, however, is to teach the student better and more efficient ways of controlling others than by throwing tantrums.

Dropping Blocks into a Bucket

Dropping blocks into a bucket has been found to be helpful in establishing cooperation during the early hours of treatment. Nonetheless, shifting to the teaching of a new response in these early stages of treatment is likely to reinstate or increase tantruming. If you ignore tantrums while continuing with the new task, however, the tantrums will most likely decrease in strength and duration with the introduction of subsequent tasks.

Before teaching the student to drop a block into a bucket, select blocks the student can hold easily in his hand. Place one block on the table within easy reach of both you and the student. Choose a large-mouthed bucket and place it close to and slightly under the table or between your legs so the student does not miss placing the block into the bucket. It also helps to use a bucket made of a material (e.g., metal or plastic) that produces to a distinct noise when the block falls into it. Similar to the tactile feedback provided by the task of sitting in the chair, the block-in-bucket task gives auditory feedback that facilitates the student's forming an association between his behavior and the reinforcing reward.

To begin teaching this new task, instruct in a loud and clear voice, "Drop block," while prompting the dropping response. Prompt by taking the student's hand, placing it over the block, and helping him grasp it. Guide the student's hand to the top of the bucket and release the student's grip on the block. Once the block is dropped, provide massive reinforcement. Over the next few trials, slowly fade the prompt. Fade the prompt by gradually decreasing the physical grip of your hand, guiding the student's hand to the block for him to grip onto it by himself, then slowly fade to just tapping the student's hand, then to gesturing toward the block with your hand, and finally to just looking toward the block when you instruct, "Drop block." Eventually fade all prompts completely such that the verbal request to drop the block (while looking at the student and not toward the block or bucket) is sufficient for the student to succeed. If the physical act of holding the block is difficult for the student, simply prompt the student to shove a block from the table into a bucket placed partly underneath the table. Repeat the instruction while fading the prompt over subsequent trials.

Once the student drops the block into the bucket upon your unprompted request, gradually increase the difficulty of the task by requiring the student to drop more than one block in order to be reinforced. This may be done by giving the instruction "Drop block" and withholding reinforcement contingent on the student dropping into the bucket not only one block, but two, then three, and then up to five or six blocks. The task can also be made more difficult by slowly increasing the distance between the blocks on the table and the bucket. As the number of trials conducted grows, some students spontaneously use both hands to place more blocks into the bucket and more forcefully drop the blocks into the bucket. Perhaps these students gain additional reinforcement from the noise generated from the blocks' hitting the bucket. In any case, such appropriate extra behaviors should be amply reinforced.

"Come Here"

Once the student learns any two of the skills presented previously, you may introduce the task of coming to the parent when a parent says to the student, "Come here." It is unlikely that the student will master this task within the first few hours of treatment given that many students tantrum so severely in these first hours that prompting "Come here" is made difficult. In addition, out-of-the-chair behaviors, such as coming to a parent upon request, may instigate other interfering behaviors, such as running away. For most students, it may be optimal to postpone this task until 3 to 4 hours into treatment. If the "Come here" task turns out to be too difficult for the student, go on to the Matching and Sorting Program (Chapter 12), the Nonverbal Imitation Program (Chapter 13), or both. Return to teaching the "Come here" task after some progress is made in one or both of those programs.

To teach the "Come here" task, one of the student's parents (or teachers) should sit in a chair or sofa 5 to 7 feet away from the student. Upon completion of a task at the table (e.g., dropping blocks into a bucket), turn the student to face the parent who, with outstretched arms, says in a loud and clear voice, "Come here." Prompt the student to go to the parent by having a second adult physically move the student to the parent. The behavior of going to the parent allows the student to leave the teaching situation contingent on completing a task (e.g., sitting in the chair or dropping blocks into a bucket), thereby reinforcing and strengthening these tasks. As soon as the student reaches her parent, the student receives immediate and abundant reinforcement both by leaving an initially unpleasant teaching situation and by gaining the opportunity to be cuddled by her parent. The student may also receive reinforcement by being able to hold her favorite book or toy while sitting on her parent's lap.

Note that the instruction ("Come here") must be loud and succinct to gain the student's attention. Also note that the parent should maximize the likelihood of the student's success by facing the student and reaching for her, adding a visual prompt to the verbal instruction. The physical prompt provided by the second adult further serves to maximize the student's success. Remember that all prompts must be *gradually* faded over time. If prompts are faded too quickly, the student may not respond correctly because the student is not as of yet "hearing" and understanding the parent. As prompts are faded over trials, trials involving less prompting should receive more reinforcement than trials requiring more prompting.

As the student gains familiarity with the teaching situation, the reward value of coming to the parent may decrease. Therefore, the student may choose not to come to the parent. Such behavior is acceptable at this time. In the future and in other situations, however, the student must learn to reliably come to the parent when doing so is necessary. In addition, the student must learn to come to you upon request in the teaching situation.

The following procedure is designed to help generalize the "Come here" instruction to other adults and other situations by teaching the student to approach the person who gives her the instruction regardless of the location of the person. Teaching the student to respond to the instruction "Come here" in this manner is most easily accomplished with the assistance of two adults who are referred to here as Teacher 1 and Teacher 2. The two teachers alternate roles of prompting and presenting instructions.

▶ Step 1

Teacher 1 stands or sits behind the student with his or her hands around the student's waist. Teacher 2 stands approximately 3 feet away, facing the student. Teacher 2 should have a reinforcer (e.g., a bite of food, a sip of juice, a favorite toy) in hand and in the student's plain view. Teacher 2 presents the instruction ("Come here") and prompts the response by stretching out his or her arms toward the student. At the same time, Teacher 1 physically prompts the student to walk to Teacher 2 by gently nudging the student forward. Teacher 2 may also prompt by showing the student the food reinforcer. Once the student reaches Teacher 2, she should be reinforced for coming over. The student should remain with Teacher 2 for approximately 5 seconds. Repeat the trial and fade the prompts over subsequent trials. Place mastery at 9 out of 10 or 19 out of 20 consecutive unprompted correct responses.

▶ Step 2

Reverse teaching roles: Teacher 2 turns the student to face Teacher 1, and Teacher 1 presents the instruction ("Come here") and stretches out his or her arms to prompt the student. Teacher 2 prompts the student to walk to Teacher 1 by gently nudging the student forward. Immediately reinforce the student after she meets Teacher 1. Set mastery at 9 out of 10 or 19 out of 20 unprompted correct responses.

▶ Step 3

Continue switching between Teachers 1 and 2, fading the prompts over trials. For example, each teacher begins hiding the food (if that was used as a prompt), stretching out his or her arms to the student for shorter time intervals, and providing less manual prompting (nudging the student forward) on each subsequent trial. With the alternation between teachers, the number of unprompted correct trials required should systematically decrease until the student is able to independently come to either teacher upon his or her first request.

▶ Step 4

When the student responds to the instruction ("Come here") to both teachers without prompting, increase the distance between teachers to approximately 5 feet and then gradually up to 9 or 10 feet or across the room. Reintroduce the prompt of outstretched arms each time the distance is increased and fade the prompt over subsequent trials.

▶ Step 5

This step is introduced to teach the student to come to the chair upon the teacher's request. This step is important for learning to perform the various programs in this manual which are, for the most part, taught to the student while sitting in a chair. To begin, place the student 4 to 6 feet away from a chair positioned directly across from Teacher 1. As Teacher 1 presents the instruction ("Come here"), Teacher 2 prompts the student to come to the chair by gently nudging her toward the chair. Provide reinforcement immediately upon completion of the response. Continue to present trials of "Come here," gradually fading the prompt on each successive trial. The prompt may be faded by, for example, progressing from nudging the student less and less on each trial to patting the chair. When the student responds to the instruction without prompting, increase her distance from the chair to 6 to 10 feet. Prompt if necessary when the new distance is introduced, and fade the prompt over subsequent trials until the student comes to the chair upon hearing the verbal instruction only ("Come here"). Gradually generalize this skill into other areas of the house (e.g., first into the hallway adjacent to the original room, then into other rooms). Once the student masters the instruction, the teacher does not need to physically bring the student to the chair, which makes the job of teaching a little easier.

The presence of toys or other objects in the room that invite self-stimulatory behavior may interfere with the student's response to "Come here" and other instructions. To maximize the student's early success, remove these objects. As the student's behavior of coming to the teacher increases in strength and the teaching environment acquires positive reinforcing properties, gradually introduce such objects into the room.

Up to this point, some 3 to 10 hours into instruction for most students, the student has learned to sit down, to perform a task such as dropping a block into a bucket, and to come to a parent and other adults upon request. Avoid teaching any two of these behaviors at the same time; for example, do not teach "Sit" and "Drop block" concurrently. Instead, simplify the response requirement by teaching each task separately to mastery, and then combine them. The combination of the separate responses constitutes a chain of behaviors which flows naturally such that the instruction "Sit" comes to cue sitting, which then cues dropping blocks, followed by coming to a parent or a teacher. The last response serves as a reinforcer for the preceding responses (techniques for forming chains are provided later in this manual). From a behavioral psychology point of view, the world is full of such chains, such as when you get up in the morning, shower, dress, eat breakfast, and then go to work or school. Rudimentary forms of these complex chains can be established during the first hours of treatment.

In the remainder of this chapter, certain additional behaviors that will help the student take full advantage of the teaching opportunities offered in this manual are introduced. These behaviors are presented at this point because they can be taught without the use of discrimination learning procedures (see Chapter 16), a relatively complex set of steps necessary to teaching most of the other programs. The student need not master the following tasks before moving on to programs such as Matching and Nonverbal Imitation (Chapters 12 and 13, respectively), both of which may be taught concurrently with one another and with the tasks described below.

Increasing Cooperative Behaviors

Younger students generally have a difficult time sitting still, especially in a teaching situation. You may have to help the student remain seated while instructions are given, not talk out loud to others, not fidget, and in general pay attention to what you are saying. At other times during learning situations, the student is encouraged to move around, be spontaneous, be explorative, and interact with others. The reader will note that we use the term *attention* in a somewhat loose and general manner. It is perfectly possible for a student to sit quietly in a chair and visually fixate on your face without attending to any part of what you are saying or doing. Looking is not the same as seeing. The psychological process of attention is described in some detail in the chapter on discrimination learning (Chapter 16). Certain precursors to attention are presented here.

Many individuals with developmental delays are less compliant than typical individuals. Some present major problems when asked to sit in a chair, even for short periods of time. As demonstrated earlier in this chapter, the first hours of treatment are devoted mainly to teaching the student to sit quietly in a chair. Although the student may master sitting in a chair and the programs in this manual do not require the student to sit in the chair for prolonged periods of time, you may notice that the student fidgets with or flaps her hands excessively, moves her legs back and forth, or rocks her body while sitting in the chair. Such self-stimulatory behavior is often the cause of a student not paying attention to you. In technical terms, the student is under the control of self-generated sensory reinforcers rather than your socially mediated reinforcers.

The student has already made some progress attending to you by mastering tasks such as responding to the requests "Sit," "Put in," "Drop block," and "Come here." Next we illustrate the instructions "Hands quiet" and "Sit nice." The behaviors performed in response to these instructions are intended to further help you gain the student's attention in order to facilitate the student's progress in future programs.

"Hands Quiet"

Teaching the student to respond to the request "Hands quiet" helps focus his attention on the task being taught and reduces the impact of stimuli generated by his self-stimulatory behaviors. The student's response to the request to keep his hands quiet can be composed of (1) keeping his arms down by his sides while his hands remain still, (2) placing his hands flat with his palms down on the top of his thighs, or (3) folding his hands in his lap. Choose the position that is the most natural for the student and the most helpful to you. Children who fidget with their thumb and forefinger should be taught Position 2 because, with their palms down and fingers spread on their legs, the temptation to fidget is minimized. Position 1 or 3 may be appropriate for students who flap their hands or arms.

When the student fidgets in the chair, present the instruction "Hands quiet" and prompt the student to respond correctly by manually guiding his hands to the desired position. Immediately reinforce the student for following your instruction. On subsequent occasions of the student's fidgeting in the chair, repeat the instruction and prompt the response. Gradually fade the amount of prompting provided. For example, after several fully prompted trials of placing the student's hands in her lap, fade the prompt to guiding the student's hands halfway up to his lap, then one quarter of the way to his lap, and so on until the student performs the response without any assistance whatsoever.

Criterion for mastery is difficult to establish for the instruction "Hands quiet" and similar attempts to reduce self-stimulatory behaviors. Therefore, be prepared for many trials over several weeks or months before the student reaches mastery of this task. The slow acquisition of this response may be due to the strong reinforcing effects of the student's self-stimulatory behavior and his extensive experience in developing and strengthening such behavior. It is possible that self-stimulatory behavior is strengthened not only by the (positive) sensory reinforcement it provides but also by the (negative) reinforcement it provides through avoidance of your instructional demands.

The best strategy for reducing self-stimulatory behavior is to gradually build socially appropriate behaviors to replace the inappropriate self-stimulatory ones. Such a strategy, however, requires a good deal of time before the desired results are realized. When forms of self-stimulatory behavior appear to be triggered by easily identifiable stimulus sources (e.g., the playing of a favorite video triggers obsessive preoccupation with that video; particular patterns of light trigger gazing), we advise that such sources be removed from the teaching environment in the initial stages of teaching.

Sitting Nice

Even after a student learns to respond to the instruction "Sit," she may slump over or slide down in the chair. In this section, the student is taught to sit properly in the chair when asked to do so. When the student does not sit properly, she is probably not attending to the teacher but rather attending to the sensory feedback arising from a particular body position. The instruction "Sit nice" helps to minimize the student's reinforcement from squirming and sliding in the chair and thus helps the student attend to the task at hand.

When the student slouches or slides down in the chair, give the instruction "Sit nice" in a loud, clear voice. Immediately prompt the student to respond correctly by physically guiding her to sit properly. This may require gently nudging her shoulders back, raising her up in the chair, or turning her legs to a forward position. Immediately reward the student for sitting properly. After several trials of the instruction "Sit nice" with full prompting, fade your prompt over subsequent trials. For example, if the student slouches in the chair, place your hands on the student's waist and see if she lifts herself in the chair rather than you having to raise her yourself. Continue to provide less assistance on each trial until the student responds correctly on her own.

In response to both the instruction "Hands quiet" and the instruction "Sit nice," it is enough for the student to suppress self-stimulatory behaviors long enough (e.g., 2 to 4 seconds) for you to present the instruction in the next trial. If the student does not self-stimulate as you present the instruction, it is more likely that the student will attend to your instructions.

Areas of Difficulty

Tantrums displayed by students during the first hours of treatment can be unnerving, to say the least. Even though students eventually need to learn not to respond with severe tantrums when placed in frustrating situations, tantrums may initially be reduced or avoided by identifying and removing particularly frustrating situations while still achieving the main teaching goals. The following anecdote submitted by a behavioral aide is an example of how this can be accomplished.

Sally

Sally appeared to be extremely attached to her mother. In addition, her reinforcement history of escaping demands was great from what I had observed earlier that morning. Every time Sally whined or threw her arms back, her mother would say, "Okay, okay," and remove her demands.

I also observed that Sally was interested in about three toys. I was able to redirect her attention from her mother to the toys on the floor and play with her for a few minutes. Sally was not upset and appeared to actually enjoy this interaction between herself, the toys, and myself, tolerating being separated from her mother while I played with her. Whenever I drew attention to her mother, however, Sally would immediately jump onto her mother's lap, suck her thumb, and twirl her hair. Although going to her mother constituted a powerful reinforcer, removing her from this reinforcing situation and placing her in the chair in order to teach the instruction "Sit" caused major tantrums.

I then decided to try something different. Instead of having Sally's mom so nearby, I requested that she sit in a different part of the room where she was not easily seen by Sally. I engaged Sally in some play with toys on the floor and then transferred the toys onto the table. Sally followed myself and the toys to the table. Once she was there, I prompted her to sit down and she continued to play for a couple of seconds. I abundantly reinforced Sally with food (which she was actually willing to take from me at that moment) and then directed her onto the floor to continue playing with other toys. We continued with this procedure for about 15 minutes. We also increased the time at the table from a couple of seconds to about 1 minute. My goal was to establish a positive reinforcement history at the table. By the end of this intervention, Sally actually approached the table on her own, sat in the chair, and started to play with some toys placed there. The major changes in emotional behavior came about effortlessly.

Teachers will encounter problems in every program. Sally's severe tantruming when separated from her mother is only one example. Some students do not tantrum at all when separated from a parent, but they may show other kinds of behavioral difficulties. This becomes increasingly evident as you work through the many and varied programs presented in this manual. However, the longer you teach, the less rigid and more creative you will become in using the teaching procedures described in this manual such that the difficulties displayed by the student are alleviated.

Before beginning to teach a student a particular skill, you cannnont accurately gauge the speed at which you should increase task difficulty. We suggest that if the student appears to have reached a plateau in his rate of mastery, you should step back and simplify the response requirement to recover successful performance before introducing more difficulty. Remember, the student's experience of success in the teaching situation is critical. The student shows you how fast to proceed; you are as much under the student's control as he is under yours.

Throughout the teaching of all tasks, the team members need to agree about and be consistent in their expectations of the student. For example, when teaching "Sit," if 5 seconds of sitting on the chair is the criterion, all teachers should consistently require this period of time. No one should introduce his or her personal requirements, as in going up to 10 or 15 seconds or down to less than 5 seconds. If a team member wants to try a different task or criterion, this needs to be discussed with all team members and agreed upon prior to introducing it. No aide's solo performances are allowed in the beginning of treatment; consistency is the rule. As the student improves, however, inconsistencies are introduced in a systematic and planned manner so that the effects can be measured and failures minimized. Obviously, for the student who masters a large number of programs, inconsistencies or variations in instructions and response requirements must be introduced and mastered. The real world is not consistent, and the student eventually needs to respond appropriately to variations.

When teaching the skills outlined in this chapter, also keep in mind that connecting the reinforcer to the behavior is essential. In some tasks, such as eye contact or babbling, the response is so subtle and fleeting that the student may not initially be able to make the connection between the behavior and the reinforcer. (Technically speaking, the student does not discriminate the reinforcement contingency.) Therefore, one should not *explicitly* teach subtle behaviors such as eye contact, vocalizations, or smiling in the early stages of treatment. As you proceed with teaching, however, appropriate behaviors such as eye contact and smiles may spontaneously emerge, and they may be prompted by the reinforcers provided within the teaching situation. For example, some students smile or babble when given reinforcement such as food or a kiss. (Technically speaking, the reinforcing stimulus contains unconditioned stimulus properties, eliciting respondent or reflexive emotional behaviors.) Other students look around the room, seeking recognition (reinforcement) for completing a correct response. Amply reinforce such socially appropriate and spontaneous behaviors. As you become increasingly competent as a teacher, you will also act more natural in the sense that your prompting and reinforcing of various behaviors will flow smoothly, entering you into a dynamic relationship with the student.

Concluding Comments

The technical concepts presented in this chapter are defined in more detail in Chapter 10. We introduce these concepts here, but detailed descriptions of them may not be essential to helping the student learn to sit in a chair, reduce tantrums, put blocks in a bucket, and go to her parents and other adults. Increased exposure to such concepts, however, facilitates a complete understanding of how they can be used when teaching more advanced programs.

Although the tasks taught in the first hours of treatment may seem trivial, keep in mind that many students have never sat in a chair for an extended period of time, not even at mealtime, or have only done so inconsistently. Most students with developmental delays have not come to their parents when requested to do so. Many have given their parents a very tough time by screaming and hitting, tyrannizing them in a way. Some students may have complied in the past, off and on, when they felt like it. To succeed in the teaching environment, a student must learn to comply with what adults want. If the student does not, no one will be able to teach her what she needs to master in order to develop more typical behaviors. Thus, the beginning tasks are designed with the intent of establishing the foundation needed to learn the skills detailed in this manual and to build the student's trust in you and pride in herself.

Behaviorists do not ordinarily use terms such as trust, pride, and sense of accomplishment. This is for reasons of objectivity. Instead, phrases such as "cooperation training" and "bringing the student under instructional control of the teacher" are prevalent in behavioral literature. Such terms should not be used to obscure the importance of behavioral teaching programs in creating what is commonly referred to as pride, motivation to learn, and the many other descriptions that are familiar to everyone whether or not they are behaviorally oriented. Further, the student who begins to smile and look at others when coming to the teaching situation on her own allows parents and teachers to feel successful as well. Adults also must obtain some reinforcement; otherwise they will lose motivation and eventually quit.

Summary of Basic Treatment Steps

CHAPTER 10

The preceding chapters provide a great deal of important information. For example, Chapter 9 on establishing cooperation and tantrum reduction introduces concepts basic to behavioral intervention such as instructions, prompts, responses, reinforcement, and shaping. Certain processes such as acquisition and extinction are also introduced in previous chapters. These concepts and processes are used in all the teaching programs presented in this manual.

Before going further, we review these processes and concepts in more detail because knowledge of how they work is important in facilitating the student's success. Although the concepts and processes might seem quite abstract at this time, you will acquire firsthand practical knowledge of them as you begin teaching the student, and you will likely feel that they help you work effectively in a number of situations. Although you may feel awkward at the beginning, over time you will gradually feel more at ease.

Note that the concepts and processes introduced previously are the same ones used in subsequent chapters. To help translate these abstract ideas into effective teaching procedures, we sometimes repeat ourselves; we do this to illustrate how the concepts apply to particular programs and situations. Once you acquire a working knowledge of these concepts and processes, you may be able to generate your own teaching programs when necessary.

Learning to teach effectively is like becoming skillful at any other complex task. No one can complete a complicated task without first learning the basics and then following through with extensive practice and consultation; even the most skillful performers seek consultation and advice from others. When one observes a recognized performer, it seems as though all their moves are executed smoothly with grace and efficiency. With practice, you will become more skillful in your abilities, enhancing the interaction between yourself and the student. However, you may never lose all of your apprehension and anxiety given that so much is at stake. Remember that some level of apprehension can be constructive when used to help monitor your own performance and the performance of others while seeking a higher level of skill as a teacher.

It is extremely important to subject yourself to review by your colleagues; therefore, we place great emphasis on working openly within a treatment team. As recommended in Chapter 4, it is useful to call in an outside consultant who is skillful at delivering behavioral treatment. An experienced consultant can help you sharpen your skills and avoid a great deal of misdirected effort.

Seeking advice in a field as difficult as one-on-one behavioral treatment of students with developmental delays is a measure of one's self-confidence; persons who refuse to solicit feedback likely feel incapable of improving. Avoiding evaluation of one's skills does not allow for betterment, and this ultimately affects the student's progress. In art, athletics, and science, even the most skillful and accomplished person must subject himself or herself to feedback; otherwise, his or her performance deteriorates.

One helpful way to receive constructive feedback is to participate in weekly staff meetings (referred to in Chapter 4). During these meetings, each team member should take turns working with the student for at least a 10-minute period. By demonstrating teaching skills in front of other team members, one's strengths and weaknesses can immediately be recognized. Strengths are modeled for everyone and weaknesses are quickly identified so their deleterious effects do not persist or become magnified. In such a closely supervised and public work environment, it is important not to belittle others for mistakes because sooner or later each team member will make errors. Rather, staff meetings should be used to build skills and unity so that each member feels comfortable working with the team and wants to continue teaching the student.

Another good reason for working within a team is that a single individual cannot become expert in all areas of teaching. Some individuals are particularly good at discovering reinforcers; others excel at suggesting prompts. Some may surpass others in their ability to develop specific programs. In short, there is strength in collaboration.

Introduction to Terminology

Throughout this manual, teaching procedures based on the principles that compose operant learning are used. Operant learning evolved out of what was earlier referred to as instrumental conditioning and trial-and-error learning. Applied Behavior Analysis is a more recent and updated field of inquiry that includes, but is not limited to, the application of operant learning principles.

Two basic concepts together form the basis of the teaching programs presented in this manual: The *discrete trial* is described in this chapter, and *discrimination learning* is introduced in Chapter 16. In the remainder of this chapter, the four parts of the discrete trial are discussed in the following order: (1) the teacher's instruction, (2) the student's response to the instruction, (3) the consequence of the student's response, and (4) the prompt and prompt fading. In addition, *shaping*, a procedure used to teach new behaviors through successive approximations, and *chaining*, a procedure for building complex behaviors, are discussed toward the end of this chapter. Note that these concepts were introduced in Chapter 9 and are referred to repeatedly throughout the rest of this manual. Given that the four components of the discrete trial are interconnected and are needed for the successful shaping and chaining of behaviors, it is essential that you become familiar with this entire chapter before going on to further teach the student.

Components of a Discrete Trial

The Instruction

Each discrete trial begins with an instruction intended to cue the performance of a behavior. The instruction may be verbal, such as "Sit down" or "Come here," or nonverbal, such as when the teacher shows the student a picture for him to label or a person for him to describe. Further, the instruction may vary from the simple (e.g., "Sit down") to the complex (e.g., "You may go out and play after you put away your toys"). Regardless of its form, the instructional component of a discrete trial is referred to in the technical literature as the *discriminative stimulus* (abbreviated SD). The terms instruction and discriminative stimulus (SD) are used interchangeably throughout this manual.

As the student becomes more familiar with the teaching process, he will learn that when an instruction (SD) is presented, a reward (reinforcement) will be provided for responding correctly to the instruction. In technical terms, the SD is a stimulus that is discriminative for reinforcement (a signal for reinforcement) provided the student responds correctly.

The student no doubt has encountered many instructions, both implicit and explicit, throughout his life, but he has too often failed to understand what the instructions mean. It is now necessary to explicitly teach the student to understand and follow instructions. To facilitate the student's early learning, it is best to begin by simplifying each instruction given to the student. This simplification is accomplished in three ways. First, keep your instructions short and succinct. It is important to refrain from complicated instructions, especially at the beginning of treatment. An example of a complicated instruction is "Come sit with me for awhile." This instruction is inefficient in the beginning stages of teaching because it contains too much extraneous information. In the beginning of treatment, the SD should contain only the relevant and critical element of the instruction, which in this case is the instruction "Sit." Do not assume that the student can attend to and understand (discriminate) the part of a complex instruction that contains the relevant cues.

Second, decide on the exact wording of the instruction and use this same word or phrase consistently. Consistency in instructions minimizes the student's confusion and maximizes learning. Thus, all teachers should agree upon a consistent format for presenting instructions. Variations in instructions (e.g., "Be seated," "Have a seat," "Please sit down," "Park your rear here") can be taught later.

Third, present the instruction in a loud and confident voice, making it clearly audible to the student and everyone else in the teaching room. Instructions should not sound as if a question is being asked; reserve the questioning intonation for only those instructions that naturally require its use, such as "What is he doing?" and "What color is it?"

The Response

The student's behavior cued by an SD is called a *response* (R). There are three important considerations to make when defining the target response. First, it is essential that all team members agree upon and are consistent in their definition of the response required of the student. For example, if dropping one block in a bucket is the criterion for correct responding, this response should be consistently reinforced by all teachers. No one should be allowed to introduce his or her personal requirements, as in having the student drop three or four blocks in a bucket. When teaching the student to sit in the chair after he is asked to sit, make certain that all teachers agree upon the length of time the student is required to remain seated before reinforcement is provided. If the response requirements are altered, as in having the student sit for different lengths of time across different teachers, then those requirements should be agreed upon in advance by all team members. No solo performances of teachers are allowed at this early stage because consistency is critical to the student's learning what he has to do to gain reinforcement. Changing from one response requirement to another minimizes the effectiveness of the reinforcer and risks teaching more than one response at a time, a situation that is too complicated for students with developmental delays in the early stages of these programs. Further, having a clear definition of the response you would like the student to make allows for consistent delivery of reinforcement. The student should be reinforced when his response matches the agreed upon definition of correct responding.

Note that it is extremely important to achieve mastery of one behavior before going on to teach the next behavior within a specific program. That is, if you choose dropping a block in a bucket as the first response in the Early Receptive Language Program (Chapter 15), make sure the student masters this skill before moving on to another response, such as coming to the chair when requested to do so. The only exception to this takes place when the student fails to make progress toward mastery of the response you have chosen to teach. Altering response requirements is intended to reduce the student's frustration over failure and increase learning.

After giving an instruction, do not allow more than 3 seconds for the student to respond. In other words, the time interval between the SD and the student's response should be between 1 and 3 seconds. This is extremely important in maximizing learning given that, in order for the student to make the connection (association) between the instruction and his response, the two events must occur almost simultaneously in his nervous system. The longer the time interval between the SD and the response, the more likely it is that the student will fail to make the correct connection. Any unintended stimuli that intervene after the SD and before the student's target response may be connected or associated with the instruction.

Failing to respond at all within the 1- to 3-second time interval is considered a nonresponse. If the student fails to respond, immediately repeat the instruction. If the student again fails to respond, repeat the instruction a third time and simultaneously prompt the correct response. (Prompts and prompt fading are described later in this chapter.)

It is inevitable that the student will sometimes engage in more behaviors than the one you are trying to teach. For example, while teaching the student to sit down, he may resist doing so and simultaneously tantrum. In such a situation, you have little or no choice but to reinforce the sitting response, risking concurrent reinforcement of the tantrum. This problem may eventually resolve itself for the following reasons. First, the sitting response is the only one that is systematically reinforced, and it should therefore eventually become strong enough to replace the tantrum. Second, as the student achieves control over reinforcers by engaging in appropriate behaviors (e.g., sitting), it is likely that inappropriate behaviors (e.g., tantruming and self-stimulatory behavior) will decrease. If tantrums do not decrease or you would like to hasten their reduction, first reinforce the student for reliably sitting when asked to do so. Once this step is mastered, proceed to the next step, providing reinforcement contingent on sitting and *not* tantruming.

Some students evidence major emotional outbursts in the beginning of treatment that show no signs of extinction after 2 to 3 hours of teaching. Such a situation requires considerable ingenuity on the part of the teacher in selecting a response that may reduce or sidestep the emotional outbursts. The following two examples illustrate this problem and describe possible solutions.

Billy

After 2 hours of intensive effort on the part of the teacher, Billy continued screaming and violently protesting, making no progress in sitting. A 15-minute play break was called, and the response requirement was changed from Billy sitting to Billy holding his favorite toy (a train) which the teacher handed to him. Billy accepted this, but only if he stood close to his mother. Over the next 2 hours, the response requirement was gradually changed from the teacher handing the train to Billy to the child having to stretch out his arms to retrieve the train from the teacher's hand. Eventually Billy was required to exert more effort by taking the train from the table (where the teacher was sitting). With this gradual change in response requirements, Billy's cooperation increased and other behaviors could be taught more easily.

Gordon

Gordon tantrumed excessively and failed to make any progress sitting in the chair after 3 hours of intensive effort by the teacher. However, when Gordon sat beside his mother on a sofa and a ring stacker was placed next to Gordon, he would stack rings as they were handed to him by the teacher. The ring stacker was then placed on the floor by the teacher, still near Gordon's mom on the sofa. Gordon moved down to the floor and stacked the rings the teacher handed to him. Over several trials, the ring stacker was eventually placed on the table and Gordon willingly sat on the chair and stacked rings. He was later presented with a puzzle he liked and given puzzle pieces by the teacher.

For both Billy and Gordon, it became increasingly easier for the teacher to introduce new tasks after identifying and working with an initial response tailored for each child. Perhaps the key was helping these children succeed in responding to the teacher's initial request. This success generalized to other teaching tasks.

The Consequence

The consequence provided contingent on the student's correct response is called a *reinforcing stimulus* (S^R). A reinforcing stimulus given contingent on a certain behavior changes the likelihood of the occurrence of that particular behavior. When a positive reinforcer such as food or approval is given contingent on a behavior, that behavior increases in strength, becoming more likely to recur. Behavior also increases in strength if it results in the removal of something unpleasant, such as escaping from discomfort like tension, pain, fear, or hunger. This type of reinforcer is called a negative reinforcer because it reinforces by the removal of a negative state. Both situations are called rewards in everyday language. Chapter 9, which deals with establishing cooperation and reducing tantrums, illustrates how leaving the teaching situation contingent on sitting in the chair can function as a negative reinforcer (strengthening sitting), whereas sitting on a parent's lap and being kissed can function as positive reinforcers.

When a behavior occurs and reinforcing stimuli are provided contingent on that behavior, the behavior is strengthened. When reinforcers are withheld, the behavior is weakened. That is, presenting contingent reinforcers results in acquisition of behavior; withholding reinforcers results in extinction of behavior. These two processes are illustrated in Chapter 5 in the discussion of how self-injurious behaviors may increase or decrease depending on whether attention (a positive reinforcer) is presented or withdrawn. The intent of this manual is to guide the teacher in effectively using reinforcers to increase the student's socially appropriate behaviors while weakening socially inappropriate behaviors, hence helping the student overcome developmental delays.

Remember that each student is different; what may be rewarding for one student may not be rewarding for another student. It is therefore necessary to test reinforcers to determine their efficacy for each individual. A kiss may function as a positive reinforcer for one student but as punishment for another. As mentioned in preceding chapters, nothing is more important in behavioral intervention than gaining access to the individual student's reinforcers, thereby gaining instructional control and effectiveness.

Once you identify a reinforcer that the student accepts when it is provided, you have made the most important advance in helping him. Some students are easier to reinforce than others, but we have never failed to find some item that is reinforcing for any particular student. We usually begin by selecting food reinforcers, and test these to see if the student eats them prior to the teaching situation. If a student accepts the foods you offer, chances are that these food items will serve as effective reinforcers.

After effective reinforcers such as food are identified, explore other reinforcers. Parents typically know best what kinds of foods and activities the student likes and does not like. If the student likes to hold a particular object, let the student receive that object contingent on an appropriate response; that is, use it as a reinforcer. Other activities include matching objects, turning on a light switch, listening to a 5-second tape of a favorite song (e.g., "Its a Small World"). Do not let the reinforcer consume too much time because this can interfere with or shorten the time needed for teaching. For the most part, a 3- to 5-second duration of the reinforcer is optimal.

Always pair effective reinforcers with social reinforcement. For example, smile and praise the student (e.g., by saying "Good!" or "Super!") each time you give him more desired reinforcers (e.g., food or leaving a stressful situation). By doing so, you help the student learn to value social praise as a reward if he does not already do so. In the technical literature, praise is called an acquired, conditioned, learned, or secondary reinforcer, whereas reinforcers such as food and escape from stress are referred to as primary reinforcers. It may help to think of secondary reinforcers as social in nature and primary reinforcers as biological in nature.

Sometimes a student does not accept reinforcers in the early stages of treatment. There are three possible reasons for this. First, when food reinforcers are offered in the early stages of treatment, the student may be too upset to eat or drink. Second, the student may not want to give you control over the situation. Third, the student may not like the particular food, drink, toy, or activity used as the reinforcer. If the student does not accept a potential positive reinforcer, it is likely that he will be reinforced by being allowed to escape from the teaching situation contingent on the desired response. As mentioned previously, escape from an undesirable situation is known as a negative reinforcer and can be used to strengthen (i.e., reinforce) the behavior it immediately follows.

The student may come to find the company of his parents to be a powerful reinforcer once the student is upset by the demands placed on him. Also, once the student accepts one reinforcer, such as going to his parent(s), he is much more likely to accept another reinforcer, such as food or comfort from other persons. You will discover an enormous range of reinforcers that are effective as you get to know the particular student.

Once you identify a reinforcer, it is essential that this reinforcer be given *immediately* upon the occurrence of the behavior you are teaching. For example, if the student is to be reinforced for sitting on the chair for 2 seconds, then after the 2 seconds have elapsed, immediately present the reinforcer. The delay between the completion of a response and the delivery of the reinforcer should be minimal (1 second or less) to maximize the effectiveness of the reinforcer. The longer the delay, the more likely it is that you may inadvertently strengthen an intervening response.

The strength of any given reinforcer varies with exposure to and deprivation of that reinforcer. Weak reinforcers can gain value when the student is deprived of those reinforcers; powerful reinforcers generally lose their value as the student is increasingly exposed to them. In technical terms, the latter phenomenon is known as *satiation*.

To avoid satiation, vary the types of reinforcers used and provide only small amounts of each particular reinforcer. For example, limit the quantity of a particular reinforcer by giving the student one kernel of popcorn for a correct response rather than a handful of popcorn. Likewise, give the student a small sip or taste of his favorite drink, not half a glass. By varying the use of several reinforcers, the student is inherently allowed limited exposure to each particular type of reinforcer used and satiation is limited or avoided. Vary reinforcers by, for example, tickling the student for one correct response, giving him a favorite toy (for a few seconds) on the next correct response, and hugging him for another correct response. Make certain that the stimuli used as rewards (e.g., tickling, a favorite toy, hugging) are reinforcing for the student, not punishing.

Do not monotonously repeat "Good" after every correct response, even though it is easy to do so. The student will quickly become satiated on this reinforcer, and this may affect his motivation to learn. When giving social rewards such as smiling and saying "Good," exaggerate your expressions. Pretend you are an actor on stage in some large Broadway production.

Once the student masters a behavior and shaping it is no longer necessary, spread out reinforcement over trials by only intermittently using the most powerful ones. Continuous reinforcement (one reinforcer for each response) is used to *teach* a response; intermittent reinforcement is used to help *maintain* responding.

Another way to avoid satiation of reinforcers is by using tokens (see Chapter 7). Tokens may be given contingent on a correct response and then later exchanged for a desirable toy, snack, or activity.

To facilitate some degree of desire for reinforcers and help reduce or prevent satiation, limit their availability outside of the teaching situation. For example, if popcorn is used as a reinforcer, limit the student's access to this reinforcer by providing him with it only in the teaching situation and using it in this situation sparingly (e.g., give the student one half or one kernel per correct response). If the student is allowed to have a favorite snack any time he wants, this reinforcement may fail to motivate him during teaching sessions.

When the student responds *incorrectly*, remove all signs of reinforcers (e.g., place your hand with food in it under the table). The loss of positive reinforcers may function to reduce incorrect responses. Such a procedure is technically known as *time-out*. After the student incorrectly responds, remove the reinforcers, wait 1 to 2 seconds, and then repeat the instruction. If the student fails on the second try, provide corrective feedback (described below) and then present the instruction a third time, simultaneously prompting the student. Reinforce the correct response.

In consequating incorrect responses, you may want to establish the use of an informational "No" as corrective feedback. After an incorrect response, say, "No" in a neutral tone and at the same time look down and prevent access to all reinforcers. Removing reinforcers may serve to associate "No" with the removal of positive reinforcers and thereby help establish "No" as corrective feedback to weaken incorrect responses. This technique is the opposite of the technique used to establish verbal praise, such as saying "Good," as rewarding by associating the verbal praise with the *presentation* of a positive reinforcer or the removal of a negative situation.

To help the student learn to differentiate your feedback, do not say "No" in the same tone of voice used when saying "Good" as praise, and do not smile when you say "No." For some students, the use of "No" may pose problems because the word may accidentally have acquired positive reinforcing properties in the past; that is, some students may work hard just to hear you say "No" and watch you get upset. Conversely, some typical students and some with developmental delays react to "No" with severe emotional upsets. In such cases, the use of "No" as feedback is not warranted.

The presentation of a consequence marks the end of a single discrete trial, which begins with an instruction (SD), is followed by a response (R), and ends with a consequence (i.e., a reinforcer [S^R] for correct responding, or the removal of a positive reinforcer and/or the use of an informational "No" for incorrect responding). Before beginning another discrete trial, it is important to allow a brief pause. This pause, the *intertrial interval*, should be (a) long enough that the presentation of the instruction in the next trial is distinct but (b) not so long that the student becomes unfocused, performing alternative behaviors such as tantruming or self-stimulating. Long intertrial intervals invite self-stimulatory and drifting behaviors; thus, whenever possible, keep the intertrial interval between 1 and 3 seconds (especially in the early stages of treatment). Not only should this help to maintain the student's attention, but shorter intertrial intervals increase the number of trials (i.e., learning opportunities) possible in any given period of time.

Remember that most learning is gradual and incremental and requires several trials. One-trial learning is a rare event for most persons, particularly for those with developmental delays prior to progress in the programs presented in this manual.

The Prompt

Prompts are an integral part of facilitating responses the student may not possess in his behavioral repertoire. Without the use of prompts, the teacher may never obtain the opportunity to reinforce and strengthen certain appropriate behaviors. By definition, a prompt is any action made by the teacher that helps the student perform a correct response so that the behavior can be reinforced and strengthened. As you become more skillful as a teacher, you will discover hundreds of ways to prompt, ensuring that the student will almost always be successful and you will not be deprived of the opportunity to praise and otherwise reward him. *Regardless of the type of prompt used to teach a particular skill, the prompt should occur at the same time as or within 1 second after the presentation of the SD; if it does not occur within this interval, the instruction and the response may not occur closely enough in time to become associated.*

A wide range of prompts are suitable for use in the programs described in this manual. The following is a brief summary of the types of prompts you may employ in succeeding chapters. This summary is meant to be a short introduction to prompting; more detailed descriptions of how to specifically use prompts within particular programs are given in the chapters that follow.

Physical or Manual Prompting

In physical or manual prompting, the teacher helps the student respond correctly by providing the student with manual assistance. That is, the teacher guides the student's body through the motions of the correct response. For example, in teaching the student to drop a block into a bucket, the teacher manually guides the student's hand to retrieve a block and then moves his hand with the block in it over to the bucket, helping him release his grip from around the block. When teaching the student to sit in a chair, the teacher places the chair behind the student and the student between his or her legs, then physically moves the student to a sitting position so that the sitting behavior can be reinforced.

Modeling

Modeling helps occasion correct responding by providing a visual demonstration of the response. To use modeling as a prompt, the student should first be taught to imitate the adults' behaviors and vocalizations (Chapters 13 and 22, respectively). For example, if you want to use modeling to prompt the student to clap his hands upon your request, first teach him to imitate your various behaviors, including hand clapping. Then instruct the student to clap while you model clapping your hands. Similarly, after the student learns to imitate the adults' vocalizations, modeling can also be used to occasion verbal responses. For example, when teaching the student to identify an apple by name, show the student the apple, ask the student, "What is it?" and prompt the correct response by saying, "Apple." The student imitates your statement of the word, and you reinforce that response. In essence, when using a modeling prompt, you show or otherwise demonstrate to the student the correct response as you would in teaching any typical individual.

In the early stages of learning, the teacher models the correct responses. In later stages, the student's peers may act as models, facilitating appropriate toy play, peer play, conversational speech, and observational learning in the classroom. There are many advantages to using modeling as a prompt; most behaviors you want the student to learn are complex and cannot be helped to occur without modeling. Chapters 13 and 22 on teaching nonverbal imitation and verbal imitation, respectively, therefore contain very important programs for both the teacher and the student to master.

Position Prompting

Position prompting is used to assist the student in programs in which a display of items is presented and the student is required to select the correct item from among these items. To help occasion the correct response, the teacher positions the target item closer to the student than the other objects, thereby increasing the likelihood the student will select the correct item. For example, when teaching a student to identify an apple from a display of items (e.g., fork, shoe, cup, apple), the teacher may place the apple close to the student and the other items farther away from the student. When the SD ("Touch apple") is given, the close proximity of the apple may facilitate correct responding.

Nonspecific Prompts

Pointing to, gesturing toward, or glancing at the correct item are referred to collectively as nonspecific prompts. These prompts are similar to position prompting in that they are used to assist the student in programs in which a display of objects is presented and the student is required to select the correct object.

Recency Prompting

Recency prompting refers to prompting by linking the target response to a previously learned response. This type of prompt facilitates correct responding by presenting trials of certain SDs in close succession. In this situation, the student can use his or the teacher's response in the previous trial as a cue for the next trial. For example, if the student has difficulty naming the object "car," present the instruction "Touch car" just prior to presenting the instruction "What is it?" The student's hearing the teacher express the word *car* in the instruction "Touch car" may help prompt his verbal response ("Car") when the teacher asks, "What is it?"

Reinforcement-Elicited Prompting

Reinforcement-elicited prompting occurs when reinforcers cue emotional behaviors (as most reinforcers do). A kiss on the cheek used as a reinforcer can tickle and prompt smiling. Once prompted, the smile can be reinforced and strengthened. Food can serve the same function, and for many students the reinforcing properties of matching (see Chapters 11 and 12) prompt expressions of contentment and more rapid mastery of other behaviors that can be reinforced and strengthened.

Fading Prompts

As discussed in Chapter 9, the main advantage of using prompts is that they help the desired behavior occur, giving you the opportunity to provide reinforcement. If the student is not prompted, the target behavior may never occur. If this happens, you will not be able to reinforce the student and the student will not progress. The main disadvantage of prompting is that, when provided with a prompt, the student does not perform correctly by herself; that is, the student is not reinforced for responding to your request but rather for responding to the prompt. With time, the student may become reliant on the prompt for correct responding. Technically speaking, you may reinforce prompt dependency.

To avoid prompt dependency, you must fade all prompts, a process termed *prompt fading*. Prompts can be faded by reducing their intensity (as in reducing the decibel level of a verbal prompt or lessening the amount of manual guidance used as a physical prompt). Problems may occur when reducing the intensity of the prompt because the student, in order to be reinforced, is inadvertently taught to attend to smaller and smaller units of the prompt which is likely to interfere with her attention to your instruction. One way to resolve this problem is to gradually withhold reinforcement for prompted trials while maximizing reinforcement for unprompted trials. By reducing the intensity of the prompt while concurrently reinforcing the student's response to the SD, the prompt becomes a less reliable cue for responding than the instruction. Reinforcement for responding to the SD is maintained, allowing the SD to become the salient and relevant cue and the strength of the association between the SD and the response to increase. In other words, the student's reliance on the prompt is gradually lessened while the student's reliance on the instruction is gradually increased. In the technical literature, this is referred to as a shift in stimulus control: The transfer of control over the response is shifted from a prompt stimulus to the SD.

Another procedure for reducing prompt dependency is *probing* the necessity of continued use of a prompt by suddenly withholding the prompt altogether. This strategy determines whether the student can correctly respond to an SD without having to go through an entire prompt fading process. To perform this procedure, use a prompt until the student consistently responds correctly with the prompt, then present the SD and withhold the prompt for a trial or two. Such trials are called *probe trials* and are used to determine whether the student has already learned the response and does not require further prompting.

Keep in mind that some responses may be more difficult for the student to learn than others. The student may require minimal prompting to learn one response but may need more prompting to learn another response.

Establishing a Prompt Hierarchy

Successful prompt fading is facilitated by the establishment of a prompt hierarchy. In other words, you should determine a sequential order of prompts for a particular task, beginning with the prompt that provides the most intensive (most effective) assistance and ending with the prompt that provides the least intensive assistance. Once this hierarchy is established, it may be used to gradually and systematically reduce the intensity of the prompt until the student can correctly respond on her own (i.e., without the prompt).

For a teacher to declare that the student has learned a particular skill, the student should respond correctly without the use of prompts. If the student previously learned a certain skill but at some later point responds incorrectly in a trial involving that skill, repeat the same instruction once more to give the student another chance to respond correctly. If the student again responds incorrectly, reinstate the response by repeating the instruction and concurrently prompting the correct response on the third trial using the least intrusive prompt necessary to occasion correct responding. The guiding principle is that you should prompt after no more than two incorrect responses (nonresponses are considered incorrect responses).

In the early stages of teaching a stimulus–response relationship, both prompted and unprompted responses should be reinforced. When gradually fading a prompt, however, reinforcement for prompted responses should be minimized while reinforcement for unprompted responses should be maximized. This procedure is termed *differential reinforcement*. This term also encompasses the process of reinforcing correct trials (whether or not they are prompted, although prompted trials are reinforced to a lesser degree) and not reinforcing incorrect trials. Once a particular task is mastered, reinforcement should be withheld for trials of that task that require prompting. In this manner, the student learns that independently performed appropriate actions earn greater rewards than assisted actions. A major goal is to teach the student to become more independent and self-sufficient.

Once you become skillful at using the components of a discrete trial, the teaching session resembles an ongoing and uninterrupted dynamic interaction between you and the student. Through such an interaction, you learn, by observing the student's behaviors, how to set the optimal pace for presenting instructions, how to use prompts to help the student perform winning behaviors, and how to provide reinforcers that also act as natural prompts for expressions of positive emotions, which in turn are reinforced, allowing for the prompting of new behaviors and more reinforcement. Under ideal conditions, the teaching situation produces a flow of appropriate behaviors for which the student may be praised, kissed, or otherwise rewarded several times per minute. Such a setting benefits the student in many ways, not only because it helps create contentment, but also because it hastens the student's learning.

Illustrations from Everyday Life

We clarify the universality and importance of prompting by illustrating some uses of prompting in teaching typical individuals. In the life of a person, one usually employs the constructs and processes of prompting without any awareness of doing so. Consider the use of prompting in teaching a child to ride a bicycle. At first, a parent provides a maximum-strength prompt by holding onto the child *and* the bike to ensure that the bike remains steady and the child does not fall off. Every effort the child makes to ride is praised (reinforced) by his parents and other observers. Over time, as the child becomes more competent at balancing himself on the bike, the parent provides less physical assistance by bracing the bike with one hand rather than two, then gradually releasing the remaining hand from the bike while running alongside just in case the child falls. Finally, the child is allowed to ride without assistance.

Many other prompts are used when raising children, many of which are more subtle than physical prompts. For example, if one asks a child what time it is and the child does not respond, one often prompts by pointing to the dial of a clock. If this minimal amount of prompting is not effective, one may resort to a more intrusive prompt by giving the full answer, "It's 12 o'clock." If a child asks her mother for a favor (e.g., "I want ice cream") and the mother prompts, "Say please," this prompt may later be faded into a less intrusive prompt such as "What's the magic word?" Parents may say to their child, "Please help your sister." If the child fails to do so, a parent may prompt either by physically guiding the child through the motions or by modeling the desired behaviors. Almost all answers to questions requiring factual information (e.g., "Who is the president of the United States?" "What is the capital of France?") are prompted when first taught. If the correct responses were not prompted, the child would not know the answer.

Other prompts are less obvious, as when a mother smiles and asks her young child, "Do you love Mommy?" and the child responds with a slight echo, "Love Mommy," which is reinforced. Another example is stating, "Come give Daddy a kiss," which may be a prompt in the sense that this statement can be faded until the mere sight of Daddy occasions a kiss. We call such a kiss spontaneous. Few parents wait around for their children to show love to each other or to themselves as parents. Parents prompt and reinforce such behaviors; otherwise, they may rarely occur and one may raise a child who demonstrates little love.

What has been said about raising children can apply equally well to maintaining a happy marriage. If your partner is somewhat distant or aloof, he or she may rarely show affection. If this occurs, your marriage may not last; it may be placed on extinction or at least it may not be very happy. To remedy this problem, it helps to prompt and reinforce affectionate behaviors. For example, one may model a desired response and comment, "See, this is how you do it," or use a less intrusive prompt such as asking, "Do you really love me?" Examples of more subtle prompts can be observed in arrangements of the physical environment. Sleeping in one bed, or at least in the same room, is an example. If a husband sits on one side of the sofa intently watching football on television and his wife sits on the opposite side of the sofa, the latter may position a pillow close to her and comment, while patting the pillow, "This is better for your back." The intent is to prompt closeness without being too intrusive. You may know of many other subtle prompts. Such prompts must eventually be faded, however, or the partner's attention may not appear genuine or natural. Prompts appear everywhere in day-to-day life, facilitating the occurrence of desirable behaviors to be reinforced and strengthened.

Just as prompts occur in everyday life, constructs such as reinforcement can be observed in day-to-day living. For example, without regular reinforcement (e.g., kisses, hugs, compliments), a marriage may not last. How often should one reinforce one's partner? No doubt there are individual differences, varying from once a day to once an hour. What behaviors and attributes should one reinforce? These are easy to discover, once one starts: "Your hair is beautiful," "I like your family," "You are smart," "Good dinner," "You are so strong," "I can trust you," and thousands of other comments. Similarly, without the expression of love to children, they may not learn to love you. In the case of raising typical children, the details of how these constructs operate may not need to be known; typical children become attached to others and develop normally without caregivers knowing much about the processes underlying their learning. Parents of children with developmental delays love these children as much as they do their typically developing children. In the case of the former, however, love is not enough. The operation of learning-based constructs must be known in great detail for a parent or teacher to be of significant help.

Shaping

Shaping is a procedure used to teach new behaviors through a process of reinforcing successive approximations of a desired or target behavior. In other words, the student initially is reinforced for a behavior that is close to the target behavior. After the student consistently performs this approximation, the criterion for receiving reinforcement is gradually changed to the student's performing a behavior that is more similar to the target behavior. Over time, the criterion for receiving reinforcement is changed until only the target behavior is reinforced. The advantage of this procedure is that it allows the student to be reinforced immediately and it helps reduce frustration for the student by initially focusing on easier, more attainable goals. One of its disadvantages, however, is that by implementing this procedure, it may take a long time to teach the target behavior. The use of shaping as it applies to teaching specific skills is detailed in subsequent chapters.

Chaining

Chaining is the creation of a complex behavior through the combination of simple behaviors into a sequence that forms a single, more complex behavior. This sequence of behaviors is called a chain. The term chain is used because earlier units of behavior come to provide the cues for the subsequent units of behavior. In technical terms it can be said that the feedback generated by one response (technically known as response-produced stimulus) provides the stimulus for the next response.

A chain is created through a link of behaviors, each link being the neural associations between one response and the next. To chain behaviors, one must follow four steps: (1) identify the target behavior; (2) break down the target response into small discrete steps; (3) teach the individual steps using a separate instruction and reinforcement for each step; and (4) fade the instruction, prompt, and reinforcement for each individual step until there is only one instruction at the beginning of the chain and one reinforcement at the end of the chain.

Two types of chaining are presented in this manual: forward chaining and backward chaining. Forward chaining entails teaching and combining behaviors in a forward chronological order. Teaching begins with the first step in the chain and ends with the last step. Backward chaining involves teaching and combining behaviors in backward chronological order. The last behavior in the chain is taught first and the remaining behaviors are added in descending order. Backward chaining requires that in the beginning stages, the student complete only the last step(s) in a chain before he is reinforced, whereas forward chaining works in the opposite direction.

The extent to which a behavior needs to be chained in a piecemeal fashion and prompted manually depends to some extent on the student's mastery of nonverbal imitation (Chapter 13). For example, the adult might have to model *and* physically prompt each step for a less advanced student. For students who have acquired nonverbal imitation (Chapter 13), it is possible for the adult to model the entire behavioral sequence and "hand shape" those elements that need improvement. Chaining techniques are explained in more detail in several programs in this manual.

Using Discrete Trials

During the beginning stages of teaching, keep the teaching sessions to a maximum of five to six trials, taking short play breaks between sets of trials. Sitting in the beginning stages should not exceed 2 minutes between breaks. As the student advances through the programs in this manual, you may extend the time spent in the chair from under 1 minute to up to 5 minutes, allowing for more trials. Eventually, as done in school, the student may be required to sit for 45 to 50 minutes at a stretch. When it is time for a play break, signal the break with the instruction "All done" and concurrently help the student leave the chair to go and play. In all programs, signal a play break contingent only on a correct response (unprompted whenever possible). *Make certain that the student does not receive a break contingent on noncompliance, a tantrum, or an incorrect response.*

Purpose of Discrete Trials

The use of discrete trials in teaching students with developmental delays is beneficial for four reasons. First, discrete trials clearly delineate what you are trying to teach and help the student attend to the SD (i.e., the instruction). Second, discrete trials let you and the student know immediately whether the response is correct. Third, discrete trials help you instruct the student in a consistent manner; this comes about because each unit is specified in concrete detail. Consistency is crucial in the beginning stages of teaching because any discrepancies may cause the student to become confused, delaying her progress in learning. Fourth, discrete trials allow for quick and easy assessment of the student's advancement. A very sensitive measure of learning is the rate at which the prompt can be faded across trials. Another measure is the speed with which the student responds correctly to your instructions across new and different tasks. Chapter 33 describes techniques for collecting data to document progress in learning.

Discrete trial procedures are frequently critiqued by those who believe that such procedures fail to teach higher level skills such as language, fail to produce generalization, fail to teach functional skills, inadequately use reinforcers, place stress on parents, and are inefficient and slow moving (Koegel & Koegel, 1995). By way of rebuttal, it should be noted that discrete trial procedures form the basis for teaching abstract language, including concepts such as colors, prepositions, pronouns, time, and cause–effect relationships, as well as conversational speech and a host of other complex skills. Discrete trials also form the basis for teaching imitation and observational learning. Both of these skills help students learn on their own through attention to the behaviors of other individuals. It should be further noted that most students graduate from reliance on discrete trial procedures as they progress through the programs presented in this manual. Finally, treatments that rely on discrete trials are the only ones that are supported by favorable long-term outcomes as measured on socially and educationally meaningful and well-normed objective assessment instruments.

Some persons claim they are against behavior modification. The fact is, *everyone* continually modifies others. The challenge is to learn how and when to use behavior modification principles in a constructive manner. Many people do not know how to effectively use such principles, especially when it comes to teaching individuals (whether they are typical or developmentally delayed). However, everyone can be taught to do so. The information presented in this manual is aimed at helping you learn constructive application of behavioral intervention techniques.

Concluding Comments

When exposed to behavioral teaching programs, persons with developmental delays evidence a great deal more complexity and individual differences than can be accounted for by current clinical and educational theory or by what is presented in this and similar teaching manuals. Thus, as programs are presented, difficulties will be encountered. Solutions to examples of such problems are reviewed in most chapters as they relate to specific programs and in Chapter 35 on common problems in teaching.

As the student experiences difficulties, you will also be challenged. Thus, it is important to remember that no one becomes a master teacher overnight. One has to make a beginning; mistakes are as inevitable as progress. Progress occurs in a situation where you are open to feedback. Just remember that no errors are so detrimental that they cannot be repaired.

Introduction to Matching and Imitation

CHAPTER 11

The programs presented in Chapters 12, 13, and 22 are critical building blocks in the student's curriculum. Chapter 12 contains programs designed to teach the student to match (a) objects such as socks, shoes, and cups; (b) attributes of objects such as shape and color; and (c) letters and numbers (a skill basic to teaching the student to read and write—see Chapter 29). Chapter 12 also contains a program designed to teach the student to sort stimuli into categories, such as people versus animals or vehicles versus edibles. Chapter 13 contains a program for teaching the student to imitate the nonverbal behaviors of other persons. Chapter 22 contains a program that presents steps for teaching the student to imitate the sounds, words, and sentences generated by others.

The Matching and Sorting and the Nonverbal Imitation Programs (Chapters 12 and 13, respectively) rely on visual stimuli and are relatively easy for the adult to teach and the student to learn. The Verbal Imitation Program (Chapter 22), on the other hand, which relies on auditory stimuli, is the most difficult program to teach and one of the most difficult programs for the student to master. The common element among all these programs is that they teach the student to match stimuli. In the Matching and Sorting Program, the student learns to match items that are similar or identical in some characteristic (e.g., color, shape, size, function). In the Nonverbal Imitation Program, the student learns to match her behaviors to those of another person (e.g., the student waves in response to a wave or smiles to a smile). In the Verbal Imitation Program, the student is taught to match her vocalizations to those of the teacher (e.g., the student matches her expression of the word "mama" to the teacher's expression of "mama").

Before we describe the specifics of each program, it may be helpful to give some background information concerning their significance. The importance of imitation to development has been recognized by virtually every person who has written on the subject. Many different terms describe the subject, including observational learning, social learning, identification, copying, modeling, and matching.

We have found that two important by-products result from learning to imitate. The first by-product pertains to the rapid acquisition of complex behaviors. It is next to impossible to teach, through shaping of successive approximations, the complex behaviors needed to function in society. It is much easier to teach the student complex behaviors by helping the student learn to imitate the behaviors of typical individuals. In this way, other people serve as models, demonstrating the many complex behaviors the student needs to master. Some forms of extrinsic reinforcement, such as adult approval, may be necessary to perfect or fine tune the student's behavior, but the major acquisition is accomplished through imitation. The second by-product relates to the student's motivation. In brief, it is likely that the matching of stimuli, as done in imitation, is intrinsically rewarding. That is, when a student imitates the behavior of another person, it is likely that the student is rewarded (reinforced) by observing the *similarity* between her behavior and the behavior of the other person. When the student perceives the similarity between her behavior and that of another person, that similarity comes to function as a powerful reinforcer for the student. The closer the student matches her behavior to that of the model, the more reinforcement the student receives. Through this, the student puts herself in the position to learn on her own. Examples from behavioral research addressing the variables that maintain imitative behavior can be found in Baer and Sherman (1964); Lovaas, Berberich, Perloff, and Schaeffer (1966); Lovaas, Freitas, Nelson, and Whalen (1967); and Parton and Fouts (1969).

Another benefit to the intrinsically rewarding property of imitation is that it promises the maintenance of the student's behaviors after treatment is terminated. If a behavior depends on extrinsic reinforcement during treatment, then it is more likely that the behavior will extinguish once treatment is terminated unless extrinsic reinforcers continue to be made available in the person's everyday life. In contrast, if the behavior is based on imitation, then the reinforcer may be said to be intrinsic and the treatment gains are more likely to be maintained. This possibility is particularly important to consider when teaching the student to imitate the behaviors of her peers. Successful peer integration is a particularly important step to maintaining the student's gains and increasing her growth.

An observation pertaining to echolalic speech may be helpful in illustrating the concept of matching as a reinforcing stimulus. When we began our work, we (mistakenly) considered echolalia to represent a pathological behavior and we made explicit efforts to withdraw social reinforcers for echolalic behavior, an intervention that had helped reduce self-injurious behavior. Withdrawing social reinforcers did not reduce echolalia (Lovaas, Varni, Koegel, & Lorsch, 1977). A resolution to this problem came when we considered echolalia to be an instance of self-stimulatory behavior and the matching of the student's voice with the voice of others to be the reinforcing event. Colleagues reported instances of echolalic speech in typical individuals as well.

Just as we could make sense of echolalia when we viewed it as a matching behavior, we could make sense of the children's strong attractions to form boards and jigsaw puzzles, which had made little sense to us when we first began developing treatment programs. The majority of the children we observed played with such toys in an appropriate manner, even if most other forms of appropriate toy play were missing. The children matched a square puzzle piece to the square hole in the puzzle, a circle to the circle, a triangle to the triangle, and so on. Some children could quickly and efficiently assemble complex 50- to 100-piece puzzles, even at a very young age. Such islets of intact intellectual functioning or special skills are often observed in children diagnosed with autism.

With a better understanding of echolalic speech, we came to the realization that the matching of stimuli, a consequence of playing with puzzles, constituted the reinforcer maintaining such behavior. In echolalia, the child matched auditory stimuli. With form boards and puzzles, the matching involved visual stimuli. The challenge for teachers became one of guiding students with developmental delays to take advantage of the powerful reinforcing effects of matching and using this reinforcer to teach socially appropriate behaviors.

There are other advantages for the student who learns to match stimuli. These advantages center on the student's learning to tell apart (selectively attend to) objects, behaviors, and language elements in her environment to which she may not have paid attention previously. One cannot match two stimuli without attending to them. Matching teaches the student to attend to stimuli, and attending to stimuli is necessary for learning the skills taught through the programs presented in this manual.

Before moving on to teach matching and imitation programs, consider why matching of certain visual and auditory stimuli is rewarding for the student. What is the purpose of such a reward? We make the following proposal: Although one may occasionally observe nonhuman animal offspring imitating their ancestors (e.g., some species of birds imitate bird songs), the major contributor to their development appears to be based on instincts, which direct their behaviors in such a fashion that, with minimal learning opportunities, they can survive and reproduce provided their environment remains reasonably constant. Human beings, on the other hand, do not appear to possess an extensive stock of instincts to direct behavior. We have to learn how to behave, how to raise our children, how to build a house, and so forth. One important advantage of *not* being born with a large repertoire of predetermined instinctual behaviors is that human beings are able to adapt to different environments and different demands with greater ease than other animals. A sudden change in the environment of a nonhuman animal species is likely to wipe out most members of that species. In contrast, without a large repertoire of prewired behaviors, members of each generation of human offspring can adapt to and survive in diverse and changing environments by imitating the behaviors of their surviving ancestors and others around them. In addition to being less instinctual, the behaviors of human beings are more complex than those of other animals. Imitation allows for rather rapid acquisition of a larger and more complex set of behaviors, many of which could not be acquired through behavior shaping procedures. Imitation can therefore be viewed as a mechanism whereby one generation of human beings relatively quickly transfers behaviors and knowledge for the benefit of the next generation. Without imitation, there would be little or no continuity in culture and our children would not survive. In that sense, the matching of behaviors is probably a primary reinforcer; it is essential for survival and as important as eating, reproducing, and escaping or avoiding pain.

In sum, if a person with autism fails to imitate (fails to learn by observing the behaviors of others), that person is without an important resource for overcoming her developmental delays; therefore, a major goal should be teaching the student to imitate. Discrete trial learning can be used to accomplish this goal. Three programs that follow—Matching and Sorting (Chapter 12), Nonverbal Imitation (Chapter 13), and Verbal Imitation (Chapter 22)—help the student acquire the critical skill of imitation.

Matching and Sorting

CHAPTER 12

The matching component of the Matching and Sorting Program outlines steps necessary for teaching the student to match objects, colors, shapes, and behaviors (actions) in three-dimensional (i.e., 3-D object) and two-dimensional (i.e., 2-D picture) combinations (i.e., 3-D to 3-D, 2-D to 2-D, 3-D to 2-D, and 2-D to 3-D). The sorting component of this program teaches the student that some objects group together because they share common properties (e.g., color or size) or have the same function (e.g., utensils or vehicles). Sorting may be considered an early step in establishing abstract concepts.

The Matching and Sorting Program typically involves the presentation of one or more items displayed on the table. These items are referred to as the *sample*. The student is handed one item, called the *match*, which is identical or similar to an item on the table. The student is then given the verbal instruction "Match" and is taught to place the match on or near (e.g., in front of) the sample. Before the steps for teaching match-to-sample are presented in detail, it may be helpful to note certain advantages inherent in the program. (Note that in the technical literature, what we refer to as the match is often referred to as the sample stimulus, and the sample is often labeled the comparison stimulus.)

We noted in the preceding chapter that one advantage of exposing students to the matching of stimuli is that matching often acquires reinforcing properties for the student (i.e., matching comes to constitute a reinforcer). Another major advantage of matching is that it helps the student attend to (discriminate) a larger range of stimuli in his environment. Individuals with developmental delays, particularly those diagnosed with autism, are said to be delayed in the skill of attending, often behaving as if they cannot see or hear. Obviously these individuals learn to attend to some stimuli, such as food, puzzle pieces, twirling objects, or floating pieces of lint. However, most stimuli seem to pass them by, as may be the case with typical infants or very young persons. The philosopher William James proposed that the visual world of the infant is a "buzzing confusion." Similarly, many professionals consider that typical children at birth do not recognize their parents or "see" everyday objects. Perhaps, as is implied by these suggestions, all individuals have to *learn* to attend to their environment.

The task of directing and building attention is one of the most difficult problems adults face in teaching students with developmental delays. Even though a student may look directly at the objects you want him to respond to, there is no guarantee the student truly sees them. It is possible for a student with autism to look directly at a person's face without actually seeing that person, but rather fixating on some minute feature of the face, such as blinking eyelids. As mentioned in Chapter 9, visual orientation is not the same as seeing. Teaching a student to make eye contact with the teacher does not imply that the student is learning to see the teacher. Teaching a student to see (or hear, for that matter) is a slow process. As we understand this problem, seeing and hearing are acquired through discrimination learning. For a detailed description of discrimination learning, see Chapter 16. The way discrimination learning relates to the present program is more fully described in later portions of this chapter. Through the Matching and Sorting Program and the discrimination learning therein, one can make a meaningful step toward teaching the student to attend to visual stimuli. The student will learn to identify and label much of these stimuli in subsequent programs.

The student may make many important gains after learning to match and sort. One of these gains is learning to detect similarities between present events and future ones such that learning can be transferred (generalized) from one situation to another; the detection of similarities among diverse situations helps provide regularity in an individual's behavior. This gain is significant given that many students with autism and other developmental delays experience difficulty generalizing from one set of stimuli or learning environment to another. Mastery of the Matching and Sorting Program should help reduce such difficulties.

In addition to being useful, the matching or sorting of stimuli is relatively easy to teach. Further, most students enjoy the program and make rapid progress, perhaps because the stimuli are visual or because perceived similarities among objects or events are reinforcing for many students. As may be expected, however, one will encounter large individual differences when teaching students to sort based on abstract properties such as clothing, furniture, foods, or animals. These differences require the teacher to remain flexible when teaching.

Certain prerequisite skills should be established before beginning the Matching and Sorting Program. For one, the student should be able to sit at the table and chair for a few minutes at a time without engaging in too many disruptive behaviors. If matching is reinforcing for the student, he will sit for a longer period of time. It is also helpful for the student to be able to visually orient to the teacher and follow the basic instructions taught in the first hours of treatment (see Chapter 9). In addition, the teacher should be familiar with Chapter 16 and refer to it when and if the student encounters difficulties.

The Matching and Sorting Program can be taught concurrently with such programs as Nonverbal Imitation (Chapter 13), Early Play Skills (Chapter 19), and Reading and Writing (Chapter 29). In the present program, the matching component should be taught before the sorting component. If sorting objects on the basis of common properties is difficult for the student in the early stages of treatment, put this component on hold and reintroduce it after a delay of a few weeks or months. Interim learning about objects may facilitate the acquisition of sorting.

Matching Identical 3-D Objects

Begin the Matching and Sorting Program by teaching the student to match identical 3-D stimuli. When selecting materials for this program, choose from common household objects. We suggest using items the student is likely to have regular contact with, thereby making the skills learned more meaningful. For example, plates, silverware, and small articles of clothing such as gloves may be ideal to use in the early matching tasks. Objects that exist in identical pairs, such as shoes and socks, are also helpful in the early matching programs. In addition, it may be helpful to initially use objects that naturally nest into one another (e.g., cups, plates, spoons). The use of nesting items will remove the ambiguity of where to place the to-be-matched item. Be aware that certain familiar and naturally reinforcing items (e.g., favorite toy figurines) are often difficult to use because the student may want to hold onto and play with them rather than match them to the corresponding objects on the table. If this does *not* occur, use them.

The steps used to teach matching conform to those specified in the chapter on discrimination learning (Chapter 16). Become familiar with discrimination learning procedures because a thorough understanding of these procedures will facilitate teaching of the skills presented in the current program and every other program in this manual. The present chapter describes how discrimination learning procedures apply to matching and sorting only.

As detailed below, the student is taught SD1–R1 (e.g., matching a cup to a cup) in Step 1 (see Chapter 10 for discussion of discriminative stimulus [SD] and response [R]). In Step 2 the student is taught SD2–R2 (e.g., matching a sock to a sock). Once the student masters both SD1–R1 and SD2–R2, Step 3 is introduced in which SD1 and SD2 are subjected to differential reinforcement and random rotation to ensure that the student attends to the objects presented to her and not inadvertent cues. SD3–R3 (e.g., matching a spoon to a spoon) is then taught. Finally, the student is taught to discriminate SD3 from SD1 and SD2. Make certain that SD1 looks distinctly different from SD2, and that SD3 differs maximally from SD1 and SD2.

During the following steps, the student should sit facing the table and you should sit next to the student. Sitting next to the student makes it easy for you to manually prompt the student. Gradually, as the student requires less assistance and prompting, you may move to sitting across from the student at the table.

To facilitate the following description of the teaching steps, the letters A, B, and C represent the sample (i.e., the items on the table), and A', B', and C' represent the match (i.e., the corresponding items that you hand to the student for her to match). Your verbal instruction for this program is "Match." Do not include in the instruction the name of the object to be matched (e.g., "Match cup"). The use of the object label is irrelevant in the beginning stages and may even detract from the student's understanding of the expected response. Initially, be sure to keep the sessions short; the student should sit at the table and chair for only 1 to 3 minutes at a time in the early stages of the program.

▶ Step 1

Place one cup (Object A) on the table in front of the student. Present SD1, which involves placing an identical cup (Object A') in the student's hand and stating, "Match," in a loud and clear voice. As the SD is given, manually prompt the student to make the correct response, placing the cup inside the cup on the table. Reinforce the correct response.

Between every trial (i.e., after the reinforcement of one trial and before the SD of the next trial), remove the stimuli from the table. In this case, remove both cups after reinforcement is given to the student. Such a procedure allows you to present the stimuli again at the beginning of the next trial, thereby maximizing the discreteness of the stimuli presentation. This discreteness increases the likelihood that the student will attend to the stimuli which, in turn, facilitates her learning. Keep in mind that leaving the stimuli on the table expedites learning for some students because it decreases the intertrial interval.

Repeat the trial and fade the prompt over subsequent trials by gradually decreasing the amount of manual assistance provided to the student. For instance, gently nudge the student's hand with A' in the direction of A on the table, then merely point to where you want her to place the object (i.e., inside the cup on the table). Gradually fade all prompts, and maximize reinforcement for unprompted trials. Place mastery at 5 out of 5 or 9 out of 10 unprompted correct responses.

Next, place the cup in different positions on the table over successive presentations of SD1. For example, place Object A on the left side of the table on one trial, on the right side of the table on the next trial, and toward the back of the table on another trial. This procedure is done so the student learns to place the cup in the cup rather than at a particular place on the table. If the student fails to respond correctly over these trials, move back a bit and introduce the least amount of prompt necessary to reinstate the correct response. Set mastery at 5 out of 5 or 9 out of 10 unprompted correct responses.

As noted in the introduction to this manual, the criterion for mastery varies across and within programs. In general, a relatively easy discrimination may be considered mastered at 5 out of 5 or 9 out of 10 unprompted correct responses, as suggested above. However, given individual differences in rates of learning, some students experience more difficulty than others and mastery may be more likely assured by placing the criterion at 9 out of 10 or 19 out of 20 unprompted correct responses. As a general rule, the first discrimination (i.e., the discrimination between SD1 and SD2) in any program tends to be more difficult to master than later discriminations. Thus, when teaching subsequent discriminations, you may want to set a less stringent criterion (e.g., 3 consecutive unprompted correct responses). If one proceeds too slowly in teaching, the student may become bored and may tantrum or self-stimulate. In addition, by presenting the same SD several times in a row, the problem arises of teaching the student to perseverate by reinforcing repetition of the same response. In contrast, by proceeding too quickly, the early steps may not become fully mastered and, thus, the student may fail at learning later, more advanced steps. The criteria for mastery presented in this manual are provided as guidelines; as you gain experience teaching the student, these guidelines may be modified to fit the student's individual needs.

▶ Step 2

Choose a second object (B) that is maximally different in color and shape from the first object. For example, if the first object was a red cup, do not choose a mug or a red toy car as the second object. Instead, a white sock might be a good choice for the second object. Remove the first object (i.e., the cup) from the table. Place one sock (Object B) on the table in front of the student and place the other sock (Object B') in the student's hand while stating, "Match," in a loud and clear voice. As SD2 is given, physically assist the student to complete R2 (i.e., placing B' on top of B). Reinforce the correct response, and then remove the stimuli from the student's view. Repeat the presentation of SD2 and begin fading the prompt. Remember to always present the SD (the object and the instruction "Match") concurrently with the prompt. Consider SD2–R2 to be mastered once the student correctly responds to 5 out of 5 or 9 out of 10 unprompted trials. After this criterion is met, move Object B to random positions on the table as was done with Object A.

▶ Step 3

Once SD1–R1 and SD2–R2 are acquired separately, SD1 and SD2 should be intermixed to help the student discriminate between them. Begin by placing the cup and the sock on the table with both objects equidistant from the student's midline to minimize position prompts. The stimuli should be clearly visible to the student. Allow an 8- to 10-inch space between the two sets of objects. If the student encounters difficulty, a position prompt may be used initially such that the target object is presented closer to the student than the other object. This position prompt should be gradually faded until the student is able to discriminate between the objects when they are presented at the same distance from the student.

We recommend starting discrimination training with SD1 and prompting the correct response (manually, by position, or both) so as to avoid a nonreinforced trial and the likelihood of a tantrum. An alternative would be to present SD2 first because this association was reinforced last; however, this presentation of SD2 technically would not require a discrimination but rather only add to the repetition of the preceding response and hence be of little instructional value.

Intermix SD1 and SD2 according to discrimination learning procedures. Because the student mastered SD2 most recently, it is likely that the student will place the cup on the sock when SD1 (the cup) is presented. To avoid a nonreinforced trial, physically prompt and reinforce the child for R1 (placement of the cup) when you present SD1 (the cup). In addition, to avoid having the student inadvertently learn to place the object in a particular position on the table, randomly interchange the left–right positions of the cup and the sock. If a position prompt is used, randomize the left–right placement of the target object while keeping it closer to the student than the other object. Fade the position prompt over trials by gradually bringing the two objects closer together on each successive trial after fading the physical prompt by providing less and less manual assistance over trials. If the student makes an error on any given trial, do not reinforce the response, but rather end the trial with an informational "No." Then repeat the presentation of the object, prompt the correct response, and reinforce.

While fading the prompt, probe with unprompted trials to help reduce prompt dependency, which is likely to occur when reinforcement is provided for prompted trials. Continued reinforcement for prompted trials will decrease the opportunity for the student to acquire the association between the SD and the correct R. Place mastery at 3 to 4 unprompted correct responses in a row with the position of Objects A (the cup) and B (the sock) interchanged and equidistant from the student. Within 2 seconds of completing mastery of SD1–R1, present SD2 (the sock) and simultaneously prompt the student's correct response. Set mastery at 3 to 4 unprompted correct responses in a row.

Over the next several trials, alternate back and forth between SD1 and SD2. With an increase in alternations between SD1 and SD2, you should require fewer and fewer correct successive responses before shifting SDs (e.g., shift after 4 unprompted correct responses in a row, then 3, then 2, then 1). Once the student is able to respond correctly to the SDs when they are presented singly (i.e., not in blocks of trials), randomly rotate the order of presentation of the objects (e.g., SD1, SD2, SD2, SD1, SD2, SD1, SD1) to help prevent the student from falling into a pattern of responding (see Chapter 16). Also randomize the positions of the objects on the table to avoid teaching the student to respond to a particular position rather than to the objects themselves.

Over successive intermixed and differentially reinforced trials, the student should make fewer and fewer mistakes as the associations between SD1–R1 and SD2–R2 are strengthened because they are reinforced and mistakes such as SD1–R2 and SD2–R1 are weakened because they are not reinforced. Once the student learns to discriminate between SD1 and SD2, we recommend that these SDs be practiced to criterion by all team members. In addition, generalize the mastery across environments by moving the sessions out of the teaching room to other rooms of the house. Cues inadvertently provided by any one teacher or room are less likely to interfere with the student's learning the correct discrimination when these procedures are employed.

▶ Step 4

The third target (Objects C and C') should be maximally different from the first two objects. For example, if you used a red cup and a white sock as Objects A and B, respectively, let C be a silver spoon. Retain the original setting, with you and the student sitting next to each other facing the table. Place one spoon (Object C) on the table in front of the student. Place an identical spoon (Object C') in the student's hand and present the verbal SD ("Match") in a loud and clear voice. As the SD is given, physically prompt the student to place the spoon (C') on top of or close to the spoon (C) that is on the table. Reinforce the correct response and then remove the objects from the student's view. Repeat the presentation of SD3 and fade the prompt over subsequent trials, remembering to present the prompt concurrently with the SD. Use the same criterion for mastery for SD3–R3 that was used for SD1–R1 and SD2–R2. Once the criterion is met, move Object C to different positions on the table as was done with Objects A and B.

▶ Step 5

After SD3–R3 is mastered when presented alone, intermix and differentially reinforce SD3–R3 first with SD2–R2 (bring to mastery at 5 out of 5 or 9 out of 10 unprompted correct responses) and then with SD1–R1. Once mastery is achieved, intermix and differentially reinforce all three matches (SD1–R1, SD2–R2, and SD3–R3) in a blocked format as done previously (i.e., switch after 4 unprompted correct responses to each SD, then after 3, then after 2, and finally after 1). Randomly rotate the presentation of the SDs (once the student can independently respond correctly to the SDs after single presentations). In addition, randomly rotate the left–right positions of the stimuli on the table to eliminate extraneous cues.

It may be helpful in the beginning to have only two samples on the table at any given time (one sample providing the correct match). Gradually, as the student acquires mastery, increase the difficulty by adding to the number of samples displayed on the table. Teach the student to match other 3-D objects by following the same procedures used to teach the first three objects. Eventually you may end up with a dozen different objects on the table (e.g., cup, sock, spoon, toy car, plastic apple, small dish, glasses, pen, toy, doll, key, plastic flower). Give the student one object at a time to match. You are likely to observe the student actively scanning the objects on the table to find the correct match and, perhaps, with a quick and determined move, complete the match.

Once the student learns to match a dozen objects, the difficult part of the matching program is completed, and it is relatively enjoyable for you and the student to progress to other matching tasks. As the student progresses through the various matching steps, you may discover that fewer food and other extrinsic reinforcements are needed to maintain the student's involvement. As is often the case with typically developing individuals, an individual must first be introduced to a certain task, sometimes against the individual's will. However, after exposure to the task, the individual may find it rewarding. The fact that many individuals come to enjoy such things as music, poetry, or sports only after trying them is a good example of the importance of initial exposure to discovering reinforcing activities. If the individual survives the first days and lessons, then she is on her way. If matching appears to be a positive reinforcer for the student you work with, consider using various formats of matching tasks as reinforcement for correct responses in other programs.

Areas of Difficulty

There are several areas in which the student may initially encounter difficulties with the matching component of the Matching and Sorting Program. For one, the student may not know where to place the to-be-matched objects handed to her. The use of nesting objects helps prevent this problem. However, once nonnesting objects are used, this problem of not knowing where to place the items may again arise. Teach the correct placement (i.e., in front of or directly next to the sample for nonnesting items) of the objects either through prompting or by defining an area of space within which to place the object. The latter may be achieved by having the student place matches onto plates or pieces of paper, each containing the correct sample object.

Other problems may be caused by inadvertent prompting. For example, if the teacher consistently uses one hand to give the student the match when the corresponding item is positioned on the left and the other hand when the corresponding placement is on the right, the student may solve the problem by responding to the hand used by the teacher rather than to the match and sample objects. Other inadvertent prompts may occur if the teacher looks at the sample object on the table while handing the student the match object. Similar inadvertent prompts may take place if the teacher signals (e.g., by smiling or shaking his or her head) correct or incorrect responding *before* the student completes her response. The teacher should wait until the student commits herself to a response (i.e., she places the object and lets go of it) before providing *any* reinforcement. If the student is unsure of how to respond, it is likely that the student will look for the teacher's inadvertent signs to help guide her to the correct response rather than attend to the target objects. Members of the treatment team should closely monitor one another for potential inadvertent prompts. If such prompts are employed, the student will not learn the skill intended by the teacher.

Matching Identical 2-D Objects

This section describes steps for teaching the student to match identical 2-D stimuli. For some students, it may be easiest to begin by teaching the student to match 2-D representations of the 3-D objects he learned to match in the first phase of this program. For example, if the student was taught to match identical cups, teach him to match photos or drawings of these same cups. Other 2-D stimuli can be obtained from flashcards depicting objects, behaviors, numbers, or letters. Later on, word cards can be used. If 2-D stimuli are taken from magazines, buy two identical magazines and cut and mount pictures in duplicate on index cards (so they are sturdy).

When using pictures, be aware of certain extraneous stimuli. For example, the student may use the borders around some pictures as cues for matching instead of the objects within the pictures. Therefore, remove any borders from pictures. Cut out the pictures as uniformly as possible because the student may match the shape or the size of the pictures rather than the pictures of the objects themselves. For many students, color is the most salient attribute of the object by which to make the match. When matching identical pictures of a dog, for example, the student may make his match on the basis of a patch of color on the dog (ending up matching color to color) rather than characteristic features of the dog itself.

Although it is virtually impossible to eliminate all irrelevant stimuli, you can work around their interference by following the procedures detailed for introducing nonidentical matching presented later in this chapter. What is likely to happen through these procedures is that irrelevant stimuli become unreliable predictors of reinforcement. Hence, attention to these stimuli is weakened while attention to the essential features gain strength because they are consistently associated with reinforcement. It is prudent to keep in mind, however, that the cues you intend for the student to use in solving problems are not necessarily the cues the student will attend to.

Teaching the student to match 2-D stimuli proceeds in the same manner outlined for teaching the matching of 3-D objects. When matching 2-D stimuli, have the student place the picture to be matched on top of the corresponding picture on the table. Some students take great care in making the placement of the picture as exact as possible, pausing to line up the sides and corners in a most precise manner. Such attention to detail is a good sign. It is also evidence of the reinforcing properties of matching.

Matching Colors and Shapes

The procedures for teaching the matching of colors and shapes are identical to those outlined for teaching 3-D and 2-D matching. The stimuli for teaching color matching should be cards made out of different colored construction or cardboard paper. Cut the stimuli cards so that they are 5 × 5 inches in size. Because the student already mastered the matching of objects and pictures, color matching may proceed relatively quickly.

Once the student learns to match color cards, 3-D objects to be matched by color may be introduced. These objects should be identical in *all* aspects except color (e.g., large plastic beads or brand new crayons) to avoid ambiguities in the dimension by which the objects are to be matched. If the student has considerable difficulty learning to match colors and makes no progress over several days, the student may be color blind. Before reaching such a conclusion, however, make sure that other factors such as the stimuli used, teaching techniques, reinforcement, and prompting are optimal. This is consistent with the suggestion made earlier in this manual to examine the adequacy of teaching methods before attributing failures to the student.

To teach the student to match shapes, cut out various similarly sized shapes from construction or cardboard paper. It is important that all of the shapes are identical in color so that inadvertent color cues are not introduced. When beginning to teach shapes, choose two initial shapes that are dissimilar from one another when contrasted (e.g., a circle and a square). Once squares are contrasted with circles, squares may be contrasted with triangles, triangles with diamonds, circles with ovals, and so on, in graduated steps of difficulty.

Numbers, letters, and words are other examples of shapes that can be introduced at this time. Remember, however, that these forms of matching should be introduced systematically; not all three forms should be introduced and targeted at the same time.

Matching 3-D Objects with Identical 2-D Representations

In this section, the student is taught to match objects to pictures of those respective objects. In other words, the student is taught to identify symbolic representations (pictures) of concrete, real-life objects, a skill that is considered by some to be a higher level cognitive process.

This part of the matching program may be of interest for two reasons. First, many professionals propose that higher level cognitive processes cannot be taught on the basis of the learning paradigm (reinforcement theory) set forth in this book. Second, students with autism, pervasive developmental disorder, and similar delays are considered to be deficient in cognitive processes involving abstract reasoning. We mention this here not only because you will enjoy observing the student learn this task, but also because she will do so in spite of what many professionals have proposed. (Adversity often brings out the best in us.) As you progress through this manual, you will learn that higher level cognitive processes can slowly but surely be taught.

Although matching objects to their symbolic representations is basic to the educational process and an important task for the student to learn, making the connection between a 3-D item and its 2-D counterpart is difficult for some students. To facilitate the acquisition of 3-D to 2-D matching, start with objects the student learned to match in previous formats. Because the teaching steps in this section are identical to those presented earlier in this chapter, they are outlined here in relative brevity.

► **Step 1**

Place the 2-D item (e.g., a picture of a cup) on the table and hand the student the corresponding 3-D object. Say, "Match," while prompting the placement of the 3-D object on top of its 2-D counterpart. Set mastery at 5 out of 5 or 9 out of 10 unprompted correct responses. Remove the stimuli between trials.

► **Step 2**

Place another 2-D item (e.g., a picture of a sock) on the table, and then give the student the corresponding 3-D object. Follow the same procedures described in the preceding step to bring this match to mastery.

► **Step 3**

Intermix and differentially reinforce the stimuli used in Steps 1 and 2. Once mastered (5 out of 5 or 9 out of 10), continue adding new stimuli as done in previous sections of this program.

After the student learns to match 3-D objects to their 2-D counterparts, teach her to match 2-D pictures to their 3-D counterparts using the same procedures just described. Generalize across teachers and environments.

Matching Objects by Class

Matching Nonidentical Stimuli of the Same Dimension

In this part of the program, the student is taught to match objects to their nonidentical counterparts. In other words, the student is taught to identify classes of objects and learns that certain objects have some common property even though they may look different (e.g., a shoe is a shoe whether it is brown, white, a loafer, or a sandal). Technically speaking, the student is taught stimulus generalization (i.e., to generalize a response from a particular example of an object to objects that appear similar to the original).

For this task, gather multiple examples of the same object. For instance, use many different exemplars of cups (plastic, paper, and ceramic cups), socks (in assorted colors, sizes, and textures), spoons (metal and plastic), shoes (brown loafers, white sneakers, black sandals, shoes with Velcro, and shoes with laces), and so on. Initially it is a good idea to use nonidentical items that are very similar (e.g., a white tennis shoe with Velcro adhesives and a white tennis shoe with laces) instead of nonidentical items that are very dissimilar (e.g., a white tennis shoe and a red high-heeled shoe). The goal is to be able to gradually decrease the physical similarity between the items the student matches until the student can match very dissimilar objects belonging to the same class of objects. Once the student learns to match nonidentical 3-D objects, teach him to match nonidentical 2-D stimuli.

Teaching should proceed in the same manner described in earlier match-to-sample procedures.

Matching 3-D Objects to Nonidentical 2-D Representations

In this section, the student is taught to match groups of objects to their nonidentical symbolic (2-D) representations. All of the objects and pictures used in the two previous tasks are needed for teaching this task. Select one item from one class and one item from a different class of 2-D objects and place these two items on the table (e.g., place a picture of a cup and a picture of a tennis shoe on the table). Hand the student a 3-D object belonging to one of the classes of objects and instruct him to "Match" (e.g., hand the student a mug and have him match it to the picture of the cup on the table). Rotate the position of the pictures on the table so as to avoid teaching the student a particular position for placement (e.g., left, right, center) rather than a match. Once this initial step is mastered (5 out of 5 or 9 out of 10 unprompted correct responses), hand the student a different 3-D object belonging to the class represented by the other item on the table, and teach the student to match it to the appropriate picture.

In practice, teaching may proceed as follows: Place a picture of a man's shoe and a picture of a metal spoon on the table in front of the student. Next, hand the student a woman's shoe while stating, "Match." Prompt the correct response if necessary and reinforce the student. Fade the prompt over subsequent trials, randomly rotating the left–right positions of the pictures on the table. Next, give the student a plastic spoon to place, then a white baby's shoe, then a sandal, then a baby spoon, and so on, making sure that all prompts are faded for each object before introducing a new object. When the student learns to match 3-D to 2-D nonidentical stimuli, teach him to match 2-D to 3-D nonidentical stimuli following procedures similar to those just described.

Throughout all matching tasks, make sure that the stimuli do not become ambiguous. For example, if a yellow cup and a brown shoe are on the table and the student is given a brown cup to match, he might think that he is supposed to match colors (a salient characteristic of the stimuli) and may therefore match the brown cup to the brown shoe. This would be an incorrect response if the student was supposed to match nonidentical objects, yet it would be a correct response if he was supposed to match colors. Therefore, make sure the items selected in the early stages of learning are clear in the characteristic by which they are to be matched.

Category Matching

A more advanced aspect of the matching program than matching on the basis of identical or near-identical appearances consists of matching stimuli into groups on the basis of some attribute other than identical or near-identical appearances. That is, objects can be matched on the basis of some common and abstract function, such as things you eat (food), items you put on your body (clothes), or objects that facilitate travel (vehicles). An enormous number of such groupings exist, given that groups can be formed on the basis of one or more common features or attributes. Be aware that learning to match members into groups defined by a common function is difficult and may require some prior conceptual (language) skills. Therefore, the next two sections may be optimally started after the student makes some progress in language.

In this section, teach the matching of commonly occurring categories of objects, such as foods, clothing, vehicles, people, furniture, and animals. It may help to begin with members of categories that differ only slightly from one another. For example, in teaching the student to match the category of animals, start with horses, cows, and dogs, as opposed to chickens, pigs, and whales. Begin with very similar items, gradually extending the concepts you teach to include many heterogeneous members forming one category. Also in the early stages, the categories contrasted should differ maximally from one another. For example, initially refrain from matching fruits versus vegetables.

In illustrating the following steps, the category of animals is taught first and clothing is taught second. Throughout each step, the left–right positions of the stimuli sets should be randomly shifted to help avoid inadvertent position cues.

► **Step 1**

Place one example of an animal (e.g., a horse) on the table in front of the student. Present SD1, which involves placing another item of the same category (e.g., a cow) in the student's hand and stating, "Match," in a loud and clear voice. As the SD is given, prompt the student to make the correct response (placing the cow next to the horse that is on the table). Reinforce the correct response. Remove the stimuli between trials, repeating the trials while fading the prompt. Provide the most amount of reinforcement for unprompted trials. Place mastery at 5 out of 5 or 9 out of 10 unprompted correct responses.

Next, hand the student another example of the animal category (e.g., a goat). Prompt the student to place the goat next to the horse on the table and then reinforce the correct response. Repeat the trial, fading all prompts over the next few trials. Place mastery at 5 out of 5 or 9 out of 10 unprompted correct responses. Continue to teach, one at a time, up to five different exemplars of the same category by following the procedures used to teach the first two exemplars.

► **Step 2**

Place one example of clothing (e.g., small pants) on the table in front of the student. Place SD2, another clothing item (e.g., a small shirt), in the student's hand and state, "Match," in a loud and clear voice. As SD2 is given, physically prompt the student to complete R2 (i.e., placing the shirt on top of the pants on the table). Reinforce the correct response, removing the stimuli between each trial. Repeat the presentation of SD2 and begin fading the prompt. Use the same criterion for mastery for SD2–R2 as was used for SD1–R1. Teach up to five other exemplars of the clothing category, one at a time, using the procedures described in the previous step.

► **Step 3**

Once SD1–R1 and SD2–R2 are acquired separately, you must help the student discriminate between the two sets of stimuli by adhering to discrimination learning procedures. Place the horse and pants on the table with both objects equidistant from the student's midline and clearly visible to the student. Allow an 8- to 12-inch space between the two sets of objects. Intermix SD1 and SD2 first by presenting repeated trials of SD1 (matching items of the animal category) while fading prompts. Place mastery at 3 to 4 unprompted correct responses in a row. Within seconds after completing mastery of SD1–R1, present SD2 (matching items of the clothing category) and simultaneously prompt the student's correct response. Set mastery at 3 to 4 unprompted correct responses in a row. Over the next several trials, alternate back and forth between blocks of SD1 and SD2 in the same manner, gradually decreasing the number of correct responses in a row required to reach mastery (e.g., 3 unprompted correct responses in a row, then 2, and then 1). Once the student independently responds correctly to each SD when presented directly after the alternate SD, randomly rotate their presentations.

After the student learns to discriminate between SD1 and SD2, we recommend that the SDs be practiced to the criterion for mastery by all team members. Teach other categories using the same procedures described in this section. As always, generalize across teachers and environments.

Sorting

In this section, the student is provided with multiple objects and taught to sort these objects, one at a time, first into groups of identical objects, then into classes based on some common attribute, and finally into categories. This component of the program is similar to those components described earlier, but it is slightly more difficult because the student is confronted with several objects at a time.

Teach the student to select stimuli (objects or pictures) from items presented to her and to place these items into a certain number of containers (e.g., plates) corresponding to the number of sets contained in the stimuli. The initial sorting is based on identical appearances. Begin by finding multiple identical exemplars of objects (e.g., several identical blue blocks and several identical blue socks). Place an example of one object in one container and an example of the other object in another container. The containers should be placed 8 to 12 inches apart and equidistant from the student's midline. Place the remaining blocks and socks together in a pile on the table (no more than three of each item in the beginning) and give the SD ("Sort"). Immediately physically prompt the student to place each of the items into the correct container. Reinforce the correct response, repeat the trial, and begin fading the prompt. Place mastery at twice placing the six items in their respective containers without assistance. Gradually increase the number of objects handed to the student to 10. If the student sorts an item into an incorrect container, make sure to deliver an informational "No" at the moment the response occurs so it is clear to the student that she sorted that item incorrectly. Do *not* wait until the student sorts all the items before providing a consequence.

After the student masters sorting identical 3-D objects, replace these objects with identical 2-D stimuli. To teach identical 2-D sorting, follow the same procedures used for teaching the student to sort 3-D stimuli. Next, after the student learns to sort identical stimuli, use the stimuli from nonidentical matching of objects and pictures to teach the student to sort by class. Finally, the stimuli used for category matching should be reintroduced to teach the student to sort stimuli by category.

Concluding Comments

Matching is a powerful educational tool as there is virtually no end to the kinds of concepts one can begin to teach using the matching procedures outlined in this chapter. The Matching and Sorting Program can be used, for example, to teach the student to discriminate among various emotions and behaviors. That is, the student may be taught to match pictures of expressions of different feelings (e.g., happy, sad, angry faces) or activities (e.g., eating, sleeping, driving). Similarly, the student may be taught numerical values by matching cards displaying particular numerals with cards depicting quantities of dots equivalent to those numerals. The dots can later be replaced by objects. Note that certain matching tasks can be very subtle, requiring considerable intellect on the part of the student. Thus, we recommend that parts of this program be maintained and expanded upon throughout the teaching of the remaining programs presented in this manual.

Nonverbal Imitation

CHAPTER 13

Typical individuals acquire many complex behaviors, such as social, recreational, and language skills, by observing and imitating the behaviors of other persons. Individuals with developmental delays, however, often fail to imitate the behaviors of others. This failure to learn through imitation constitutes a major source of developmental delays. Shaping and chaining behaviors (as discussed in Chapters 9 and 10) can help students with developmental delays acquire certain simple behaviors such as sitting in a chair, dropping blocks in a bucket, and following elementary instructions (e.g., "Come here"). Shaping and chaining will fail, or be too impractical, however, to help the student acquire complex behaviors such as toy play, receptive language, and social skills. Teaching students with developmental delays to imitate is a major step toward helping them overcome their delays.

The ultimate goal of the Nonverbal Imitation Program is to teach the student *generalized imitation*. Generalized imitation takes place when the student learns to imitate novel behaviors without specifically being taught to do so. The practical advantage of imitation can be seen in one-trial learning, whereby a person merely demonstrates a new behavior and the student immediately performs that behavior without any assistance but the model. In an upcoming volume on advanced programs, the Observational Learning Program is presented in which the student is taught how to learn through the observation of other students learning from a teacher in a regular classroom environment. In the technical literature, such forms of newly acquired behaviors are referred to as social learning. It has been proposed that this sort of learning cannot be explained by the use of separate learning principles. However, this appears not to be the case.

Research has demonstrated that such imitative behavior can be learned and that the teacher can rely on operant learning principles (presented as discrete trials in this manual) to teach this skill. As with other matching programs, the perceived similarity in the student's and other person's behaviors may become inherently reinforcing to the student. In popular literature this is referred to as the establishment of an imitative tendency or capacity.

As for all the other programs in this manual, the skills gained through the current program are taught in a stepwise manner. The student is first taught, through prompting and reinforcement, to imitate simple behaviors of an adult, such as dropping a block in a bucket or waving a hand. Slowly and systematically, the student is taught to imitate more complex behaviors, such as playing with toys, writing, and playing preschool games. Specifically, the student is first taught to imitate certain simple gross motor behaviors, when the teacher says, "Do this," and concurrently demonstrates an action (e.g., dropping a block in a bucket, pushing a car back and forth, tapping a table top). Newly established imitative behaviors can be extended for learning imitation of basic self-help behaviors (e.g., drinking from a glass, brushing hair, washing hands), early and appropriate play and sports (e.g., Red Light–Green Light, Follow the Leader, shooting baskets, doing somersaults), preschool skills (e.g., drawing, writing, cutting, pasting), and appropriate social skills (e.g., crying when others cry, smiling when others smile). Through this program, the student learns to pay more attention to other people and becomes motivated to learn by watching how others behave. In short, learning to imitate the behaviors of others can do much to enhance the overall social, emotional, and intellectual development of the student.

All students can learn nonverbal imitation to some degree, but there are large individual differences in both the rate of progress and the end product. For example, all students can learn to imitate simple behaviors, such as many self-help skills, and most students with developmental delays can learn to imitate typical children playing simple preschool games, such as Ring Around the Rosie. However, a small minority of students will fail to imitate even the simplest behaviors from the program as it is now devised.

Nonverbal imitation training can be started when the student has learned to sit down in a chair without engaging in too many disruptive behaviors. It may also help if the student can visually orient to the teacher. Acquisition of nonverbal imitation is further facilitated by the student's being able to follow certain basic instructions as taught in Chapters 9 and 15. Both the Nonverbal Imitation Program and the Matching and Sorting Program (Chapter 12) may be started during the first 2 to 3 full, 6- to 8-hour days of treatment.

After 1 hour into training of the present program, it should become apparent whether the student is improving or standing still (see Chapter 33). Progress is shown when the student begins to imitate one of the adult's behaviors, or at least when the prompt fading process has begun. If the student does not improve, team members need to help each other identify potential problems in their use of discrete trials, prompts, or reward delivery (see Chapter 35). Lack of progress may also mean that the kinds of tasks being taught need to be revised. For example, a limited motor skill level may not allow the student to perform the behaviors demonstrated by the teacher.

Before moving on, it is important to comment on the need for the teacher to become familiar with discrimination learning procedures (see Chapter 16). The steps involved in teaching nonverbal imitation conform to those specified in the chapter on discrimination learning.

Gross Motor Imitation Using Objects

The teaching of nonverbal imitation should be introduced by using objects (e.g., teach the student to imitate the teacher dropping blocks into a bucket, pushing a toy car, placing rings on a ring stacker, hitting a drum with a drumstick). It does not matter whether the student has already learned to use some of these objects because the Nonverbal Imitation Program teaches the student to imitate the *teacher's* use of these objects.

We have three reasons for recommending that the teacher use objects when beginning to teach nonverbal imitation. First, most students are reinforced by actions involving toys or come to discover the reinforcing properties after exposure to such actions. Second, behaviors that involve handling an object may be more discriminable than behaviors that involve only the body. Third, actions involving objects often create noise, providing distinct feedback that facilitates discrimination of (attention to) the association between the student's behavior and the reinforcement provided for that behavior (technically speaking, distinct feedback helps the student discriminate the reinforcement contingency).

When the student learns to imitate the first few of the teacher's behaviors, it may appear to the casual observer that the student has learned to imitate. However, in the majority of instances, the student has not learned to imitate, as demonstrated by the fact that many new and different behaviors performed by the teacher will probably not be imitated but rather cue already established behaviors from the student at this early stage of learning. With increased exposure to imitation training, however, the student will learn to attend to very specific nuances in the teacher's behaviors.

During the beginning stages of teaching, keep each sitting to a maximum of 5 to 6 trials, and take about 30-second play breaks between sets of trials. Sittings in the early stages of teaching should not exceed 2 minutes between breaks. As the student advances through the programs in this manual, the teacher may extend the length of sittings from 1 to 5 minutes, allowing for more trials. When it is time for a play break, signal the break with the instruction "All done" and concurrently help the student to go and play. In all programs, signal a play break contingent only on a correct response (unprompted whenever possible). *Make certain that the student does not receive a break contingent on noncompliance, a tantrum, or an incorrect response.*

In the beginning of training, the student should sit next to the teacher at the table. This seating arrangement makes it easier for the teacher to manually prompt the student to imitate actions with toys. By sitting next to the student, the teacher also can better control the student's behavior in other ways, such as preventing the student from running away. After both the student and the teacher have acquired more experience, some tasks may be easier taught by positioning the teacher and the student across from one another. Later on, the teacher and student can move away from close physical arrangements, such as sitting by a table, and instead imitation can be taught in the student's everyday environment. An advantage of starting at the table is that it allows the teacher to have better control over the teaching environment. This control helps the student attend to the behaviors the teacher models, thereby facilitating the student's rate of mastery.

The teacher needs the following materials for the first behavior modeled to the student: two identical blocks and a large bucket made of a material that creates noise when a block is dropped into it. The second behavior involves use a ring stacker with a flat bottom and two identical rings. Two identical toy cars are used for the third behavior.

▶ Step 1

Place two identical blocks about 1 foot apart side by side in front of the bucket and on the table. Place one block in front of you, the other in front of the student. For some students it may be helpful to initially place the bucket between your knees, making it easier for the student to reach (in this scenario, you and the student should be positioned across from one another rather than side by side).

Present SDl, which consists of your saying, "Do this," in a loud and clear voice while concurrently retrieving the nearer block from the table and dropping it into the bucket. It may be helpful to present the SD while the student is oriented toward the teaching material. Passing the block in front of the student's eyes may also facilitate this orientation. Immediately after giving SD1, prompt R1. Since the student already mastered R1, dropping a block into a bucket during earlier programs, it is likely that only minimal prompting will be needed. You may prompt either by instructing the student, "Drop block," or by manually taking her hand, helping her to grasp the block, and moving it to the bucket. After the response is completed, reinforce the student. Repeat the trial and begin fading the prompt by gradually decreasing the amount of verbal or manual prompting. The manual prompt may be decreased by gradually providing less and less physical assistance until the manual prompt is gradually shifted to a less intrusive visual prompt (e.g., pointing to the block while presenting SD1). The verbal prompt may be faded by lowering its volume or by systematically eliminating words from the prompt, beginning with the last word. Place mastery at 9 out of 10 or 19 out of 20 unprompted correct responses.

With successive presentations of the SD, place the bucket in different positions on the table so that inadvertent position prompts (e.g., the block can only be dropped in the bucket provided the bucket is in a specific location) may be avoided. Eventually try placing the bucket on the floor, on one side of the student's chair, and then on the other side. If the student fails to respond or responds incorrectly, introduce the least amount of prompt necessary to reinstate the correct response. During prompt fading, remember to occasionally probe unprompted trials to determine whether further fading of the prompt is necessary. If the student fails to respond correctly, immediately prompt, reinforce the correct response, and then resume prompt fading. Abundantly reinforce the student if she responds without a prompt, guarding against reinforcing prompt dependency. With the bucket placed in different positions, set mastery at 5 out of 5 or 9 out of 10 unprompted correct responses and then go on to Step 2.

▶ Step 2

To facilitate the discrimination between SD1 and SD2, the behaviors used as SDs should be maximally different from each other. Placing a ring on a stacker is a good target behavior for SD2. Remove the bucket and blocks from the table and place the ring stacker on the table with two identical rings in front of it. Present SD2, which consists of your saying, "Do this," while concurrently placing a ring on the stacker. Manually prompt the correct response (concurrently with or no later than 1 second after the SD) by taking the student's hand, helping her to grasp the ring, and moving it to the stacker. Reinforce, then repeat the presentation of SD2. Again, prompt the response and reinforce. Over the next few trials, gradually fade the prompt by, for example, decreasing the amount of manual guidance over trials until eventually a mere tap on the student's hand ora point to her ring occasions R2. After 9 out of 10 or 19 out of 20 unprompted correct responses, begin a block of trials that involves moving the ring stacker to different positions on the table.

Once SD1–Rl and SD2–R2 are acquired separately, you must help the student discriminate between the two actions by using discrimination learning procedures. Begin by placing the bucket with the two blocks in front of it and the ring stacker with the two rings in front of it on the table in front the student. Allow a 12-inch space between the two sets of objects.

▶ Step 3

Intermix SD1 (dropping a block in the bucket) and SD2 (placing a ring on the stacker). Because

SD2 was mastered last, it is likely that the student will give R2 when SD1 is presented. To avoid a nonreinforced trial, prompt and reinforce R1 when SD1 is presented. Present mass trials of SD1 while fading the prompt. Place mastery at 3 unprompted correct responses in a row. Within 2 seconds of completing mastery of SD1 (dropping a block in the bucket), present SD2 (placing a ring on the stacker) and simultaneously prompt the student's correct response. In an attempt to decrease the number of prompted trials, probe with unprompted trials. Set mastery at 3 unprompted correct responses in a row. Over subsequent blocks of trials, alternate back and forth between the two instructions. If the student makes an error, as in giving R2 to SD1, do not reinforce but rather provide an informational "No" and immediately present SD1 again while prompting the response. Reinforce, and continue presenting the SD until all prompts have been faded.

With subsequent shifts between SD1 and SD2, require fewer and fewer successive correct responses before presenting the alternate SD (e.g., 3 in a row, then 2, and then eventually 1). It is important to switch between SD1 and SD2 after 1 unprompted correct response to each SD to help establish the discrimination. Over successive intermixed and differentially reinforced trials, the student will make fewer and fewer mistakes and eventually show that she has mastered the discrimination. This comes about because the associations between SD1–R1 and SD2–R2 are reinforced and thereby strengthened, whereas mistakes, such as SD1–R2 and SD2–R1, are weakened because they are not reinforced but rather placed on extinction. Eventually the student will respond correctly without prompts the first time the instructions are presented when contrasted with one another.

The student may learn to perseverate (adopt a win–stay strategy) when several trials of a particular SD are presented in a row. Also, the student may acquire a win–shift strategy when SD1 and SD2 are systematically alternated. It is important to introduce random rotation as described in the discrimination learning chapter (Chapter 16) to counteract these and other problems. The student has mastered the discrimination once she correctly responds in 9 out of 10 or 19 out of 20 unprompted trials with the SDs randomly presented.

The first discrimination is usually the most difficult and should be considered a major accomplishment by the student. As such, it is important to strengthen it. Therefore, once the student learns to discriminate between SD1 and SD2, we recommend generalizing the discrimination as follows: (a) move the position of the objects to different places on the table; (b) have all team members practice giving the SDs; (c) practice the discrimination across different environments; and (d) practice the discrimination off and on over the next 4 to 5 days. Be aware that a shift in environments and teachers is likely to result in the student's making errors. To maximize the student's success, change to new teachers and environments in small steps. For example, place a familiar teacher beside a new and unfamiliar teacher during the first trials, and then gradually increase the distance of the familiar teacher from the unfamiliar teacher. When changing environments, slowly move the table and chairs to other positions in the teaching room, then gradually move into other rooms of the house or to the floor.

Given that the student has mastered the SD1–SD2 discrimination, you may want to conduct generalization sessions in a little more playful and informal manner than that in which the training sessions were conducted. If the student loses the discrimination during this time, return to earlier steps and reestablish mastery before going further.

The third imitation, SD3–R3, should be maximally different from the first two imitations. Pushing a car back and forth may be used as SD3. To teach SD3, retain the original setting with you and student sitting next to each other facing the table. Place two identical cars about 12 inches apart in a horizontal line on the table. One car should be placed in front of each person.

▶ Step 4

Present SD3, which consists of your saying, "Do this," while concurrently pushing the nearest car back and forth. While performing this behavior, manually prompt the student's response by placing her right hand on her car and helping her push the car back and forth. Reinforce the correct response. Fade the prompt by gradually lessening the amount of manual guidance. Then, instead of actually taking the student's hand and directing it toward the car, fade to a visual prompt such as pointing to the car while presenting SD3. If the prompt is faded too rapidly, the student will fail to respond correctly and you will need to go back and introduce the least amount of prompting necessary to reinstate the correct response. Remember to completely fade all prompts and to save the best reinforcers for unprompted trials. Set the criterion for mastery at 9 out of 10 or 19 out of 20 unprompted correct responses.

▶ **Step 5**

Once SD3–R3 is mastered in mass trials, teach the student to discriminate between SD3 and SD1 (dropping a block in the bucket) and then between SD3 and SD2 (placing a ring on the stacker). Remember to rehearse the earlier SD1–SD2 discrimination. If this discrimination is partially lost during the teaching of the other SDs, go back and reestablish it through prompting, prompt fading, and random rotation. Once the student achieves mastery, responding correctly to the random presentations of SD1, SD2, and SD3 (for 9 out of 10 or 19 out of 20 unprompted correct responses), introduce SD4.

▶ **Step 6**

Tapping a drum may be used as SD4. Retain the original setting with the student seated next to you facing the table. Place a drum and two sticks on the table. Present SD4, which consists of your saying, "Do this," while concurrently picking up the nearest stick and tapping the drum. Simultaneously prompt the student's correct response by manually helping the student to pick up her stick and tap the drum. Reinforce the correct response. Fade the prompt gradually over the next several trials by decreasing the amount of manual guidance. If the student fails to respond or responds incorrectly, go back and introduce the least amount of prompting necessary to reinstate the correct response. Completely fade all prompts. Set mastery at 9 out of 10 or 19 out of 20 unprompted correct responses.

▶ **Step 7**

Once SD4 (tapping the drum) is mastered in mass trials, teach the student to discriminate between SD4 and SD1 (dropping a block in the bucket), then SD4 and SD2 (placing a ring on the stacker), and finally SD4 and SD3 (pushing a car back and forth). Once these discriminations are mastered (for 9 out of 10 or 19 out of 20 unprompted correct responses), intermix all four SDs at once. If the table size does not allow for simultaneous presentation of all four sets of objects, present two or three sets of objects at a time. Remember, however, to randomly rotate the presentation of all four SDs.

Additional Imitations Using Objects

Once the student masters the first four imitations, try adding novel imitations by relying on the experience gained from establishing the earlier ones. The following are examples of possible choices for the next several imitations:

Additional Imitations Using Objects

SD	"Do this"
5	pretend drinking from a cup
6	pretend eating toy food
7	throwing a crumpled napkin in a wastebasket placed next to the table
8	putting a doll in a crib (use two identical dolls)
9	putting on a hat (avoid the loose, floppy kind)
10	pushing a toy car down the ramp of a toy garage
11	galloping a toy horse across the table
12	turning the handle on a jack-in-the-box
13	tapping a xylophone (any keys) with drumsticks
14	shaking a tambourine
15	banging a toy hammer
16	placing two animals inside a pen (use four identical animals)
17	brushing hair
18	pretending to read a book
19	vacuuming the floor with a toy vacuum cleaner

The imitations are listed in order of apparent level of difficulty. Given the large individual differences that exist among students, however, what may be easily mastered by one student may be difficult for another student. If little or no progress is made on any particular imitation after 1 hour, try another action and return to the difficult imitation later.

Note that any one of the imitations listed can be used as a springboard for teaching similar imitations. For example, SD5 (drinking from a cup) may be extended to picking up a spoon and placing it in a dish, picking up a napkin and wiping one's mouth, and a host of other actions associated with eating at the table. Given the supply of reinforcers and models of appropriate behaviors readily available at mealtimes, there are abundant opportunities for extending the Nonverbal Imitation Program to this everyday setting (see Chapter 21 on self-help skills).

Just as SD5 provides for an extended range of learning opportunities, SD8 (putting a doll in a crib) may also be extended. For example, teaching the child to imitate kissing a doll, patting a doll on its back, stroking a doll's hair, feeding a doll, and placing a doll in a crib helps establish appropriate play behavior (see the section on playing with dolls in Chapter 19). Such appropriate play behavior may be begun by requesting, "Do this," while modeling the behavior. Later this request could be transferred to the instruction "Play with dolls" as the model is faded out (see Chapter 15).

Another example of how a single SD can be extended to develop new behaviors may be illustrated by teaching the student, through imitation, to push a car down the ramp of a toy garage (SD10). This behavior may lead to going up the ramp with the car, driving the car onto the car elevator, turning the handle to move the car up to the top of the garage, driving the car up to the pump, and filling up the tank with gasoline (see the section on playing with cars in Chapter 19). This kind of play may later be extended to larger units of play in which the student pretends her tricycle is a fire engine, which she fills up with gas before driving off to put out an imaginary fire.

SD7 (throwing a crumpled napkin into a wastebasket) may easily be extended to teaching the student to tidy up after snacks. SD9 (putting on a hat) could be the beginning of teaching the student to dress independently. SD13 (tapping a xylophone) may be extended to imitating the use of other instruments (e.g., triangle, tambourine, tone blocks, rhythm sticks). SD17 (brushing hair) could be extended to the student's brushing teeth, washing face, and similar personal hygiene behaviors.

Note that it is virtually impossible, or at least highly impractical, to shape each of these behaviors separately; however, shaping comes in handy as an additional step for fine-tuning the student's play and self-help skills so they become closer to those of typical individuals. It should be further noted that if you target several behaviors within one area (e.g., doll play), the student is more likely to acquire generalized imitation of behaviors within the same area. Generalized imitation is less likely to occur with a radical change in the SDs, such as moving from self-help to doll play.

You may notice that some imitations require two relatively complex behaviors. These may be referred to as two-part imitations. For example, mastery of imitating your feeding a doll requires that the student retrieve both the doll and the bottle and then put the bottle to the doll's mouth. Given this complexity, some students fail to imitate such behaviors. Students who experience difficulty may be taught in a two-step process: First, the student should be taught to imitate the behaviors separately. Second, the behaviors should be chained together. It is to the student's advantage for you to delay the imitation of complex behaviors until a relatively large number (50 to 100) of simpler imitations are mastered. See "Chaining Two-Part and Three-Part Imitations" later in this chapter for specifics on how to teach complex imitations.

It may seem to some that training such as that described in this section (e.g., in the case of table manners) is unduly intrusive. However, it must be remembered that typical persons acquire many socially appropriate behaviors through similar procedures, although to a less intense degree. For example, it is not unusual to observe parents of typical children modeling appropriate eating behaviors for their children and correcting and shaping eating, dressing, and similar behaviors for years to come.

Maintenance and Generalization

Keep mastered imitations maintained on a schedule adapted to the student's particular needs. For some students, the various imitations must be worked through at least once per day. Other students maintain their skills when they are practiced once per week. As the schedule is thinned out, the student's performance demonstrates whether mastery of the imitations is maintained.

Generalize imitative skills across objects by introducing nonidentical exemplars of target items. For example, imitating drinking with various kinds of cups should be introduced, as should putting different kinds of hats on one's head, pretending to read a number of different books, and so on. Not only does such a procedure facilitate generalization, it also tends to keep students motivated and less likely to become bored and noncompliant. Remember, generalization should be done across persons, environments, and target stimuli.

Gross Motor Imitation Without Objects

We recommend starting with gross motor behaviors because they tend to be more discriminable than fine motor behaviors. Examples of gross motor movements include standing up, sitting down, tapping a knee, clapping one's hands, raising a foot, raising one's arms, and waving. We also recommend starting with motions related to parts of the body the student can readily observe, as well as motions that you can readily and manually prompt (e.g., motions that can be demonstrated with one hand and prompted with the other).

Tapping a knee is used as SD1 for illustrative purposes. You and the student should sit facing each other with your knees slightly touching the student's. Note that the table is not necessarily involved in this kind of imitation. Other than that, the teaching procedures for gross motor movements are virtually identical to those presented earlier for imitating actions done with toys.

▶ Step 1

Present SD1, which consists of saying, "Do this," while tapping your left knee twice with your left hand (to allow prompting using your right hand). The hand movements should be exaggerated, as in lifting your hand at least 10 inches above your knee between taps. Exaggerated movements may help the student orient to SD1. Once SD1 is presented, immediately and manually prompt the correct response by taking the student's right hand (with your right hand) and assisting him in tapping his right knee twice. Reinforce the correct response.

Fade the prompt over subsequent trials by gradually reducing the amount of manual guidance provided to the student. Fading may be initiated by merely guiding the student's hand toward his knee. In fading the prompt over the next several trials, let go of the student's hand halfway to his knee, then just pull his hand out of his lap and in the general direction of his knee. If the student fails to respond correctly on any given trial, go back and introduce the least amount of prompting necessary to reinstate the correct response. Remember to eventually fade all prompts and save the best reinforcement for unprompted trials. Set mastery at 5 out of 5 or 9 out of 10 unprompted correct responses (the criterion for mastery is reduced based on mastery of earlier imitations using toys). If the student is unable to imitate without the use of prompts, use the procedures described in "Areas of Difficulty" presented later in this chapter

In illustrating the following step, raising a foot is used as SD2. Raising a foot is different from SD1 (tapping a knee) and is therefore likely to facilitate the student's discrimination. Like SD1, raising a foot makes manual prompting and the presentation of the SD possible to do simultaneously. To make the SD and the prompt as clear as possible for the student as well as the teachers, agree as to whether the student should lift the left, the right, or both feet as the correct response (the left foot is used here as the correct response to SD2).

▶ Step 2

You and the student should sit on chairs facing one another, with the student's left foot on top of your right shoe. Present SD2, which consists of saying, "Do this," while simultaneously raising your right foot at least 20 inches off the floor. Immediately prompt the correct response by raising your right foot, thus lifting the student's foot up. By doing this, both your hands are free to reinforce the student or to be used for additional prompting, if necessary. Be sure to reinforce the student while his foot is raised high. If reinforcement is postponed until the student's foot is back on the floor, lowering his foot may be accidentally reinforced (a behavior incompatible with raising his foot).

Fade the prompt gradually, by first lifting the student's foot halfway up, then by merely giving his foot a little upward push with the tip of your shoe. If the student fails to respond correctly on any given trial, go back and introduce the least amount of prompting necessary to reinstate the correct response. Remember that all prompts must be faded and the best reinforcers should be saved for unprompted trials. Once the student achieves mastery of SD2 (5 out of 5 or 9 out of 10 unprompted correct trials), go on to Step 3.

▶ Step 3

Begin discrimination training between SD1 and SD2. Present SD1 (tapping a knee) first. Because SD2 was mastered most recently, it is likely that the student will give R2 (raising a foot) when SD1 is presented. To avoid a nonreinforced trial, prompt and reinforce R1 when SD1 is presented. Remember to probe unprompted trials so as to possibly decrease the number of prompted trials and help reduce prompt dependency. Place mastery at 2 unprompted correct responses in a row. Within 2 to 3 seconds of completing mastery of SD1 (tapping a knee), present SD2 (raising a foot) and simultaneously prompt the student's correct response. Set mastery at 2 unprompted correct responses in a row. Over the next few trials, switch back and forth between the two instructions while fading the prompt and differentially reinforcing correct responses (i.e., provide greater reinforcement for correct unprompted trials than for prompted trials, and provide an informational "No" for incorrect responses). Switch after 2 unprompted correct responses in a row, then after 1. Finally, subject SD1 and SD2 to random rotation. Once this stage is reached, place mastery at 9 out of 10 or 19 out of 20 unprompted correct responses.

Once the discrimination between SD1 and SD2 is mastered, we recommend that this discrimination be practiced across team members and gradually introduced across different locations. This is consistent with our earlier recommendation regarding the first discrimination: The first discrimination should become firmly established so as to facilitate the student's learning of subsequent discriminations.

SD3 is illustrated as raising an arm. Raising an arm is perceptually different from SD1 (tapping a knee) and SD2 (raising a foot) and is therefore likely to facilitate discrimination. Raising an arm also allows for a manual prompt to take place simultaneously with the presentation of the SD. To help make the trial as discrete as possible, agree as to whether the student should lift the left or the right arm, or both, as the correct response to SD3. For illustration, the left arm will be used as the correct response to SD3.

▶ Step 4

You and the student should sit on chairs facing each other. Present SD3, which consists of saying, "Do this," and concurrently raising your right arm while simultaneously prompting the student's correct response. Prompting may be done by taking hold of the student's left hand with your right hand and raising the student's hand up with yours. Remember to reinforce the student while his arm is still raised high, not while he lowers it (which would reinforce a response that is incompatible with raising his arm). Fade the prompt over the next several trials by removing your manual assistance when the student's arm is halfway up, then fading the prompt to merely giving the student's arm a push upward. Finally, fade the prompt to giving the student's elbow a push upward with your right hand as you raise your arm. If on any trial the student does not respond appropriately, go back to a stronger prompt. Once SD3 is mastered (5 out of 5 correct or 9 out of 10 unprompted correct trials), go on to Step 5.

▶ Step 5

Before intermixing SD1 (tapping a knee), SD2 (raising a foot), and SD3 (raising an arm), rehearse the earlier SD1–SD2 discrimination, which may have been partially lost while establishing SD3. Next, reintroduce SD3. Prompt if necessary and set mastery at 2 unprompted correct responses in a row. Within 2 seconds of completing mastery of SD3, present SD1 (tapping a knee). Over successive intermixed and differentially reinforced trials, the student will make fewer and fewer mistakes and eventually show he has mastered the discrimination between SD1 and SD3. After this occurs, reintroduce SD2, intermixing SD2 and SD3. Finally, intermix the three SDs, one at a time, according to the random rotation paradigm. Place mastery at 9 out of 10 or 19 out of 20 unprompted correct responses.

Touching tummy may be used as SD4 because the action is different from the three earlier instructions, it may be observed by the student, and it is easy to prompt. Use the same procedures for teaching SD4 as were described for teaching SD3. Remember to intermix SD4 with the other SDs after it has been mastered separately. The intermixing of the various SDs rehearses and thereby maintains the accuracy of the earlier mastered imitations. When introducing new SDs, the teacher may receive some guidance from the following list of behaviors.

Additional Gross Motor Imitations

SD	"Do this"	SD	"Do this"
5	tapping table next to you	25	flexing upper arm muscles (showing how strong you are)
6	standing up	26	waving bye-bye
7	touching head	27	clapping hands
8	turning around	28	holding arms out to sides
9	stamping feet	29	touching feet
10	touching shoulders	30	patting side of bottom
11	crossing ankles	31	touching elbow
12	putting arm out to side	32	touching ears
13	touching chin	33	standing on knees
14	opening/ shutting hands	34	touching neck
15	touching toes	35	slapping thighs
16	jumping up and down	36	standing on one foot
17	shading eyes with hand	37	doing a somersault
18	marching on the spot	38	rocking body back and forth
19	touching cheeks	39	sitting Indian style
20	folding arms	40	throwing kisses
21	shaking hands loose	41	walking on knees
22	touching back	42	covering eyes with hands
23	rolling on floor	43	touching throat
24	moving body from side to side	44	touching heel

Imitation of finger games and songs (e.g., Itsy-Bitsy Spider, Roly-Poly; Head, Shoulders, Knees, and Toes; Five Little Monkeys) may also be taught to help prepare the student for participation in group settings, such as preschool. Some of these games and songs appear to have intrinsically reinforcing properties for many students, suggesting that they will be maintained by little or no extrinsic reinforcement (e.g., social approval, food).

Maintenance and Generalization

By now the student may have learned more than 50 single nonverbal imitations involving objects and gross motor activities. We recommend that you organize the SDs into two schedules, a Maintenance Schedule and a Current Schedule. The Current Schedule should identify the more recently mastered SDs as well as the SDs on acquisition. The SDs on the Current Schedule need to be practiced every day. A senior team member should be assigned the responsibility of keeping the Current Schedule up to date with weekly adjustments (e.g., the status of prompts) for each item. Another team member should be given the responsibility of updating and assigning the regular work-through of items on the Maintenance Schedule. The Maintenance Schedule should contain the SDs mastered and frequently practiced in the past and should be done on a regular schedule so as to ensure these items are not forgotten. The frequency of work-through for each program on a maintenance schedule has to be adjusted for each student you work with as the amount of practice required to maintain skills varies from student to student. Note that a maintenance schedule is helpful for most or all of the programs presented in this manual.

What To Expect

The nonverbal imitation skills presented thus far are mastered by almost all students. Most students make rapid progress and seem to enjoy this program, and some students begin to spontaneously imitate adults' gross motor behaviors. For example, a boy may begin to imitate the way some males walk, with their legs apart and with large arm movements ("walking big"), whereas a girl may begin to walk more gracefully. Such imitation suggests the early beginnings of sex-role differentiation. At this time boys may be introduced to a larger proportion of imitations with boy-oriented objects (e.g., trucks, tools, and male Disney figurines such as Peter Pan, Aladdin, Quasimodo, Woody, and Buzz), whereas girls may receive a larger proportion of imitations dealing with girl-oriented objects (e.g., dolls, dollhouses, toy stoves, and female Disney figurines such as Belle, Wendy, Pocahontas, the Little Mermaid, and Esmeralda). Given the large overlap in gender roles, parents are advised to use their own judgment as to whether and to what extent the imitation programs should be differentiated.

Considering individual differences and difficulty predicting what will be easy or difficult for any one student, you are advised to be flexible in deciding which imitations to introduce. For example, raising one's arms may seem an easy imitation to master, yet many students show difficulty acquiring this behavior. Or, the response may be imitated but weakened into a partial and minimal response, making it difficult to decide whether to reinforce. It is as if students are extremely efficient at minimizing efforts while maximizing gains, a trait common to all humans. If any particular imitation creates an unusual amount of effort to teach, postpone teaching it until later.

You may encounter problems helping the student discriminate between behaviors that appear similar. For example, imitations involving adjacent body parts (e.g., touching shoulders vs. touching tummy) require more training than distinct acts (e.g., touching head vs. jumping up and down). The same problem may occur when teaching behaviors the student cannot observe herself performing (e.g., touching teeth vs. touching lips, or touching chin vs. touching throat). The imitation of subtle and minute body movements (e.g., smiling vs. frowning) should be undertaken only after the student masters 20 or more larger body movements.

Tasks for Improved Finger–Hand Dexterity

Fine motor imitations, such as pointing, picking up tiny objects, holding a pencil correctly, and stringing beads, are likely to be difficult for the student to imitate because these behaviors require the student to attend to (discriminate) very subtle visual stimuli. Also, the motor movements involved may not be well developed in some students. Many students need separate training to improve their hand and finger dexterity in order to progress to learning skills in programs that require mastery of fine motor skills (e.g., pointing to objects, drawing, writing, cutting). We strongly recommend diligent practice of the following tasks before or concurrent with the teaching of fine motor imitations. Nonverbal imitation may be used to prompt dexterity tasks (e.g., say, "Do this," while demonstrating the target action). The exercises are ordered in apparent degree of difficulty.

Finger–Hand Dexterity Imitations

SD "Do this"

1. pouring beans/rice/water from small mug into wide then narrow container
2. spooning rice/flour from one bowl to another and then to a cup, changing from a big spoon to a smaller spoon
3. putting cylindrical blocks into a shape sorter (tape the other holes shut)
4. pulling apart two blocks of Legos
5. removing the tops of big markers
6. putting the tops back on big markers
7. crumpling tissue paper
8. turning the dial on a toy telephone
9. pinching Play-Doh
10. opening and closing the Velcro on a shoe
11. unzipping a zipper (finding a reinforcer inside)
12. picking M&Ms/raisins/beads/pennies out of an egg carton
13. picking party toothpicks from a pile of Play-Doh/Styrofoam and placing them into a cup/bottle
14. picking up party toothpicks from the table and placing them in a pile of Play-Doh or piece of Styrofoam
15. picking up pennies from the table and putting them into a piggy bank
16. stringing beads (starting with big wooden beads and gradually moving to smaller ones)
17. lacing cards (starting with a few large holes and gradually moving to several small holes)
18. picking up small objects with kitchen tongs and dropping them into a container
19. squeezing/pulling the trigger of a toy gun
20. placing hair clips in a doll's hair
21. placing clothespins around a paper plate
22. twisting nuts onto large bolts, then smaller bolts
23. unscrewing a lid (finding a reinforcer inside)
24. tracing stencils
25. stringing rubber bands on a peg board
26. unbuttoning a pocket (finding a reinforcer inside)

Fine Motor Imitations

We suggest starting fine motor imitations with exercises that are functional for the student and ones the student is likely to succeed at performing. We have chosen making a fist as SD1 and pointing as SD2 for two reasons. First, it is relatively easy to manually prompt making a fist. Second, pointing is a functional behavior given that the student must point in most receptive language programs when asked to identify target items.

In the following steps, the student should sit facing you so he can easily observe your actions. Note the similarity between these teaching steps and those presented earlier.

▶ Step 1

Present SD1, which consists of saying, "Do this," while raising your left hand and making a fist. Slow and exaggerated motions may help the student orient to the SD. Immediately and manually prompt the student's response by raising his right hand with your right hand while curling his fingers into a fist. Reinforce the correct response. Fade the prompt in gradual steps until you eventually only need to nudge the student's knuckles with your fingers, then just give his elbow a little push upward, and so on. If on any trial the student does not respond appropriately, go back to a stronger prompt. Place mastery at 5 out of 5 or 9 out of 10 unprompted correct responses. After this criterion is met, go on to teach SD2.

▶ Step 2

Present SD2, which consists of saying, "Do this," while making a fist with your left hand then stretching your index finger out to a pointing position. Immediately prompt the student to respond correctly. This may be done by placing your right hand on the student's fist and teasing out his index finger with your index finger. Fade all prompts gradually over the next several trials. Set mastery at 5 out of 5 or 9 out of 10 unprompted correct responses.

▶ Step 3

Intermix and differentially reinforce SD1 (making a fist) with an already mastered gross motor imitation. Then randomly rotate SD1 with one or two other mastered gross motor imitations. Next, intermix and differentially reinforce SD2 (pointing) with an already mastered gross motor imitation and then randomly rotate SD2 with one or two other mastered gross motor imitations. The gross motor imitations serve as contrasting stimuli and are introduced to facilitate the discrimination of (attention to) SD1 and SD2. When mastery is achieved (i.e., the student responds correctly in 9 out of 10 or 19 out of 20 unprompted trials), go on to Step 4, which involves intermixing SD1 and SD2 with one another.

▶ Step 4

Present SD1. Prompt and reinforce the response. Fade the prompt and place mastery at 2 unprompted correct responses in a row. Within 2 to 3 seconds of completing mastery of SD1, present SD2 and simultaneously prompt the student's correct response. Set mastery of SD2 at 2 unprompted correct responses in a row. Over the next several trials, alternate back and forth between the two instructions (SD1 and SD2) while fading the prompt and differentially reinforcing correct responses. Remember to occasionally probe unprompted trials to ascertain whether the student can respond correctly without further prompting. Switch SDs after 2 correct responses in a row, then 1. Over successive intermixed and differentially reinforced trials, the student will make fewer and fewer mistakes. Once the student is able to respond correctly without prompts the first time the instructions are contrasted, randomly rotate the presentations of SD1 and SD2. Place mastery at 9 out of 10 or 19 out of 20 unprompted correct responses in trials with the SDs randomly rotated.

The following are examples of additional fine motor imitations, listed in apparent degree of difficulty.

Additional Fine Motor Imitations

SD "Do this"

1 pointing with both index fingers in the air

2 "walking" across table with index and middle fingers

3 repeatedly bending and stretching index finger(s)

4 pointing to nose
5 putting tips of index fingers together
6 putting tips of thumbs together
7 tapping the tips of the index finger and thumb on same hand together (making a "talking beak")
8 folding hands
9 pointing to lips
10 folding hands then "winging" fingers up and down like a flying bird
11 pointing to eyelids
12 placing the tip of the thumb on your nose then fanning out the other fingers (as done when teasing someone)
13 pointing to teeth
14 making a peace sign
15 drumming on the table with fingers
16 making a fist and then, one at a time, fanning out fingers starting with the thumb (as if counting from 1 to 5)
17 fanning out fingers on the left hand, then with right index finger pointing to one fanned-out finger at the time (as if counting the fingers)

If it is difficult for the student to differentiate pointing to or touching parts around the head that cannot be observed (e.g., pointing to nose vs. pointing to mouth, touching cheeks vs. touching chin), postpone such discriminations until additional imitations are mastered.

Maintenance

Up to this point, the student has acquired a variety of nonverbal imitations involving objects, as well as gross and fine motor imitations without using objects. Gradually transfer all mastered imitations to the Maintenance Schedule and continue to practice them according to the individual student's needs. Note also that mastered nonverbal imitations should be intermixed with difficult discriminations (e.g., fine motor discriminations), as well as the skills involved in more difficult programs (e.g., the Verbal Imitation Program, Chapter 22). This will help maintain the student's attention and motivation.

Imitation of Facial Motions and Expressions

Motions involving the mouth (e.g., blowing, smacking lips, sticking out one's tongue) and facial expressions (e.g., smiling, frowning, pretend crying) require the student to attend to (discriminate) visual stimuli that are even more subtle than those presented in the previous section. Further, because the student cannot observe her own responses when performing imitations involving the face, it may be difficult for the student to acquire the discrimination of separate motions. Consequently, we recommend postponing teaching the imitation of facial motions until after the student has acquired a number of gross and fine motor imitations, after more functional behaviors have been taught (e.g., early receptive language), and after the teacher has gained more teaching experience.

Imitation of oral-motor motions helps the student gain strength and control over mouth and tongue muscles, which in turn may facilitate prompting and acquisition of correct articulation during verbal imitation training. Imitation of facial motions and expressions helps the student become more aware of your expressions and her own facial expressions. We suggest starting with blowing (SD1), opening mouth (SD2), and sticking out tongue (SD3), motions that are relatively easy to prompt. When mastered, these imitations may facilitate the imitation of other more difficult facial motions. If any one of these first responses seems particularly difficult for the student to learn, substitute it with another response from the Additional Facial Imitations list, provided later.

Begin by sitting on the floor at face level with the student. This positioning optimizes the student's opportunity to attend to (discriminate) the visual stimuli presented to her.

▶ Step 1

Present SD1, which consists of saying, "Do this," and then blowing. Do not blow in the student's face, as she might find this aversive. If the student responds incorrectly or fails to respond within 5 seconds, provide a consequence (e.g., an informational "No") and then repeat the SD, prompting the correct response. For example, with a neutral face and as little lip movement as possible say, "Do this." Then open your mouth wide, draw in air, and let out a long, audible blow. Such an exaggerated demonstration may help the student attend to the SD. Gradually fade the visual prompt over the next several trials. If the student fails to respond with this prompting procedure, try the prompt suggested later in the "Areas of Difficulty" section. Shape stronger blowing by using differential reinforcement. Set mastery at 5 out of 5 or 9 out of 10 unprompted correct responses.

▶ Step 2

Present SD2, which consists of saying, "Do this," and then opening your mouth. If the student does not imitate the behavior within 5 seconds, repeat SD2 and prompt the correct response. For example, with a neutral face and as little lip movement as possible, say, "Do this," and then suddenly open your mouth wide. Keep your mouth open for 3 to 5 seconds. Opening one's mouth is a subtle as well as soundless behavior, and if the student does not pay close attention to your face, she may not notice the action or discriminate the difference between a closed and an open mouth. If necessary, try to prompt the student's mouth open with your fingers. If the student resists a manual prompt, try the prompting procedure suggested later in the "Areas of Difficulty" section. When the student masters SD2 (responding correctly in 5 out of 5 or 9 out of 10 unprompted trials), go on to Step 3.

▶ Step 3

Intermix and differentially reinforce SD1 (blowing) with a contrasting stimulus, such as an already mastered gross motor imitation (e.g., touching tummy). Once that discrimination is mastered, intermix and differentially reinforce SD2 (opening mouth) with a contrasting stimulus, such as a gross motor imitation that is mastered but different from the one intermixed with SD1 (e.g., clapping). The gross motor imitations serve as contrasting stimuli and are introduced to facilitate the discrimination among SD1 (blowing) and SD2 (opening mouth), which are difficult to tell apart given that both instructions involve facial motions. Once both discriminations are mastered, go on to Step 4, intermixing SD1 and SD2.

▶ Step 4

Present SD1 (blowing after saying, "Do this"). Prompt and reinforce the correct response. Fade the prompt over subsequent trials. Place mastery at 2 unprompted correct responses in a row. Within 2 to 3 seconds of completing mastery of SD1, present SD2 (opening your mouth after saying, "Do this") while simultaneously prompting the student's correct response. By quickly prompting, you help prevent the student from making an error. Set mastery of SD2 at 2 unprompted correct responses in a row. Over the next several trials, alternate in blocks of trials between the two instructions (SD1 and SD2) while fading the prompt and differentially reinforcing correct responses. Switch SDs after 2 correct responses in a row, then after 1. Over successive intermixed and differentially reinforced trials, the student will make fewer and fewer mistakes and eventually respond correctly without prompts the first time the instructions are contrasted with one another. As always, if the student fails to respond or responds incorrectly, reinstate the least intrusive prompt that establishes correct responding. The student has mastered the discrimination when she responds correctly in 9 out of 10 or 19 out of 20 unprompted and randomly presented trials.

▶ Step 5

Present SD3, which consists of saying, "Do this," and then sticking out your tongue. If the student responds incorrectly or does not respond within 5 seconds, provide a consequence and prompt the correct response on the next trial. For example, with a neutral face and as little lip movement as possible, say, "Do this," and then stick out your tongue as far as you can, keeping your tongue out for 3 to 5 seconds. If the student does not correctly imitate the action, try the prompting procedure described later in the "Areas of Difficulty" section. Set mastery at 5 out of 5 or 9 out of 10 unprompted correct responses. Next, intermix SD3 with a contrasting stimulus, such as a previously mastered gross motor imitation. Once this discrimination is mastered, intermix SD3 (sticking out tongue) with SD1 (blowing) and SD2 (opening mouth) following the procedures described in Step 4.

After the student learns to imitate blowing, opening mouth, and sticking out tongue, teach the student to imitate following the behaviors.

If any one of these behaviors seems particularly difficult for the student and the task becomes too time-consuming, teach a different behavior from the list. Use your own experience with the student you are teaching when developing and fading prompts for subsequent imitations.

Additional Facial Imitations

SD "Do this"

1 smacking lips
2 biting lower lip
3 pressing lips together (start from open mouth)
4 tapping teeth together (open and close several times)
5 placing tongue between teeth and blowing
6 moving tongue straight out and up and down, left to right, or in and out
7 biting upper lip
8 pursing lips tight and kissing
9 puffing out cheeks with air and then letting air out
10 sucking in cheeks (making a "fish mouth")
11 placing tip of tongue behind lower teeth
12 opening mouth, placing tip of tongue behind upper teeth, and then moving tongue up and down (as in slow, soundless la-la-la)
13 making "raspberries"
14 sticking tongue out and curling it like a tube
15 drawing upper and lower lips in over teeth
16 biting lower lip, then blowing air
17 licking lips
18 nodding head "yes"
19 shaking head "no"
20 sneezing
21 coughing
22 laughing
23 pretending to cry
24 looking angry (exaggerate)
25 looking happy (exaggerate)
26 looking sad (exaggerate)
27 looking surprised (exaggerate)
28 looking scared (exaggerate)

Maintenance

At this time, we suggest merging the four groups of imitations into two lists, one list consisting of mixed imitations for the Current Schedule (i.e., recently mastered SDs with one to three SDs on acquisition being practiced daily) and one list consisting of mixed imitations for the Maintenance Schedule (i.e., previously mastered SDs being practiced less often but regularly). The variety inherent in mixed imitations should help the student stay focused and motivated.

By now the large number of imitations transferred to the Maintenance Schedule probably requires a considerable amount of time to be reviewed. To help make it practical to maintain these SDs, we suggest grouping them. For example, if the student has a maintenance schedule of 70 SDs, we suggest that the SDs be arranged in mixed groups of 10 and that one group be practiced every day such that all 70 SDs are practiced in a week.

Areas of Difficulty

Some students need stronger prompts to learn a task than the prompts described previously. In this section, we suggest particular prompts for some gross, fine, and facial imitations that have proven to be effective when the usual prompting procedures fail.

Gross Motor Imitations

Suppose the student experiences problems with gross motor imitations even with the use of physical prompts. For example, the student may not make progress (the prompts are not able to be faded) at imitating your tapping a knee. If this occurs, an object should be added to the imitation. To illustrate a prompt for the example just given, both you and the student could use a block to tap knees. The visual cue provided by the block is likely to help focus the student's attention on the movements.

For this prompting procedure, use two identical blocks of a size comfortable for the student to grab and hold. The student should be seated facing you in such a fashion that the student's right knee is touching the inside of your left knee. Put a block in the student's hand and then, holding his hand with the block in it, pick up the other block and present the SD ("Do this") while tapping both blocks two to three times on *the student's knee*. Reinforce. Fade the prompt gradually by first switching the tapping of your block from the student's knee to your own knee while still manually prompting the student to tap his knee with his block. Next, slowly move your leg away from the student's leg. Then fade the manual assistance of holding and tapping the student's block on his knee until he taps the block without a physical prompt. Discard your block and tap your knee with your hand. Finally, remove the student's block. If the block cannot be removed at this stage, gradually fade in the use of a smaller block and then proceed again with the fading process. When mastery is achieved (9 out of 10 or 19 out of 20 unprompted correct responses), return to the next step in the main program section.

You may use the same block prompt procedure when teaching other imitations, such as touching head, touching tummy, touching nose, and touching ear.

Fine Motor Imitations

Some students have problems with fine motor imitations, such as imitating making a fist. To help remedy this problem, use a long pencil (or similar stick) for the student to hold. Present the SD ("Do this") while grabbing the upper end of the pencil with your left hand and holding it up in front of the student. With your right hand, take the student's right hand and curl his fingers around the lower part of the pencil so he makes a fist around the pencil. Reinforce. Fade the pencil prompt gradually over the next several trials by having the student grab the pencil himself and placing your hand further and further down so that the student's end gets shorter and shorter and less and less of his fist is made around the pencil. Or, replace the pencil with a thinner pencil or stick, then with a twist tie, and then with a thin piece of wire. If you fade the prompt too quickly, go back and introduce the least amount of prompting necessary to reinstate correct responding. Remember to occasionally probe unprompted trials to ascertain whether the student can respond without a prompt. Set mastery at 5 out of 5 or 9 out of 10 unprompted correct responses, then return to the next step of the main program section.

Facial Imitations

Some students have problems with certain facial imitations. Suppose a student has a problem imitating blowing. To help prompt blowing, you may employ a toy instrument that makes a sound when blown into (e.g., harmonica, whistle, flute). Present the student with a number of such instruments to choose from in order to maximize the probability that the student will find one she likes. Do not present the verbal part of the instruction ("Do this") if it makes demonstration of the action and the prompting unnecessarily complicated. Place the instrument in the student's right hand and manually move it to her lips. With your left hand, raise your own instrument to your mouth, draw in air, and blow into the instrument. Blow softly if the student reacts negatively to loud noises. Reward the student even if she only holds the instrument against her lips, for a partial imitation is a good start. Repeat this step until sound, no matter how feeble, is heard from the instrument. From this point on, use the technique of shaping to build stronger blowing. If the student's blowing is slow in coming, you may want to introduce novel instruments to help maintain her motivation. When the student can make sound with the instrument, discard your own instrument and demonstrate blowing without it. Let the student continue to blow into her instrument. When the student's sound is strong, fade her instrument and keep it as a reinforcer for blowing without it. Set mastery at 5 out of 5 or 9 out of 10 unprompted correct responses.

If musical instruments are ineffective as prompting devices, try blowing tiny pieces of tissue paper placed in a large shallow bowl. We suggest postponing teaching imitation of blowing bubbles or blowing out a lit candle because these actions require the student to aim at a small target in addition to blowing with a certain strength in order to succeed, which may result in frustration rather than success.

If the student has difficulty opening her mouth, use a variety of the student's favorite foods for prompting mouth movements. This may be done by holding the student's favorite food (e.g., cookies) in front of your mouth and saying, "Do this," while opening your mouth wide and taking a bite of your cookie while moving another cookie toward the student's mouth. If the student opens her mouth just a tiny bit, praise her instantly, and then give her a bite of the cookie. Holding the cookie somewhat above the student's mouth instead of directly in front of it may facilitate her opening her mouth wider. Repeat this step for several trials. Begin fading this prompt by discarding your cookie but keeping hers and use differential reinforcement for further shaping of a wide-open mouth. Probe to see if the cookie can be faded as a prompt while keeping the cookie as a reinforcer for the student opening her mouth. Then fade the sight of the cookie altogether. Once mastery is reached (5 out of 5 or 9 out of 10 unprompted correct responses), return to the next step in the main program section.

If the student has difficulty sticking out her tongue, help to remedy this by using one of the student's favorite "licking" foods (e.g., lollipop, Popsicle, cotton candy, ice cream cone, jam placed on the tip of a Popsicle stick). A lollipop is used in this example. Tilt your head forward a little so the student can easily catch sight of your tongue when it moves out of your mouth. Say, "Do this," stick your tongue out as far as you can, move the lollipop up, and lick it. Simultaneously move the student's lollipop up for her to lick. As soon as the student's tongue sticks out a tiny bit, reinforce her by moving the lollipop to her tongue for a lick. Repeat this step while gradually fading your lollipop but keeping the student's and use differential reinforcement for further shaping of the imitation. Then fade the student's lollipop as a prompt but continue to use it as reinforcement. Finally, change the reinforcer to something that would not be used as a prompt for licking. Set mastery at 5 out of 5 or 9 out of 10 unprompted correct responses. Once this behavior is mastered, return to the next step of the main program section.

Chaining Two-Part and Three-Part Imitations

Up until now the student has learned to attend to and imitate single behaviors. From the following sections, the student is taught to imitate two and later three behaviors in a chained sequence. This is often a difficult task, but it is essential to establishing complex behaviors. You may take some comfort in knowing that once this technique is mastered, it can be used in the teaching of many subsequent programs (e.g., learning to follow complex instructions involving several parts, such as "Close the door, then turn on the light, and sit down"). For younger students, one goal of teaching the imitation of chains is for the student to eventually attend to other children playing and imitate them in parallel play and in play interaction. It is impossible to separately shape the various and complex behaviors the student needs to learn in order to play with other children. However, the student can be taught to imitate chains of behaviors, a skill that enables him to later imitate chains of novel behaviors demonstrated by his peers.

The following prerequisite skills and stepwise procedures facilitate the acquisition of chaining tasks and should be followed closely: (1) The student should have mastered at least 50 single gross and fine motor imitations. (2) The student should have mastered the imitation of the separate behaviors that compose particular two- or three-part imitations. (3) There is some reason to believe that mastery of tasks that require the student to attend to a series of stimuli can facilitate mastery of two- and three-part imitations. These tasks are presented in the Matching and Sorting Program (Chapter 12) and the receptive language programs (Chapters 15, 17, and 18). Examples include matching rows of visual stimuli and retrieving several objects when instructed to do so.

In chaining, once the student engages in one response, this response provides the cue for him to engage in a second response. For example, if you demonstrate putting a block in a bucket (SD1) immediately followed by tapping a drum (SD2), the student must learn to imitate SD1 which in turn cues R2. The fact that such a response requires learning is evidenced by the observation that when the teacher demonstrates two behaviors in a row to students who have learned to imitate only single behaviors, these students typically imitate R2 and skip R1. Most likely, these students imitate the teacher's presentation of SD2 because that stimulus is the most recent one and hence the most likely one for them to respond to. Part of the task becomes one of teaching the student to respond to the *temporal ordering* of the teacher's two behaviors (responding with R1 *before* R2).

To facilitate the acquisition of chained imitations, start with chains that consist of two short and maximally different in-the-chair behaviors (e.g., imitating putting a block in a bucket, then tapping a drum). For some students, it may be more effective to first teach the chaining of gross motor behaviors as opposed to behaviors involving objects. If you decide to start by using gross motor behaviors without objects, begin with two behaviors related to body parts that are relatively far from one another (e.g., imitating tapping head, then stomping feet). Such behaviors should be easier for the student to attend to (discriminate) than two behaviors that involve body parts in close proximity to one another (e.g., imitating touching neck, then touching shoulders).

After a few short in-the-chair chains are mastered, introduce chains consisting of one short and one longer in-the-chair behavior (e.g., imitating throwing paper into the wastebasket, then building a pretend tower out of blocks). Once the student masters a number of such chains, go on to chains consisting of two relatively long in-the-chair behaviors (e.g., imitating completing a four-piece shape puzzle, then stacking rings on a ring stacker). Once the student masters the imitation of several in-the-chair chained behaviors, introduce chains consisting of one in-the-chair behavior and one out-of-the-chair behavior, again starting with the imitation of two short behaviors (e.g., imitating closing a book, then putting it on the shelf) and then gradually moving on to responses that require longer periods of time to complete. Finally, teach the imitation of two out-of-the chair behaviors, again starting with two short behaviors (e.g., turning off a light, then putting a ball into a toy basketball hoop) before teaching the imitation of two longer and more complicated behaviors. Procedures demonstrating how to teach two-part chains follow.

Two-Part Imitations

We illustrate the following procedures using a two-part chain consisting of having the student imitate you tapping your head and then stomping your feet. In the steps that follow, the student should sit facing you (no table is needed). Let SD1 be your demonstration of tapping your head and R1 be the student's correct imitation of SD1. Let SD2 be the demonstration of stomping feet and R2 be the student's imitation of SD2.

Phase 1

▶ Step 1

Present SD1, which consists of saying, "Do this," while tapping your head. Prompt R1 if necessary. *While the student is engaged in R1*, present SD2 (stomping feet). Thus, while the student taps his head, you should remove your hand from your head, place your hand in your lap, and quickly present SD2 (stomping feet). It may be necessary to manually prompt the student's stomping his feet. If a manual prompt is needed, fade it over the next few trials. Do not reinforce the student until both R1 *and* R2 are completed.

Note that there is an overlap between the two imitations (R1 and R2, tapping head and stomping feet). This is referred to as a response overlap, which functions as a prompt because it prevents the student from performing only R2 when both SD1 and SD2 are presented in a sequence. Stated differently, the prompt allows the student to engage in the R1–R2 sequence, which then can be reinforced and strengthened.

Once the manual prompt is faded, fade the response overlap prompt by decreasing the time interval between the presentations of SD1 and SD2. That is, initially say, "Do this," while tapping your head and then, when the student just begins to tap his head, quickly go on to stomping your feet. Next, begin fading the prompt by, for example, stomping your feet as the student lifts his hand to touch his head. If you fade the response overlap prompt too quickly, the student will skip R1 and emit only R2. If this occurs, go back and reinstate the minimal amount of response overlap necessary to restore R1. Eventually demonstrate both behaviors before the student begins either of his responses. Remember to probe unprompted trials so as to decrease the number of prompted trials, if possible. Place mastery at 5 out of 5 or 9 out of 10 unprompted correct responses.

When you demonstrate SD1 followed by SD2 without a delay and the student responds correctly with R1 and R2, a new SD and a new R are created. The new SD is the SD1–SD2 combination, and the new R is the R1–R2 chain. Once the student masters the first chained two-part imitation, consider this to be a major and significant achievement. We recommend that this mastery be strengthened by all team members and practiced across different environments before the second chain is introduced. To help maintain the student's motivation, keep the teaching sessions short and intersperse other programs, such as Matching and Receptive Identification of Objects, between sessions of Nonverbal Imitation.

The response overlap prompt may help most students achieve mastery of chained imitations, but it may not be sufficient for all students. If the student continually responds with R1 and does not go on to complete the chain with R2, use a visual or verbal prompt as follows: Present the SD1–SD2 stimulus. If the student responds with R1 and then stops, wait for a moment, thereby giving the student a subtle prompt of expecting her to go on to R2. If this prompt fails, repeat the trial using a stronger prompt, such as looking at the student's feet, pointing to them, manually moving them, or whispering, "Stomp feet" (if the student has mastered this instruction). Remember to reinforce prompted trials, otherwise the student will eventually stop imitating and may tantrum. The student's favorite reinforcers, however, should be saved for unprompted trials.

It is sometimes difficult to fade the overlap prompt because the student may start R1 as soon as you present SD1. The student, however, must learn to *wait* while you complete the SD1–SD2 sequence. This may require some additional prompting. The simplest procedure for teaching the student to wait while you demonstrate a two-part behavior is to choose chains that can be demonstrated with one hand. With one hand free, you can hold the student's hands in his lap while presenting the SD combination. For example, while presenting the SD1–SD2 combination, place your right hand over the student's hands in his lap, preventing him from engaging in R1. With the completion of SD2, let go of the student's hands to allow him to engage in the R1–R2 chain, giving him a slight physical prompt if necessary.

► **Step 2**

You may anticipate that, as the student masters responding to the SD1–SD2 combination with R1–R2, this response may not be the same as *imitating* the SD1–SD2 combination. Such an occurrence may be observed if you demonstrate any behavioral combination and that combination triggers the R1–R2 chain. To help prevent this, you should establish another chain to be imitated (e.g., raising an arm, then tapping a knee) and then intermix these two chains as well as additional chains as done in discrimination learning. Suggestions for new two-part imitations are provided in the following list.

Additional Two-Part Body Imitations

SD	"Do this"
1	raising an arm, then tapping a knee
2	touching an elbow, then raising a foot
3	crossing legs, then tapping tummy
4	folding arms, then waving
5	touching ears, then rocking from side to side
6	touching back, then touching feet
7	touching neck, then crossing ankles
8	"drinking," then touching shoulders
9	holding up a hand in a "stop" gesture, then stomping one foot
10	blowing, then shading eyes with one hand
11	raising both arms, then clapping
12	opening mouth, then stretching arms to sides
13	sticking out tongue, then wiggling fingers
14	folding hands, then making a fish mouth

Phase 2

Slowly increase the difficulty of two-part imitations by introducing two-part imitations in which one imitation is conducted in the chair and the other is done out of the chair. Examples of such two-part imitations are given in the following list. These chains should be taught by following the teaching procedures described in the section "Two-Part Imitations." When teaching chains that contain out-of-chair behaviors, call the student back to the chair after each chained response in order to keep him focused.

In-Chair, Out-of-Chair Two-Part Imitations

SD	"Do this"
1	standing up, then walking around a chair
2	blowing nose, then throwing tissue in a wastebasket
3	drinking juice, then putting on shoes
4	looking at a book, then putting the book on a shelf
5	doing a simple puzzle, then putting it away on a shelf
6	scribbling on paper, then putting crayons in a drawer
7	putting blocks in a bin, then walking over to sit on the couch
8	stringing two beads, then crashing two cars on the floor
9	putting five beans into a bottle, then opening a door

Once mastery is achieved in Phase 2, introduce two-part imitations containing two out-of-chair behaviors. Follow the same teaching procedures described in Phase 1. Call the student back to the chair after each two-part chain in order to keep him focused.

Out-of-Chair, Two-Part Imitations

SD	"Do this"
1	turning off a light, then shooting a basket
2	closing a door, then jumping on a trampoline
3	throwing a beanbag over a chair, then turning on the radio
4	shooting a basket, then walking around the room
5	picking shoes up from the floor, then putting shoes in the closet
6	getting a pile of blocks, then building a tower on the floor
7	knocking the tower down, then putting the blocks in a bin
8	getting a doll from a crib, then feeding the doll on the couch
9	doing a somersault, then jumping on a trampoline
10	getting a cup from the kitchen, then setting it on the table

Maintenance and Generalization

Once the student masters approximately 15 two-part imitations, transfer the first 10 and most frequently practiced chains to a Maintenance Schedule. Review maintenance chains as often as necessary to keep them mastered. Generalize chains across teachers and to everyday environments. It is particularly important to practice and generalize imitations that are functional for the student. One by one, introduce novel two-part imitations to the Current Schedule and move mastered and frequently practiced chains to the Maintenance Schedule.

Three-Part Imitations

Given that the acquisition of three-part imitations is difficult for most students, you should plan ahead, combining behaviors the student is most likely to master. We recommend that the following prerequisite skills be mastered before introducing three-part imitations: (1) The student should be proficient at chaining *novel* two-part imitations (i.e., two-part chains not specifically taught) and should have achieved mastery of 30 to 40 two-part chains. (2) The student should have mastered 20 to 30 single imitations that will compose the first three-part imitations to be taught. (3) The student should have mastered a number of receptive language programs (and expressive programs if the student is verbal), including identification of objects, colors, shapes, letters, and numbers; single and two-part receptive instructions; and prepositions.

Three-part imitations should be taught by following the same procedures described for teaching two-part imitations. If the student does not make progress in learning the first three-part imitation after 1 week of practice, temporarily place this format of the Nonverbal Imitation Program on hold. It may be reintroduced at a later stage in teaching.

Before beginning to teach three-part imitations, remember that it is easy to get carried away when teaching programs like the Nonverbal Imitation Program because many students excel in such programs. However, it is just as important to broaden the student's curriculum as it is to teach specific skills within certain programs. Suppose the student is 6 months into the treatment program by the time two-part imitations are mastered. In this case, the student may also be involved in programs ranging from Early Play Skills to Early Abstract Language, skills that may be of more benefit to the student than further advances in imitation at this time.

Three-Part Imitations

SD "Do this"

1 emptying out a puzzle, then completing the puzzle, and then putting it away
2 getting a cup, then sitting down, and then pouring juice into the cup
3 getting a car, then driving it down the garage ramp, and then parking the car in the garage
4 building a tower, then knocking it down, and then putting the blocks into a bin
5 taking off shoes, then taking off socks, and then sitting down on the couch
6 blowing, then clapping, and then crossing legs
7 touching head, then touching knees, and then touching toes
8 waving, then stomping feet, and then folding arms
9 jumping, then pointing to nose, and then sitting down
10 pretending to cry, then pointing to teeth, and then folding hands
11 standing up, then walking around a chair, and then sitting down
12 marching, then flapping arms, and then turning on a light

Maintenance and Generalization

Follow the same procedures for maintaining mastery of three-part imitations that are suggested for the maintenance of two-part imitations. Generalize functional chains to everyday situations when appropriate.

Concluding Comments

As progress is made in teaching the student to chain imitative behaviors, you make an important step toward extending nonverbal imitation into meaningful, everyday behaviors. We illustrate this extension by presenting programs for teaching art and preacademic skills in the Arts and Crafts Program (Chapter 20) and reading and writing skills in the Reading and Writing Program (Chapter 29). Nonverbal imitation also forms a basis for acquiring play skills (see Chapter 19) and self-help skills (see Chapter 21).

Introduction to Language Programs

CHAPTER 14

Before describing programs designed to teach language, we provide some brief comments about the language delays typically seen in individuals with developmental delays such as autism, the important role language plays in human development, and behaviorists' approaches to the task of remedying language delays, with examples of outcome data from early and intensive intervention and individual differences in rates of progress.

Language Delays in Individuals with Autism

When parents are asked what area their child needs the most help at developing, almost all parents specify language. Some parents report that their child never spoke; others describe that their child made progress in language somewhere up to 16 to 24 months of age, at which point the child stopped talking over a period of a few weeks. Almost all individuals with autism vocalize, but most of these individuals are mute in the sense that they do not express words. Those individuals who do express words most often echo them either immediately or with a delay, using these words with little or no meaning. In short, individuals with autism have little or no *expressive* language. When asked how much the individuals understand what is said to them, it soon becomes apparent that there is a considerable delay in *receptive* language as well. There are exceptions to this in that some individuals with autism have relatively well-developed language skills, both expressive and receptive. Such occurrences, however, are rare. It is best to be prepared for much work when helping a student with developmental delays acquire language.

When asked what they consider to be the second most important problem, most parents refer to their child's tantrums. Tantrums often start in the first year of life. By the age of 3 or 4, one may observe the first signs of self-injury, as in head banging, and aggression toward caretakers, such as biting and scratching. From what is written about tantrums in Chapters 5 and 6, it seems likely that the delay in language acquisition and the excessive amount of tantrums are interrelated in that the individual's tantrums are a form of nonverbal communication based on an inadequate mastery of language.

Parents and teachers who become familiar with research related to autism and mental retardation are likely to learn of opinions to the effect that language development is mediated by some innate neurological structure, that this structure is damaged in individuals with autism and other developmental delays, and that language cannot be taught but rather develops according to neurologically regulated maturational processes. In short, parents and teachers receive the impression that there is nothing much one can do to help individuals with developmental delays learn language.

The language programs in this teaching manual will help all students develop language. Some students will acquire language that appears indistinguishable from that of typical individuals. We call these students auditory learners. Others, labeled visual learners, will not progress as well with the language programs as they are now designed. We attempt to help these latter students communicate as well, by emphasizing visual forms of communication as in the Reading and Writing Program (Chapter 29) and the Picture Exchange Communication System Program (Chapter 30).

The information we provide concerning establishing and strengthening language behaviors illustrates that the same learning principles used in the first hours of treatment (see Chapter 9) can be employed as building blocks when teaching the student communicative language. An additional teaching process that is essential to teaching complex language, discrimination learning, is described in detail in Chapter 16.

The Importance of Teaching Language

One may infer that a person who experiences severe delays in vocally or visually mediated language will be placed outside so many social influences that it will be difficult or impossible for that person to grow up and develop as a typical individual. How can a parent or teacher help an individual develop to his maximum potential if that individual cannot comprehend what is said to him or understand what he reads in books? How can a person develop emotionally when he is unable to describe his feelings to others or understand what others describe about their own emotions? How can a person develop relationships with peers if he cannot converse with them? If a person's "public language" eventually becomes the building block for that person's own "private language," how can a person without language skills evaluate and plan actions on a day-to-day basis? When parents state that their first priority is to help develop their child's language, they are in full agreement with most professionals that the acquisition of language is a critical contributor to a person's development. It is in recognition of the importance of language that the majority of our programs help teach language.

Typical persons acquire language without anyone knowing exactly how this acquisition occurs. We do know, however, that typical individuals acquire language in part by interacting with others who speak, and that this acquisition occurs during most of the individual's waking hours, 7 days a week, year after year. We also know that the process is gradual and stepwise. If language is learned, then the learning process of even a typical individual must be described as slow. Using a typical individual as a model, one may infer that teaching language to an individual who is delayed in language development will be a piecemeal process and require a great deal of time even if the individual practices language most hours of the day, 7 days a week for many years.

Accounts about language development, as written by developmental psychologists and linguists, have been largely descriptive and highly theoretical, allowing for no specific guidelines on how to teach language. Some 35 years ago, behavioral psychologists began to explore procedures for teaching language. The teaching procedures developed were based on sound scientific data and were described in sufficient detail so as to be replicable by others. Many of these procedures generated very advanced use and understanding of language. We have been able to take advantage of the discoveries of these investigators in presenting the language programs in this manual. The field of behavioral psychology has developed knowledge in a gradual and incremental manner, and, although there is still much that needs to be discovered, the future looks brighter now for those individuals who need help in learning to talk.

Overview of the Language Programs

The language programs presented in this manual have been arranged in order of difficulty, with receptive language programs preceding expressive language programs. Examples of how to teach receptive language are presented in Chapters 15, 17, and 18. These chapters are followed by Chapter 22, which outlines procedures for teaching students to imitate the speech of other persons. Acquisition of verbal imitation is essential to mastering subsequent programs emphasizing expressive language, as in the labeling of objects and behaviors (Chapters 23 and 24, respectively). Expressive and receptive language programs go hand in hand and start with the identification and labeling of objects in the student's immediate environment. Programs that help the student describe the behaviors of others as well as her own behaviors are then introduced, followed by programs that teach the student to obtain what she desires. The language programs in this manual also include procedures for teaching abstract concepts such as color, size, and shape (Chapter 25), and prepositions (Chapter 27). Procedures for teaching the beginnings of grammar are presented in Chapter 26.

More advanced language programs will be described in an upcoming volume, which includes procedures for teaching the student pronouns, cause–effect relationships, an understanding of time, how to converse with others, how to describe her own and other people's feelings, and how to describe events that have happened in the past as well as what may happen in the future. Other programs in the advanced volume help the student listen to stories told by others, tell her own stories, and use language to facilitate imagination. Emphasis is placed on the social and functional aspects of language. All language programs are generalized from the one-on-one teaching situation to family, peers in the community, and especially school environments.

Although there is no clear-cut division between early and advanced language, we decided to make the division after prepositions (which are in this volume) and prior to pronouns (which are in the upcoming volume). We placed the division at this point because most visual learners encounter significant problems acquiring personal pronouns and other advanced and abstract *vocal* language. Nevertheless, visual learners have made major progress when taught how to read and write (Chapter 29).

Note that in this manual, language programs are intermixed with programs that are intended to help the student obtain a necessary context for and better comprehension of language. For example, the Matching and Sorting Program (Chapter 12) helps the student identify (discriminate, attend to) objects in her environment, a skill critical to learning early receptive and expressive labels. The Nonverbal Imitation Program (Chapter 13) teaches the student to imitate the actions of other persons and is important for several reasons, one of them being that imitation can be used to prompt (i.e., model) the correct nonverbal response to verbal requests made by the teacher.

Every attempt has been made to intermix language and nonlanguage programs in a way that should help accelerate the student's learning, although we do not claim to have the final answer on how to sequence these programs optimally. It is reasonable to plan the student's program schedule according to a developmental sequence for no reason other than that, in development, simple behaviors precede the more complex ones. However, a typical developmental sequence may not always be ideal. For example, although there appears to be general agreement in scientific literature that receptive language (understanding) precedes expressive usage of language, recent data suggest that the opposite may occur in many students with developmental delays; that is, some of the students learn expressive labels before they master receptive counterparts. To illustrate, we have observed that some students make no progress in learning receptive identification of objects even after 2 months of intensive training. When expressive labeling of objects is first introduced, however, some of these same students acquire this skill within a day. All of this underscores the necessity of being flexible, willing to explore alternatives, and, most important, adhering to scientific procedures whereby data from language programs are tested and reviewed. If one proceeds according to scientific paradigms, one will be in a position to continuously update and improve upon the treatment presently available.

A Learning Model of Language Acquisition

It may be helpful to illustrate how language, when divided into expressive and receptive components, can fit into the learning model that forms the basis of our treatment programs. Consider that in receptive language, introduced in Chapter 15, the student receives the adult's message. The stimulus is verbal and the response is nonverbal; the teacher speaks to the student and the student behaves in accordance with the adult's request. For example, the adult may ask the student to stand up (a verbal stimulus). When the student does as requested (the student stands up, a nonverbal behavior), one may infer that the student has acquired part of the meaning of the words stand and up.

We illustrate expressive language, introduced in Chapters 23 and 24, as the flip side of receptive language by considering the stimulus to be nonverbal and the student's response to be verbal. For example, the adult may hold up a glass of milk (a nonverbal stimulus) and teach the student to say, "Milk" (a verbal response). Receptive and expressive language components may, at a later stage in teaching, become related by intermixing them. For example, the student may be asked to sit and, while seated, then be taught to label the behavior by saying, "I am sitting." Mastery of such relationships gives further evidence that the student's language is acquiring meaning. In everyday terms, the student is beginning to know what he and others are talking about. Another relationship occurs when both the stimulus and the response are mostly verbal. For example, the adult may ask, "What is your name?" and teach the student to answer, "John." Verbal interactions are often considered to be the basis of conversational speech.

The language relationships just described are summarized in Table 14.1 as three basic discriminations. In Discrimination 1, the student must learn to discriminate (attend to) an adult's speech in order to master receptive language. The student may not comprehend what is said to him in the beginning of treatment, behaving as if he cannot hear. By selective use of reinforcement (as presented in Chapter 16), one can teach the student to attend to (discriminate) what other people say. The adult knows that the student comprehends what is said to him when the student behaves in accordance with the adult's requests. Discrimination 1 may be simple, such as when the student learns to point to a doll (a nonverbal response) when the teacher requests, "Point to doll" (a verbal stimulus). Or, the discrimination may involve a complex stimulus, such as "Place the milk in the refrigerator after you have filled your glass." If the student behaves correctly in response to this request, he understands a complex sentence involving a preposition (*in*), pronouns (*you* and *your*), and a temporal arrangement (*after*).

TABLE 14.1
Three Basic Discriminations in Language Training

Discrimination	Stimulus	Response	Language Type
1	Verbal	Nonverbal	Receptive
2	Nonverbal	Verbal	Expressive
3	Verbal	Verbal	Conversational

In Discrimination 2, the student must learn to attend to a particular object or nonverbal event and then signal to the adult that he is attending to that event by describing it correctly. As with Discrimination 1, Discrimination 2 may consist of a simple discrimination, such as responding with "Apple" when shown an apple. The discrimination may also be complex; for example, the student may describe his morning activities by saying, "I got up and brushed my teeth, then I had breakfast and went to school."

Both the input and the response are verbal in Discrimination 3 (e.g., conversational speech such as "What is your name?" "My name is Lisa," and "Where do you live?" "I live in Washington"). Like the other two discriminations, the stimuli in Discrimination 3 may be simple or complex. Complex stimuli may consist of the student saying, "I want to play with Power Rangers," and another individual responding, "You don't have Red Ranger."

All three discriminations contain mixtures of both verbal and nonverbal stimuli. For example, an adult may ask the student, "What is your name?" To answer that question correctly, the student must discriminate (attend to) both verbal and nonverbal stimuli (the question and himself as a person). A more comprehensive definition of these discriminations would note that the presence of vocal versus nonvocal stimuli is a matter of degree (e.g., in Discrimination 1, the stimulus is largely auditory but may contain visual components).

It is essential that the teacher become familiar with discrimination learning procedures (see Chapter 16). If the teacher does not learn to apply such procedures, the student cannot be taught to overcome his language delays. This manual provides many concrete illustrations of discrimination learning. It is our experience that once the adult begins to practice the programs contained in this manual, technical terms such as *discrimination learning* will be readily understood and used in a constructive and creative manner. This is true not only for language, but also for most of the behaviors the student must learn in order to overcome his behavioral delays.

Overall Outcome of Language Programs

As mentioned earlier in this manual, there are significant differences among individuals within the same diagnostic category. We have found it helpful to classify students with developmental delays as being either visual or auditory learners. Auditory learners perform well on both auditory and visual tasks, and they are the ones who progress the furthest in the language programs as they are currently constructed. Perhaps the earliest sign that the student is an auditory learner is the student's relatively rapid rate of acquisition of verbal imitation (Chapter 22) and expressive language (Chapter 23). About 45% of a sample of students with autism acquired vocal language skills comparable to those of typical persons (McEachin, Smith, & Lovaas, 1993).

Visual learners vary considerably in their mastery of vocal language. Most visual learners make some progress in vocal language but have difficulty expressing themselves clearly. The expressive language of visual learners often appears stilted and is sometimes difficult to understand. Although many of these students can learn to express basic needs, some fail to master even the simplest vocal language skills. To help such students, we developed the Reading and Writing Program (Lovaas, Koegel, Simmons, & Long, 1973). The 1960s saw the inception of this program when we taught sight reading to echolalic children. This effort paralleled the endeavors of Hewitt (1964) and Sidman (1971). We hoped that, by learning to read, the children would acquire knowledge about the world through newspapers and books. No such development took place; the children did not attach meaning to what they read. They were individuals without experience, much like infants. It was as if the world had passed them by. This point is emphasized because we find it necessary to place the Reading and Writing Program in the context of the other programs in this and similar teaching manuals that help students attach meaning to the words they encounter. The meaning of a word, phrase, or sentence is provided by the stimulus context, and that context cues a response. This is consistent with the information provided in Table 14.1. Without a broad context or range of meaning, the student is likely to use a newly acquired printed word (or some other symbol, such as a picture) to facilitate only the simplest form of meaningful communication.

In our studies, we had the advantage of working inductively without significant reliance on widely available theory, which almost always emphasized irreversible pathology. The value of inductive empirical work is the objectiveness of such work; the data accumulated from inductive research closely guides the investigation. Through our studies we observed that students who failed to master vocal language still performed well in programs involving visual stimuli, such as Matching and Sorting and Nonverbal Imitation (Chapters 12 and 13, respectively). We therefore found it appropriate to use the distinction between visual and auditory learners to replace the grouping that some have referred to as low functioning versus high functioning. At this time, the failure to adequately teach visual learners can most profitably be attributed to our failure as teachers to develop more effective programs.

A distinction is also made among people in the typical population with respect to individual differences in preferences in modes of presentation. Some persons acquire and retain educational material more readily by visual rather than auditory modes of presentation; others prefer to learn by hearing rather than seeing educational material. Such observations help erase the idea of a qualitative difference existing between individuals with and without developmental delays, prompting us once more to look at the average environment for guidance in constructing educational environments for the nontypical person. Future research may well identify interactions among visual and auditory language programs which, in turn, will facilitate the acquisition of vocal language for visual learners.

Early on in our work with students with developmental delays, we hoped that the acquisition of language would result in a major personality reorganization; we hoped that language would function as a pivotal behavior. For example, we anticipated that, once language was mastered, the students we worked with would come out of their "autistic shells" and start to behave more like typical individuals. We found this not to be the case. In technical terms, there appeared to be little or no evidence of response generalization (e.g., the acquisition of prepositions did not result in the mastery of pronouns). This was a bitter disappointment because we counted heavily on the role of language as facilitating a major leap forward. We found it discouraging that the students possessed little native knowledge, and that each student was instead a tabula rasa onto which experience had yet to be written. Despite these disappointments, we did find that the students' newly acquired language skills facilitated interactions with parents and peers, leading to less frustration on all sides. These language skills also helped the students learn more independently from their everyday environments and not only from explicitly designed teaching programs. In short, it was easier to teach the students the many cognitive, social, emotional, and self-help skills that were necessary for development once progress had been made in their understanding and use of language.

There is great efficiency in the learning processes introduced in this manual. We recognize that parents and other adults who work with students with developmental delays need to learn a great deal about teaching and be prepared for much hard work. In the future, there will be many more teachers and other professionals who will be knowledgeable in the effective teaching of students with developmental delays, lessening the burden on parents. We apologize for the 20- to 30-year delay in the application of effective treatment by the professional community.

Early Receptive Language

CHAPTER 15

In the first hours of treatment (Chapter 9), the student was taught the beginnings of receptive language, namely to respond appropriately to the teacher's verbal requests to "Sit," "Come here," and "Drop block." These exercises are referred to as receptive language tasks because the student is taught to receive the teacher's verbal messages and act appropriately in response to those messages. In technical terminology, the student is presented with verbal stimuli and is taught to make the correct nonverbal response to those stimuli.

The present chapter is aimed at teaching more elaborate receptive language than that introduced in the beginning hours of treatment. The student will need to acquire thousands of receptive language messages in order to function adequately in society. Some of these messages are relatively easy for the teacher to teach and for the student to learn, such as "Come here" and "Sit." Others are more difficult, such as "Finish eating before you put on your coat" and "We are going to Grandma's house." Most students are able to learn at least some receptive language as it is presented in this chapter. A smaller portion of students master all of the receptive language programs presented in this manual. The teacher will not know how much receptive language a student will master until some time into the program.

Instructions such as "Sit," "Come here," and "Drop block" are ideal to introduce first because the student's responses to these instructions can be manually prompted; that is, the teacher can physically guide the student through the desired responses. Several other early responses can be prompted in a similar manner. These include responses to requests such as "Clap hands," "Push car," "Drink juice," "Hands quiet," and "Give me hug." Procedures for teaching the student to respond to such instructions are presented later in this chapter.

In teaching the student to respond to requests that require complex behaviors, manual prompting becomes cumbersome or impossible. In such instances, modeling the behavior is a more practical and efficient prompt. A model prompt is a demonstration of the behavior for the student to imitate. Examples of responses that are easily prompted by modeling range from relatively simple behaviors, such as sticking out tongue, smiling, blowing, and stomping feet, to more elaborate behaviors, such as writing letters, drawing pictures, playing with toys, combing hair, and playing games (see Chapter 13, which describes how to teach the student to imitate the adult's behaviors).

In this chapter, we progress from simple receptive language (e.g., "Sit," "Come here") to the very complex skill of requiring the student to respond to novel instructions consisting of three actions each. If the student begins to learn the first two receptive language instructions during the first hours of treatment, she will likely master three-part instructions 1 year into treatment. It is important, therefore, that concurrent with the teaching of these skills, the teacher balances the student's curriculum by practicing a number of other programs, such as Matching and Sorting, Nonverbal Imitation, Verbal Imitation, Early Play Skills, Arts and Crafts, and Self-Help Skills.

Assessing Receptive Language

The three instructions learned in the first hours of treatment may be easy for the student to tell apart. However, you may have unknowingly helped the student respond correctly by adding visual prompts, such as looking toward the bucket or block when instructing, "Drop block," or stretching out his or her arms when stating, "Come here." One way to determine whether such inadvertent prompts are used is for you to fixate on the student's face and refrain from gesturing when giving instructions. An additional procedure involves generalizing the student's mastery across other teachers and adults, because others are unlikely to employ the same inadvertent prompts. If the student responds correctly without the presence of inadvertent prompts to the verbal instructions taught in the first hours of treatment, then go on to Step 1 in the next section. If the student responds incorrectly, teach her to respond appropriately to these instructions by fading inadvertent prompts.

There is no reason to expect that a student with developmental delays can differentiate between two instructions without being taught to do so. To test whether the student can tell the difference between two instructions, present an instruction such as "Sit" while a block and bucket are on the table and, making certain that inadvertent prompts have been removed, observe the student's response. If the student responds in any way other than sitting down, it is likely that she has not learned to discriminate the instruction to sit from the instruction to place the block in the bucket. When the student can correctly respond to two or more instructions when presented randomly and without prompting, it is said that the student is able to discriminate between these stimuli (i.e., the verbal instructions). In layperson's terminology, it is said that the student gives evidence of paying attention to the differences between these instructions.

Although the understanding of discrimination learning procedures is facilitated by the practical experience of working through the Early Receptive Language Program, it is critical that you first become familiar with discrimination learning procedures as they are presented in Chapter 16. Discrimination training contains important procedures used in all programs, language or otherwise. In this chapter, we describe discrimination learning procedures only as they apply to early receptive language.

The First Two Instructions

Instructions for behaviors requiring object manipulation are generally taught first because the objects help provide clear-cut visual cues for the student and because behaviors that involve objects are easy to prompt. To begin teaching, you and the student should sit next to the student's table and face one another. The student's dominant hand should be nearest the table. In illustrating the following steps, SD1 is "Drop block," and SD2 is "Car."

▶ Step 1

Follow the procedures described in Chapter 9 to establish the student's correct response R1 (dropping block in bucket) to your instruction SD1 ("Drop block"). Remember to always reinforce correct responses. Place mastery at 5 out of 5 or 9 out of 10 unprompted correct responses.

▶ Step 2

Remove the bucket and block from the table and place a toy car on the table such that it is within easy reach of the student. Avoid selecting a car that makes noises or flashes lights as such distractions may detract the student's attention from the task at hand. Present SD2 ("Car"), keeping the instruction short and simple. The correct response, R2, is for the student to push the car back and forth on the table. Say the instruction clearly and in a voice slightly louder than normal conversational tone. Note that, to maximize the discriminability between the two instructions, we recommend using the SD "Car" instead of "Push car." This is done because the use of two-word phrases for each instruction might lessen discriminability.

Up to this point, the student has had no prior experience with this instruction; hence he most likely does not understand what you are asking him to do. You should therefore prompt and reinforce the correct response. Concurrently with or immediately after presenting SD2 ("Car"), place your hand over the student's dominant hand and physically guide the student to push the car back and forth three to four times (enough times to make the response discriminable). Reinforce immediately after the prompted correct response. Repeat this procedure approximately five times, making sure you allow a distinct pause of 1 to 3 seconds between trials.

Systematically fade the physical prompt by gradually reducing it in subsequent presentations of SD2. For example, after the student responds correctly with a full physical prompt for 5 successive trials, physically guide the student's hand to the car and push his hand forward once, then let go. The student must still push the car back and forth to receive reinforcement. If the student does not give the required response, the prompt may have been faded too quickly. If this occurs, provide a full physical prompt in 3 to 5 more trials, then try to fade the prompt again by gradually reducing the prompt in each subsequent trial. Begin the fading process by physically guiding the student's hand on top of the car, then letting go. If this prompt is successful, guide the student's hand to a short distance above the car on the next trial. On subsequent trials, lift the student's hand until it is halfway between his lap and the car, then lift it several inches from his lap, and so on until no prompt is provided at all. If the student cannot follow the instruction independently, return to using the least amount of prompt necessary to reinstate the correct response, and then fade it systematically once more. For students who have made progress in nonverbal imitation, you may prefer to use a model prompt, which is less intrusive than a physical prompt and easier to administer.

As described in Chapter 10, it is sometimes helpful to see if the student can respond to the SD without having to go through the entire prompt fading process. Probe by presenting the SD and withholding the prompt for a trial or two after the student is responding consistently with the prompt. Also, recall that in the early stages of teaching a particular task, both prompted and unprompted responses should be reinforced. When gradually fading a prompt, however, differential reinforcement should be employed such that reinforcement for prompted responses is minimized while reinforcement for unprompted responses is maximized.

After the student responds to SD2 at the criterion of 5 out of 5 or 9 out of 10 unprompted correct trials, begin discrimination training between SD1 and SD2 by intermixing, differentially reinforcing, and randomly rotating the SDs as described in the next section.

Intermixing SD1 and SD2

Having just finished teaching SD2 ("Car") to mastery, if you were now to give SD1 ("Drop block") with the car *and* the block and bucket displayed on the table, the student would most likely incorrectly respond by pushing the car. Such a response would signify that the student cannot yet distinguish the difference between the two instructions and that he will simply perform the last behavior that received reinforcement. This is a reasonable mistake given that the student has been reinforced for pushing the car over several preceding trials. At this point, all the student hears you say to him is noise; the student understands that you want him to perform an action after you say something. Your task now is to teach the student that the two instructions "Car" and "Drop block" have different meanings. In other words, you must now teach the student to discriminate between the two instructions. You can be confident that the student has learned to discriminate between the two instructions when the student can correctly respond to these instructions presented in a random order. The following procedure outlines the steps that lead to such a discrimination.

▶ Step 3

Place the materials required for both responses, dropping and pushing car, on the table. Present SD1 ("Drop block") in mass trials (i.e., provide multiple trials using the same SD). Because the student was most recently reinforced for pushing the car, it is likely that he will make a mistake and push the car when instructed "Drop block." If this mistake occurs, the student misses out on a reinforcer. To avoid this, prompt the correct response as soon as SD1 is given. The prompt used should be just intrusive enough to occasion the correct response. In other words, use a partial prompt rather than a full prompt if the partial prompt is effective at occasioning the response. Once the student responds correctly to SD1 in at least 2 consecutive prompted trials, fade the prompt as you did in Step 1. Continue teaching until the student responds correctly in 4 consecutive unprompted trials of SD1. Remember to reinforce correct responses.

▶ Step 4

Present SD2 ("Car") in mass trials. Prompt the student on the first trial so that he gives the correct response. Fade the prompt. After the student responds correctly without a prompt in 4 consecutive trials, go on to Step 5.

▶ Step 5

Present SD1 ("Drop block") in mass trials. Prompt the correct response on the first trial. Fade the prompt until the student responds correctly in 3 unprompted trials in a row. Reinforce each response.

▶ Step 6

Present SD2 ("Car"). Prompt the correct response in the first trial and fade the prompt over subsequent trials. Go on to Step 7 after 3 successful trials without prompting. Reinforce as done above.

▶ **Step 7**

Reintroduce SD1 ("Drop block"). On the first trial, test for mastery by withholding the prompt altogether. If the student responds correctly, reinforce him amply and present one more trial of SD1, then go on to Step 8 if he again responds correctly. If the student responds incorrectly, prompt the correct response on the next trial. Fade the prompt over subsequent trials until the student responds correctly in 2 consecutive trials without prompting. Reinforce as done above.

▶ **Step 8**

Switch to SD2 ("Car"). On the first trial, probe for mastery by withholding the prompt. If the student gives the correct response, reinforce amply and present 1 more trial of SD2, then go on to Step 9 if he again responds correctly. If the student does not respond correctly, prompt the next trial and fade the prompt over subsequent trials. After 2 consecutive unprompted correct responses, go on to Step 9.

▶ **Step 9**

Present SD1 ("Drop block"). On the first trial, probe by withholding the prompt. If the student responds correctly, reinforce and then present SD2. If the student responds incorrectly, provide the least intrusive prompt necessary to occasion correct responding. Fade the prompt and switch to SD2 after 1 unprompted correct response. Follow the same procedure for SD2. Continue alternating between SD1 and SD2 until the student is able to respond correctly without prompting when the SDs are directly contrasted with one another (i.e., SD1, SD2, SD1, SD2).

As the SD1–R1 and SD2–R2 relationships are reinforced and the SD1–R2 and SD2–R1 relationships are not reinforced, the SD1–R1 and SD2–R2 relationships become strong enough to successfully compete with the SD1–R2 and SD2–R1 associations. Over successive alternated trials involving differential reinforcement, the student should make fewer errors.

As mentioned in the discrimination learning chapter (Chapter 16), there is one problem with systematically alternating between instructions, as in presenting SD1, SD2, SD1, SD2, and so on. The problem is that the student may learn that if SD1–R1 was reinforced on the preceding trial, then he should switch his response on the next trial when SD2 is presented. That is, the student may acquire a win–shift strategy. To avoid such an outcome, introduce random rotation as presented in the next section. For a more complete description of random rotation, refer to Chapter 16.

Random Rotation

▶ **Step 10**

Present SD1 and SD2 in random order. For example, first ask the student to drop the block two times in a row, then ask the student to push the car once, then drop the block once, then push the car three times, and so on. It is important to keep changing the sequence and the frequency of the instructions such that the student cannot discern a pattern and then use this pattern rather than the instruction as a basis for responding. For example, if you present the same instruction many times in a row and reinforce the same response, it may seem to you that the student has learned the correct response. Most likely, however, the student is taught to perseverate; that is, the student is taught to repeat the response that was reinforced on the preceding trial. Students are often very adept at figuring out ways to be successful without having to listen to the teacher's instructions. Make certain that your procedures allow the student to use only your instructions (i.e., your words) to cue responding. Continue to present instructions in a random order until the student responds to the criterion of 9 out of 10 or 19 out of 20 unprompted correct responses.

Mastery of the first discrimination (i.e., the discrimination between SD1 and SD2) constitutes a major achievement for both you and the student in any program. Generalization across teachers and environments is critical in any treatment program, including the present one. We therefore recommend that mastery of the first discrimination be generalized across teachers; that is, these instructions should be practiced by all of the student's teachers so as to reduce idiosyncratic effects of a particular person and thereby help eliminate the effects of potential inadvertent prompts or irrelevant cues. In addition to generalizing across teachers, the SD1–SD2 discrimination should be practiced across different settings by gradually extending the teaching into different parts of the house and outside of the house. If the student makes errors at any time during such generalization training, go back to using the least intrusive prompt necessary to reestablish correct responding before proceeding.

The Third Instruction

To maximize the student's success, select stimuli that are as dissimilar as possible in the *early* stages of teaching. In *later* stages, introduce instructions that are similar to each other because the student must eventually learn to respond to subtle details in order to understand much of spoken language. "Clap" is an appropriate third instruction (SD3) to teach because it sounds and looks different from SD1 ("Drop block") and SD2 ("Car"). We use the instruction "Clap" to illustrate the introduction of SD3, but keep in mind that your student may have greater success with instructions requiring her to manipulate objects.

▶ Step 1

Present SD3 ("Clap") and mass trial this SD as you did the first two instructions taught. Let R3 be two to five claps so as to make the response reliably recognizable by all teachers and discriminable to the student. If the student previously learned to imitate clapping, you may prompt by clapping concurrent with or immediately following SD3. If the student fails to imitate your action, prompt by physically holding onto the student's hands and moving them together and apart. Reinforce and gradually fade the prompt. To fade a model prompt, start with your hands at your sides and then bring your hands toward each other until they are about 1 inch apart. Further fading can be accomplished by moving your hands to the level of your chest, then waist, and so on until no visual prompt is provided. When fading a model prompt, it is likely that the student will imitate your behavior, clapping less and less. To prevent this, do not reinforce the student for partial responses; only reinforce complete responses. To fade a physical prompt, gradually provide less and less manual guidance.

After the student can clap to criterion (5 out of 5 or 9 out of 10 unprompted correct responses), begin random rotation as described in Step 2.

▶ Step 2

Intermix the third instruction with the first two instructions. Begin by providing differential reinforcement and gradually moving the third instruction (SD3) into random rotation with the first instruction (SD1; as done in Steps 3 through 9 of the previous section "Intermixing SD1 and SD2"). Place mastery at 9 out of 10 or 19 out of 20 consecutive unprompted correct responses when SD3 and SD1 are randomly intermixed. Then proceed to intermix and randomly rotate SD3 with SD2 to the same criterion for mastery. Finally, use differential reinforcement and random rotation to build the discrimination among all three instructions, setting mastery at 9 out of 10 or 19 out of 20 unprompted correct responses. Generalize this discrimination across teachers and environments.

Additional Instructions

After the student masters three instructions, additional instructions may be taught, such as "Drink juice," "Give me hug," "Stand up," and "Pat tummy" (additional instructions are listed in Table 15.1). The fourth instruction (SD4) should look and sound as dissimilar from the first three instructions as possible. Teach SD4 following the same procedures used to teach SD1 through SD3. That is, present SD4 in mass trials, using a full prompt on the first trial to help prevent errors and maximize the student's success. Continue to teach SD4 in mass trials until prompts are completely faded and the student responds correctly to criterion. Then gradually intermix this new instruction, with previously taught instructions, following the differential reinforcement and random rotation procedures described earlier. Teach additional instructions in the same manner, introducing them first in mass trials and then gradually mixing each instruction with the instructions taught earlier. Next, generalize the instructions across teachers and environments. After mastery of the first few discriminations, the student should acquire subsequent discriminations with increasing ease.

TABLE 15.1
Additional Instructions for the Early Receptive Language Program

Gross Motor—Seated in the Chair		
Sit down	Hands quiet	Raise arms
Touch nose	Clap	Wave
Stomp feet	Stand up	Cross arms
Cross legs	Pat tummy	Slap table
Shake head	Cough	Give me five
Blow kisses	Touch (body part)	Blow
Laugh	Sneeze	
Gross Motor—Out of the Chair		
Turn around	Jump	March
Walk around chair	Knock on door	Turn on/off light
Hop	Dance	Close/open door
Give me the (object)	Give me a hug	Kiss me
Throw away		
Fine Motor and Facial Expressions		
Point	Thumbs up	Make a fist
Open mouth	Stick out tongue	Blink
Smile		

In selecting new instructions, make them as functional for the student and as practical for you as possible. "Open door," "Drink juice," "Turn on light," "Read book," "Feed doll," and "Do puzzle" are examples of receptive instructions the student may find enjoyable and functional. The student's newly acquired understanding of language should be to his entertainment and benefit, facilitating adjustment to his social and physical environment.

Teaching "Drop block," "Car," "Clap," and other simple instructions may seem trivial unless it is remembered that, by the teaching of these instructions, the student learns to attend to you and suppress self-stimulatory behaviors. Both are critical achievements for the student. At the same time, you gain valuable experience, acquiring certain basic teaching skills essential to effectively teaching more advanced programs.

Areas of Difficulty

Large individual differences exist among students in their rate of mastery of vocal instructions. Some students move quickly and acquire 20 different instructions over a 3-week span of time; others fail to make even minimal progress in learning receptive language, yet they make rapid progress in acquiring expressive language.

Some students demonstrate difficulty acquiring a particular instruction but make significant progress in learning other instructions. If this occurs with the student you work with, place the particularly difficult instruction on hold (i.e., stop practicing it) for a period of time, replacing the difficult instruction with an alternate instruction to test whether the alternate instruction is easier for the student to learn. It is better to temporarily move away from difficult instructions so as to facilitate success rather than frustrate the student by persisting with instructions that are difficult for her.

Some students experience serious difficulty discriminating SD1 from SD2, making little or no progress after 1 week of training. In such a case, intermix SD1 ("Drop block") with an SD that does *not* have a verbal component (e.g., use an SD from the Matching and Sorting Program or the Nonverbal Imitation Program). When an SD is used in this manner, it is referred to as a contrasting stimulus. This step should be considered a pretreatment exercise, giving the student further experience discriminating (attending to, telling apart) the teacher's instructions. This procedure is described in detail in Chapter 16. After the student learns to discriminate SD1 from a contrasting stimulus, reintroduce the previously difficult discrimination.

Some students tantrum a great deal when the teacher intermixes stimuli. If the student has been recently reinforced for responding correctly to SD1 and you now present SD2, it is likely that the student will respond with R1 rather than R2. Withholding reinforcement for R1 (the response that was previously correct but is now incorrect given the new SD) is likely to be its own SD—a frustrating stimulus that cues tantrums. To avoid a nonreinforced trial and an ensuing tantrum due to frustration, prompt the correct response (R2). Although the student needs to learn to tolerate frustration, it may be better to reserve lessons in frustration tolerance for a later time. However, although we have suggested that prompts be used to avoid nonreinforced trials and errors in discrimination learning, there are reasons to believe that errorless learning (which prompting procedures can produce) may result in less robust discriminations than discriminations acquired through both successful and unsuccessful trials. Further, as mentioned earlier, the only way to test whether the student can discriminate among instructions is by observing whether she correctly responds at least 90% of the time to randomly intermixed instructions given without prompts. Therefore, do not be afraid to intermittently probe for mastery by withholding prompts.

As the student masters several receptive instructions and you introduce additional instructions and move on to programs in other areas, make certain that all previously mastered instructions are rehearsed. *If previously mastered instructions are not practiced, they will be forgotten.* One effective way to ensure rehearsal of previously mastered material is to practice mastered items on an intermittent schedule between new items introduced in other programs. By interspersing previously mastered instructions (which are considered to be easy for the student) with novel items, frustration is reduced and success is maximized.

Instructions Requiring the Student To Leave the Chair

After the student masters approximately 15 to 20 instructions at the table, teach him to respond to instructions that require him to leave the chair. Because some time elapses between the instruction and the student's completion of the response in this format of receptive instructions, the student will have to retain (remember) the instruction. Such retention facilitates the acquisition of skills taught in more advanced programs.

Select a first instruction, such as "Turn on light." Teach this instruction as you did the earlier instruction, and maximize success by placing the student directly in front of the light switch. Present the instruction first in mass trials, prompting and then fading the prompt until criterion is reached (5 out of 5 or 9 out of 10 unprompted correct responses). Once this step is mastered, gradually increase the distance between the student and the light switch. Prompt when necessary, and fade the prompt. Eventually the student should be given the instruction while seated at the chair placed across the room from the light switch, requiring that he retain the instruction for several seconds in order to successfully complete the response.

Once the first instruction is mastered when presented alone, intermix it with previously mastered instructions such as "Drop block." After the student responds to criterion for this new instruction when it is presented randomly with other mastered instructions, introduce another out-of-chair instruction such as "Knock on door." Teach the second instruction using the procedures presented earlier. Continue to teach additional instructions that require the student to leave the chair (e.g., "Get book," "Touch bed," "Bring me doll") until the student masters approximately 10 out-of-chair responses.

The instruction "Come here" may be added to an out-of-chair instruction to create a chain of two behaviors. For example, you could instruct the student to turn on the light and return to you. The completion of the first response (i.e., turning on the light) becomes the SD for the second response (i.e., coming to you). This chain is created by providing reinforcement contingent on the completion of *both* behaviors and is prompted by giving the instruction "Come here" after completion of the first part of the chain.

Two-Part Instructions

After the student masters simple instructions, including those that require leaving the chair and then returning, begin chaining additional behaviors. Do not begin this step until the student masters imitating two-action chains as presented in the Nonverbal Imitation Program (Chapter 13).

Start with a simple two-part instruction, such as "Clap and stand up," provided the student has mastered each of the actions composing this instruction when presented separately. Break up the instruction ("Clap and stand up") into two components: Present the first part of the instruction ("Clap") and, just as the student completes the appropriate response, present the second part of the instruction ("and stand up"). This technique is referred to as a pause prompt or a time delay prompt. Fade this prompt by presenting the second half of the instruction closer and closer in time to the first half of the instruction until no delay remains. Provide reinforcement only after the student completes both responses. Should the student engage in the first response and fail to engage in the second response, withhold reinforcement and wait approximately 5 seconds for the second response to occur. If this kind of prompt fails, move to a more intrusive prompt, such as repeating the last part of the instruction ("and stand up") or manually prompting the second response. Continue to teach the two-part instruction until the student can perform both actions in the correct order without beginning either action until the entire instruction has been presented.

A common problem is the student's beginning to respond *before* the teacher finishes the instruction. For example, the student may clap her hands as soon as the teacher says, "Clap," not waiting for the teacher to complete the instruction. Or, if the teacher hurries the instruction by quickly saying, "Clap and stand up," the student may stand up without first clapping (the last part of the instruction is the most recent stimulus and therefore the portion the student will most likely respond to). If the student begins her actions before you present the entire instruction, hold the student's hands lightly in her lap and then release her hands as soon as the entire instruction is completed. Holding the student's hands should be considered a prompt, which needs to be faded over time. You can also help the student withhold responding until you complete the two-part instruction by using actions that require object manipulation (e.g.,

"Push car and drop block"). Using object manipulation tasks as the first action in response chains allows you to control the timing of the student's response by limiting the student's access to the objects until after the instruction is completed.

Once the student masters the first two-part instruction (i.e., the student reaches the criterion of 5 out of 5 or 9 out of 10 unprompted correct responses), teach a second two-part instruction (e.g., "Stand up and shake head"). Teach the second instruction in the same manner the first was taught, placing mastery at 5 out of 5 or 9 out of 10 unprompted correct responses.

There is reason to believe that the student may merely learn to perform two actions in a particular sequence rather than listen to the order in which the teacher verbally presents the actions. This is a reasonable outcome given that the teacher reinforces instructions containing a particular order of actions. A good rule of thumb is to suspect that if the student can solve the problem without having to attend to your verbalizations, then it is likely that the student is not attending to the verbal instructions. To help overcome this problem, at some stage in the program, you should make the first action presented in a two-part instruction the same action presented in another two-part instruction. For example, if one instruction is "Clap and stand up," another (later) instruction may be "Clap and touch head." Teach two-part instructions, keeping the first action in the instruction the same and varying the second action (e.g., "Clap and drink juice"), until the student responds correctly to the first and second actions of *novel* instructions without prompting.

Next, continue to teach two-part instructions, but vary the first action while holding the second action constant. For example, use "Stomp feet" as the second action for the next several instructions while varying the first action (e.g., "Touch nose and stomp feet," "Wave and stomp feet"). Teach subsequent instructions following the same procedures used to teach the first instructions, and place mastery at the same criterion.

To help the student attend even more closely to your instructions (acquire even finer discriminations among your speech), vary the order of any mastered behavior by sometimes presenting it as the first behavior and sometimes presenting it as the second behavior in a two-part instruction. Such instructions are often highly difficult for the student, making it necessary to go back to intrusive levels of prompting when beginning this stage. For example, the second behavior may need to be presented as the student begins to perform the first behavior, or the student may need to be given a reminder to wait by having her hands lightly held in her lap. Teach two-part instructions in this format until the student can respond to any novel two-part instruction on the first trial.

Varying the order of the instructional components allows the student's responses to be brought under the control of fine nuances in your instructions. The goal is to teach the student to attend to your verbal instruction rather than memorize the order of or anticipate the instruction. Mastery of two-part instructions that contain varying components provides some reassurance that the student is not merely learning to chain actions but is listening to the specific parts of the instruction and the order in which its components are presented.

The next step is to present two-part instructions that take more time to complete than earlier instructions (e.g., "Do puzzle and drink juice"). In the beginning, make sure that the second behavior is simpler (in this case, not as time consuming) than the first behavior since the student will have to retain the information as she completes the first behavior. As the student becomes proficient at this skill, the second behavior can gradually be made to be more time consuming (e.g., "Do puzzle and put away toys").

Three-Part Instructions

After the student masters two-part instructions, begin teaching three-part instructions. Do not start this portion of the program until the student masters the imitation of three-action chains because you will use modeling to prompt three-part instructions.

Begin teaching three-part instructions as you taught two-part instructions. Present the first two parts of the instruction and, just as the student completes the second action, present the last (third) part of the instruction. The overlap between the response and the presentation of the last part of the instruction should be faded as was done with two-part instructions. It may be necessary to remind the student to wait by holding his hands lightly in his lap until the instruction is completed. This should also be considered a prompt and, as such, should be faded.

Areas of Difficulty

Regardless of the teacher's skill, a variety of problems can be expected. For example, some students may not make appreciable progress in receptive instructions that require action on the part of the student, such as clapping or stomping feet. However, the same students may make progress in mastering receptive identification of objects, numbers, or letters. Other students may master identifying actions before learning to identify objects. Some students encounter problems "storing" instructions that have multiple components, only to make progress after gains are made in verbal imitation, particularly if the Verbal Imitation Program produces echolalic repetition of the teacher's instructions. In such a case, the echolalia may facilitate storage of the auditory stimulus through the student's rehearsal of the instruction. Such individual differences require that the teacher be considerably flexible, a skill that comes only with experience in teaching.

Other problems are of a less comprehensive nature. For example, the teacher may find that, as additional responses are taught, the student frequently confuses two particular responses. If this occurs with your student, try to reduce the confusion as follows: First, analyze the instructions to determine if they are similar in some way (e.g., "Cross arms" and "Raise arms"). If the two instructions are similar, change one of the instructions to create a dissimilar pair (e.g., change "Raise arms" to "Raise hands"). As the student gains proficiency in this program, she will learn to attend to finer nuances in your instructions. During this process, instructions should gradually be made more similar until the student is able to discriminate between such instructions as "Cross arms" and "Raise arms." A second solution to this problem is placing one of the responses on hold for a short time and focusing on teaching a different response. This step should be considered if one of the responses is newly acquired and confusion between the two responses is halting the student's progress in learning additional instructions.

Generalizing Receptive Language

There are four ways to facilitate generalization of the student's mastered receptive language. First, practice the instructions learned in the teaching environment, across settings. Begin by giving the student instructions in the hallway next to the treatment room, then in rooms close to the treatment room, and then move to rooms farther away from the original setting. Go on to practice these instructions in less formal environments, such as in the backyard, at the park, and in the grocery store. As the instructions are moved away from the initial setting and into the community, the student must learn to ignore or suppress all new and distracting cues. For example, if the student self-stimulates on certain features of the bathroom or the grocery store, he must now learn, however gradually, to reduce the impact of such distracting stimuli.

Second, teach instructions that have practical applications in new and varied environments. For example, the instructions "Get your shoes," "Put on table," and "Throw away" can be used frequently while spending time with the student around the house. Being creative and using instructions such as "Put in" (the shopping cart) while at the grocery store or "Wipe mouth" in restaurants helps the student acquire socially appropriate behaviors.

Third, receptive language may be generalized by the introduction of new teachers. Make certain that these new teachers replicate the original teacher in terms of instructions used and reinforcement delivery. In other words, new teachers should be familiar with the teaching procedures presented in this manual. During generalization, there are bound to be different tones of voice and gestures. Thus, be prepared to step in and regain mastery if there is a loss in correct responding. Learning to respond to many persons increases the probability that the student will respond to novel persons rather than only to familiar teachers. Generalizing instructions across novel persons (i.e., other adults and peers who are unfamiliar with behavioral teaching procedures) is an important criterion for mastery.

Finally, the teacher should eventually vary the delivery of the instructions so the student learns to respond to different versions of the instructions. For example, the mastery of one-part instructions such as "Clap" may be generalized by gradually adding extra words to form the instruction "Clap hands" and eventually "Show Mommy clap hands." Mastered two-part instructions may be generalized in the same manner. Similarly, the teacher can introduce new versions of instructions that do not necessarily include part of the original wording, such as varying "Sit" to "Have a seat." This instruction may be taught by combining the two instructions into "Sit, have a seat." Later, the "Sit" component may be faded by lowering the volume in which it is spoken, changing the stimulus control to "Have a seat." In gradual steps, the instructions may be modified to "Please come have a seat," "Take the weight off your shoulders," "Park it," and so forth. If the student fails to respond correctly, introduce each new version as you would a new instruction by first presenting mass trials of the instruction and then mixing it in with other mastered instructions. Vary instructions based on instructions understood by individuals similar in age to the student. It is better to find commonly occurring phrases to use as variations than to provide exercises involving nonnatural phrases just for the sake of generalization.

Early Learning Concepts

SECTION 3

Discrimination Learning

CHAPTER 16

This chapter on discrimination learning is the most important chapter in this manual. Although every effort is made to present discrimination learning in a detailed and stepwise manner, the procedures involved in discrimination learning can be difficult for the teacher to master. Therefore, be patient with yourself and proceed in small steps. It is helpful to read this chapter more than once and to review it before beginning any new program. The payoff for doing so is that discrimination learning procedures will facilitate the student's acquisition of all the programs presented in this manual.

Discrimination learning is a process essential to helping the student acquire complex and flexible behaviors. In describing the various teaching programs in this manual that depend on discrimination learning, we review the basic steps involved in using discrimination learning as they apply to the particular tasks contained within those programs. We are especially conscientious and detailed in our presentation of discrimination learning in those programs that are difficult for the student to master, such as verbal imitation and prepositions. It is, however, to the teacher's advantage to be presented with these steps in a more general and abstract format, as done in this chapter.

Discrimination learning forms a basic teaching process that helps the student attend to (discriminate), and therefore learn about, all the subtle and complex stimuli to which human beings must respond in order to survive and develop. Over time, typical individuals learn to attend to an enormous range of stimuli without anyone having to explicitly and carefully teach them how to attend. Individuals with autism and other developmental delays, however, evidence extreme delays in learning to attend and must be taught to do so. This heightened attention gained through the use of discrimination learning procedures increases the student's rate of progress in the teaching situation.

Attention is considered a higher level mental process by most psychologists and educators, which speaks of its central role in the development of complex behaviors. It is by the use of discrimination learning that students with developmental delays and autism learn to attend to and imitate the behaviors of others, develop language, and acquire the concepts of such complex events as identifying and describing spatial relationships, differentiating between feelings within themselves and others, learning about the causes of different emotions, and much more.

In this chapter, we describe how to optimize discrimination learning by selecting appropriate teaching materials and achieving consistency across teachers. We then describe how to use differential reinforcement to help the student discriminate between different instructions, whether verbal (vocal, auditory) or visual. This is followed by a procedure called random rotation, which describes how to order the presentation of teaching material so as not to mislead the student but rather to help the student focus on the important parts of the teacher's instructions. Finally, we examine some of the problems teachers encounter in conducting discrimination learning and how these problems may be prevented or resolved. First, however, we illustrate how important it is for the teacher to be familiar with discrimination learning.

If you present the student with a particular instruction (vocal or visual) and teach the student to respond to that instruction, you may encounter two problems. First, there is no guarantee the student is attending to the salient or critical elements in your instructions. Although we use vocal instructions to illustrate the procedure, visual instructions (e.g., printed words) could just as well be used. If you reinforce the student for pushing a toy truck when you instruct him to "Push truck," and he eventually responds according to your instruction, it may seem as if he has learned to attend to your instruction. However, a simple test of whether the student responds to the critical elements of your instruction ("Push truck") can be made by instructing him to "Clap hands." If the student responds by pushing the truck, he may be responding to your instructions as undifferentiated auditory input (as vocal noise). Similarly, you may teach the student the appropriate response to "Clap hands." If you then ask the student to "Push truck," he may clap his hands. In technical terms, the student is not attending to (discriminating) the critical stimulus elements of the instructions.

The second possibility is that the student may not respond to your vocal instructions (the auditory stimuli), but rather to some visual cue. For example, when instructing, "Push truck," a teacher may inadvertently look in the direction of the truck and this visual cue may lead the student to seem to respond correctly. Similarly, if a teacher instructs the student to "Clap hands" while looking at the student's hands, then this visual cue may guide his response. A test of whether the student responds to the auditory stimuli may be performed through the elimination of visual cues by fixating your gaze at the student's forehead while presenting verbal instructions. If the student is attending to the visual rather than the auditory cue, it is most likely that the student will either not respond or alternate between responses while looking at the teacher's face, searching for a significant visual cue. Some students learn to read lips, and this illustrates a similar problem. If the teacher's lips are covered while the instructions are provided, the student may fail to respond correctly, if at all.

Many persons with developmental delays seem to attend better to instructions that possess visual rather than auditory stimuli. There could be many reasons for this. One possibility is that auditory stimuli are of such short duration that they terminate the moment the teacher finishes the instructions. In contrast, visual stimuli, such as a teacher's gaze and pictures or printed material, last longer. Perhaps because they last longer, the student is given more of an opportunity to attend, and this may help him associate visual instructional input with behavior. We introduced a similar possibility in Chapter 1, where we considered the student's echolalia to be a form of rehearsing instructions and prolonging the duration of auditory stimuli, thereby facilitating the student's acquisition of verbally transmitted information.

It is important to remember that it is easy for students to learn things that teachers do not intend for them to learn. Whenever a teacher delivers an effective reinforcer contingent on some behavior, the student learns. A skillful teacher is aware of potential teaching mistakes, how to avoid them, and how to teach the student in an effective and productive manner (see Chapter 35). Every teacher can learn to become skillful.

Instructions

We illustrate the basic steps of discrimination learning by using one of the first programs the student will learn: receptive language. Specifically, we use as an example the discrimination between the receptive instructions "Clap hands" and "Touch table." Note that these are only examples, and that these examples help illustrate not only programs that teach receptive language but also nearly all programs in which a teacher presents stimuli, be these auditory (as in the Verbal Imitation Program) or visual (as in the Nonverbal Imitation, Expressive Language, and Reading and Writing Programs).

The great majority of students need to be exposed to discrimination learning to master correct responses to even simple instructions, and, in our experience, all students with developmental delays have to undergo discrimination learning when exposed to the more advanced programs in this manual. It is important to abide by the following guidelines before beginning to teach discrimination learning:

▶ Guideline 1

Start with two instructions that are maximally different. For example, "Clap hands" and "Touch table" appear to be more separate and different sounding than instructions such as "Push truck" and "Push car," or "Touch her nose" and "Touch my nose." The instructions "Clap hands" and "Touch table" differ in two important ways. First, the two instructions require actions that are different from one another (i.e., one involves an object whereas the other involves the body only). Second, the instructions sound different from each other. To further increase the dissimilarity of the instructions, you may abbreviate "Touch table" to "Table" and contrast this with "Clap hands," which renders the instructions different in length as well. If length is a prompt, make sure to fade it. During the early steps, use only the part of the instruction that is salient and critical for the student's mastery; avoid extra elements that are superfluous and may interfere with the student's solution. "Please be so kind as to touch the table for me" is an example of a sentence with considerable redundancy that interferes with the student's learning to attend to the relevant stimulus element, namely "table." Although it is important to eventually generalize and teach subtle differences among instructions, it pays to start with the simple instructions and help the student learn to attend to *gradually* more subtle variations.

▶ **Guideline 2**

Initially simplify the setting in which teaching occurs rather than trying to use naturally occurring situations such as a classroom environment. The more control you exercise over the stimulus presentation and the simpler this environment is, the less likely it is that distracting stimuli will interfere with learning and the more likely it is that the student will learn to respond to your instructions.

▶ **Guideline 3**

Use instructions that involve different and distinct behavioral topographies when appropriate. For example, touching a table requires a very different response from clapping hands, in contrast to similar behaviors such as pushing a toy truck and pushing a toy car. Pointing to one's eye and pointing to one's nose is another example of a difficult discrimination because both the instructions and the two responses are similar, and the student receives little differential feedback (in this case visual) from her responses. The response to the instruction "Look at me" is more difficult to effectively reinforce than previously considered because the sensory feedback from the response is subtle and difficult for the student to discriminate (i.e., it is difficult for the student to connect the response to the reinforcing event). Vocalizations such as babbling may also be difficult to strengthen by reinforcement for the same reason. In short, start with maximally different stimuli and use responses with distinct proprioceptive feedback, which are easier to bring under reinforcement control.

▶ **Guideline 4**

Specify in detail what constitutes the correct response before beginning to teach, and decide exactly what your instruction is for that particular response. For example, if you decide to reinforce the student for clapping her hands, do not arbitrarily change the response requirement from one or two to several claps. If you are teaching the student to touch a table, it is enough for the student to touch the table with any part of her hand for 2 to 3 seconds. If that response is reinforced, do not arbitrarily alter the response requirement by, for example, teaching the student to touch the table with her finger, which will most likely interfere with mastery of either task. As another example, suppose you decide to teach the student to clap her hands, and the student stands up in response to your instruction. If you then instruct, "Sit down and clap hands," you may be unwittingly attempting to teach two tasks at the same time. It is better to separate the tasks, teaching one at a time, to simplify the learning situation. Later in the program, the student will need to learn more than one response at the same time and how to deal with inconsistencies, ambiguities, and differences in teaching styles. However, such skills should not be taught during the beginning stages.

▶ **Guideline 5**

Make certain that all members of your team understand the requirements for instructions and responses. If team members are not consistent or if a teacher shows hesitancy about what and when to reinforce, then correct these mistakes before going any further. Otherwise, the student is likely to become confused, and this will delay her mastery. Remember that it is important to have other team members present their teaching skills on a regular basis, as done in weekly meetings and visits to the house by senior team members, so that feedback and advice on how to proceed can be given. It is difficult or impossible for any one person to know how to proceed, and it is easy for any one team member to drift off criterion. We will provide numerous examples of potential teaching mistakes later in this chapter, in Chapter 35, and within each program, and suggest ways by which these mistakes can be remedied or avoided.

The first step in discrimination learning is teaching each instruction separately until the student masters the response to the instruction. This is termed *mass trials* and is done by the teacher helping the student achieve mastery through the presentation of several trials of a particular task in a consecutive and repetitive manner. After two separate tasks are mastered in this manner (e.g., "Clap hands" and "Touch table"), the teacher intermixes and alternates between these two tasks so that they are contrasted with each other, thereby helping the student tell them apart. This process of intermixing is likely to lead to a temporary loss of what the student has already mastered because the student cannot discriminate between the two instructions when they are first intermixed. This problem is solved by introducing the student to differential reinforcement and, later, random rotation. These procedures are described in detail in the next several sections.

Differential Reinforcement

One important teaching technique that was introduced in Chapter 10 concerns the use of differential reinforcement. Differential reinforcement helps direct the student's attention to the relevant aspects of the teacher's instructions. By definition, differential reinforcement consists of a procedure in which the teacher differentiates between the student's correct and incorrect responses by reinforcing and thereby strengthening correct responses while not reinforcing and thereby weakening incorrect responses. It is by the use of differential reinforcement that the student learns to tell the difference (discriminate) between the teacher's instructions.

It may be helpful to illustrate the process of differential reinforcement in the form of a diagram. Using the two instructions "Clap hands" and "Touch table," let SD1 (Discriminative Stimulus 1) represent the instruction "Clap hands" and SD2 (Discriminative Stimulus 2) represent the instruction "Touch table." Let R1 (Response 1) represent the student's clapping his hands and R2 (Response 2) represent the student's touching the table. If these two tasks have been taught separately, it is highly likely that the student will be unable to tell the instructions apart and will sometimes respond to SD1 ("Clap hands") with R2 (touching table) and make similar errors (e.g., clapping hands) when SD2 ("Touch table") is presented. In Figure 16.1, let the arrow represent the bond or association between the SD (the teacher's instruction) and the R (the student's response).

If the association between SD1 and R2 is as strong as the association between SD1 and R1, the student will respond to SD1 with R2 as often as he does with R1. This is a common occurrence prior to the use of differential reinforcement. However, if the teacher continues to reinforce the SD1–R1 relationship ("Clap hands" and the student claps his hands) and withholds reinforcement when SD1–R2 occurs, it is likely that the SD1–R1 association will be strengthened and the SD1–R2 association will be weakened. In technical terms, the SD1–R1 relationship is placed on acquisition while the SD1–R2 relationship is placed on extinction. With such a procedure, the SD1–R1 association eventually grows strong enough to block out errors.

In addition to withholding the reinforcer, the teacher may give an informational "No" upon the student's incorrect response. For some students, however, the word no, may be neutral (i.e., have no effect) or be a positive reinforcer (e.g., the student seems to enjoy the teacher's informational "No"). Regardless, by combining (associating) the informational "No" with the withholding (withdrawal) of a positive reinforcer (e.g., food), it is likely that the informational "No" will eventually become an aversive stimulus, which will help to inhibit the incorrect response.

Once the SD1–R1 association becomes strong, the SD2–R2 association is practiced in the same manner as SD1–R1. The discrimination between SD1 and SD2 is accomplished by intermixing and contrasting the two associations as described in the later section "Intermixing Stimuli." Once the student gives the correct responses to SD1 and SD2 when they are randomly intermixed, it can be said that the student has learned to attend to the two instructions through the teacher's use of differential reinforcement.

Consider an illustration of a more difficult discrimination: At some stage into treatment, you teach the student pronouns such as *my* and *your*. Suppose the student is asked, "What is *your* name?" in contrast to the question,

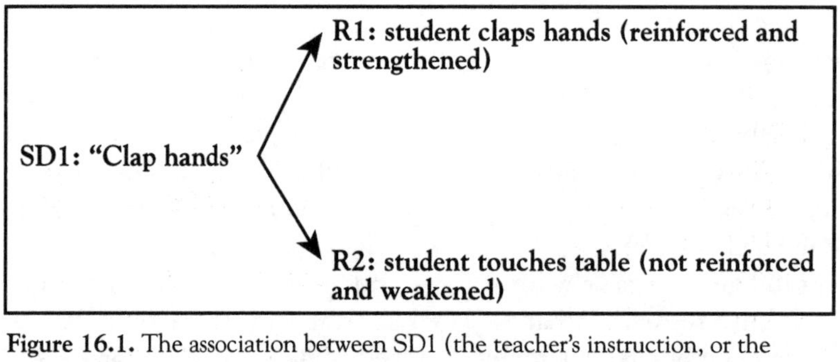

Figure 16.1. The association between SD1 (the teacher's instruction, or the discriminative stimulus) and R1 (the correct student response) or R2 (the incorrect response).

"What is *my* name?" For the student to answer correctly, he must attend to (discriminate) the relevant and significant elements in the question which center on the use of the pronouns *my* and *your*. Consider more elaborate instructions, such as when a teacher asks, "What animal gives us milk?" or "Can you tell me what you did today?" There is no reason to believe that people are born with the ability to answer such questions, but there is every reason to believe that the answers can and have to be taught, and that differential reinforcement plays a major role in this process. Although parents and other adults must provide corrective feedback, typical children learn such discriminations without anyone having to pay too much attention to the teaching processes; questions are asked and feedback is delivered in a more or less informal manner. However, individuals with developmental delays need specific teaching programs to acquire such discriminations. When provided with such programs, these students master many of the discriminations taught to them and some master all of them.

Mass Trials

As mentioned earlier, the first step in discrimination learning is the individual presentation of instructions in a mass trials format. In the mass trials procedure, repeated presentations of the same instruction are delivered to the student, and the student is prompted and reinforced for the correct response. Within a block of mass trials, the prompt is gradually faded, and mass trials are terminated when the student responds correctly without the prompt for a certain number of trials (the criterion for mastery).

The receptive instructions "Clap hands" and "Touch table" are again used for illustrative purposes. Let SD1 be "Clap hands" and SD2 be "Touch table." In other chapters throughout this manual, we provide detailed information on how to apply discrimination learning procedures to the various programs.

▶ Step 1

Present SD1 ("Clap hands") in mass trials; that is, repeatedly go through the process of presenting the instruction, waiting up to 3 seconds for the response, and then consequating the response. If the student does not respond correctly (which includes a failure to respond), repeat the instruction, prompt simultaneously with the instruction, and then reinforce the correct response. The reason for prompting simultaneously with the presentation of the instruction is so that the temporal interval between the SD and the response can be as short as possible (ideally a second or less). A longer time interval is not optimal for the teaching of an association between the instruction and the response. For example, if you prompt the correct response after the student fails to respond within 3 seconds of the SD, the association between the prompt and the response is strengthened rather than the association between the instruction and the response.

Clapping may be prompted by placing your hands on the student's wrists and moving her hands together and apart. If the student has mastered clapping hands in the Nonverbal Imitation Program (Chapter 13), simply prompt the correct response by clapping your hands as a model for her to imitate. Continue mass trialing "Clap hands." Gradually fade the prompt over subsequent trials (by providing less and less assistance or by providing less and less of the model). Continue with mass trials until the student meets the criterion of 9 out of 10 or 19 out of 20 unprompted correct responses.

▶ Step 2

Present SD2 ("Touch table"). Mass trial SD2 and prompt the student to respond correctly by placing her hand on the table or by modeling the correct response. Gradually fade the prompt and continue reinforcement over subsequent trials. When the student responds correctly without a prompt, continue with mass trials until she meets the criterion of 9 out of 10 or 19 out of 20 unprompted correct responses.

Note that a round of mass trials resulting in mastery (e.g., 9 out of 10 correct) is unlikely to be achieved in one session of sitting. Although some students master this criterion in one session, most students require several separate sessions across several days (with different programs intermixed so as to reduce boredom and facilitate recall).

Intermixing Stimuli

Now that the student can correctly respond to both instructions when presented separately, intermix and differentially reinforce the instructions so the student can learn to discriminate between them. Intermixing is essential to ensuring mastery. It is a common mistake to believe that a student has mastered two labels when they are presented separately. To maximize the student's success when stimuli are intermixed, present each instruction in a strong, clear voice and set the intertrial interval at 2 to 3 seconds initially, then gradually decrease the interval to 1 to 2 seconds. The closer the time interval between the two instructions, the closer the contrast between them and the more likely it is that the discrimination between the two instructions will be mastered. Moreover, by using a short intertrial interval, you give the student little opportunity to self-stimulate. Do not present instructions while the student is engaged in self-stimulatory behavior, such as gazing at lights, squinting his eyes, or flapping his hands. Rather, try to capture the student's attention before you present the instruction by showing the student the reinforcer he may earn. Or, present a warm-up trial of a simple task he knows well (e.g., imitating stomping feet). Remember that the student has mastered Steps 1 and 2 but may have temporarily lost either or both of the skills mastered in these steps because of an intervening activity. Once you have the student's attention, quickly move on to Step 3.

▶ **Step 3**

Present SD1 ("Clap hands"). Because the student was most recently reinforced for touching the table (in Step 2), it is likely that he will make a mistake and touch the table when instructed "Clap hands." If the student makes a mistake, he loses out on a reinforcer and may tantrum. To avoid this, prompt the correct response as soon as the instruction "Clap hands" is presented. Reinforce upon completion of the correct response. Present mass trials of SD1 while fading the prompt. Place mastery of Step 3 at 4 unprompted correct responses in a row.

▶ **Step 4**

Within 3 seconds of completing mastery of SD1 ("Clap hands"), present SD2 ("Touch table") in a loud and clear voice and simultaneously prompt the student's correct response. By quickly prompting the correct response, the student is prevented from making an error (e.g., clapping hands). Set mastery at 4 unprompted correct responses in a row.

▶ **Step 5**

Reintroduce SD1 ("Clap hands"). If the student is not prompted, the most likely result is that the student will respond by touching the table because he has not yet learned to discriminate between the two instructions. Therefore, prompt the clapping of hands before the student makes a mistake. Use the minimal amount of prompting necessary to obtain the correct response. Fade the prompt and go on to Step 6 after 3 unprompted correct responses.

▶ **Step 6**

Reintroduce SD2 ("Touch table") and again prompt, reinforce, and fade the prompt. After 3 unprompted correct trials, go on to Step 7.

▶ **Step 7**

Reintroduce SD1 ("Clap hands"). This time, test for mastery by suddenly withholding the prompt altogether. The prompt is removed to avoid reinforcing the student for prompt dependency as discussed in Chapter 10. If the student responds correctly without the prompt, present one more trial and then go on to Step 8. If the student responds incorrectly, use the minimal amount of prompting necessary to reinstate the correct response. Fade the prompt over subsequent trials. After 2 unprompted correct responses in a row, go on to Step 8.

▶ **Step 8**

Reintroduce SD2 ("Touch table"). Test for mastery by suddenly withholding the prompt altogether. If the student responds correctly, present one more trial and then go on to Step 9. If the student responds incorrectly, present a minimal prompt on the next trial. Fade the prompt over subsequent trials. Minimize or withhold reinforcement for responding on prompted trials while maximizing reinforcement for correct responding on unprompted trials. After 2 correct responses without prompting, repeat Steps 7 and 8.

▶ **Step 9**

Continue to alternate between the two instructions until the student responds correctly to each of them the first time they are presented in contrast with one another. Provide differential reinforcement by maximally reinforcing correct responses and withholding reinforcers for incorrect responses by acting as if the response did not occur. If acting as if the response did not occur fails to reduce errors, consequate incorrect responses with an informational "No" (not a harsh "No") and remove reinforcers from the student's view (e.g., by placing them under the table). "No" paired with the temporary removal of food or other reinforcers may eventually establish "No" as corrective feedback. However, an informational "No" may act as a reward for some students. Likewise, the teacher's looking down contingent on incorrect responding may also be rewarding for some students because it may signal a momentary escape from the teaching situation. The type of consequence used for an incorrect response should not be rewarding and should not last for more than 3 seconds.

If the student responds incorrectly on any given trial, reintroduce the least amount of prompting necessary to reinstate correct responding on the next trial and then gradually fade the prompt. Over successive intermixed and differentially reinforced trials, the student will make fewer and fewer mistakes until he responds correctly without prompts the first time the instructions are contrasted with one another. This process occurs for two reasons. First, as the prompts are faded and minimized in strength, they become less and less reliable as cues while the instructions remain reliable and accrue strength. Second, as correct responses are rewarded and strengthened, incorrect responses are not rewarded and are weakened. If discrimination training is done correctly, the student has no choice except to succeed in making the discrimination (i.e., telling the two instructions apart).

In Step 7 we recommended testing for mastery by suddenly withholding the prompt instead of slowly fading it. Remember that this is a test and that some but not all students are likely to respond correctly without a prompt at this early stage of learning. We have also recommended that the teacher switch between instructions, moving from SD1 to SD2 after a gradually decreasing number of trials on any one instruction until the student can respond correctly without a prompt when the instructions are presented singly (as opposed to presented in blocks of 4, 3, and 2). There are three reasons for these recommendations. First, the teacher wants to avoid establishing prompt dependency. Second, the teacher wants to reduce perseveration by not reinforcing the student for merely repeating the same response. Finally, there may be some value in letting the student make a mistake, such as SD1–R2, in the sense that a nonreinforced trial is mildly aversive and thereby helps to speed up the discrimination.

The numerical values specified earlier (e.g., switching after 3, then 2, then 1 correct response) are based on our experience with the average learning rate of students with developmental delays. If the student has required several hours to master the first or second instruction (SD1 or SD2), or both, when presented in mass trials, the criterion should be increased (e.g., to 5 unprompted correct responses in a row or 9 out of 10). As the student's mastery increases, reduce the criterion to 4 in a row, then to 3, and so on, before switching instructions. A number of subtleties in the constructive use of instructions and prompts are unique to particular teaching programs and will be discussed in subsequent chapters.

Students with developmental delays typically experience difficulty learning to discriminate between the first two instructions in any program. However, additional instructions are usually acquired with increasing ease. It is as if the student learns how to learn.

Areas of Difficulty

One helpful step for students who experience problems differentiating two particular instructions (e.g., "Clap hands" and "Touch table") is to change one or both instructions. For example, introduce "Block in bucket" instead of "Touch table" or "Clap hands." Another possibility is changing instructions to those that contain a more substantial and direct payoff (reinforcer), such as the instruction "Drink juice" if the student likes juice or "Light switch" if the student likes to turn on and off lights and a light switch is handy. These are examples of instructions the student may have already learned, and this prior learning may facilitate mastery of the discrimination.

If difficulties continue, try contrasting one of the SDs (e.g., SD1) with a *contrasting stimulus* (SDCS) from another program, such as the Nonverbal Imitation Program. That is, intermix SD1 with SDCS (e.g., from nonverbal imitation, give the SD "Do this" and model stomping feet). The SD1–SDCS discrimination should be easier for the student to discriminate because it involves a contrast between a visual stimulus and an auditory stimulus instead of two auditory stimuli. Thus, this discrimination could be used as a warm-up trial for the SD1–SD2 discrimination.

A few students (1 out of 10 or 15) may respond to two or three elementary instructions when presented separately (e.g., "Sit down," "Drop block," or "Drink juice") but fail to learn to discriminate between any two verbal instructions when intermixed despite teachers' most extensive efforts using what is now known about discrimination learning. These students may be referred to as visual learners, and they may excel at acquiring discriminations among visually presented instructions such as those introduced in the Nonverbal Imitation Program (Chapter 13), the Reading and Writing Program (Chapter 29), and the Picture Exchange Communication System Program (Chapter 30). The discrimination learning procedures described in this chapter are just as important to teaching responses to visual instructions as they are to teaching responses to vocal instructions. If the student has difficulty learning, examine the teaching style before attributing failure to the student.

Random Rotation

The intermixing and differential reinforcement of instructions (or any stimuli) have been subjected to much scrutiny by psychologists with special interests in learning processes in order to find a way to maximize the number of correct responses and minimize the number of errors made by an organism when learning discriminations. In working out an optimal procedure for intermixing presentations of instructional stimuli, the field has developed a procedure that we label *random rotation* (technically termed *random stimulus presentation*). Random rotation of instructional stimuli may be considered a safety check and a strengthening measure that ensures the student has acquired the correct discrimination through the employment of differential reinforcement procedures. It is absolutely essential that you become familiar with this procedure.

Random rotation is a procedure in which presentations of two or more SDs are intermixed in a nonspecific, random order. An example of a random sequence of two SDs follows: SD1, SD2, SD2, SD1, SD1, SD2, SD1, SD2, SD2, SD2, SD1, SD1, SD2, SD1, SD1, SD1, SD2, SD1. The sequence is called random because it does not allow the student to predict which SD will appear next. To illustrate random rotation in the Early Receptive Language Program, let SD1 represent "Clap hands," SD2 represent "Touch table," and SD3 represent "Block in bucket."

An illustration of a random sequence of trials follows. Let the correct response to SD1 be R1 and the correct response to SD2 be R2. Remember, if the student fails to provide a correct response when the SDs are switched (as in going from SD1 to SD2, or vice versa), the teacher should prompt to establish correct responding, and then fade it before moving on.

Trial	Stimulus–Response	Result
1	SD1–R1	Correct, reinforce
2	SD2–R1	Incorrect, extinction or "No"
3	SD2	Prompt R2 and reinforce
4	SD2–R2	Reinforce
5	SD2–R2	Reinforce
6	SD1–R2	Extinction or "No"
7	SD1	Prompt R1 and reinforce
8	SD1–R2	Extinction or "No"
9	SD1	Prompt R1 and reinforce
10	SD1–R2	Extinction or "No"
11	SD1	Prompt R1 and reinforce
12	SD1	Prompt R1 and reinforce
13	SD1–R1	Reinforce
14	SD1–R1	Reinforce
15	SD2–R2	Reinforce
16	SD1–R1	Reinforce
17	SD2–R2	Reinforce
18	SD2–R2	Reinforce
19	SD1–R1	Reinforce

Note that in Trials 4 and 5, the teacher repeats SD2 twice before switching to SD1. This is done to strengthen the SD2–R2 association because the intermixing has just begun and the SD2–R2 may need strengthening. In Trial 6, the student loses the SD1–R1 association, perhaps because she had been reinforced for SD2–R2 in the preceding trials (4 and 5). In both Trials 8 and 10, the student again loses the SD1–R1 association. The teacher responds to this error by prompting twice (Trials 11 and 12) and repeating reinforceable trials twice (Trials 13 and 14) so as to strengthen the association before going on to SD2. Intermixing SD1 and SD2 (Trials 15, 16, 17, and 18) indicates that the discrimination may have been mastered unless the student learned a certain pattern of alternating between responses, a problem we describe in more detail in the next section. The correct response in Trial 18 is an early test of whether this problem exists, and the student's correct response suggests that it may not. The student would have given R1 in Trial 18 had she been alternating and not attending to the teacher's instruction.

Before we proceed, it may be helpful to comment further on the loss of the correct response in Trial 8, which occurred after the student had been prompted and reinforced for the correct response in Trial 7. The same loss occurred in Trial 10. The teacher went from Trial 7 to 8 and from Trial 9 to 10 abruptly, withholding the prompt to probe whether the student had achieved mastery. It is impossible to probe without withholding prompts, and it is not possible to predict the exact point at which to suddenly withdraw the prompt to test whether the student has achieved mastery. However, the teacher will become more proficient at determining when to probe as he or she gains experience. Note that the teacher went on to establish the correct SD1–R1 association in Trials 11 through 14.

Common Problems When Intermixing Instructions

It is important to help ensure that the student is not misled when taught to discriminate among stimuli. As illustrated in this section, it is easy to mislead a student when intermixing instructions.

▶ Win–Shift Strategy

If the teacher systematically alternates instructions, as in SD1, SD2, SD1, SD2, SD1, SD2, and so on, it may seem that the student should learn to tell the two instructions (SDs) apart. Such a systematic alternation was described previously when SD1 ("Clap hands") and SD2 ("Touch table") were intermixed. Some students may acquire the discrimination under this condition, but others will not. From the student's point of view, instead of attending to the auditory stimuli, it may be easier to solve the problem by learning that if he was reinforced for responding correctly on one trial, he needs to switch responses on the next trial to get reinforcement. In technical terminology, reinforcement of R1 ("Clap hands") rather than the teacher's instruction becomes the SD for R2 ("Touch table"). This is called a win–shift strategy. In short, such a procedure is not conducive to helping the student attend to the teacher's instructions.

▶ Win–Stay Strategy

If the teacher repeats the same instruction across numerous trials, as in SD1, SD1, SD1, SD1, SD1, and so on, a procedure similar to the mass trials phase used during the acquisition of a response, the teacher's intent may be to strengthen the student's response to the instruction provided. However, the student may be reinforced for merely repeating what he did the last time and not for listening to the teacher's instructions. He may learn that if he responds the same as the last time he was reinforced, he will again be reinforced. The student is taught to perseverate. This is called a win–stay strategy. In technical terminology, the SD for the student's response is the reinforcement received for the performance of the same response done in the preceding trial and not the teacher's instruction. Random rotation of SDs is critical to preventing this.

▶ Lose–Shift Strategy

If the teacher presents SD1 ("Clap hands") and the student responds with R2 (touching the table) and is not reinforced, and the teacher then repeats SD1 ("Clap hands") and the student responds with R1 (clapping hands) and is reinforced, the student may learn that if reinforcement was withheld for touching the table in the last trial, he needs to switch to clapping in next trial. This is called a lose–shift strategy in which the loss of a reinforcer becomes the SD for shifting to an alternate response. One way to break up such a strategy is to insert an already mastered SD–R trial after the reinforced SD1–R1 trial. The contrasting stimulus should consist of an instruction to which the student can already respond, such as "Stand up," or a nonverbal imitation trial as in waving in response to a model. The sequence of SDs may then proceed in the following manner:

Trial	SD and Result
1	SD1–incorrect R, do not reinforce
2	SD1–correct R, reinforce
3	Present a contrasting stimulus and reinforce correct R.
4	Present SD1. If the student responds with R1, the teacher may be more confident that the student's correct response is associated with SD1 and not the loss of a reinforcer on a preceding trial.

Another example of inadvertently teaching a lose–shift strategy occurs when the teacher lets the student self-correct. Self-correction may be helpful for typical individuals and for those who master advanced programs, but it may lead to serious prolems for students with developmental delays in the early stages of learning. Self-correction is discussed later in Mistake 12 of the section "Areas of Difficulty."

The illustrations provided in this section show that it is easy for the student to learn the wrong associations. He seems efficient at gaining reinforcers, perhaps because he is expending less effort than would be needed for paying attention to what the teacher is saying. Maximizing gains while minimizing effort is not only characteristic of students with developmental delays, but of all living organisms.

Introducing the Third Discrimination

Mastery criterion when SD1 and SD2 ("Clap hands" and "Touch table") are randomly rotated may be set at 9 out of 10 or 19 out of 20 unprompted correct responses. At that point, we strongly advise teachers to further strengthen mastery of the discrimination between these two instructions by actively rehearsing the discrimination over the next 2 or 3 days, generalizing it across teachers and across different physical locations (e.g., across rooms of the house), and intermixing other programs such as Matching and Sorting (Chapter 12) and Nonverbal Imitation (Chapter 13). Intermixing the discrimination with other tasks helps strengthen recall, a phenomenon more fully discussed in Chapter 31. The discrimination between the first two stimuli (SD1 and SD2) is the most difficult, and success should be considered a great achievement for both the student and the teacher. Once the first discrimination is firmly established, new stimuli may be added at a faster rate and with less likelihood that the first discrimination will be lost.

Once you feel assured that the SD1–SD2 discrimination is mastered, a third instruction (SD3, such as "Block in bucket") can be introduced. Mass trial SD3, then intermix and differentially reinforce SD3 with SD1. Once SD3 is randomly rotated with SD1 and mastered, intermix SD3 with SD2. Follow up with random rotation. Use the same procedures to introduce new SDs.

A typical outcome from discrimination learning is that, with the introduction of SD3 and for each new SD thereafter, there is a concomitant decrease in the number of errors the student makes. This happens because the student learns to attend to (discriminate) the teacher's instructions. This is an inevitable outcome when the correct response is reinforced and thus strengthened and incorrect responses are not reinforced and thus weakened. Eventually the student may become so attentive to the teacher's instructions that one prompt of the correct answer is sufficient for learning. This is known as one-trial learning.

Areas of Difficulty

The student may demonstrate little or no progress in learning a discrimination after several trials. For example, the student may not master the discrimination between the first two instructions after 3 hours of instruction even though you adhere to correct discrimination learning procedures. It is *very* easy to make mistakes when teaching children with developmental delays. Mistakes are likely to reinforce behaviors that will hinder or block new and appropriate learning. Consider the following teaching mistakes:

- **1.** The stimuli being contrasted are too similar. If this could be the problem, reexamine whether the teacher is in fact beginning with stimuli that are maximally different and that require maximally different responses (when appropriate).
- **2.** Members of the team are inconsistent in what and how they teach. Check consistency at the weekly team meeting by having each teacher demonstrate his or her skills with the student.
- **3.** The particular task the teacher employs is especially difficult for the student. If this is a possibility, try another task for contrast. For example, if the student mastered SD1 ("Clap hands") but continuously makes errors when this instruction is mixed with SD2 ("Touch table"), then shift to another instruction such as "Block in bucket." Reintroduce "Touch table" later.
- **4.** There are problems with reinforcers and motivation. If the student reaches a plateau or begins to lose mastered tasks, try the following possible remedies: (a) If this problem is caused by ineffective reinforcers, search for new and more powerful reinforcers or avoid satiation on older ones. It is a common mistake for teachers to repeatedly use consequences, such as saying, "Good," "Nice job," "Fine," "Splendid," "Fantastic," "Super," "Right on," "Excellent," and "Yes," all to no avail. (b) If self-stimulatory behaviors have shown a marked increase, engage the stu-

dent in attention exercises (also known as wake-up exercises) for a 10- to 15-second duration by rapidly alternating between SDs of already mastered tasks (such as "Sit down," "Stand up," "Turn around," or nonverbal imitation tasks) and then suddenly presenting the SD you are training. (c) Make certain the reinforcement is immediate; there should be no delay between the student's response and the reinforcement. The effectiveness of the reinforcer decreases exponentially over the time elapsed between a response and the delivery of reinforcement. Data suggest that a 1-second delay between the response and the reinforcer is only 25% as effective in strengthening a response as a .5 second delay (Reynold, 1968). If the delay is longer than .5 second, the student is likely to have started doing something else and that behavior will inadvertently be the one that receives reinforcement (i.e., the behavior performed immediately before the delivery of reinforcement will be strengthened). If a teacher uses a reinforcer that cannot be delivered immediately (e.g., food), it is recommended that the teacher bridge the delay by immediately giving verbal praise while reaching for and providing a food reinforcer. Through such a procedure, verbal praise (e.g., "Good") is likely to acquire reinforcing properties because it signals (becomes associated with) an already powerful reinforcer (i.e., food consumption). (d) Make sure the consequences for incorrect trials do not inadvertently function as positive reinforcers and thereby increase incorrect responding. This could happen if the student receives a pause in teaching by, for example, the teacher talking to the student ("I know you are trying hard and you are getting upset, but we have to continue"). (e) Do not reinforce the student before she completes her response. If you do so in your eagerness to help the student, the student is reinforced before she commits to a response. If this occurs, the student does not have the opportunity to complete, be reinforced for, and learn the correct response. (f) Be sure not to overwork the student. If the student makes rapid progress, she has reinforced the teacher for introducing an ever-increasing number of new and perhaps more difficult tasks. The student, however, often cannot vocally communicate to the teacher when it becomes too much and may fall back on an earlier, well-practiced strategy of tuning out or tantruming. If this occurs, simplify the program, reinstate motivation, and then move forward at a slower pace. (g) If the student's entire curriculum, not only a specific program, is too academically oriented, behaviors such as tantruming toward the end of the day and nonresponsiveness across programs may become evident. To help avoid these problems, introduce play breaks between sittings and intersperse other reinforcing activities between academically oriented programs.

▶ **5.** The teacher may give inadvertent prompts, such as looking at the student's hands when asking the student to "Clap hands" or looking at the table when asking the student to "Touch table." If the student is reinforced for responding to inadvertent prompts, she will not learn the desired association between the teacher's request and her response. Also, if the student is not inadvertently prompted in the same way at another time or by other teachers, then she will fail to respond correctly. Other kinds of inadvertent prompts also may delay mastery. For example, the instructions may differ in length, as when a one-word SD such as "Table" is contrasted with a two-word SD such as "Clap hands." Length of the instructions may help prompt the correct response, but the teacher must be aware of such prompts and must fade them by changing the instructions to make them of equal length.

▶ **6.** The student responds to some element of the instruction not intended to be solely responded to, such as the first part of the instruction (e.g., "clap" in "Clap hands" or "touch" in "Touch table"). To check for this possibility, merely present the instructions as "Hands" and "Table." Place the instructions "Hands" and "Table" into discrimination training if the student fails to respond correctly. Once mastered, fade in "Clap" and "Touch" by first presenting these words at a very low decibel level (whispering them) and then gradually increasing their volume until they are stated as loudly as "hands" and "table." Note, however, that is the student is more likely to respond to the last part of the instructions than the first part because the last part is the most recent stimulus element. Therefore, in the case of "Clap hands" and "Touch table," it is more likely that "hands" and "table" will become associated with the correct response than "clap" and "touch." The student is taught to "store" instructions of increasing length as she progresses through language programs.

▶ 7. The teacher shifts to a new SD after a prompted response on the preceding trial. For example, in Trial 1 the teacher presents SD1 and the student responds with R2 (an incorrect response) or not at all. In Trial 2, the teacher presents SD1 once more, prompts, and reinforces the correct response, R1. The teacher then goes on to Trial 3 and presents SD2 with the intent of contrasting SD1 with SD2. The mistake occurs in Trial 3, where the prompt was not faded for SD1. The student was not reinforced for responding to SD1 with R1, but rather for responding with R1 to the prompt. In such a situation, SD2 is contrasted with a prompt instead of SD1. This situation does not help the student learn to discriminate between the relevant stimuli (SD1 and SD2 in this example). In other words, very little learning occurs if the student simply gives responses to prompts. It is easy to make this mistake in one's eagerness to help the student move along.

▶ 8. The teacher inadvertently reinforces incorrect responses by, for example, providing encouragement to the student when she gives a mistaken response. Examples of such encouragement include "Good try," "Almost right," "Try again," and "We don't want to do that, do we?" If the student responds to such consequences as rewarding, the teacher may inadvertently strengthen incorrect responses. A typical individual may know the meaning of such feedback and not respond as if being reinforced for an incorrect response. However, it is best not to assume that a person with language delays comprehends such comments. As mentioned earlier, even a consequence such as "No," which is aversive for many students, may serve as a positive reinforcer for some students. If in doubt, withhold any and all potential reinforcers for incorrect responses so as to avoid reinforcing errors.

▶ 9. An extended time interval occurs between trials. For example, the teacher talks too much between trials as in commenting, "That is good clapping hands. Let's try it one more time, you are doing so well." Or, the teacher takes time away from teaching to record whether the student made the correct response. Too much time may also pass if the student is given a chewy food or a large amount of food that takes a long time to consume. In each instance, time between trials may result in the student drifting off into self-stimulatory behavior, making it difficult for the teacher to regain her attention to the appropriate stimuli. Short intertrial intervals allow for the presentation of more trials than is possible when intervals between trials are longer. In general, the more trials, the more often a response is reinforced and the stronger that response becomes. The practice of lengthening intertrial intervals should be employed only when introducing the procedures intended to maintain already mastered material (Chapter 31).

▶ 10. The time interval between the teacher's instruction and the student's response is too long. This interval should be as short as possible (not exceeding 3 seconds). Avoid prolonged intervals by providing feedback (informational "No") if the student does not respond 3 seconds after the instruction, and then immediately start another trial, prompting the desired response if necessary. Technically speaking, for a stimulus–response association to be made, the two events should occur concurrently (i.e., overlap) in the student's nervous system. If a teacher presents an instruction and the student delays responding, other intervening stimuli may become associated with the response instead of the teacher's instruction.

▶ 11. The SD and the prompt do not overlap. Rather, the SD is presented, 2 or more seconds pass, and then the teacher prompts the correct response. For the SD to take control over the student's response, the SD and the prompt must occur simultaneously (overlap) in the student's nervous system. If the student does not respond to the SD, repeat the SD and simultaneously present the prompt.

▶ 12. The teacher allows the student to self-correct. That is, the student makes the incorrect response (either in whole or in part), hesitates for a brief moment as if waiting for the teacher's reaction, and then, if no reinforcement is forthcoming, switches to the correct response. Reinforcement of the correct response may seem like the appropriate strategy except that the correct response may now be associated with the teacher's withholding of reinforcement for the aborted incorrect response. This is similar to the lose–shift strategy, which was discussed earlier, and to the problem discussed in the paragraph numbered 7. If the student self-corrects, quickly end that trial and then provide the SD again, prompting the correct response to avoid self-correction.

▶ 13. A variation on intermixing SD1 with SD2 for the student who experiences serious problems during acquisition is to intermix SD1 with an already mastered SD from another program, such as Nonverbal Imitation (this was earlier referred to as the use of a contrasting stimulus). This step should be considered a pretraining step or a warm-up. Mastery of such a discrimination should not be accepted in place of the target discrimination; it is intended to facilitate the student's mastery of subsequent discriminations. There are three advantages to a procedure that intermixes different kinds of SDs: (1) The student is more likely to acquire a discrimination between two instructions when one is auditory and the other is visual; (2) SDCS may have reinforcing properties, thereby helping to maintain the student's cooperation with the teaching situation; and (3) inserting SDCS helps improve recall of SD1 (see Chapter 31).

▶ 14. The discrimination learning procedures described in this chapter use prompts that are ideally suited to help teach discriminations in programs containing auditory instructions or simple visual stimuli, such as in the Early Receptive Language, Matching and Sorting, Nonverbal Imitation, and Verbal Imitation Programs. The prompts are reasonably simple, such as moving the student's hand to help execute the appropriate action or emphasizing a critical element in the teacher's instruction. However, several of the programs outlined in this manual require the student to make a selection from several visual stimuli, such as in the Receptive Identification of Objects and Receptive Identification of Behaviors Programs. For example, in the Receptive Identification of Objects Program, the teacher names an object and teaches the student to select that object from among several objects placed on the table in front of the student. To facilitate correct responding in such a program, certain additional prompts must be introduced in discrimination learning procedures to help the student make the association between a particular verbal or printed label and the object that the label denotes. Prompts specific to particular programs are described as each program is introduced.

Other Problems

If one has exhausted all known possibilities and the student still makes little or no progress, consider the possibility that the student may have a neurological deviation that makes it difficult for her to associate certain kinds of stimuli, such as auditory stimuli, with behaviors. In our experience, 1 out of 10 to 15 students appears to experience this problem to an extreme degree, acquiring a reliable response to only one or two verbal instructions after a month or more of instruction. Such students appear to be primarily visual learners and are likely to make progress in programs involving visual stimuli, including the Matching and Sorting, Nonverbal Imitation, Reading and Writing, and Picture Exchange Communication System Programs (Chapters 12, 13, 29, and 30, respectively). The student's exposure to visual instructions may later facilitate her recognition of verbally presented material.

Another possibility is that the student has a hearing or visual impairment. Most parents have already suspected such impairments and have taken their child for a comprehensive neurological evaluation. It is recommended that a neurological evaluation be scheduled as part of the intake (pretreatment) assessment. If this has not been addressed, it should be at this point.

In the context of obtaining a comprehensive neurological examination, we raise a warning against "over-pathologizing" because one can risk handicapping both the student and the teacher. Most teachers have been exposed to alternate treatment approaches (see Chapter 2). Various instructional sets or philosophies may have been acquired through this exposure and could interfere with the effective use of the teaching principles advocated in this manual. Although rewarding correct responses and withholding rewards for incorrect responses may sound reasonable, basic, and commonsensical, many adults find it difficult to follow such advice because individuals with developmental delays have historically been conceptualized as qualitatively different from typical individuals—as extremely frail, anxious, and the like. Therefore, qualitatively different treatments, such as noncontingent love and acceptance, have been applied, often independent of how the person behaves. Gentle Teaching, Options, Holding Therapy, and psychodynamic intervention illustrate such treatments. Research has indicated that many persons, even when not adhering to any of these philosophies, have a tendency to reinforce any responses of individuals with developmental delays, including incorrect ones (Eikeseth & Lovaas, 1992).

Teachers may also have been taught to rely on theories that place an emphasis on the idea that development unfolds according to maturational stages. Such theories have been influential in determining education for both typical persons and persons with developmental delays. Some of these theories are based on developmental psychology and include the views of Chomsky, Piaget, and Kohlberg. These theories imply that a teacher may have to wait for certain maturational stages to manifest themselves and then, with minimal exposure to language and educational material, competence will occur. Whether or not these theories are true of typical children is a matter of heated debate, but they clearly have been found to be inapplicable to children with developmental delays.

Finally, there are those who propose that the goal of a teacher is to free a frightened little person out from behind an autistic shell, a person capable of understanding what the teacher may be communicating. Once out of the shell, the person would be expected to speak or write in full sentences and otherwise behave like a typical individual. Such were the theories of Bettelheim (1967). What this and the theories presented earlier have in common is that they are well known; sound attractive, comforting, and humanistic; can be mastered by a teacher attending a workshop of a 1-week or less duration; and allow the teacher to assume a more passive role toward the individuals with developmental delays. Although all of these interventions may be well meaning, none of them have demonstrated effectiveness, and several seem to cause more harm than good (see Chapter 3). A less speculative approach is to assume that the individual has a potential for learning and that there is not a qualitative difference between the processes by which individuals with developmental delays and typical individuals learn. However, with a learning-based behavioral approach, the teacher will need a great deal more training to become competent and the child, the teacher, and the parent will have to work much harder.

Receptive Identification of Objects

CHAPTER 17

The Receptive Identification of Objects Program is designed to teach the student to identify objects and persons encountered in her everyday life. This is a skill that may be taught regardless of whether the student possesses expressive language skills. The teacher's familiarity with the procedures presented in this chapter and the student's success at learning to receptively identify objects may help the student acquire new concepts such as color, shape, and size (see Chapter 25).

Prior to starting this program, the student should have been working on the Matching and Sorting, Nonverbal Imitation, and Early Receptive Language Programs (Chapters 12, 13, and 15, respectively), with the beginning stages at or near mastery. Further, it is essential that the teacher be familiar with discrimination learning procedures (see Chapter 16).

To teach the student to receptively identify objects, the teacher needs a large number of common household objects (e.g., cup, shoe, block, cookie, crayon) with which the student has frequent contact, photos of these same household objects, photos of the student's parents and siblings, pictures of objects cut from magazines or other sources and mounted onto 3 × 5-inch index cards, and a table for placement of the objects and pictures. To help ensure that the student can tell the objects and the pictures apart (i.e., discriminate among the 3-D objects and the objects depicted in the pictures), it is helpful for the student to have mastered matching of the stimuli to be employed in this program (see Chapter 12).

We present this program in considerable procedural detail to facilitate the teacher's learning of correct treatment techniques. Obviously, the better the teaching techniques, the more rapidly the student will acquire the skills taught. As the teacher gains experience, future programs will be presented in a less detailed, step-by-step format.

Identifying the First Two Objects

The first two objects the student is taught to identify should be ones the student frequently encounters in his everyday environment and ones that are easily held by the student. We illustrate the procedures for teaching the student to identify the first two objects by using a cup and a shoe. It is important to choose objects with minimally distracting features; thus, in our example, small, solid-colored objects without pictures or designs are used. Other objects the teacher could use include a toy truck, a plain doll, a solid-colored ball, or a food item such as a cookie or an apple.

If the student can identify a particular object (e.g., by touching it, pointing to it, or going to get it when asked to do so) before he receives any formal instruction, begin teaching with that object. We recommend first establishing instructional control over the objects the student can already identify so that the student's success can be maximized and teaching time can be minimized. In addition, if the student already knows how to identify one or a few objects but often fails to demonstrate this skill when requested to do so, the task now is to obtain more consistency.

► **Step 1**

Place the cup about 1 foot in front of the student and on the table and concurrently say, "Cup." Enunciate the word "cup" in a succinct and clearly audible manner. The presentation of the cup and your verbalization of "cup" constitute SD1. If the student fails to respond correctly, repeat the instruction and, *immediately* after presenting SD1, physically prompt the student's response by gently taking his hand and placing his palm on the cup. (Touching the appropriate object is illustrated in these steps as the correct response. The student may be taught, however, to point to the correct object on the table or hand you the correct object.) If the student has made sufficient progress in nonverbal imitation, simply model the correct response (a less intrusive prompt) while giving the SD. If the prompt is not performed concurrent with or immediately after the SD, the time interval between the SD and the correct response will be too long to form the SD1–R1 association.

Reinforce the student immediately after he performs the prompted response. Next, remove the cup from the table, replace it on the table, and say, "Cup." This starts a new trial, and the removal and replacement of the cup ensures a discrete and succinct stimulus presentation, facilitating the student's attention to the stimulus. Keep the interval between trials at 1 to 3 seconds. After 3 to 4 successful prompted trials, gradually and systematically fade the prompt in subsequent trials by, for example, performing less and less of the model or pulling more and more lightly on the student's hand and releasing his hand sooner and sooner before it reaches the cup. Next, slowly transfer from a manual or model prompt to a less intrusive prompt such as pointing to the cup. Then fade this prompt as well. Reinforce each correct response whether or not it is prompted, but maximize reinforcement for unprompted trials. When the student responds correctly without prompting in 5 out of 5 or 9 out of 10 trials, proceed as described below.

Continue to present mass trials of SD1, repeatedly presenting the same SD in each trial. Introduce a slightly more difficult component by placing the cup in a different location on the table on each trial. Vary the position of the cup in relation to the student so that the cup is placed on the left side of the table on one trial, the right side of the table on another trial, and so forth. This step is introduced to help avoid position cues and facilitate the student's scanning for the object. After 3 to 4 unprompted correct responses in a row, go on to Step 2.

Keep in mind that at this point the student has yet to learn to identify a cup as a cup. The student might touch any object when instructed, "Cup." The steps that follow are introduced to help the student discriminate (attend to the differences) among objects. To facilitate this discrimination, the second object taught to the student should look different from the first object taught and it should have a name that sounds different from the label of the first object. For example, a glass would *not* be an ideal second object to use because it looks similar to a cup. Likewise, a cat would not be ideal as a second object because its label sounds similar to the word *cup*. A shoe may be a good second object to teach because it looks different from a cup and its label sounds different as well.

▶ Step 2

Clear the table of all stimuli. Present SD2 by placing the shoe on the table in front of the student and concurrently stating, "Shoe." Prompt the student to respond correctly (i.e., touch the shoe) by guiding his hand on top of the shoe or by modeling the behavior. Reinforce. Remove the shoe between trials to make its presentation discrete. Continue to present SD2 ("Shoe") in mass trials, gradually fading the prompt over subsequent trials. When the student successfully responds without prompting in 5 out of 5 or 9 out of 10 trials, continue to present mass trials of SD2 ("Shoe"), placing the shoe in a different location on the table at the start of each trial to avoid position cues and facilitate scanning. When the student is successful without prompting in 5 out of 5 or 9 out of 10 trials, go on to Step 3.

▶ Step 3

Intermix SD1 ("Cup") and SD2 ("Shoe") according to discrimination learning procedures. Present SD1 with a full position prompt by placing the cup in the middle of the table and the shoe in the back corner of the table away from the student. The placement of the cup close to the student facilitates the correct response (touching the cup), whereas the placement of the shoe away from the student helps to inhibit the student's touching the shoe. If the student fails to respond correctly, repeat SD1 ("Cup") and further prompt the next trial by physically guiding the student, pointing to the cup, or modeling the response. Fade the physical, point, or model prompt first, and then fade the position prompt over subsequent trials by reducing the distance between the two objects until they are aligned on the table and about a foot apart, equidistant from the student. Remember to randomly rotate the left–right positions of the objects (cup and shoe) on the table throughout this step to help avoid inadvertent cues. When the student responds correctly without prompting in 9 out of 10 or 19 out of 20 consecutive trials, go on to Step 4.

▶ Step 4

Present SD2 ("Shoe") with the shoe placed in front of the student and employ a full position prompt by placing the cup on the back corner of the table. Present mass trials of SD2 ("Shoe"). Fade the position prompt over trials until the cup and shoe are placed linearly, about 1 foot apart and equidistant from the student. Remember to randomly rotate the left–right positions of the objects (cup and shoe) on the table throughout this step to help avoid inadvertent cues. Set mastery at 9 out of 10 or 19 out of 20 unprompted correct responses.

▶ Step 5

Reintroduce SD1 ("Cup") using a full position prompt. Fade the position prompt while reinforcing correct responding. Because the SD1–R1 relationship has been strengthened, the prompt can be faded more quickly; that is, the two objects can be brought closer together more quickly without causing errors. If errors do occur, reintroduce the least amount of position prompt necessary to occasion correct responding. Place mastery at 5 out of 5 or 9 out of 10 unprompted correct responses. (With each reversal of SD1 and SD2, a lesser number of correct responses is necessary.)

▶ Step 6

Switch back to mass trials of SD2 ("Shoe"). Start with a full position prompt, and then fade the prompt over subsequent trials. When the student independently responds correctly in 4 consecutive trials, go on to Step 7.

▶ Step 7

Return to mass trials of SD1 ("Cup"). Begin with a reduced position prompt: Place the cup in the middle of the table and the shoe halfway between the back corner of the table and the cup. Fade the position prompt over subsequent trials. When the student independently responds correctly in 4 consecutive trials, go on to Step 8.

▶ Step 8

With the cup and shoe on the table, begin alternating between SD1 and SD2, gradually lessening the number of consecutive correct responses needed before switching SDs. If the student responds incorrectly on any given trial, reintroduce the least amount of prompting that reinstates the correct response. Fade all prompts completely before switching to the alternate SD, giving maximal reinforcement for unprompted trials. When the student responds correctly to each SD when directly contrasted (i.e., SD1, SD2, SD1, SD2, etc.), begin random rotation of SD1 and SD2 as described in the discrimination learning chapter (Chapter 16). Place mastery at 9 out of 10 or 19 out of 20 unprompted correct responses with the SDs randomly rotated.

Because the first discrimination is the most difficult one for the student to master as well as an important achievement, it is recommended that this discrimination be generalized in blocks of 5 to 10 trials across teachers and environments 4 to 5 times per day over the next 3 to 4 days before teaching identification of additional objects. Distributing practice of the discrimination across various times of the day will also help the student remember (retain) what has been learned.

In introducing new persons and environments, be aware that it may take weeks for some students to master the transfer of newly acquired skills. The reasons why some students experience this lag are difficult to ascertain. Perhaps moving from a highly controlled environment into one with several distracting stimuli contributes to the problem. In any case, generalize skills in a careful and systematic manner. For example, in generalizing environments, move slowly and in a stepwise fashion from the treatment room to the door, then to the hallway, and then to other rooms.

Identifying the Third Object

Teach the student to identify a third object by following the steps in the previous section. Make sure this object is perceptually different from the first two objects. After the student masters identifying the third object when presented in mass trials, teach the student to discriminate between SD3 and SD1 and then SD3 and SD2. Then teach the student to discriminate between all three SDs, subjecting them to random rotation.

Identifying Additional Objects

Once the student is able to identify and discriminate among three objects, teach identification of additional objects by following the same procedures used to teach the first three.

That is, teach each new object to mastery one at a time, then intermix the objects to establish discriminations among them. Initially the objects selected should be common items the student encounters in her everyday environment, and they should be chosen carefully to avoid similarities in appearance and sound of the labels. As the student gains experience in the program, however, items that look and sound more similar should gradually be introduced.

As the student learns to identify a larger number of objects, you may find that it is not necessary to follow all of the steps listed in the standard discrimination learning procedures to establish mastery. Mastery of the identification of earlier objects may enable some students to discriminate between a new object and any mastered object without having to employ an elaborate intermixing of objects and prompting techniques for each new SD.

Areas of Difficulty

If the objects chosen to teach are too similar in appearance or their labels are too similar in sound, the student may have difficulty making the discrimination. Keep in mind that two object labels may sound quite different to you but very similar to the student. For example, the words *sock* and *book* are different in terms of initial sounds and vowel sounds. However, their final sounds (*k*) are identical. If the student retains only the final sounds of words in his memory (which also are the most recent sounds), the student will have difficulty learning to discriminate between these objects despite their different appearances.

Inattention is also very likely to lead to difficulty making discriminations. Several factors may contribute to the student's inattention. As mentioned in Chapters 6 and 8, a student may not attend to the task at hand because of his engaging in self-stimulatory behavior, which competes with reinforcers the teacher offers. Inattentive behavior may also result if a teacher presents too many trials in a single sitting and the student resorts to inattentive behavior to avoid or escape the teaching situation. During the beginning stages of teaching, try to limit the number of trials to 5 or so in a single sitting, reinforcing the student by ending the sitting and engaging in a short break. Also, try to quickly intersperse 3 to 4 trials of already mastered material, such as nonverbal imitation. Such trials may serve as wake-up exercises and help motivate the student to continue with the more difficult task. Another factor that may contribute to a student's inattention is a slow pacing of trials. Long intertrial intervals allow the student to engage in alternative behaviors between trials and lose focus on the task being taught. In contrast, short intertrial intervals may block self-stimulatory behavior and reinforce attending to the teacher.

The student may have difficulty discriminating between objects because the presentation of materials is not optimal. The procedure of displaying objects on a table requires the student to attend to the table and scan the objects to make a correct response. Some students have greater success when objects are held in front of them by the teacher at eye level. However, there are drawbacks to using this approach. One drawback is that this method of presentation automatically imposes a limit on the number of objects able to be presented at one time (one object per hand). A second drawback is that this method of presentation differs from the standard procedure used in schools and many other environments. The differences in procedures could result in reduced generalization across environments. Given these drawbacks, presenting the objects by holding them should be considered a type of prompt that must be faded over time until the objects are displayed on the table.

Again, keep in mind the different rates of learning among students within the same diagnostic category. Some students learn the first discrimination within 10 minutes and acquire identification of new objects at the extremely rapid rate of one per minute if the teacher so allows. Be careful not to proceed too fast, because such a student can easily be overloaded with labels and is likely to become noncompliant. Remember that students with developmental delays often do not possess the verbal skills necessary to inform the teacher when tasks become overly abundant or too complex. If the student learns five new labels per week and makes steady progress in other programs, consider the acquisition of 40 receptive labels in a 2-month period to be sufficient. There is much more for the student to learn than identifying objects.

On the other extreme, there are students who experience difficulty mastering the first discrimination after 1 month of teaching. If the student you work with demonstrates such difficulty, consider the following: (a) The student may acquire receptive identification of actions more easily than receptive identification of objects. If so, the identification of objects may be prompted by including receptive action labels in the SDs (e.g., "Push car," "Drink juice," "Eat cookie," "Wipe mouth"). The action labels (push, drink, eat, wipe) may then be faded until only the object labels (car, juice, cookie, mouth) remain. Such a pretraining step may help the student discriminate (attend to) the object. (b) It is a good idea in the beginning of this program to make certain the student can tell apart the objects to be taught. Demonstration of this skill may be observed through the mastery of matching pairs of these objects (see Chapter 12). (c) Some students acquire expressive labeling of objects (see Chapter 23) *before* they acquire receptive identification of objects

(Smith, 1999; Wynn, 1996). That is, some students learn to verbally label objects by, for example, saying "Cup" to the sight of a cup and "Shoe" to the sight of a shoe but have serious difficulty identifying these objects when asked to do so receptively. If this is the case for the student you work with, begin teaching where the student's strength lies. After mastering a skill by one mode, the gains acquired may transfer in part to another mode.

For those students who experience extreme difficulty making the first SD1–SD2 discrimination, there exists a remedial or pretraining step whereby SD1 is first discriminated from what we have labeled a contrasting stimulus instead of SD2. A contrasting stimulus can be any mastered stimulus that is maximally different from SD1. Intermix SD1 with the contrasting stimulus as suggested in the discrimination learning chapter (Chapter 16). In brief, the sequence of trials may proceed by first intermixing SD1 with a nonverbal imitation task. Chances are that the student will make few errors, if any. Next, proceed to a more difficult step in which SD1 is contrasted with your verbal SD for a mastered action such as "Stand up." Because your SD is verbal, the student is likely to make mistakes but may well acquire the discrimination sooner when presented in this manner than when presented as the original discrimination between SD1 ("Cup") and SD2 ("Shoe"). The purpose of using a contrasting stimulus is to make the steps toward reaching the target discrimination more gradual and successful for the student.

If the student encounters serious difficulty in acquiring receptive identification of objects despite the recommendations described in this section, we suggest placing this program on hold for a month or two. In the meantime, practice other programs and reintroduce the Receptive Labeling of Objects Program at a later stage in treatment.

Anticipate the fact that students often become frustrated and bored when subjected to a strict teaching criterion of success such as 19 correct out of 20 unprompted trials. On one hand, you want to be certain that the student masters the discrimination, which shows that the student is learning to concentrate on the task and suppress attention to interfering stimuli (e.g., self-stimulatory behaviors). On the other hand, you want the student to enjoy being taught. This situation underscores the need to be creative in finding novel and powerful reinforcers to accompany teaching sessions.

In short, there is considerable room for experimentation in the area of teaching students with developmental delays. When you reach a stumbling block, take this to mean that more must be learned about individual differences and the development of innovative methods of teaching. This is only one example of when an experienced consultant can be a great deal of help and when it pays to work within a team.

Generalizing Receptive Identification of Objects

After the student learns to identify approximately 15 different objects, begin generalization across objects of the same class. Generalization helps programs become more functional and helps ensure that the student is not solving discriminations by attending to some irrelevant feature of the stimuli. Through generalization, the student learns to identify many different examples of an object belonging to a class of objects, not only the single item initially taught. For example, after the student learns to identify a particular kind of a shoe, she should be taught to identify sneakers, high heels, sandals, and loafers as shoes. Teach new exemplars of mastered objects by varying their shape, size, and color (Stokes & Baer, 1977).

Initially, generalization should be limited to items that look quite similar to the original object to maximize the student's success. As the student progresses, gradually introduce items that look increasingly dissimilar from the original object. When introducing a new example of a mastered object, the student may need prompting. Continue to teach members of a class until the student can identify several new members the first time they are presented. After the student can correctly identify a member of a class on the first trial, the student is closer to forming a concept of that class. One assessment of the extent to which a student can identify members of a class is provided in the Matching and Sorting Program (see "Category Matching" in Chapter 12).

After the student masters identifying classes of objects in the highly structured table setting, begin teaching the student to identify objects as they occur in her everyday environment. In preparation for such generalization, teach the student the receptive instruction, "Get (object)." To facilitate acquisition of this task, start by placing a familiar object, such as a shoe, on the table in front of the student as was done earlier in the program. Present the instruction, "Get shoe" (emphasize the word "Shoe" initially), and, if necessary, prompt the student to pick up the shoe and hand it to you. Present mass trials of this SD, fading the prompt over subsequent trials. After 9 out of 10 unprompted correct responses, probe a different familiar object, such as a cup. Present the instruction "Get cup" and wait to see if the student responds correctly on her own. If the student fails, prompt and reinforce on the next trial. Fade the prompt over subsequent trials and practice this SD until mastery is reached.

Once the student shows mastery of this discrimination, place the objects farther and farther away from the table on subsequent trials and eventually require the student to *leave the chair* to retrieve the specified item. In gradual steps, teach the student to recover objects from the other side of the room, the hallway leading to a second room, and finally from another room.

After the student learns to recover objects one at a time from several different locations, return to the original teaching environment (at the student's table) and place other objects near the target item to increase the complexity of the task. Once this skill is mastered, ask for more than one item at a time. For example, present the instruction "Get shoes and socks." When introducing this step, it is helpful to place objects close to the table, thus reducing the length of time the student must keep the two items in memory before retrieving them. (Please read "Two-Part Instructions" in Chapter 15 for ideas on prompting this skill.) The goal is to increase both the number of items the student must retrieve at one time and the distance of the objects from the student.

Identifying Pictures

Once the student can easily identify a variety of objects of different classes in three-dimensional (3-D) form, teach the student to identify these objects in two-dimensional (2-D) picture form. To teach objects and persons depicted in 2-D form, follow the same procedures used to teach 3-D objects. You may want to buy stimuli by purchasing appropriate flash cards through a store that sells learning materials, or you can create the stimuli yourself by cutting out pictures from magazines and gluing them onto index cards or by taking photos of objects.

Use pictures of objects that are commonly found in the student's environment. Pictures of individual family members and friends may be introduced as well. The pictures used should be free from background clutter, roughly the same size, and mounted on same-sized cards (e.g., 3 × 5 inches). If pictures or cards of different sizes and shapes are used, the student may attend only to this size–shape dimension when discriminating among the stimuli. If the pictures have items in the background, the student may attend to these items rather than to the target objects.

Remember, what the student attends to is not always what the teacher intends for him to attend to. Therefore, after the student masters identifying approximately 15 objects in 2-D picture form, introduce pictures of different exemplars of class members to promote generalization. Do so by following the same procedures described for teaching generalization of 3-D objects.

Areas of Difficulty

If the student has difficulty identifying objects in 2-D form, it may be helpful to introduce photos of mastered 3-D objects before other pictures are introduced. If the student continues to have difficulty with the photos, try presenting the pictures vertically (as on an easel) rather than horizontally (flat) on the table so that the cards are presented closer to the student's eye level. Over time, fade the use of the vertical display.

If the student has difficulty mastering receptive identification of pictures but not objects, use the object as a prompt by placing it behind the picture. Fade the use of the object by gradually covering it with a piece of paper and then eventually removing it completely. In the reverse case, if the student has difficulty mastering receptive identification of objects but not pictures, place the object directly behind the picture and then gradually fade the picture by covering it more and more with either the object itself or an index card.

Concluding Comments

There are three major benefits to learning the skills described in the Receptive Identification of Objects Program. First, by progressing through the program, the student becomes increasingly attentive to her environment. This attention successfully competes with, and may over time replace, excessive self-stimulatory behavior. Second, the student gains increased skill in memory. The longer the instructions and the greater the physical distance between the student and the objects, the longer the student must memorize ("store") your instruction. In conjunction with increased memory, the student is taught generalization of the object identification task across environments. Third, instead of the teacher manually guiding the student to a particular object, the adult can increasingly manage the student on a verbal level. For example, the student's mother can ask the student to bring her a pair of the student's shoes from the bedroom rather than physically guiding the student to do so or having to do the task herself. The longer this skill is practiced, the more benefit you and the student are likely to receive. Through mastery of this program, the student should become increasingly easy to manage and live with, a desirable outcome that was initiated in the first hours of treatment (Chapter 9).

Receptive Identification of Behaviors

CHAPTER 18

In the Receptive Identification of Behaviors Program, the student is taught to identify common everyday actions, such as eating, standing, walking, and smiling. The same prerequisites are recommended for this program as were recommended for the Receptive Identification of Objects Program. These prerequisite skills include matching and the early parts of the programs on nonverbal imitation and receptive language, all of which will help the student attend to (discriminate) the stimuli involved in this program. It is likely that the student will experience more difficulty discriminating between behaviors than objects, perhaps because many behaviors are more similar to one another than objects are and because identification of behaviors may involve more distracting stimuli (e.g., movement) than those used in teaching objects. Take some comfort, however, in the fact that the teaching procedures employed in the present program are nearly identical to those presented in the preceding program dealing with receptive identification of objects.

To facilitate mastery in the current program, begin teaching by introducing two-dimensional (2-D) stimuli (i.e., pictures of behaviors). Pictures are useful teaching tools because distracting stimuli may be reduced and pictures can illustrate behaviors that may be difficult to perform during teaching sessions (e.g., sleeping, riding a bicycle).

The following materials should be gathered before beginning to teach the Receptive Identification of Behaviors Program: separate photos of the student, a parent, or a friend engaging in easily identifiable and commonly occurring behaviors, such as eating, bicycling, sleeping, and smiling; or pictures showing individuals performing the same commonly occurring behaviors cut out from magazines or books and mounted onto 3 × 5-inch index cards; or pictures from a prepackaged set of commercially available behavior cards that clearly illustrate the actions you want to teach the student to identify. (Most stores selling teaching materials carry such cards.)

Identifying the First Behaviors

The first behavior you select to teach the student to identify should be one that the student finds enjoyable or one that is frequently performed in his everyday environment, such as eating. It may be helpful to initially use photos of the student or other familiar person performing behaviors because such pictures may be more salient to the student than pictures of unfamiliar persons. In the early stages of this program, present behaviors that are easily discriminable visually as well as auditorily. For example, walking versus running might be a difficult discrimination early on in this program, as might sleeping versus sweeping. In illustrating the teaching steps of the present program, we use the behaviors eating and standing. Examples of other behaviors you may want to teach the student are as follows:

Behaviors	
Walking	Brushing teeth
Driving	Cooking
Riding bike	Drinking
Waving	Combing hair
Clapping	Playing
Swimming	Swinging
Jumping	Sleeping
Reading	Skating
Dancing	Fishing

To help ensure that the student can tell the pictures apart, the student should have mastered matching of the stimuli to be taught in this program.

▶ Step 1

SD1 consists of the presentation of a picture depicting a person eating while you concurrently say "Eating." Given the student's familiarity with the Receptive Identification of Objects

Program (Chapter 17), he may understand that he is supposed to respond by touching the card. If the student performs this response correctly, continue to present mass trials of SD1 until the student responds correctly in 5 out of 5 unprompted trials. Then go on to Step 2. If the student responds incorrectly or does not respond at all, prompt him by either modeling the correct response or physically guiding the student's hand on top of the card. Continue to present SD1 in mass trials, gradually fading the prompt over subsequent trials. Always remove the stimulus card between trials. When presenting SD1, move the card to a different location on the table for each trial. The student should be able to touch the card when instructed to do so regardless of where it is placed on the table. After the student responds correctly in 5 out of 5 or 9 out of 10 unprompted trials, go on to Step 2.

▶ Step 2

The behavior depicted on the second card should be different in appearance and sound from the first behavior in order to facilitate the student's discrimination between the two behaviors. If eating is the first behavior taught, drinking is *not* an ideal second behavior because of the similarities between these two actions. Also remember that the initial behaviors selected should have maximally dissimilar labels. Standing may be a good choice for the second behavior.

Begin Step 2 by placing the second behavior card (a card depicting a person standing) in the center of the cleared table in front of the student and concurrently saying, "Standing." SD2 consists of the presentation of the second behavior card and your enunciation of "Standing." If the student responds correctly by touching the behavior card, present mass trials until the student responds correctly in 5 out of 5 unprompted trials. If the student responds incorrectly or does not respond at all, prompt as you did in Step 1 and fade the prompt over subsequent trials. When presenting SD2, place the card in different locations on the table in each trial. The student should be able to touch the card when instructed to do so regardless of where it is positioned on the table. When the student responds correctly in 5 consecutive unprompted trials, go on to the next step.

▶ Step 3

Place the cards used in SD1 (eating) and SD2 (standing) on the table. To minimize errors in teaching the student to discriminate between SD1 and SD2, use a position prompt by placing the SD2 card on the far corner of the table, away from the SD1 card, which is placed close to and in front of the student. Next, present SD1 by saying, "Eating." Over successive trials, slowly minimize the position prompt by moving the SD2 card closer to the SD1 card. That is, repeatedly present the instruction "Eating" and reinforce the student's correct response as you fade the standing card into place beside the eating card. If the student fails to respond correctly, reintroduce the position prompt at a sufficient strength to reinstate correct responding to SD1, and then again proceed to fade the prompt until the cards are side by side and equidistant from the student. Throughout this presentation, the left–right positions of the SD1 and SD2 cards should be randomly rotated to eliminate potential position cues. When the student responds correctly to SD1 in 4 consecutive unprompted trials with the positions of the two cards randomly rotated, go on to the next step

▶ Step 4

Present mass trials of SD2 (standing). Begin by using a full position prompt as done in the previous step, and fade this prompt over the next few trials. When the student responds correctly in 4 consecutive trials without prompting, go on to Step 5.

▶ Step 5

Present mass trials of SD1 (eating), starting with a partial position prompt: Place the eating card in front of the student and the standing card 1 to 2 feet away from the eating card. Fade the position prompt over trials, randomly alternating the left–right positions of the cards. After 3 consecutive correct responses without prompting, go on to Step 6. Reduce the number of required correct responses with each successive switch from SD1 to SD2. This is done in gradual steps on the assumption that the SD1–R1 and SD2–R2 associations become increasingly stronger with each reinforcement for correct responding.

▶ **Step 6**

Switch back to mass trials of SD2 (standing), starting with a partial position prompt. Quickly fade this prompt over the next few trials. Go on to the next step after 3 consecutive unprompted correct responses.

▶ **Step 7**

Switch to mass trials of SD1 (eating), beginning with a minimal position prompt. Quickly fade this prompt over the next few trials. When the student responds correctly in 2 unprompted consecutive trials, go on to Step 8.

▶ **Step 8**

Continue to alternate between SD1 and SD2, gradually fading the position prompt within blocks of trials until the student responds correctly to SD1 and SD2 when presented alternately with the behavior cards placed equidistant from the student and their left–right positions interchanged in a random manner. If the student responds incorrectly on a trial, use the minimum position prompt necessary to reinstate correct responding. Fade the prompt as soon as possible. The student has mastered the discrimination between eating and standing when he responds correctly in 9 out of 10 or 19 out of 20 unprompted and randomly rotated trials. As with the first discrimination in the Receptive Identification of Objects Program, we recommend firming up this important achievement and generalizing it across teachers and environments before moving on to SD3.

As new behavior cards are introduced and mastered in mass trials, intermix trials of the new SD with trials of SDs learned earlier. For example, once SD3 is mastered when presented alone, intermix SD3 with SD1, then intermix SD3 with SD2, then intermix all three SDs. This procedure becomes difficult and impractical to implement after the student acquires the identification of several behaviors. Once this point is reached, the new SD need only be intermixed with three or four already mastered SDs. As always, place the student's achievements on a maintenance schedule, and intermix the Receptive Identification of Behaviors Program with other programs. This helps reduce boredom and is essential to maintaining mastery.

Areas of Difficulty

Some students have difficulty identifying the correct behavior as position prompts are faded. If the student gives an incorrect response as the cards are positioned closer together, go back and reinstate the previous level of prompt that helped the student respond correctly. When the student responds correctly for at least 3 consecutive unprompted trials, try again to gradually fade the position prompt until the two cards are presented such that they are equidistant from the student. If the student continues to have difficulty identifying the correct card, present the cards vertically (e.g., against a board) rather than flat on the table. As with the Receptive Identification of Objects Program, the vertical presentation may make the cards more visible and thus facilitate the discrimination. Vertical presentation of cards, however, should be considered a prompt and faded as such.

It is possible for some students to acquire the discrimination between 2-D stimulus presentations without first learning to match the cards to identical cards. If this step has been deleted and if the student fails to acquire a particular discrimination in the present program, check to see if the student can match pairs of cards. Note that some students are able to discriminate large features of behaviors (e.g., eating vs. standing) but more subtle differences (like smiling vs. frowning) prove to be too difficult. If this is true for the student you work with, go back and subject the difficult stimuli to matching (see Chapter 12). If the student can match the behavior cards but fails to learn to identify the behaviors, some other factor may be contributing to the student's difficulty with this task. Consider placing the cards depicting the difficult discriminations on hold and introducing new behavior cards to see if the student's performance improves. The difficult behaviors can be reintroduced at a later stage.

Learning the discrimination between two behaviors, especially early on in the program, may be too difficult for the student. The student may be helped by the pretraining exercise of discriminating SD1 from a contrasting stimulus. Replace SD2 with a contrasting stimulus (e.g., a blank card) and use the procedures described previously to teach the discrimination. In brief, start by placing the SD1 card in front of the student and the contrasting stimulus on the far corner of the table. Present SD1 until the student responds correctly in 9 out of 10 or 19 out of 20 unprompted trials, and then go on to intermixing SD1 with SD2.

Some students have extreme difficulty discriminating behaviors when they are presented in 2-D form. However, these students may master receptive identification of behaviors in vivo with relative ease (see the later section "Identifying Behaviors In Vivo"). As with all programs, begin teaching in the area where the student's strength lies. The learning of receptive identification of behaviors in vivo may facilitate the acquisition of receptive identification of behaviors presented in 2-D form.

Generalizing Receptive Identification of Behaviors

It is critical that the student applies what he learns about a specific behavior to varied representations of the same behavior. Sometimes it is helpful to probe new pictures of mastered behaviors to see if the student generalizes on his own. If the student does not independently generalize, teach new exemplars following the procedures outlined earlier in this chapter, and periodically probe additional pictures to test for generalization. For example, show the student a novel picture of a person eating. If the student correctly responds to this behavior card, move on to another exemplar of the same action. If the student responds incorrectly, teach him to respond correctly to the novel exemplar by following the steps described in the earlier section "Identifying the First Behaviors." The larger the number of exemplars of behaviors the student masters, the more likely it is that the student will conceptualize the behavior.

Identifying Behaviors In Vivo

Some students master receptive identification of behaviors in vivo (behaviors demonstrated by real-life persons) with more ease than receptive identification of behaviors presented in pictures. As mentioned earlier, the teaching of three-dimensional (3-D) stimuli should precede the teaching of 2-D stimuli if the student's strength lies in learning behaviors in vivo.

If the student began this program by identifying behaviors presented in 2-D form, teach in vivo identification of behaviors after the student learns to identify approximately 20 behaviors in their 2-D form. When teaching in vivo behavior identification, use real-life models by asking two adults on the team to engage in the behaviors the student previously learned to identify in pictures. If the in vivo format is the student's first exposure to the Receptive Identification of Behaviors Program, follow the guidelines presented earlier in the section "Identifying the First Behaviors," which outlines how to go about choosing stimuli.

► **Step 1**

Position two adults (Adult 1 and Adult 2) 3 to 4 feet apart and about 4 to 6 feet in front of the student. Present mass trials of SD1, in which Adult 1 demonstrates a behavior (e.g., clapping for 5 to 8 seconds) and the teacher concurrently says, "Clapping" (if the behavior chosen is clapping). Prompt and reinforce R1, which consists of the student pointing to the adult who claps. Bring to mastery (5 out of 5 or 9 out of 10 unprompted correct responses).

► **Step 2**

Present SD2, which consists of Adult 2 jumping up and down five to eight times and the teacher concurrently saying, "Jumping." Bring to mastery as done in Step 1. Because the student may learn merely to point to the adult rather than to the adult's behaviors, it is necessary to introduce Step 3.

► **Step 3**

Intermix SD1 and SD2 according to discrimination learning procedures until the student responds correctly in 9 out of 10 or 19 out of 20 unprompted trials. To help rule out inadvertent prompts, the two adults should randomly alternate positions and behaviors. For example, Adult 1 should demonstrate clapping twice in a row, jumping once, clapping once, jumping three times, and so forth, and randomly alternate his or her left–right position. Bring to mastery (5 out of 5 or 9 out of 10 trials correct). Adult 2 should then be introduced and perform the behavior Adult 1 is not performing at the same time. Such a task requires the student to make increasingly fine discriminations between behaviors and begin to generalize identification of behaviors across persons. Once the first two behaviors are mastered, new behaviors can be introduced by following the same procedures outlined in this section.

At some point the student should be taught to respond to slightly more elaborate requests, such as "Point to clapping" and "Point to jumping." To reduce errors when additional words are introduced into the instruction, prompt the correct response by maximizing the volume and enunciation of the significant parts of the sentence while expressing the less important words softly and quickly (e.g., "Point to CLAPPING"). Fade the prompt by gradually increasing the volume and lessening the pace of the least important words while decreasing the volume and increasing the pace of the most important component of the instruction until the entire SD is spoken at an equal volume and consistent rate.

Areas of Difficulty

Some students encounter serious difficulty mastering 3-D (in vivo) stimuli but proceed rather quickly at mastering 2-D stimuli. You may facilitate discrimination of 3-D stimuli by providing 2-D stimuli as prompts (e.g., by the adult positioning the corresponding 2-D behavior card in front of himself or herself and then gradually fading the use of the card as a prompt). Some students give evidence of transfer between formats, with the learning of 2-D stimuli facilitating the acquisition of 3-D stimuli, or vice versa.

Concluding Comments

Movement is a primary means of exploration for most individuals. It is also often a source of enjoyment. Thus, teaching the student to identify her own movements and the movements of others may be an ideal means to advancing her receptive language. Some of the programs presented later in this manual use procedures similar to those outlined in this chapter to teach the student to verbally describe her own behaviors and the behaviors of others (see Chapter 24).

Early Play Skills

CHAPTER 19

A delay in toy play is one of the defining features of autism and other forms of developmental delays. When toy play is present, it is often stereotyped and unique to the point of appearing inappropriate. For example, an individual with developmental delays may turn a toy truck upside down and spin its wheels, carry a doll around and suck on its feet, or repeatedly bang a hammer on a toy xylophone.

Typical individuals seem to develop toy play spontaneously, with adult assistance limited to modeling and preventing damage to toys. Certain salient features of toy play among very young typical children may be worth noting. First, such toy play seems autonomous and requires little, if any, social reinforcement by adults to be maintained. In that sense, it has some of the properties of the high-level self-stimulatory behavior outlined in Chapter 6. Second, toy play quite often has a social symbolic component, as when a child pretends to take care of a baby doll by feeding it, putting it to bed, and so forth. Similar symbolic components can be observed in children playing with toy cars, as when a child pretends there is an engine in a car or pretends the car smashes into a wall by making noises appropriate to these actions. Such pretend play has obvious origins in the child's social or interpersonal exposures from which a person with developmental delays may not have benefited. Given these prerequisites, it seems reasonable to predict a delay in pretend play demonstrated by individuals with autism and other developmental delays; however, one would be expected to observe the individual with developmental delays catch up on such toy play as she is taught to benefit from social interactions. One may infer from this that teaching a child to play with toys is facilitated by the child's learning about social behaviors through observation and interaction with adults and peers. Chapter 13 on nonverbal imitation introduces certain aspects of play as an extension of the student's progress in imitating adults and, subsequently, peers.

Toy play can make at least two important contributions to the student's development. First, an increase in toy play is critical to helping the student interact with typical peers because much of peer interaction, including conversational speech among peers, centers around play with toys. Second, an increase in appropriate toy play is accompanied by a decrease in socially inappropriate, self-stimulatory behavior. This decrease in inappropriate behavior makes it easier for the student to be integrated into a least restrictive environment and makes it more likely for the student to be accepted by peers and adults.

In this chapter, we introduce the following kinds of toy play: completing puzzles; using a shape sorter; and playing with cars, dolls, and balls. Also included in this chapter are examples of how to teach preschool games and action songs. The Early Play Skills Program contains teaching principles that may be used to construct many additional programs for forms of play the student needs. The Arts and Crafts Program (Chapter 20) also contains information helpful for developing play.

Once a play skill is taught, the question remains as to how it should be maintained. In the case of students with developmental delays, adults may have to reinforce appropriate play in order to maintain it. At other times, exposure to various kinds of play sensitizes students to particular reinforcers involved in certain types of play. Needless to say, if students are not exposed to such reinforcers, then the reinforcers cannot acquire value. Thus, given that individual students differ largely from one another, it pays to expose the student to several kinds of play in hopes that some forms of play are easily acquired by or reinforcing for the student. An example from everyday life illustrates this idea. Many individuals resist initial exposure to activities such as playing a musical instrument, engaging sports such as basketball and skiing, reading a novel, drawing a picture, or playing with other children. Nevertheless, these persons often learn to enjoy the same activities they first resisted. Without exposure to a particular activity, one does not know what one is missing.

Prior to teaching basic toy play, the student should have made some progress in the following programs: Matching and Sorting, Nonverbal Imitation, and Early

Receptive Language (Chapters 12, 13, and 15, respectively). For example, the student should be able to match three-dimensional (3-D) objects, imitate simple actions with objects (e.g., putting a block in a bucket, holding a doll, moving a toy car), and follow basic instructions (e.g., "Sit down"). Keep in mind the importance of using these programs as means toward facilitating and extending toy play, as in teaching the student to work with Lincoln Logs, build towers, draw letters or pictures, and otherwise engage in more constructive activities than socially inappropriate forms of self-stimulatory behavior.

The current program begins with the teaching of puzzles. However, some teachers may choose to start the toy play program by teaching the preschool games described toward the end of the chapter. For some students, preschool games are easier to teach and more enjoyable (reinforcing) than the other forms of play introduced in this chapter. In any case, we advise intermixing various kinds of play as the student progresses in learning appropriate play skills.

Playing with Puzzles

Although some students may already excel at completing puzzles, others need to be specifically taught to acquire this skill. For those who have not yet mastered puzzles, further exposure to matching stimuli (matching is inherent to completing puzzles) may help establish playing with puzzles as reinforcing in and of itself. To teach the student to complete puzzles, the adult needs two to three items from each of the following sets of materials: (a) inset puzzles with pegs on the pieces (i.e., each piece has a defined location on the board and has a plastic handle on top), (b) inset puzzles without pegs on the pieces, (c) noninterlocking frame tray puzzles (i.e., there is a tray in which to assemble the puzzle and the pieces touch, but do not interlock), (d) interlocking frame tray puzzles (i.e., there is a tray in which to assemble the puzzle and the pieces interlock), and (e) jigsaw puzzles (i.e., puzzles with interlocking pieces and no tray in which to assemble the puzzle).

The First Puzzle

Begin by teaching the student to complete inset puzzles with pegs. This type of puzzle is generally the easiest to teach because each piece has a defined location on the board, none of the pieces touch or interlock, and the pegs on top of the pieces often make it easier for the student to manipulate the pieces. Although some students use the pegs to pick up the pieces without any prior teaching, other students need to be taught this strategy. If the student does not use the peg independently, he can be taught to do so through the use of nonverbal imitation.

Before starting, select a simple four-piece peg puzzle. Start with a puzzle that (a) has pieces that are common shapes (e.g., circle, triangle, square, diamond) and (b) does not have pictures on the board or frame, as pictures may distract the student from the task of completing the puzzle. A shape puzzle is ideal to teach first because each piece in the puzzle has a small number of sides; thus the student will not have to spend a great deal of time trying to fit each piece into place.

▶ Step 1

You and the student should sit directly across from each other at the table or at adjoining sides of the table. Place the puzzle on the table in front of the student and begin teaching by using a backward chaining procedure. That is, place all the pieces in the puzzle except one (e.g., the circle). Hand the student the missing piece (circle) and present the SD ("Do puzzle"). Prompt the response by physically placing your hand over the student's hand and moving his hand with the puzzle piece in it to the correct location. Reinforce the student's correct response. Repeat the trial and gradually fade the prompt over subsequent trials. If the student fails during prompt fading, go back to the least amount of prompt necessary to reestablish correct responding, then resume fading the prompt. Once the manual prompt is completely faded (the student is able to insert the piece into the puzzle on his own), place the piece on the table rather than handing it to the student and prompt by immediately pointing to the puzzle piece after giving the SD. Be sure to reinforce the student as soon as he fits the piece into the proper location. Continue trials using the same piece until the student picks it up and inserts it independently into the proper location in 5 out of 5 or 9 out of 10 trials.

▶ Step 2

Once the student learns to place the first piece in the appropriate location without assistance, remove from the puzzle the piece he just learned to insert and a new piece. Place the pieces on the table beside the puzzle and present the instruction, "Do puzzle." If the student stops after inserting only one piece, prompt him by pointing to, touching, or handing him the second piece. Use the prompt that is effective while being least intrusive. Reinforce the student only after he correctly inserts the two pieces. Repeat the trial and fade all prompts over subsequent trials. Place mastery at the same criterion used in Step 1.

▶ **Step 3**

Remove a third piece from the puzzle, present the SD ("Do puzzle"), and prompt the placement of all three pieces. Place mastery at the same criterion used in Steps 1 and 2.

▶ **Step 4**

Following the procedures described in the preceding steps, provide reinforcement contingent on the student's completing the placement of all the pieces of the puzzle. That is, withhold reinforcement until the student completes the entire puzzle. If the student pauses before inserting all the pieces, prompt if necessary to resume the chain (e.g., by pointing to the form on the board). The procedure of delivering reinforcement contingent on the completion of a gradually increasing number of connected responses is crucial to chaining individual responses into a single response.

▶ **Step 5**

Once the student completes the entire puzzle after you remove all the pieces and place them on the table, teach the student to take out the puzzle pieces on his own. Place the puzzle on the table, present the SD ("Empty"), and then physically prompt the student to turn the puzzle over and dump out the pieces. Repeat the trial and fade the prompt over the next few trials. After the student learns to empty the puzzle independently, teach him to reinsert the pieces. If needed, prompt the student by pointing to a piece or tapping the puzzle. Gradually fade this prompt so that the student can remove the pieces on his own and then replace them without assistance. Reinforce upon the student's emptying and then completing the entire puzzle.

Teaching puzzles may seem like a boring task both for the teacher and the student. Nevertheless, do not forget to be enthusiastic when delivering the reinforcer. Keep in mind the long-range goal that some day your student may learn to enjoy completing puzzles and use this skill to replace lower level forms of self-stimulation.

The Second Puzzle

Introduce a second inset puzzle with pegs that is at a slightly higher level of difficulty than the previous one. For example, the puzzle may now contain pieces that are animals, vehicles, fruit, and the like. Note that such puzzles require a skill similar to that taught in matching (Chapter 12). You will recognize that a puzzle is too difficult if the student verbally protests, shows a high rate of non-responsiveness, or tantrums. Remember, you want to keep the student successful so he enjoys engaging in the activity. Engagement in this activity will help to replace socially inappropriate forms of self-stimulatory behavior. Therefore, choose your targets carefully and be very reinforcing.

The second puzzle should be taught by proceeding through the same sequence of steps used for teaching the first puzzle. Again, using a backward chaining procedure, remove one piece from the completed puzzle and then place it on the table in front of the student. If the student requires some initial assistance placing the piece into the correct location, use a pointing prompt to direct the student to the appropriate space on the puzzle. Continue removing one additional piece at a time and gradually deliver reinforcement contingent upon the student's completion of a larger portion of the puzzle. Finally, present the student with the puzzle and teach him to dump out the pieces and then complete the puzzle as was done with the first puzzle.

Before moving on to more difficult puzzles, give the student other inset puzzles with pegs to ensure that he can be successful with new targets. When you say, "Do puzzle," and present a new puzzle, the student should be able to first dump out the pieces and then complete the puzzle. Keep in mind that, as new puzzles are introduced with pieces that are more detailed than those that compose the initial puzzles, the student may require more time to fit the pieces into place. Therefore, be sure to allow sufficient time for the student to insert each piece. If necessary, provide some form of prompting to help the student complete the puzzle.

Additional Inset Puzzles

Additional inset puzzles should be taught by using the backward chaining procedure described earlier. Once the student masters approximately five inset puzzles with pegs, teach him to do inset puzzles without pegs. This type of puzzle is typically more difficult because it requires the student to maneuver each piece using more of his hand than just his fingers. The student may exhibit some initial difficulty because the pieces are harder to manipulate, but mastery should be reached more quickly in this and subsequent puzzles because the basic skills are the same. Make sure to provide adequate prompting so the student does not become frustrated.

Noninterlocking Frame Tray Puzzles

Once the student becomes proficient at completing inset puzzles (with and without pegs), introduce simple noninterlocking frame tray puzzles. In this type of puzzle, the edges of the pieces touch but do not interlock. These puzzles are assembled within a tray, but the pieces do not have an obvious location on the board (i.e., there is one large space in which to fit together all the pieces as opposed to an individual space for each piece). The student must learn to attend to the pictures on the pieces to successfully complete the puzzle.

▶ **Step 1**

As in earlier programs, start with a puzzle that has relatively few pieces (e.g., four to five pieces). Using the backward chaining procedure, remove one to two pieces and then present the SD ("Do puzzle"). Gradually increase the number of pieces removed, one to two at a time, until the student is able to insert all of the pieces on his own. Proceed through this sequence until the student is capable of completing the puzzle independently by first emptying out all the pieces and then replacing them one at a time.

▶ **Step 2**

Once the student is successful at completing one noninterlocking puzzle, introduce a second noninterlocking puzzle and then a third. When choosing new puzzles, select puzzles that are slightly more difficult than previous ones (i.e., select puzzles with more pieces or more complex pieces). Proceed through the same sequence of steps presented previously until the student can take out the pieces and complete the entire puzzle on his own.

Interlocking Frame Tray Puzzles

After the student masters inset and noninterlocking puzzles, introduce simple interlocking puzzles. Like noninterlocking puzzles, interlocking frame tray puzzles contain a tray in which to assemble the puzzle. However, unlike noninterlocking puzzles, interlocking puzzles have pieces that fit into one another. These puzzles closely resemble jigsaw puzzles in that each piece connects with others and has several sides and indentations. The pieces of interlocking puzzles, however, are larger than jigsaw puzzles and interlocking puzzles are assembled within a framed tray.

Begin with a puzzle that has three or four pieces. As previously recommended, start by removing one piece and then present the SD ("Do puzzle"). If the student has difficulty inserting the piece (e.g., he attempts to fit the piece upside down or backward), prompt the response and then fade the prompt over subsequent trials. Continue removing one to two pieces at a time until the student is able to finish the puzzle without help. Next, teach the student to empty out the pieces on his own as was done with earlier puzzles. Introduce several more interlocking frame tray puzzles, gradually increasing their complexity.

Jigsaw Puzzles

Jigsaw puzzles are the most challenging puzzles, in part because there is no tray in which to assemble the puzzle. The student must make his own border using the outer pieces of the puzzle. As done before, begin with a puzzle that has a relatively few number of pieces (e.g., 4 to 6) and, as the student becomes more proficient, gradually introduce puzzles that contain a greater number of pieces (e.g., 7 to 20). Teach jigsaw puzzles by using the backward chaining procedure presented earlier.

As the puzzles become more difficult, you may want to provide the student with a visual aid such as the picture on the cover of the puzzle's box. This will enable the student to use the picture as a reference for assembling the puzzle and see what the completed picture should look like. When doing jigsaw puzzles, the student needs to use some of the matching skills learned in Chapter 12; that is, to finish the puzzle, the student must fit the pieces together (i.e., match) according to their color and shape.

Areas of Difficulty

Some students are distracted by the puzzle pieces themselves and become preoccupied by playing with them instead of assembling the puzzle. To proceed with teaching puzzles, you must block or otherwise reduce these behaviors and reinforce correct behaviors.

Playing with Shape Sorters

The student should have already gained some exposure to shape matching through the Matching and Sorting Program (Chapter 12) and may enjoy this kind of play because of the intrinsically reinforcing properties of matching. Also, in learning nonverbal imitation involving objects (refer to Chapter 13), the student may have learned to pick up a block and insert it into a shape sorter after the action is modeled by the teacher. The goal of this section is to teach the student to complete the shape sorter independently.

The First Shape Sorter

Select a shape sorter that has three or four shapes (e.g., sphere, cube, pyramid). The first sorter should have holes to insert the shapes only on its top surface so that the student is not required to maneuver the sorter to find the appropriate locations. A sphere is the best shape to teach the student to insert first. This shape is easiest because it should fit into the sorter with less manipulation than, for instance, a pyramid or a star.

▶ **Step 1**

The student should sit at the table beside or across from the teacher. Remove all the blocks from the shape sorter and hand the student the sphere as you present the verbal request (e.g., "Do sorter"). If the student responds correctly by placing the sphere in its appropriate location in 5 out of 5 or 9 out of 10 unprompted trials, move on to Step 3. If the student does not respond correctly or fails to respond, go to Step 2.

▶ **Step 2**

Repeat the SD and immediately prompt the student by pointing to the correct location on the shape sorter. If this prompt does not lead to the correct placement of the shape, use a more intrusive physical prompt in the next trial by placing your hand over the student's hand and guiding it to the correct location on the sorter. Reinforce and gradually fade the physical prompt to a pointing prompt, then fade the prompt completely. Place mastery at the same criterion used in Step 1.

▶ **Step 3**

Once the student masters inserting the sphere into the sorter without assistance, place the sphere beside the shape sorter rather than handing it to the student. Present the instruction ("Play") and physically prompt the correct response. Fade the prompt to a pointing prompt on subsequent trials. Continue to fade the prompt until the student picks up the sphere and places it into the shape sorter unassisted. Again, place mastery at 5 out of 5 or 9 out of 10 unprompted correct responses.

▶ **Step 4**

Remove the first shape from the table before starting Step 4. Now that the student has learned to pick up the sphere and insert it into the sorter after hearing your instruction, introduce a second shape. To maximize the student's success, choose a shape that looks different from the first shape. For example, if the first shape was a sphere, a good next target would be a cube. Present the SD ("Play") and immediately provide the student with a prompt by pointing to the correct location (i.e., square hole) on the shape sorter. This prompt should prevent the student from trying to insert the cube into the hole where the sphere fits. Allow the student some extra time to fit the cube through the hole since this may be her first exposure to these stimuli. Physically prompt the placement of the cube into the sorter if necessary.

Once the student masters inserting the second shape, teach her to insert a third and then a fourth shape, one at a time, following the same procedures used to teach the first two shapes. Before teaching each new shape, clear the table of all other stimuli, putting aside previously taught shapes. Proceed to teach the student to correctly insert each shape into the sorter one at a time, making sure that she learns to independently pick up the shape from the table and insert it before moving to the next stage.

▶ **Step 5**

Position two shapes on the table beside the shape sorter (e.g., cube and sphere) and teach the student to place the two shapes into the shape sorter, one after the other. If the student inserts one of the shapes and then stops, prompt her response by pointing to the remaining shape. Gradually increase the number of shapes presented on the table (e.g., place three shapes on the table, then four, etc.) and provide reinforcement contingent upon the student inserting an increasing number of shapes in each trial; that is, instead of reinforcing the student after she inserts one shape, delay reinforcement contingent on her inserting two shapes, then three shapes, and so on. Mastery is achieved when all of the shapes are presented at once and the student inserts each shape without assistance after given the SD ("Play").

The Second Shape Sorter

The second shape sorter should be taught by proceeding through the same sequence of steps used to teach the first shape sorter. This sorter should have a few more shapes than the first sorter, or the shapes may have more sides (e.g., hexagons, stars, and crosses as opposed to spheres, cubes, and pyramids). In addition, the second shape sorter should have holes on more than one side of it. The student must now learn to turn the cube to find the holes that correspond to the shapes.

Although it is likely that you will need to teach the student to turn the sorter to search for the correct holes, let the student independently try to insert one of the new shapes instead of immediately prompting her response. If prompting is necessary to teach manipulation of the sorter, first prompt by pointing to different sides of the sorter. If this level of prompt is not sufficient, use a more intrusive prompt by physically guiding the student's hands, helping her turn the sorter to reveal the other sides. As you prompt the student, provide a verbal instruction such as "Turn it." By doing this, the student may learn to associate your verbal instruction with the physical action of turning the cube. Gradually fade out the amount of physical prompt provided while continuing to give the instruction and ample reinforcement for completing the response.

Teach the student to insert the shapes one shape at a time as done previously. Withhold reinforcement in gradual steps until the student can insert all of the shapes into the shape sorter. If necessary, continue to verbally prompt the student to turn the sorter. Remember, however, that all prompts must eventually be faded.

Areas of Difficulty

Some students are easily distracted by the shapes and become preoccupied by playing with them instead of inserting them into the cube; the shapes may "invite" self-stimulatory behavior (e.g., gazing at the shapes, placing them in mouth, or spinning them). The student, however, needs to be attentive to your instructions and not engage in self-stimulation if she is to learn to play appropriately with a shape sorter. You may reduce self-stimulatory behaviors by using the techniques described in this section.

Assume you have just presented the SD ("Play") and, instead of inserting a shape into the cube, the student spins it on the table or twirls it in front of her eyes. Consequate this behavior by giving an informational "No" and removing the shape from the student's hand. Present the SD again and hand the shape to the student. If the student spins the shape again, provide another informational "No" and take away the shape. Because the upcoming third trial was immediately preceded by two incorrect responses, you should prompt the student's response. Present the SD, hand the student the block, and simultaneously prompt by tapping the shape sorter or physically guiding the student's hand to the sorter. It is important that you prompt the student immediately after the SD so that she does not have time to self-stimulate with the shape. As soon as the student inserts the shape into the sorter, reinforce her. Perform mass trials of inserting one shape into the shape sorter, prompting the desired response, and gradually fading the prompt over the next few trials.

Remember, the correct response for this task is the student's picking up a shape and then inserting it into the shape sorter. If the student picks up a shape and attempts to twirl it before inserting it, this is an incorrect response and should therefore receive an informational "No" while you withhold the reinforcer. Make sure that the consequence (i.e., "No") occurs as soon as the student begins engaging in the self-stimulatory behavior and not as she inserts the shape into the sorter.

If the student continues to have difficulty, it may be necessary to prompt the correct response by modeling it. To perform a model prompt for this task, two identical shape sorters need to be present on the table. Place one shape sorter in front of you and the other in front of the student. Present the instruction ("Do this") and simultaneously pick up a shape and drop it into the sorter. The student should imitate your action by picking up a shape and inserting it into the sorter. Continue to model the correct response but change the instruction to "Play." Once the student responds correctly (i.e., the student does not play with the shape before inserting it), gradually fade the modeling prompt.

You may also stop the student from engaging in self-stimulatory behavior by providing the student with SDs that are incompatible with the self-stimulatory action. That is, SDs may be presented that require the student to stop engaging in the self-stimulatory behavior in order to make the correct response to the SD. For example, if the student twirls the shapes in front of her eyes, present an SD that requires the student to use her hands (e.g., "Clap" or "Touch toes"). Such SDs allow you to reinforce the student for appropriate behaviors, getting her back on track.

Be sure that the SDs presented do interfere with the self-stimulatory behaviors and are well mastered by the student; they should be instructions with which the student is familiar and to which she has learned the appropriate responses. A variety of SDs may be used from the Early Receptive Language Program (e.g., "Clap," "Wave," "Touch ears") or the Nonverbal Imitation Program (e.g., "Do this" as you clap hands). Keep in mind that you may need to present several mastered SDs in a row; that is, it may be necessary to give a series of receptive instructions or nonverbal imitation tasks in order to get the student back on track. These tasks can be referred to informally as wake-up tasks. As the student correctly responds to these SDs, reinforce her quickly and then immediately reintroduce the target SD ("Play").

Playing with Cars

In the Nonverbal Imitation Program, the student may have learned to imitate pushing a car back and forth on the table. The student may also have learned to perform this behavior upon your request in the Early Receptive Language Program. In this section, the student learns to expand his play with cars through the introduction of additional items such as people, a garage, and road tracks.

To teach car play, the following materials are needed: two identical toy cars with places for toy people, two little toy people that fit in the cars, one toy car garage with a ramp, and a set of plastic pieces that connect into a 2- to 6-foot long track. In selecting appropriate stimuli for this program, begin by choosing cars and people that are limited in detail so that distractions are minimized. For example, do not begin by using cars that have doors that open or people with movable arms and legs.

Before beginning this component of the Early Play Skills Program, the student should have learned to imitate single and chained actions with and without objects and he should have made some progress in the Early Receptive Language Program (Chapter 15).

Playing with a Car and a Garage

▶ Step 1

Seat the student across the table from you or at an adjacent side. Place one car in front of you and another in front of the student. Place a toy person next to each car. Present the SD ("Do this") as you pick up your person, place it in the car, and then push the car back and forth on the table. If the student imitates your actions, immediately reinforce. If he fails to respond correctly, prompt by physically guiding the student to put the person into the car and push the car back and forth on the table. Gradually fade this prompt by providing less assistance on each trial.

If the student is verbal, you can teach him to imitate sounds as he pushes the car (e.g., "Beep-beep" or "Vroom"). Make sure the sounds you choose are ones the student can successfully imitate in the Verbal Imitation Program (Chapter 22). If the student has difficulty combining the physical actions and the verbalizations, these behaviors should be taught separately by first teaching the student to place the toy figures in the car, then to push the car, and then to push the car while vocalizing appropriately (the vocalizations should be brought to mastery in verbal imitation before they are added to the physical action). Finally, these behaviors should be chained into the sequence of actions described previously. Have the student practice the complete response until criterion is achieved (5 out of 5 or 9 out of 10 unprompted correct responses).

▶ Step 2

Set up the materials in the same format used in Step 1. For this step, add a toy garage to the stimuli and place it on the table either between you and the student or off to the side of the table. Then proceed to teach the student to imitate a chain of three actions. Present the SD ("Do this") as you place the person in the car and push the car back and forth on the table. Immediately after the student imitates these actions, quickly reinforce him and then present the SD ("Do this") again, placing your car at the top of the garage ramp and rolling it down. If the student imitates these actions, reinforce him. If the student does not imitate your actions, assist him with a prompt on the next trial. Begin with the least intrusive prompt possible by first pointing to the top of the ramp. If this does not occasion the desired response, use a physical prompt by gently guiding the student's hand to the top of the ramp as he holds the car and then help him to roll the car down. Gradually fade this prompt and place mastery at the same criterion used in Step 1.

▶ Step 3

Continue to present mass trials of the action sequence described in Step 2 (i.e., place the person in the car, push the car back and forth, and then roll the car down the garage ramp). This time, however, instead of giving the SD twice, present it once at the beginning of the sequence (i.e., as you put the person in the car). Gradually withhold reinforcement until the student imitates all the actions in the sequence. Thus, instead of reinforcing the student after he picks up the person and places it in the car, wait until he has completed the response by rolling the car down the ramp of the garage. After the student responds to criterion, proceed to the next step.

▶ Step 4

In this step, teach the student to engage in the chain presented above after being verbally instructed to do so. Position the materials in the same manner as done before. Present the SD ("Do this") and simultaneously model the response. After the student has completed one successful trial, change the SD from "Do this" to "Play with garage" and model the sequence again (i.e., put the person in the car and then roll the car down the ramp of the garage). Gradually fade the modeling sequence as a prompt so that the student learns to play with the car and garage when you say to the student, "Play with garage," without first showing him what to do.

Connecting Road Tracks

Connecting road tracks is an activity that is similar to assembling puzzles, described earlier. It is important to begin with road tracks that are relatively easy to assemble. Tracks that require the student to hold them at a certain angle to fit them together or that require precise placement before they connect are likely to frustrate the student. Therefore, select large tracks the student can connect with relative ease. Also, ensure that the toy cars used with the tracks are sized so they fit easily on the tracks. Initially avoid tracks that have grooves designated for wheels.

▶ Step 1

You and the student should sit at the table across from one another. Place two pieces of track in front of you and two pieces in front of the student. Present the SD ("Do this") and connect your two pieces of track. If the student imitates your actions and connects his tracks, reinforce him. If the student responds incorrectly or fails to respond, prompt on the next trial by placing your hands over his, physically guiding the student to connect the tracks. Gradually fade the amount of assistance provided on subsequent trials. After approximately two consecutive successful trials, change the SD from "Do this" to "Play with tracks" and continue to model the correct response. Gradually start to fade the modeling sequence as a prompt. The goal is to have the SD ("Play with tracks") occasion the appropriate response independent of prompting. Be ready, however, to assist the student by saying, "Do this," and modeling the response. Once the student is able to connect the tracks without prompting when presented with the instruction "Play with tracks," proceed to the next step.

▶ Step 2

One at a time, increase the number of tracks placed on the table. Begin by placing three tracks in front of the student and presenting the SD ("Play with tracks"). If the student successfully connects the tracks, continue to introduce one additional piece of track at a time, up to approximately five or six pieces. For a few trials, moderately reinforce the student each time he connects a piece of track and save the big reinforcer for the end of the chain. Gradually begin to withhold all reinforcement until the student successfully connects all of the tracks as a single response.

If the student has difficulty connecting additional pieces of track or stops after connecting the first two pieces, prompt him to continue by tapping the remaining pieces of track while saying, "Keep going" or "Finish." By repeatedly pairing the verbal prompt with the nonverbal cue (in this case, the tap), the student may eventually learn to follow the instruction when presented without the visual component.

▶ Step 3

Place several pieces of track on the table along with a car, and present the SD ("Play with tracks"). After the student assembles the track, present the SD ("Do this") and model pushing the car along the tracks. If the student responds correctly and pushes the car along the tracks, reinforce him. If the student responds incorrectly or fails to respond, provide a physical prompt on the next trial by gently placing your hand over his hand, helping him to push the car along the tracks. Remember to gradually fade this prompt and any additional prompts so that the student learns to connect the tracks and then push the car along them when he hears the SD ("Play with tracks").

Extending Car Play

You can teach the student a variety of additional car play skills through the use of nonverbal imitation. This extension may progress in several different directions. First, the student can be taught new actions using the toys with which he has already mastered actions. For example, the student may be taught to put "gas" in the car, park the car in the garage, or push the car around on the floor. Second, the student can be taught to perform actions similar to those already mastered but use different toys to perform these actions. For example, the student may learn to push a train (instead of a car) along a new set of tracks. Third, different toys, such as airplanes, can be used to teach the student new actions such as flying an airplane and then landing on a runway.

When teaching the student new activities or play with novel toys, remember to proceed in a manner similar to the steps described previously. That is, begin by breaking down each new task into separate components and then gradually build up to the entire sequence. If the goal is to teach the student to assemble train tracks, put people in a train, and then push the train along the track, remember to first teach each of these tasks individually.

Areas of Difficulty

The student may engage in self-stimulatory behavior with the cars instead of playing with them appropriately. For example, the student may prefer to turn the car upside down and spin its wheels instead of pushing it along the table. Similarly, the student may self-stimulate by lowering his head until the car is at eye level, and watching the wheels turn as he pushes the car back and forth.

Each new response the student is to learn should be taught in small steps to help replace self-stimulatory behavior. For example, if the student self-stimulates by spinning the car's wheels, teach him to push the car back and forth along the table without self-stimulating *before* you teach him to roll it down the ramp of the garage. Then, once the self-stimulatory behavior has been successfully reduced, move on to teaching additional actions.

As with other toys and activities, the student may not initially enjoy playing with cars. However, it is important to provide the student with an adequate amount of prompting and reinforcement to appropriately test whether he finds this kind of play reinforcing. If, despite your best teaching efforts, the student shows no interest in playing with cars, switch to another form of toy play. The student may acquire an interest in car play at a later time.

Playing with Dolls

The following materials are needed to teach doll play: two baby dolls, two baby bottles, a crib, and a small blanket. Prior to beginning this component of the Early Play Skills Program, the student should have learned to imitate actions involving objects and two-action chains. The student should also have gained some exposure to receptive instructions.

As with many other play programs, doll play is initially taught through imitation; you model playing with a doll and teach the student to imitate the actions. As the student becomes proficient at imitating different actions with dolls, the student is taught to engage in these actions in response to a receptive request (e.g., "Rock baby"). It is important to emphasize the facilitating effect of real-life interactions with their symbolic counterparts (e.g., toys). For example, toy play with dolls may transfer to congruent actions with babies and small children. Because a common language unites the two counterparts, learning the language associated with certain actions will help to mediate the transfer of skills from the symbolic to the actual. Early play skills that are established at this time will be intermixed, extended, and elaborated as the student grows older and learns more about parallel events in her everyday environment. It is then that the student's play becomes more consequential.

Patting a Doll

▶ **Step 1**

You and the student should sit facing one another in front of the table. Place both dolls on the table, one next to yourself and one next to the student. Present the SD ("Do this") as you pick up the doll, hold it up to your chest, and pat it on the back. If the student responds correctly and imitates your actions, reinforce. If the student fails to respond or responds incorrectly, simplify the task by teaching only the first behavior in the sequence (i.e., picking up the doll) and physically prompting the response. Fade the prompt and gradually add additional behaviors and reinforce contingent on the longer chain (sequence of behaviors). Place mastery at imitation of the entire chain (i.e., picking up the doll, holding it against the chest, and patting its back) in 5 out 5 or 9 out 10 unprompted trials.

▶ **Step 2**

Change the SD from "Do this" and the model to the instruction "Pat baby" by gradually fading out the model prompt. Set mastery at the same criterion used in Step 1.

Rocking a Doll

▶ **Step 1**

Maintain the physical arrangement above. Present the SD ("Do this") as you pick up the baby and then rock it back and forth in your arms. If the student responds correctly and imitates your actions, reinforce. If the student fails to respond or responds incorrectly, prompt her as you did previously and then fade this prompt over time. Once the student is able to imitate rocking the doll in 5 out of 5 or 9 out of 10 unprompted trials, proceed to the next step.

▶ **Step 2**

Repeat Step 1. However, this time change the SD from "Do this" to "Rock baby." Gradually fade the model prompt so that the student learns to respond to the receptive instruction "Rock baby" without prompting.

Additional Doll Play Skills

A variety of doll play skills may be taught through imitation. For instance, the student may be taught to place a doll in a crib and then pretend to feed it with a bottle and cover it with a blanket. These actions should first be taught through imitation. Then, once the student masters the actions with a model, the student may be taught to play when given instructions appropriate to the behavior (e.g., "Feed baby" or "Dress baby").

As with car play, the student may eventually be taught to perform a series of interrelated behaviors when given a general instruction such as "Play with dolls." However, anticipate that it will take a great deal of prompting and reinforcement to build a chain of behaviors that create complex forms of doll play. Remember to first teach each behavior separately and then proceed to chain more elaborate sequences by providing reinforcement contingent on an increasingly longer series of behaviors.

Areas of Difficulty

As with other toy play activities, the student may self-stimulate with the dolls instead of playing appropriately. To help remedy this problem, become familiar with the guidelines presented under the "Areas of Difficulty" section of "Playing with Cars." It is also possible that the student may not find doll play reinforcing and cease playing with dolls when not extrinsically reinforced. However, it is important to remember that peers may eventually be able to provide the extra reinforcement necessary for maintenance of this skill. If, despite your best teaching efforts, the student continues to show no interest in playing with dolls or finds this type of play aversive, switch to another form of toy play. The student may acquire an interest in doll play at a later time when gaining behaviors relevant to real-life events.

Playing with Balls

To teach the student basic ball play skills, such as rolling, throwing, and catching, you need a large, soft, inflatable ball (e.g., a beach ball). Using a soft ball will prevent the student from getting hurt, which in turn will help prevent him from fearing and cowering from the ball when it is thrown to him. Also, a large ball will aid in the student's acquisition of catching because large balls are generally easier to catch than small balls. In the future, however, balls of varying size and weight should be introduced for the purpose of generalization.

Rolling a Ball

▶ **Step 1**

Two teachers are needed for this program. One teacher and the student should sit on the floor facing each other, approximately 4 to 5 feet apart, with their legs open in a V position. A second teacher should sit directly behind the student to prompt the correct sitting position and appropriate responses to the first teacher's SDs. Once both adults and the student are positioned, the first teacher presents the SD ("Catch") while rolling the ball to the student. The adult seated behind the student physically prompts the student to catch the ball by holding the student's arms out in front of him and clasping his hands around the ball. Both adults immediately reinforce the student for catching the ball. Continue to roll the ball to the student and gradually fade the amount of assistance provided. For example, fade the full physical prompt by lessening the intrusiveness of the prompt until just a tap on the student's elbows occasions the correct response. Once this level of prompting is reached, fade the prompt completely until the student catches the ball independently in 5 out of 5 or 9 out of 10 trials. After this criterion is met, go on to Step 2.

▶ **Step 2**

Assume the same positions taken in Step 1. The first teacher presents the SD ("Catch") while rolling the ball to the student. Immediately after the student catches the ball, reinforce him. Next teach the student to reciprocate the action by prompting the student to roll the ball back to the teacher. The first teacher presents the SD ("Roll") and the second teacher (seated behind the student) prompts the response by helping the student push the ball toward the teacher. Reinforce the response. Continue taking turns rolling the ball back and forth, gradually fading the amount of prompting provided on each trial. Place mastery at 5 out of 5 or 9 out of 10 unprompted correct responses.

▶ **Step 3**

Continue rolling the ball back and forth. However, in this step, instead of providing an SD for each trial (i.e., "Catch" and "Roll"), state a more general SD at the beginning of the trial (e.g., "Let's play ball") and begin chaining the two behaviors (catch and roll). Fade the SDs "Catch" and "Roll" by providing these SDs on every second trial, then every third trial, and so on until only the more general SD ("Let's play ball") is provided. If the student fails to respond appropriately (e.g., he does not roll the ball back to the teacher), reintroduce the least intrusive prompt that is effective at producing the correct response. Fade this prompt as quickly as possible. Once the skill is mastered (5 out of 5 or 9 out of 10 unprompted correct trials), slowly fade out the adult's assistance from behind the student. This may be done by having the adult move from sitting directly behind the student to sitting 1 to 2 feet back, then kneeling behind the student, then standing, and so on. The first teacher should continue to provide SDs while the distance between the student and the second adult is gradually increased until the second adult is completely removed.

▶ **Step 4**

Deliver reinforcement contingent on the student's rolling *and* catching the ball as one response. Also, gradually increase the distance between the teacher and the student approximately 1 to 2 feet at a time. Set mastery at 5 out of 5 or 9 out of 10 unprompted correct responses.

Catching and Throwing a Ball

▶ **Step 1**

The teacher and student should stand facing one another at a distance of approximately 2 to 3 feet. A second adult should stand behind the student and provide prompting. Once the student and both adults are positioned, give the SD ("Catch") and lightly toss the ball into the student's outstretched arms (held in place by the second teacher). Over trials, gradually fade the amount of physical prompting and increase the distance from 3 to 5 feet. Reinforce the student once he independently catches the ball in 5 out of 5 or 9 out of 10 trials.

▶ **Step 2**

Now that the student can catch the ball, teach him to throw the ball back to the teacher. One adult should stand directly behind the student and the other adult should face the student and stand approximately 2 to 3 feet away. Once the adults and student are positioned, present the SD ("Throw"). If necessary, prompt the response by physically helping the student throw the ball underhand back to the teacher. Reinforce the response. Fade the prompt by providing less assistance on each successive trial.

▶ **Step 3**

Continue to throw the ball back and forth as done in Step 2, but now start to shape the behavior so that the student throws the ball back to the teacher immediately after catching it (i.e., chain the behaviors). Gradually fade the individual SDs ("Catch" and "Throw"), as done previously in Step 3 for rolling a ball. Shift the reinforcement until it becomes contingent on completing both behaviors (catching and throwing). Finally, once the student is able to catch and throw the ball with little or no assistance, increase the distance between the teacher and the student and gradually remove the adult from behind the student.

As the student becomes more proficient at throwing and catching, begin introducing different balls. Each time a ball is introduced, it should be only slightly heavier and smaller in size than the one that directly preceded it.

Areas of Difficulty

Some students are unable to hold onto the ball once it is thrown to them and try to compensate by catching the ball using their arms instead of their hands. Pretraining exercises may be used to remedy this problem. Begin by having one adult hold the ball while a second adult prompts the student to pull the ball out of the other adult's hands (SD is "Get ball" or "Pull"). By doing this, the student learns to use his hands to grasp the ball. After the student practices pulling the ball out of the teacher's hands, reintroduce catching and use a full physical prompt. As the student becomes more adept at catching the ball with his hands, fade the prompt and increase the distance between the teacher and the student.

If the student continues to have difficulty catching the ball, try using a large balloon instead of an inflatable ball. A balloon should be easier for the student to catch because it stays airborne longer than a ball. Thus, the student will have a longer period of time in which to prepare to catch the balloon.

Given that students vary greatly in their gross motor abilities, the acquisition of ball play skills will be more difficult for some students than others. Similarly, whereas some students demonstrate an immediate interest in ball play, others react indifferently. However, by providing ample reinforcement and adequate prompting, most students learn to enjoy ball play.

Preschool Games

Prior to being taught to play basic preschool games, the student should have mastered a variety of behaviors in nonverbal imitation (e.g., stand up, pat legs, touch head, clap, jump) and simple receptive instructions (e.g., "Stand up," "Clap"). It is important that the student has previously mastered instructions and imitative actions that require moving around the room in addition to those performed while seated in a chair. Because the majority of preschool games require a circle-time format, the student must be able to sit on the floor with a group of people for at least 1 minute. It is helpful but not necessary for the student to have some verbal ability (e.g., verbal imitation, expressive labeling of objects). If the student is not verbal, she will still be able to participate by performing actions.

The student may be taught any of numerous preschool games (e.g., Hot Potato, Duck Duck Goose, Musical Chairs, Tag) and action songs (e.g., Ring Around the Rosie, Itsy Bitsy Spider). Keep in mind that, as with other play skills, some students may not initially find these games and songs to be reinforcing; however, others may enjoy the self-stimulatory properties of songs such as Itsy Bitsy Spider. It is important that everyone in the group enthusiastically reinforces the student for playing or singing, making the experience as much fun as possible.

Hot Potato

We use the game Hot Potato as an illustration because this game is relatively easy to teach and the skills involved are basic and relatively easy to prompt. If the student has limited verbal ability or is unable to imitate words or sounds, this section can be taught by eliminating the verbal component.

Before proceeding, an object that can serve as the hot potato must be found. It is not necessary to use a real potato, and it is actually preferable to use an object that is softer and lighter than a potato (e.g., a beanbag or small ball). A lighter object may be easier for the student to pass and no one in the game will be injured if the object is accidentally thrown too vigorously.

At least three people (the student, a teacher, and another person) are needed to begin teaching the game; however, a group size of approximately four to six is ideal. In the future, siblings or other individuals may be included in the group, but only adults who have experience teaching the student should participate initially.

► **Step 1**

The student and other participants should sit on the floor in a circle. One person should be designated as the teacher and lead the game. The student should sit immediately to the teacher's right, being the last person to have a turn in the circle. The person on the other side of the student (i.e., the person immediately to the student's right) functions as the prompter.

► **Step 2**

The teacher presents the SD ("Hot potato!") and passes the item representing the potato in a clockwise direction. Upon receiving the potato, the second person says, "Hot potato!" and passes the object to the next person in the circle, and so on. When it is the student's turn to be given the potato, the prompter may need to assist the student to respond correctly. If necessary, the prompter should provide the SD ("Hot potato!") and physically prompt the student to catch the "potato" and pass it to the teacher. If the student fails to respond correctly, present an SD with which she is familiar (e.g., "Catch") and physically prompt her to respond correctly. Gradually fade all prompts

► **Step 3**

Repeat Steps 1 and 2 until the student is able to pass the potato without any assistance. Gradually increase the speed with which the potato is passed until the student learns to toss the potato quickly after receiving it. Also, vary the student's location within the circle so she does not always receive the potato last.

Additional preschool games can be taught by following steps similar to those described above. Simplify various components of the game as much as necessary to keep the student successful. As elementary games are mastered, more difficult games should be introduced.

Singing Action Songs

Most students enjoy singing songs, which is helpful when preparing them for preschool. As with games, the student does not have to be verbal to participate in action songs. If the student is unable to sing along with the group, she can participate by performing the appropriate actions. Action songs may be taught in a one-on-one setting (i.e., with the teacher and student) or in a circle-time format. All participants should sing the songs and perform the behaviors that correspond to the lyrics.

To keep the student successful, some of the actions may need to be simplified or the song's pace slowed down. If at any time the student does not imitate your behaviors or stops singing, provide her with a receptive instruction (e.g., "Clap" or "Sing") or prompt her to imitate your actions (i.e., say, "Do this," as you model an action). As you may know, the words of the songs should cue various behaviors. Sets of words to three of the more popular action songs follow. Note the self-stimulatory properties of rhymes such as "stout," "spout," "shout," "trout," "out," or repetitions as in "round," "round," and "round." "Edited echolalia" may be a fitting description for such socially acceptable and self-reinforcing behaviors.

I'm a Little Teapot

I'm a little teapot short and stout,
Here is my handle and here is my spout.
When I get all steamed up, hear me shout.
Tip me over and pour me out.

Wheels on the Bus

The wheels on the bus go round and round, round and round, round and round.
The wheels on the bus go round and round, all through the town.
The people on the bus go up and down, up and down, up and down.
The people on the bus go up and down, all through the town.
The wipers on the bus go swish, swish, swish. Swish, swish, swish. Swish, swish, swish.
The wipers on the bus go swish, swish, swish, all through the town.
The babies on the bus go waa, waa, waa. Waa, waa, waa. Waa, waa, waa.
The babies on the bus go waa, waa, waa, all through the town.
The driver on the bus says, "Move on back," "Move on back," "Move on back.
The driver on the bus says, "Move on back," all through the town.

If You're Happy and You Know It

If you're happy and you know it, clap your hands.
If you're happy and you know it, clap your hands.
If you're happy and you know it, and you really want to show it, if you're happy and you know it, clap your hands.
If you're mad and you know it, stomp your feet.
If you're mad and you know it, stomp your feet.
If you're mad and you know it, and you really want to show it, if you're mad and you know it stomp your feet.

Arts and Crafts

CHAPTER 20

The six portions of the Arts and Crafts Program presented in this chapter are intended to help students with developmental delays adjust to preschool and prekindergarten environments, as well as to help them engage in socially appropriate arts and crafts play behaviors during their free time. The portions of the program that constitute this chapter are presented in the following order: (1) block building, (2) drawing, (3) cutting with scissors, (4) gluing, (5) painting, and (6) writing longhand. Each portion consists of one or more phases, and each portion and phase within the program is laid out in order of apparent difficulty.

Certain portions of the Arts and Crafts Program may be introduced in the beginning stages of treatment by, for example, teaching imitation of simple block building as an extension of the Nonverbal Imitation Program. As the student progresses through treatment, various portions of the Arts and Crafts Program appropriate to the student's skill level may be continued into the teaching of such programs as the Prepositions Program (Chapter 27) and the Reading and Writing Program (Chapter 29). Thus, although teaching the student to build with blocks is somewhat elementary and may be accomplished very early in treatment, teaching a student to write his own name (see Chapter 29) is relatively difficult and may best be introduced after the student has shown extensive mastery of Matching and Sorting (Chapter 12), Nonverbal Imitation (Chapter 13), and Receptive Language (Chapters 15, 17, and 18).

Given the large individual differences among students, you must be sensitive not only to variations in the particular student's overall rate of learning but also to the variability the student may show across and within certain types of programs. For example, in this program, the student may excel at block building and painting but experience considerable difficulty with drawing and cutting. Given such complexity, it is our advice to work as a team with other teachers and invite and be open to feedback regarding this and all of the other programs presented in this manual.

Block Building

Most preschoolers enjoy building with blocks alone or in interaction with others. Younger children typically stack blocks, whereas older children build complex structures such as houses, fortresses, bridges, and mazes. Typical children often imitate others' moves when they build with blocks and tell each other how and what they are building. Many students with developmental delays learn to become ardent block builders as well, and some learn to build intricate and complex structures. Others may find block building less reinforcing at first, but deserve a fair chance at finding out whether they will learn to enjoy this activity over time.

Block building is a relatively easy task for the teacher to instruct and for the student to learn. It provides an opportunity for the student to generalize matching and nonverbal imitation skills into an area of play while learning to attend to increasingly complex visual stimuli. Through an increase in sharpness of attention, the student acquires creativity and problem-solving skills. In addition, block building is an ideal facilitator of conversational speech among students, adults, and peers.

Block building should initially be taught at the table, because it is easier to structure tasks at the table than on the floor given that the table and chair setting provides for more control over the student's behavior and, thus, acquisition of new skills. You may extend block building to the floor after the student becomes proficient at building at the table. Trials of block building may be performed efficiently by placing a bin containing the blocks on a chair next to the table, facilitating quick placement of the blocks on the table as needed.

In choosing the initial stimuli, keep in mind that the student may experience less success in early stages of block building if all the blocks used are identical in color, size, and shape. You should therefore use such stimuli as Tootsie Toys 100 Blocks, which come in various colors, sizes, and shapes. Tootsie Toys 100 Blocks are available in major toy and department stores.

The progression of block building is described through the following nine phases: (1) imitating the teacher building on and around a base block, (2) imitating the teacher building a structure one block at a time, (3) imitating the teacher building a structure without a prepositioned base block, (4) imitating the teacher chaining blocks, (5) copying the teacher's prebuilt block structure, (6) copying the teacher's block structure built behind a screen, (7) copying block structures in photographs, (8) building a block structure upon the teacher's request, and (9) building with different kinds of blocks.

Phase 1: Imitating the Teacher Building On and Around a Base Block

You may facilitate the student's initial imitation of block building by using two blocks only: a base block and a placement block. Two identical sets of blocks (i.e., two identical base blocks and two identical placement blocks) are needed for Phase 1. In this phase, you position the two base blocks on the table such that one is in front of the student and the other is in front of you. You then demonstrate positioning the placement block in various locations in relation to the base block. The student is to respond by imitating the arrangements of the placement block. You may position the placement block *on top of* the base block, *next to* the base block, *in front of* the base block, or *behind* the base block.

For the sake of illustration, let the base blocks be two identical relatively big, red, rectangular blocks placed flat on the table, one in front of the student and one in front of yourself. Let the placement blocks be two yellow blocks that are otherwise identical in size and shape to the base blocks. Position one placement block to the right of the student (if the student is right handed) and about 6 to 8 inches from the student's base block. Position the other placement block 6 to 8 inches to the left of your base block, and then go on to Step 1. The placement block should be removed from the table between each trial.

▶ Step 1

Mass trial SD1 to mastery (e.g., placement of the yellow block *on top of* the base block). Present SD1, which consists of the instruction "Do this" while picking up, moving, and placing the yellow placement block on top of the base block. Prompt the student's response by, for example, manually prompting her to pick up her yellow placement block and place it on top of her base block. Reinforce the response and remove the blocks from the table. Over the next few trials, gradually fade the physical prompt to a less intrusive prompt such as pointing to the student's placement block, then fade all prompts completely. Set mastery at 5 out of 5 or 9 out of 10 unprompted correct responses.

▶ Step 2

Mass trial SD2 to mastery (e.g., placement of the yellow block *in front of* the base block). Present SD2, which consists of the instruction "Do this" while picking up, moving, and placing the yellow placement block in front of the base block. Following the teaching procedures described in Step 1, set mastery at 5 out of 5 or 9 out of 10 unprompted correct responses.

▶ Step 3

Intermix SD1 (i.e., placement of the yellow block on top of the base block) and SD2 (i.e., placement of the yellow block in front of the base block) according to the discrimination learning paradigm (see Chapter 16). Begin by presenting SD1 and set mastery at 3 consecutive unprompted correct responses in a row. If prompts are needed initially, fade them over subsequent trials and maximize reinforcement for unprompted trials. Two seconds after the student reaches mastery of SD1, present SD2. Prompt the student's correct response if needed. Again set mastery at 3 unprompted correct responses in a row. Over successive trials, gradually reduce the number of consecutive unprompted correct responses from 3 to 2 and finally to 1 before alternating between SDs. If the student makes an error, such as responding with R2 to SD1, immediately interrupt the response by retrieving the placement block and withholding reinforcement while giving an informational "No." Repeat SD1, prompt R1, reinforce the response, and then fade the prompt over the next few trials. Over successive intermixed, randomly rotated, and differentially reinforced trials, the student will make fewer and fewer mistakes and eventually master the discrimination (i.e., responding correctly in 5 out of 5 or 9 out of 10 trials). This discrimination occurs as the associations between SD1–R1 and SD2–R2 are strengthened because they are reinforced, and mistakes such as SD1–R2 are weakened because they are not reinforced.

▶ **Step 4**

Mass trial SD3 to mastery (e.g., placement of the yellow block *next to* the base block) by following the procedures outlined in Step 1. Once SD3 is mastered separately, intermix SD3 first with SD1 and then with SD2, adhering to the discrimination learning paradigm outlined in Step 3. Set mastery at 5 out of 5 or 9 out of 10 unprompted correct responses.

▶ **Step 5**

Mass trial SD4 to mastery (e.g., placement of the yellow block *behind* the base block) by following the procedures outlined in Step 1. Once SD4 is mastered separately, intermix SD4 first with SD1, then with SD2, and finally with SD3, according to discrimination learning procedures. Set mastery at 5 out of 5 or 9 out of 10 unprompted correct responses. Finally, gradually generalize the student's building skill from building exclusively with the yellow rectangular placement block to building with novel placement blocks.

Phase 2: Imitating the Teacher Building a Structure One Block at a Time

In this phase of the program, the student learns through imitation to build a small structure with two placement blocks (e.g., a yellow block and a blue block) identical in size to the base block. As done in the previous phase, position one base block in front of the student and one in front of yourself. Horizontally line up two placement blocks approximately 6 to 8 inches to the right of the student's base block and two to the left of your base block.

Once the blocks are in position, pick up the placement block closest to the base block and instruct, "Do this," while placing the block *next to* the base block so that the two blocks are equal in height. Manually prompt the response if necessary. Once the student places her block, pick up the second placement block and say, "Do this," while placing the block *on top of* the two adjoining blocks. If necessary, prompt the student's response and fade the prompt over successive trials. After reinforcing the correct response, remove the placement blocks and return them to their original positions on the side of the table. Set mastery at 5 out of 5 or 9 out of 10 unprompted correct responses.

To reduce inadvertent prompts and facilitate generalization to other structures, begin randomizing the shape and color of the placement blocks and the shape and color of the base blocks. In addition, position the placement blocks in various locations relative to the base block. Systematically increase the number of placement blocks from two to six and then vary the number of placement blocks used in each structure. Also, randomly rotate the position of the placement blocks in the lineup next to the base block, remembering to choose the placement block nearest the base block each time a placement block is arranged in the structure.

Phase 3: Imitating the Teacher Building a Structure Without a Base Block

In Phases 1 and 2, a prepositioned base block helped simplify the task for the student. Similarly, the placement blocks were arranged in a horizontal line at the side of the table, helping the student to select the correct blocks. To aid the student's mastery of block building in a more natural setting, both kinds of prompts are removed in this phase.

Begin this phase by placing on the table two identical "piles" of two blocks, one pile for the student and one pile for yourself. Present SD1 by saying, "Do this," while picking up a block from the pile closest to you and placing it on the table in front of yourself. Slow and exaggerated motions may facilitate the student's attending to the SD. If necessary, prompt the student's correct response by, for example, pointing to the identical block in the student's pile or separating the block out from her pile and positioning it closer to her. Reinforce the student's correct response. Then follow up by picking up a second block and placing it in somewhere in relation to the first block. Prompt as needed. Fade all prompts over subsequent trials.

After the student masters building with two blocks using the procedures outlined for this phase, add a third block to each pile. Once the student masters building from a pile of three blocks, gradually continue to add blocks to each pile. As the student learns to build from a larger pile of blocks, vary the number of blocks used in each structure, teaching the student that not every block needs to be used in every structure. Eventually place all the blocks—yours and the student's blocks—into a bin located on the side of the table and teach the student to choose the correct blocks from the bin. Some students will learn to build structures (e.g., bridges and fortresses) consisting of 10 to 15 blocks when modeled in a one-by-one stepwise fashion. When the student can build complex structures in this manner with ease, proceed to the next phase.

Phase 4: Imitating the Teacher Chaining Two Blocks

Thus far the student has built structures following your model. In the present phase, the student learns to be less dependent on your prompts and begins to initiate building, establishing her own steps as the stimuli for the next steps.

Place two sets of blocks consisting of two identical but random blocks on the table, one set for the student and one set for yourself. Instruct, "Build this," while picking up and positioning one block on the table and immediately picking up and placing the other block *next to* the first block. If necessary, manually prompt the student to pick up and position her blocks such that they duplicate your structure. Repeat the SD and fade the manual prompt over trials. Although both prompted and unprompted correct responses should be reinforced, reinforcement for *unprompted* correct responses should be maximized. Make sure that reinforcement is withheld, however, until the student completes the placement of both blocks, as this chain of responses constitutes the correct response. Eventually the student's placement of the first block will provide the stimulus for the placement of the second block. Once mastery is achieved (5 out of 5 or 9 out of 10 unprompted correct responses), generalize to novel sets of two blocks. In the following phase, expand upon the chaining learned in the current phase by presenting prebuilt block structures of more than two blocks.

Phase 5: Copying the Teacher's Prebuilt Block Structure

In this phase, the student is taught to duplicate a structure you build in its entirety while the student watches. Begin this phase by piling two identical sets of three blocks on each side of the table, one set for the student and one set for yourself. Build a simple structure (e.g., two blocks placed side by side and the third placed on top of the first two to make a bridge). Point to the structure and say, "Build this." If necessary, prompt the student's response. Gradually fade prompts over subsequent trials, maximizing reinforcement for unprompted correct responses. The student has mastered this phase once she responds correctly in 5 out of 5 or 9 out of 10 unprompted trials. Once mastery is reached, increase the complexity of this phase by adding blocks to the piles and modeling gradually more elaborate structures. Increase the number of blocks in the structures to a maximum of 10 to 15 blocks, depending on the student's rate of success. Eventually place the blocks used in the structures plus any distracter blocks (i.e., extra blocks) in a container next to the table.

Phase 6: Copying the Teacher's Block Structure Built Behind a Screen

In this phase, you build a structure behind a screen (e.g., a sheet of paper or the lid of a container), remove the screen, and then teach the student to duplicate the structure. The student's responses should initially be facilitated by presenting her with the exact number of blocks she needs to build the structure. Begin with three to four blocks and build a structure behind the screen. Once the structure is completed, remove the screen, point to the structure, and say, "Build this." Teach the student to copy three to four different structures in this manner before adding blocks to the structure. Once the student can imitate different structures consisting of 10 to 12 blocks picked from a bin containing the blocks needed plus several additional distracter blocks, move on to the next phase.

Phase 7: Copying Block Structures in Photographs

Present photographs or well-drawn colored representations of block structures as models. The stimuli must clearly show each block in the structure, and photographs should be taken against a white or neutral uncluttered background. Start with a photograph or colored drawing of a two-block structure and present the student with the exact number of blocks needed to copy the model structure. Show the student the picture of the structure and say, "Build this." Facilitate the student's response by positioning the picture upright. Gradually fade this prompt by lowering the picture until it is positioned flat on the table. Pointing to the blocks in the picture and to the corresponding blocks on the table may also be helpful. Fade all prompts gradually over trials. Set mastery of each structure at 5 out of 5 or 9 out of 10 unprompted correct responses. The number of blocks in each structure should not exceed 10 to 12.

Once the student can build a number of structures from pictures, present pictures of structures that mimic objects, such as tables, chairs, and couches. A block table can be built by positioning a rectangular block (the tabletop) on top of two smaller square blocks (the legs). A chair can be built by positioning a square block upright (the backrest) behind another square block (the seat). A couch may be build much like a chair only with long rectangular blocks. Once several such structures are mastered, teach the student to build these block structures in response to your verbal request as described in the next phase.

Phase 8: Building a Structure upon the Teacher's Request

At some point in the block building program, the student should be taught to build a certain structure when asked to do so. Before being taught this skill, the student should have learned to label the objects to be built either in their 3-D or 2-D form as taught in the Receptive Identification of Objects Program (Chapter 17).

The process for teaching the student to build structures in response to your instructions may proceed as follows. Say to the student, "Build chair" (SD1), and prompt by displaying a model such as a prebuilt structure of a chair or a picture of a chair built out of blocks. Next, fade the model by gradually giving the student shorter and shorter amounts of time to view it, bringing the student's building under the control of your verbal request. Once the first structure is mastered, introduce "Build table" (SD2) using the same procedure. Then alternate between presentations of SD1 and SD2 according to the discrimination learning paradigm.

Once the student masters discrimination between SD1 and SD2, gradually add distracter blocks to the pile of blocks presented and teach the student to find, among many blocks, those needed for building a structure that corresponds to the instruction. We recommend that the student be taught to expressively label the structures she builds as well. Teach expressive labeling of the structures by adhering to the procedures described in the Expressive Labeling of Objects Program (Chapter 23).

Phase 9: Building with Various Kinds of Blocks

At this point, new types of blocks, such as colored cubes, Duplos, Legos (if the student's fine motor skills allow for their introduction), and big cardboard blocks, should be introduced. Along with big cardboard blocks, introduce extra materials that may make building with the blocks more fun. For example, blankets or sheets may be used to make a house that the student can play in alone or with a sibling or friend. Big Bird, Barney, Winnie the Pooh, Woody, Buzz, Esmeralda, Barbie, or other favorite characters would be great to bring to a tea party in the block house. Introduce cars and animals when building with Duplos or Legos and create places where people live, play, and go to work. Some students with advanced block building skills enjoy building Lego structures from the instructions that come in the Lego boxes.

Areas of Difficulty

Although most students learn to build with blocks, individual differences are apparent in that some students learn quickly with little or no prompting, whereas others need extra help throughout every phase of this portion of the program. As you gain teaching skills and acquire knowledge of the student's idiosyncrasies, it becomes easier to identify remedies for difficulties that may arise in teaching as a result of the student's unique characteristics. It is impractical to describe all possible problems that may arise and their potential solutions, but two common difficulties are identified in this section as illustrations.

Some students experience difficulty lifting the placement block and putting it into position relative to the base block as described in Phases 1 and 2. If this occurs, help the student by demonstrating and prompting her to *slide* (instead of lift) the block first to random positions on the table and later to various positions in relation to a base block. For example, place two identical blocks on the side of the table. Slide your block to a random position on the table and manually prompt the student to grab her block and then slide it such that the two blocks end up side by side. Reinforce the response. Gradually fade the manual prompt over subsequent trials. Work on this skill until the student can slide her block unprompted to any random position on the table in imitation of your placements. Next, teach the student to imitate sliding the placement block *in front of*, then *next to*, and finally *behind* the base block on the table, following the stepwise teaching procedures described in Phase 1. Once sliding is mastered, transfer from sliding to lifting the placement block into position. Initially use slow and exaggerated movements when lifting the block to facilitate the student's attention to the SD.

When you first demonstrate chaining the placement of two blocks, some students may begin their response as soon as you place the first block. Such an error is reasonable because it is consistent with the response learned up to that point in teaching. Solve the problem by withholding the student's blocks until your chain is complete.

Drawing

Persons with developmental delays, like typical individuals, differ widely in their interest in drawing. Some students appear to find drawing reinforcing in and of itself, whereas others need external reinforcers for their efforts. Many students, however, *learn* to like drawing after they have gone through the phases presented in this program.

Drawing is an elaborate behavior that can be taught as an extension of the student's progress in the Matching and Sorting and Nonverbal Imitation Programs. It is to the student's advantage to have mastered fine motor imitations and the exercises for building and strengthening finger–hand dexterity described in the Nonverbal Imitation Program before beginning the current portion of the Arts and Crafts Program.

In the first phase of this portion of the program, the student is taught to hold the crayon correctly and imitate your straight lines. Next, the student is taught to draw basic shapes, such as circles, rectangles, squares, and triangles. After learning this skill, the student is taught to combine shapes to create figures and then to draw these recognizable figures upon your request. The student also is taught to color inside the lines of shapes and simple figures. Later the student may draw original and creative pictures; however, it is unlikely that he will do so without first being explicitly taught to draw in imitation of your drawings. An occasional student is extremely creative in drawing and produces intriguing figures and interesting artwork from the start.

Large sheets of construction paper, jumbo crayons, and thick water-soluble markers are needed to teach drawing. The crayons should leave a strong colored line on the paper as opposed to a barely discernible trace (the latter has a less reinforcing effect for most students). If the student seems more reinforced by using markers than crayons, begin with markers and introduce crayons at a later time, teaching the student to put more force behind his strokes. The teacher and the student should use identical drawing utensils in the initial stages of imitation.

If the student does not demonstrate a hand preference, teach him to draw consistently with his right hand from the beginning. If the student is 3 years old or older, teach him to hold the writing utensil correctly. A younger student may use a fist grip. To teach a correct grip, the following procedure may be used: Place the crayon or marker with the tip pointing toward the student next to or on the paper. Give the instruction "Pick up marker" and manually prompt the student to pick up the marker between his thumb and index finger, then adjust his grip. Practice this procedure until the student can pick up and hold the marker correctly without your prompt. Allow the student to scribble on the paper while he is practicing holding the marker with a correct grip. As the student learns to draw in imitation, remind him when necessary to hold the crayon or marker correctly by, for example, saying, "Hold marker right" or "Fix marker." Combine the instruction with a manual prompt if needed.

Note that when you move from simple instructions such as "Do this" to more complex instructions such as those just presented, you should not assume that the student understands and thus can respond appropriately to such instructions. In short, complex instructions may not initially function effectively. Rather, when the instructions are combined with effective prompts, they may be gradually mastered if associated through procedures presented in the Early Receptive Language Program (Chapter 15).

When beginning to teach drawing, you should sit behind the student at the table as this position facilitates manual prompting. Keep in mind, however, that sitting behind the student makes it difficult to observe whether he is attending to the SD. Therefore, shift to a side-by-side position once the consistent use of manual prompts is faded. Keep sessions short initially (e.g., around 1 minute) and use the student's favorite reinforcers.

Phase 1: Imitating the Teacher Drawing Straight Lines

In Phase 1, the student learns to draw straight lines in imitation of your drawing. For the purpose of illustration, let drawing a vertical line be SD1, drawing a horizontal line be SD2, and drawing a diagonal line be SD3. After sitting behind the student, place the paper on the table and then introduce Step 1.

▶ Step 1

Present SD1, which consists of your saying, "Do this," while drawing a vertical line about 8 to 12 inches long on the left side of the paper. Immediately prompt the student's response by manually guiding him through the motions of drawing a vertical line on the right side of the paper. A black dot placed on the top of the page, indicating the line's starting point, may be added as an additional prompt. Alternatively, a dotted line between a big beginning dot and an end dot may be provided as a prompt. Gradually fade the manual prompt to a pointing prompt that indicates where the student should begin his stroke, and gradually erase the dotted line between the dots. Finally, decrease the size of the dots until all prompts are eliminated. During the prompt fading process, be sure to probe unprompted trials to help reduce the number of prompted trials and avoid prompt dependency.

In the early stages, you may reinforce slightly rounded or crooked lines as acceptable approximations of your straight line. By the use of differential reinforcement, such approximations should gradually be shaped to closer approximations of your straight vertical line. Once the student masters drawing a straight vertical line in imitation of your line by responding correctly in 5 out of 5 or 9 out of 10 unprompted trials, introduce drawing a horizontal line.

► **Step 2**

Present SD2, which consists of your saying, "Do this," while drawing a horizontal line on the paper. Imitating a horizontal line is a new experience, and the student will most likely require prompting to respond correctly. If he does, follow the same prompting procedure used in Step 1. Once the student masters drawing a horizontal line in imitation of your line, go on to the next step.

► **Step 3**

Intermix SD1 and SD2 according to the discrimination learning paradigm. Begin with mass trials of SD1 (saying, "Do this," while drawing a vertical line). If necessary, prompt the response and fade the prompt over mass trials. Set mastery of SD2 at 3 unprompted correct responses in a row. Within 2 to 3 seconds of completing mastery of SD1, present SD2 (saying, "Do this," while drawing a horizontal line) and prompt the student's correct response, if necessary. Fade the prompt and, after 3 consecutive correct responses, shift back to SD1. Over the next few trials, set mastery at 2 consecutive correct responses then 1 correct response before alternating SDs. Set mastery at 5 out of 5 or 9 out of 10 unprompted correct responses presented in random rotation.

► **Step 4**

Mass trial SD3 (saying, "Do this," while drawing a diagonal line). Teach SD3 to mastery by following the procedures outlined in Step 1. Once SD3 is mastered separately, intermix it first with SD1 and then with SD2 according to the discrimination learning paradigm.

Once the student can draw and discriminate vertical, horizontal, and diagonal lines in imitation of your lines, go on to Phase 2.

Phase 2: Imitating the Teacher Drawing Basic Shapes

In Phase 2 of the drawing portion of the Arts and Crafts Program, the student learns to imitate your drawings of circles, triangles, rectangles, and squares. Initially divide each shape into separate components. As the student becomes proficient at imitating each component, gradually chain the components together to create a shape. Let SD1 be a circle which tends to be the least difficult shape to imitate.

► **Step 1**

Present SD1 (saying, "Do this," while drawing a circle). Immediately provide the student with a manual prompt. If necessary, draw a dotted circle for the student to trace and fade the dots gradually from clear sharp dots to less and less visible dots. If the student completes the circle but continues by drawing spirals, prompt him to stop as he closes the circle by saying, "Stop," while lifting his marker from the paper. Marking the beginning and the end of the circle with an obvious dot may also be helpful in prompting the student from making spirals. Reinforce correctly drawn circles that are prompted or unprompted, but remember to save the student's favorite reinforcers for unprompted trials. Occasionally probe unprompted trials to reduce the number of prompted trials and help avoid prompt dependency. Once the student masters drawing a circle (5 out of 5 or 9 out of 10 unprompted correct responses), go on to Step 2 and teach the student to imitate an isosceles triangle (i.e., a triangle in which two sides are of equal length). This behavior should be broken down into three separate components, which are then gradually chained together.

► **Step 2**

Present the first component of SD2 (drawing an isosceles triangle) by instructing, "Do this," while drawing a diagonal line as the left side of the triangle. Upon completion of the student's correct response, present the second component by saying, "Do this," and drawing a diagonal line as the right side of the triangle. Immediately upon the student's correct response, present the last component by saying, "Do this," and drawing the base line of the triangle from left to right. If prompting is necessary, manually guide the student through the motions or draw a dotted triangle for the student to trace. To fade the former prompt, gradually provide the student with less and less assistance on subsequent trials. To fade the latter prompt, gradually erase the dots.

Once the student can draw the triangle unprompted in response to your three separate instructions, start chaining the sides of the triangle together. Begin by saying, "Do this," while first drawing the left side of the triangle and then immediately drawing the right side of the triangle. Prompt the correct response and fade the prompt over successive trials. Provide reinforcement contingent on the student's completion of both sides of the triangle. Add the base line last and reinforce this response separately. After the student can draw the two sides of the triangle in response to a single SD, chain all three sides together by saying, "Do this," while drawing the left side, the right side, and then the baseline of the triangle. The student should be provided with reinforcement contingent upon his completion of the entire triangle in response to a single SD. Set mastery at 5 out of 5 or 9 out of 10 unprompted correct responses.

▶ **Step 3**

Intermix SD1 (drawing a circle) and SD2 (drawing a triangle) according to the discrimination learning paradigm.

▶ **Step 4**

For the sake of illustration, let SD3 be the drawing of a square. Teach this skill by following the procedures described in Step 1. Once SD3 is mastered, intermix it first with SD2 and then with SD1 according to discrimination learning procedures.

Other shapes that should be taught include a semicircle and an oval. If the student's motivation wanes a bit while drawing, vary the task by, for example, letting the student trace stencils of the shapes he is learning to draw.

Phase 3: Imitating the Teacher Drawing Figures

Once the student learns to draw basic shapes, he may go on to learning to draw simple figures, such as a house, a tree, an ice cream cone, a train, a happy face, a stick person, a cat, a dog, a giraffe, and so on, by combining mastered single shapes in various ways. It may facilitate the student's learning if he masters matching 2-D pictures of the figures he is to learn to draw and receptive labeling of the 2-D figures prior to beginning this phase of the program.

To teach these prerequisite skills, draw two sets of clear pictures of the figures and then, according to the procedures described in Chapter 12 (Matching and Sorting), teach the student to match the like figures. By matching the figures, the student learns to attend to the similarities and differences among the stimuli. Once the matching task is mastered, teach the student to identify the figures by following the procedures outlined in the Receptive Labeling of Objects Program (Chapter 17). By teaching the student these skills prior to this phase, the 2-D figures may be used as visual prompts when teaching the student to draw the figures, and the labels of the figures may be used as verbal prompts. Descriptions of the arrangements of each figure are provided below. The figures are sequenced in order of apparent level of difficulty, and we recommend teaching one figure at a time to mastery before introducing the next figure.

Drawing a House

Drawing a house consists of imitating your drawing of a square (the main portion of the house) with a triangle on top (the roof). Because the student has already learned to draw these two components separately, they may be easily chained into a single response by your modeling the second shape immediately after modeling the first shape and providing reinforcement contingent on the student's imitating the drawing of *both* shapes in correct relation to one another. You may use the picture of the figure as a prompt by, for example, covering the second part of the house until the student finishes drawing the first part, then revealing the whole house. Once the imitation of the main house is mastered, two square windows and a rectangular door may be added.

Drawing a Tree

The drawing of a tree consists of a triangular top and a rather long and narrow rectangular trunk stemming from the middle of the triangle's base. You should follow the same procedures described for drawing a house, combining the two already learned component parts into a single response.

Drawing an Ice Cream Cone

The drawing of an ice cream cone consists of a semicircle (the ice cream) on top of a triangular cone. As done before, teach the task first as two separate responses and then chain the components into a single response.

Drawing a Train

The drawing of a train consists of a narrow, vertical rectangle (the cab), then a wide, horizontal rectangle attached to the cab (the engine), then a small vertical rectangle on top of the front end of the engine (the smokestack), and finally one circle underneath the cab and another circle underneath the engine (the wheels). Once the student masters imitating the train drawn in five separate components, use backward chaining to teach him to draw the entire train as one response to a single SD. Start by drawing the cab, engine, and smokestack as separate SDs, then draw both wheels as a two-part chain with one SD. Once this chain is mastered, chain the two wheels and the smokestack together, drawing them onto the predrawn cab and engine. Continue with this chaining procedure until the student can draw the entire train in imitation of a single SD.

Drawing a Happy Face

The drawing of a happy face consists of a circular head, two dotted eyes, and a single curved line as the mouth. Once again, first the components are taught separately, then they are chained together. To teach this imitation, a forward chaining procedure (see Chapter 10) may be used. That is, teach the student first to draw the head and one eye as one response, finishing the face using separate SDs for the remaining components. Next, chain the head and both eyes into one response, then combine the head, eyes, and mouth into one response, until the student is able to imitate drawing the entire face after being given only one SD.

Drawing a Stick Person

The drawing of a stick person consists of a happy face (the head), a long vertical line for the neck and the body, a horizontal line for the arms, and two diagonal lines for legs that stem from the vertical midline. Prior to learning to draw this figure, the student should have learned to draw a happy face as a chained imitation. The other components should be taught as separate imitations before they are chained. Once the student can imitate the separate components, use a forward chaining procedure to combine the responses. The teacher may, depending on the student's drawing skills, teach the student to elaborate upon this drawing by adding simple hands, feet, ears, and hair to the person.

Drawing a Cat's Profile

The drawing of a cat's profile consists of a small circular head, a larger circular body, a vertical line as a tail, one small triangular ear, a happy face with whiskers, and four stick legs. Once the student has learned to imitate the separate components, employ backward chaining procedures to combine the responses.

Drawing a Dog's Profile

The drawing of a dog's profile consists of a triangular head (tilted so that the triangle's baseline makes up the dog's neck), a rectangular body attached to the neck, a tail drawn as a single horizontal line from the corner of the body, one small triangular ear, and four vertical lines (legs) extending from the body. Once the student has learned to imitate the separate components, employ backward chaining procedures to combine the responses.

Drawing a Giraffe

The giraffe drawing consists of an oval head, a long narrow rectangular neck, a large horizontally oriented oval (or rectangular) body, four legs as single vertical lines or long narrow rectangles, a single line as a tail, and a small triangular ear. Drawing a dot and a curved line on the oval head gives the giraffe a happy face. To teach the student to draw a giraffe, follow the procedures employed for drawing a cat and a dog.

Once the student masters imitation of these basic figures, you may add more detail. Novel figures may also be introduced, such as other vehicles (e.g., a car, a bus, a boat), animals (e.g., a snake, a lion, an elephant), and objects (e.g., the sun, the moon, stars, grass, flowers, ocean waves, mountains). These figures may, in turn, be used as prerequisite skills for learning to draw complete scenarios, such as a house with a person and a dog playing in the yard, a boat sailing on the ocean, and a train moving through a landscape on a sunny day with a mountain range in the background.

Once the student learns to draw several figures through imitation, shift the SD from being imitative in nature to being receptively cued. That is, teach the student to draw figures in response to verbal requests (e.g., "Draw a house," "Draw a boat"). Prompt by using the pictures of the figures as models, then gradually fade these models either by covering more and more of them or by presenting them for shorter and shorter durations over subsequent trials. Later, some students may learn to draw when given nonspecific requests such as the SD,

"Draw a picture." At this stage, it should become apparent whether the student takes an interest in drawing particular pictures. For example, the student may show an affinity for drawing animals or he may show an interest in drawing landscapes (e.g., hills, a sun, and a rainbow). A strong enough interest in drawing is likely to reflect that the student finds the visual feedback from his drawing reinforcing. If this occurs, the student's drawing behaviors may be maintained with little or no extrinsic reinforcement. Drawing may, in fact, prove to be so pleasurable for the student that he may occupy his free time by appropriately drawing pictures rather than engaging in other inappropriate forms of self-stimulatory behaviors. For the majority of students, however, we recommend incorporating drawing into their daily schedule even if doing so requires explicit instructions and extrinsic reinforcement. Consistent with our model, it is to the student's advantage to engage in a higher level form of socially appropriate self-stimulation than in socially inappropriate forms such as rocking, hand flapping, or spinning.

Phase 4: Coloring Inside the Lines of Shapes and Simple Figures

Once the student can draw basic shapes, you may introduce coloring inside the lines of these shapes. Adjust the demand for accuracy to the student's fine motor capabilities. The thickness of the lines around the shapes may be increased to make coloring within the lines easier. You may prompt the student to stay within the lines by saying, "Color inside." To establish the student's response to this verbal prompt, combine it with a manual prompt and then gradually fade the manual prompt until only the verbal component of the prompt remains. Most students need verbal reminders to stay within the lines for quite awhile, but you should be able to gradually reduce frequency of these reminders.

Once the student learns to color simple shapes, you may introduce coloring books. You should initially choose coloring books with simple figures, avoiding intricate details. If coloring books with few details are difficult to find, create a coloring book by cutting out single figures from overcrowded coloring books and photocopying these figures onto clean sheets of paper.

After the student masters coloring in a nonverbal imitation format, introduce coloring in a receptive instructions format. For example, teach the student to color a circle when you request, "Color the circle." Nonverbal imitation may be used as a prompt in the receptive instructions format. To teach the receptive format, follow the procedures described in the Early Receptive Language Program (Chapter 15).

As in all other programs, individual differences become evident in that some students learn to color nicely inside the borders of shapes and figures within a short time and with minimal prompting, whereas others require days or even months to reach the same level of perfection. Many students need a good deal of extrinsic reinforcement for quite some time before the task becomes reinforcing in and of itself. For others, however, coloring, like drawing, provides its own reinforcement from the very beginning.

Areas of Difficulty

For students who experience difficulty in the early phases of learning to draw, using a slanted work surface such as an easel may make it easier for the student to see your drawings as well as his own responses. Some students like to draw on dry erase sheets (clear plastic) or dry erase boards, and some are motivated (reinforced) by erasing lines contingent on correct drawings.

If the beginning phase of the drawing portion of the program (imitating a vertical line) seems too difficult for the student, place this task on hold and introduce the pretraining step of teaching the student to scribble when you scribble. You should scribble on one side of the paper and the student on the other side. Although the student may have already acquired this form of drawing, this pretraining step may teach the student to pay attention to your actions, which may facilitate learning to imitate drawing lines when this task is reintroduced.

When imitation of drawing a vertical line is reintroduced, the student may be reinforced by being allowed to scribble contingent on correct responding. If the student is reinforced by scribbling, use two sheets of paper, one sheet for imitation of straight lines and the other for scribbling. Scribbling used as a reinforcer may be implemented by quickly switching to the scribbling sheet contingent on the student's correct imitation of your SD.

If the student insists on drawing his line over your line, let him do so in the beginning stages. A visual prompt, such as a thick line down the middle of the paper dividing the student's side from your side, may later be introduced.

Cutting with Scissors

Cutting with scissors is an important skill in a preschool student's repertoire. Drawing, cutting, pasting, and painting are interrelated activities and are included in any preschool curriculum. For example, after drawing and coloring a picture, the student may cut it out, paste it onto paper, and take it home to her parents, giving them an important item for the student's first art portfolio.

Like drawing, cutting with scissors is a task at which some students become proficient without much structured training. Most students, however, need a step-by-step curriculum such as the one presented here. In Phase 1 of the cutting portion of the Arts and Crafts Program, the student learns the very basic step of picking up and holding a pair of scissors correctly. In Phases 2, 3, and 4, the student learns to cut on straight, angled, and curved lines, respectively. In Phase 5, cutting out shapes and simple figures is introduced.

In some instances, the student's level of fine motor ability may prevent her from starting with regular scissors, and pretraining with spring-loaded scissors is recommended. If the student's dexterity allows her to use regular scissors from the beginning, use quality scissors (e.g., Fiskars) as it is extremely frustrating for both you and the student if the scissors do not cut properly or do not open and close smoothly. The scissors should have a small loop for the thumb and a larger loop to fit the index and middle fingers.

Some students are reinforced by watching pieces of paper fall to the floor as they are cut. These students should be taught to cut while sitting on a chair facing you and away from the table so they can see the pieces fall. If such feedback holds no special reinforcement value for the student, prepare other reinforcers and sit behind the student at the table until manual prompts are faded. Then sit next to the student, where it is easier to present less intrusive prompts such as pointing.

Phase 1: Learning To Cut with Scissors While Holding the Paper

Begin by teaching the student to hold the scissors correctly. A model prompt should be attempted initially, as some students succeed with this kind of prompt. Most students, however, are only partially successful with a model prompt and need shaping and more intrusive prompting to be successful. If a hand-over-hand manual prompt is needed, you should practice the following prompt procedures on another adult prior to introducing it to the student because the prompt is somewhat cumbersome and takes practice to use effectively.

Position yourself behind the student and help the student hold the scissors correctly with her thumb through the small loop and her index finger, middle finger, and perhaps ring finger through the large loop of the scissors. The back surface of the student's thumb should always face upward when she cuts. Support the student's hand by cupping your left hand under the big loop of the scissors and around the student's hand. With your left thumb wedged between the handles of the scissors, pry them apart. Quickly put a ½-inch wide strip of index card between the blades using your right hand. (Index cards are thick and small and therefore easy to hold and control.) A ½-inch wide strip should be used in the initial stages because it can be cut in half with a single snip. Immediately shift the position of your thumb from being wedged between the handles to being placed on top of the small loop with the student's thumb inside, then push the handle down to cut the paper in half. Concurrent with the manual prompt, you may say, "Open," while the student opens the blades and, "Cut," while the student cuts the paper. Fade the prompt gradually by providing less and less manual assistance on subsequent trials. Remember to probe with unprompted trials to decrease the number of prompted trials if possible and help avoid prompt dependency.

Once the student can pick up the scissors, hold them correctly, and cut a ½-inch wide index card strip in half while you hold the strip, start teaching the student to hold the strip herself. Teach this step as follows: Instruct the student to pick up the scissors, then give her the strip to hold onto with her free hand. Manually prompt correct responding initially. Fade the prompt gradually by providing less and less assistance on each subsequent trial. Once the student can hold and cut a ½-inch wide strip of index card independently, gradually widen the strip so that two snips, then three snips, and so on are needed to cut the strip in half. When the student can cut a 3 × 5-inch index card in half across the short side (approximately five to six consecutive snips), proceed to Phase 2.

Phase 2: Cutting on Straight Lines

Prior to teaching Phase 2, the student should have learned in Phase 1 to pick up and hold the scissors correctly as well as to cut an index card in half without your help. For the current phase, draw a ⅛-inch thick black line across a 1-inch wide strip of index card and teach the student to cut on the line. Place the card strip and the scissors on the table and instruct, "Cut line." If necessary, prompt the response by manually steering the student's hand such that the scissors cut on the line. Fade the prompt over the subsequent trials. Once this skill is mastered, gradually increase the length of the line until the student can cut a line drawn across the short side of a 5 × 8-inch index card while holding the card herself. Gradually reduce the thickness of the line until the student can cut on a line drawn with a standard marker.

Phase 3: Cutting on Angled Lines

To cut on an angled line, the student will have to adjust the card as she cuts the angle. Adjusting the card while cutting takes practice. We recommend starting with only one angle, which requires only one adjustment of the card. Draw a ⅛-inch thick, black, angled line across the shorter side of a 3 × 5-inch index card. Instruct, "Cut line," while manually prompting the student to adjust the card when the scissors reach the corner of the angle. Fade the prompt. Once this skill is mastered, use a larger index card and add a second angle and then a third. Gradually reduce the thickness of the line until the student can cut angled lines drawn with a standard marker.

Phase 4: Cutting on Curved Lines

Cutting on a curved line requires continuous small adjustments of the card. Therefore, we recommend that the student master cutting lines with angles prior to starting Phase 4. Draw a ⅛-inch thick black, wide, curved line across the shorter side of a 3 × 5-inch index card, and follow the same teaching procedures described in Phase 3. Gradually increase the bend in the curve after the student has mastered the initial curve. As the student progresses, introduce larger index cards with more compressed curves and then multiple curves.

Phase 5: Cutting out Simple Shapes and Figures

With the cutting skills the student has acquired up to this point, cutting out simple shapes and figures should be introduced. Draw, for example, a triangle in the middle of a 4 × 6-inch index card and follow the same teaching procedures described in Phase 3 for cutting angled lines. Once the student can cut out triangles, teach her to cut out squares, rectangles, and circles. Finally, teach the student to cut out shapes she draws herself. Generalize the student's skills to cutting out shapes drawn onto 5 × 8-inch index cards, then onto 5 × 8-inch pieces of construction paper, and finally onto thick art paper. Later, teach the student to cut out pictures from magazines.

Gluing

Gluing may be taught concurrently with cutting or after the student learns to cut out simple shapes. It may be helpful to provide the student with a visual prompt by using white (e.g., Elmer's) glue on colored paper, making the glue clearly visible. Relatively large pictures should be made available for gluing, as smaller pictures may be difficult for the student to pick up.

To teach the student to glue, have the following supplies available: white glue, colored paper, a paper plate or shallow bowl, and two paint brushes. Begin by pouring some glue onto the plate or bowl, dipping the brush into the glue, and then applying it to the paper. Concurrent with these actions, instruct, "Brush," and immediately provide a manual prompt if needed to help the student pick up the brush, dip it into the glue, and apply the glue onto the paper. Next, give the instruction "Glue" and prompt by giving the student a picture and indicating to her (e.g., by pointing) where to attach the picture. The student may need prompting to position the picture face up on the paper (to some students it is not initially obvious which side of the picture should touch the glue).

It may be easier for some students to glue objects other than pictures onto the paper. If this is true for the student you work with, use materials such as cotton balls, colored strings, ribbons, confetti, buttons, glitter, feathers, and macaroni. The student may also be taught to use various kinds of glue sticks, starting with the application of glue from colored glue sticks onto white paper and then progressing to the application of clear glue from glue sticks onto any kind of paper. In addition, the student can be taught to use glue when decorating figures she has drawn herself. For example, the student may decorate a person she has drawn by gluing on cotton for hair and applying glitter to the person's clothing.

Painting

Painting is a fun activity for most young students and is in and of itself a loosely structured activity. Students usually apply paint freely onto paper, mixing colors in the paint jars as well as on the paper. To maintain some organization and help the student stay in control of his play with paint, you must usually introduce some structure into the activity. This may be done by, for example, teaching the student to match brushes with paint on them to jars or plates with corresponding colors. This type of discrimination does not come without practice for any individual. You must decide whether each particular student is ready to learn this type of discrimination at the start of this portion of the Arts and Crafts Program, or whether the student should first be taught to use a brush and apply paint to a sheet of paper. In this section, we describe a way for you to instruct the student to keep the brush with the paint it was paired with initially and apply the paint to paper.

To teach the student to match brushes to their corresponding paint jars, start with a format similar to that used in matching colors (see Chapter 12). Place two to three plates or wide, shallow jars containing paints of different colors on the table. Dip the tips of the brushes into the paint jars, present the instruction "Match," and give the student one brush at a time to match to each respective plate or jar. After these discriminations are mastered, teach the student to respond to the instruction "Paint." Place a large sheet of white paper in front of the student, give the instruction, then prompt the correct response, which is to pick up a clean brush, dip it into the paint, apply the paint to the paper, and return the brush to the correct jar. You may prompt by using modeling (i.e., nonverbal imitation). If a model prompt is insufficient, however, the skill may be taught through backward chaining. To use this procedure, teach each behavior separately, beginning with the last behavior in the sequence, placing the brush in the correct jar. Then chain the second and third behaviors, applying paint to paper and returning the brush to the correct jar. Finally, chain the first behavior to the already combined last two behaviors such that all three behaviors (picking up the brush, painting, and returning the brush to the jar) are cued by the instruction, "Paint." If necessary, prompt the student to put the brush back in the correct jar by saying, "Match" or "Put with same."

Once the student masters painting at the table, teach him to apply paint to paper on an easel. Appropriate painting for a preschool-age student is to apply paint freely to the paper, "expressionist" style. The student may later be taught to paint figures in the same manner he was taught to draw figures.

Writing Longhand

It is not uncommon for students with developmental delays to show a special interest in letters. Some students enjoy letter puzzles, others line up plastic letters on magnetic boards in the correct alphabetical order without being specifically taught to do so, and still others are fascinated by letters displayed on television or videotapes and in books (in technical terms, certain visual forms possess reinforcing properties). Such students are often more motivated to learn to write letters than students who do not display an interest in letters. However, many students develop an interest in letters as they become directly exposed to them through the various programs in this manual (technically speaking, exposure to the stimuli sensitizes the student to the reinforcing properties of the stimuli).

Note that, although learning to write letters and words is initiated in this portion of the Arts and Crafts Program, learning the meaning of written words is largely postponed until the Reading and Writing Program (Chapter 29) is introduced. We recommend teaching the student to write uppercase letters in the early stages of this portion of the program because uppercase letters are typically easier to write than lowercase letters.

Before beginning the current portion of the Arts and Crafts Program, we recommend that the student acquire the following prerequisite skills: First, the student should learn to attend to and discriminate among the letters of the alphabet as demonstrated through mastery of uppercase letter-to-letter matching (see Matching and Sorting, Chapter 12). Second, the student should master the nonverbal imitation of two-part chains (at least) because you will model chaining separate lines of a letter together in this portion of the program. Third, the student should master the receptive identification of letters (see Receptive Identification of Objects, Chapter 17). Lastly, the student should be proficient at generalized imitation of single behaviors (i.e., the student can imitate novel motions with little or no prompting).

In the phases presented below, the writing tasks are sequenced in order of apparent difficulty, with drawing of straight-lined uppercase letters first (i.e., E, F, H, I, L, T), letters with curved lines next (i.e., B, C, D, G, J, O, P, Q, R, S, U), and letters with diagonal lines last (i.e., A, K, M, N, V, W, X, Y, Z). Many letters of the alphabet may be taught by the use of forward chaining procedures. Prompts that tend to be effective for teaching the student to write longhand are common to all phases of this portion of the program and are described at the end of this chapter in the section "Areas of Difficulty."

Phase 1: Writing Letters with Straight Lines

Uppercase letters composed of vertical and horizontal straight lines (i.e., E, F, H, I, L, T) should be taught first. We suggest starting with the letter "T" and breaking it down into two separate components (i.e., a horizontal line and a vertical line). Present the instruction "Do this" while drawing a short horizontal line from left to right. Prompt if necessary. Once the student correctly imitates the horizontal line, present the second SD by instructing,

"Do this," while drawing a vertical line down from the center of the horizontal line, completing the letter "T." Prompt if necessary.

Once the student masters the letter "T" as two separate imitations, chain the two imitations together by following the procedures described in the section of the Nonverbal Imitation Program on chaining two-part imitations. Specifically, give the instruction, "Do this," while drawing the short horizontal line and then immediately draw the longer vertical line down from the center of the horizontal line. Prompt if necessary and fade the prompt over subsequent trials. Remember to probe with unprompted trials in an attempt to decrease the number of prompted trials and help avoid prompt dependency. Reinforce the student contingent on her completion of *both* lines. Teach the second letter in the same manner, followed by intermixing the first and the second letters according to the discrimination learning paradigm.

Teach the remaining letters composed of horizontal and vertical lines, focusing on one letter at a time and using the same procedures described above. Once the student can imitate your writing of uppercase letters with straight horizontal and vertical lines, move on to Phase 2.

Phase 2: Writing Letters with Curved Lines

By following the procedures outlined in this phase, the student is taught to write letters with curved lines (i.e., B, C, D, G, J, O, P, Q, R, S, U). We suggest starting with the letter "C." Present the SD ("Do this" while writing a "C"). Placing large dots where the "C" should begin and end may reduce the likelihood that the student will overextend her stroke and write an "O." Gradually fade all prompts over trials. Intermix writing "C" with letters already mastered in Phase 1. Teach the remaining letters in Phase 2 in the same manner, using chaining procedures when necessary.

Phase 3: Writing Letters with Diagonal Lines

In this phase, letters that have diagonal lines are taught (i.e., A, K, M, N, V, W, X, Y, Z). We recommend beginning with the letter "K." Start by breaking the "K" down into three components (i.e., a vertical line and two diagonal lines). Present the SD by saying, "Do this," while drawing the vertical line of the "K" from the top down. Once the student learns to correctly imitate this line unprompted, present the second SD by saying, "Do this," while drawing the upper diagonal line down to the center of the vertical line. After the student correctly imitates this line without prompting, present the next SD, which consists of saying, "Do this," while drawing the last diagonal line down from the center of the vertical line, completing the letter "K." Provide the amount of prompting needed for the student to respond correctly.

Once the student correctly imitates the letter "K" when presented as three separate components, begin chaining the SDs. Start this procedure by presenting the SD for the first two behaviors ("Do this" while drawing the vertical line and the upper diagonal line). Once you complete both lines, the student should begin drawing her lines in imitation. Upon the student's correct drawing of both lines completed as one response, present the next SD, which consists of saying, "Do this," while drawing the lower diagonal line, completing the letter. Finally, chain all three lines together with the presentation of one SD ("Do this" while writing the entire letter "K"). Provide reinforcement contingent on the student's completion of the entire letter as one response. Intermix writing "K" with letters already mastered in Phases 1 and 2. Teach the remaining letters in Phase 3 using the procedures described above, focusing on one letter at a time.

Phase 4: Writing Letters in Response to the Teacher's Receptive Instruction

Prior to the introduction of Phase 4, the student should have mastered receptive labeling of letters (in accordance with the procedures described in Receptive Labeling of Objects, Chapter 17) and writing letters through imitation (as described in the previous three phases). In this phase, teach the student to write letters in response to your receptive instruction (e.g., "Write A"). Prompt by either modeling the response or by showing the student an "A" printed on a card. The former prompt may be faded by gradually lightening the letter over subsequent trials; the latter prompt may be faded by providing the student with less and less time to view the card or by gradually sliding a blank card over the letter card until the letter is completely covered.

Phase 5: Writing Words

Teach the student to write words, starting with short words such as "UP," "ON," and "TO." After saying, "Do this," while writing a word such as "UP," prompt the student to copy the word from left to right. If the student starts with the last letter, interrupt her response immediately and prompt the correct sequence on the next trial by pointing to each letter from left to right or by placing a blank card over the word and uncovering it one letter at a time from left to right. Once the student can copy several two-letter words independently, go on to three-letter combinations such as "MOM," "DAD," "CAT," and "DOG."

Phase 6: Writing the Student's Name

Once the student can write letters by following your receptive instructions as described in Phase 4 and imitate writing short words as taught in Phase 5, teach the student to write her own name through imitation. If, after you give the SD ("Do this" while writing the student's name), the student starts her response by imitating the last letter or any letter other than the first one, interrupt her response immediately and prompt the correct sequence. Provide a visual prompt for the correct sequence of the letters in the student's name by pointing to each letter from left to right. If necessary, cover all the letters in the student's name except the first letter and disclose the remaining letters one by one as the student writes. Fade the former prompt by gradually pointing to fewer and fewer letters; fade the latter prompt over trials by exposing two letters, then three letters, and so on, until the student's full name is finally exposed.

Phase 7: Writing in Response to the Teacher's Receptive Instruction

After the student can copy a number of short words and her name correctly from left to right, teach her to write these words in response to receptive instructions, such as "Write *cat*" or "Write your name." This skill may be taught by presenting the verbal instruction while visually prompting the correct response through use of a card with the word printed on it. Fade the prompt card using the procedure described in Phase 4.

Once the student masters the writing tasks presented in this section, her writing skills will be equivalent to those of a typical 5-year-old. Procedures for teaching advanced writing skills will be presented in an upcoming volume on advanced programs.

Areas of Difficulty

Many students need visual prompts such as predrawn dotted letters for quite some time when they learn to write letters. If the student has problems restricting the size of her letters once the dotted letters are faded, prompt the appropriate size (e.g., 5 inches tall) by teaching the student to write within squares made of thick black lines predrawn on the paper. Gradually fade the thickness of the lines to regular pencil lines. Once this skill is acquired, reduce the distance between the lines to 3 inches or less, depending on the student's age and fine motor ability. Eventually fade the lines completely.

Self-Help Skills

CHAPTER 21

It is not uncommon for individuals with developmental delays to be behind in their acquisition of basic self-help skills. Nor is it unusual for them to require considerable assistance and effort from their parents and other adults to accomplish even basic tasks such as dressing and toileting. Nonetheless, with patient, systematic instruction, many students with developmental delays learn quite intricate self-help skills. Once the student becomes more self-sufficient, she will be happier with herself and easier to care for. Also by learning to become self-sufficient, the student will be more likely to enter a less restrictive placement in school and the community. For instance, students who are toilet trained are more likely to be accepted for enrollment in mainstream classes than students who do not know how to use the toilet.

This chapter presents programs for teaching the student to eat with a spoon, expand her diet, eat when requested, dress and undress, brush hair, brush teeth, wash hands, and use the toilet. Obviously, the skills discussed in this chapter do not encompass all those the student needs to know; however, a sufficient number of teaching principles are illustrated to allow for adequate generalization of these principles when constructing additional programs. The programs presented in this chapter are examples of programs presented in more detail by other investigators. Research into the area of helping individuals with developmental delays acquire self-help skills has been active over the past 30 years. Relevant materials are included among the References at the end of this manual.

Other programs presented in this manual should not be taught at the expense of teaching self-help skills. In one's attempt to comprehensively normalize the student's behaviors, the teaching of self-help skills is critical. Plan on completing most or all of the programs presented in this chapter in approximately 2 years. However, do not attempt to teach too many skills at one time; select a single skill and, before going on to the next skill, work regularly with the student until she makes significant progress with the target skill. Such a procedure helps to maintain the teacher's motivation and build the student's self-esteem.

Teaching many of the skills described in this chapter requires use of the shaping and chaining procedures described in Chapter 10. That is, several self-help skills are taught by reinforcing approximations of the target response, breaking down various complex behaviors into smaller elements, or both. As the individual elements of a particular self-help skill are learned, the teacher gradually combines these elements into a chain of behaviors occasioned by a general verbal instruction.

Most of the skills or skill elements are prompted physically (i.e., by manually guiding the student through the desired motions) or by modeling (i.e., demonstrating the behaviors). If the student is able to imitate the adult, modeling prompts rather than more intrusive physical prompts should be used. If the student needs prompting so as to follow a particular verbal instruction, the student gives evidence that she does not understand the teacher's instruction. Over time, however, the student will acquire some receptive language simultaneously with self-help skills through the combination of verbal instructions and prompts.

The program to teach feeding may be started after the student masters the first steps in nonverbal imitation using objects. Other more complex skills, such as brushing hair, dressing, hand washing, tooth brushing, and toileting, are best begun after the student masters the Nonverbal Imitation Program (Chapter 13) and is able to follow several verbal instructions.

Eating with a Spoon

Eating with a spoon is typically taught first because spoons are easier to manipulate than other eating utensils. Because eating is a complex behavior, it should be broken down into several small discrete steps. A backward chaining technique is recommended to teach eating with a spoon.

To begin, select a spoon the student can easily manipulate. If the student's hands are too little for a typical adult spoon, try a child-sized spoon. The student will learn to independently feed himself more quickly if he does not have to struggle with holding a spoon that is awkward for him to manipulate. Use soft foods, such as applesauce, oatmeal, mashed potatoes, or yogurt. Soft foods are easier to put on a spoon and tend to be more reinforcing than dry cereal or small bites of meat or vegetables. The foods used should be ones the student prefers and should be placed in a bowl, making it easier for the student to secure the food onto the spoon.

Backward Chaining the Steps Together

The target behavior is for the student to pick up a spoon placed next to a bowl of food, put the spoon in the food, move the spoon with food on it to his mouth, eat the food, and place the spoon back on the table. To teach the target behavior using backward chaining, break down the behavior into the following discrete steps:

1. Removing the spoon from the student's mouth and placing it on the table.
2. Placing the spoon in the student's mouth.
3. Lifting the spoon from the bowl.
4. Placing the spoon under a portion of food.
5. Moving the spoon to the bowl.
6. Picking up the spoon.

▶ Steps 1–2

Place the spoon with food on it in the student's mouth after giving the general instruction "Eat." Using a manual prompt, help the student take the spoon out of his mouth and place it on the table. Provide the student with verbal reinforcement. By placing the spoon on the table, each trial is kept discrete from other trials. In addition, placing the spoon on the table helps the student learn to pause between bites. Gradually fade the physical prompt over subsequent trials. After the physical prompt is faded, give the general instruction "Eat" again and hand the student the spoon (with food on it). Manually prompt the student to grip the spoon and place it in his mouth. Reinforce the student by letting him eat the food on the spoon. Have the student complete the chain by placing the spoon back on the table. After the student successfully places the spoon in his mouth and then removes it and puts it on the table with assistance in four to five trials, fade the prompts and reinforcement for placing the spoon in his mouth. Provide reinforcement contingent on the completion of *both* responses. Once Steps 1 and 2 are mastered (5 out of 5 or 9 out of 10 unprompted correct responses), go on to Step 3.

▶ Step 3

Hand the student the spoon (with food on it), give the general instruction "Eat," and manually prompt the student to lift the spoon from an empty bowl. Reinforce the response. If fading of prompts was successful in Steps 1 and 2, the student should complete the chain of behaviors. Verbally reinforce the student after he places the spoon on the table. After the student successfully completes the entire sequence of behaviors, fade the prompts and reinforcement for the behavior of lifting the spoon from the bowl. Continue to fade the prompts and reinforcement from this behavior until the student completes the entire chain following presentation of the general instruction "Eat." Once Step 3 is mastered (5 out of 5 or 9 out of 10 unprompted correct responses), go on to Step 4.

▶ Step 4

Place the spoon under a portion of food in the bowl and give the general instruction "Eat." Manually prompt the student to lift the spoon from the bowl, keeping only a small portion of the food on it. (Soft, sticky foods such as pudding or yogurt are much easier than other foods for the student to keep on the spoon.) Reward the student for picking up the spoonful of food and placing it into his mouth by letting him eat the food and by providing verbal reinforcement. If the fading of prompts was successful in previous steps, the student should place the spoon in his mouth and then remove it and place it on the table. Verbally reinforce the student after he places the spoon on the table. Provide any necessary prompts to complete this chain of behaviors. After the student successfully lifts the spoon from the bowl, eats the food, and places the spoon on the table for a few trials, fade the prompts and verbal reinforcement for lifting the spoon. Continue to fade the prompts and verbal reinforcement for this behavior until the student completes the entire chain following presentation of the general instruction "Eat." Once Step 4 is mastered (5 out of 5 or 9 out of 10 unprompted correct responses), go on to Step 5.

▶ **Step 5**

Hand the student the spoon and give the general instruction, "Eat." Manually prompt the student to move the spoon to the bowl. Provide social reinforcement for moving the spoon toward the bowl. The student should then complete the remainder of the chain without assistance. If the student does not complete the chain, provide the least amount of prompt necessary to reinstate correct responding. Verbally reinforce the student after he places the spoon on the table. After the student successfully completes the sequence of behaviors, starting with moving the spoon to the bowl, fade the prompts and verbal reinforcement for the behavior of moving the spoon to the bowl. Continue to fade the prompts and verbal reinforcement provided for this behavior until the student completes the entire chain following presentation of the general instruction "Eat." Once the student reaches criterion, go on to Step 6.

▶ **Step 6**

Place the spoon next to the bowl and give the general instruction "Eat." Manually prompt the student to pick up the spoon and then provide social reinforcement for his performance of the behavior. The student should then complete the remainder of the chain without assistance. When the student successfully completes the sequence of behaviors, fade the prompts and verbal reinforcement for the behavior of picking up the spoon. Remember to provide verbal reinforcement contingent on completion of the entire chain, starting with picking up the spoon following presentation of the general instruction "Eat."

After the student masters Steps 1 through 6, you may want to prompt and reinforce him for pausing between bites without having to put the spoon on table each time he finishes a bite. However, if the student tends to eat quickly, continue to have him put the spoon on the table after each bite to slow down his eating.

Note that this chain of behaviors is not illustrated with an adult model of appropriate spoon use. Instead, the student is manually prompted through each step. It is better, however, to teach these behaviors by providing assistance through the use of both modeling and physical prompting. If the student is able to imitate all of the individual behaviors that make up the skill, teach by using modeling exclusively to save time and energy.

Areas of Difficulty

Rather than postponing gratification (which is what the student must learn to do in order to eat appropriately with utensils and in small portions), the student might revert to earlier ways of eating when faced with a bowl of one of his favorite foods. Or, the student might use the spoon to self-stimulate (e.g., by flipping the spoon while gazing at the light reflecting off of it). If the student engages in self-stimulatory behavior with either his hands or the spoon, or if he frequently attempts to place his hands in either the food or the bowl, instruct him by saying, "Hands quiet," if he acquired this skill earlier in treatment (e.g., during the first hours of establishing cooperation and tantrum reduction). When given this instruction, the student should keep his hands in his lap between trials. If he does not, brush up on the instruction "Hands quiet" by prompting and reinforcing the student for placing both hands in his lap until the next instruction to eat is given. Remember to provide the student with reinforcement for keeping his hands in his lap between bites *and* for using the spoon appropriately.

If the student experiences difficulty manipulating the spoon, first teach him to use the spoon without feeding himself. Begin by teaching the student to correctly pick up a large spoon using the handle. When he masters this skill, teach the student to use the spoon to make a scooping motion inside an empty bowl and then to scoop a small amount of sticky food such as pudding or yogurt out of the bowl. Use an undesired food if you are not going to allow the student to eat the food at this point. After the student masters this skill, generalize to a smaller spoon and then return to the sequence of steps outlined earlier to teach the student to feed himself with the spoon.

If the student masters feeding himself with a spoon when sticky foods are used but experiences difficulty generalizing to bite-size pieces of solid food, teach the student to scoop small objects out of a bowl using a large spoon. Place small objects such as little plastic beads into a bowl. Teach the student the motions involved in scooping up some of the objects and dropping them back into the bowl. When the student masters the scooping motion, teach him to balance the objects on the spoon long enough to transfer them to an adjacent bowl. After this skill is mastered, generalize to a smaller spoon and then to scooping up bite-size pieces of solid food.

Finally, if the student experiences serious difficulty in mastering eating with a spoon when taught through the use of backward chaining procedures, try forward chaining procedures as described in the next section.

Forward Chaining the Steps Together

The steps in forward chaining are virtually identical to those in backward chaining except they are presented in the reverse order. To aid the teacher, the steps are presented in detail. Note that these steps are illustrated with the use of both verbal instructions and manual prompts. This is done with the intent of helping to teach receptive language. If the combination of both manual and verbal prompts does not facilitate mastery of the receptive instructions used in this program, delete the verbal component.

▶ **Step 1**

Place the spoon next to the bowl and give the general instruction "Eat." Manually prompt the student to pick up the spoon and then reinforce either by verbally praising the student or by giving him a small portion of the food from the bowl (use a separate spoon). Fade all prompts. When the student picks up the spoon unprompted in 5 out of 5 or 9 out of 10 trials, go on to Step 2.

▶ **Step 2**

Place the spoon next to the bowl of food and give the general instruction "Eat." After the student successfully picks up the spoon, give the instruction for the next response in the chain ("Spoon in bowl"), manually prompt the student to move the spoon to the bowl, and reinforce the student's response. Repeat trials while fading the manual prompt. When the student successfully places the spoon in the bowl without manual prompting, fade the instruction "Spoon in bowl" (e.g., by deleting it one word at a time or by gradually lowering its volume). After this step is mastered (5 out of 5 or 9 out of 10 unprompted correct responses), go on to Step 3.

▶ **Step 3**

Place the spoon next to the bowl of food and give the general instruction "Eat." After the student picks up the spoon and moves it to the bowl, give the instruction "Get food" while physically prompting him to place the spoon under a portion of food by turning his wrist to make the spoon dip inward. Reinforce and fade the prompts over subsequent trials. After the student successfully moves his spoon under a portion of food without assistance, fade the specific instruction "Get food." When the student masters this step (i.e., he responds correctly in 5 out of 5 or 9 out of 10 unprompted trials), go on to Step 4.

▶ **Step 4**

Place the spoon next to the bowl of food and give the general instruction "Eat." After the student independently picks up the spoon, moves it to the bowl, and places it under a portion of food, give the instruction "Lift spoon" and guide his hand so that he lifts the spoon upward toward his mouth. When the student successfully lifts the spoon toward his mouth without prompting, fade the specific instruction "Lift spoon." After Step 4 is mastered (5 out of 5 or 9 out of 10 unprompted correct responses), go on to Step 5.

▶ **Step 5**

Place the spoon next to the bowl of food and give the general instruction "Eat." After the student successfully picks up the spoon, moves it to the bowl, places it under a portion of food, and lifts it toward his mouth, give the instruction "Put in mouth" and guide his hand to place the spoon in his mouth. The student may open his mouth to accept the spoon without additional prompting. The student is reinforced by eating the food on the spoon and by your verbal reinforcement. Fade prompts and then fade the specific instruction "Put in mouth." After the student masters Step 5, go on to Step 6.

▶ **Step 6**

Place the spoon next to the bowl of food and give the general instruction "Eat." After the student independently picks up the spoon and moves it to the bowl, places it under a portion of food, lifts it toward and places it and the food in his mouth, give the instruction "Spoon on table," prompting him to take the spoon out of his mouth and place it on the table. Provide verbal reinforcement, and fade the prompts over subsequent trials. Finally, fade the specific instruction "Spoon on table."

Note that in these steps, you rely upon manual prompting to teach the student to eat with a spoon. If the student you work with is proficient in nonverbal imitation, it is better to teach by using a combination of modeling and physical assistance or, if possible, modeling alone.

Generalizing the Use of Eating Utensils

Once the student successfully feeds himself soft foods using a spoon, switch to small quantities of solid foods. This should only require a prompt to help the student to spoon the food and perhaps to hold the spoon steady before placing it into his mouth; the student should be capable of performing the remaining steps on his own.

After the student is able to use a spoon to eat different kinds of food, teach the student to eat with a fork and a knife. Use pieces of food small enough for the student to eat in one bite but large enough that they can be easily cut with a knife and then picked up with a fork. As done when teaching the student the behaviors needed to eat with a spoon, reduce the task into separate steps. Following backward or forward chaining procedures, begin teaching by using prompting, specific instructions (if using forward chaining procedures), and reinforcement for each step, and then slowly fade out the prompting, specific instructions, and reinforcement until the student can perform the chain of behaviors when given a general instruction.

Increasing Variety in the Student's Diet

Many individuals with developmental delays eat a very limited number of foods. A restricted diet is often of great concern for parents who fear their child may suffer from malnutrition. If you have such concerns, it is a good idea to consult a pediatrician to examine the student's physical health. At the same time, you may want to create a list of the foods the student eats and those she prefers not to eat to help ascertain whether certain nutrients are missing from the student's diet. In addition, if you notice that certain foods have detrimental effects on the student's behavior, include this information when consulting the pediatrician. For example, food allergies (e.g., allergies to milk or wheat products) and large amounts of sugar can cause major behavioral disturbances in some individuals.

There are times when food preferences seem incorporated into an individual's ritualistic behaviors. When such rituals are interrupted, the individual may tantrum. We mentioned earlier in this manual that a certain student would eat only perfectly shaped Cheerios and would throw major tantrums when he encountered ones that were not perfectly shaped. This behavior required that the student's parents go through every box of Cheerios they bought and carefully scrutinize the contents for imperfectly shaped Cheerios. While typical individuals sometimes show similar idiosyncrasies, more often than not such persons outgrow them over time. Whether individuals with autism follow a similar pattern is not known. In any case, for those parents who risk exposing their child to a restricted diet or forever seem to have to prepare special meals separate from those served to other family members, it may be helpful to increase the variety in the child's diet.

The present program describes steps whereby the student is helped to eat a larger variety of foods. Once the student eats novel foods in special teaching sessions, the student is taught to eat specific foods when you so request. Finally, to facilitate generalization, introduce these foods into regular mealtimes with family members.

In preparation for this program, create a list of foods the student already eats and note those that are highly preferred. Then create a list of foods that the student does not eat but that may be of benefit to the student. The general rule is to use favorite or highly preferred foods as reinforcers for eating nonpreferred foods. For example, if the student has a strong preference for a particular cracker, find a cracker slightly different from the preferred one in terms of appearance, taste, or shape, and then use the preferred cracker as the reinforcer for taking a small bite of the new cracker. Similarly, if the student eats only a certain brand of chicken nuggets, select a second brand that is similar in appearance and taste and use small bites of the preferred brand of nugget as a reinforcer for taking a small bite of the novel one. It is also helpful to have access to powerful food reinforcers, such as chocolate frosting or ice cream, and to provide small tastes of those treats as reinforcers for exploring new and nonpreferred foods. This is not all that different from what parents do with typical children, such as when a child is served dessert only after she finishes her vegetables. The teaching program for students with developmental delays, however, proceeds in relatively small steps (which help ensure success). Based on findings in empirical research, there are reasons to believe that one can change food preferences by following such procedures.

Using Modeling To Teach Eating a Nonpreferred Food

The student and the adult should sit in chairs across the table from each other. Place two very small portions (about the size of a quarter) of a nonpreferred food in the middle of the table. Place a favorite food reinforcer (e.g., chocolate frosting or ice cream) on the table next to you.

▶ Step 1

Present the instruction ("Do this") and use a finger to touch the *small* piece of nonpreferred food on the table in front of you. If necessary, physically prompt the student to do the same. Reinforce the student with a *small* bite of her favorite food for having touched the nonpreferred food. (Small bites are used to avoid early satiation). Fade the prompt and place the criterion for mastery at 5 out of 5 unprompted correct responses.

▶ Step 2

Present the instruction ("Do this") and pick up the food from the table, then place it back. Physically prompt the student to perform the same behavior if necessary. Reinforce, fade the prompt, and bring to mastery.

▶ Steps 3–5

Present the instruction ("Do this") and pick up the food, touch it to your nose, and then put it back down. Continue until mastery is reached. In Step 4, repeat the instruction, pick up the food, touch it to your lips, and then place it back on the table. In successive steps, increase the level of exposure to the food by holding the food to your lips for 1 second, gradually increasing to 5 seconds, before placing it back down on the table. Then proceed to Step 5, teaching the student to pick up the food and touch it to her tongue.

If the student becomes upset during any step presented above, immediately go back to an earlier step and reinforce her for completing the imitation of your action with the food. Then gradually increase the student's exposure to the nonpreferred food until she masters Step 5.

▶ Steps 6–7

Present the instruction ("Do this"), place a very small piece of the food in your mouth, and prompt the student to imitate your action. Should the student swallow the food, immediately reinforce with a small bite of her favorite food (e.g., ½ teaspoon of ice cream or a small sip of a favorite beverage). If the student does not swallow the food, help remove the food from her mouth and then, over several trials, increase the time interval the student must hold the food in her mouth from 1 to 5 seconds. In Step 7, you should model chewing and swallowing the food after the student places the food in her mouth. Try prompting the student to swallow the food by giving her a sip of her favorite beverage to swallow or a bite of a favorite food to eat. This immediate reward not only serves to reinforce the chewing or swallowing but also serves to remove the taste of the nonpreferred food. (In the technical literature, if a mildly aversive stimulus is systematically paired with a highly preferred stimulus, the first stimulus loses its aversive properties and begins to resemble the preferred one).

As the student advances through this program, introduce foods that are progressively more dissimilar to those the student presently eats. For example, introduce foods that differ in texture and color from the student's usual foods. Each new dimension may have to be introduced separately and in a stepwise fashion. Use very gradual steps when introducing multicolored and multitextured foods, such as pizza or spaghetti with tomato sauce, because such foods may look very different from those on the student's original food list. When introducing pizza, for example, begin with a small piece of crust only, then add a small amount of sauce, then cheese, and then gradually increase the portion to a regular-size piece of pizza. Keep in mind that some items (e.g., mushrooms, green pepper) may be more aversive than other items. If the student has a strong aversion to particular accessory foods, remove these food items for the time being.

Teaching the Student To Eat When Requested To Do So

Typical individuals learn to eat certain foods at certain times when requested or expected to do so. There are several reasons for teaching the student with developmental delays to do the same, one of which is to help the student eat some or all of the foods presented at mealtime. Another reason is to teach the student to restrict his food intake between meals. As it may be difficult to teach the student to eat a nonpreferred food when so requested, you may want to begin by teaching him to eat a favorite food or a neutral food upon your request. At the same time, you may want to teach the student *not* to eat a favorite food when it is available (e.g., when it is on the table or in the refrigerator).

The student may have already been taught to eat certain foods as part of the Early Receptive Language Program (Chapter 15). For example, the student may have been taught to respond appropriately to such requests as "Drink juice" and "Eat cookie." Follow the same steps described in Chapter 15 to teach the student to eat a particular food upon your request. If possible, begin by using a neutral or not strongly preferred food item. For illustrative purposes, we use cheese.

▶ **Step 1**

Place two small pieces of cheese on the table, one in front of the student and one in front of yourself. Present the instruction "Eat cheese," prompt by modeling the behavior, and reinforce the student's imitation with a favorite food. Gradually fade the model prompt until the student eats the small portion of the food without prompting and without becoming upset. Note that many students become upset at the prospect of eating a food when requested to do so even if they accepted the food when the teacher modeled the behavior. In our experience, with practice and with the preferred food reinforcer in view, most students overcome their emotional response to this situation.

▶ **Step 2**

Slowly increase, in an incremental and stepwise fashion, the portion of food the student is expected to eat. For example, introduce a piece of food cut into half the size of a sugar cube, then increase the portion to the size of a full sugar cube, then to a cube and one half, and so forth. It is important that you show the student the special food item to be used as a reinforcer for his eating the food when requested. If the student becomes too upset at the sight of a larger portion of food, go back to earlier steps by having the student touch the larger portion of food in imitation of your action, then move it toward his nose, then move it to his mouth, and then touch it to his tongue. Should the student continue to be upset, reinstate the student's cooperation by interspersing a few nonverbal imitation or receptive instruction trials unrelated to eating the food item. Remain at any given portion size for several trials (10 to 20 or more) before increasing size. Take your time and proceed in small steps until the student can eat a regular portion of the food.

Should the student's progress be very slow when using a neutral food item, switch to a highly preferred food and establish instructional control using that food. Place the preferred food item on the table and teach the student to eat the food when you request him to do so. This setting is also helpful for teaching the student *not* to eat the food on the table until asked to do so. The steps for teaching this skill may involve placing a preferred food on the table and instructing the student, "Do *not* eat." Prompt the student to withhold reaching for the food until he is given the instruction "Eat (food)" (or some similar instruction). Note that all individuals must learn when to eat and when not to eat and to comply with others' requests in this regard.

Introducing Foods into the Student's Mealtime[1]

After the student masters eating a regular portion of food in a structured setting, gradually introduce that food into the student's mealtime. Proceed in a stepwise fashion as follows: At mealtime, place on the student's plate a small portion (e.g., bite-size) of the nonpreferred food the student just mastered eating. The special reinforcer the student will receive contingent on eating the new food item should be in full view. Follow your regular mealtime rules about leaving the table if the student eats most or all of the meal. In other words, if the student must eat a certain amount of her regular meal before being excused from the table, continue to follow these guidelines. Remember that the student should not receive the special reinforcer

[1] We would like to thank our client E. K. and his family and staff for helping to develop this program.

unless she at least tries the new food item. If the student refuses the new food item as part of her regular meal, return to earlier steps to establish the new food as more appetizing and reintroduce the item to the table during her regular mealtime at a later date. In gradual steps, slowly increase the size of the portion the student must eat before receiving her special reinforcement. Once a student eats what her parents consider to be a reasonable amount of the new food, slowly remove the special reinforcer and continue to supply this new food as part of the student's regular meal.

A program like the one outlined in this section may take several months to accomplish. Remember, however, there are large individual differences among students in their rates of progress in this and every other program. Keep in mind that for students who have gained skills in receptive language, you may verbalize certain contingencies (e.g., if the student eats a certain food, she will receive a reinforcer; conversely, if she does not eat the food, she will not receive a reinforcer). In any case, maintain an appropriate perspective by considering the length of time it takes for typical children to learn to eat the kinds of foods their parents want them to eat. Also keep in mind that some typical individuals go for days hardly eating anything at all, seeming to live on oxygen alone. Despite parents' fears, it is unusual for such children to suffer from malnutrition.

Undressing and Dressing

Undressing

The skills required to undress oneself are taught more easily than those required to dress; consequently, undressing is targeted first. The goal of this program is for the student to remove certain pieces of clothing after being asked to do so. The steps for removing a pair of pants are outlined first, as this undressing skill is often the easiest for the student to learn and for the teacher to instruct. Backward chaining procedures are used in teaching this skill and can be applied to the steps involved in teaching the student to take off his shirt, socks, shoes, and jacket. Prior to learning to undress independently, the student should have achieved some mastery in imitation of object manipulation, gross motor imitation, and receptive language.

Removing Pants

When first teaching the student to remove pants, choose a pair of pants that do not fit too snugly on the student. The pants should have an elastic waistband that does not require unbuttoning or unzipping and should fit easily over the student's hips and legs. A loose-fitting pair of shorts are also a suitable choice when teaching this program. The target behavior of removing pants can be broken down into the following discrete steps presented in the order in which they should be taught:

1. Pulling off the pants from around the student's feet while he is sitting.
2. Pulling off the pants from around the student's ankles while he is sitting.
3. Pulling off the pants from around the student's shins while he is sitting.
4. Pulling off the pants from around the student's knees while he is sitting.
5. Pulling off the pants from around the student's thighs while he is standing.
6. Pulling off the pants from around the student's hips while he is standing.
7. Pulling off the pants from around the student's waist while he is standing.

► **Step 1**

Seat the student on the floor or on a chair and position the waistband of his pants around his feet. Give the general instruction "Pants off" and physically prompt the student to grip the waistband of his pants by hooking his thumbs inside the waistband, pulling them off from around his feet, and placing them on the floor. Reinforce and fade the prompt over successive trials. Set mastery at 5 out of 5 or 9 out of 10 unprompted correct responses.

► **Step 2**

Seat the student on the floor or on a chair and position the waistband of his pants around his ankles. Proceed as described in Step 1.

► **Steps 3–4**

Steps 3 and 4 are analogous to Steps 1 and 2 except the waistband of the student's pants is placed around his shins in Step 3 and around his knees in Step 4.

► **Steps 5–7**

In Steps 5 through 7, the response requirements are gradually increased in succinct steps from placing the waistband around the student's thighs to around his hips and then to around his waist. Beginning with Step 5, the student should stand to facilitate removing his pants. Prompt the student to remove the pants from around his thighs and then reinforce as done in earlier steps. Once Step 5 is mastered, go on to Step 6, which is equivalent to Step 5 except that the student's pants are positioned around his hips. Once Step 6 is mastered, go on to Step 7, having the student remove the pants from around his waist.

Removing a Shirt

When teaching the student to remove his shirt, use a loose-fitting short-sleeved shirt without buttons or zippers. The shirt should have a large opening at the top so it easily fits over the student's head. Using the same procedures described above for teaching the student to remove his pants, teach the student to remove his shirt. Removing a shirt can be broken down into the following steps:

1. Pulling off the shirt from around the crown of the student's head.
2. Pulling off the shirt from around the student's ears.
3. Pulling off the shirt from around the student's chin.
4. Pulling off the shirt from around the student's neck.
5. Pulling off the shirt with one of the student's arms through an armhole.
6. Pulling off the shirt from around the student's chest with both of his arms through the armholes.
7. Pulling off the shirt with the body of the shirt pulled down to the student's waist.

Removing Socks

When beginning to teach the child to remove socks, use an older child's or adult's sock and gradually decrease the size of the sock as the student becomes proficient at removing socks. Removing socks can be broken down into the following steps and taught by following the backward chaining procedures described above:

1. Pulling off a sock from around the student's toes.
2. Pulling off a sock from around the middle of the student's foot.
3. Pulling off a sock from around the student's heel.
4. Pulling off a sock from just above the student's heel.
5. Pulling off a sock from around the student's lower ankle.
6. Pulling off a sock from around the student's calf.

Removing Shoes

Shoes of a larger size than the student's own shoe size should be used when first teaching this portion of the program. As with removing socks, start by using an older child's or adult's shoe (ideally without laces) and gradually decrease the shoe size as the student becomes proficient at removing shoes. This skill can be broken down into the following steps and then combined using backward chaining procedures:

1. Pulling off the student's shoe from his toes.
2. Pulling off the student's shoe from halfway around his heel.
3. Pulling off the student's shoe from his entire foot.
4. When using shoes with laces, buckles, or Velcro, teach undoing of these fasteners last.

Removing a Jacket

A loose-fitting jacket should be used when beginning to teach the child to remove a jacket. Removing a jacket can be broken down into the following steps and then chained in the corresponding order:

1. Taking the second arm out of the jacket with the sleeve around the student's elbow.
2. Taking the second arm out of the jacket with the sleeve around the student's shoulder.
3. Taking the first arm out of the jacket with the sleeve around the student's elbow.
4. Taking the first arm out of the jacket with the sleeve around the student's shoulder.
5. Taking the jacket off with the front two sides of the jacket together but not fastened.

Dressing

In this program, the target response is for the student to dress himself when the teacher requests for him to do so. Except for the instruction (e.g., "Dress") given to the student, teaching a student to dress should be done in the same manner as undressing. In other words, the final step in the chain of behaviors is taught first and the preceding steps are added in descending order until the first step in the chain is reached. The distinct steps for putting on pants, a shirt, socks, shoes, and a jacket are presented below, in the order in which they should be taught. Follow the backward chaining procedures outlined earlier to combine the steps listed for each dressing behavior.

Putting on Pants

A loose pair of pants or shorts with an elastic waistband that fits easily over the student's legs and hips should be used. Putting on pants can be broken down into the following steps:

1. Positioning the waistband of the pants at the student's waist.
2. Pulling the pants up from the student's hips to his waist.
3. Pulling the pants up from the student's thighs to his hips.
4. Pulling the pants up from the student's knees to his thighs.
5. Pulling the pants up from the student's ankles to his knees.
6. Pushing the second foot through pant-leg hole to get pants around the student's ankles.
7. Positioning the pants over the student's second foot (when someone is holding the pants).
8. Pushing the student's first foot through the pant-leg hole.
9. Positioning the pants over the student's first foot (when someone is holding the pants).
10. Picking up the pants.

Putting on a Shirt

A loose-fitting short-sleeved shirt with a large opening at the top should be chosen when first teaching this portion of the program. Putting on a shirt may be broken down into the following steps:

1. Pulling the body of the shirt down from under the student's arms to his waist.
2. Putting the student's second arm through the sleeve.
3. Putting the student's first arm through the sleeve.
4. Turning the shirt to position the armholes.
5. Pulling the shirt from the student's chin to his neck.
6. Pulling the shirt from the student's ears to his chin.
7. Pulling the shirt from the top of the student's head to his ears.
8. Placing the shirt on the crown of the student's head (with someone holding the shirt).
9. Picking up the shirt.

Putting on Socks

A loose-fitting pair of socks should be used in the initial stages of this portion of the program. Putting on socks can be broken down into the following steps:

1. Pulling the upper edge of the sock up from the student's lower ankle to his calf.
2. Pulling the top of the sock up from just above the student's heel.
3. Pulling the top of the sock up from around the student's heel.
4. Correctly positioning the heel of the sock.
5. Pulling the sock up to the student's heel from around his toes.
6. Placing the opening of the sock on the student's toes.
7. Holding the opening of the sock in front of the student's toes (with someone initially holding the sock).
8. Picking up the sock.

Putting on Shoes

Shoes of a size larger than the student's own shoe size should be used when beginning to teach this program. Putting on shoes can be broken down into the following steps:

1. Pushing the student's heel into the shoe's heel.
2. Pulling the shoe's heel with the thumbs, from the middle of the foot.
3. Pushing the front of the foot into the shoe, with the toes just inside the opening of the shoe.
4. Placing the opening of the shoe over the student's toes (with someone initially holding the shoe).
5. Holding the opening of the shoe in front of the student's toes.
6. Grasping the shoe.

Putting on a Jacket

Use a loose-fitting jacket when teaching this skill. Putting on a jacket can be broken down into the following steps:

1. Pulling the front two sides of the jacket together.

2. Putting the second arm through the sleeve with the student's hand placed in the opening of the sleeve.
3. Placing the second hand in the opening of the sleeve.
4. Pulling the jacket over to the second hand from the opposite side of the student's back.
5. Putting the first arm through the sleeve with the student's hand placed in the opening of the sleeve.
6. Placing the first hand in the opening of the sleeve.
7. Holding the opening of the sleeve in front of the first hand.
8. Picking up the jacket.

Wait until a later time to target fastening skills, such as zipping, buttoning, and snapping, given that these tasks require finger dexterity and are often difficult for students to learn. When you do teach fastening skills, you may want to begin with fasteners that are attached to a board or large piece of fabric. These skills can later be generalized to the student's own clothing.

Brushing Hair

The ultimate goal of this program is for the student to brush her hair when you say, "Brush hair." A combination of imitation, shaping, and chaining should be used to teach the student to brush her hair. You may want to teach the student to brush her hair while seated at a mirror as this may facilitate acquisition of the target behavior.

▶ Step 1

Place one hairbrush in front of the student and one in front of yourself. Give the instruction "Brush hair" while picking up your brush. If the student does not pick up the brush after you model the response, consequate the nonresponse and verbally prompt her on the next trial by saying, "Do this," again picking up the brush. If the student does not respond correctly, physically prompt her to pick up the brush in the next trial immediately after you model the behavior. Reinforce the response and fade the physical prompt until the student independently imitates picking up the brush in 5 out of 5 or 9 out of 10 trials. If you cannot fade the physical prompt, wait to introduce this program until you are sure that the student has mastered imitation involving object manipulation. Once Step 1 is mastered, go on to Step 2.

▶ Step 2

Again model the behavior of picking up the brush. Once the student imitates the action, move your brush up until it touches the top of your head and prompt the student to imitate the action if necessary. Reinforce the correct response. Once Step 2 is mastered (5 out of 5 or 9 out of 10 correct responses), go on to Step 3.

▶ Step 3

Model the behaviors taught in Steps 1 and 2. After the student places the brush on top of her head, move your brush in a downward stoke to the base of your head. Repeat the entire sequence (i.e., pick up the brush, move it to the top of your head, and then stroke the brush through your hair to the base of your head) several times until the student imitates the sequence in a continuous and flowing manner so that there is little to no pause between each individual movement. Once Step 3 is mastered (5 out of 5 or 9 out of 10 correct responses), go on to Step 4.

▶ Step 4

The goal of Steps 4 and 5 is to teach the student to imitate multiple strokes following the instruction "Brush hair." Begin by giving the instruction, moving your brush to the top of your head, and performing two downward strokes. Prompt the student to imitate the complete response if necessary. Provide reinforcement only after the student imitates two strokes with the brush. Once Step 4 is mastered, go on to Step 5.

▶ Step 5

Step 5 is analogous to Step 4 except that in this step you gradually increase the number of strokes the student is required to make before receiving reinforcement. Present the instruction "Brush hair" and complete three downward strokes. After the student masters completing three strokes, increase the number of strokes to four. Continue adding strokes one at a time until the student completes enough strokes to brush her entire head of hair. Once Step 5 is mastered, go on to Step 6.

Step 6

The goal of Step 6 is to fade all the modeling prompts so the student can independently brush her hair when given the instruction "Brush hair." Gradually decrease the amount of prompting by providing less and less of your model. Begin by fading the last downward stroke first, then the second to last stroke, and so forth until you only model picking up the brush. Continue to fade your prompt until the student no longer requires a prompt to pick up the brush and brush her hair when given the instruction "Brush hair."

The steps described for brushing hair may be modified depending on the student's particular haircut. The teaching steps may include grasping the brush with the dominant hand, brushing the hair beginning at the part and moving downward on both sides, and grooming the hair at the back of the head. Further steps might address brushing the hair from underneath in order to groom long hair.

Brushing Teeth

Brushing teeth is a complex skill and should not be attempted until well into the second year of the Self-Help Skills Programs. Note that a typical individual may not acquire this skill until 5 to 6 years of age.

For this program you need the following materials: a toothbrush, toothpaste, a toothbrush holder, a cup, and a towel (have a duplicate of each of these items if modeling is to be used as a prompt). Similar to eating and dressing, the target behavior of brushing teeth is composed of several discrete elements. A forward chaining procedure is used to teach and combine each of the elements in a forward chronological order. By the end of this program, the student should be able to brush his teeth after given the instruction "Brush teeth."

As with the teaching of any behavior, modeling is the preferred prompt provided the student has mastered modeling. Some students advance relatively quickly in learning to imitate a model; others, however, advance at a slower pace and need more physical prompts. Also, some behaviors such as brushing teeth and washing hands are quite complex, consisting of several steps. More complex behaviors are likely to need a larger proportion of manual prompting. On the other hand, complex behaviors such as brushing teeth are likely to be introduced later in a student's program, after the student has made additional advances in the Nonverbal Imitation Program. We recommend that the teacher probe with modeling prompts before using manual prompts when introducing this program. Remember that a complex behavior such as brushing teeth could, and perhaps should, be used to extend the nonverbal imitation skills acquired in Chapter 13.

This program may be begun at the table or some other convenient place. When the first five steps are mastered, move the program to the bathroom and have the student stand in front of the sink. The following chain of steps is suggested as a guide for instructing the student to brush teeth. This is an abbreviated list and does not encompass all possible steps or additional steps the student may need later as he grows older and more accomplished with his self-help skills. The behaviors to be taught can be broken down as follows:

1. Grasping the toothbrush.
2. Brushing the teeth on the left side of the mouth.
3. Brushing the teeth on the right side of the mouth.
4. Brushing the front teeth.
5. Laying the toothbrush down.
6. Picking up a cup with water in it.
7. Taking a sip of water.
8. Rinsing out the mouth.
9. Putting down the cup.
10. Turning on the faucet.
11. Rinsing the toothbrush.
12. Putting the toothbrush away.
13. Turning off the faucet.
14. Drying off the hands.
15. Drying the outside of the mouth.

As mentioned earlier, forward chaining is used to teach the student to brush his teeth. Modeling, as opposed to manual prompting, should be used as a prompt whenever possible.

Step 1

Until the student masters Steps 1 through 5, you may want to use a toothbrush without toothpaste. Present the instruction "Brush teeth," immediately prompt the student (using nonverbal imitation or manual guidance) to pick up his toothbrush, and reinforce the correct response. When the student correctly imitates your behavior in 5 out of 5 or 9 out of 10 trials, go on to Step 2.

▶ Steps 2–5

Steps 2 through 5 involve teaching the student to brush his front teeth and the teeth on the left and right sides of his mouth. In Step 2, the student should imitate your picking up the toothbrush after presentation of the instruction "Brush teeth." Next, give the instruction "Brush in" and prompt the student to put the brush in the left side of his mouth and then to brush the teeth on that side. Reinforce. After the student masters Step 2, teach Step 3 by following the completed sequence with the instruction "Other side" and prompt the student to brush the teeth on the right side of his mouth. Reinforce. When the student masters Step 3, teach Step 4 by following the completed sequence with the instruction "Front." Prompt the student to brush his front teeth and follow this action with reinforcement. After the student masters Step 4, teach Step 5 by following the completed sequence with the instruction "Brush down" and prompt the student to lay down the toothbrush. Follow this behavior with reinforcement.

When the student masters Steps 1 through 5, fade the individual instructions, beginning with the instruction "Brush in." Fade this instruction one word at a time until the student picks up the toothbrush and brushes the teeth on the left side of his mouth (Steps 1 to 2) after presentation of the instruction "Brush teeth." After this goal is met, gradually fade the instruction "Other side" one word at a time until the student complete Steps 1 through 3 following presentation of the instruction "Brush teeth." Finally, fade the instruction "Front" and then "Brush down" in a similar manner until the student completes Steps 1 through 5 following presentation of the instruction "Brush teeth." Continue practicing Steps 1 through 5 for approximately 1 to 2 weeks before moving on to Step 6.

▶ Steps 6–9

After the student masters Steps 1 through 5, teach Steps 6 through 9, which involve teaching the student to rinse his mouth with water. Present the instruction "Brush teeth" and, after the student completes Steps 1 through 5, present the instruction "Get cup" and prompt the student to pick up the cup. Reinforce the response. Continue to practice Steps 1 through 6 until Step 6 is mastered. Next, teach Step 7 by following the completed sequence with the instruction "Take a sip." Prompt the student to take a sip of water and follow this action with reinforcement. When the student masters Step 7, teach Step 8 by following the completed sequence with the instruction "Rinse." Prompt the student to rinse out his mouth and spit out the water. Teach Step 9 by following the completed sequence with the instruction "Cup down." Prompt the student to put down the cup and then reinforce the behavior.

After the student masters Steps 1 through 9, fade the individual instructions given in Steps 6 through 9 by following the fading procedures outlined above for Steps 2 through 5; that is, fade the instruction for Step 6 ("Get cup") first and continue to fade the instructions in forward chronological order until the student completes Steps 1 through 9 following presentation of the instruction "Brush teeth." Continue practicing Steps 1 through 9 for approximately 1 to 2 weeks before moving on to Step 10.

▶ Steps 10–15

When the student masters Steps 1 through 9, proceed with Steps 10 through 15, which involve teaching the student to rinse his toothbrush and then dry his hands and mouth. Present the instruction "Brush teeth." After the student completes Step 9, present the instruction "Water on" and prompt the student to turn on the cold water. Follow this action with reinforcement and continue to practice Steps 1 through 10 until Step 10 is mastered. Next, teach Step 11 by following the completed sequence with the instruction "Wash brush," prompting the student to rinse his brush under the water. Follow this action with reinforcement. When Step 11 is mastered, teach Step 12 by following the completed sequence with the instruction "Put away" and prompt the student to put the brush in a holder. Follow this action with reinforcement. When Step 12 is mastered, teach Step 13 by following the completed sequence with the instruction "Water off" and prompt the student to turn off the water. Reinforce the correct response. After the student masters Step 13, teach Step 14 by following the completed sequence with the instruction "Dry hands," prompt the student to dry his hands with a towel, and follow this action with reinforcement. When Step 14 is mastered, teach Step 15 by following the completed sequence with the instruction "Dry mouth." Prompt the student to dry his mouth with the towel and follow this action with reinforcement.

When the student masters Steps 1 through 15, begin to fade the individual instructions given for Steps 10 through 15 by following the fading procedures outlined above for Steps 2 through 5. Fade the instruction for Step 10 ("Water on") first and continue to fade in forward chronological order until the student completes Steps 1 through 15 following presentation of the instruction "Brush teeth." Finally, gradually fade out the use of prompts, transferring control to the general instruction.

Areas of Difficulty

If the sequence of 15 steps for brushing teeth appears too complex for the student's current level of functioning, it may be taught in a more gradual or simplified manner first and then shaped into the entire sequence at a later time. As recommended earlier, the motions involved in brushing teeth may be taught first in the student's teaching room with you and the student seated across from each other. Without toothpaste, you may teach the student to imitate brushing motions in this controlled environment. Similarly, you may teach imitation of drying motions with a towel for both the hands and mouth in a controlled environment before teaching the previously outlined sequence of steps in the bathroom.

If you encounter difficulties fading out the individual verbal instructions for each step, you may want to use a picture sequence to help the student achieve independence with his brushing routine. Using symbols or photographs of the student engaging in each of the steps, create a chart that depicts each step in a left-to-right or top-to-bottom fashion. Teach the student to follow this chart by prompting him to complete a step for each picture, then gradually fade yourself out as the student masters following the steps depicted on the chart. Consult the Reading and Writing Program and the Picture Exchange Communication System Program (Chapters 29 and 30, respectively) for more ideas about teaching the student to follow visual sequences.

Washing Hands

For this program, you need a bar of soap and a towel (have duplicates of these items available if modeling is to be used as a prompt). The target response is for the student to wash her hands when you say, "Wash hands." Similar to brushing teeth, the target behavior of hand washing is composed of several discrete steps that may be combined in forward chronological order. This program may be taught with the student standing in front of the sink in the bathroom or kitchen.

The following sequence of steps is recommended as a guideline for teaching the student to wash her hands:

1. Turning on the cold water.
2. Putting both hands under the water.
3. Picking up the soap.
4. Rubbing the soap between the student's hands.
5. Putting the soap away.
6. Rubbing the student's hands together.
7. Rinsing off the student's hands.
8. Turning off the water.
9. Picking up the towel.
10. Drying the student's hands.
11. Putting the towel away.

As mentioned earlier, forward chaining is used to teach and combine the individual steps. Modeling as opposed to manual prompting should be used whenever possible.

▶ **Step 1**

Give the general instruction "Wash hands" and immediately prompt the student to turn on the water. Provide reinforcement for this action. When the student masters Step 1 by independently performing the target action in 5 out of 5 or 9 out of 10 trials, go on to Step 2.

▶ **Steps 2–7**

Steps 2 through 7 involve teaching the student to put her hands under the water, wash them with soap, and then rinse them. Begin by presenting the instruction "Wash hands." After the student turns on the water, present the instruction "Hands wet." Prompt the student to put her hands under the water and then reinforce the behavior. When the student masters Step 2, add Step 3 to the sequence by presenting the instruction "Get soap" following the completed sequence (turning on the water and putting her hands under it). Prompt the student to pick up the soap, and provide reinforcement for this action. When the student masters Step 3, teach Step 4 by following the completed sequence of steps with the instruction "Rub the soap" and prompt the student to rub the bar of soap between her hands. Follow this action with reinforcement. Once the student masters Step 4, teach Step 5. Following the completed sequence of steps, present the instruction "Put soap away" and prompt the student to put the soap back in its proper location. Reinforce the response. When the student masters Step 5, teach Step 6 by presenting the instruction "Rub hands," prompting the student to rub her hands together. Follow this action with reinforcement. Next, teach Step 7 by following the completed sequence of steps with the instruction "Hands wet." Prompt the student to put her hands under the water and rinse them. Reinforce.

When the student masters Steps 1 through 7, begin fading the individual instructions by following the fading procedures outlined for Steps 2 through 5 in the Brushing Teeth section. That is, fade the instruction for Step 2 ("Hands wet") first and continue to fade in forward chronological order until the student completes Steps 1 through 7 following presentation of the instruction "Wash hands." Continue to practice Steps 1 through 7 for approximately 1 to 2 weeks before moving on to Step 8.

▶ Steps 8–11

When the student masters Steps 1 through 7, teach Steps 8 through 11, which involve teaching the student to turn off the water and dry her hands. Following the same teaching procedures outlined previously, use the instructions "Water off" and "Get towel" to complete the chain. Prompt as necessary. When the student masters Step 9, teach Step 10, which involves the instruction "Dry hands" and prompting the student to dry her hands. When Step 10 is mastered, teach Step 11 by presenting the instruction "Towel away" after the student completes the above sequence of steps. Prompt the student to put the towel away and then provide reinforcement.

After the student masters Steps 1 through 11, begin fading the individual instructions given in Steps 8 to 11 by following the fading procedures outlined in Steps 2 through 7; that is, fade the instruction for Step 8 ("Water off") first and continue to fade instructions in forward chronological order until the student completes Steps 1 through 11 following presentation of the instruction "Wash hands." Finally, gradually fade out the use of your prompts, transferring control to the general instruction.

Areas of Difficulty

As discussed in the section on brushing teeth, if the sequence of steps appears too complex for the student's current level of functioning, it may be taught in a more gradual or simplified manner. These behaviors may later be shaped into the sequence described. The motions involved in hand washing may be taught while the student is in the controlled environment of the teaching room. Here the student may be taught to imitate the motions of rubbing her hands together and drying her hands with a towel.

As mentioned earlier, you may also come across difficulties fading out the individual verbal instructions for each step. If this occurs, you may want to consider using a picture sequence to help the student become less prompt dependent. As with all self-help skills, remember that time is on your side; typical individuals also require a considerable amount of time before they master these skills.

Daytime Toilet Training

The following materials are needed to teach toileting skills: a potty seat or chair, a stool, cloth training pants, a watch or timer, a book to record toileting events, a large supply of the student's favorite drinks and salty snacks, and a variety of the student's favorite tabletop toys or activities. Before you teach this program to the student, the student should have mastered dressing and undressing with his pants. Toilet training the student initially requires a significant investment of time on your part; be prepared to devote several hours addressing this skill with the student. Remember, however, that after the student is toilet trained, both you and your student will be happier.

The procedures described in this program are adapted and modified from Azrin and Foxx (1971). As they discussed, it is possible to successfully teach some students toileting skills in 1 day of intensive toilet training. After 1 day of 10 hours of training, the student should be able to hold his urine until instructed by the adult to use the bathroom. The procedures outlined in this section do not teach the student to *initiate* using the bathroom; initiating is taught separately in procedures described toward the end of this chapter. Initiation is taught after the student learns to control his bladder and is successful in that respect over several weeks.

In Preparation

A full day should be set aside to focus exclusively on toilet training (the intensive toilet training day). As a pretraining step, teach the student to go through the motions of going to the bathroom. Instruct the student, "Let's potty." If the student is verbal, prompt him to make a statement such as "Potty" as you enter the bathroom. If the student is nonverbal, prompt him to give you a picture of a toilet or perform some other nonverbal gesture. Take the student into the bathroom and prompt him to pull down his pants (if the student already learned this skill from the previous section on undressing skills, merely ask him to take off his pants). Then prompt the student to sit on the toilet. If the student is big enough, it is preferable to use a regular toilet or a toilet with a potty seat rather than a potty chair. By doing so, toileting skills will not have to later be transferred from a potty chair to the toilet. When using a regular toilet, provide the student with a stool on which he can rest his feet as he sits on the toilet.

Once the student sits on the toilet, have him remain there for 3 to 5 minutes. While the student is sitting, reinforce him by allowing him to look through books, listen to music, do puzzles, or engage in some other favorite activity so he learns that sitting on the toilet is a pleasant activity. If the student happens to urinate while seated on the toilet, give him a very special treat and abundant verbal praise, and then let him leave the bathroom. The special treats should consist of items (e.g., ice cream or chocolate chips) the student especially enjoys but is not allowed access to on a regular basis.

The pretraining procedure described should be conducted for approximately 3 to 5 minutes every hour and should be continued for 2 or 3 weeks prior to the day set aside for intensive toilet training. Two or 3 days prior to the intensive training day, increase the frequency of these trips to the toilet to every 15 to 20 minutes. This provides the student with extra exposure to the bathroom.

The Intensive Training Day

Before beginning the intensive training day, keep in mind that most but not all students are successful on their first day. If the student is successful, it is likely that this success will be restricted to bladder training as bowel training takes much longer to teach and learn. Also, even if the student is taught to urinate into the toilet by the end of the first day, it is likely that accidents will still occur. It takes some extra time to teach a boy to stand up and urinate after he masters urinating while sitting down. On top of that, it also takes some extra effort to help a boy aim his urine inside the toilet rather than on the seat or floor. We provide suggestions on how to teach such accuracy. Keep in mind that typical persons also need help aiming, avoiding accidents, and the like. The reason for having one intensive toilet training day is to mass trial this skill in order to get off to a good strong start.

To maximize the student's success on his day of intensive training, adhere to the following guidelines. First, increase the student's intake of liquids so he urinates frequently. Doing so provides the student with many successes (i.e., reinforced trials) on the toilet. Second, decide in advance which correction procedure you will use in the event of an accident. For example, you may have the student wash his wet pants in a sink for 2 minutes or wipe the floor with a wet cloth for 3 to 4 minutes. Keep in mind that the correction procedure chosen should not be an activity the student will enjoy but rather one that will require some effort. Third, keep the student entertained and engaged in activities throughout the day in the bathroom to help make toilet training a positive experience.

Following are the major steps involved in toilet training the student. To make the day more tolerable for the adults, have as many team members present as possible to take turns helping the student and providing food, drinks, happy conversations, and the like.

▶ Step 1

Early in the morning, just after the student wakes up, seat the student on the toilet after prompting him to say, "Potty," or to nonverbally demonstrate the need to go to the bathroom (e.g., by handing the teacher a picture of a toilet). This step may serve as a pretraining step to help the student initiate toileting and should be performed before each trip to the bathroom. Provide the student with many liquids and salty foods that will make him thirsty. The large amount of liquids serves as a prompt to urinate. During this step, the student should sit on the toilet for approximately 30 minutes. The student should not wear any undergarments or pants at this point to avoid the possible confusion of having to remove such garments. Allow the student to look at books, do puzzles, and so forth, to keep himself occupied while sitting on the toilet. When the student urinates, provide abundant verbal praise and a special treat selected just for potty training. Also provide the student with ample liquids as a reinforcer, which will serve to prompt future urination.

Let the student off the toilet for a 5-minute play break (make this break shorter if the student is likely to urinate during the break).

When the break is over, place the student back on the toilet for another trial. Even if the student does not urinate, give praise approximately every 3 minutes for sitting nicely and provide more liquids to drink. If the 30-minute period elapses without the student urinating, give the student a 5-minute play break. Stay near the bathroom during this break and keep the student undressed from the waist down. If the student begins to urinate during the break, quickly place him back on the toilet and then reinforce him for urinating into the toilet. If the student does not urinate during the break, allow him to play for the full 5 minutes and then return to the toilet for the next 30-minute session.

▶ Step 2

After the student successfully urinates into the toilet three or four times and is consistently accident free during his breaks, decrease the amount of time on the toilet to 25 minutes and increase the break time to 7 minutes. The student should still be undressed from the waist down and returned to the toilet if an accident occurs during the break. As the student consistently urinates in the toilet and is accident free during breaks (three to four times in a row), continue to increase the break time to 15 minutes and *gradually* shorten the interval the student must sit on the toilet to 5 minutes.

If the student is not successful during longer breaks (i.e., if breaks cannot be increased to any substantial interval without incurring accidents) by the late afternoon of the first day, this may not be the right time for the student to learn the toileting skills presented in this section. Consider postponing the training for another 2 to 4 months; it is less frustrating for all involved to wait until the student is ready to learn a particular skill before beginning or resuming training.

▶ Step 3

Dress the student in a pair of training pants after mastery of Step 2. Remove the training pants when the student is placed back on the toilet.

▶ Step 4

If the student remains accident free during breaks while wearing training pants and consistently urinates in the toilet, the break time should be further increased. The amount of time seated on the toilet should be proportionally decreased. Periodically check the student's training pants and verbally reward the student for having dry pants during break time. If an accident occurs, show the student the wet pants, state an informational "No," and have the student perform a correction procedure (e.g., have the student wash the pants for 2 minutes). The presence of wet pants may help the student discriminate (become aware of) accidents. After the student completes the correction procedure, return student to the toilet for 5 minutes.

▶ Step 5

For the remainder of the day, gradually increase the student's break time and proportionately decrease the amount of time required on the toilet. Continue to reinforce the student for urinating into the toilet and for having dry pants during break time. Implement the correction procedure if the student has an accident during a break. The student should continue to eat salty foods and drink plenty of liquids during the remainder of the day.

A realistic goal to strive for on this first day is 30-minute accident-free break periods interspersed with 2- to 3-minute intervals of being seated on the toilet with one or more successful urinations. The student should be allowed to leave the bathroom contingent on successful urination to enjoy the 30-minute break. It is crucial to continue this schedule until the student goes to bed. At that point, you may dress the student in a diaper to be worn overnight. If the student is placed in a diaper in the daytime, however, the diaper is likely to serve as a cue for urination. The diaper provides a stronger cue for urinating than the toilet in the early stages of training.

▶ Step 6

The day after intensive training, return to the student's regular routine (i.e., an intermingling of teaching time and play time) but take the student to sit on the toilet at specified time intervals (i.e., the longest interval mastered the previous day). In other words, continue with the student's teaching sessions during time off the toilet but take the student directly to the toilet as soon as the time interval passes even if this time falls during a formal teaching situation. The student should remain dressed only in training pants and a shirt for a few days to make the bathroom routine easier to complete. It is often helpful to use a timer to time the intervals so as to help reduce accidents. Intermittently check for dry pants during the intervals in which the student is not seated on the toilet. Reinforce the student if pants remain dry and use a correction procedure for accidents.

▶ Step 7

Over the next several weeks, gradually increase the break interval. For most students, the interval may be extended to a 1- or a 1½-hour period between trips to the bathroom. For example, if at the end of the intense potty training day the student was successful with 30-minute breaks and sat on the toilet for 5 minutes or less, continue with this schedule for a couple of days, then increase the break interval to 35 minutes. Continue to increase in 5-minute intervals every couple of days. If at any time the student repeatedly has accidents, consequate the accidents with correction procedures and go back to a shorter interval until the student is again successful. Remember that the correction procedure should not be enjoyable; if the procedure is enjoyable, it will inadvertently reinforce accidents.

Additional Toileting Skills

The toileting skills that follow may be addressed after the student masters the steps presented previously.

Aiming

Boys are notorious for missing the toilet. If this occurs with the student you work with, place Fruit loops (the cereal) inside the toilet as targets to improve the aim (Fruit loops are better than cereals such as Cheerios because Fruit loops are more discriminable given their bright colors). The prompt provided by the Fruit loops may be faded over trials by gradually reducing the number of cereal pieces placed in the toilet at a time. As always, reinforce correct behavior.

Wiping

Instruct the student to get some toilet paper (e.g., by saying, "Get paper"), helping him to take an appropriate amount. Reinforce the student, then help him to correctly grab the paper and prompt him through the motion of wiping himself after you give the instruction "Wipe." Provide the student with reinforcement for wiping, then instruct and prompt him to drop the paper into the toilet.

Flushing

After the student uses the toilet, instruct, "Flush." You may physically prompt this behavior by guiding the student's hand to the handle and pushing down firmly or by modeling the behavior if the student has mastered the imitation of gross motor movements. Praise the student for flushing the toilet and fade the prompt over successive trials. Many students enjoy flushing toilets; thus, this skill may eventually be used as reinforcement for eliminating in the toilet.

Teaching the Student To Initiate Using the Toilet

After a successful month or so with 1- to 2-hour periods between trips to the bathroom, slowly increase the interval in 5-minute increments. The purpose of increasing the time interval is to make the student aware of (discriminate) the need to urinate, which may help the student learn to initiate going to the bathroom by expressing, "Potty," or performing a nonverbal indication (e.g., gesturing or handing you a picture of a toilet). As the time interval grows increasingly long, help the student go into the bathroom by conducting treatment or playtime near an open bathroom door (especially as the end of the interval nears). You may further help the student by walking the student toward the bathroom door should you observe signs of his needing to urinate. You may also use a partial prompt by saying all or part of the word "potty" or motioning the student to nonverbally indicate the need to go to the bathroom. Continue to increase the interval and fade prompts until the student independently initiates going to the bathroom when needing to urinate.

Defecating in the Toilet

Most students are successful at learning to urinate into the toilet but still have accidents with their bowel movements. Although controlling the bowels is often more difficult to acquire than controlling the bladder, the same basic procedures may be used to teach this skill as those used for teaching the student to urinate in the toilet. One of the major problems encountered when teaching the student to use the toilet for bowel movements centers on the infrequency of elimination and the virtual absence of prompts such as the liquids used to prompt urination. The fewer opportunities there are to prompt, the lower the frequency of the behavior and opportunities to reinforce. Hence the slower rate of acquisition.

Perhaps the best way to go about teaching the student to defecate in the toilet is to anticipate when the student is likely to have a bowel movement. The student may defecate at a certain time of the day or go to a certain place in the house to defecate. If you can anticipate when the student is likely to have a bowel movement, prompt sitting on the toilet for 5 to 15 minutes to probe whether or not success follows. If the student is successful, provide abundant verbal praise and special edible treats. If the student is not successful, provide praise for sitting nicely on the toilet, remove the student from the toilet, and later place him back on the toilet for a short time. If you catch the student in the act of defecating in his pants, immediately place the student on the toilet in an attempt to provide him with a successful bowel movement in the toilet. If the student completes the bowel movement in the toilet, provide abundant verbal praise and a special edible treat. This phase will most likely take much more time and effort than training the student to urinate in the toilet. Try not to become discouraged with the student, however, as learning to defecate in the toilet is a difficult step and takes many students with developmental delays a long time to acquire.

Areas of Difficulty

As with the other programs in this manual, the toilet training program was developed to suit the learning characteristics of most students with developmental delays. Despite these procedures, a variety of unique problems may manifest themselves, and you will have to improvise solutions for these problems.

A common problem is the student's withholding defecation when on the toilet. Some students may refrain from defecating for 4 or more days, causing much anxiety in their parents and team members. Some typical individuals "hold on" as well, especially if only unfamiliar bathrooms are nearby. One solution to this problem is to wait it out; another solution is to consult the student's pediatrician to obtain a fast-acting laxative, which should produce results within 1 to 2 hours. The latter solution serves as a prompt. If it is fear that causes the student to withhold defecation, use a student's potty chair and take steps unique to the student to reduce his fear (e.g., play music, have her hold a favorite toy).

Some students refuse to eliminate in the bathroom but may eliminate in other rooms of the house or outside in the yard. If this occurs, begin toilet training in the area where the student is comfortable eliminating and gradually move the potty chair inside in incremental steps.

Numerous teaching manuals are available for helping children with developmental delays acquire self-help skills. Such manuals include the guidebook by Baker et al. (1997) and the detailed program for toilet training by Azrin and Foxx (1971).

Expressive Language

SECTION 4

Verbal Imitation

CHAPTER 22

The skills taught in the Verbal Imitation Program are important for all students with developmental delays, including students who do not currently speak and those who are echolalic. Through this program, the student learns to enunciate sounds, words, phrases, and sentences. Enunciation is the first step toward learning to use words in a meaningful manner, because once verbal imitation is mastered, this skill can be used to prompt responses in other programs that require verbal responses (e.g., Chapters 23 and 24). Verbal imitation training also aids the teacher in gaining control over the timing of an echolalic student's repetition of words and phrases. Whether the student is echolalic at the beginning of treatment or becomes echolalic as a result of the Verbal Imitation Program, echolalic responding may be so excessive that it interferes with the student's acquisition of vocal language. If the student you work with acquires this tendency, the interference of excessive echolalic responding may be reduced by using the techniques described in the section "Managing Echolalia" toward the end of this chapter.

Gaining instructional control over the student's vocalizations accomplishes two goals. First, in shifting control over the student's vocalizations from the student's own sensory feedback (as in self-stimulatory behavior) to the teacher's externally mediated reinforcers, the teacher is in a better position to subsequently influence and shape the student's vocalizations into recognizable and meaningful speech. In contrast, if the student's vocalizations are not effected by the teacher's use of extrinsic reinforcement, they are less likely to be brought under instructional control and less likely to be modified by the teacher. Second, once the student learns he can gain some control over his social environment by vocalizing, he makes a major step toward developing socially appropriate behaviors that may replace tantrums and self-stimulatory behaviors.

Given that parents and teachers tend to prioritize language skills, they may try to work quickly through the steps in this program. In teaching verbal imitation, the teachers need to constantly remind themselves that *haste runs the risk of making language aversive to the student*. This is a very difficult program to teach and a very difficult program for the student to master. Hence, everybody must be patient and move forward in small steps.

As a prerequisite for the current program, you should have established instructional control as described in Chapter 9. Specifically, the student should have learned to comply with elementary requests, such as sitting in a chair when asked to do so and should display few tantrums and self-stimulatory behaviors while in the teaching situation. The student should have also made progress in his mastery of matching and nonverbal imitation (see Chapters 12 and 13) prior to beginning this program. Although there appears to be no discernible generalization between nonverbal imitation and verbal imitation, the prior learning of mouth movement imitations (e.g., closing lips, blowing, sticking out one's tongue) helps to prompt certain sounds. Finally, it is very important that you become proficient at employing discrimination learning procedures (Chapter 16), as these procedures are essential to teaching verbal imitation.

There are as of yet no data (e.g., regarding student characteristics) that allow teachers to predict whether the student is an auditory or a visual learner, a distinction that was described in Chapter 3. The only advice we have is to start teaching verbal imitation and see how well the student learns to imitate your vocalizations. If the student fails to learn to imitate speech or demonstrates extreme difficulty learning to do so, introduce Chapter 29 (Reading and Writing), Chapter 30 (Communication Strategies for Visual Learners), or both. Some preliminary and informal data suggest that some children learn to verbalize once progress is gained in the Reading and Writing Program.

The Verbal Imitation Program is divided into several phases, ranging from the relatively simple to the very complex, and can be outlined in brief as follows: In Phase 1, the student is taught to increase the amount of his vocalizations. This increase marks the first attempt to gain reinforcement control over the student's spontaneous and random vocalizations (e.g., babbling, humming) by shifting control from self-produced sensory reinforcers (as in self-stimulatory behavior) to extrinsic reinforcers that you provide. Phase 1 is the first step toward allowing you to influence and later shape the student's vocalizations into recognizable words.

Phase 2 builds upon Phase 1 and is a little more demanding in that the student does not obtain reinforcement simply for vocalizing but rather for vocalizing *after* you vocalize. That is, you make a sound, and if the student vocalizes shortly thereafter, the student is reinforced. In everyday language, the student is taught to listen and respond to your vocalization in order to be reinforced (in technical terms, the student is taught a temporal discrimination).

Phase 3 is complex because reinforcement in this phase is given only if the student's vocalizations match your vocalizations. For example, if you vocalize the sound "ah," the student is reinforced for imitating the sound "ah." If you then introduce another sound "mm," the student is provided with reinforcement contingent on his imitating the new sound "mm." These sounds (e.g., "ah" and "mm") are then subjected to discrimination learning procedures. This phase in particular marks the beginning of true verbal imitation and requires you to have thorough knowledge of discrimination learning principles.

Phase 4 goes beyond the imitation of isolated sounds and teaches the student to imitate a combination of sounds, such as those that compose simple words like "dada" and "baby." Phase 5 teaches the imitation of complex words, and Phase 6 introduces strings of words as used in phrases and sentences (e.g., "I want up"). Phase 7 teaches the student to imitate your use of volume, pitch, and speed.

Although we are reasonably confident in recommending that Phases 3, 4, 5, 6, and 7 be taught in consecutive order, there are no scientific data to indicate that Phase 1 must precede Phase 2 or that Phase 2 must precede Phase 3. Indeed, there are substantial individual differences among students. In our experience, some students have serious difficulties with Phase 1 but master Phase 2 relatively quickly. The sequence of phases in this chapter is the best guide we currently have to help you start verbal imitation training, aid in the student's success, and increase the student's motivation to talk. However, it is certainly not universally successful.

Because of the difficulty involved in teaching verbal imitation, we recommend that one or two teachers be appointed to specialize in this program. They should confer closely with one another and ask advice from the remaining team members and consultants. They should also inspect for inadvertent variations in teaching style across teachers, making sure that such variations do not occur and delay the student's mastery, especially in the early stages of verbal imitation training.

Phase 1: Increasing Vocalizations

To increase the frequency of the student's vocalizations, all you should do in Phase 1 is reinforce the student for vocalizing. A vocalization may be defined as any audible sound or word made by the student and includes grunting, laughing, coughing, babbling, "ah," "ee," "baba," recognizable words such as "mama," and the like. Within less than 1 second after the occurrence of a vocalization, a reinforcer should be delivered. Make sure that the reinforcer is powerful and discriminable. For most students, we recommend food reinforcement (small bites of easily chewed food) and pronounced smiling, verbal approval, and clapping on the part of the teacher and other people present. In short, the student should cause quite an audience reaction based on her attempts to vocalize. Keep in mind, however, that some students are hypersensitive to sounds and may react with fear or anger to too much gusto, so set the volume accordingly.

If the student has a favorite food, it should be reserved for the Verbal Imitation Program. A small bite of a favorite food not only can serve to reinforce vocalizations but, as discussed later in this section, can prompt them as well, which paves the way for further opportunities to reinforce. The student's favorite food may make her content, and vocalizations are more likely to occur during periods of contentment. In short, the delivery of reinforcement (e.g., kisses, food, and tickles) often cues emotional behaviors, which in turn prompt more vocalizations. (Technically speaking, the reinforcing stimulus may possess unconditioned stimulus properties that may cue vocal respondent behaviors. These behaviors may later be brought under reinforcement control and become operant behavior.)

Although the procedure in Phase 1 may seem relatively simple, you may encounter one or more of the following problems. First, the student's spontaneous rate of vocalizations may be quite low, giving you few opportunities to reinforce. Second, you may find it very difficult to prompt more frequent vocalizations. Third, given that vocalizations are fleeting responses, it may be difficult for the student to connect her response with the reinforcing stimulus. Technically speaking, it may be difficult for the student to discriminate the reinforcement contingency (the connection between the vocalization and the subsequent reinforcer), which makes it difficult for you to gain reinforcement control over the student's vocal behavior.

Phase 1 should begin by having the student sit across from you, provided that such a situation does not make the student anxious. Whether and how long the student should remain seated should be contingent on her degree of comfort in such a situation. Perhaps 1- to 3-minute sessions interspersed with other programs and play may be optimal in the beginning.

There is no reason why the student should sit in the chair during Phase 1 except that such close proximity to the student gives you the opportunity to immediately reinforce each spontaneous vocalization. You may explore other physical arrangements that may be more conducive to eliciting vocalizations, such as having the student sit on your lap, on the floor or a couch with you, or on a swing or seesaw. Some students love taking baths and may vocalize readily there. Others may vocalize while watching videos or looking at books. All of these are examples of prompts.

Keep in mind that different students respond in varied ways to certain settings. For example, some students may be afraid of taking baths and stop vocalizing in such a setting. However, if you discover environments that promote vocalizations, there is no reason not to use such opportunities and later transfer gains back to the chair. In general, we recommend reinforcing spontaneous vocalizations throughout the day and then returning to the chair prior to beginning Phase 2.

It is often difficult to find prompts for vocal behavior, and methods that work for one student may not work for another. It may be tempting to request vocalizations by saying such things as "Talk," "Speak," or the like. However, the student probably does not know the meaning of such requests at this stage into teaching. Therefore, these requests are likely to be ineffective and perhaps aversive because the student may have encountered such requests in the past and been frustrated by her failure to respond appropriately. Instead, use prompts such as saying, "Hello," while waving a hand and smiling, or holding a food reinforcer in front of the student while vocalizing (such as saying, "Hello"), testing to see whether this gesture increases the probability of the student's vocalizing. If the student can imitate songs, she may be prompted to complete the words of a song after the teacher sings the first three or four words and then stops. If the student continues the song, such vocalizations should be reinforced.

Some prompts may be inherent in noncontingent use of positive reinforcers. Therefore, we advise that small bites of food be provided ("for free") every half minute or so during sessions of Phase 1 in hopes that these reinforcers cue contentment, and hence vocalizations, which should be reinforced with both social and food reinforcers. Also, try to prompt vocalizations by tickling the student, kissing the student on the neck, or stroking the student's cheeks or hair. Try activities such as helping the student jump up and down and turn upside down only if these are likely to make that particular student happy and more likely to vocalize (some students may become frightened). Smiles, cooing, gently poking the student's stomach, and otherwise giving signs of happiness may also be used as potential prompts. These behaviors may be similar to what adults employ in talking to very young typical children. The difference is that these behaviors are used in this case as prompts or as reinforcers that are given immediately after and contingent on the student's vocalizations.

Consult the student's family members for help in discovering effective prompts. Speech therapists also often possess useful information concerning methods for prompting speech. Some speech therapists are likely to recommend that the student be shown a favorite toy or similar object and then be required to vocalize in order to receive that toy. If done in a playful and nondemanding manner, this technique may prove useful.

For the skills learned in Phase 1 to be useful in subsequent phases, it seems reasonable to define mastery as two or more vocalizations per minute across 5 or more days in the setting where the training takes place (ideally this setting is the student sitting in the chair across from you at the table). We suggest working up to sessions of a 5- to 10-minute duration once an hour over the course of the day. There should be a noticeable increase in the student's rate of vocalizations over the level demonstrated prior to beginning Phase 1. Remember that the goal of Phase 1 is to increase the rate of vocalizations so that these vocalizations can be used in Phase 2.

If Phase 1 is successful, you have gained some control over vocalizations by the use of extrinsic reinforcers and are thereby in a better position to influence future language development. Keep in mind what was said earlier: It is difficult to gain reinforcement control over vocalizations because vocalizations are fleeting and thus the connection between the reinforcer and the behavior may be difficult to make. Therefore, some students may not form the connection and hence may not make progress in Phase 1. Nevertheless, for reasons that are not understood at this time, some of the students who fail in Phase 1 succeed in Phase 2 or Phase 3. Whether or not the student makes notable progress in increasing her rate of vocalizations after a 2- to 3-week period, go on to Phase 2.

Phase 2: Bringing Vocalizations Under Temporal Control

In the Early Receptive Language Program (Chapter 15), the student is taught to respond with nonverbal behaviors to your verbal requests. That is, the student learns to listen to you and behave as you ask him to behave. In Phase 2 of the Verbal Imitation Program, the student is taught to listen to your vocalizations and respond not with nonverbal behaviors but with vocalizations. This is similar to early baby talk when a parent talks to the new baby and pretends that the two are in a conversation.

Some readers may expect that if the student has made progress in the Early Receptive Language Program (i.e., the student has learned to respond to your vocal instructions by engaging in nonverbal responses), he should also have learned to respond to your vocalizations with vocal responses and should therefore master Phase 2 quickly. However, we have no clear evidence demonstrating that such a transfer occurs between these two programs. Listening to instructions and responding in the visual mode may not transfer to listening to instructions and responding in the auditory mode.

Phase 2 involves temporal discrimination learning in that you present the student with a vocal SD and reinforce any of the student's vocalizations that fall within a 5-second period following the SD. Any vocalizations that fall outside of this period during a sitting of Phase 2 should *not* be reinforced so that mastery of the temporal discrimination is facilitated. Technically speaking, your vocalization plus 5 seconds constitute the SD; the absence of this SD constitutes S Delta (the nonreinforced or negative stimulus). This procedure applies only to Phase 2 of the Verbal Imitation Program and does not mean that you should withhold reinforcement for the student's spontaneous vocalizations during other programs or free time.

Begin Phase 2 by sitting face to face with the student so the student can see your facial expressions. These visual cues may help the student make the discriminations, as well as prompt the student's vocalizations. Also, you should sit close to the student given that close proximity helps you provide immediate reinforcement for the student's correct responses.

▶ Step 1

Present the SD (e.g., "Hello") and reinforce the student if he produces *any* vocal response within 5 seconds of the SD. Any and all of the student's vocalizations qualify as correct responses provided they fall within a 5-second period immediately following your vocal SD. If the student responds correctly, present the SD again about 2 to 3 seconds after the student receives the reinforcer from the preceding trial. If the student fails to respond, present the SD once every 2 to 3 seconds after the 5-second response interval. That way, the student will have approximately 20 opportunities to respond every minute. With such a high frequency of trials, it is likely that the student will learn to vocalize within the 5-second interval, especially if Phase 1 was mastered and the student's rate of vocalizations is high. If the student continues not to respond, pair the SD with a prompt as done in Phase 1 and fade the prompt over trials.

Sittings of Phase 2 should be set at a similar duration to those of Phase 1. Intersperse other programs between sittings, including rehearsing and reinforcing already mastered programs so as to maintain the student's motivation. Mass trial the SD in Phase 2 until the student responds correctly in 9 out of 10 or 19 out of 20 unprompted trials.

▶ Step 2

One way to sharpen the temporal discrimination is by slowly decreasing the reinforcement contingency from responding within 5 seconds to responding within 4 seconds, then 3 seconds, and finally 2 seconds or less, provided mastery is met for each previous time interval. The reason for tightening the contingency to 1 or 2 seconds is that it gives clear evidence, for both you and the student, that mastery of the discrimination has been achieved.

We strongly recommend that you rehearse the mastery of Phase 2 for the next week or two in order to solidify the discrimination and help the student establish self-confidence and trust in you. During this time, the student's mastery should be generalized across teachers and environments.

Phase 3: Imitating Sounds

Phase 3 is designed to teach the student to imitate specific sounds. For example, if you say, "ah," the student should respond, "ah"; likewise, if you say, "mm," the student should respond, "mm." This phase is important because the sounds that the student learns to imitate in this phase will be combined in subsequent phases to help the student imitate words and, later, phrases and sentences.

Deciding Which Sounds To Start With

There is typically some difficulty deciding with which sounds to begin teaching. We can offer three suggestions: (1) use sounds or words the student frequently vocalizes, (2) use sounds or words that can be prompted, and (3) use sounds or words that are commonly overheard and that often occur early in the development of typical children.

Start by listing the sounds or words the student made in Phase 2 and those overheard to be made by her in her everyday environment. Some of these sounds may be simple, as in "ooh" and "ah," or more complex, as in "winnie poo," "up," "no," "agogoo," "get out," and "dada." Although the student is unlikely to imitate these sounds initially, you should begin with them, as the student may be more likely to imitate them than other sounds. The fact that these sounds are more likely to occur gives the student more opportunity for reinforcement and thus makes these sounds more likely to be imitated later on in this phase.

Most vocal sounds are difficult to prompt. Thus, teachers have fewer opportunities to reinforce and the student has fewer opportunities to learn in this program than in programs that do not require vocal responses. To complicate matters, the prompts used must facilitate one or more *specific* sounds. Because of the problem finding effective prompts, we discuss how to search for potential prompts.

Some students occasionally label letters or numbers printed on cards. Others complete words to parts of songs sung by their parents. Others may label items such as "doggie," "cookie," and so on, when these items appear as pictures in a book. In such instances, you may use the cards, songs, or pictures as prompts when presenting the SD, and later fade the printed material or songs to bring the student's vocalizations under the control of your vocalizations.

This strategy was effective for Robert, a boy diagnosed with autism. After several weeks of making no progress in making separate sounds, Robert's mother reported that he would spontaneously label letters shown in an alphabet book. The teachers used these letters (written on cards) as prompts for verbal imitation. The teachers gave the SD "A" and simultaneously showed Robert a letter card with A written on it. With this prompt he was able to say, "A." The teachers then slowly faded out the word card until Robert imitated the teachers' verbal SD ("A") rather than responding to the visual prompt. A similar procedure was later used to prompt and teach the imitation of other letters.

If the student "sings along" to certain songs, use the song as a prompt. For example, if a student already imitates a word like "round" in the song "The wheels on the bus go round and round," present this song as the prompt and gradually reduce the number of words until only the word "round" remains. "Round" then become the SD. Reinforce any approximations of "round" such as "roond" or "ound" and modify the SD to fit that approximation in the initial stages.

With many or most students, the teacher may fail to observe instances of spoken sounds or words whether they occur spontaneously or in response to specific stimuli such as songs, pictures, letters, and numbers. For such students, the sounds or parts of sounds may have to be manually prompted or prompted through nonverbal imitation. For example, a "mm" sound may be prompted manually by the teacher gently closing the student's lips while presenting the SD "mm" or by the teacher modeling closed lips (as taught in the Nonverbal Imitation Program, Chapter 13). Reinforcement should be provided while the student's lips are closed. Physical assistance and nonverbal imitation can also be used to occasion an open mouth, which may prompt an "ah" sound. The prompt can then be faded by providing less and less physical assistance (for a manual prompt) or by performing less and less of the behavior (for a modeling prompt). The teacher should use the partially correct responses of mouth closing (part of "mm") and mouth opening (part of "ah") as the starting point for shaping the sounds that correspond with these oral movements.

A relaxed and playful mood is likely to help prompt vocalizations, as was mentioned in the discussion of prompts for Phases 1 and 2. Remember that the student's contentment typically elicits vocal behavior. In contrast, a student who is apprehensive and anxious may inhibit vocalizations (although these states may also increase instances of echolalia).

If you start with sounds that have visual components that can help prompt vocalizations (sounds such as "ooh," "ah," "ee," "buh," "mm," "b," and "p"), it is likely that the student will lip read rather than respond to your sounds. Therefore, if such sounds are used, gradually fade the visual prompts until the sounds are presented when the student is not looking at you, your face is turned away from the student's line of vision, or your lips are covered with one hand or a piece of tissue. Remember to fade prompts gradually to maintain the student's correct responding.

Sounds that do not have clear visual components are difficult to prompt and may be more difficult for the student to discriminate than sounds that have visual components. However, once the student masters imitating vowels and consonants with visual components that can be partially prompted, the student may be more likely to master sounds (vowels and consonants) in which the visual components are harder to detect, as in "g, "c," "s," and "k." One way to prompt "k" is by first teaching the student to imitate your cough, and then using differential reinforcement to separate out the "k" sound from the cough sound. Labial–dental consonants such as "d" and "t" are easier to teach because they can be prompted through the imitation of tongue and mouth positions. Although easier to teach separately, however, they are difficult to discriminate from one another. Note that "l," "r," "f," and "th" sounds are usually not correctly enunciated by typical children until quite a bit of language is gained. Therefore, postpone teaching these sounds until the student progresses further into this program. Even if the student does not master imitating all consonants, hundreds of useful words can be taught in this program (see Phase 5).

In determining which sounds to teach the student, consider the usual progression of typical children in addition to the suggestions made above. Early vowel sounds include "aah," "ooh," "ee," and "uh." Early consonant sounds include "mm," "buh," "puh," "duh," and "tuh." Intermediate vowel sounds include "ay" (as in "say") and "i" (as in "ice"). Intermediate consonant sounds include "ss," "zz," "sh," "guh," "buh," "wuh," "yuh," "juh," and "ch." More advanced sounds and discriminations include consonants such as "fuh," "vuh," "lah," "ruh," and "th."

Keep in mind that there are exceptions to the recommendations made in this section. Occasionally one encounters a student who quickly acquires mastery of guttural consonants such as "k" and "g" and slowly masters frontal vowels such as "ah" and "oh." There are also some students who quickly acquire imitation of complex words or sound combinations (e.g., "agogoo," "cookie," "helicop") even prior to their mastery of simple sounds.

Imitating Sounds

Arrange yourself and the student in a position in which the student was successful in Phase 2 of this program, preferably sitting across from each other in chairs. Remember, you want the student not only happy and relaxed, but also close enough to see your face in order to receive prompts as well as immediate reinforcement. Have your best reinforcers ready. It is a good idea to reinforce the student for coming to the chair and to let the student have one or two reinforcers for free while sitting nicely in the chair.

For illustrative purposes, we start with teaching the student to imitate the sounds "ah" and "mm." "Ah" and "mm" sound different as well as look different when you present them (allowing visual cues to serve as prompts). However, "ah" and "mm" may not be ideal beginning sounds for the particular student you work with, and thus you should be flexible in your choice of early sounds to teach. For example, if the student regularly responds with "eeh" to your "ah," then accept that response and change your SD1 to "eeh." If the student responds to "mm" with "beh," then use "beh" as SD2. The fact that both "ah" and "mm" (and "eeh" and "beh") sound and look different should facilitate the early discrimination. It is the discrimination between sounds that is key to successful imitation because it enables the student to attend to the similarity between her and your vocalizations. That is, the training helps the student match the two stimulus inputs, which requires that the student hear (discriminate, attend to) both her own *and* your vocalizations and learns to associate the two, a task that is not easily mastered and should not be taken for granted.

Because the first imitation tends to be particularly difficult for the student to master, leading to several nonreinforced trials and resulting frustration, occasionally intermix (e.g., every five to seven trials) mastered tasks that can be reinforced, such as imitating waving. Tantrums are not a bad sign unless the tantrums seriously interfere with the student's vocalizations or your attempts to prompt vocalizations. Make certain that you do not reinforce tantrums, as in letting the student's tantrum allow her to escape from the teaching situation. Verbal imitation is a difficult skill to acquire, and tantrums may indicate that the student is involved in the learning task.

In illustrating the following steps, SD1 is "ah," and the student's correct imitation of "ah" is R1. SD2 is "mm," and the student's correct imitation of "mm" is R2. We advise you to avoid prefacing the SD with "Say," as in "Say, 'ah,'" and, "Say, 'mm.'" There are three reasons for this. First, the stimulus "say" is common to both SDs and therefore serves to lessen the distinction between the SDs, making the discrimination more difficult for the student. Second, some students imitate "say" along with the correct response (e.g., "Say, 'ah'"), and then "say" must eventually be removed so that it does not interfere with the student's acquisition of appropriate imitations. Third, the student may not know the meaning of the word "say." Hence the word may be extraneous.

▶ Step 1

Present the SD1 ("ah") and mass trial R1 (the student's "ah") using prompts, prompt fading, and differential reinforcement. Set mastery at 9 out of 10 or 19 out of 20 unprompted correct responses. To be reinforced, the student's R1 should sound close enough to your SD1 so that attending adults recognize it as an imitation, and it should occur shortly (i.e., within 5 seconds) after your SD1.

▶ Step 2

Present the SD2 ("mm"), prompt, and mass trial R2 to mastery (9 out of 10 or 19 out of 20 unprompted correct responses). Anticipate that when switching to SD2 ("mm"), the student may respond with R1 ("ah") because this response was most recently reinforced. It is important that R2 ("mm") is a close approximation to your SD2 and maximally different from R1 ("ah"). If the sounds are not clearly distinguishable, take the time to shape their clarity rather than rushing to new sounds. If the vocalizations are not shaped to sound different from one another, they may combine into a sound such as "mah." If this occurs, the discrimination between R1 and R2 will be difficult in Step 3. Note that Step 3 requires firsthand and working familiarity with discrimination learning procedures (Chapter 16).

▶ Step 3

Intermix and differentially reinforce SD1–R1 and SD2–R2. If SD2–R2 ("mm") was presented and reinforced last, it is likely that the student will give R2 when you present SD1 ("ah"). To avoid this error, prompt and reestablish correct imitative responding to SD1 (3 unprompted correct imitations in a row), then switch to SD2, prompt, and reestablish R2 (3 unprompted correct imitations in row). Switch back to SD1 and reestablish R1.

As you shift back and forth between SD1 and SD2 and employ differential reinforcement, the student gradually learns to discriminate between the two SDs as evidenced by fewer errors made and fewer prompts needed each time you shift from one SD to the other. In other words, with each successive contrast of SDs, the student becomes increasingly able to tell the sounds ("ah" and "mm") apart through the reinforcement of SD1–R1 and SD2–R2 and the nonreinforcement of SD1–R2 and SD2–R1. As the strength of the correct associations increases, you can set mastery criterion at decreasing numbers of successive correct responses, such as moving from 3 in a row to 2 in a row and finally to 1, before switching SDs. This is done to avoid inadvertently reinforcing the student for repeating the same response (perseverating), a pattern of responding that interferes with the student's mastery of the contrast (discrimination) between SD1 and SD2. To ensure that the discrimination between SD1 and SD2 is accomplished, introduce random rotation after the student correctly responds to systematic alternation between SD1 and SD2 after single trials of each SD. Random rotation must be done to eliminate extraneous cues that may result in the student's learning a win–stay, lose–shift strategy rather than the discrimination.

Keep in mind that this first discrimination between sounds is the most difficult for the student to master. Therefore, once mastery of the discrimination between SD1 and SD2 is accomplished (9 out of 10 or 19 out of 20 unprompted correct responses with the SDs presented in random rotation), we recommend that this discrimination be practiced once every hour of formal teaching over the next 4 to 5 days, allowing the student access to a good deal of reinforcement. After this, generalize the discrimination across teachers and then situations. Teaching in different parts of the house, outside, and so forth, allows the gains to be spread to environments other than the original teaching setting. With each new situation (teacher or setting), a loss in mastery may occur, necessitating some prompting to reestablish mastery. To help reduce a loss in mastery, make sure that each teacher consistently adheres to the teaching procedures collectively agreed upon, and make certain that effective reinforcers are always employed. Continue generalization of this portion of the program for 2 to 3 weeks.

▶ Step 4

After 2 to 3 weeks of rehearsing the discrimination between SD1 and SD2 across teachers and environments and intermixing this discrimination with other tasks, introduce the third sound, SD3. SD3 should be as different from SD1 and SD2 as possible, while at the same time being a sound the student can master. As already stated, individual differences among students precludes our identifying a particular sound for all students. It may be safest to pick the third sound from the list of sounds made in Phases 1 and 2. "Duh," "oh," and "puh" are examples of sounds that fulfill criteria of differing in both visual and auditory stimulus properties from the SDs used in our illustration of teaching the discrimination between "ah" and "mm."

► **Step 5 Onward**

Teach SD3 as the first two SDs were taught. Once SD3 is mastered in mass trials, systematically intermix SD3 with SD1 and then with SD2 while maintaining the SD1–SD2 discrimination. Begin random rotation of the SDs once the student correctly responds to each SD with systematic alternation after single trials. Bring all three discriminations to mastery before SD4 and other new sounds are introduced.

Areas of Difficulty

If you use a *visual prompting* procedure (from the Nonverbal Imitation Program) by exaggerating mouth movements when vocalizing sounds, the student may imitate your movements but not the exact vocalizations by, for example, enunciating "eh" rather than "ah" in response to SD1. If this occurs, shift your SD1 to "eh" in order to match the student's sound. The discrimination between SD1 and SD2 is important in this phase, not the actual sounds used. Make certain to remove (fade) the visual prompt.

It is difficult to specify when you should discontinue teaching a particular sound (e.g., SD1 "ah," or some other sound) and move on to another sound. However, no progress toward mastery after 100 to 200 trials is typically a safe criterion. By no progress, we mean no approximations. You may return to the difficult sound at a later stage. If you fail to make progress with SD1 using visual prompting, discontinue that SD for the time being and go on to a sound that can be manually prompted. For example, switch to a sound like "mm," which you can manually prompt part of by holding the student's lips together when she vocalizes. You may also test for the student's ability to imitate other sounds by using different prompts.

If the student can imitate one sound (e.g., "ah" or "eh") but fails to make progress in imitating a second or third sound, shift to a contrasting stimulus such as blowing bubbles in imitation of your blowing bubbles. Fade the bubbles and use this remedial SD as the contrasting SD in discrimination learning procedures. As individual differences are enormous, it is a good idea to remain flexible in the sounds targeted and the means by which these sounds are prompted. For example, blowing bubbles did not serve as an effective prompt for a student who instead liked to blow out lit matches (perhaps the visual feedback from a flickering flame constituted a sensory reinforcer). The training steps proceeded as follows: (a) The teacher blew and concurrently presented the lit match for the student to blow out. The teacher reinforced the student's blowing with social approval. (b) The teacher continued to present trials but faded the prompt, presenting the match to the student without the flame. The student blew and was reinforced. (c) Over successive trials the teacher's hand was still presented, but the match was gradually faded behind the teacher's fingers. The student continued to blow and was reinforced. Finally, the teacher's hand was faded, bringing the student's blowing under the control of the teacher's SD. That is, the student learned to imitate the teacher's blowing and this response was then used as a contrasting stimulus in teaching imitations of sounds. Remember, it is the student's discriminations among the teacher's and her own vocalizations that are critical, and remedial (or pretraining) procedures may be helpful in the student's acquisition of these discriminations.

Shaping

As the student progresses in imitation training, it becomes increasingly important that the student's imitations match your vocalizations as closely as possible. It is highly likely that the accuracy of the imitation will vary over trials. Therefore, after the student shows a reliable but rough approximation of your SD, begin shaping that response to more closely match the SD. Specifically, on a given trial, reinforce the student's response only if it approximates your SD more closely than the last reinforced response. If the student fails to match the SD closely enough to be reinforced over 3 or 4 trials, backtrack and reinforce a less accurate approximation to keep the student's vocalization from being placed on extinction and to help prevent the student from losing interest in the imitation task. Also, if the student receives too little reinforcement, she is likely to tantrum. Be careful when providing informational "No's" as consequences in this program because such consequences used early on in the Verbal Imitation Program may result in discouraging the student's vocalizations. If the student's approximations are not accurate enough to be positively reinforced, consider withholding reinforcement and repeating the SD.

Motivation

The Verbal Imitation Program may be stressful for the student. Therefore, intersperse SDs from mastered programs such as Matching, Nonverbal Imitation, or Receptive Language every 5 to 7 trials so as to amply reinforce the student for cooperating and to help ensure maintenance of the student's involvement. Try not to exceed five nonreinforced trials in a row before introducing a mastered task and keep the sessions short (they should not exceed 5 minutes). Remember to vary the reinforcers used within each sitting, especially if no one reinforcer is particularly strong. End each sitting with reinforcement for a correct response. Ending a sitting contingent on a correct response will provide two reinforcers: leaving a difficult situation and gaining access to a favorite edible, toy, or activity. Ending a sitting contingent on an incorrect response may serve to reinforce, and thus strengthen, incorrect responding.

Keeping Up a High Rate of Vocalizations

Remember to reinforce spontaneous vocalizations from Phases 1 and 2 to maintain the student's production of these sounds. Thus, should the student vocalize between sittings of Phase 3 of verbal imitation training or during other programs, reinforce such vocalizations by, for example, stating, "Good talking," while smiling. The best reinforcers, however, should be saved for correct imitations to keep the student motivated to perform the more difficult task of imitating rather than spontaneously vocalizing.

Loss of Mastery When Generalizing

Anticipate that some students may either stop responding or start making errors when a new teacher is introduced or when the teaching situation is changed to a different environment. If difficulties occur when a new teacher is introduced, gradually fade in the new teacher by having him or her sit beside the familiar teacher who presents the SDs. Next, with both teachers sitting next to one another, have the new teacher give the SDs at the same time as the familiar teacher. Then, if mastery is maintained, completely fade out the familiar teacher. If the relative abruptness of the last step results in incorrect responding by the student, fade the original teacher more gradually by having him or her move a foot or two away from the initial position after every few SDs.

To avoid deterioration in correct responding when attempts are made to generalize responding across new environments, change the environment in gradual, incremental steps. This can be done by moving away from the original arrangements of the chairs and table by first leaving the table but keeping the chairs, then moving to other chairs, then onto the floor, then to different parts of the original room, then to the adjoining hallway, and so on. Keep in mind that students with developmental delays are not the only ones who have difficulty generalizing; typically developing persons evidence problems in generalizing behaviors across environments as well. Children do not always behave in public the way they behave at home. A way to guarantee discontinuity in any individual's behavior is by quickly changing the persons and physical environments that surround her.

What To Expect

Prepare for the imitation of the first two sounds to be the most difficult, with a gradual increase in the rate of mastery over the next sounds introduced. For those students who enter the Verbal Imitation Program with previous (although perhaps occasional) expression of words or imitations of sounds or words, the rate of mastery tends to be more rapid than for those who have no history of vocalizations. If a student can express a word prior to imitation training, then that student already demonstrates evidence of being able to listen to and match verbal responses. There is currently no evidence that those students who imitated their parents' vocalizations and then stopped when they were approximately 18 to 24 months of age learn to master verbal imitation sooner than those who never imitated vocalizations.

One of the most promising signs occurs when, some time into verbal imitation training, the student begins to spontaneously imitate words she hears in everyday settings or the teacher's instructions in other programs that may run concurrently with the present program, such as "sit down" or "point to knee." This gives evidence that the student is becoming echolalic and that the matching of the student's and the teacher's speech has acquired reinforcing properties for the student.

Note that some people become concerned about the emergence of echolalic speech and try to discourage it because it is considered a symptom of autism. It is a mistake to discourage or otherwise attempt to change echolalia until much later into treatment when the presence of echolalia is likely to hinder mainstreaming and other peer integration. It is likely that all persons echo the speech of others, but do so subvocally (as in private speech), having been taught not to think out loud. For now, consider imitation as having become its own reinforcer; the student likes to talk and has become less dependent on the adult's use of extrinsic reinforcement.

Some students may be echolalic and thus already able to imitate words and strings of words upon entering treatment. However, such students may not echo (imitate) the teacher's words when asked to do so and may experience significant problems in learning to imitate the teacher's words when presented with these words in the Verbal Imitation Program. Perhaps spontaneous echolalia does not share the same properties as the vocal imitation taught in the present program.

An encouraging sign can be found in the Verbal Imitation Program, however, when examining the nature of the errors the student makes because these errors point to rational, learning-based origins. For example, suppose the student practices the three imitations "ah," "mm," and "eeh." Prior to mastery, the student "mixes up" her answers such that if the teacher presents SD1 ("ah"), the student may not respond with R1 ("ah") but rather with R2 ("mm") or R3 ("eeh"). That is, the student makes the wrong associations. This occurs because SD1 ("ah") exercises some power (associative strength) over "mm" or "eeh." This is known in the technical literature as *stimulus generalization*. In everyday language, it can be said that the student attempts, in a trial-and-error fashion, to hit upon the correct response. This should be considered a normal phenomenon. Through the continuation of discrimination training, the teacher withholds reinforcement for the incorrect associations (e.g., SD1–R3, SD3–R2) and thereby weakens them. At the same time, the teacher reinforces and strengthens the correct associations (SD1–R1, SD2–R2, and SD3–R3) to compete with the incorrect associations. Often, with each new imitation mastered, the number of total errors decreases until imitations of the teacher's vocalizations are made without error upon their respective first presentations. Technically speaking, this is referred to as *generalized imitation*.

When To Teach and How To Progress

Reserve the majority of the verbal imitation sessions for the morning hours when most students' rates of learning appear to be maximized. Conduct sittings of an approximately 1- to 5-minute duration, with mastered tasks intermixed within the sitting. Give the student a 2- to 3-minute play break between sittings and intersperse sittings of programs that teach skills the student may more easily master than those involved in the Verbal Imitation Program (e.g., Nonverbal Imitation or Receptive Instructions).

Once the student can imitate between 5 and 10 sounds consistently, you may begin using an informational "No" and withholding reinforcement if the student does not imitate the sounds you make or if the approximations the student gives are below the standard criterion the student previously attained. Do not make the "No" loud and aversive. It should be given calmly and should not sound angry, frustrated, or disappointed, but rather should be given as informational feedback to let the student know that her response was incorrect and that she needs to try again after the next SD in order to obtain reinforcers. After the student masters the imitation of approximately 8 to 10 sounds (e.g., 5 vowels such as "ooh," "eeh," "ah," "u," "oo," and 2 to 3 consonants such as "m," "d," and "b"), begin Phase 4, shaping the first simple syllables and words. At the same time, intersperse trials from Phase 3 to introduce new sounds. It is important to teach each new sound to mastery, one at a time, rather than introducing a number of sounds at once.

Phase 4: Imitation of Consonant–Vowel Combinations

Imitating the First Combination

Once the student learns to imitate his first 8 to 10 sounds, including vowels and some consonants, teach the student how to connect these sounds together into simple words or to combine consonants and vowels in ways that will later be needed to build words. Consonant–vowel combinations and simple words such as "ma," "mu," "bah," "duh," "mama," and "dada" are examples of SDs you might start with. In the following steps, the procedures of imitation, shaping, and chaining are reviewed so as to help you use them interactively to build consonant–vowel combinations.

Shaping

A few students successfully imitate a consonant–vowel combination the first time the teacher gives the SD. Other students make an approximation to the combination on the first few trials, and the teacher can then use *shaping* on the later trials to help the student more closely approximate the teacher's SD. Most likely there will be imperfect imitations during training, and you will have to use shaping procedures to help the student improve certain imitations. For example, you may express "muh" to your "mah" or express "deh" to your "dah." To begin shaping, repeat the SD over several trials and reinforce the student's response on a given trial if it approximates your combination as closely as or more closely than the last reinforced response. It pays to shape in steps no larger than those that keep the student reinforced and successful. Prompt the student whenever possible, facilitating the approximation. Continue the shaping procedure until the student's approximation of the combination is consistently clear enough to be understood by other people. Remember that the student's response needs to be as close to your SD as possible. Otherwise, the student will not succeed in learning to match your SD or to discriminate between your SDs. Also remember that exposure to similarity among auditory stimuli (yours and the student's) will help establish similarity as a reinforcing event for the student and help develop generalized and spontaneous imitations.

Shaping procedures work only if there are some initial similarities between the student's and your vocalizations. In most instances, and especially with complex SDs, the student's response will not approximate your SD closely enough to allow for shaping. In such cases, your word or sound combination will have to be broken down into parts the student can imitate and then combine through chaining.

Chaining

In chaining, a teaching process introduced in Chapter 10, two or more responses are "chained together" in such a fashion that when one response occurs, it cues a second response to follow. Technically speaking, one response generates stimuli for a second response. The chain can consist of simple units, as when "m" provides the cue for "a" to form the syllable "ma." In an example involving somewhat more complex stimuli, the response "ma" may come to cue the student to repeat "ma" to create the word "mama." Through the use of chaining procedures, separate words are later built into increasingly complex combinations such as phrases and sentences.

To chain sounds, a particular sound combination should be divided into component sounds that the student can already imitate, and then each sound should be presented as a separate trial. Thus, the combination "mah" may be broken down into "m" and "ah." The student should imitate each component when it is presented, and should be reinforced for repeating each component. Then slowly shorten the amount of time separating the presentation of each component and eventually provide reinforcement contingent on the student's completion of both components as one response.

In illustrating the following steps, SD1 and R1 represent "m" and SD2 and R2 represent "ah." It is assumed that the student has already learned to correctly imitate your SD1 and SD2.

▶ **Step 1**

Present SD1 ("m") and reinforce the correct response.

▶ **Step 2**

Present SD2 ("ah") and reinforce the correct response.

▶ **Step 3**

Present SD1 and move to the next step (4) *just as* the student begins to respond.

▶ **Step 4**

Present SD2 and reinforce the correct response.

In Step 3 do *not* reinforce after the student's correct R1 but rather immediately present SD2. Withholding the reinforcer for R1 and immediately presenting reinforcement for correct responding to SD2 should help the combination "m-ah" occur. Reinforcement can then be delivered contingent on gradually decreasing amounts of time between the two sounds ("m" and "ah") until the student is able to respond correctly to the sounds given as a single SD ("mah").

The fact that the student learns to respond with "mah" to your "mah" does not mean that the student actually imitates your "mah." By contrasting "mah" with another sound combination, you can determine whether the student is imitating the SD or merely memorizing a response. Again, discrimination learning is the key to your success as a teacher and to the student's mastery.

Imitating the Second Combination

The second consonant–vowel combination should be maximally different from the first combination in terms of both your sounds and your mouth movements. For example, if "mah" is the first combination taught, "beebee" is a good choice for the second combination. The second combination, like the first, should come from your list of frequently heard sounds and should be composed of sounds the student can imitate separately. This combination should be taught in the same way the first combination was taught. Be sure to continue rehearsing mastered combinations as each new combination is introduced, helping to maintain those responses while working on new combinations.

After mastery of the second combination presented alone, begin discrimination training with the first two combinations. Achieve mastery of SD1–R1 ("mah"), then proceed to Step 2 and achieve mastery of SD2–R2 ("beebee"). In Step 3, intermix SD1 and SD2 using differential reinforcement until the SDs are presented in random rotation. Continue to intermix the SDs until the student responds correctly in 9 out of 10 or 19 out of 20 unprompted trials. As done previously, solidify the discrimination among SD1 and SD2 by generalizing it across teachers and environments over the next 4 to 5 days.

Combinations 3 Through 8

Introduce the next six combinations (e.g., "da" or "dada," "up," "pa" or "papa," "me") the same way the first and second combinations were introduced. Each time a new combination is acquired, this combination should be randomly rotated with all of the previously mastered combinations. For example, if the student mastered seven different combinations and his eighth combination is ready for random rotation, intermix the eighth combination with Combinations 1 through 4 the first time you randomize presentations, Combinations 5 through 7 the second time the SDs are randomized, and so on. This helps maintain the earlier mastered combinations or reestablish them.

Once the student masters six to eight combinations, move on to build words by following the procedures presented in Phase 5. The combinations the student practices in the current phase may already contain recognizable words (as in "me") or they may be helpful in teaching words (e.g., by using "mah" as a building block for teaching the word "mama"). Although imitation of most words is more extensive than the combinations taught in this phase, the principles involved in teaching the student to imitate words are the same as those used to teach imitation of sounds and combinations.

To facilitate the student's acquisition of imitating words, it may be helpful to differentiate between homogeneous and heterogeneous chains. "Mama," "papa," and "dada" are examples of homogeneous chains (the same combinations are repeated). "Cookie," "table," and "baby" are examples of heterogeneous chains (different sounding components are combined). Homogeneous chains are likely to be easier to master; therefore, it is recommended that this type of combination be introduced first.

Note that when we refer to words, we do not imply that the student knows the meaning of the words he imitates. For example, if the student acquires imitation of the word "mama," he probably does not know what that word means. The meaning of words is taught separately in the receptive and expressive language programs.

Areas of Difficulty

If the student experiences difficulty acquiring a chain (e.g., the chain "mah"), try the following variation. Present SD1 ("m"). After the student responds with "m," do not present SD2 ("ah") but rather pause and look expectantly at the student, waiting for R2 ("ah") to occur. The pause may operate as a prompt. If R2 occurs within 5 seconds of SD2, *abundantly* reinforce the student. The reason you present only "m" instead of the combination "mah" is that doing so increases the likelihood that the student will respond to the SD with "m" and the pause with "ah" and decreases the likelihood the student will respond to "mah" as an SD with only "ah." Because "ah" is the most recent sound the student hears when you say "mah," it is the most likely sound to be emitted. In other words, the "ah" in "mah" is likely to block the student's "m." The pause makes it more likely that the student will express both the "m" and the "ah," saying, "mah."

The pause after "m" may be considered a prompt for the student's "ah." If the pause (i.e., the time delay prompt) fails, add a visual prompt after "m" by opening your mouth while looking expectantly at the student. Slowly fade out the visual prompt and shift to a pause prompt. Fade the prompt over subsequent trials until the student responds correctly in 9 out of 10 or 19 out of 20 unprompted trials. By the end of this step, your SD should be "m" and a short pause. The student's correct response should be "m-ah."

Once the previous step is mastered, change the SD to "mah." To minimize errors, loudly present "m" and then immediately present "ah" in an almost inaudible volume. By presenting "ah" quickly and at a low volume and not reinforcing the student for merely repeating "ah," the student is taught not to skip "m" and merely repeat "ah." Abundantly reinforce the student for emitting "m-ah" to your loud "m" and barely audible "ah." Gradually increase the volume of "ah" over subsequent trials until the student is eventually presented with the entire combination ("mah") stated at a constant volume. The speed with which "ah" is increased to a normal volume is determined by the student; ideally it should be increased gradually enough that the student does not make errors but quickly enough that the student does not become prompt dependent.

Phase 5: Imitation of Words

The First Word

Use three criteria in selecting the initial word for the student to imitate. First, choose a word composed of sound combinations that will facilitate the student's mastery of imitation of the word. For instance, "mama" or "dada" should be chosen only if the student can imitate the component sounds of the word. Likewise, "cookie" should be chosen only if the student can imitate "koo" and "key." As mentioned earlier, because "cookie" represents a heterogeneous chain, it may be more difficult to teach than "dada" or "mama," which are homogeneous chains. Second, choose a word that will sound different from the second word to be taught so as to facilitate the student's discrimination (and subsequent imitations). Third, whenever possible, select a word the student can use in her everyday environment to get things she wants. For example, "open" can be used by the student to ask an adult to open a door. Similar functional use can be made of "play" to leave the work table, "mama" to go to her mother, "up" to be lifted in the air, and the names of foods (e.g., cookie, bacon) to get her favorite snacks. It is not unusual to observe some students utter with great fidelity those words that lead to powerful reinforcers such as food or removal from the teaching situation.

The following words are examples of sound combinations that may be helpful to start with: "mama," "papa" or "dada," "bye-bye," "up," "baby," "tummy," "doggy," "cookie," "shoe," "nose," and "cup." Note that words with sibilants (as in "shoe"), guttural consonants (as in "cookie"), and those requiring heterogeneous chains are relatively difficult to master.

Shaping

Start by exploring words or approximations of words the student has already mastered. For example, for the first few trials, give an SD (e.g., "mama") and shape by reinforcing any approximations that include the main sounds of the word. Thus, "ma," "mam," "am," or "mum" are adequate initial approximations of "mama." Likewise, an adequate initial approximation to "dada" is "daddy," to "doggy" is "gogo," and to "baby" is "baba." To develop an approximation, you may want to break a word down into combinations the student has already mastered and practice these combinations separately. For example, if the student continues to imitate "baba" when the teacher presents "baby," select out the "bee" sound in "baby" and practice it separately, later adding it back into the word "baby."

To shape words, follow the same procedures used to shape the combinations in Phase 4: Reinforce the student's response on a given trial only if it approximates your word as closely as or more closely than the last reinforced response. For example, if the target response is "mama" and the student initially responds with "mah," reinforce her. If on the next trial the student responds only with "m," withhold reinforcement because "m" is less close of an approximation than "mah." Once "mah" is established, try withholding reinforcement to test for a closer approximation like "mam," "mom," or "maha." The withholding of the reinforcer is likely to occasion an increase in vocalizations. If a closer approximation occurs, reinforce the student. Withholding reinforcement for inadequate approximations can lead to the student's trying harder to come closer to the target response. If the student's performance deteriorates, go back and reinforce earlier sounds (like "m") to reinstate the student's responding. It is almost inevitable that the student's performance will show ups and downs during shaping, but you must use reinforcement in a manner that ensures more ups than downs.

Continue the shaping procedure until the student's approximations of the words are consistently clear enough to be understood by most people. The student's responses need not be perfect at first, but they should be shaped to be as close to perfect as possible. For imitation training to achieve the maximum benefit, the similarity between the student's and your pronunciations must be very close. Otherwise, similarity will not become a reinforcing event for the student, and the student may then depend on extrinsic reinforcement such as food and praise to maintain language gains. If shaping fails to produce closer approximations of words, go on to chaining.

Chaining

The student may fail to approximate your SDs, providing insufficient opportunities for you to shape the student's responses. For example, the student may fail to imitate one or more of the component sounds that make up a word, inadequately approximating the word (e.g., the student may say, "ah," to "papa" or "doggy"). In such a case, the word must be built using a chaining procedure. Divide the word into its component sounds and present each sound as a separate trial as done with sound combinations. For example, "papa" should be divided into "p" and "ah," then "pah," then "pah-pah," and finally "papa." That is, chain "p" and "ah" together to form "pah" (make SD1 "p" and SD2 "ah"). Then chain "pah" and "pah" together to form "papa" (make SD1 "pah" and SD2 "pah"). It may be helpful to provide the teaching steps in detail even though there is considerable overlap from the steps described in Phase 4.

▶ Step 1

Present SD1 ("p") and reinforce the correct response.

▶ **Step 2**

Present SD2 ("ah") and reinforce the correct response.

▶ **Step 3**

Present SD1 and move to the next step *just as* the student begins to respond.

▶ **Step 4**

Present SD2 and reinforce the correct response.

Repeat this sequence until virtually no pause prompt is left between the "p" and the "ah." Once the student masters "pah," chain "pah" and "pah" together as follows:

▶ **Step 5**

Present SD1 ("pah") and reinforce the correct response.

▶ **Step 6**

Present SD2 ("pah") and reinforce the correct response.

▶ **Step 7**

Present SD1 and move to the next step *just as* the student begins to respond.

▶ **Step 8**

Present SD2 and reinforce the correct response.

▶ **Step 9**

Present SD3 ("papa"). If the student responds correctly, reinforce. If the student fails to respond correctly, repeat Steps 7 and 8, gradually reducing the latency between the two "pah" sounds until there is virtually no latency left between the first "pah" and the second "pah," such that the student imitates "papa."

The Second Word

The second word chosen should be maximally different from the first word. For instance, if "papa" is the first word taught, "baby" may constitute an appropriate second word (even though it constitutes a heterogeneous chain). If possible, the second word, like the first, should come from your list of frequently heard words from the student or should be composed of sounds the student can imitate independently.

The second word should be taught in the same way the first word was taught. It may help to rehearse mastered words in separate sittings as each new word is introduced to help maintain the old responses and reduce confusion when working on new words. After the student correctly imitates the second word to mastery criterion, begin discrimination training with the first two words. That is, present SD1 (e.g., "papa") and reinforce the student's R1 ("papa"). Prompt if necessary. Place mastery at 5 out of 5 or 9 out of 10 unprompted correct responses. Once mastery of SD1 is reached, present SD2 ("baby") and bring it to mastery. Next, intermix SD1 and SD2 using differential reinforcement and eventually place them into random rotation. Place mastery at 9 out of 10 or 19 out of 20 unprompted correct responses. At this point, generalize the discrimination across teachers and environments over the next 5 to 6 days.

Areas of Difficulty

Building the first word is a difficult procedure to write out in detail, and you may have to improvise a bit to help a particular student along. Some students may persist in making slight pauses between the component parts of a word for quite some time (e.g., "pah" [pause] "pah" rather than "papa"). These pauses can be eliminated by the use of shaping such that you provide reinforcement for decreasing lengths of pauses.

Despite the most extensive efforts by well-trained teachers, many students fail to progress beyond imitation of separate sounds to imitation of words. In this regard, it is important to know that occasionally a student acquires vocal imitation of some words after mastering the matching of words as done in the Reading and Writing Program (Chapter 29). Similar observations have been reported by the use of the Picture Exchange Communication System (PECS) Program (Chapter 30). Whether these informal observations will hold up when subjected to an objective scientific inquiry remains to be seen. Nevertheless, it may be worthwhile to try either program to test for such advances.

Words 3 Through 8

Teach the next several words (e.g., "mama," "doggy," "go," "cookie") the same way the first two were taught.

Once each new word is mastered, this word should be randomly rotated with all the previously mastered words. For example, if the student has seven different words mastered and her eighth word is ready for random rotation, we advise that you intermix this new word with Words 1 through 4 during the first randomization; with Words 5 through 7 during the second randomization; with Words 2, 3, 6, and 7 during the third randomization; and so on. Such intermixing helps the student to both discriminate new words from already established ones and rehearse and thereby maintain the mastery of established words.

So far we have limited the student's curriculum to short or relatively easy words. The teaching of more complex and polysyllabic words such as "dinosaur," "umbrella," "caterpillar," and "helicopter" may be delayed for a month or more into training of this phase to avoid placing too much stress on the student. When such words are introduced, use shaping if the student accomplishes close approximations of the words. If the student does not produce close approximations, use chaining procedures as described previously.

Use the best reinforcers you have at your disposal for unprompted correct responses and extinction or informational "No's" when the student is incorrect. It is tempting to move quickly once the student masters 8 to 10 word imitations given the importance of the mastery of verbal imitation. Although you receive a great deal of reinforcement for teaching efforts when the student progresses rapidly, it is important not to push the student too far too fast or to teach skills within this program at the expense of skills taught in other programs. We warn against moving too fast since the student cannot inform you, by language, that the load is too heavy. One risks losing progress gained because of the student's becoming noncompliant or nonresponsive, tactics many students have mastered to perfection in the past.

Imitation of 8 to 10 words should be considered a major achievement and marks the occasion for you to increase the intermixing of other programs between sessions of the Verbal Imitation Program to expand the student's competence and reduce her stress level. Expressive language programs (Chapters 23 and 24) should be introduced to teach the student to use her newly acquired vocabulary to obtain a larger range of reinforcers in a more efficient manner than before (i.e., through the use of language; see Chapter 26 for methods of teaching the student to verbally indicate her desires). At the same time, gradually proceed through the Verbal Imitation Program, teaching new single sounds, combinations of sounds, and recognizable words to increase the student's vocabulary.

What To Expect

After the mastery of the first 10 to 20 words, many students begin to spontaneously echo the teacher's words. For example, in a receptive language program, the teacher may ask the student, "Point to mommy," and the student may echo some or all of the instruction. We refer to such students as auditory learners in contrast to visual learners. Auditory learners may be identified after 4 to 5 months of 40 hours per week of one-on-one intervention by a qualified teacher or after 9 to 12 months for a student who was less than 30 months old when the program began. Students who fail to master generalized verbal imitation (i.e., they do not become echolalic or beome only partly so) vary widely in their progress in the Verbal Imitation Program. Some continue to acquire new words, although at a slow rate (e.g., they acquire one or two words every month). Others do not acquire any more words or acquire them sparsely and express these words only with considerable effort. The difficulties these students experience should be rightfully attributed to inadequacies in the Verbal Imitation Program rather than to hypothetical deficiencies of the student (e.g., apraxia, low muscle tone, central auditory processing deficits). The teaching of verbal imitation is a relatively new field; only since the mid-1960s has research been done on this very complex task.

Auditory learners proceed at a faster rate through the programs described in this manual. Most, but not all, of these students reach "normal" functioning as defined by measures of treatment outcome (McEachin, Smith, & Lovaas, 1993), provided they receive 40 hours of one-on-one treatment by persons qualified to administer the UCLA treatment model.

Students who are primarily visual learners benefit mainly from visual forms of communication as described in the Reading and Writing Program (Chapter 29) or the PECS Program (Chapter 30). Nevertheless, we recommend continuing with the Verbal Imitation Program, although at a less intense rate. This is particularly important for students for whom the teacher discovers different and unique ways of teaching verbal imitation. For example, some students fail to make progress in verbal imitation as it is presented here, yet they imitate the voices of cartoon characters (e.g., from Disney's *The Lion King*). Many questions need to be answered to help isolate more effective ways of teaching verbal imitation than the methods presented in this chapter.

Even though the adaptation of visual forms of communication for students with developmental delays is in its infancy, you are likely to observe visual learners make extensive progress in communication through programs emphasizing visual stimuli. It should be noted that auditory learners also benefit from learning to read and write.

Phase 6: Imitation of Simple Phrases and Sentences

While teaching expressive language programs and maintaining and building upon earlier phases of the current program, teach (in separate sessions) a more complex imitative skill by introducing phrases and simple sentences. The student's imitation of the teacher's phrases and sentences can best be described as mastery of elaborate word chains or word strings and should not be understood to mean that the student has mastered sentences and phrases as grammatical units. Rather, the student's imitation of word strings can later be used to teach grammar. Procedures for teaching the student grammar and the use of sentence form to generate new and spontaneous sentences are presented in Chapter 26.

Phase 6 of the Verbal Imitation Program presents procedures for teaching the student to imitate phrases and sentences consisting of increasingly longer strings of words. Once the student acquires this skill, you can use such imitations to prompt correct answers in other programs and in everyday life. For example, when teaching an item in the Expressive Labeling of Objects Program (Chapter 23), the teacher may ask, "What is it?" while pointing to a toy dog and prompt the student to answer, "Brown dog," through imitation. In a different program, the teacher may ask, "What do you want?" and prompt the student to answer, through imitation of the teacher's vocalization, "I want cookie." To benefit from such prompts, the student must master imitation of the teacher's phrases and sentences.

Remember to teach the imitation of phrases and sentences that are functional for the student; that is, teach phrases and sentences that can be used by the student to secure immediate reinforcement. The following are examples of phrases and sentences that are helpful to start with. The words "want" and "juice" can be chained into the phrase "Want juice." The word "I" can later be added to form the sentence "I want juice." Similarly, the words "me," "big," "bird," and "give," can be expanded to "big bird" and later to "Give me big bird." The separate words "I," "want," "play," and "to" can be expanded to the sentence "I want play" and later to "I want to play," a sentence that the student can be taught to use to go outside and play.

Imitating the First Phrase and Sentence

Shaping

Introduce the first phrases and short sentences following the same basic procedure used to introduce the first word. Begin by presenting SD1, which may consist of the teacher expressing two-word combinations for the student to imitate. For example, give the SD "Want eat" or any other two-word sequence for the student to approximate. Reinforce any approximations that include the main sounds or words of the phrase. You may want to explore ("probe") different short phrases and sentences and select the ones the student can match the closest. If the student can approximate imitating a three-word sentence (e.g., "I want play"), select that sentence to teach first. Some two-word phrases may contain words that are more difficult for the student to approximate than simple three-word sentences. Start with combinations the student has the most success with and hence the most opportunity to be reinforced for and learn.

If the student makes adequate approximations of your SD on the first five or six presentations of that SD, use shaping on later trials to help the student more closely approximate your verbalizations. When shaping, reinforce the student's response on a given trial only if it approximates your phrase or sentence as closely as or more closely than the last reinforced response. If necessary, prompt by exaggerating sounds that are weak in the student's responses. If the student has problems with a three-word sentence (e.g., "I want play"), simplify it to two words (e.g., "Want play"). Continue the shaping procedure until the student's approximation of the two-word SD is consistently clear enough to be understood by most people, and then add the third word. If shaping does not produce closer approximations of your verbalizations, go on to chaining.

Chaining

For some phrases and sentences, the student may fail to even roughly approximate your SD on the first trials. For example, the student may fail to imitate more than one of the words that make up the phrase or sentence. If this occurs, you must build the phrase or sentence using one of two chaining procedures: forward chaining or backward chaining. As students differ in their responses to the two types of chaining procedures, deciding whether to use forward chaining or backward chaining requires a little experimentation. Try out both procedures to see which works best for the student you work with.

Forward Chaining. Divide the phrase or sentence into its component words and present each word as a separate trial. In teaching a three-word chain, simply chain the first two words together and then add the third word. For example, the sentence "I see ball" should first be divided into "I," then "I see," and finally "I see ball." Follow the same steps used to chain simple sounds into words. Chain together "I" and "see" (making SD1 "I" and SD2 "see"), then chain together "I see" and "ball" (making SD1 "I see" and SD2 "ball") as follows.

▶ **Step 1**

Present SD1 ("I") and reinforce the correct response.

▶ **Step 2**

Present SD2 ("see") and reinforce the correct response.

▶ **Step 3**

Present SD1 ("I") and go on to Step 4 *just as* the student begins to respond.

▶ **Step 4**

Present SD2 ("see") and reinforce the correct response.

▶ **Step 5**

Present "I see," and prompt by providing a short latency between the two words. Fade the prompt by gradually decreasing the latency between the two words until the phrase "I see" is given as a single SD.

By following Steps 1 through 5, the student learns to express the response chain "I see." Once the student masters imitation of this phrase, chain "I see" and "ball" together to form a sentence.

▶ **Step 6**

Present SD1 ("I see") and reinforce the correct response.

▶ **Step 7**

Present SD2 ("ball") reinforce the correct response.

▶ **Step 8**

Present SD1 and go on to the next step *just as* the student begins to respond.

▶ **Step 9**

Present SD2 and reinforce the correct response. Repeat Steps 9 and 10 until there is virtually no latency prompt left between "I see" and "ball" (e.g., "I see [pause] ball," then "I see [less pause] ball," and finally "I see ball" [without a pause]).

Backward Chaining. Backward chaining is beneficial for those students who tend to jump ahead, completing the response rather than imitating the teacher's sentence when forward chaining is used. For example, when using forward chaining to teach the sentence "I see ball," some students may say "ball" when you ask them to imitate "I see," essentially completing the phrase you started. Backward chaining helps to eliminate this problem. To begin, chain together "ball" and "see" (make SD1 "ball" and SD2 "see"). Then chain together "see ball" and "I" (make SD1 "see ball" and SD2 "I"). The following is an example of backward chaining. Pay special attention to the order in which the SDs are presented.

▶ **Step 1**

Present SD1 ("ball") and reinforce the correct response.

▶ **Step 2**

Present SD2 ("see") and reinforce the correct response.

▶ **Step 3**

Present SD2 and move to the next step *just as* the student begins to respond.

▶ **Step 4**

Present SD1 and reinforce the correct response. Repeat Steps 3 and 4 until there is virtually no latency left between the presentations of "see" and "ball." Once the phrase "see ball" is mastered, chain "I" and "see ball" together.

▶ **Step 5**

Present SD1 ("see ball") and reinforce the correct response.

▶ **Step 6**

Present SD2 ("I") and reinforce the correct response.

▶ **Step 7**

Present SD2 and go on to the next step *just as* the student begins to respond.

▶ **Step 8**

Present SD1 and reinforce the correct response. Repeat Steps 7 and 8 until there is virtually no latency left between the word "I" and the phrase "see ball" (e.g., "I [pause] see ball," then "I [less pause] see ball," and finally "I see ball" [without a pause]).

Imitating the Second Phrase and Sentence

The second phrase or sentence to be imitated should be maximally different from the first phrase or sentence. For instance, if "I see ball" is taught first, "Pick me up" is an appropriate second sentence to teach. The second phrase or sentence, like the first, should be composed of sounds and words the student can imitate on his own.

The second phrase or sentence should be taught in the same way the first phrase or sentence was taught. Be sure to continue working on the first phrase or sentence during separate sittings of verbal imitation as the second phrase or sentence is introduced. This helps maintain the mastered phrase or sentence and may reduce confusion when working on the new phrase or sentence. After the student correctly imitates the second phrase or sentence, begin discrimination training between the first and second phrases or sentences by following the discrimination training procedures described earlier.

Phrases and Sentences 3 Through 8

Teach the next six phrases or sentences (e.g., " I love you," "I like juice," "I want cookie," "Long cold day," "Big red flower") the same way the first two were taught. As with the procedures used for teaching the imitation of words, you should include a number of mastered phrases and sentences in random rotation as each new phrase or sentence is ready to be randomly rotated. For example, if the student has seven different phrases or sentences mastered and the eighth is ready for random rotation, intermix this phrase or sentence with Phrases or Sentences 1 through 4 during the first randomization; with 5 through 7 during the second randomization; with 2, 3, 6, and 7 during the third randomization; and so on. While practicing skills from this phase of verbal imitation, remember to continue teaching new sounds and sound combinations from Phases 3 and 4 in separate sittings.

It is best to move rather slowly through the imitation of phrases and sentences. Try intermittently testing for generalized imitation by probing new word combinations after the student masters three-word combinations. Starting with a *mean length of utterance* (on average, the number of words the student can say in a chain) of three words, do not move on to four words until the student demonstrates mastery of 8 to 10 three-word chains across different settings and persons. Once the student gives evidence of imitating your presentation of novel three-word combinations, start teaching four-word combinations following the same procedures used to teach two- and three-word combinations. Use forward chaining (chaining Word 1 to Word 2 to Word 3 to Word 4) or backward chaining (chaining Word 4 to Word 3 to Word 2 to Word 1) or chain Word 1 to Word 2 and Word 3 to Word 4 separately, then chain the two groups of words together (chain the combination of Words 1 and 2 to the combination of Words 3 and 4).

Once the student masters imitating six to eight four-word phrases or sentences consistently, move on to Phase 7 to teach imitation of volume, pitch, and speed. Concurrently, the student should be taught to imitate new sounds, combinations, words, phrases, and sentences, including the names of people with whom the student interacts regularly and any other labels that are functional and useful for him in his everyday life.

Areas of Difficulty

The student may persist in making slight pauses between words in a sentence for quite some time (e.g., "I see . . . ball"). These pauses should gradually diminish with increased training in other language programs. If they do not, they can be corrected by procedures outlined in Phase 7.

Some students may jump the gun by starting to imitate before you finish the sentence. If this occurs, it sometimes helps to stop the trial immediately and give an informational "No" or to place your fingers on the student's lips until the SD is completed. If this fails, some sort of cue may be introduced as a prompt to help pace the student. For example, tapping out each word in a sentence with a block and then giving the block to the student to tap while completing his sentence is often an effective prompt. Another prompt can be provided by laying out three blocks in a row (if you are working with a three-word chain) and then pointing to one block with the expression of each word. For example, using this prompting procedure, if you say, "I see ball," you would touch the first block while saying, "I," the second block while saying, "see," and the third block while saying, "ball." The student is provided access to a similar row of blocks to help pace and prompt his sentence. Note that whether or not these prompts are effective, the student's learning to *read* sentences may help establish the concepts of pacing and chaining.

Do not add new phrases and sentences so quickly that the student has difficulty maintaining clear enunciation of each component word. Remember, for you to use the student's imitation of phrases and sentences as prompts in subsequent programs, the student's close match of your verbal prompts must be maintained. Two problems arise if this recommendation is ignored. First, you may find it necessary to correct the student's imitation of a particular word after he completes his sentence. As a result, the student's sentence is not reinforced and you may thus inadvertently place the student's imitation on extinction. If you need to sharpen the imitation of a particular word, take time to focus on this word in a separate session. Second, it is important to ensure a close imitation of the student's correct response in later programs so that no ambiguity in when or what to reinforce arises. For example, if the student is asked to label a picture "Mommy and a baby," and is prompted to do so but expresses the response as "Me and baby," the teacher will be uncertain as to whether to reinforce the response. Note that although typical children may be hard to understand when they are just beginning to talk, their behaviors do not extinguish as quickly as the appropriate behaviors gained by students with developmental delays. In short, it is in the student's best interest for you to secure adequate performance of early and basic steps rather than hurry forward to new and more complex programs.

Phase 7: Imitation of Volume, Pitch, and Speed

As the student makes progress in the earlier phases, problems may occur in the enunciation of volume, pitch, and overall speed of verbalizations. It is not unusual for some students, even after acquiring mastery in Phase 6, to express themselves very softly and almost inaudibly. Others may speak in a very monotonous voice, not changing expressions with variations in the content of sentences. Some students may space out their words, taking an unusually long time to complete a sentence. Some may hurry through a sentence so that it sounds like one word. Suggestions for overcoming these problems are presented in the sections that follow. Note that correction of these dimensions of speech should be introduced only after the student makes considerable progress both in verbal imitation and in expressive language programs (Chapters 23 and 24).

Imitation of Volume

To increase the volume of the student's responses, it may be helpful to teach her to discriminate between loud and soft voices. When teaching the student to imitate volume, use words or phrases that the student can already imitate and that are conducive to a loud or a soft voice. For example, "roar" or "yahoo" may both be good loud words, whereas "baby" or "kitty" may be good soft words. For the sake of illustration, let SD1 be "Roar" stated in a loud voice and SD2 be "Baby" stated in a whisper. Try prompting the word "roar" to be said in a loud volume by actively gesturing like a cheerleader and by getting the student excited and moving around the room. Toy microphones also work well if you need a little help increasing the student's volume; many students are reinforced by hearing themselves speak into a microphone.

▶ **Step 1**

Present SD1 ("Roar") and use shaping procedures to help the student match your loudness. That is, over successive trials, reinforce the student only if she imitates the word correctly *and* if the volume of her response is as loud as or louder than the volume of the last reinforced response. Set mastery at a criterion in which the student's loudness comes close to yours or distinctively above her earlier level of speaking.

▶ **Step 2**

Present SD2 ("Baby") at a very low decibel level, as in a whisper. Prompt the low volume by being very quiet and gentle, settling down yourself and the student. Put your hand or finger on the student's lips to help prompt a low volume. Reinforce the volume level if it was as soft as or softer than the loudness of the last reinforced response. Continue this procedure until the student closely matches your whisper. If the student does not exactly match your whisper, accept a difference in loudness between R1 and R2 that is pronounced enough to help the student to learn to discriminate between her own two levels of volume.

► **Step 3**

Intermix SD1 and SD2 according to the discrimination learning paradigm. Set mastery at 9 out of 10 or 19 out of 20 unprompted correct responses with the SDs presented in random rotation. Remember to fade the physical prompts (e.g., gestures) for both volume levels.

Once imitation of each word with its respective volume level is achieved, you cannot guarantee that the student can discriminate loudness per se. Rather, the student may have reached mastery in Step 3 on the basis of responding to the two different words or some other cue. To ensure that the student can discriminate and imitate loudness, proceed as follows.

► **Step 4**

Select a new word (e.g., "hello") and present that word in a loud voice (as SD1), and then present the *same* word in a low voice (SD2). Prompt the initial trials, fade the prompts over successive trials, and then intermix the two SDs according to the discrimination learning paradigm. Finally, teach new words one at a time in a loud or a soft volume and then intermix the loudness of each word. For example, teach the word "car" as a loud yell and then as a whisper, relying on discrimination learning procedures.

Bringing Volume Under Instructional Control

Once the student learns to imitate the volume of the teacher's voice across many words, teachers, and environments, bring the loudness of the student's speech under instructional control. The goal of this step is for you to be able to tell the student to "Speak louder" or "Speak softer" as the situation demands (e.g., at home, in church, in restaurants). To accomplish this task, it is helpful to prompt by presenting the instructions in loud versus soft volumes. In brief, present the instruction "Speak louder" with the word "louder" at a high decibel level. Subsequently, the decibel level of your "louder" is faded as a prompt while the student's loudness is maintained. The instruction "Speak louder" is then contrasted with the instruction "Speak softer" according to the following steps.

► **Step 1**

Present SD1 ("Speak louder") and prompt the correct decibel level by stating "louder" very loudly for the student to imitate (the student imitates the word "louder" and its volume). When the student responds correctly in 5 out of 5 or 9 out of 10 trials, go on to the next step.

► **Step 2**

Present SD2 ("Speak softer") and prompt the student's correct response by stating the word "softer" in a whisper. After the student reaches mastery criterion (5 out of 5 or 9 out of 10 correct responses), go on to the next step.

► **Step 3**

Intermix SD1 and SD2 according to the discrimination learning paradigm. This step should proceed relatively quickly because the student already mastered loudness discrimination through the procedures in the previous section. Bring the discrimination among SD1 and SD2 to mastery at 9 of 10 or 19 out of 20 correct responses.

► **Step 4**

Gradually remove volume as a prompt, bringing the student's loudness under the control of your SD (i.e., "Speak loud" or "Speak soft" without any difference in volume among the two instructions). By maintaining differential reinforcement during prompt fading, the student is likely to learn to speak according to the instruction. That is, after you state, "Speak loud," in a conversational tone, the student should say, "Loud," loudly. Similarly, the student should respond with the appropriate decibel level when you instruct, "Speak soft." Set mastery at 5 out of 5 or 9 out of 10 unprompted correct responses for each instruction.

► **Step 5**

Generalize the instructions "Speak loud" versus "Speak soft" across new words and sentences. For example, if you instruct the student, "Say loud hello," the student should pronounce the word "hello" loudly. To help the student refrain from imitating the "say loud" component of the instruction, quickly and almost inaudibly state,

"Say loud," while immediately prompting a loud "hello" for the student to repeat. Gradually over the next several trials, fade in a normal volume of the words "say loud" while maintaining, with differential reinforcement, the student's loud expression of the word "hello." Set mastery at 5 out of 5 or 9 out of 10 correct responses for each new instruction.

▶ **Step 6**

Using the same techniques presented in Step 5, teach the student to express words in a low decibel level when you give new instructions such as "Say soft bye-bye." Set mastery at 5 out of 5 or 9 out of 10 correct responses for each new instruction.

▶ **Step 7**

Intermix two of the new SDs according to the discrimination learning paradigm. Set mastery at 9 out of 10 or 19 out of 20 unprompted correct responses. As with all programs that rely on discrimination learning, make certain that random rotation is included to avoid perseveration; win–stay, lose–shift; or other patterns of responding.

Over time, change the initial instructions to more typical expressions such as "I can't hear you" or "You are too loud" by slowly fading out the earlier instructions while gradually fading in the new instructions one word at a time.

Areas of Difficulty

It is difficult to maintain the student's volume level when volume is faded as a prompt (as in Step 4 of the previous section). This comes about because the student has been extensively reinforced for imitating several aspects of verbalizations, including volume. Nevertheless, with patience and practice, the student should master this program. If the student has extreme difficulty with volume training, however, hold off on teaching this skill unless the student speaks so softly that she cannot easily be heard by the teacher.

Imitation of Pitch and Contour

The portion of the program for teaching the student to modulate pitch and contour in an appropriate fashion is also taught through imitation and may be appropriate to introduce here, even though the implementation of this program should be delayed until substantial progress in expressive language is demonstrated. Pitch refers to the frequency with which sound waves are produced and is analogous to what are called deep versus high voices (as in a bass vs. a soprano voice). Contour refers to the modulation of pitch across parts or types of sentences (such as a question, which ends in a rising pitch). The speech of persons with autism is often characterized as monotone and lacking in contour or expression; the teaching of pitch and contour modulation helps eliminate this characteristic.

The procedures for teaching appropriate variation in pitch are similar to the procedures used for teaching loudness imitation. When teaching the student to imitate pitch, use words or phrases the student can already imitate and those that may help prompt a high or a low pitch. For example, "hi," "wee," or "cook" may help generate high pitches, whereas "cow," "no," or "daddy" may facilitate low pitches. You may also attempt to prompt a high pitch by sitting up tall and raising your arms while smiling. You may prompt a lower pitch by slouching or changing your facial expression to a frown. As with all vocal imitations, you may find it difficult to isolate effective prompts and may have to rely heavily on shaping. To illustrate the steps that follow, let SD1 be "Wee" stated in a high-pitched voice and let SD2 be "Daddy" stated in a low-pitched voice.

▶ **Step 1**

Present SD1 ("Wee") in a high-pitched voice. Over a series of trials, shape the student's response to match your high pitch by reinforcing closer and closer approximations of your pitch.

▶ **Step 2**

Present SD2 ("Daddy") in a low-pitched voice. Shape the student's pitch to resemble your pitch. It is unlikely that the student will achieve a perfect match of your pitch in Steps 1 and 2. Perfection in pitch imitation is not necessary, however, as long as the adults who are present agree that the student's pitch of SD1 is noticeably different from that of SD2. By noticeably different, we mean that the difference is large enough to enable the student to make the discrimination in Step 3.

▶ **Step 3**

Intermix SD1 and SD2 according to the discrimination learning paradigm. Place mastery at

9 out of 10 or 19 out of 20 unprompted correct responses.

► **Step 4**

Begin generalization training across words. That is, replace "Wee" in SD1 and "Daddy" in SD2 with new words and train to criterion as done in Steps 1 through 3. Later, present the same word as both SD1 and SD2 but change the pitch in which the word is stated. Both procedures help generalize pitch across words by separating particular pitches from particular words.

► **Step 5**

After the student imitates the pitch of words the first time they are given, present a three-sound SD1 such as "da-dee-da," expressing the sounds at different pitches (e.g., low–high–low). Shape the student's response until she imitates the pattern of pitches you make. When the student masters SD1, present SD2 with a different pattern of pitches and shape the student's pitches to match yours. Next, introduce new three-part sounds and shape the student's responses until the student imitates patterns of pitches the first time they are presented. The final step is to take one three-part SD and change it randomly. For example, take SD1 ("da-dee-da") and change the pitch of that SD (e.g., high–high–low, then high–low–high, then low–low–high, etc.).

Use these procedures to teach the student to imitate questions ("What is it?" "What did you say?" and "How are you?"), which require a rising pitch across words. In the same manner, the student may be taught to express declarative statements (e.g., "I don't want that" and "My name is Ben") with a falling pitch.

Imitation of Speed

Some students speak very slowly and do not adjust the speed of their expression to contexts. As with volume and pitch, speed of utterances may have to be taught separately as follows.

► **Step 1**

Present SD1, which consists of any mastered three-syllable word or a word sequence expressed at a rapid rate. An example is "da-da-da" stated so that it consumes approximately 1 second. Shape the student's speed of expression to closely resemble that of your speed. Speed may be prompted by the use of visual cues such as gesturing in rhythm to your speech. Set mastery at 5 out of 5 or 9 out of 10 unprompted correct responses.

► **Step 2**

Present SD2, a sequence of syllables or words similar in length to SD1 but different in sound (e.g., "tee-tee-tee"). Say SD2 at a rate that lasts approximately 3 seconds. Maximize the difference between SD1 and SD2 by exaggerating the slow versus fast speed. Prompt and shape the student's slow rate to approximate yours. Set mastery at 5 out of 5 or 9 out of 10 unprompted correct responses.

► **Step 3**

Intermix SD1 and SD2 and bring to mastery (9 out of 10 or 19 out of 20 unprompted correct responses), adhering to the discrimination paradigm.

In subsequent steps, generalize speed to different syllable or word combinations. Once this is mastered, bring the student's rate of speech under your instructional control by teaching her to respond correctly to the instructions "Speak faster" versus "Speak slower." This may be accomplished by following procedures similar to those presented under the section "Bringing Volume Under Instructional Control."

Areas of Difficulty

Be aware that the student may regress during the Verbal Imitation Program. The student may start to tantrum and self-stimulate more than he did before this program was started, or the student may achieve a level of mastery one week that may not be improved upon the following week, or he may lose some of the previous week's gains. Do not be alarmed by such occurrences. Verbal Imitation is one of the most elaborate programs to teach and one of the most difficult programs for the student to learn. Hence, this program can be very frustrating for the both you and the student. We know of no program in which the student continuously improves from session to session without occasional setbacks. If regression does occur, simply ease back into the program and return to a stage the student can master and thus be reinforced for so as to regain his confidence and feeling of success. You may also want to consider cutting in half the length of time you keep the student in the chair. Intersperse various instructions from other programs the student can successfully perform to help him regain the feeling of success and break up the monotony brought on by the repetition of a single program. You may also try changing reinforcers or teaching in a different room of the house.

As the student's imitative speech is subjected to programs involving grammar and meaning, it is likely that the clarity of his enunciation will suffer. It may become increasingly difficult to understand the student and decide whether to reinforce an utterance. In such cases, one must go back to the Verbal Imitation Program to reinstate adequate enunciation.

There are several ways to help the student maintain and achieve well-enunciated speech. One such procedure consists of teaching the student to read (see Chapter 29). The visual cues involved in reading may help improve the student's enunciation. Teaching the student to be the teacher (while you play the student) is another way to maintain and achieve well-enunciated speech; it is quite common to observe a student give instructions to the attending teacher in a most precise manner and with adequate volume. Perhaps this is because the student is reinforced by taking control.

Managing Echolalia

Imitation is a basic mechanism by which to learn. Typical students often learn the correct answers to questions by listening to and reproducing the teacher's answers or other students' answers. For example, if a teacher asks a typical student, "When is Washington's birthday?" and the student fails to answer, either the teacher or other students in the class will prompt the answer, "February 22." The teacher may then again ask the question to the student who failed to answer and teach the student to repeat the answer ("February 22"). In contrast, an echolalic student will repeat the question, "When is Washington's birthday?" and fail to associate the correct answer. For example, suppose the teacher asks the student, "What is your name?" and the student echoes the entire question or only a portion of the question, such as "Name" or "Your name." The teacher may try to prompt the correct answer by stating the student's name (e.g., "Michael") in hopes that when the question is repeated, the student will answer correctly. In all likelihood, the student will again repeat the teacher's question and not the correct answer. The student's repetition of the teacher's question serves to block or prevent learning of the correct answer.

The following procedures are recommended for helping the student inhibit inappropriate echolalic responding. One procedure consists of using a volume prompt as a way to help the student discriminate between what to repeat and what not to repeat. For example, if the teacher asks, "What is your name?" and wants to prompt the student to answer appropriately (e.g., "Michael"), the teacher may quickly whisper the question, "What is your name?" and then immediately and loudly prompt "Michael." Directly after the student says, "Michael," the teacher should provide the student with abundant reinforcement. In subsequent trials, the teacher should fade the prompt by slowly raising the volume and decreasing the speed of the question while slowly lessening the volume of the correct answer.

Generalize the student's imitation of correct answers by introducing new questions that must be prompted in order to be answered correctly. For this procedure to be effective, you must present numerous short, simple questions that require one-word answers. The loudness of the correct answer to each question should be faded over trials. Contemporaneous with the presentation of novel questions, the student is likely to generalize imitation of the correct responses rather than merely repeat your questions. Should the student fail, return to earlier steps by lowering the volume of the question while raising the volume of the answer. Reinstate the prompt fading process once correct responding is established.

A second procedure consists of teaching the student to answer "I don't know" in response to questions that are unfamiliar to her. To illustrate, the teacher may ask, "What is the capital of France?" and then immediately prompt the student to repeat "I don't know." Present the question in a low volume and the answer in a high volume, and immediately reinforce the student for repeating the correct answer (i.e., "I don't know"). In gradual steps, increase the volume of the question and decrease the volume of the prompted answer. Repeat this question-and-answer sequence until the student answers correctly five times in a row without your prompt. Then go on to additional questions, such as "Where does dad work?" "Why do we have firefighters?" and "Why do we eat food?" Once the student's responses to several such SDs are mastered, help the student discriminate between what she knows and does not know by intermixing questions she can already answer. Adhere to discrimination learning procedures when teaching this skill.

Further aid the student by teaching her to say, "What is the answer?" "Help me," or "Tell me" in response to unknown SDs. One way to accomplish this is by prompting the statement "Tell me" after the student responds with "I don't know" to a question such as "Why do we eat food?" This sequence should be repeated until the student can answer with "Tell me" without being prompted. The completed, mastered sequence would proceed as follows:

TEACHER: Why do we eat?

STUDENT: I don't know, tell me.

TEACHER: To live.

Over successive trials, the student is provided with the opportunity to generalize this kind of verbal interchange. The rate of acquisition varies across students; some students master and generalize this task after three or four questions, whereas others show little or no progress.

Concluding Comments

The procedures described in this chapter are complex, may seem tedious to apply, and may seem to achieve limited gains. It is important to remember, however, that once the student masters most of the beginning steps in this program, it takes relatively less work to expand the student's mastery across new and advanced programs. Furthermore, once gains are made, teaching can be taken out of the highly structured setting necessary for mastery of the first discriminations, and new skills can be taught and expanded in less formal environments. As the student's imitations become more generalized and inherently reinforcing, you should observe the student learning from the volume, inflection, and speed expressed by adults and typical peers in his everyday environment.

Keep in mind that the student cannot maintain and generalize what he learns in the Verbal Imitation Program unless these skills are practiced outside of scheduled teaching sessions. Therefore, provide many informal rehearsals of the skills taught to the student through this program. Present instructions in a playful and enjoyable context, increasing the likelihood that the student will learn to like to imitate speech. If the student learns to enjoy imitating speech, he may become echolalic, which is good in the early stages of teaching. The student may then "play" with speech, even if he does not know the meaning of what he says. Meaning can be taught later. There are reasons to believe that students who echo the teacher's instructions learn how to respond to such instructions sooner than students who do not echo. Apparently, the student who echoes is able to "store" the teacher's instructions and thus is better able to respond to those instructions; the instructions are not gone the moment the teacher finishes them. It may be helpful to consider that we all tend to echo questions to which we do not know the answer, or to questions that are complex with answers not immediately available. We often echo these questions subvocally, rehearsing them to give us time to formulate the correct answer.

The Verbal Imitation Program tends to remain a focus of teaching for a relatively long time as this program helps increase vocalizations and fix enunciation problems. Verbal imitation is also used to prompt answers to questions throughout much of the student's early years. It is therefore important for both the student and the teacher to become proficient at this program.

The teaching skills learned in the current program help the teaching of most, if not all, of the other programs presented in this manual. With mastery of the procedures presented in this program, the teacher takes a giant step toward becoming an expert at teaching the student with developmental delays.

Expressive Labeling of Objects

CHAPTER 23

In this program, the student is taught to identify objects by stating their respective labels. Prior to being taught expressive labels, the student should have learned to receptively identify approximately 15 to 20 objects as taught in the Receptive Identification of Objects Program (Chapter 17). Acquisition of the skills taught in this labeling program may also be facilitated by the student's learning to match the objects to be labeled. By following the procedures detailed in the Matching and Sorting Program (Chapter 12), the student's discrimination of the target objects will be strengthened. Prior to beginning the Expressive Labeling of Objects Program, the student should have learned to imitate the words to be labeled in the current program, such as "juice," "ball," and "cookie" (see Verbal Imitation, Chapter 22). Such imitations are used as prompts in this program.

When choosing prospective objects for the student to label, make certain that the student's enunciation of the labels are clear enough that other adults can understand what she is saying. Clarity is particularly important in helping to avoid such difficult situations as when teachers disagree on whether to reinforce a particular response given by the student. Clarity in enunciation may first be established by practicing labels through verbal imitation. It should then be decided which labels are the most uniformly understood across team members. Monosyllabic words (i.e., words containing only one syllable) may be easier to master in verbal imitation than polysyllabic words (i.e., words containing several syllables); therefore, monosyllabic words make good candidates for the initial expressive labels to be taught to the student.

In addition to using labels the student can pronounce clearly, use labels that are highly discriminable and, if possible, useful and practical for the student in her everyday life. This may be accomplished by considering the vocabulary of a typically developing young individual. Such a vocabulary normally consists of words used to communicate needs and desires. For example, labels such as "car," "water," "spoon," "cup," "mommy," and "milk" are more meaningful to most 3-year-olds than labels such as "map," "fan," "shelf," and "stone." Similarly, the practicality of the labels taught may be established by using the student's favorite food, drink, and toy reinforcers as the first labels. Once the student receives the labeled item as a reinforcer, she is more likely to label it again. Later, single labels may be used to build simple sentences. For example, the word "milk" may be used to receive milk, then a verb such as "want" may be added to produce the phrase "want milk," then this phrase may be expanded to "I want milk" (see Chapter 26).

Keep in mind that the student may learn to label an object expressively before she learns to identify it receptively. When this is the case, the learning of expressive labels often facilitates the learning of receptive labels. Most often, however, generalization occurs the opposite way such that the receptive identification of an object facilitates its expressive identification. For example, the student's learning to touch a cookie when requested to do so may help the student label the cookie upon the teacher's request.

The procedures for teaching expressive labels follow those described in earlier programs involving discrimination learning (see Chapter 16). However, although earlier programs in this manual largely employ nonverbal prompts to teach new skills, the Expressive Labeling Programs employ primarily verbal prompts. Nonetheless, the principles of prompting and prompt fading remain the same. To simplify the following text, we use the object labels "cup," "ball," and "shoe" to represent SD1, SD2, and SD3, respectively. Note that these labels sound sufficiently different and the objects look sufficiently different to facilitate the student's discrimination.

Labeling the First Objects

You and the student should sit facing each other. As described in previous chapters, you should sit close enough to the student to allow for clear presentation of instructions and immediate reinforcement delivery. The use of a table is not necessary in this program. Present each three-dimensional object to be labeled by holding it in front of the student, approximately 1 foot away from him.

▶ Step 1

Present SD1, which consists of your asking, "What is it?" while simultaneously moving a cup distinctively in front of the student's eyes. A correct response is defined as the student stating, "Cup," at the time you present the cup. After giving the SD, prompt the response by stating, "Cup," and reinforce the student for imitating the label. Remember that the prompt must occur immediately after the SD (within 1 second). Present the verbal portion of the SD ("What is it?") quickly and at a low volume and then immediately express the prompt ("Cup") loudly and succinctly as an additional prompt. By doing this, the student may be prevented from repeating your question ("What is it?") rather than simply responding with "Cup." Gradually increase the volume of the question while fading the volume of the prompt. While fading the prompt, monitor the student's rate of correct responding and reduce the prompt at a pace that maintains a clear enunciation of the label. Present mass trials of SD1 until the criterion for mastery of 9 out of 10 or 19 out of 20 consecutive unprompted correct responses is reached.

One problem that may occur when fading the prompt by reducing its volume is that the student may imitate the volume you use. There are three possible solutions to this problem. One is to teach the student to maintain the volume of his label even though the volume of the prompt is lowered. This may be done by reinforcing only those responses that are adequately loud. Another way to solve this problem is by probing for a correct response by suddenly eliminating the prompt. Precede the probe trial with a series of fully prompted trials in close succession, delivering reinforcement immediately after the student's response and beginning each trial within 1 second after the delivery of reinforcement in the prior trial. After the student correctly responds across 3 to 5 trials, eliminate the prompt completely and continue to present the next few trials in close succession. A third solution may be employed by systematically reducing the length of the prompt. By gradually excluding the final sounds of the object label, the label is eventually eliminated as a prompt (e.g., begin with "Cup," then reduce the prompt to "Cu," then to "C," and then eliminate the prompt completely). Make sure the student expresses the label in its entirety (even though the prompt is reduced) by reinforcing only the student's enunciation of the complete label.

Clearly expressed responses are critical to the team's agreeing upon which responses are to be considered correct and hence reinforced. If the student is reinforced for stating the label while lowering his volume in imitation of a fading prompt, it becomes difficult for the student to decide what component of the response is being reinforced. (Technically speaking, the reinforcement contingency is not discriminable.) That is, the student may not know whether you are reinforcing him for stating the label, lowering the volume of his speech, or both. It is therefore crucial that reinforcement be given contingent only upon labels that are clearly enunciated in a proper volume. It is also important to remember not to inadvertently prompt the student's responding to such cues as your mouth movements rather than the auditory input. Observation by other team members can help reduce such prompts, as can saying the word while covering up your mouth or presenting the instructions when the student is facing the table rather than you.

▶ Step 2

Present SD2, which consists of your asking, "What is it?" while concurrently moving a ball in front of the student's line of vision. Immediately (within 1 second) prompt the correct response by stating, "Ball." The prompt helps prevent the student from stating, "Cup," which is a likely response given that this label was heavily reinforced in Step 1 and the student has yet to learn that different objects have different labels. (Technically speaking, the student demonstrates a flat generalization gradient; different stimuli cue the same response.) Reinforce the correct response and gradually fade the prompt. Mass trial SD2 and set mastery at the same criterion used for SD1.

To facilitate the student's attention to the SD, you may first state, "Look," while moving the ball in front of the student's visual field. This may help temporarily inhibit certain self-stimulatory behaviors that could block the student's attention to the SD; however, a disadvantage in adding this statement in that the distinctiveness of the SD may be decreased, thus making the discrimination more difficult. Therefore, it may be more effective to engage the student in three or four successive presentations of a well-mastered task (e.g., nonverbal imitation or receptive instructions) and then quickly switch to the target SD once the student's attention has been gained.

▶ Step 3

Intermix SD1 and SD2 according to the discrimination learning paradigm. Set mastery at 9 out of 10 or 19 out of 20 unprompted correct responses. Once mastered, practice the discrimination between SD1 and SD2 for approximately 1 week across different teachers and environments so as to help solidify and generalize this discrimination.

This first discrimination is an extremely important achievement because it provides some evidence that the student can speak and may go on to more elaborate expressive language. To be able to express such things as wants, impressions, and observations in the quick and efficient medium of language is critical for facilitating development. It is important to keep in mind the significance of the first discrimination given that this discrimination is almost always difficult to achieve and requires enormous patience and diligence from both you and the student.

▶ Step 4

Present SD3, which consists of your asking, "What is it?" while showing the student a shoe. Follow the same procedures used for teaching SD1 and SD2. After the response to SD3 is mastered in mass trials, systematically intermix SD3 with SD1 and then with SD2 according to the discrimination learning paradigm.

Up to this point, direct prompting techniques have been demonstrated (i.e., in this case, stating the label of the object as the SD is presented). A less direct but potentially useful prompt is the combination of receptive and expressive labels such that the receptive identification of the object provides the prompt for the expressive identification of the object. For example, if you instruct the student to "Point to cup," you may ask, "What is it?" while or immediately after the student performs the action. The "cup" portion of the receptive instruction may prompt the student's expressive labeling of the object. Receptive identification may also facilitate the student's attention to the object to be labeled.

Generalizing Expressive Labeling of Objects

After the student learns to label 20 to 25 objects presented in 3-D form, teach her to label other exemplars of these same items (e.g., if the student learned to label a white shepherd as a dog, now teach her to label a brown collie as a dog). By varying characteristics (e.g., size, color) of the objects, the student learns to group particular features associated with classes of objects. Remember that this step is crucial to the student's development given that she must learn to associate common abstract elements among objects in order to form concepts rather than simply know isolated labels for particular objects. Certain early steps in this direction were introduced in Chapter 12, Matching and Sorting.

Once the student learns to label a variety of objects of different classes or categories in a structured one-on-one teaching situation, begin to generalize this mastery to new situations. For instance, place items around the living room (e.g., a cup on a coffee table, a doll on the floor, a ball on a chair) and ask the student to label them. As teaching is extended to several parts of the student's daily life, the student learns to generalize skills she first acquired in the more structured treatment setting to the less structured real world.

An important step toward the generalization of labels is teaching the student to label objects when they are presented in their 2-D form (e.g., objects depicted in books, magazines, and movies). After the student learns to label 20 to 25 various exemplars of objects presented in their 3-D form, teach her to label these objects when presented in their 2-D form. It may be helpful to begin by using photographs of previously learned 3-D objects. The photos should be clear and unambiguous (e.g., to generalize the label "car," use a clear picture of a car without background clutter). The procedures for teaching expressive labels presented in 2-D form are the same as those used for teaching expressive labels shown in their 3-D form. Simply present SDs, one at a time, by showing the student the pictures of the objects, prompt, bring to mastery, and finally employ discrimination learning procedures.

When the student learns to expressively label 20 or more pictures of separate objects, teach her to label these objects as they appear in picture books. Begin by using books that contain only a few pictures per page. Such simplicity facilitates the student's success at correctly labeling the target items. Systematically introduce books that contain more and more items per page and teach labels of novel objects as they are presented in the books. This format of teaching marks the beginning of more informal and natural teaching, and it extends the student's description of her environment.

Areas of Difficulty

One problem that may occur in the student's responding is excessive echolalia. The student may echo the SD in part or in whole instead of imitating the prompt or in addition to imitating the prompt. This problem was touched upon earlier in this chapter, but because it is a common problem, it may be helpful to further discuss how it can be resolved. If echolalia occurs during responding, ask the question in a low volume, stating the object label in a louder volume than the volume of the question. For example, ask the student, "What is it?" quickly and in a low volume while presenting a toy car, then quickly state the prompt "car" loudly and clearly before the student can echo "What is it?" Reinforce the student for repeating the prompt and withhold reinforcement for repeating the question. Gradually increase the volume of the question "What is it?" while maintaining reinforcement for *not* echoing. If the volume is increased too quickly, the student may go back to repeating the question. Use the amount of volume necessary to block the student from repeating the question and increase the volume of the question at a rate that helps the student *not* to repeat the instruction but rather to repeat your label.

Echolalia is likely to occur when the student does not know the answer to your question. Once the answer is mastered, the student is likely to cease echoing the question. For example, if a student does not know the answer to a question such as "What is the capital of France?" the student is likely to echo that question. If the student knows the answer, he is less likely to do so. We proposed in Chapter 1 that echolalia may serve as a way of storing auditory input so as to give a person time to evaluate or prepare an answer. If this proposal is true, then echolalia is a useful strategy. It is also a strategy used by typical persons. For example, if a typical adult is asked, "What is 2 times 2?" the adult is likely to answer, "4," without echoing the question. In contrast, if a person is asked a question such as "What is 2 times 2 plus 5 minus 7?" the person is likely to echo the question, although subvocally because the person has been taught not to think out loud (Carr, Schreibman, & Lovaas, 1974).

Another difficulty that may arise is that the student may master labeling certain 3-D objects but encounter problems in labeling representations of these objects when they are presented in a photograph or picture. If this occurs, prompt the student by presenting the 3-D objects beside or behind their 2-D representations. After the student consistently responds correctly to the instruction, slowly fade the 3-D objects from the student's view, shifting the labels from the 3-D objects to their 2-D representations. Note that some students learn rather quickly to label 2-D objects but experience difficulty with labeling 3-D objects. Begin teaching in the area where the student's strength lies.

Some students (approximately 1 out of 10) fail to label any objects despite the most extensive teaching efforts. Some of these students may learn to label behaviors before learning to label objects. If this is the case with the student you work with, introduce the Expressive Labeling of Behaviors Program (Chapter 24), and return to the Expressive Labeling of Objects Program after the student masters labeling behaviors.

Expressive Labeling of Behaviors

CHAPTER 24

In the Expressive Labeling of Behaviors Program, the student is taught to identify behaviors by verbalizing their respective labels. To learn how to expressively label behaviors, the student should possess the same prerequisite skills required for teaching the Expressive Labeling of Objects Program (Chapter 23). To review, the student should have mastered the matching of pictures of the behaviors to be labeled (Chapter 12), the imitation the behaviors to be labeled (Chapter 13), and the receptive identification of these same behaviors (Chapter 18). (Keep in mind that some students acquire expressive labels before receptive labels.) The student should also be able to verbally imitate a variety of action verbs in their gerund form (e.g., "swimming," "running," "eating," "smiling"). In addition, it is recommended that you begin with words the student learned to imitate with clarity in the Verbal Imitation Program (Chapter 22).

For ease in presentation, the term *action labels* is used instead of *labels of behaviors*, and *action pictures* replaces *pictures of behaviors*. In all programs requiring the use of physical stimuli, perceptually dissimilar stimuli are likely to facilitate mastery of the discriminations among those stimuli. Therefore, start with action pictures that differ considerably in physical appearance. For example, pictures of a person eating versus a person waving appear to be more distinctive than pictures of a person eating versus a person smiling or pictures of a person waving versus a person clapping. More subtle differences among stimuli (e.g., the difference between smiling and frowning) may be introduced in later stages.

You may begin the Expressive Labeling of Behaviors Program by using 2-D representations (i.e., pictures) of behaviors rather than behaviors performed in vivo (3-D), given the relative ease in presenting 2-D as opposed to 3-D stimuli. Some students, however, master the 3-D format of this program with much less difficulty than the 2-D format. Therefore, if you encounter serious problems when teaching action labels using pictures, switch to 3-D stimuli.

The sequence of steps used to teach this program is identical to the sequence presented in Chapter 23, Expressive Labeling of Objects. The only distinction is that the stimuli used in this program represent actions rather than objects. To illustrate the progression of teaching the student to expressively label behaviors, the action labels "waving," "eating," and "sleeping" are used.

▶ Step 1

Present SD1, which consists of asking, "What is she (or he) doing?" emphasizing the word "doing" and displaying a picture of a person waving. Immediately prompt the correct response by stating, "Waving." Should the student echo the instruction as part of his response, say the SD in a low volume and immediately present the prompt ("Waving") in a loud voice. If the student continues to echo, merely state, "Doing," as the SD and fade in the rest of the question ("What is she") at a later time. Reinforce the student for each correct response. Gradually decrease the volume of the verbal prompt and intermittently probe withholding the prompt altogether. As discussed in the preceding chapter, be sure to remove inadvertent prompts and completely fade partial prompts (e.g., mouthing the word or any part of the word "waving"). Mass trial SD1 to the criterion of 5 out of 5 or 9 out of 10 unprompted correct responses.

Note that the correct response at this stage in teaching is a one-word response. In later stages (after the student masters several action labels, pronouns, and verbal imitation of phrases), the student may be taught to respond using full sentences (e.g., "He is waving").

▶ Step 2

Present SD2, which consists of asking, "What is he (or she) doing?" (emphasizing the word "doing") while displaying a picture of a person eating. Immediately prompt the correct response by loudly stating the action word "eating." Reinforce correct responses and systematically fade the use of the verbal prompt. Mass trial SD2 until the criterion of 5 out of 5 or 9 out of 10 unprompted correct responses is met.

▶ **Step 3**

Intermix SD1 and SD2 as described in the discrimination learning chapter (Chapter 16). After systematically alternating between SD1 and SD2, intermix these SDs according to the random rotation paradigm. Place mastery at 9 out of 10 or 19 out of 20 unprompted correct responses.

▶ **Step 4**

Present SD3, which consists of asking, "What is he (or she) doing?" (emphasizing the word "doing"), while displaying a picture of a person sleeping. Teach SD3 following the same procedures used to teach SD1 and SD2. When the response to SD3 is mastered in mass trials, systematically intermix SD3 with SD1 and then SD3 with SD2 according to the discrimination learning paradigm. Finally, intermix all three SDs. Teach the next 7 to 10 action labels following the same training procedures used in Steps 1 through 4.

Generalizing Expressive Labeling of Behaviors

After the student learns to label 10 to 15 actions presented in 2-D form, teach her to label other exemplars of these actions. That is, teach the student to label pictures that depict the same actions but that vary the persons portrayed. For example, after the student learns to label a picture of a girl jumping, teach her to label pictures of a man jumping, a woman jumping, and a boy jumping. Such generalization is important because the student must learn to label a particular action regardless of who performs the action. Similarly, the student must learn to label particular behaviors even though the forms of the behaviors may differ slightly from one picture to the next. Remember to generalize labeling across pictures in magazines, posters, and books. Also generalize across environments by moving out of the treatment room to other rooms of the house. Eventually generalize to environments outside of the house by, for example, labeling pictures in advertisements on store windows or along a street. Keep in mind that distracting stimuli in these new environments may interfere with correct labeling. If this occurs, proceed gradually from relatively simple to more complex contexts.

Labeling Actions in Vivo

After the student learns to label 15 to 20 actions in the formats described above, move on to teaching the student to label these same actions performed in vivo. Teach the student to respond to the question, "What am *I* doing?" Ask this question while you are simultaneously performing the target action. For example, ask the student, "What am I doing?" and simultaneously wave one hand. The student should be immediately prompted to say, "Waving." In this format, the student must attend to the action of a real person rather than a picture of a person. Once one in vivo action is mastered in mass trials, introduce a second action label (e.g., jumping), bring it to mastery in mass trials, and then intermix the labels according to the discrimination learning paradigm. Once mastered, go on to introduce another action label. Because the action labels taught in this format have already been mastered in another format, acquisition of the correct labels should occur relatively quickly, and it is likely that only slight prompting will be needed to achieve mastery.

Describing His Own Behaviors

Begin teaching the student to describe his own behaviors by modeling an action previously mastered in another format of this program. While the student is imitating the action, ask him, "What are you doing?" The student should then be taught to state the appropriate action label by following the steps presented above. To illustrate an example, say to the student, "Do this," while knocking on the table. While the student is knocking, ask him, "What are you doing?" and immediately prompt his response by saying, "Knocking." Repeat the trial and fade the verbal prompt over subsequent trials. If the student has mastered performing the behavior through the skills taught in Chapter 18, you may instruct the student to engage in the behavior (e.g., "Knock") instead of using modeling as a prompt. Note that your instruction may help prompt the correct answer ("Knocking"). Proceed through discrimination training by introducing new behaviors in mass trials, then intermixing these behaviors until random rotation is achieved. Once the student masters labeling your and his own behaviors, generalize the labeling across other persons such as parents, grandparents, siblings, and neighbors. Also, generalize across environments.

The pronouns *he*, *she*, *I*, and *you* are included in some of the instructions presented in this chapter. There is no evidence that the student understands pronouns at this stage in teaching or that he will acquire the use of pronouns based on the present program (pronouns will be taught in an upcoming manual on advanced programs).

Labeling Actions and Objects in Books

Teach the student to expressively label 15 to 20 different behaviors in 2-D form, then go on to teaching the student to label these same behaviors in picture books. Start with books that have only one person pictured per page. Later, move on to books with two and then three or more persons per page. If there are items on the page that detract the student's attention from the persons performing the target behaviors, initially cover such items or point to the target persons. Systematically fade all prompts while maintaining the student's description of the behaviors. Once this format is mastered, it should be extended to the student describing what she sees (objects *and* behaviors) in various picture books. This task helps the student develop a prerequisite skill for later and more complex mastery of language (see Chapter 26).

Areas of Difficulty

If the student echoes your question "What is she doing?" present the question at low volume (as in a whisper) and prompt the correct response quickly and loudly. Provide reinforcement contingent on responding to the prompt and not the question. Over successive trials, gradually increase the volume of the question and decrease the volume of the prompt until the student responds appropriately to the question only.

When you are teaching the student to expressively identify several actions (and object labels) in books, magazines, and the like, the student may demonstrate difficulty scanning a picture to identify only one action. To help remedy this problem, use a homemade poster that initially depicts one action. When the student masters labeling this action, add an object, then include two actions and one object, and so on. If needed, prompt by pointing to the different items. Fade all prompts and provide reinforcement contingent on the student's labeling an increasing number of items. To further facilitate spontaneity, help the student examine pictures by displaying items in a row, and teach the student to label the items by scanning from left to right. Gradually increase the number of rows. Once the student can label most or all of the items in such a display, gradually remove the prompting effect of the rows.

Some students experience considerable difficulty labeling the actions of persons in vivo. This may occur even if the student previously mastered labeling the actions of 2-D representations of the same persons. A helpful prompt in such a circumstance is to hold a mastered picture of the behavior in front of yourself while engaging in the same behavior, then fading the picture. The student's learning to label actions in vivo may also be facilitated if you stand behind a picture frame while performing the actions to be labeled (e.g., smiling, eating). The use of a picture frame may help the student focus on the relevant stimuli. Such a tactic is a prompt that obviously needs to be faded.

As in all other programs, individual differences become apparent in the Expressive Labeling of Behaviors Program. Over time, you will gain more flexibility and creativity in learning how to deal with the uniqueness displayed by the student.

Early Abstract Language: Teaching Color, Shape, and Size

CHAPTER 25

The programs in this chapter are designed to teach the student to identify and label certain abstract properties of objects. Specifically, the student is taught to identify and label the color, shape, and size of objects independent of the objects. In the case of color, the student is taught that there are blue cars, blue clothing, blue cups, a blue sky, a yellow sun, yellow cups, yellow clothing, and so on. The same is true of size and shape, as there exist both small and large persons, trees, and houses, and round and square signs, windows, and mirrors.

These are complex tasks for the student to learn, but because they are a part of everyday life, the student will benefit from mastering them. The student who understands a question such as "Do you want the red or the blue shirt?" or comprehends an instruction such as "Go get the little cup" or can express the phrase "I want the big cookie" is likely to live a less frustrating life than a student who cannot make such distinctions. There is also a less obvious benefit in that the student who can discriminate and attend to environmental stimuli such as color, shape, and size is more likely to be aware of and truly see her external environment and less likely to remain isolated.

The order in which these programs are introduced (i.e., color first, then shape, and finally size) represents their apparent degrees of difficulty, from easier to more difficult, based on informal observation. There are also some a priori reasons to believe that learning about the size of objects is more difficult than learning about the color or shape of objects, given that size discrimination requires the student's attention to the *relationship* between two or more stimuli, whereas color and shape discriminations do not.

Colors

The Colors Program consists of both receptive and expressive components. In the receptive component, the student is taught to touch, point to, or otherwise identify colors when you state the respective labels of those colors. In the expressive component, the student is taught to label colors by stating their respective names.

Before beginning to teach the student to identify and label colors, gather basic color swatches (red, orange, blue, yellow, green, black, brown, white, purple, and pink) that are identical in all dimensions except color (i.e., same size, shape, and texture). The color swatches may be made out of construction paper cut into identically sized squares or rectangles for each color. They may also be obtained from a paint store. Choose vivid colors as opposed to dull colors. Depending on the durability of the construction paper, you can use the swatches just as they are, glue them onto index cards, or laminate them. If a particular color card becomes marked as it is used (e.g., by smudges), replace it so irrelevant cues are not introduced. Otherwise, the student may learn to identify a card based on some impertinent cue rather than its color.

Receptive Identification of Colors

Prior to beginning instruction in the receptive component of the Colors Program, the student should have mastered the matching of colors (see Chapter 12) and receptive identification of objects (see Chapter 17). The procedures for teaching receptive identification of colors are similar to those outlined for teaching receptive identification of objects. After the basic teaching steps are presented in the current program, we explore problems that may be encountered in the course of learning and pose possible solutions to these problems.

Identifying the First Two Colors

Begin by selecting two targets that are highly discriminable from one another. The colors you choose should not only look different, but their labels should sound different as well. For example, blue and black would not be an ideal first pair of colors to teach because the labels sound alike. Likewise, red and orange would not be an ideal first pair because these colors look quite similar. A good pair of colors to teach first may be red and blue.

Throughout the following steps, the student should be seated at the table across from you or at an adjacent side of the table. To illustrate the teaching the steps, we select red as the first color (SD1) and blue as the second color (SD2). The correct response to SD1 is the student's pointing to (or touching) the red card. The correct response to SD2 is the student's pointing to (or touching) the blue card.

▶ Step 1

Clear the table of all items. Present SD1 by saying, "Red," immediately after placing the red color card on the table in front of the student. Prompt and reinforce the correct response. Prompt by pointing to the color or, if the pointing prompt is not effective, use a physical prompt. Gradually fade the prompt until the student can respond to the SD without assistance. Over the next few trials, move the red card to various positions on the table to avoid position cues. Place criterion at 5 out of 5 or 9 out of 10 unprompted correct responses. Then go on to Step 2.

▶ Step 2

Repeat Step 1 but use "Blue" as SD2. Once SD2 is mastered according to the same criteria used in Step 1, go on to Step 3, using discrimination learning procedures to teach the student to identify the red card from a display that includes both the red and the blue cards.

▶ Step 3

Place both cards on the table and use a position prompt, placing the red card close to the stu-dent and the blue card at the far end of the table. Present SD1 ("Red") and add a pointing or manual prompt if necessary to occasion the correct response. Fade the position prompt by slowly moving the blue card in line with the red card until the cards are aligned with one another, approximately 6 inches apart. To help avoid inadvertent position cues, randomize the left–right positions of the two color cards on the table throughout the prompt fading process. Set mastery at 9 out of 10 or 19 out of 20 unprompted correct responses. Once the student masters the correct response to SD1 ("Red") when both colors are placed on the table and their positions are randomly rotated, go on to the next step.

▶ Step 4

Position the two colors on the table such that the blue card is close to the student and the red card is placed at the far end of the table (i.e., use a full position prompt). Present SD2 ("Blue"). Further prompt if necessary and reinforce the correct response. Begin fading the position prompt by slowly moving the red card closer to the blue card until the two cards are placed side by side on the table. Randomize the left–right positions of the color cards throughout the prompt fading process. Place mastery at 9 out of 10 or 19 out of 20 unprompted correct responses.

▶ Step 5

Place both colors on the table and present SD1 ("Red"). Prompt if necessary, either by touching the correct color card or using a position prompt. Reinforce. Fade all prompts and randomize the left–right positions of the cards. Place mastery at 5 out of 5 or 9 out of 10 unprompted correct responses. Then go on to Step 6.

▶ Step 6

Follow the same procedures used in Step 5 except present SD2 ("Blue"). Go on to Step 7 after the student responds correctly in 5 out of 5 or 9 out of 10 unprompted trials.

▶ Step 7

Place the red and blue cards on the table and then present SD1 ("Red"). Prompt if necessary and reinforce correct responding. Randomize the left–right positions of the cards on the table. After the student responds correctly in 4 unprompted trials in a row, present SD2 ("Blue"). Because it is likely that the student will respond with R1 (touching red), given that this response was most recently reinforced, prompt to avoid an error. Fade the prompt over subsequent trials. After the student responds correctly in 4 unprompted trials in a row with the positions of the cards randomized, go back to SD1, prompt, and secure 3 unprompted correct responses in a row before returning to SD2.

With each differentially reinforced alternation between SD1 ("Red") and SD2 ("Blue"), it is likely that the student will make fewer and fewer errors. This is because SD1–R1 (your stating the word "red" and the student's pointing to the red card) is strengthened through reinforcement while SD1–R2 (your stating the word "red" and the student's pointing to the blue card) is not reinforced and therefore weakened. In a similar fashion, SD2–R2 is strengthened while SD2–R1 is weakened. The two correct associations, SD1–R1 and SD2–R2, become separate and robust entities. Such an outcome is anticipated for all skills that rely upon discrimination learning.

As the correct associations (i.e., SD1–R1 and SD2–R2) are strengthened, reduce the number of consecutive correct responses from 4 to 3 to 2 before switching SDs. As a final step in systematically alternating between SD1 and SD2, switch between these instructions after 1 correct response to either instruction. The advantage of doing so is that such a procedure avoids your reinforcing the student for perseverating on a single response. The disadvantage of this procedure is that it reinforces a win–shift pattern of responding. Therefore, place SD1 and SD2 in random rotation once systematic alternation after 1 trial involving each SD is reached, and place mastery of the discrimination at 9 out of 10 or 19 out of 20 unprompted correct responses.

Learning to respond to color implies that the student must learn to attend to the wavelength of a particular color, a highly complex neurological phenomenon. In Steps 3 through 7 you help the student solve this task by enabling the student, through the use of discrimination training, to attend to color. Once the student masters Steps 3 through 7, other colors should be acquired with increasing ease. Therefore, consider the mastery of the first discrimination to be a major achievement. To solidify this achievement, generalize the discrimination across teachers and environments. This will help make it more functional and eliminate inadvertent prompts that may have interfered with the correct discrimination.

Identifying Additional Colors

Teach the identification of additional colors in the same manner as the first two were taught. In selecting the third target, choose a color that looks and sounds different from the first two colors. If red and blue were used as the student's first targets, a good third target choice would be yellow. Once the next target is selected, proceed through the same steps described in the previous section. When the student meets mastery criterion for the third color, teach him to discriminate the third color from each of the first two colors. Over time, increase the difficulty of the discriminations by, for example, contrasting blue with black or pink with red. Gradually increase the number of colors placed on the table at one time, moving from two to three or more cards. Between trials, remember to randomize the positions of the cards on the table. Less common colors may be taught intermittently once the basic colors are mastered, allowing you to focus on the skills taught in other programs.

Generalizing Receptive Identification of Colors

Thus far the student has learned to discriminate among various colors when these colors are presented as swatches. This does not imply that the student can identify a particular color as distinct from other colors if this color is displayed as a characteristic of an object. To accomplish such a task, the student must learn to *abstract* a common feature or property, such as redness or greenness, from several different kinds of objects. To do this, the student must be taught to recognize several forms in which the color may be exemplified, hence the need for generalization training.

When beginning to teach generalization, continue to present the stimuli in 2-D form but replace the original stimulus cards with felt pieces similar in color and size to the original stimuli. The student's success will be maximized if the new stimuli are initially close in hue to the original colors. Once the student masters the discriminations among these stimuli, vary their size by enlarging or reducing them. After the student is able to identify colors with the new 2-D stimuli, extend generalization by introducing 3-D objects identical in all aspects except color. For example, use blocks that vary in color but have a constant size and shape. Then slowly extend the concept of color in graduated steps to nonidentical toys, food, furniture, and so on. Do not use objects that have several colors (e.g., a multicolored beach ball); instead, each object introduced should be colored uniformly (e.g., a banana or a pen).

As new exemplars of colors are introduced, there will inevitably be some variation in their shades. For example, the original shade of blue taught from the color card will not be identical the blue shades of jeans, toys, books, and so forth. Through such generalization, the student learns that there are many examples of a single color (e.g., light blue, dark blue, royal blue). This type of generalization should be carried out gradually to facilitate the student's success at forming the concept of color.

It may be tempting to teach colors intensively throughout the day and over several successive days given that there are many colors and thus many items to be mastered. This program could consume a great deal of time at the expense of teaching other skills. To avoid this, be certain to intermix other programs with the current program to extend the students' competence and break up the monotony.

Areas of Difficulty

If the student has difficulty identifying colors or learning to discriminate among various colors, try presenting the stimuli vertically as opposed to horizontally. That is, instead of placing the colors flat on the table, display them perpendicular to the student's line of vision such that they are at his eye level and therefore easier to see. This type of display may be accomplished by placing the colors on a felt board or easel. The vertical display should be considered a prompt and, as with all prompts, it must be faded over time.

If any given pair of colors (e.g., red and blue) is unusually difficult for the student to discriminate, switch to another pair of colors (e.g., orange and green) or contrast one of the original colors with white (e.g., teach red vs. white instead of red vs. blue). If this fails, go back to SD1 ("Red") and compare SD1 with a contrasting stimulus the student has already learned to receptively identify, such as pointing to a shoe. When the student masters this discrimination, reintroduce Step 3 (the red–blue discrimination). Finally, if no progress is made after 3 or 4 days of training (broken up by play breaks and other programs), place the Colors Program on hold for a month or two, resuming color training after the student makes progress in other areas. If serious difficulties continue after the program's reintroduction, consider the possibility that the student is color blind. Because this condition is sex-linked recessive, it occurs very rarely in females. However, approximately 1 in 10 males are color blind to some degree.

Some students successfully learn to identify colors in 2-D form but have difficulty identifying colors in 3-D form. In this case, a student may be able to identify a variety of colors when presented as colored construction paper or felt pieces but unable to identify colors when they are a characteristic of a 3-D object. If the student experiences this problem generalizing the concept of color, try having him match 3-D objects to their corresponding 2-D colors. For example, place on the table two of the 2-D colors first taught (e.g., yellow and green cards). Hand the student a 3-D object that is the same color as one of the colors on the table (e.g., a yellow ball) and present the SD ("Match"). (The student should already be familiar with this SD from earlier matching programs.) After the student places the object on top of the correct color, reinforce him and then immediately present the SD ("Yellow") while the ball is still on top of the yellow card and physically prompt the correct response. Once the student is able to point to (or touch) the requested 3-D color while the 2-D color is underneath it, fade the 2-D color as a prompt. This may be done by gradually decreasing the size of the color card so the object covers a greater portion of it over successive trials until only the object is left on the table.

If difficulties persist, introduce the expressive component of the Colors Program, as some students master expressive components of programs before they master receptive components, and sometimes the acquisition of the expressive component generalizes to the receptive component. If the student continues to have difficulty, temporarily put this program on hold and teach the student shape discrimination, returning to the Colors Program at a later stage in treatment.

Expressive Labeling of Colors

In the expressive component of the Colors Program, the student is taught to identify colors by stating their respective labels. Prior to reaching this level of instruction, the student should have mastered verbal imitation of color labels such as "blue," "red," "orange," and so on. The student may have echoed various color labels as he learned to identify them receptively (e.g., after hearing the SD ["Red"], the student said, "Red," as she pointed to or touched the red card or object). If this occurred, the student may master expressive labeling of colors at a relatively quick rate.

Labeling the First Two Colors

Select as the first target a color label that is easily pronounced by the student, choosing words that the student mastered with good enunciation in the Verbal Imitation Program (Chapter 22). If the student has difficulty pronouncing two or more color labels (e.g., the student has difficulty pronouncing the "r" in "red" and says "ed" instead, or the student has problems with the "gr" sound in "green," pronouncing it "een"), go back and practice color labels in the Verbal Imitation Program prior to beginning expressive labeling of colors. If necessary, accept one or two imperfectly pronounced labels on the condition that all the team members agree upon exactly what response to reinforce. Then, over time, shape up clearer enunciation. It is not out of the ordinary to observe typical children mispronounce certain words when first beginning to talk and later have these words shaped up to match the speech of other persons.

Throughout the following steps, you and the student should sit across from one another. Present each stimulus by holding it in front of the student, approximately 1 foot away from him. Remember that the display should be succinct and discrete so as to facilitate the student's attention to each stimulus presentation. In the following steps, we use "Red" as R1 and "blue" as R2.

► **Step 1**

Present SD1 ("What color?") and simultaneously move the red color card in front of the student's eyes. Immediately prompt the correct response by saying, "Red." When presenting the SD, say the word "red" in louder volume than the question "What color?" to facilitate correct responding. As soon as the student says, "Red," reinforce him. Continue to present SD1 while gradually fading the prompt so the student learns to respond independently. The prompt may be faded by either lowering its volume or by stating less and less of the label over successive trials, or probe with abrupt removal of the prompt. Set criterion at 5 out of 5 or 9 out of 10 unprompted correct responses.

► **Step 2**

Introduce a second color following the same procedures used in Step 1. That is, present SD2 ("What color?") and simultaneously move the blue card in front of the student's eyes. Prompt the correct response immediately by saying, "Blue." Reinforce the correct response and fade the prompt over subsequent trials. Set criterion at 5 out of 5 or 9 out of 10 unprompted correct responses.

► **Step 3**

Intermix SD1 and SD2, presenting one color at a time according to the discrimination paradigm. Bring SD1 to mastery at 4 unprompted correct responses in a row, and then bring SD2 to mastery using the same criterion. Next, alternate between SD1 and SD2, switching after 3 unprompted correct responses in a row to each SD, then 2, then 1; then present SD1 and SD2 according to the random rotation paradigm. When SD1 and SD2 are presented in random rotation, set the criterion for mastery of the discrimination at 9 out of 10 or 19 out of 20 unprompted correct responses. Once the student masters the discrimination between SD1 and SD2, focus on generalizing the discrimination across other teachers and environments.

As with any mastery of intermixed SDs (as in Step 3 above), consider mastery of the first discrimination between two expressive color labels a major accomplishment. In all likelihood, additional discriminations will be acquired with increasing ease. Also remember to generalize this and all other discriminations across persons and environments.

Labeling Additional Colors

Once the student is able to expressively label the first two colors, teach him to label additional colors. The third color introduced should look different from the first two colors and should have a label that sounds different from the first two labels (e.g., white). It is also important to select a color label the student can pronounce clearly. The procedures for teaching additional colors are the same as those used to teach the first two colors. Remember, only one additional color should be taught at a time. After the student successfully labels the third color when presented alone, implement discrimination learning procedures, intermixing SD3 and SD1, then SD3 and SD2, and finally alternating among all three SDs. Place mastery at 9 out of 10 or 19 out of 20 unprompted correct responses to randomly rotated SDs. Once the student successfully discriminates among all three colors presented in random rotation, continue to introduce new colors according to the same procedures.

Generalizing Expressive Labeling of Colors

Follow the same procedures used to generalize receptive color labels to generalize expressive color labels (see the previous section "Generalizing Receptive Identification of Colors").

Areas of Difficulty

The methods used to address problems in the receptive component of the Colors Program can also be used to rectify problems that arise in the expressive component. For example, if the student has difficulty generalizing color labels from their 2-D to their 3-D form, place the target 3-D object on top of its corresponding 2-D color. Point to the object (e.g., a banana) while it is on top of the color card and present the SD ("What color?"). Be sure to gradually fade the 2-D color as a prompt.

Another difficulty that may occur while generalizing the concept of color to 3-D stimuli is that the student might become distracted by the 3-D stimuli. Minimize this problem by introducing neutral objects (e.g., blocks) and withholding favorite objects (e.g., toys) in the early stages of generalization.

An effective prompt for many students who demonstrate difficulty learning to expressively label colors is combining receptive labels with expressive labels, allowing your receptive instruction to prompt the student's expressive label. For example, you may instruct the student, "Point to blue" (emphasizing "blue"), and then quickly ask, "What color?" while pointing to the blue card on the table.

Shapes

Receptive Identification of Shapes

In the receptive component of the Shapes Program, we outline procedures for teaching the student to identify various shapes such as triangles, circles, and squares. The following materials are needed to teach the Shapes Program: pairs of basic shapes (circle, triangle, square, rectangle, oval, heart, diamond) identical in all dimensions except shape (i.e., same size, color, and texture). As done in the Colors Program, shapes may be cut out from construction paper. Before teaching this program, it is important that the student previously master the matching of shapes.

Identifying the First Two Shapes

To maximize the student's success in learning to identify the first two shapes, the shapes should look different from one another and their labels should sound different as well. Because the shapes circle and rectangle look different from one another and their labels sound different, they make a good pair of shapes to teach first. In illustrating the following steps, your saying "Circle" is SD1 and the correct response to SD1 is R1, the student's pointing to (or touching) the circle. SD2 is your saying, "Rectangle," and the student's pointing to (or touching) the rectangle is R2. In the steps that follow, you and the student should be arranged at opposite or adjacent sides of the table.

▶ **Step 1**

Clear the table of all items. Place the circle on the table in front of the student, present SD1 ("Circle"), prompt the correct response, and reinforce. Prompt first by pointing to the shape. If this prompt fails, move to a more intrusive prompt such as a physical prompt on the next trial. Fade the prompt over subsequent trials. After the student correctly responds to SD1 without prompting, avoid position cues by moving the circle into various positions on the table with each presentation of SD1. Remember to remove the shape between trials to maximize the distinctiveness of the stimulus presentation. Place criterion at 5 out of 5 or 9 out of 10 unprompted correct responses. Then go on to Step 2.

▶ **Step 2**

Step 2 is taught in the same manner as Step 1 except that SD2 ("Rectangle") is used. Begin this step by removing all objects from the table. Present SD2 ("Rectangle") immediately after placing the second target shape on the table in front of the student. Once the student responds correctly to SD2 in 5 out of 5 or 9 out of 10 unprompted trials, go on to Step 3.

▶ **Step 3**

Present SD1 ("Circle") and use a position prompt by placing the circle close to the student. Position the rectangle at the far end of the table to minimize errors during the transition from SD2 to SD1. Given the full position prompt, it is unlikely that the student will make an error in responding. However, if an error does occur, provide a more intrusive prompt such as a physical prompt in addition to a position prompt on the next trial. Fade the physical prompt first and then fade the position prompt by moving the rectangle in line with the circle while randomizing the left–right placements of the two shapes to avoid position cues. Once the position prompt is faded, the shapes should be placed approximately 6 inches apart in line with one another. If the shapes are placed too close together, the student's response may not be distinct and you may then have difficulty deciding whether to reinforce. Place mastery at 9 out of 10 or 19 out of 20 unprompted correct responses with the two shapes in line with one another and their left–right positions intermixed. Then go on to Step 4.

▶ Step 4

Change the position of the two shapes such that the rectangle is close to the student and the circle is placed at the far end of the table (i.e., in a full position prompt). Present SD2 ("Rectangle"), prompt if necessary, and reinforce. Begin the fading process by gradually moving the circle closer to the rectangle on each trial, remembering to randomly alternate the left–right positions of each shape. After the circle and rectangle are placed side by side with their left–right positions randomized and the student responds correctly in 9 out of 10 or 19 out of 20 unprompted trials, go on to the next step.

▶ Step 5

Place both shapes on the table and present SD1 ("Circle"). If necessary, prompt either by touching the correct shape or by using a position prompt, reinforce the correct response, and fade the prompt over successive trials. Place mastery at 5 out of 5 or 9 out of 10 unprompted correct responses with the left–right positions of the shapes randomized. Then go on to Step 6.

▶ Step 6

Follow the same procedure outlined in Step 5 except present SD2 ("Rectangle"). Place mastery at the same criterion used in Step 5 and then move on to the next step.

▶ Step 7

Present SD1 by saying, "Circle," immediately after placing the circle and the rectangle on the table. Prompt if necessary, and reinforce. Randomize the left–right positions of the shapes. After mastery is reached (4 unprompted correct responses in a row), present SD2 ("Rectangle"). Because the student will likely respond with R1 instead of R2 given that touching the circle was most recently reinforced, prompt the response to avoid an error and then fade the prompt.

After the student responds correctly in 4 unprompted trials in a row with the positions of the shapes randomized, go back to SD1, prompt, and secure 3 unprompted correct responses in a row. With the intermixing of SD1 and SD2, gradually alternate SDs after 3 unprompted correct responses in a row, then 2, and finally 1. Recall that the advantage of systematically alternating between responses is that it avoids the student's being reinforced for perseverating on the same response. The disadvantage of reinforcing systematic alteration is that it tends to produce a win–shift pattern of responding. To avoid such a strategy, place the presentations of SD1 and SD2 in random rotation. After the SDs are randomly rotated, set the criterion for mastery of the discrimination at 9 out of 10 or 19 out of 20 unprompted correct responses. Consider mastery of this initial discrimination to be a major achievement. Solidify it by generalizing the discrimination across teachers and environments.

Identifying Additional Shapes

Teach each additional shape in the same manner the first two were taught. Remember that the shape selected as the third target should look different from the first two shapes and its label should sound different as well. A star or square may be a good choice for the next shape. After the student responds to criterion for the third shape, teach the student to discriminate the third shape from each of the first two shapes. Over time, gradually increase the difficulty of the discriminations by, for example, contrasting an oval with a circle or a rectangle with a square. At the same time, gradually increase the number of shapes presented on the table at a time from two to three or more. Eventually the student should be able to identify a shape (e.g., a circle) when that shape is placed on the table among several other shapes (e.g., a triangle, oval, rectangle, and star). Be sure to randomize the positions of the shapes as well as the presentation of the SDs. As is the case with teaching colors, the initial focus when teaching shapes should be limited to the commonly occurring shapes. The teaching of additional shapes should then be intermittently performed. This will allow for the teaching of other programs and will aid in strengthening recall (Chapter 31).

Generalizing Receptive Identification of Shapes

Begin generalization training by presenting drawings of the stimuli as ¼-inch thick black lines on separate pieces of identically sized and shaped white paper. Then proceed with discrimination training, following the procedures outlined earlier. It may be helpful to use the original set of stimuli as prompts for the line drawings by placing the drawn forms next to the cutout forms. The prompt provided by the original stimuli can be faded by gradually decreasing the size of the original shapes or by gradually sliding the original stimuli under the new stimuli.

Once the discrimination of line drawings is mastered, gradually move to variously shaped 3-D objects such as dishes, pots, pans, and foods (e.g., circular vs. rectangular-shaped cookies). Through the procedures outlined thus far, most students learn to abstract the attributes that form the concept of shape.

Areas of Difficulty

Although most students master the receptive component of the Shapes Program, individual differences in acquisition of this skill invariably come into play. Should the student encounter significant problems discriminating between, for example, a circle and a rectangle, try contrasting a circle and star or moving on to a completely different pair of shapes. If problems continue with the student's learning to identify shapes, consider once more subjecting the shapes to the matching component of the Matching and Sorting Program to ensure that the student attends to (can discriminate) the shapes. After the student masters this skill, reintroduce the receptive component of the Shapes Program.

Another procedure that may be helpful in facilitating discriminations is the introduction of a contrasting stimulus as outlined in the discrimination learning procedures (Chapter 16). The use of a contrasting stimulus is considered a pretraining step and can be done by contrasting SD1 ("Circle") with a 3-D object such as a shoe or a sock. Because these stimuli are so different, it can be assumed that their contrast constitutes an easier discrimination than the original one. Thus, the student should more quickly learn to point to or touch the circle when SD1 ("Circle") is presented. If necessary, use position prompts and fade in the prominence of the contrasting stimulus over trials. In learning theory terminology, the student learns to inhibit the response to the second object when SD1 ("Circle") is presented. To state it differently, the student learns *not* to respond with R2 as the SD1–R1 association is strengthened.

Expressive Labeling of Shapes

Before beginning the expressive component of the Shapes Program, the student should have mastered 15 to 20 labels of objects and behaviors (Chapters 23 and 24) and the verbal imitation of at least two shape labels (e.g., "circle" and "rectangle"). If the student has difficulty clearly enunciating certain shape labels, try words of comparable meaning, such as "round" instead of "circle." It is best to select those labels that are most clearly enunciated in verbal imitation and then, if necessary, shape their enunciation in pretraining sessions. Accept the student's verbal approximations only if they sound close to the correct pronunciation of the target label. Remember that the student's enunciation of the label must be clear enough for each team member to agree upon whether to reinforce the student's response.

Labeling the First Two Shapes

The procedures for teaching the expressive labeling of shapes is virtually identical to those used in teaching expressive labeling of colors; however, in the present program, the shape stimuli replace the color stimuli. In the expressive component of the Shapes Program, teach the student to label the same shapes identified in the receptive component of this program. For example, if the student mastered receptive identification of the circle and rectangle, teach the student to expressively label these shapes as long as the student can clearly enunciate their labels. For illustrative purposes, let SD1 consist of the question "What shape?" and the presentation of a circle, and let SD2 consist of the question "What shape?" and the presentation of a rectangle. In the steps that follow, you and the student should sit on chairs opposite each other.

▶ **Step 1**

Present SD1 ("What shape?") while holding up the circle, verbally prompt the correct response, reinforce, and fade the prompt by lowering its volume or saying less and less of it over subsequent trials. After the student responds correctly in 5 out of 5 or 9 out of 10 unprompted trials, move on to the next step.

▶ **Step 2**

Present SD2 ("What shape?") while holding up the rectangle. Prompt the correct response, reinforce, and fade the prompt over subsequent trials. Move on to Step 3 after the student responds correctly in 5 out of 5 or 9 out of 10 unprompted trials.

▶ **Step 3**

Intermix SD1 and SD2 according to the discrimination learning paradigm. Place mastery at 9 out of 10 or 19 out of 20 unprompted correct responses with the stimuli presented in random rotation. Once the student's responses reach mastery criterion, strengthen the discrimination over the next 3 to 4 days while generalizing the task across team members and environments. Later, generalize the discrimination across different exemplars of circular and rectangular shapes by presenting these shapes as line drawings and then as characteristic of 3-D objects. Next, go on to teach two or three additional shapes, one at a time, over the next 4 to 5 weeks.

Areas of Difficulty

It is important to maintain correct and clear enunciation of the shape labels; otherwise the task becomes too difficult for the student (the discrimination becomes unclear) and the teacher (whether to reinforce becomes unclear). It is not unusual to observe a student who tries to combine two different labels into one label, as in combining "rectangle" and "circle" into "reccir." On the one hand, this is a clever strategy on the student's part since it may maximize reinforcement and minimize effort. On the other hand, it puts the teacher at a loss as to whether to reinforce the student. If reinforcement is provided contingent on such responding, it may serve only to strengthen errors.

Size

Receptive Identification of Size

The Size Program is designed to teach the student the concept of size using the words "big" and "little." The procedures for teaching size are exactly the same as those used for teaching colors and shapes; therefore, the teaching steps presented in this section are condensed. Once the basic teaching steps of the Size Program are introduced, special problems that may arise in teaching the concept of size are discussed and ways in which these problems may be solved are suggested.

Before being taught receptive size identification, the student should master the matching of various sizes. In addition, given that acquisition of the concept of size requires a complex abstraction and comparison among objects, the student should master the less complex concepts of color and shape prior to the introduction of the Size Program.

The following materials are required to teach the Size Program: pairs of 3-D objects identical in all respects except size (e.g., big and little red plastic apples, big and little blue rectangular blocks), 3-D nonidentical objects of different sizes (e.g., big and little cars that are not exactly the same in aspects such as color and shape), and pictures of big and little objects on flashcards and in books.

Keep in mind that size is probably the most abstract and complex concept the student is presented with at this point in her learning because mastery of size requires that the student discriminate (attend to) relationships between objects (as in the Prepositions Program introduced in Chapter 27, which is similarly demanding). To help maximize the student's success in acquiring the concept of size, the first pair of objects selected should exaggerate size differences. For example, introduce a baby's tennis shoe versus an adult male's tennis shoe. In illustrating the following teaching steps, the correct response to SD1 (your saying, "Big," and presenting an adult-size tennis shoe) is R1 (the student's pointing to or touching the adult-size shoe) while the correct response to SD2 (your saying, "Little," and presenting a baby-size shoe) is R2 (the student's pointing to the baby-size shoe). For each of the following steps, sit across from the student at the table and clear all items from the table before each trial.

Before going on, note that the student is not likely to learn anything about size in Step 1. Rather, the student may learn to identify a tennis shoe in response to your vocalization "Big." This process is similar to the Receptive Identification of Objects Program (Chapter 17), in which the student learned to identify a shoe when you requested, "Shoe." The same result can be said to occur in Step 2 below, when the student learns to identify a tennis shoe when you say, "Little." However, Steps 1 and 2 are considered to be essential for the introduction of Step 3, where the student does in fact learn about size.

▶ Step 1

Place an adult's tennis shoe on the table in front of the student and say, "Big." Prompt the correct response and reinforce. Prompt by pointing to the big object or use a manual prompt if pointing is inadequate. Fade the prompt over subsequent trials. Once the student independently responds correctly, move the big object to various positions on the table with each subsequent presentation of SD1 in this step. When the student responds correctly without prompting in 5 out of 5 or 9 out of 10 trials, go on to Step 2.

▶ Step 2

Remove SD1, the adult shoe, from the table, and then present SD2 by saying, "Little," and placing an item identical to the big item except in size (i.e., in this case, a baby's tennis shoe) on the table in front of the student. Once the student meets the criterion for SD2 (5 out of 5 or 9 out of 10 unprompted correct responses), subject SD1 and SD2 to discrimination learning procedures as described in Step 3.

▶ **Step 3**

State, "Big," while placing the adult's tennis shoe close to the student and the baby's tennis shoe at the far corner of the table. If the position prompt does not occasion the correct response, provide a manual or pointing prompt in addition to the position prompt on the next trial. Fade the manual or pointing prompt first and then fade the position prompt by moving the little object in line with the big object over subsequent trials. Randomize the left–right positions of the two objects on the table throughout the fading process to avoid irrelevant position cues. Place mastery at 9 out of 10 or 19 out of 20 unprompted correct responses when the two objects are positioned linearly approximately 6 inches apart with their left–right positions randomly intermixed.

▶ **Step 4**

State, "Little," positioning the baby's tennis shoe in front of the student and the adult's tennis shoe at the far end of the table in a full position prompt. Provide additional prompts if necessary and reinforce correct responding. If additional prompts are used, fade these first, and then proceed to fade the position prompt. Randomize the left–right positions of the objects on the table throughout the fading process. Go on to the next step after the student responds correctly in 9 out of 10 or 19 out of 20 unprompted trials.

▶ **Step 5**

Present SD1 with both objects on the table. Prompt if necessary, reinforce the correct response, and fade the prompt over subsequent trials. Set the criterion for mastery at 5 out of 5 or 9 out of 10 unprompted correct responses with the left–right positions of the objects randomized. Then go on to Step 6.

▶ **Step 6**

Present SD2 and follow the same procedures outlined in Step 5. After the student responds correctly in 5 out of 5 or 9 out of 10 unprompted trials, go on to Step 7.

▶ **Step 7**

Place the big and the little objects on the table in line with each other. Present SD1, prompt if necessary, and reinforce the correct response. Randomize the left–right positions of the objects over trials. Place mastery at 3 unprompted correct responses in a row. When this criterion for mastery is reached, present SD2 and prompt the response to avoid an error. Fade the prompt. After the student performs 3 unprompted correct responses in a row, return to SD1, prompt, and secure 2 unprompted correct responses in a row first to SD1 and then to SD2. Next, alternate between SD1 and SD2 after 1 unprompted correct response to each SD. Present SD1 and SD2 in random rotation as soon as possible in order to avoid reinforcing systematic alternation between R1 and R2. Place mastery at 9 out of 10 or 19 out of 20 unprompted correct responses.

Generalizing Receptive Identification of Size

After the student masters identifying big and little objects using one set of 3-D objects similar in all properties except size, introduce additional sets of 3-D objects by following Steps 1 through 7 of the preceding section. Stimuli such as stacking cups or stacking dolls seem ideal for such a task. Remember to teach only one pair of identical objects at a time. Set the criterion for mastery at 5 out of 5 or 9 out of 10 successful identifications of novel (i.e., untaught) pairs of identical objects. To help the student reach this criterion, it may be helpful to teach approximately five pairs of identical objects and then probe with a new pair of objects. If the student can successfully identify the big and little objects from this new pair without teaching, generalize this skill across other objects, teachers, and environments. If the student is not successful with identifying big and little objects when presented as novel pairs of objects, continue to teach pairs, probing new pairs of objects periodically to test for generalization.

After the student masters the receptive identification of 3-D objects identical in all properties except size, introduce nonidentical 3-D objects. Start by presenting objects that are very similar but not identical. For example, introduce a little stuffed toy horse versus a big plastic horse. Gradually introduce increasingly different objects such as a little cup versus a big bucket and, eventually, a pen versus a pillow. Set the criterion for mastery of generalized nonidentical objects at 5 out of 5 or 9 out of 10 unprompted correct responses.

Once the student meets the criterion for mastery of nonidentical 3-D objects, introduce objects in 2-D form. It may be helpful to first introduce objects depicted in 2-D form that are identical in every respect except size (e.g., present photographs of the objects initially used in this program). Initially probe for generalization by withholding prompts. If the student does not respond correctly to the probed trial, follow Steps 1 through 7 described in the previous section to teach the 2-D object discrimination. Set the criterion for mastery at 5 out of 5 or 9 out of 10 unprompted correct identifications of big and little identical (except in size) objects depicted as 2-D stimuli. Then introduce nonidentical pictures of objects followed by pictures in books.

As a final test for generalization, reverse the SDs of the objects taught. In other words, present an object the student learned to identify as little in a context in which the object is big, and vice versa. Keep in mind that this is a difficult step for almost all students to master, so be patient with yourself and the student.

Areas of Difficulty

If from the start the student has difficulty learning to receptively identify size, introduce a different set of objects and place the original pair of objects on hold. The student's difficulty may be specific to the first set of objects. If the student continues to have difficulty and is unable to make progress in identifying size after several weeks of teaching, consider temporarily postponing this program and reintroducing it at a later stage in treatment.

When reintroducing the program, follow Steps 1 through 7 using a different set of objects from the set(s) with which the student experienced failure. Also, you might try an alternative teaching procedure: Teach "big" using one pair of objects, then generalize to other pairs of objects. Next, teach "little" using a different pair of objects, later generalizing to other pairs of objects. Finally, work toward random rotation of big and little objects, focusing on one pair of items at a time. This teaching procedure allows the student to gain more experience in identifying big and little objects separately before requiring discrimination among sizes. Some students are more successful when size is taught in this manner. If the student is not able to discriminate size among big and little objects after several weeks of teaching using this procedure, discontinue the receptive task and introduce expressive labeling of size.

Expressive Labeling of Size

Before teaching expressive labeling of size, the student should master verbal imitation of the words "big" and "little." If words of comparable meaning are easier for the student to enunciate (e.g., "large," "small"), then use these words instead. As mentioned in earlier chapters, students most often learn receptive identification tasks before they learn expressive labeling tasks. However, keep in mind that the student you work with may more easily learn to expressively label size than receptively identify size. Nonetheless, as a general guideline, make an effort to teach the receptive task first.

Begin teaching expressive labeling of size using 3-D objects identical in all respects except size. If the student previously mastered receptive sizes, introduce objects mastered from that component into this component of the program. For example, teach the student to label the size of the baby tennis shoe and adult tennis shoe she was previously taught to receptively identify.

The expressive component of the Size Program is most easily taught when you and the student sit across from each other at the table. This format allows you to present two objects on the table simultaneously. We recommend starting with the instruction "Big or little?" because this SD contains some prompt properties. Later this instruction may gradually be switched to "What size?" once the student masters the response to the original instruction. In illustrating the following steps, let R1 consist of the student's stating, "Big," and R2 consist of the student's stating, "Little."

▶ Step 1

Place on the table a pair of objects identical in all properties except size. Position these objects approximately 6 inches apart and present SD1, which consists of your saying, "Big or little?" while simultaneously pointing to or lifting and replacing the big object. Prompt the correct response by stating, "Big," and reinforce the student for imitating the verbalization. Gradually fade the prompt over subsequent trials. Continue with mass trials until the student meets the criterion of 5 out of 5 or 9 out of 10 unprompted correct responses.

► **Step 2**

Place the same pair of big and little but otherwise identical objects approximately 6 inches apart on the table. Present SD2, which consists of the teacher saying, "Big or little?" while simultaneously pointing to or lifting the little object. Immediately prompt the correct response by stating, "Little." Reinforce the correct response and fade the prompt. Mass trial SD2 and set mastery at the same criterion used in Step 1.

► **Step 3**

Intermix SD1 and SD2 according to the discrimination and random rotation paradigms, setting mastery at 9 out of 10 or 19 out of 20 unprompted correct responses. Once the student masters the discrimination between SD1 and SD2, generalize this task across teachers and environments to help solidify the discrimination.

Generalizing Expressive Labeling of Size

After the student masters labeling the objects of one pair of 3-D objects as big and little, introduce additional sets of 3-D objects following Steps 1 through 3 outlined in the preceding section. Teach one pair of objects at a time until the student successfully labels novel (i.e., untaught) objects as big and little the first time they are presented. It may be helpful to first teach approximately five pairs of objects following Steps 1 through 3 and then probe a new pair of objects. If the student successfully labels the size of the novel objects, generalize this skill across other new objects, teachers, and environments. If the student does not successfully label the size of the objects in a new pair, continue to directly teach other pairs of objects identical in all aspects except size, probing new pairs of objects periodically to test for generalization. Once the student generalizes to several novel pairs of identical objects, gradually introduce objects with less obvious size differences. Finally, reverse the SDs for taught objects. In other words, present an object the student learned to label "little" in a context in which the object is now big, and vice versa. Use stimuli such as stacking cups or stacking dolls for this purpose.

When the student masters expressive labeling of 3-D objects identical in all aspects except size, introduce nonidentical 3-D objects. Begin this phase by presenting objects that are similar but not identical. For example, introduce a small saucer made of china versus a large paper plate. Gradually introduce increasingly dissimilar objects until the student can label the size of such objects as a big toy car versus a little cookie. Set the criterion for mastery of generalization to novel nonidentical 3-D objects at 9 out of 10 or 19 out of 20 unprompted correct responses.

Once the concept of size when presented in 3-D form is mastered, introduce objects in 2-D form. It may be helpful to first introduce flashcards depicting objects identical in all aspects except size. If necessary, follow the previous Steps 1 through 3 to teach this skill. Set the criterion for mastery at the successful labeling of several novel 2-D stimuli that differ only in size. Then introduce nonidentical 2-D depictions of objects and, finally, pictures in books. When the student generalizes the concept of size to untaught pictures, gradually shift the instruction from "Big or little?" to the question "What size?" by adding on the latter to the former first as a whisper. Gradually increase the volume of the new question over trials while proportionally decreasing the volume of the original question until only the new question remains as the SD.

Areas of Difficulty

Some students become confused when they hear the words "big" and "little" in the same SD. The typical response for students who demonstrate this difficulty is "Big–little." Several teaching techniques may help solve this problem. First, try using the receptive task as a prompt for the expressive task by placing the big and little objects on the table and presenting an instruction that contains properties of the target response (e.g., "Touch big"). Immediately after the student responds correctly, point to the correct object and ask, "What size?"

Another helpful prompt is reversing the order of the instruction to "Little or big?" when asking for the big object since the last word ("big") is likely to be the one that the student will repeat or remember because of its recency. If the student continues to have difficulty with the expressive component of the Size Program, the following alternative SD may be introduced in place of "Big or little?": Place two different objects on the table and, depending on the target, present the instruction "What's big?" or "What's little?" The student's response should be naming the object with the target property. If this strategy works for the student, prompt the student by introducing "What's big?" as SD1 and "What's little?" as SD2. Follow the standard procedures for discrimination learning.

Early Grammar: I Want, I See, I Have

CHAPTER 26

This chapter describes procedures for teaching the student to use elementary forms of grammar, such as noun–verb combinations. The three programs used to accomplish this task are titled I Want, I See, and I Have. From these programs, the student is taught to generate such sentences as "I want play," "I see Big Bird," and "I have pizza." These programs may be taught as extensions of the skills introduced in the Expressive Labeling of Objects Program (Chapter 23).

As part of the I Want Program, the student is taught to verbalize choices when confronted with desired versus undesired items and to become more spontaneous in his requests. In the I See Program, the student is taught to describe what he observes in his surrounding environment and to do so in an increasingly spontaneous manner. In the I Have Program, the student is taught to describe his possessions. This program also includes steps describing how to begin early conversational speech between the student and the teacher, as in making reciprocal statements. Each of the programs presented in this chapter should help facilitate social communication.

I Want

We recommend that you begin the I Want Program by teaching the student to request her favorite foods, objects, and activities. The reasons for such a recommendation are twofold. First, such favorites almost invariably involve reinforcers, strengthening "I want" sentences. Second, the student's mastery of an efficient way of expressing her desires is likely to result in a reduction of tantrums.

Note that the response in this program is a full sentence that incorporates the label of the preferred item. Because the sentence "I want (item)" must be prompted by the teacher, the student should have mastered verbal imitation of the sentence "I want (item)" prior to introducing it into this program. For example, if you wish to choose Big Bird as the stimulus for SD1, the student should have mastered imitation of the sentence "I want Big Bird." Be certain that the student can imitate several "I want" sentences before beginning the present program (e.g., "I want cookie," "I want juice," "I want Barney").

The steps involved in teaching "I want" sentences are similar to those in all other programs that involve discrimination learning. For the first three steps in teaching "I want" statements, choose three items the student would delight in receiving as reinforcement for a correct response. These items may include a favorite toy, a special food, or a favorite activity.

▶ Step 1

Present SD1, which consists of asking, "What do you want?" while displaying a highly favored food or toy distinctly in front of the student's eyes. For example, if the student likes juice, present a cup of juice, and ask, "What do you want?" Prompt the correct response by immediately stating, "I want juice." To avoid having the student echo your question, present the question quickly and in a low voice while emphasizing the prompt in a louder voice. Because the student is unlikely to know the meaning of the question "What do you want?" it may be more efficient simply to present the SD as "Want?" in the beginning and then fade in the rest of the question as the student gains experience in this program. Reinforce the student's response by giving her a *small* amount of the item named in her response (i.e., if the item is a beverage, pour a small sip into the cup and give the student the small sip as a reinforcer; if the item is food, give her a piece half the size of a sugar cube; if the item is a toy or activity, allow her approximately 5 seconds to play with the toy or engage in the activity). Fade the prompt ("I want juice") by gradually saying less and less of the sentence or by lowering the volume of the sentence while maintaining the student's complete and audible response. Intermittently probe unprompted trials to reduce, if possible, the number of prompted trials and help avoid prompt dependency. Remember that the student should receive as reinforcement the same item she requests. Mass trial to the criterion of 9 out of 10 or 19 of 20 unprompted correct responses.

► **Step 2**

Present SD2, which consists of asking, "What do you want?" or merely "Want?" while displaying a second desired item (e.g., a chip) distinctly in front of the student's eyes. Prompt the correct response by stating, "I want chip." Fade the prompt while maintaining the student's correct response. Reinforce the student by giving her a *small* amount of the item she requests. Set the criterion for mastery at 9 out of 10 or 19 out of 20 unprompted correct responses.

► **Step 3**

Intermix SD1 and SD2. That is, alternate between presenting the chip and the juice, differentially reinforcing and moving to random rotation of the SDs as described in the chapter on discrimination learning (Chapter 16). Set mastery at 9 out of 10 or 19 out of 20 unprompted correct trials. As recommended in earlier programs, generalize this achievement across teachers and environments (e.g., mealtimes) for the next 3 to 4 days before going on to SD3.

If the first two SDs involve food-related items, it may be helpful in establishing the next discrimination to use a preferred nonfood item for SD3, such as "up" (if the student likes to be lifted), "tickle," or a favorite toy. After SD3 is mastered in mass trials, intermix it first with SD1 and then with SD2 while maintaining the SD1–SD2 discrimination in different sittings.

Areas of Difficulty

Should you choose a nonpreferred item or activity to teach the student to request, it is reasonable to expect that the student's requesting will deteriorate. Similar deterioration may be observed should the student satiate on the preferred items (i.e., the reinforcers). If the student's requests show a marked decrease, add a second reinforcer to back up correct responding in an effort to maintain her skills. For example, should the student master the phrase "I want Big Bird" and lose interest in Big Bird over trials, reinforce the student with food for merely retrieving Big Bird. If the student refuses an item in the early stages, replace that item with one the student desires. In the section that follows, steps are made to help prevent the difficulties described in this section.

Presenting the student with a large amount of the reinforcer (e.g., a full cup of juice) but allowing the student to consume only a small amount of the reinforcer (e.g., a sip) is likely to cause a struggle for the larger portion. The ensuing tantrum is likely to reduce the effectiveness of your efforts; therefore, provide the student with reinforcement that is preportioned.

Verbalizing Choices

It is a great accomplishment for a student to learn to verbalize preferences. Unfortunately, not every student acquires this skill. For those students who encounter serious difficulties expressing their choices verbally, however, the Reading and Writing Program and the Picture Exchange Communication System (PECS) Program (Chapters 29 and 30, respectively) offer alternatives. By adhering to the following steps, the student may learn to verbalize choices.

► **Step 1**

Present SD1, which consists of asking, "Which one?" while showing the student two items. The student should have previously learned to label both items. One of the items presented should be a highly desired item (e.g., a preferred food such as ice cream) and the other a less desired or undesired item (e.g., a nonpreferred food such as a pickle). As soon as the objects are presented on the table, prompt the student to say, "I want (ice cream)." Reinforce by providing the student with the preferred item. Systematically fade the prompting. This task typically is mastered relatively quickly, in part because the student is unlikely to request an item she does not want. If the student makes an error, withhold reinforcement or present the student with the nonpreferred item. Place mastery at 5 out of 5 or 9 out of 10 unprompted correct responses.

► **Step 2**

Present SD2, which consists of asking, "Which one?" while presenting a new preferred item (e.g., a preferred toy) and a new undesired item (e.g., a washcloth if the student does not like her face wiped). Immediately provide a prompt, and then fade it systematically. Remember to reinforce the student with the item she labels in her response. If she requests the nonpreferred item, present her with that item. Place mastery at 5 out of 5 or 9 out of 10 unprompted correct responses.

▶ **Step 3**

Teach the student to discriminate between SD1 and SD2 by following discrimination learning procedures. That is, the stimulus display should eventually vary between the preferred items presented in a random order and always in contrast with one of the undesired items (e.g., ice cream in contrast with either a pickle or a washcloth, a favorite toy in contrast with either a pickle or a washcloth).

After the student learns to choose desired items over undesired or nonpreferred items, show two desired items and an undesired item when presenting the SD. For example, ask the student, "Which one?" while presenting ice cream, a favorite toy, and a pickle. If the student verbally chooses both of the favorite items, reinforce by giving her both items. Withhold reinforcement for selecting the nonpreferred or undesired item, or give the student the item as a consequence for requesting it.

As the student masters this task, you may extend the SD to produce the question "Which one do you want?" You may also make several new choices available to the student, such as choices among preferred behaviors versus nonpreferred or undesired behaviors rather than items. By modifying the teaching program outlined above, it is possible to teach the student to choose between two behaviors of different desirability, such as a kiss and a pinch. For example, you may ask, "Want a kiss or a pinch?" If the student says, "I want kiss," she should be kissed. If she says, "I want pinch," you may want to pinch the student just enough to make it unpleasant for her and then present another trial, prompting the response that receives the preferred behavior. New choices (e.g., bath vs. television, play vs. work) should be introduced in proportion to the student's comprehension of language. Suffice it to say, there are endless variations of the original question "What do you want?"

At some later point into treatment, the student may be taught yes/no responses to volitional items (e.g., "Do you want a kiss?" "Do you want a pinch?"). Extensions of volitional questions will be introduced in an upcoming volume on advanced programs in which yes/no answers to factual questions ("Is the sky blue?") are introduced.

Making Choices When No External Stimuli Are Present

Following the steps described in the preceding section, present SD1 ("Do you want [Item 1] or [Item 2]?"). The items involved in this question should not be within the student's view but should be readily accessible so the student may be provided with a consequence immediately upon her response. Directly following the SD, prompt the student to say, "I want (object label)." Quickly present the item named in the student's response. For example, ask the question, "Do you want ice cream or pickle?" and quickly prompt, "Ice cream." Reinforce the student by providing her with a taste of ice cream. After mastering SD1, introduce a second pair of items in SD2 (e.g., a favorite toy such as Woody or Buzz vs. mustard or salad dressing). Prompt as done before and fade the prompt over subsequent trials. When the student reaches mastery criterion for SD2, subject SD1 and SD2 to discrimination training.

Although it is advisable to use the preferred item as the reinforcer for correct responding, you must decide whether to use the undesired item as the consequence for incorrect responding. For example, you may present the student with the pickle if she requests it. Most likely, such a consequence is mildly aversive and may therefore facilitate the discrimination. To help the student make choices among less extreme stimuli, pair highly desired items with mildly desired items (e.g., ice cream vs. pretzels).

Spontaneous Requesting

The goal of this portion of the I Want Program is to help the student spontaneously request items she wants. By spontaneous, we mean that you do not ask or otherwise prompt the student to request something.

▶ **Step 1**

Present a desired object on the table. The correct response is the student's requesting the item on the table (e.g., saying, "I want juice," if juice is on the table and is a preferred item). If necessary, prompt the correct response by providing a relatively unintrusive prompt, such as an expectant look toward the student. If this fails, try mouthing the word "I" or the phrase "I want." If necessary, provide a full verbal prompt. To make this skill spontaneous, all prompts must be faded. Set mastery at 5 out of 5 or 9 out of 10 unprompted correct responses. At a later stage in teaching, the correct response can be extended from "I want juice" to "I want juice, please."

▶ **Step 2**

Present more than one object on the table, such as a glass of juice and a washcloth. Prompt the correct response and immediately reinforce the student. Fade the prompt over subsequent trials. Once this response is mastered, present more than one desirable item plus an undesirable item on the table (e.g., the display may consist of juice, ice cream, and raisins) and prompt the student to ask for both of the preferred items. After this skill is mastered, generalize the student's requests to the family's mealtime when many desired items may be available.

Continue to introduce items until the student can express "I want" sentences involving items, activities, or behaviors that have not been specifically taught in this portion of the program. These are spontaneous or self-generated sentences. Once the student has given evidence of early mastery in this area, extend the teaching of "I want" sentences to her everyday environment so as to maintain this skill and expand upon her expressive language.

Areas of Difficulty

At any given point in the I Want Program, some students will encounter *serious* problems when attempting to verbally communicate their requests. If this occurs, introduce the Reading and Writing Program (Chapter 29), the PECS Program (Chapter 30), or both. Progress in either or both of these programs may facilitate the student's progress in the present (vocal) program.

Spontaneous verbal communication is an area of difficulty for most students with language and other developmental delays. To maximize the effectiveness of the Early Grammar Programs, it is essential that the instructional format be practiced in all environments. If a parent or other caregiver consistently provides a student with desired foods and activities even though the student has mastered requesting these items, the student is reinforced for *not* requesting. It is therefore important to monitor the frequency with which the student's desires are satisfied if she is to learn to communicate them independently. Rather than merely giving the student a desired item, place it and other items in front of her and give her an expectant look. Be sure the student does not pick up the item and take it away; she should receive the item only after she has requested it in an appropriate manner. Also, do not reinforce nonverbal gestures if the student has learned to request items verbally. If necessary, prompt the student to use the most advanced level of communication she has mastered.

Remember that for many years and thousands of occasions, a parent may have provided all kinds of help and favors to the student in part because the student could not talk or otherwise communicate appropriately. Remember also that parents and teachers may have been told that the student was helpless, sick, and in need of noncontingent love and affection. It is often very difficult for a parent or teacher to relearn such attitudes and relationships even when the student has mastered certain more appropriate and age-related forms of communication.

I See

The goal of the I See Program is to teach the student to begin describing what he observes. In a sense, the I Want Program benefits mostly the student. The I See Program may be viewed as primarily benefiting persons other than the student because, through this program, the student tells others of his experiences, providing reinforcement to someone other than himself. Prior to beginning the current program, the student should have mastered the expressive labeling of 15 to 20 objects presented in both their 2-D and 3-D forms (see Chapter 23). The student should also have mastered verbal imitation of "I see" phrases that include mastered object labels (e.g., "I see balloon").

A variety of items used in the Expressive Labeling of Objects Program should be gathered for use in the I See Program. This set should include objects in both their 2-D and 3-D forms.

▶ **Step 1**

Present SD1 ("What do you see?") after placing an object (e.g., a cup) in its 3-D form on a table that is free from all other stimuli and reinforcers.

Immediately prompt and reinforce the correct response ("I see cup"). Repeat this SD and reinforcement for correct responding over trials while gradually fading the prompt. Note that the correct response in this program is the statement of three discrete words that form a complete sentence. If the student omits one or more words, you should conduct more trials that include prompting the full response. All prompts should then be systematically faded until the criterion for mastery is met. Set the criterion for mastery at 5 out of 5 or 9 out of 10 unprompted correct responses.

▶ **Step 2**

Present SD2 ("What do you see?") after showing the student a second object (e.g., an apple). Again, place this item on an otherwise empty table. Immediately prompt the correct response ("I see apple"). Gradually fade this prompt over trials while continuing to reinforce subsequent correct responses. Continue to present SD2 until the student independently responds correctly in 5 out of 5 or 9 out of 10 trials.

▶ **Step 3**

Intermix and differentially reinforce SD1 and SD2 according to the discrimination learning paradigm. Given the student's previous mastery of labeling the cup and apple, the criterion for mastery may center on his providing a full three-word response. Should the student fail to complete the entire response to either SD1 or SD2, additional prompting may be necessary. Often a partial prompt (e.g., "I") is all that is needed to reinstate the correct response. As always, systematically fade all prompting until the student can respond independently. Place mastery at 9 out of 10 or 19 out of 20 unprompted correct responses when SD1 and SD2 are randomly intermixed.

▶ **Step 4**

After the student masters the discrimination between SD1 and SD2, introduce a third item, SD3 ("What do you see?"), and teach the student to respond with, "I see (e.g., hat)." Follow the procedures outlined in Step 1. After the student masters SD3, intermix SD3 with SD1 and then SD3 with SD2 until each discrimination is mastered. Maintain the SD1-SD2 discrimination throughout this process in different sittings.

Subsequent responses should be taught using Steps 1 through 4. After the student masters a new SD (SD4, SD5, etc.) when presented alone, intermix it with three to four already mastered SDs.

At some point, most students generalize "I see" sentences to all the objects they can label. Such generalization may occur relatively early in the learning of the skills involved in the I See Program (e.g., after the student has mastered five SDs). Other students may demonstrate generalization relatively late or not at all. You will know the student has begun to generalize when the student responds correctly to objects presented that have not been specifically taught in this program. For example, if you present the student with an object that has not been used in this program but that the student can label (e.g., a banana) and then ask, "What do you see?" and the student answers, "I see banana," without being prompted, then the student has made progress in generalizing this skill. When the student has begun to generalize or after the student has mastered 15 SDs in the I See Program, begin Step 5 in which the student is taught to label several objects using the "I see" phrase.

▶ **Step 5**

Place two objects on the table. For example, place a sock on the left side of the table and a toy tiger on the right side of the table (from the student's perspective). Place the objects approximately 1 foot apart and equidistant from the student. Present the SD ("What do you see?") and prompt the response "I see sock and tiger." If necessary, add a prompt by pointing to the objects or, if the student misses an object, pointing to the missed object.

Note that the object to the student's left should be stated first. This may be the student's first exposure to the skill known as sequencing, an important skill necessary for successfully completing several types of tasks. Patterning, filling in a calendar, storytelling, writing, and reading are all activities that rely on the use of sequencing in a left-to-right manner. At this stage into the I See Program, the order in which the student states each object label is incorporated into the criterion for mastery.

In adding more demands on the student (naming both the stimuli and naming them in the correct order), be careful not to expose the student to too many nonreinforced trials. If the student's responses show signs of extinction, go back and reestablish the number of objects labeled, and then the order of labeling. Remember that the order is imposed to help the student scrutinize the entire stimulus display and provide a foundation for using the skill of sequencing in later, more advanced programs.

▶ **Step 6**

Once the student responds correctly in 5 out of 5 or 9 out of 10 trials using the first two objects (sock and tiger), add a new pair of objects (e.g., pencil and cup) and teach to mastery. Continue introducing new pairs of stimuli until the student generalizes the "I see..." response to every label in his repertoire.

Using the same procedures described earlier, teach the student to label three to five objects in a field. The first part of the response (i.e., "I see") should remain the same. What changes are the number of labels stated in the response and the length of the statement needed to gain reinforcement. For example, after the student has learned to generate a sentence containing any two known object labels, place a fire engine, a strawberry, and a toy mouse on the table and present the SD ("What do you see?"). The student's response should be "I see fire engine and strawberry and mouse." It is, of course, acceptable for the student to insert the article "a" in front of the object labels.

The student who has mastered three object labels may quickly move to five object labels. When he has generalized the production of this type of response, objects presented in their 2-D form should be used as program stimuli.

▶ **Step 7**

Follow the same steps of instruction when teaching the student to respond with the "I see" phrase to stimuli presented as pictures of objects (i.e., in their 2-D form). Systematically increase the number of objects presented in this format until the student can label as many as five objects within one response.

The use of a photo album allows the teacher to manipulate the number of items presented on a single page. Systematically increase the number and complexity of items shown per page until the student can label five or more items in a single response. At this time, picture books or posters may be introduced as program stimuli. Each picture used should contain between two and approximately eight objects to be labeled. Mastery is achieved when the student can use the phrase "I see" in expressing all object labels he knows, and when many or most of these sentences are novel (i.e., not specifically taught). It is ideal to generalize this task to informal settings, such as having the student describe to his mother pictures from a book while sitting on the sofa.

Areas of Difficulty

The student may experience difficulty when the program stimuli are shifted from pictures presented on the table to pictures presented in a photo album or on a poster. This means that the teacher may need to prompt more heavily and simplify the presentation and orientation of stimuli by, for example, placing the pictures in sequence from left to right. Later, the pictures may be gradually placed in a less ordered format. This latter stage will help to prepare the student for labeling pictures in a book as these pictures are usually presented in idiosyncratic arrangements.

A second area of difficulty is dealing with incomplete responses. For example, it is quite common for students to complete the last part of a verbal prompt rather than repeat all the words presented within the prompt. That is, should the teacher prompt by saying, "I see cup and hat," the student may delete the "I see" portion and say only, "Cup and hat." To alleviate this problem, review the use of backward chaining as described in the Verbal Imitation Program (Chapter 22).

I Have

This chapter ends with the teaching of rudimentary conversation. In the I Have Program, the student is taught to state a parallel phrase in response to an SD. The statement of analogous or complementary phrases is an important part of conversation. At this stage, the SD is not a question, but a statement.

Before beginning instruction in this program, the student should have gained the following prerequisite skills: (1) expressive labeling of 15 to 20 objects presented in 3-D and 2-D forms, (2) some mastery of "I want" and "I see" sentences, and (3) verbal imitation of "I have" phrases that incorporate object labels (e.g., "I have pizza," "I have banana"). The article "a" as in "a pizza" is deleted to simplify the sentence; it can be introduced at a later stage.

The First Object Labels

▶ **Step 1**

Present SD1 by giving the student an object (e.g., a duck) and asking, "What do you have?" Verbally prompt the student to state the response "I have duck." Some students use the article "a" correctly with little or no instruction to do so. If the student responds in this way, the article "a" may be used to complete the sentence. If not, this portion may be taught in later stages of language acquisition. Fade the use of the prompt while continuing to present this instruction in mass trials. After the student has responded correctly in 5 out of 5 or 9 out of 10 unprompted trials, go to the next step.

▶ **Step 2**

Present SD2, which consists of giving the student an object different from the one presented in Step 1 (e.g., a crayon) and presenting the verbal instruction "What do you have?" Use a verbal prompt to assist the student in stating the correct response (i.e., "I have crayon"). Fade the prompt gradually until the student gives 5 out of 5 or 9 out of 10 independent correct responses.

▶ **Step 3**

Intermix SD1 and SD2 according to the discrimination learning paradigm. After the student masters the discrimination between SD1 and SD2, additional objects should be introduced systematically.

Multiple Object Labels

After the student learns to generate an accurate sentence in the format described in the previous section, teach her to include two objects in a single response. The steps described previously should be followed exactly; however, in this step, the teacher should present the student with two objects rather than one object. It may be necessary to prompt the student to insert the word "and" between the object labels (e.g., "I have horse *and* wagon"). This and other verbal prompts should gradually be faded until the student can state the correct response independently in 5 out of 5 or 9 out of 10 trials. After the student meets this response criteria for the first pair of objects, present the instruction for a second pair of objects. Introduce new pairs systematically. The student has mastered this sentence structure when she can include any two mastered object labels she is presented with.

The teacher may already have anticipated how "I have" sentences can be generalized to the student's experiences. For one, the student may be taught to describe hurt, happiness, and other emotional states (see Chapter 28). For example, it is inevitable that a child will get scratched or bruised by falling down. When such an event occurs, it provides an opportunity to label the hurt "Boo-boo" and teach the student to say, "I have boo-boo." In a similar manner, a student can be taught to describe holding onto her mother by saying, "I have Mommy." Limitless opportunities for creative teaching exist in this area.

Reciprocal Statements

As mentioned in the introduction to this chapter, the I Have Program lends itself to the early stages of conversational speech. This comes about because the presence of objects helps prompt the student's "conversation." An upcoming book that includes programs on advanced language will contain programs for advanced conversation. Note that the kind of early sharing of information described in this section is similar to show-and-tell sessions in typical schools.

▶ **Step 1**

Present SD1, which consists of the student's holding an object (e.g., a book) and your holding an object that is different from the student's object (e.g., a shoe) while stating, "I have shoe." R1 is the student's stating, "I have book." Prompt the student's correct response by asking, "What do you have?" immediately after giving SD1. Gradually and systematically fade the prompt by saying less and less of it or by reducing its volume. Move on to the next step after the student responds correctly in 5 out of 5 or 9 out of 10 unprompted trials.

▶ **Step 2**

Present SD2 by giving the student a new object (e.g., a toy bus) and holding a new object of your own (e.g., a flower) while stating, "I have flower." Once again, prompt the response as necessary. Fade all prompts as soon as possible. Begin Step 3 after the student responds correctly in 5 out of 5 or 9 out of 10 unprompted trials.

► **Step 3**

Intermix SD1 and SD2 using discrimination learning procedures. After the student has learned to discriminate between SD1 and SD2, introduce SD3. After the response is mastered when presented in mass trials, it should be brought into discrimination training.

Generalizing "I Have" Sentences

Following mastery in the formal teaching environment, all instructional formats should be practiced in several different settings and across different persons. Facilitate natural interactions by presenting SDs when the student happens to be holding one or more objects in settings less structured than the controlled environment provided at the table (e.g., while walking through the house and handling objects or joining an adult shopping in a supermarket). Also, present SDs while engaging in parallel or interactive play with the student. Instructions from the I Have Program should be intermixed with those from other programs to ensure discrimination and generalization. To help prepare a younger student for a classroom environment, a show-and-tell type of format may be introduced by having the student and several adults (playing children) sit in a circle. Some children become very spontaneous in this type of setting.

Areas of Difficulty

The student may echo the question "What do you have?" and not respond to the prompt. If this should occur, it may be necessary to present several trials with the question "What do you have?" as the SD, establishing correct responding to this SD. After the student responds correctly to the question three or four times, start the conversation by stating, for example, "I have puzzle" in a very soft voice and then adding the question "What do you have?" in a louder voice. Over several trials, increase the volume of the statement and decrease the volume of the prompt.

Prepositions

CHAPTER 27

Up to this point in teaching, the student has made several gains. Some of these gains, such as being able to identify and label concrete objects, may be viewed as relatively simple, whereas other gains, such as learning to express basic wants and needs and using language as it applies to abstract concepts such as color, shape, and size, are considered more complex. Now, in acquiring prepositions, the student is taught certain abstract spatial relationships among objects or events. The Prepositions Program is potentially one of the most difficult programs for the student to master.

By means of the Prepositions Program, most students eventually learn that two objects can be described in terms of the spatial positions they possess relative to one another. For example, the student may learn to understand statements such as "Place the pillow *on* the bed," "Put the milk *inside* the refrigerator," or "Please put a plate *under* your sandwich." Many students also learn to express prepositional relationships, such as "He is *inside* the house," "Trees have roots *below* ground," "Planes fly *above* the ground," and "I am standing *on top* of the stairs." Equally important, many students learn to request certain arrangements, such as telling another person to sit *close* to her or to place a doll *inside* the toy house.

Psychologists and educators attribute many advantages to the acquisition of prepositional relationships. The acquisition of prepositions can help students orient themselves in space as well as in relation to other persons. These gains may aid in the student's development of individual boundaries, such as self-image or personal identity. Although behavioral psychologists do not use terms like self-image and personal identity, the concepts they represent are often used in everyday conversation such as when a person speaks of "seeing herself in relation to another," "feeling outside the family," and the like. An individual who is familiar with relationships among objects, individuals, and personal boundaries will converse more easily with others than persons who are not familiar with such relationships. Another advantage of learning prepositions is that prepositional relationships may later facilitate mastery of temporal or causal relationships

We begin this program by teaching the receptive identification of prepositional relationships. Once the receptive portion of the Prepositions Program is mastered, students are taught to express, or verbally describe, such relationships. The strategy of introducing novel material using receptive language prior to expressive language is a model adhered to in the preceding chapters. However, maintaining flexibility is important given that some students learn novel material more readily through the expressive format than the receptive format.

It is of the utmost importance that each team member working with the student acquire a thorough knowledge of discrimination learning procedures (Chapter 16) before the current program is introduced.

Receptive Prepositions

In the initial steps of this program, the student is taught to position an object in relation to another object. For example, the student is taught to respond correctly to your instruction "On top" by placing an object, such as a block, on top of another object, such as a box or a bucket positioned upside down. The following materials are needed to teach prepositions: a small block, various small items (e.g., a toy car, figurines, a beanbag), a box or a bucket, two chairs, and a table of a size such that the student can place objects on top of it, climb on top of it, and fit underneath it.

Begin by having the student sit in front of the table and across from the teacher. Place a 12- to 20-inch tall bucket or box upside down on the table in front of the student. Note that the following steps all conform to the steps outlined in discrimination learning. Because it is difficult for most students to master prepositions, the steps involved in this program are described in some detail.

► **Step 1**

Hand the student a block and mass trial SD1 ("On top"). Prompt the correct response by manually guiding the student to pick up the block, move the block toward the top of the upside-down bucket, and then release the block on top of the bucket. Reinforce. Begin fading the prompt by guiding the student's hand until it is positioned above the bucket and then letting go of the student's hand so that he releases the block independently. Fade the prompt further by guiding the student's hand toward the bucket and then letting go of his hand such that he needs to raise the block above the bucket *and* release it independently. Continue fading the prompt until the student picks up the block from the table and completes the entire action without assistance.

For some students, the teacher may want to employ a pointing prompt to aid the student's correct placement of the block. Do this by presenting SD1 ("On top") while pointing to the top of the bucket. The pointing prompt may help to bridge the gap between manually prompted trials and unprompted trials. If the student fails during prompt fading, go back a few steps and reinstate the level of prompting necessary to regain the student's success. Then begin the prompt fading process again. Be careful not to use inadvertent prompts such as looking at the top of the bucket while giving the SD or during the student's response. Place mastery at 5 out of 5 or 9 out of 10 unprompted correct responses.

► **Step 2**

Perform mass trials of SD2 ("Beside") following the same procedures used for SD1 ("On top"). The use of the word "beside" as SD2 should help to facilitate the discrimination between SD1 and SD2 because these SDs are composed of words that sound different from one another and consist of a different number of words. The placements of SD1 and SD2 are physically distinct from one another as well, which will further aid the student's discrimination between SD1 and SD2.

Immediately after presenting SD2, prompt the student's correct response by manually guiding him through the motions of placing the block beside the bucket. If further prompting is necessary after the manual prompt is faded, prompt by pointing to the correct location. Once the student performs 5 out of 5 or 9 out of 10 unprompted correct responses, go on to Step 3.

► **Step 3**

Within 2 seconds of completion of a correct response to SD2 ("Beside"), present SD1 ("On top") and simultaneously prompt the student's correct response. Fade the prompt and, after 3 correct responses in a row, switch to SD2 ("Beside"). Prompt the response, fade the prompt over successive trials, and secure 3 unprompted correct responses in a row before switching back to SD1 ("On top"). Next, alternate between SD1 and SD2 after 2 successive unprompted correct responses and then after 1 unprompted correct response. Provide an informational "No" and withhold reinforcement for errors. As the teacher alternates between SD1 and SD2 and reinforces correct responses while not reinforcing incorrect responses, the SD1–R1 and SD2–R2 associations are strengthened and the SD1–R2 and SD2–R1 relationships are weakened. As the correct associations strengthen, randomly intermix SD1 and SD2 to prevent a win–stay or lose–shift pattern of responding. Set mastery at 9 out of 10 or 19 out of 20 unprompted correct responses.

Once mastery of the discrimination between SD1 and SD2 is achieved, we recommend that this discrimination be generalized across several team members and different locations around the house over the next 3 or 4 days. This is consistent with earlier recommendations concerning the first discrimination and newly established discriminations achieved within a program. This first discrimination should be solidified because doing so facilitates the student's acquisition of new prepositional relationships.

Select a third preposition that is as different from the first two as possible. "Next to" may not be easily discriminated from SD2 ("Beside") due to its similarity in positioning. "Under" may be more discriminable although the student may be distracted by the need to use two hands to complete the response to this SD: one hand to lift up the bucket and the other hand to put the block underneath the bucket. Finally, "Behind" is not a good choice for SD3 given that it sounds fairly similar to SD2 and the student cannot observe the eventual placement of the block. "In front" may be the best choice for SD3 given that only one hand is required for performing the response, the words composing the SD sound different from the former SDs, and the placement of the stimuli will be observable and relatively discriminable from SD1 and SD2.

▶ **Step 4**

Present mass trials of SD3 ("In front"). Prompt the correct response (placing the block in front of the bucket) and reinforce as done in Steps 1 and 2. Gradually fade the prompt(s). Once SD3 is mastered (5 out of 5 or 9 out of 10 unprompted correct responses), intermix SD3 with SD1 ("On top"). Once the intermixing of SD3 with SD1 is mastered (9 out of 10 or 19 out of 20 unprompted correct responses), move on to intermixing SD3 with SD2.

In addition to practicing these new discriminations, be sure to practice the SD1–SD2 discrimination, which may have been partially lost in establishing SD3. Note also that we recommend stopping at three prepositions at this time and further strengthening the student's mastery of these prepositions by introducing the next phase of the Program: Generalizing Prepositions Across Objects.

Generalizing Prepositions Across Objects

Up to this point, the student has gone through several steps of the Prepositions Program. The student first learned to place an object (a block) on top of another object (a bucket). The student was then taught to position the block beside the bucket and discriminate between placing the block on top of and beside the bucket. The student was also taught to place the block in a third position ("In front") in relation to the bucket. Finally, the student learned to discriminate the third position from the first two.

Despite all this training, it is likely that the student will need further help in discriminating prepositions when different objects are used and different teachers present the instructions. That is, the student may have been inadvertently reinforced for attending to a very specific and idiosyncratic feature of a particular object or to certain auditory or visual cues unique to a particular teacher. To avoid such a narrow understanding of prepositional relationships, we recommend introducing new teachers (e.g., family members) and extending the number and variety of objects to be placed and objects to be referenced for placements. To facilitate the illustration of steps needed to accomplish this skill, we use the term *placement object* to refer to the object that is placed (moved into position) and the term *target object* to refer to the object that receives the placement object. In the previous section, the block was the placement object and the bucket was the target object. In the following steps, the target object may be varied by using such items as a different looking bucket, then a shoebox, and then a big coffee mug. Similarly, the original placement object (the block) may be varied by using such items as animal figures, toy cars, spoons, and beanbags.

Prior to beginning the steps presented below, the student should have been taught to identify (e.g., point to or touch) the new target and placement objects by following the procedures described in the Receptive Identification of Objects Program (Chapter 17).

▶ **Step 1**

Generalize placement objects. Using the bucket as the target object, change the placement object to, for example, a toy car, then a beanbag, and then an animal figurine. Once the student is able to position novel placement objects on top, beside, and in front of the target object on the first trial, move on to the next step.

▶ **Step 2**

Position two or more placement objects in front of the student (e.g., a toy car and the original block) so they are side by side, about 8 to 10 inches apart. As a pretraining step, make certain the student can correctly identify (by pointing to or touching) each object when they are displayed concurrently on the table. Next, instruct the student to place one of these two objects on top of the bucket. For example, instruct, "Car on top," emphasizing the word "car" to facilitate the student's correct response. Prompt if necessary (e.g., with a position prompt), reinforce, and fade the prompt. Once the student achieves mastery (5 out of 5 or 9 out of 10 unprompted correct responses) with "Car on top" as the SD, change the SD to "Block on top" and establish correct responding. Finally, randomly rotate "Car on top" and "Block on top" by following discrimination learning procedures.

▶ Step 3

Slowly increase the number of placement objects displayed concurrently on the table from two to five or six, first making certain that the student can identify each one of them receptively. Vary the instructions as needed to form the appropriate SDs for each of the different objects.

▶ Step 4

Teach the second and third prepositions ("Beside" and "In front") while retaining the same placement objects and target objects used in Steps 1 and 2 of this section. The student now must identify the correct placement object *and* discriminate among prepositions. This is an example of a simultaneous discrimination and shows how the program progresses in complexity in a gradual manner, which is an appropriate manner considering the difficulties most students experience when attempting to master prepositional relationships. Set mastery at 5 out of 5 or 9 out of 10 unprompted correct responses in trials that involve the random rotation of the placement objects and the three locations ("On top," "In front," and "Beside").

▶ Step 5

Generalize target objects. Using the same placement objects introduced in previous steps, change the target object by removing the bucket and replacing it with a box. Note that the student should have previously mastered receptive identification of both the bucket and the box. Once mastery is achieved (5 out of 5 or 9 out of 10 unprompted correct responses) using the box as the target object, go on to Step 5.

▶ Step 6

Position two target objects (the bucket and the box) side by side on the table (about 1 foot apart) and place one of the placement objects (e.g., the block) on the table such that it is equidistant from both the bucket and the box. Teach the student to place the block on top of the box in contrast to on top of the bucket, emphasizing the words "bucket" and "box" in their respective instructions to help facilitate the discrimination.

After mastery is reached using the block as the placement object, add a second placement object (e.g., a toy car) and teach the student to discriminate among the four possibilities: SD1 ("Block on top of bucket)," SD2 ("Car on top of bucket"), SD3 ("Block on top of box"), and SD4 ("Car on top of box"). Once the student masters the discriminations among these SDs, teach the second preposition ("Beside"). At this stage, there are eight discriminations ("Block on top of bucket," "Block beside bucket," "Block on top of box," "Block beside box," and the same positions but involving the car). Further discriminations may be taught by introducing the third preposition ("In front"). Mastery of these discriminations necessitates that the student make a triple discrimination; that is, the student must choose between target objects, placement objects, and prepositions.

It was earlier advised that generalization training should be employed across teachers and environments after the first discrimination (between "On Top" and "Beside") was mastered. The same advice should be followed after each discrimination. With increasingly large numbers of prepositions, there is a concomitant increase in risk of interference from idiosyncratic expressions and teaching styles across teachers. Be patient and proceed gradually. Generalization training will solidify the discriminations, facilitate their functional and practical properties, and improve the student's recall.

Areas of Difficulty

With this program, the student is confronted with very difficult learning tasks. It is important to keep in mind that even for those students who move relatively quickly through the beginning stages of this program, mastery of the discriminations may take some time.

Sometimes a teacher gets carried away when teaching a particular program, such as prepositions, and involves the student in that program at the expense of other programs. A fast-moving learner may make a promising (and, to the teacher, reinforcing) start, only to become overwhelmed by all the various combinations and permutations involved in using several placement objects, several target objects, and several prepositions. It is therefore important to set aside a limited amount of time for teaching prepositions once the basic steps are mastered. It is essential to intermix sessions of prepositions with sessions of easier tasks, such as nonverbal imitation and matching, as well as tasks placed on the maintenance schedule. Through the intermixing of programs that help the student succeed, a high level of motivation is maintained, boredom is averted, and frustration is reduced.

Individual differences among students are as pronounced in the Prepositions Program as they are in any other program. Students vary enormously in their rate of acquisition of the receptive prepositions presented thus far. Our experience is that a small minority of students master the use of receptive prepositions by the end of 1 month. Many students, however, do not master receptive prepositions even after 2 years of intensive teaching.

Some students experience considerable difficulty with the initial discrimination in the Prepositions Program. If this occurs, intermix SD1 ("On top") with a contrasting stimulus that may later facilitate the SD1–SD2 discrimination. The contrasting stimulus could be chosen from the Nonverbal Imitation Program or any of the receptive language programs. In addition, the response to the contrasting stimulus should be kept simple (e.g., imitating your clapping hands or touching the table).

To use a contrasting stimulus to facilitate the student's discrimination, first present SD1 ("On top") and reinforce the correct response. Then introduce a contrasting stimulus (SDCS) that is nonverbal in nature (e.g., imitation of your clapping hands), intermixing SD1 and SDCS according to the discrimination learning paradigm. Once the student masters the intermixing of SD1 ("On top") and SDCS in random rotation, you may want to further facilitate the acquisition of the target discrimination by introducing an SDCS that, like SD1, has a verbal component. For example, contrast SD1 with an SDCS such as "Touch nose." This contrast should be more difficult than the contrast between SD1 and the nonverbal imitation SDCS because both SDs contain auditory cues. Subject SD1 and the new SDCS to discrimination learning procedures until the student performs correctly in 5 out of 5 or 9 out of 10 unprompted trials. Once the student can discriminate SD1 from a contrasting stimulus, return to the SD1–SD2 discrimination.

Another potentially helpful procedure for the student who has difficulty with the initial discrimination is using two different placement objects for each of the first two prepositions and then fading out one of these objects. For example, use a red block for "On top" and a white block for "Beside," or use a block for "On top" and a beanbag for "Beside." The target object (a bucket) should be kept constant. Any deviation (of color, size, or shape) in stimuli that may facilitate the student's discrimination is considered to function as a prompt. As always, the disadvantage of using prompts involves teaching prompt dependency. Therefore, fade all prompts as soon as possible and remember to keep an eye out for inadvertent prompts. For example, after giving the SD, do not inadvertently prompt the correct response by looking toward the area in which the placement object should be positioned. Although it may be tempting to encourage the student through the use of such prompts, remember that, once mastery of a skill is reached without prompts, it is easier for the student to acquire new skills within the program.

A problem that can occur when only two responses are targeted at a time is that the student may fall into a win–stay and lose–shift pattern of responding. In other words, if the student gets one response wrong and misses out on reinforcement, the student may switch to the other response on the next trial without listening to your instructions. To prevent such a pattern from occurring, adhere to random rotation once this step is reached in discrimination learning.

Other problems may occur because of the stimuli themselves. For example, a particular toy used as a placement object may invite self-stimulation. Another possibility is that the response the student learned with the block and bucket in the first hours of treatment (placing a block in the bucket) may interfere with correct responding in future programs that involve these same stimuli. If either of these problems occurs, replace the block with a beanbag, change the bucket to a box, or both.

For some students, it may be easier to position *themselves* in relation to an object rather than position two objects in relation to each other (see the later section, "Receptive Prepositions In Vivo"). For example, the student may have less difficulty learning to place himself on top of or under a table than placing a block on top of or under a bucket.

If all else fails, withdraw the Prepositions Program for a month or more and then reintroduce it at a later time. This is good advice for students who encounter serious difficulty in any program. Sometimes intervening programs facilitate mastery of later or reintroduced programs.

Expressive Prepositions

We advise that you begin teaching receptive prepositions in vivo as the receptive prepositions using objects format nears mastery. However, we introduce the early stages of the expressive format at this point because the prior mastery of receptive prepositions may facilitate the student's acquisition of expressive prepositions. Regardless of which format is started first, we suggest that you practice receptive prepositions in vivo between sessions of expressive prepositions.

The student should have mastered verbal imitation and made significant progress in expressive labeling (Chapters 22, 23, and 24, respectively) before beginning the expressive component of the Prepositions Program. Begin by teaching the student to verbalize the prepositional relationships taught in the receptive format, and initially keep the expressive labels simple (e.g., "On top"). Later, by adding verbs such as "is," you can start teaching sentence structure (e.g., "Block is on top of bucket"). These sentences can then be built upon through the addition of pronouns, extended to an in vivo format, and generalized to everyday life as expressed in sentences such as "I am standing *on top* of the table," "I am sitting *between* Mom and Dad," and "My school is *next to* the park."

There are at least two ways to approach the teaching of expressive prepositions. You can give the receptive instruction first (e.g., "On top") and then ask the student, "Where is it?" and teach the student to answer, "On top." Alternatively, you can delete the receptive phase and present the student only with the physical arrangement (e.g., with the block on top of the bucket) and then ask, "Where is it?" prompting the correct verbalization and reinforcing as described in the expressive labeling programs. We outline the steps for teaching the latter procedure first.

▶ Step 1

Start the expressive component of this program by arranging the teaching environment in the same manner and with the same stimuli used in teaching receptive prepositions. Distinctly place the block *on top* of the bucket and then give the verbal SD ("Where is it?"). Immediately after giving SD1, prompt and reinforce the student for responding with a short label (e.g., "On" or "On top"). Mass trial SD1 and systematically fade the prompt. Place mastery at 5 out of 5 or 9 out of 10 unprompted correct responses.

▶ Step 2

Place the block beside the bucket and give the instruction "Where is it?" Immediately after giving SD2, prompt the correct response "Beside." Mass trial SD2 while systematically fading the prompt. Place mastery at 5 out of 5 or 9 out of 10 unprompted correct responses.

▶ Step 3

Intermix SD1 and SD2 according to discrimination learning procedures. Place mastery at 9 out of 10 or 19 out of 20 unprompted correct responses. Once the discrimination is established between SD1 and SD2 in this controlled environment, strengthen the discrimination over the next 2 to 3 days by extending it across persons and environments. Also, generalize the first expressive prepositions by using different objects as was done in the receptive format. Once the student demonstrates mastery of the SD1–SD2 discrimination, introduce SD3 using the procedures described in Steps 1 and 2. Once SD3 is mastered in mass trials, intermix it first with SD1 and then with SD2. Finally, teach the student to discriminate among all three SDs.

Up to this point, a maximal prompt has been used: You have directly prompted the correct response by stating, "On top," "Beside," and so on. As mentioned earlier, however, your receptive instruction may also prompt the student's expressive label. At some point into the program, you may probe such a prompt by giving the student the placement object and presenting the receptive SD "On top" in a loud voice. Immediately after the student's correct placement, quickly ask, "Where is it?" If the student fails to respond correctly, consequate the response and then prompt the next trial by saying, "On top," fading this prompt over subsequent trials. We recommend using receptive instructions as prompts at some stage in learning since this kind of prompt is less intrusive than a full verbal prompt and is more likely to be used in everyday life.

A minority of students (approximately 2 out of 10) master an additional three to four expressive prepositions within the same week of having mastered the first two prepositions. However, for the majority of students, we recommend holding off on new prepositions, introducing them one at a time and intermixing them after the first three prepositions are generalized across persons and environments and practiced in vivo. By following this advice, the gains made are transferred to a student's everyday environment and serve the functional purpose of helping the student achieve better adjustment in day-to-day living. This adjustment, in turn, will likely reinforce and maintain the student's mastery of prepositions.

Receptive Prepositions In Vivo

We recommend that you start the Prepositions Program with a "contrived" environment (with a block, a bucket, and the student seated at a table) in order to simplify the teaching environment and achieve better control over the variables involved in the teaching situation. For this part of the program, the student should participate more actively in prepositional relationships. Start this task in the receptive format by asking the student to position herself in relation to some object. For example, the student may be asked to place herself on top of the table, beside the table, in front of the table, and under the table. This skill is then extended to other items, such as a bed, a chair, and another person. To start, you and the student should stand approximately 2 to 3 feet apart, side by side, in front of the student's table.

▶ **Step 1**

Present SD1 ("On top") and physically prompt the student to climb on top of a low table. Reinforce the response. Help the student down from the table. Then repeat SD1, fading the prompt over subsequent trials. It may be helpful to gradually transfer to a less intrusive prompt, such as pointing to the top of the table, which is easier to administer and fade than a physical prompt. Mass trial SD1 and place mastery at 5 out of 5 or 9 out of 10 unprompted correct responses.

▶ **Step 2**

Present SD2 ("Under") and prompt the correct response as done in Step 1. Fade the prompt. Place mastery at 5 out of 5 or 9 out of 10 unprompted correct responses.

▶ **Step 3**

Intermix SD1 and SD2 according to discrimination learning procedures. Place the criterion for mastery at 9 out of 10 or 19 out of 20 unprompted correct responses. Once the two prepositions "On top" and "Under" in relation to the table are mastered, generalize these prepositions from the table to other target objects. For example, teach the two prepositions in relation to a chair, a bed, and other objects in the house that allow for the teaching of "On top" and "Under." We recommend solidifying the mastery of these two receptive prepositions over the next several days, generalizing them across team members, before going on to additional in vivo receptive prepositions (e.g., *beside*, *behind*, *in front*). Some students enjoy being actively involved in learning and thus may be more motivated to learn through in vivo formats.

Expressive Prepositions In Vivo

Once the student masters two or three receptive prepositions in vivo, begin teaching their expressive counterparts. The SD for expressive prepositions in vivo consists of the question "Where are you?" and the student's position in relation to a target object, such as a piece of furniture (e.g., a table). The teaching situation should be arranged in the same manner that was used to teach receptive prepositions in vivo.

▶ **Step 1**

Give the receptive instruction "On top" in a loud and clear voice or place the student on top of the table. Once the student is in position, present the verbal component of SD1 ("Where are you?"). If necessary, prompt the correct response by using a full verbal prompt, requiring only the short verbal response "On top" at this point. Reinforce the response. Repeat the trial. Remember to remove the student from the table between trials and position him on top of the table with each presentation of SD1. Bring to the mastery criterion of 5 out of 5 or 9 out of 10 unprompted correct responses.

▶ **Step 2**

Instruct the student, "Under," or place him under the table. Next, present the verbal component of SD2 ("Where are you?") and immediately prompt the student's response. Reinforce. Set mastery at 5 out of 5 or 9 out of 10 unprompted correct responses.

▶ **Step 3**

Intermix SD1 and SD2 according to discrimination learning procedures. Once discrimination between SD1 and SD2 is mastered, generalize it across teachers. Then introduce the third expressive preposition (e.g., "Beside") using the procedures just described.

In the beginning stages of teaching the student to label prepositions, do not require a complex answer. An example of a complex response is "I am standing on top of the table." By requiring such an answer, you may inadvertently attempt to teach two behaviors at the same time (i.e., expressive prepositions *and* sentence construction), a procedure that is likely to interfere with the student's mastery of prepositions. It is the prepositions themselves (e.g., *on top, under, beside*) that are targeted in the Prepositions Program; sentence construction should be taught separately. Thus, in the initial stages, require only the most important element (i.e., the actual preposition) and teach the student to elaborate on the answer in sentence form at a later stage.

Generalizing In Vivo Prepositions

When generalizing prepositions, the student should be taught to answer questions such as "Where are you?" while she is in various environments. To achieve generalization, walk the student to different positions in relation to individual objects (e.g., a table, a chair, a bed, a car) and give the SD ("Where are you?"). Prompt the correct answer if necessary. It may be helpful at this point to use the receptive mode as a prompt for the expressive mode. For example, give the SD ("Sit *inside* the car") and, once the student is in position, present the SD ("Where are you?"). Verbally prompt the correct answer if necessary. Again, remember that all prompts must be systematically faded. That way, when asked, "Where are you?" in everyday situations, the student is able to provide the correct answer independently. Generalize prepositions one at a time and teach the student to discriminate among them in different settings by following the methods described earlier in this chapter and in the discrimination learning chapter.

Concluding Comments

We have advised teaching two or three prepositions involving everyday objects in the receptive, expressive, and in vivo formats. Once these few prepositions are mastered, we recommend teaching one new preposition per month so that ample time is left to solidify the student's mastery of these prepositions and to teach the many other programs the student needs to master. Prepositions are abstract concepts, and mastery of prepositions may conceivably facilitate the student's later acquisition of other abstract concepts, such as pronouns and cause–effect relationships. No empirical data as of yet, however, suggest that such transfers of learning occur.

Emotions

CHAPTER 28

It has been postulated that persons with autism have blunted or inappropriate emotions and that they are unable to understand mental states and the causes of mental states as experienced by themselves and others. In short, it has been proposed that persons with autism lack "Theory of Mind" (see Frith, 1989). Like the areas of intellectual functioning and language, the emotional domain of persons with autism has been viewed by many as damaged beyond repair. The reader, however, must not be misled by such speculations. Most students who receive intensive early behavioral intervention develop richer and more varied emotional lives than individuals who do not receive such intervention.

The program in this chapter, which describes how to teach students to identify feelings and the diverse causes of feelings, should pose no particular problem for many of the students taught. *Complete* mastery of the current program, however, requires considerable mastery of expressive language, including the labels of various facial expressions, such as smiling and crying. In addition, the student's ability to use pronouns in sentences such as "He is angry" and "We are happy" is essential for full mastery of the Emotions Program. It is possible, however, to help the student make a start at identifying certain feelings both interpersonally and intrapersonally without elaborate expressive language provided the student has achieved some mastery of receptive identification of the visual stimuli commonly used to signal basic emotions, such as a smile (see Chapter 18). It is also possible to aid the student who has limited expressive language by teaching him to use written language (see Chapter 29) to label certain emotions.

Before we present the beginning steps of the Emotions Program, it may be helpful to comment briefly on how people often approach the subjects of emotions and emotional development. Let us begin by stating that how one feels about oneself, one's family, one's work, and so forth, is often used as the criterion for whether or not that person has made a successful adjustment. A supportive family life, good friends, and a good job are often cited as causes for feeling happy. When favorable situations are lost or absent, people may describe themselves as unhappy, depressed, or lonely. Further, we often judge other people in terms of whether they make us happy or sad as reflected in such statements as, "You make me so happy; I could not ask for more," in contrast to, "You hurt me; I feel angry and depressed." Parents are often asked how they feel about their children and may describe that their children give rise to all kinds of feelings, ranging anywhere from extreme love to hurt to anger, depending on how their children behave.

Clinical psychologists and psychiatrists have placed a major emphasis on trying to understand the feelings of their clients, and they guide much of their therapeutic work toward achieving this goal. One often hears of therapies that aim to alleviate feelings of depression, anger, and fear, with the goal often being described as an attempt to help the client reach a feeling of satisfaction and competence. A great deal of effort in clinical training institutions is also placed on helping incoming individuals develop the ability to identify the feelings of others and themselves. It may be said that when one understands how a person really feels, then one can be in a better position to help that person.

Anyone familiar with persons with developmental delays inevitably observes a delay in the growth of many emotions. Some kinds of emotions, such as angry outbursts, may be quite evident, whereas other emotions, such as joy, affectionate attachment, sadness, and grief, may occur relatively rarely. However, the more one learns about individuals with developmental delays, the more one comes to realize that the delay in emotional development is one that can best be described as different in degree and frequency of expression rather than in quality of expression.

Developing Feelings

Given the importance people assign to emotions and the delay in emotional development of the students we serve, it may seem surprising that of the many programs introduced in this manual only one explicitly addresses the student's emotions. There are two reasons for such a brief account. First, for many years we had assumed that emotional development could be taught or shaped up in a way similar to the way we shape up language and other behaviors. In one of the first programs we developed, children were taught to hug each other and the adults who took care of them. After mastering this program, the children demonstrated they had learned to hug others. We had hoped that when the children learned to accept and return hugs, these skills would open up an avenue for more elaborate emotional expressions. In other words, we had hoped that the hug would generalize to other emotional expressions of affection. This was not the case when we began in 1963 and it appears not to be the case now either. We were pleased to be hugged, and the children sometimes seemed pleased as well. But many times the embraces seemed more like the children were merely going through the motions without "real feelings." We referred to these hugs as operant hugs. At the same time, it became apparent that it was impossible to teach the children to laugh or cry when it was appropriate to express such feelings. It was as if we had reached a standstill.

The problems involved in teaching genuine and varied emotions solved themselves, however, without the need for specific teaching programs. It took some time before we realized that the development of such emotional behaviors came as a result of progressing through the teaching programs detailed in this manual. In other words, the development of emotional behaviors occurred spontaneously as a consequence of the children's successes and failures in acquiring new and varied behaviors and reinforcers. The emotional development of the children we worked with became more and more like that of typical children, which was one of the strongest signs that we were on the right track.

The strong correlation between the reinforcing properties of an event and the capacity for that event to concurrently elicit emotional behaviors relates back to the old hedonistic interpretation of rewards and punishment. A reward is something that makes you feel happy, and a punishment or loss of a reward is something that makes you feel sad or anxious. Positive feelings are elicited when one's behaviors gain positive reinforcers, such as love, food, and freedom. Positive feelings also arise when one reduces or eliminates negative events by escaping or avoiding unpleasant situations, such as fear, pain, and embarrassment. In contrast, feelings of unhappiness, such as depression and fear, seem elicited by the frustration involved in the loss of a positive reinforcer or the presentation of a negative event. The self-injurious and tantrumous behaviors reviewed in Chapter 5 are often triggered by just those kinds of consequences: Interruption of the student's self-stimulatory behavior removes a positively reinforcing event, and, similarly, the presentation of an aversive event, such as an instruction the student fails to understand, often causes anger and discomfort.

Two important gains were made when we recognized these relationships. First, we did not have to separately teach emotional expressions because they occurred spontaneously as a consequence of the students' acquisition of more varied behavioral repertoires. Second, the emotions that emerged seemed genuine, sincere, and basic, and looked similar to those of typical individuals. Their genuine appearance most likely reflects that these emotions are inborn or reflexive expressions common to all human beings. A full explanation of these relationships would require an exposition of what has been called classical (respondent) conditioning, which is beyond the scope of this book. Perhaps all that is necessary to know at this point is that the presentation or removal of many or most reinforcers possesses unconditioned stimulus properties that elicit affective–emotional behaviors.

If we now attempt to explain why individuals with autism are delayed in emotional development, we can provide two observations. First, given the individuals' limited behavioral repertoires prior to treatment, in addition to the limited reinforcers available to those individuals, it is reasonable to expect a restriction and delay in expression of emotional behaviors. In contrast, as the student acquires an increasing range of behaviors, the stage is set for the student to come into contact with and acquire a growing range of reinforcing consequences. Second, there is always the possibility that, as reinforcers are gained, they can also be withdrawn or lost for the simple reason that many or most reinforcers are controlled by others. Given this scenario, all kinds of feelings ranging from happiness to sadness should emerge with the delivery or loss of external reinforcers. On the other hand, a student who is heavily involved in self-stimulatory behaviors has control over her own limited range of reinforcers (see Chapter 6). She has nothing or little to lose, for what is reinforcing to her is not controlled by others but rather by herself. The less a person has to gain or lose, the less that person is likely to demonstrate emotional expressions of happiness, depression, sadness, and grief. If a person is not attached to others and is not reinforced by their presence, the departure of a person would not cause much anxiety and sadness. Perhaps this is the reason why many autistic persons do not seem upset when their parents leave them alone or when they are lost. One may compare such a person to a meditating guru, who may experience a continual state of peace and serenity provided that such a person is divorced from the everyday world and instead engaged in ritualistic behaviors. Indeed, individuals with developmental delays and autistic features historically have been acclaimed as saints or mystics.

It may help to illustrate the correlation between gaining and losing reinforcers on the one hand and the development of various emotional states on the other hand through examples of excerpts from two popular songs. The song called "Only You" (Reed, 1955) is about acquisition: obtaining the positive reinforcers associated with love and losing the negative states associated with loneliness. These states are basic to being a happy individual. In contrast, many other songs illustrate the opposite, such as the song from the Beatles called "Yesterday" (McCartney, 1965). This song is about depression and loneliness associated with extinction and the loss of reinforcers. Songs frequently illustrate feelings caused by the gaining and losing of all sorts of reinforcers.

Once emotional behaviors are triggered, they need to be modified in their expression so as to fit the cultural mode of acceptance. The modification of tantrumous behavior (Chapter 5) is an example of altering an emotional expression. Tantrumous and angry behaviors have to be modified in typical children as well. Adults contribute in this effort, shaping emotional behaviors such as anger, affection, and sadness into acceptable expressions corresponding to the culture in which the children live. At this point into teaching, you are likely to know enough about reinforcement operations to shape appropriate expressions.

One of the first steps in shaping emotional behaviors is teaching the student to recognize and identify expressions. We start by teaching the student to identify outside or external expressions of emotions. We then teach the student how such external expressions correspond to internal states or feelings. For example, we may teach the student to label external emotional expressions such as smiling and crying and then help the student label the underlying feelings of happiness and sadness. Finally, we teach the student to identify the causes of various feelings (e.g., "She is happy because you are patting her" or "He is sad because you are hitting him").

Receptive Identification of Emotional Expressions in a 2-D Format

Some students progress faster when the current program is initiated through the expressive labeling component instead of through the receptive identification component. However, for most students, receptive identification of emotional expressions tends to be easier to acquire than expressive labeling of emotional expressions; therefore, we recommend that you begin the Emotions Program with receptive identification. In addition, some students progress faster when persons displaying expressions are used rather than pictures of facial expressions. For other students, however, the opposite occurs. Therefore, be flexible with what kinds of stimuli are used.

Prior to beginning this program, the student should have mastered the matching of facial expressions (e.g., smiling, crying, scowling) depicted on photographs as described in the Matching and Sorting Program (Chapter 12). Such matching will facilitate the student's discrimination of and attention to emotional expressions. When using 2-D stimuli, select one picture of a person expressing readily identifiable signs of happiness (e.g., smiling) and another picture of the *same* person expressing readily identifiable signs of sadness (e.g., crying). Note that the procedures for teaching the student to identify these expressions are identical to those employed in the receptive language programs and thus are outlined only briefly here.

▶ Step 1

Present SD1, which consists of your saying, "Point to smiling," while presenting a picture of a person smiling. Prompt and reinforce. Over successive trials, fade the prompt. Place mastery at 5 out of 5 or 9 out of 10 unprompted correct responses.

▶ Step 2

Present SD2, which consists of your saying, "Point to crying," while presenting a picture of a person crying. Prompt and reinforce. Over successive trials, fade the prompt. Place mastery at 5 out of 5 or 9 out of 10 unprompted correct responses.

▶ Step 3

Intermix the two SDs according to discrimination learning procedures. Because the pictures of persons smiling and crying may differ in several stimulus dimensions not related to either expression, the student may learn to attend to these irrelevant stimuli instead of the emotional expressions. The identification of emotional expressions should therefore be generalized across different pictures of persons displaying the same expressions until the student is able to extract the expressions regardless of who exhibits them.

Once mastery is achieved in Step 3 (9 out of 10 or 19 out of 20 unprompted correct responses across novel stimuli), generalize from 2-D stimuli (pictures) to 3-D stimuli (in vivo) as described below.

Receptive Identification of Emotional Expressions In Vivo

When teaching this task, it is helpful to have two additional adults (Adult 1 and Adult 2) present to demonstrate emotional expressions. The student, the teacher, and the two extra adults should sit facing each other in a rectangular configuration with approximately a 2- to 3-foot space in the center. The teacher should have previously instructed the adults to model exaggerated expressions on cue and to maintain a neutral expression between trials. In general, the more exaggerated the expressions, the easier it is for the student to discriminate between them. When exhibiting such expressions, it pays to think of oneself as a performer on stage.

▶ Step 1

Present SD1, which consists of instructing Adult 1 to smile broadly and asking the student to "Point to smiling" (or simply "Smiling"). Prompt if necessary, reinforce, and fade the prompt over trials. If you experience problems fading the prompt, try prompting by presenting the 2-D stimulus card used in the previous section. Place the 2-D card on the adult (or have the adult hold it) to prompt the correct response. Fade the card by moving it in gradual steps under the adult's seat or underneath the adult's shirt. Place mastery at 5 out of 5 or 9 out of 10 unprompted correct responses. Generalize to Adult 2, placing mastery at 3 out of 3 or 4 out of 5 unprompted correct responses. Next, alternate between Adults 1 and 2, setting mastery at 5 out of 5 or 9 out of 10 unprompted correct responses.

▶ Step 2

Present SD2, which consists of Adult 1 presenting an exaggerated expression of crying (a sad face and "sobbing") and your asking, "Point to crying." Prompt, reinforce, and fade the prompt. Generalize to Adult 2 so that the emotional expression is not associated with a particular adult.

▶ Step 3

Intermix SD1 and SD2 according to the discrimination learning paradigm, placing mastery at 5 out of 5 or 9 out of 10 unprompted correct responses. Remember to randomly rotate between adults at all stages during this step and, once the random rotation phase of discrimination procedures is reached, also randomly rotate presentations of SD1 and SD2. At this point, you may want to include yourself as well as other adults for generalization purposes.

Expressive Labeling of Emotional Expressions in a 2-D Format

▶ Step 1

Present SD1, the initial picture of smiling used in the receptive identification component, while asking, "What is he doing?" (or just "Doing?"). Expressively prompt the response ("Smiling") or use receptive identification ("Point to smiling") as a prompt to help occasion the expressive label. Reinforce each correct response, and fade the prompt over the next several trials. Set mastery at 5 out of 5 or 9 out of 10 unprompted correct responses.

▶ Step 2

Present SD2, which replaces smiling with crying.

▶ Step 3

Intermix SD1 and SD2 according to the discrimination learning paradigm, setting mastery at 5 out of 5 or 9 out of 10 unprompted correct responses. Generalize across other pictures.

Expressive Labeling of Emotional Expressions In Vivo

Because verbally describing emotional expressions in vivo is basic to learning to label underlying feelings of emotional expressions, the current portion of the Emotions Program is presented in some detail. Retain the setting used in the previous section "Receptive Identification of Emotional Expressions In Vivo."

► **Step 1**

Present SD1, which consists of cueing Adult 1 to smile and then ask the student, "What is she doing?" Expressively prompt the answer "Smiling" for the student to imitate or use receptive identification to help occasion the expressive label. The latter prompt may be arranged by your saying, "Smile," to Adult 1 and, once the adult smiles, asking the student "What is she doing?" Make certain that both adults assume a neutral facial expression between the trials and that the onset of the smile is distinct and exaggerated and occurs concurrently with the instruction. Over successive trials, fade all prompts until the student independently responds by saying, "Smiling." A single-word response ("Smiling") is sufficient in the early parts of this program. In later steps, the student may be taught to respond in a complete sentence (e.g., "She is smiling"). Place mastery at 5 out of 5 or 9 out of 10 unprompted correct responses, then generalize to Adult 2.

► **Step 2**

Present SD2, in which Adult 1 presents an exaggerated expression of crying (a sad face and "sobbing") and you ask, "What is she doing?" Prompt the answer "Crying," following the same procedures used in Step 1. Set mastery at 5 out of 5 or 9 out of 10 unprompted correct responses, then generalize to Adult 2.

► **Step 3**

Intermix SD1 and SD2 according to discrimination learning procedures. Set the criterion for mastery at 9 out of 10 or 19 out of 20 unprompted correct responses. To facilitate the student's acquisition of the initial discrimination, both adults should maintain a neutral facial expression between trials, and the onset of the adult's exaggerated expressions should occur concurrently with your SDs so as to facilitate the student's attending to (discriminating) what you want the student to respond to.

Generalize the first two emotional expressions across several adults in vivo as was done in the receptive component of this program. Although you could introduce more labels of emotional expressions at this point, we prefer to teach the underlying feelings that correspond to the first two expressions. Once this skill is mastered, additional expressions may be introduced. Be aware that not all students master this component of the Emotions Program. For those students who have difficulty with vocal expressions, the Reading and Writing Program may prove to be an effective format for teaching emotions.

Teaching the Underlying Feelings of Emotional Expressions

Teaching the student the underlying feelings of particular emotional expressions proceeds as follows:

► **Step 1**

Present SD1, which consists of asking, "What is he doing?" as the adult smiles. The student should have previously mastered the answer, "Smiling." As soon as the student labels the facial expression and while the adult is still smiling, present the question "How is he feeling?" and immediately prompt the response "Happy." Reinforce the student for imitating the prompt. To further facilitate the student's response, you should enunciate the words "feeling" and "happy" clearly and loudly to help the student discriminate (attend to) the relevant parts of the questions. Both prompts should be faded over subsequent trials. Consider the response mastered when the student responds correctly to the adult's smile and your question, "How is he feeling?" in 5 out of 5 or 9 out of 10 unprompted trials.

We recommend that the student respond with the two separate answers "Smiling" and "Happy" to the respective questions "What is he doing?" and "How is he feeling?" on the assumption that the student will learn to associate the words "smiling" and "happy." However, if responding to two different questions proves too difficult, simply require the word "happy" in response to the question "How is he feeling" and the adult's smile (see Step 4 for more detail on implementing this format).

▶ Step 2

Repeat the procedures described in Step 1 using crying rather than smiling as the visual component of the stimuli. In this step, the response to SD2 "How is he feeling?" should be "Sad." Place criterion at 5 out of 5 or 9 out of 10 unprompted correct responses.

▶ Step 3

Teach the student to discriminate between the emotions happy and sad by intermixing SD1 and SD2 according to discrimination learning procedures. Both SD1 and SD2 are complex given that they each consist of three components: the adult's smiling or crying, the student's label "smiling" or "crying," and the question "How is he feeling?" It can be expected that the student will respond incorrectly upon transitions from SD1 to SD2, and vice versa, during the early stages of discrimination learning. The correct answers should therefore initially be prompted by using the least intrusive prompt that is effective. Place mastery at 9 out of 10 or 19 out of 20 unprompted correct responses. As mastery of the SD1–SD2 discrimination strengthens, you may want to extend the responses from "Happy" and "Sad" to "He is happy" and "He is sad." Note that such responses require mastery of pronouns. To minimize confusion, you refrain from attempting to teach pronouns at the same time as emotions (i.e., do not try to teach two skills at the same time). An upcoming volume on advanced programs outlines procedures for teaching the student to use pronouns.

It may seem unduly elaborate to present such complex instructions in teaching the student to label the underlying feelings of the overt expressions smiling and crying as "happy" and "sad," respectively. The reasoning behind using this procedure is that it often helps students associate the words "crying" and "sad" and the words "smiling" and "happy." The verbal labels are likely to mediate generalization between different physical expressions of the corresponding emotions. Should this procedure be too difficult for a particular student, and to test whether the student acquired the appropriate discrimination through this procedure, go on to Step 4, which may serve to establish or test the correct discrimination between the two emotions.

▶ Step 4

Through Steps 1 to 3, the student may have learned to associate the words "happy" and "sad" with the words "smiling" and "crying," respectively, rather than with the expression on the adult's face and your question, "How is he feeling?" Step 4 helps to correct this problem if it occurs. Begin by presenting SD1, which consists of having the adult smile without being verbally instructed to do so. While the adult is smiling, ask, "How is he feeling?" The correct answer is "Happy." If the student responds incorrectly or fails to respond, repeat the question, prompt, and then fade the prompt over subsequent trials. Place mastery at 5 out of 5 or 9 out of 10 unprompted correct responses.

▶ Step 5

Present SD2 by cueing (but not verbally instructing) the adult to cry and asking, "How is he feeling?" If necessary, prompt the correct response, "Sad." Place mastery at 5 out of 5 or 9 out of 10 unprompted correct responses.

▶ Step 6

Intermix SD1 and SD2 according to discrimination learning procedures. Mastery is reached when the student correctly responds to the SDs presented in random rotation in 9 out of 10 or 19 out of 20 unprompted responses.

Solidify this discrimination by generalizing it across different adults and environments over the next 1 to 2 weeks, extending it into everyday situations. Include in this generalization the student's parents and siblings, and involve the teaching of sentences as illustrated in answers such as "Mommy is happy" and "Baby is sad."

The Causes of Feelings

Once a minimum of two different expressions of emotions and their respective underlying feelings are mastered, teach the student to label the causes of feelings.

▶ **Step 1**

Present SD1 by cueing the second adult to smile and asking the student, "What is she feeling?" Immediately after the student gives the correct response "Happy," affectionately pat the adult on the back; ask, "Why is she happy?"; and then prompt, "Patting." The prompt should be faded until the student responds correctly without prompting in 5 out of 5 or 9 out of 10 responses.

▶ **Step 2**

Present SD2 by cueing the second adult to look sad and asking, "What is she feeling?" Immediately after the student gives the correct response, "Sad," look angry and mock slap one of the adult's arms; ask, "Why is she sad?"; and then prompt, "Hitting." Fade the prompt and place mastery at 5 out of 5 or 9 out of 10 unprompted correct responses.

▶ **Step 3**

Intermix SD1 and SD2 according to discrimination learning procedures. Place mastery at 9 out of 10 or 19 out of 20 unprompted correct responses.

▶ **Step 4**

It is essential to generalize the student's achievements from the formal teaching setting to everyday life. To generalize SD1 and SD2, first replace the original adults with new persons (including family members and friends) who have somewhat different ways of expressing the facial manifestations of happy and sad emotions. Next, generalize the causes of feelings. For example, take food away from an adult or yell at an adult to cue crying and feelings of sadness. Tell another person how smart and pretty she is or give her a present to cue smiling and happiness. If the student has a baby brother or sister, opportunities for teaching about feelings are numerous (e.g., before and after the baby is given the bottle, before and after a nap).

Once begun, training should proceed with increasing ease and be extended to everyday life. At some point into generalization, the student should be able to master the causes of various emotions after having them pointed out just one time. This is called one-trial learning (sometimes referred to as incidental learning). Once the student masters basic actions or causes after one trial, gradually shape his responses into phrases (e.g., "Because you are patting her" or "Because you are hitting him").

There are no hard and fast rules established concerning when the next emotion should be introduced. We suggest that the student be taught additional emotions depending on how quickly he mastered the discrimination between the first and second emotions. If the student mastered the first discrimination quickly (i.e., the student acquired the first discrimination in both the receptive and expressive components of the Emotions Program in 1 week of teaching with a total of 2 hours per day focusing on this program), then additional emotions may be introduced at the rate of one every other week. If the student mastered receptively and expressively identifying the first two emotions with moderate difficulty (e.g., after 20 days of practice with a total of 2 hours per day focusing on this program), do not teach a third emotion right away, but rather place the original two emotions on a maintenance schedule and teach the third emotion a month or two later. If the student required more than 20 days (or 40 hours) to achieve the receptive discrimination between the first two emotions, it may not be to the student's advantage to pursue the Emotions Program at the expense of teaching other skills at this point. Instead, we recommend introducing and expanding upon other programs, returning to the Emotions Program after a couple of months, or teaching emotions through the Reading and Writing Program (Chapter 29).

Teaching the Student To Label Her Own Feelings

It is of the utmost importance for the student to learn to generalize her understanding of others' feelings to her own feelings. Once the two basic feelings (i.e., happy and sad) are taught in reference to other persons, it is appropriate to teach the student to label her own emotional expressions and their underlying feelings.

This portion of the Emotions Program parallels the portion used to teach the student to label the emotions of others. Modify the present portion such that the student rather than the adult is prompted to smile (e.g., by being tickled or fed) and taught to answer the questions "How do you feel?" and, later, "Why are you happy?" After the student is taught to describe her happiness, she may be taught to describe her feelings of being sad. This may be done by frowning and mocking a spank to cue a crying response prompted through imitation of your wiping off pretend tears and moaning. Discrimination learning procedures should then be introduced. Once this initial discrimination is established in a controlled learning situation, the meaning of these feelings will be more fully acquired in the student's everyday environment as she encounters situations that naturally give rise to smiling and happiness or crying and sadness in other persons and herself. The student's learning to describe her own feelings marks a giant step in her development.

Once the student learns to discriminate and generalize the associations between smiling and being happy and crying and being sad, a third basic emotion such as anger may be introduced. Anticipate difficulties when teaching more complex feelings in which the cues are subtle and thus hard to discriminate, such as the distinction between sadness and guilt. Keep in mind that feelings are complex, and even a typical individual can spend an entire lifetime learning about them without ever achieving mastery.

What To Expect

Students differ widely in their rates of mastery of the Emotions Program. Some students master the discrimination between smiling and crying, the underlying feelings of these expressions, and the causes of the underlying feelings in less than 1 hour of one-on-one teaching. Others master the receptive discrimination between smiling and crying but fail to progress beyond that stage. Some of these same students, however, demonstrate progress when emotions are taught through the Reading and Writing Program.

The Emotions Program is one of the most recently developed programs. There is obviously a great need for objective outcome data on this and similar programs, as well as a need for systematic research to help identify more effective teaching procedures. We hope that the presentation of this program will facilitate such research.

Strategies for Visual Learners

SECTION 5

Reading and Writing: A Brief Introduction

CHAPTER 29

Nina W. Lovaas and Svein Eikeseth

The Reading and Writing (R&W) Program is the most recently developed program in this manual, hence the program most in need of more research and subsequent revisions. Despite this state of affairs, we judge it appropriate to introduce the program in part because experienced parents and aides have worked through preliminary drafts and offered many improvements. We hope that the R&W Program will stimulate empirical research, making it even more efficient to teach and thus more beneficial for students. Watthen-Lovaas and Lovaas (2000) describe in detail the portions of the R&W Program briefly introduced in this chapter, along with many additional reading and writing tasks, such as color, shape, and size concepts; writing short phrases, observations, and requests (e.g., "I see . . . ," "I have . . . ," "I want . . ."); and typing object labels and short sentences using a desktop or laptop computer (see Watthen-Lovaas & Lovaas, 2000).

Many or most students with developmental delays have difficulty acquiring vocal language and may be called visual learners as opposed to auditory learners Auditory learners usually acquire the language skills of typical individuals. In contrast, most visual learners acquire some vocal language, but they often obtain scores within the delayed range on language scales such as the *Reynell Developmental Language Scales* (Reynell & Gruber, 1990). Visual learners also typically obtain relatively low scores on scales of intelligence containing many verbal items (e.g., the *Wechsler Intelligence Scale for Children–Third Edition* [Wechsler, 1991]), but perform better on nonverbal scales of intelligence (e.g., the *Merrill-Palmer Scale of Mental Tests* [Stutsman, 1984a, 1984b]). Even though the R&W Program is likely to be particularly helpful for visual learners, auditory learners and typical individuals must learn to read and write as well. Thus, although the present program was developed for teaching students with developmental delays who have difficulty acquiring vocal language, it may also be useful for teaching auditory learners and typical individuals.

Certain informal observations of visual learners who possess little or no receptive or expressive language may give rise to optimism regarding their ability to attend to certain stimuli. For example, some students enjoy looking at books and pointing to pictures contained therein, anticipating sequences of visual material as the pages are turned. Others are interested in letters and memorize the order of the alphabet, and many are able to complete age-appropriate puzzles. Some have the capacity to memorize complex visual stimuli, such as printed strings of numbers and specific routes of travel. On a more dramatic scale, some students who otherwise seem oblivious to their surroundings are observed absorbing complex information when they watch certain videos. For example, a student may watch a certain video for the first time and observe a frightening scene, such as a bad animal attacking a good animal. When this student watches the same video in the future, she may anticipate the frightening scene and back away from the television set, cover her ears, or leave the room, returning as soon as the scary scene passes. This sort of scenario suggests that even visual learners with little or no vocal language skills are capable of assimilating certain kinds of information.

Prior to introducing the R&W Program to students, teachers should be made aware of the large range of differences among visual learners, differences that become apparent through the extent of mastery of the program. For instance, out of 20 visual learners exposed to the R&W Program, an estimated 5 may learn to read and write messages using a computer and communicate sentences such as "I want juice"; type the answer, "My name is (student's name)," to their parents' typed question, "What's your name?"; and request outings such as, "Let's go to the zoo." This level of communication may be observed in students who have made significant progress in nonverbal programs (such as those described in Chapters 12 and 13) but who have failed to acquire even the simplest forms of vocal receptive and expressive language despite months of intensive one-on-one intervention implemented by highly qualified teachers. In contrast, some students fail to master even the most elementary reading and writing skills (e.g., word-to-word matching and object-to-word associations) despite extensive teaching efforts. At present, we are unable to predict at onset to what extent a particular student will succeed in the R&W Program. No current theory of autism or other developmental delays can account for these differences, but leads may be found in future research on language disorders.

The R&W Program is not the first program proposed for helping individuals with autism and other developmental delays communicate by means of visual stimuli. In the mid-1960s, O. K. Moore's "Talking Typewriter" was designed to help meet this need. More recently, strong sentiments were expressed for the benefits of Facilitated Communication (Biklen, 1991, 1992; Biklen, Morton, Gold, Berrigan, & Swaminanthan, 1992; Biklen et al., 1991; Crossley & Remington-Gurney, 1992; Spake, 1992). The claims made by proponents of these programs, however, were not supported by empirical research (Eberlin, McConnachie, Ibel & Volpe, 1992), possibly because of the many misleading assumptions that exist regarding individuals with autism. For example, in the case of Facilitated Communication (and psychodynamic theory), the assumption is made that an informed and knowledgeable individual is hidden within a shell of autism. Little or no evidence supports such an inference. In contrast, the R&W Program is based on scientifically sound learning-based research on teaching students with developmental delays to communicate by visual means (see Dube, McDonald, McIlvane, & Mackay, 1991; Hewitt, 1964; Mackay, 1985; Sidman, 1971; Stromer & Mackay, 1992).

The R&W Program, as introduced in this chapter, takes the reader through the progression of the following tasks: (1) matching printed letters, (2) matching printed words, (3) associating printed words with objects and objects with printed words, (4) using a R&W Board to facilitate early reading and writing skills, and (5) using letters to spell words. Note that throughout this chapter, letters and words printed on cards are denoted by placing them inside brackets. For example, **[i]** refers to a card with the letter *i* printed on it, and **[banana]** refers to a card with "banana" printed on it. The word *banana* without brackets (and without quotation marks) refers to a 3-D banana or a picture of a banana.

The R&W Program closely parallels the vocal language programs described in this manual. For example, in the Verbal Imitation Program (Chapter 22), the student is first taught to verbally imitate (i.e., match) the teacher's expressions of sounds such as "ah" and "m," then spoken words, and finally combinations of spoken words. In the R&W Program, the student is first taught to match the same units but presented as visual rather than vocal stimuli, such as matching printed letters and, later, printed words. In the receptive portion of the vocal language programs, the student is presented with a vocal stimulus and taught to act upon it. For example, the student is taught to identify (e.g., by pointing to or touching) a picture of a banana after the teacher says, "Banana." Analogously, in the R&W Program, the student is shown the printed word **[banana]** and then taught to identify the object or the picture of a banana. In the R&W Program, the printed word replaces the teacher's vocal word. In the expressive portions of the vocal language programs, the teacher presents a visual stimulus, for example, a cup, and the student is taught to vocalize the correct response, saying, "Cup." In the expressive portion of the R&W Program, the teacher presents the same visual stimulus, a cup. The student is taught to describe the cup by selecting the corresponding printed response **[cup]** from a display of several word cards. Later the student learns to spell out the word "cup" longhand or type it on a computer keyboard. The written or typed response replaces the vocal response.

It is entirely possible, however, for a student to learn to read words and strings of words without knowing their meanings. Such behavior is referred to as "testing" in contrast to "reading." Hewett (1964) referred to this problem in teaching his student to read. The meanings of words are acquired by learning the environmental context with which they are associated. The more a student is taught to interact with and attend to the environment, the more extensive and useful the R&W Program will become. Consequently, we recommend that the R&W Program be taught in conjunction with other programs in this teaching manual.

It is important to read the entire chapter and become familiar with its overall progression before going on to teach the skills introduced in it. In addition, experience with programs presented earlier in this manual (including programs with an emphasis on vocal language) will help you administer the R&W Program more effectively. It may also help you to practice some of the teaching steps presented in this chapter on an adult before introducing the student to the program.

Prerequisites for the introduction of the first phases of the R&W Program (Matching Letters and Matching Words) consist of the student's ability to cooperate with you and mastery of basic matching and nonverbal imitation tasks (Chapters 12 and 13, respectively). In addition, you must show that you can teach these tasks successfully.

Matching Letters

The materials needed to teach letter matching consist largely of 3 × 5- or 4 × 6-inch index cards with letters printed on them.

Learning to match letters may be facilitated by presenting relatively large letters, at least 1 inch high, whether handwritten or typed (e.g., in point size 72, bold font). If the letters are handwritten, all the letter cards should initially be written by one person and later generalized to other persons' handwriting.

To facilitate the student's discriminations, begin with letters that are maximally different in appearance. For illustrative purposes, the letters [S], [I], and [O] correspond to SD1, SD2, and SD3, respectively. Note that in the following steps, the letters [S], [I], and [O] displayed on the table represent the samples. Duplicate letters [S], [I], and [O] represent the matches that are handed to the student one by one to be matched with (placed with) the corresponding samples on the table. Throughout the following steps, you and the student should be seated across from each other at the table (assuming you have good control in this situation).

▶ Step 1

Mass trial SD1–R1 to mastery (the student matches [S] to [S]). Place the sample [S] on the table in front of the student, then hand him the match [S] while stating, "Match." Prompt the correct response immediately either by pointing to the sample [S] or by manually guiding the student to place his [S] (the match) on top of the sample. Reinforce the correct prompted response. While mass trialing SD1, place the sample in random positions on the table. Remove the stimuli between trials, presenting the stimuli again at the beginning of each trial. This procedure maximizes the discreteness of the stimuli presentation and thus the likelihood that the student will attend to them. Keep the intervals between trials at less than 5 seconds to help inhibit self-stimulatory and other off-task behaviors. Over the next several trials, fade all prompts and maximize reinforcement for unprompted correct responses. Set mastery at 5 out of 5 or 9 out of 10 unprompted correct responses.

▶ Step 2

Mass trial SD2–R2 to mastery (the student matches [I] to [I]). Place the sample [I] on the table and then give the student the match [I] while saying, "Match." Adhere to the same teaching procedures and criterion for mastery described in Step 1.

▶ Step 3

Intermix SD1 and SD2. Place both samples, [S] and [I], on the table, equidistant from the student's midline. Allow approximately 4 to 6 inches between the two letters. Present SD1 [S] and immediately prompt R1 in order to avoid a nonreinforced trial. Mass trial SD1 while fading all prompts, including removal of the match from on top of the sample after each trial. Place mastery of SD1 at 3 unprompted correct responses in a row with the left–right positions of the samples [S] and [I] randomly interchanged and equidistant from the student. Within 2 seconds of the student's achieving mastery of SD1–R1, present SD2, the match [I], with both samples [S] and [I] on the table. Immediately prompt the student's correct response. Mass trial SD2 while fading all prompts. Set mastery of SD2 at 3 unprompted correct responses in a row. Over the next several trials, alternate back and forth between blocks of SD1 [S] and SD2 [I], requiring 2 unprompted correct responses before shifting SDs and then 1 correct response before shifting SDs. Randomly interchange the left–right positions of the samples [S] and [I] throughout this process. Place mastery at 5 out of 5 or 9 out of 10 unprompted correct responses with the presentation of the SDs and the left–right positions of the samples randomly rotated.

▶ Step 4

Mass trial SD3–R3 to mastery (matching [O] to [O]). Follow the teaching procedures described in Step 1. Once SD3–R3 is mastered in mass trials, go on to Step 5.

▶ Step 5

Intermix and differentially reinforce SD3–R3 (matching [O] to [O]) and SD1–R1 (matching [S] to [S]), adhering to the discrimination learning procedures described in Step 3. Once the SD3–SD1 discrimination is mastered, intermix SD3 with SD2 (matching [I] to [I]), adhering to the same procedures. Finally, intermix SD1, SD2, and SD3. Remember, to eliminate extraneous and inadvertent cues, you must randomly rotate the positions of the three samples on the table and the presentation of the matches.

Once the student can place five or more matches with their samples displayed simultaneously on the table (preferably in two parallel rows), alternate between giving the student one match at a time and handing the student a stack of two and then three letter cards to be matched. With an increasing number of matches in hand (maximum four) and samples on the table (e.g., 12 displayed in three rows), the student's attention to the task (i.e., persistence) is likely to increase. Keep in mind that increased attention and work output are functions of how reinforcing the particular task is for the student. For most students, matching becomes very reinforcing.

After the student masters the matching of uppercase letters, teach the student to match lowercase letters by following the teaching procedures just presented for uppercase letters. After the student masters lowercase and uppercase letter matching separately, it may be appropriate to teach the equivalence of lowercase and uppercase letters. However, it is likely that the student will make larger educational and functional gains by learning this skill concurrent with typing. Procedures for teaching the equivalence of lowercase and uppercase letters as well as the skill of typing are described in detail by Watthen-Lovaas and Lovaas (2000).

Matching Words

In this phase of the R&W Program, the student learns to match printed words; that is, she learns to attend to (discriminate among) words. Later, printed words will be placed in context with objects and actions, making the words meaningful and functional.

Use approximately 1-inch tall words typed or handwritten in lowercase letters on 4 × 6-inch index cards. The first four to six words should be maximally different from one another in appearance (e.g., **[cat]**, **[dinosaur]**, **[apple]**) to facilitate the student's discrimination among them. The teaching procedures are the same as those detailed in the previous section on letter matching and are simply summarized in this section to reduce redundancy.

During mass trial procedures in Steps 1 and 2, teach the student to place the match **[cat]** with the sample **[cat]** (Step 1) and to place the match **[dinosaur]** with the sample **[dinosaur]** (Step 2). During discrimination learning procedures in Step 3, teach the student to match **[cat]** to **[cat]** and **[dinosaur]** to **[dinosaur]** with the left–right positions of the samples **[cat]** and **[dinosaur]** randomly interchanged on the table and equidistant from the student. Hand the student the match cards one at a time in random order. Set mastery at 5 out of 5 or 9 out of 10 unprompted correct responses for each step. New words should be introduced and intermixed according to these same procedures.

Once the student masters matching 10 to 15 words that have obvious perceptual differences, gradually increase the complexity of the task by reducing these differences (e.g., **[milk]** and **[mom]**, **[book]** and **[bottle]**, **[swing]** and **[frog]**). Eventually, teach the student to discriminate between words such as **[car]** and **[cat]** and **[truck]** and **[duck]**. Once such discriminations are mastered, words that play more functional roles for the student should be introduced. For example, introduce words denoting favorite foods (e.g., spaghetti, muffin, juice, chips, cracker), close persons (e.g., mom, dad, names of siblings and teachers), common clothing (e.g., shirt, shorts, pants, dress, shoes, hat), common furniture (e.g., table, chair, couch, bed, dresser), and animals the student shows interest in (e.g., cat, dog, horse, duck, giraffe, lion, monkey). Also introduce words such as crayon, marker, paper, scissors, glue, paint, and brush (if the student is learning art skills) and actions such as open, tickle, kiss, eat, and swing (if the student enjoys engaging in these behaviors). Keep in mind that even if the student is able to match words (whether in their auditory or visual form), there is no reason to believe that the student knows the meanings of the words. The skills of associating printed words with their corresponding objects and associating objects with their respective labels are introduced under the later section "Associations."

Areas of Difficulty

Discriminating between words of similar appearance may be difficult for some students. Visual prompts such as underlining the letters that mark the difference between the words (e.g., underline the "r" in "car" and the "t" in "cat") may prove helpful in such a situation. Marking the discriminative letters with different colors or printing discriminative letters in a larger font may also facilitate the student's attention to them. Remember, all prompts must be faded for the student to establish the correct discrimination.

Associations

In an attempt to facilitate the student's success in subsequent stages of the R&W Program and his acquisition of more flexible reading and writing skills, we have constructed two preliminary steps: (1) Associating Printed Words with Objects (which later extends into reading) and (2) Associating Objects with Printed Words (which later extends into writing). At this point, we do not have enough data to ascertain whether these preliminary steps are necessary for progressing toward the more advanced reading and writing stages; however, by establishing these associative skills, you are provided with an effective means of prompting the student's progress in subsequent portions of the R&W Program, thereby facilitating his discriminations.

Associating Printed Words with Objects

In the preliminary steps of early reading, place objects on the table and teach the student to place a word card directly below the object denoted by the printed word. As previously advised, the stimuli involved in the initial discriminations should be as different from one another as possible to facilitate the student's acquisition of these discriminations. In illustrating the following steps, SD1 is an airplane, SD2 is a sock, and SD3 is a pig. The teaching steps are virtually identical to those described in the previous section on matching letters and are therefore described in relative brevity below.

▶ **Step 1**

Mass trial SD1–R1 to mastery (the student places **[airplane]** with the 3-D airplane). With the airplane (as the only object) positioned on the table, state, "Match," while handing the student **[airplane]**. Prompt the correct response (i.e., the placement of **[airplane]** directly below the airplane). Reinforce. Fade the prompt over subsequent trials. Set mastery at 5 out of 5 or 9 out of 10 unprompted correct responses. Once mastery is achieved, go on to Step 2.

▶ **Step 2**

Mass trial SD2–R2 to mastery (the student places **[sock]** with the sock). The sock is the only object on the table. Follow the procedures described in Step 1 until mastery of SD2–R2 is reached.

▶ **Step 3**

Begin with the objects airplane and sock placed on the table equidistant from the student's midline, allowing a space of about 4 to 6 inches between the two objects. Intermix SD1 and SD2 according to discrimination learning procedures (see Step 3 of the section "Matching Letters"), and set mastery at 5 out of 5 or 9 out of 10 unprompted correct responses.

If the student makes an error during discrimination training in Step 3 (e.g., by placing **[airplane]** with the sock), interrupt the response by retrieving the match and give an informational "No." Immediately repeat the SD, prompting and reinforcing the correct response. Over successive intermixed and differentially reinforced trials, the student should make fewer and fewer mistakes and eventually master the discrimination. That is, the associations between SD1–R1 and SD2–R2 are strengthened because they are reinforced, whereas mistakes such as SD1–R2 and SD2–R1 are weakened because they are not reinforced. Set mastery at 5 out of 5 or 9 out of 10 unprompted correct responses.

Areas of Difficulty

A student may experience difficulty associating printed words with 3-D objects, particularly when the associations involve 3-D objects with which the student has a history of learning. It may be that such objects cue behaviors (e.g., retrieving or manipulating the objects) that are incompatible with the placement of a printed label below the objects. Introduce new and unfamiliar objects to help avoid this problem. If the problem persists with entirely new objects, place the task on hold and introduce an alternative task: associating words with 2-D objects. To create the stimuli needed for this format, photograph the target 3-D objects against a neutral, solid-colored background. All photographs should be of equal size (e.g., 4 × 6 inches). To facilitate this requirement, choose relatively small objects and photograph them close-up. To maximize the benefit of using 2-D stimuli, teach the student to match picture to picture and then pictures to their corresponding 3-D objects as prerequisite requirements to associating words with their corresponding 2-D pictures.

Associating Objects with Printed Words

In the preliminary steps of early writing, the words and the objects used as stimuli should be maximally different in appearance. For example, if the object car placed with the printed word **[car]** is the first association, then dinosaur with **[dinosaur]** may be a good choice for the second association, and baby associated with **[baby]** would be appropriate for the third association. Discriminations may also be facilitated by presenting objects in which the student has shown some prior interest. The discrimination learning procedures are the same as those described in the previous section "Matching Letters." Steps 1, 2, and 3 are summarized below.

In Step 1, teach the student to place the object car below the word **[car]**. Position the word **[car]** in random positions on the table across trials. In Step 2, teach the student to place the object dinosaur with the word **[dinosaur]** that is randomly positioned on the table across trials. In Step 3, teach the student according to discrimination learning procedures to place the objects car and dinosaur with their corresponding word cards, **[car]** and **[dinosaur],** both displayed simultaneously on the table and in random positions.

Introduce and intermix new associations (e.g., associating the object baby with **[baby]**) according to these same procedures. Once the student masters 10 to 12 associations among 3-D objects and their corresponding printed words, teach generalization from 3-D objects to 2-D representations of objects, followed by generalization across nonidentical 3-D objects (i.e., keep the classes of the objects consistent but vary their size, shape, and color). Continue to teach new associations between 3-D and 2-D objects and their corresponding printed words. Gradually increase the number of word cards displayed on the table to six or more placed in two parallel rows.

Areas of Difficulty

If the student excessively manipulates any of the 3-D objects, select other objects that are less interesting to him. If the student is confused as to where to place the objects, prompt correct placement as follows: Place a white sheet of paper on the table and position the word card (e.g., **[car]**) on the upper half of the paper. With a pencil, draw a dotted outline of the object car on the paper directly below **[car]** to help prompt the placement of the object. Present SD1 by stating, "Match," while handing the student the car. Manually prompt the student to place the car inside the dotted area. Fade the dotted outline by gradually erasing more and more of it on each subsequent trial. Finally, remove the paper. If the student fails to respond correctly at any point, go back and introduce the least amount of prompt necessary to reinstate correct responding, then start fading the prompt again at a slower rate.

Using an R&W Board

In this phase of the R&W Program, the student is taught to use an R&W Board to facilitate early forms of reading and writing. In the Early Reading Skills section, the student learns to generalize the association of printed words with objects from the table to the R&W Board; that is, a printed word is presented at the top of the board and the student is taught to read the word and to identify the object or behavior described by the word from several alternative stimuli displayed further down on the board (in the response field). In the Early Writing Skills section, the student learns to generalize the association of objects with printed words from the table to the R&W Board. That is, an object is displayed at the top of the board and the student is taught to select the printed label corresponding to that object from a display of several words on the Board. The Early Writing Skills section is a precursor to more advanced writing programs, such as those describing how to use letters to compose words when instructed to label objects, behaviors, and desires. We have found it easier to teach writing tasks by beginning with whole words (i.e., word cards) rather than individual letters. Spelling out words is taught in the later section titled "Writing Object Labels."

A basic R&W Board can be made as follows:

1. Create an approximately 20 × 18-inch rectangular board using ⅛-inch thick white cardboard, posterboard, or dry erase board. Adjust the size of the board according to the size of the student.
2. Attach a ½-inch wide strip of black Velcro horizontally across the top of the board, 1½ inches from the top and 1 inch in from either side of the board. Attach instructions on this horizontal strip, referred to as the *instruction strip*.
3. Attach two strips of black Velcro vertically on the board 1 to 2 inches in from the sides (one strip on each side) and about 3 inches down from the top and up from the bottom of the board. From these two vertical strips, referred to as the *choice strips*, the student will choose stimuli in response to the teacher's instruction.
4. Attach a strip of black Velcro horizontally across the board about 1½ inches from the bottom of the board and 1 inch in from either side of the board. The student places the stimuli she selects in response to the teacher's instruction on this strip, referred to as the *response strip*.
5. In the middle of the board, on the area between the two black choice strips, attach two white strips

of Velcro (*prompt strips*) parallel to the choice strips and about 2 to 3 inches apart. Visual prompts may be attached to these two strips. Use the hook side of the Velcro for all strips on the board. (See Figure 29.1 for a sample R&W Board.)

Use a bold font of approximately point size 56 when making word cards to be used on the R&W Board and use cards that are 3 × 5 inches. Laminate the word cards, or use contact paper if lamination is not available. Each word card should have a Velcro dot or strip on the back so that the student can attach and remove the cards from the choice strips and response strip with ease. Use the loop (soft bushy) side of the Velcro on all word cards and other 2-D material. The board should be placed flat on the table within easy reach of the student or at an angle on an easel.

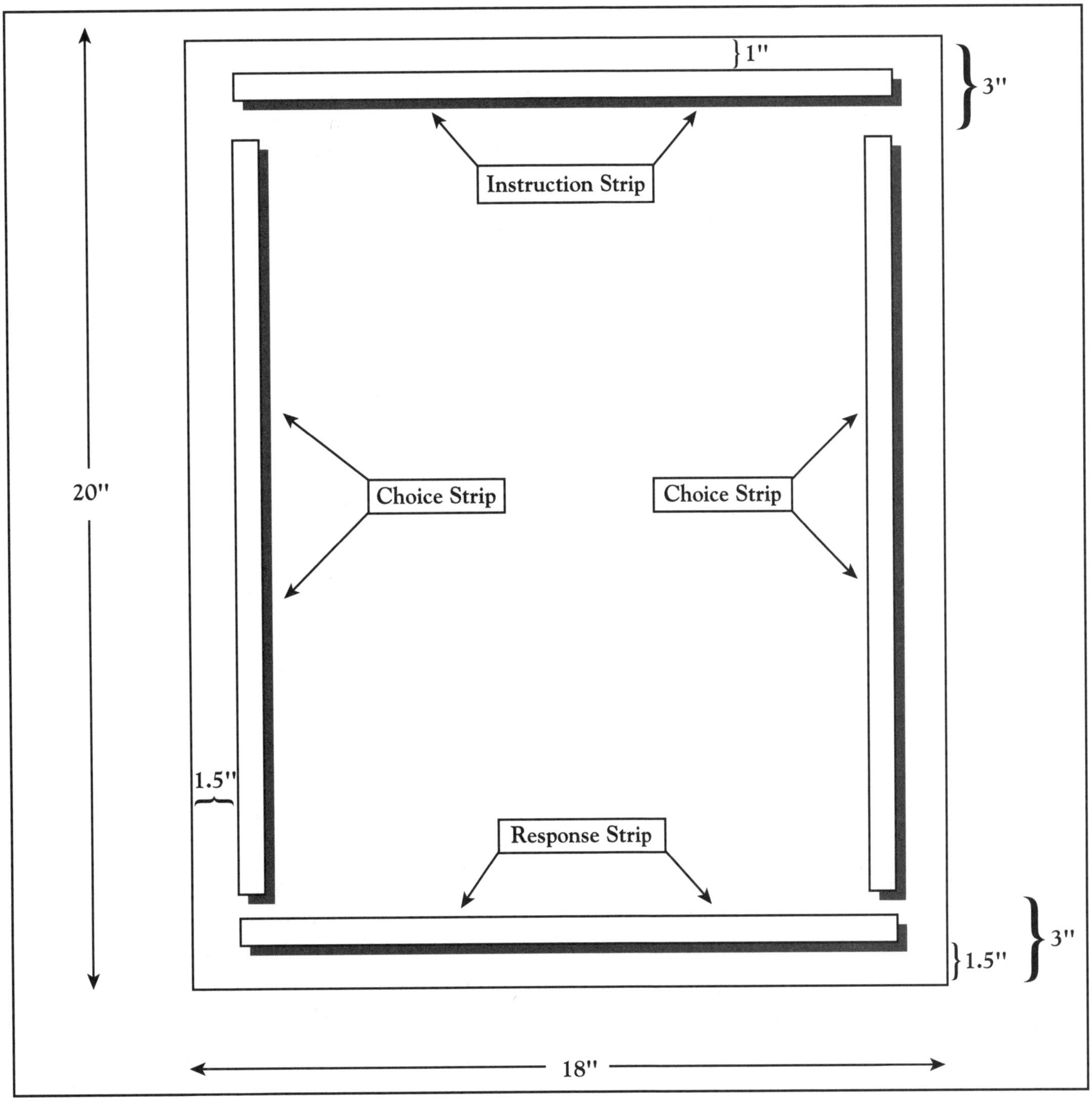

Figure 29.1. The Reading and Writing (R&W) Board.

For teaching an early reading task, a printed instruction, such as **[Touch] [duck]**, is presented on the instruction strip. A 3-D duck is displayed on the lower half of the Board (i.e., in the response field). The student is taught to read the instruction and to identify the correct object by touching it. Gradually, additional objects are displayed in the response field. When teaching an early writing task on the board, the teacher presents a printed instruction, such as **[What is it?]**, with an object, such as a 3-D duck, adjacent to it on the instruction strip. The student is taught to attend to this SD, select the word card **[duck]** that is displayed on a choice strip, and place the word card on the response strip. In a sense, the student "writes" her response using a word card. Additional word cards are gradually displayed on the choice strips while one object is presented on the instruction strip with the printed instruction **[What is it?]**. When spelling is introduced, the teacher presents the instruction **[What is it?]** and, for example, a duck on the instruction strip. The letters **[d]**, **[u]**, **[c]**, and **[k]** are displayed on the choice strips and the student is taught to spell the word by placing the letters one by one in the correct order from left to right on the response strip. Gradually, distracter letters are added to the choice strips.

Matching Words on the R&W Board

Familiarize the student with the R&W Board by generalizing her word matching skills from matching on the table to matching on the board. Place the board on the table in front of the student, and sit next to her. For illustrative purposes, SD1–R1 is matching **[cat]** to **[cat]**, and SD2–R2 is matching **[juice]** to **[juice]**.

▶ **Step 1**

Place the sample **[cat]** centered on the board and positioned just above the response strip; that is, place the word card on a prompt strip. In this position, the word card is close to the response strip and, therefore, facilitates a correct response. Hand the match **[cat]** to the student while saying, "Match." Prompt the student to place the match on the response strip directly below the sample. After this stage is mastered, position the match word **[cat]** on a choice strip instead of handing it to the student, and teach her to remove the word card from the choice strips and then place it on the response strip directly below the sample word **[cat]**. Over trials, gradually move the sample up to the instruction strip while the student continues to use the response strip for placement of the match. Display the match card in random positions on either choice strip. Place mastery at 5 out of 5 or 9 out of 10 unprompted correct responses.

▶ **Step 2**

Follow the procedures described in the previous step to teach the student to pick the match **[juice]** from a choice strip and place it on the response strip with the sample **[juice]** on the instruction strip. Place mastery at 5 out of 5 or 9 out of 10 unprompted correct responses.

▶ **Step 3**

Present the samples **[cat]** (SD1) and **[juice]** (SD2) one at a time on the instruction strip, starting with **[cat]**, and display the matches **[cat]** and **[juice]** simultaneously and in random positions on the choice strips. Intermix SD1 and SD2 according to discrimination learning procedures. After mastery is reached (5 out of 5 or 9 out of 10 unprompted correct responses), teach the student to match additional words, gradually increasing the number of word cards (matches) displayed on the choice strips to 6 to 12 cards (while only one sample card is presented on the instruction strip at a time). After each completed correct response, you should return the match to a random place on one of the choice strips to limit inadvertent prompts.

Once the student learns to match 15 to 20 words on the R&W Board, begin teaching the student early reading skills as outlined in the next section.

Early Reading Skills

There is a great deal of overlap between the Early Reading Skills section of the R&W Program and the Receptive Identification of Objects Program presented in Chapter 17, and we recommend that you become familiar with the procedures used in that chapter before introducing this section. In the vocal language program in Chapter 17, the student is taught to identify (e.g., point to or touch) an object after you verbally request the student to do so. In the present section, you replace the verbal request with a printed request; effectively, the student is taught to generalize the skills taught in the previous section "Associating Printed Words with Objects."

When you present printed instructions in this section, we recommend verbalizing them in addition to pointing to them. This recommendation is based on the *informal* observation that some students begin to understand your vocalizations when they are combined with their visual counterparts. That is, over time, some students learn to identify the target objects without the written word present. Although such incidental teaching is often effective for typical students, little formal research has shown its effectiveness for children with autism or other developmental delays. Nonetheless, informal observations warrant use of this procedure unless it becomes apparent that your vocalizations actually interfere with the student's learning to read. For students who have mastered Receptive Identification of Objects (Chapter 17) prior to the introduction of this section, however, we advise that you say, "Read," while pointing to the printed instruction *without* verbalizing the printed SD. The steps that follow are illustrated using this format. In this case, the printed SD should be verbalized only when used as a prompt; otherwise, there is no reason for the student to attend to the printed word. Fade the verbal prompt over trials to ensure that the student actually learns to read.

Stimuli from discriminations mastered in earlier sections of the R&W Program may facilitate the discrimination tasks taught in this section. To further facilitate the student's acquisition of early reading skills, we recommend beginning with 3-D objects. Note, however, that some students have difficulty learning when 3-D stimuli are used. If this is true for the student you work with, shift to 2-D stimuli, but continue to proceed according to the following steps.

For illustrative purposes, SD1, SD2, and SD3 correspond to the printed word card **[Touch]** in addition to **[airplane]**, **[sock]**, and **[pig]**, respectively.

▶ Step 1

Mass trial SD1–R1 to mastery (the student reads **[Touch] [airplane]** then touches the 3-D airplane). Begin by placing the airplane in a prompted position 2 inches below the instruction strip (i.e., on a prompt strip). Next, place the printed instruction **[Touch]** approximately 3 inches from the word card **[airplane]** on the instruction strip, positioning the word card **[airplane]** directly above the airplane. Point to the word card **[Touch]** while saying, "Touch," then immediately point to **[airplane]**. Manually prompt the student to touch the airplane as she attends to **[airplane]**. Remove the stimuli between trials and fade the manual prompt over the next few trials. Note that the close proximity of the airplane to the word card **[airplane]** functions as a prompt. Fade the prompted position of the airplane by gradually increasing the distance between the airplane and the instruction strip both in vertical and horizontal directions, eventually randomizing its position in the response field. This prompt fading procedure teaches the student to search for the airplane once she reads the word **[airplane]**. In this way, irrelevant stimuli are reduced while scanning for the correct object is facilitated. Set mastery at 5 out of 5 or 9 out of 10 unprompted correct responses. Once this step is mastered, go on to Step 2.

If the choice strips, vertical prompt strips, and response strip interfere with the placement of the 3-D objects on the board, turn the board over and use the back for reading tasks. Place a black Velcro instruction strip lengthwise at the top of the board and two white prompt strips parallel to the instruction strip and spaced about 3 to 4 inches apart for the display of 3-D stimuli.

▶ Step 2

Mass trial SD2–R2 (the student reads **[Touch] [sock]** then touches the 3-D sock). Follow the teaching procedures described in Step 1. Set mastery at 5 out of 5 or 9 out of 10 unprompted correct responses.

▶ Step 3

Center the airplane and the sock on the lower half of the board in the response field and begin with presentations of SD1. Intermix SD1 and SD2 according to discrimination learning procedures.

Once the student can discriminate between SD1 and SD2, generalize mastery of this discrimination across all teachers before introducing SD3. SD3–R3 (reading **[Touch] [pig]**, then touching the pig) should initially be taught in mass trials and then intermixed with SD1 and SD2 as previously described.

As the student masters new SDs, increase the number of object choices presented at one time in the response field from three to six or seven, depending on the student's rate of progress and the size of the board. With several objects placed randomly on the board, it is likely that irrelevant and interfering stimuli will be reduced or eliminated, thereby solidifying the student's mastery of the discriminations. Once the student learns to discriminate among the printed labels of 10 to 15 objects, introduce 2-D representations of the 3-D stimuli (see the following section, "Areas of Difficulty," for guidelines on teaching this skill). As the student learns to generalize to 2-D stimuli, continue to teach new 3-D objects. Once the student has established mastery of approximately 25 discriminations in the original format, generalize to nonidentical 3-D and then nonidentical 2-D stimuli. Teach 15 to 50 object identifications, depending on the student's rate of learning.

Areas of Difficulty

When you verbalize the entire SD in addition to presenting the printed material (e.g., you say, "Touch airplane," while pointing to the word cards **[Touch]** and **[airplane]**) and use the word "touch" across many objects, there is no reason to believe that the student learns the meaning of the word "touch." In fact, the introduction of the word "touch" may interfere with or block the student's acquisition of the meaning of the word identifying the object.

If the student encounters difficulty with instructions such as **[Touch] [airplane]** when contrasted with other instructions such as **[Touch] [sock]**, increase their discriminability by removing the **[Touch]** word card. Once the discriminations are made between the most relevant portions of the instructions (i.e., **[airplane]** vs. **[sock]** in this example), reintroduce **[Touch]**.

Some students experience difficulty associating 3-D objects with printed words. If this is true for the student you work with, try using 2-D pictures instead of 3-D objects (see Figure 29.2). A visual prompt (similar to the prompt described in the earlier section "Associating Objects with Printed Words") may be helpful, and is described in the following steps.

▶ **Step 1**

Mass trial SD1–R1 to mastery (reading **[Touch] [airplane]**, then touching the picture of the airplane). Begin by placing **[Touch]** and **[airplane]** on the instruction strip. Display a picture of the 3-D airplane in a prompted position about 2 inches below the instruction strip. Place a duplicate word card **[airplane]** (i.e., a prompt card) directly below the picture of the airplane. Point to the instruction **[Touch]**; say, "Touch"; then point to **[airplane]** on the instruction strip. Manually prompt the student to touch the picture of the airplane. Remove the stimuli between trials. Over the next several trials, increase the distance between **[airplane]** on the instruction strip and the picture of the airplane until the picture is positioned anywhere on the lower half of the board (i.e., the position prompt is faded). In addition, fade the prompt card **[airplane]** over trials by gradually sliding it under the picture of the airplane. Set mastery at 5 out of 5 or 9 out of 10 unprompted correct responses.

▶ **Step 2**

Mass trial SD2–R2 to mastery (reading **[Touch] [sock]**, then touching the picture of the sock). Follow the procedures described in Step 1.

▶ **Step 3**

Place the picture of the airplane and the picture of the sock 3 to 4 inches apart on the lower half of the board. Reinstate the prompt cards (i.e., place the prompt cards **[airplane]** and **[sock]** below the corresponding pictures). Start by presenting SD1 (**[Touch] [airplane]**) and intermix SD1 and SD2 according to the discrimination learning paradigm. First fade the manual prompt, then fade the prompt cards by *simultaneously* and in gradual increments sliding them under their respective pictures. Probe unprompted trials in an effort to reduce the number of prompted trials. Randomly rotate the positions of the pictures to avoid position prompting. Place mastery at 5 out of 5 or 9 out of 10 unprompted correct responses with the SDs presented in random rotation.

Early Writing Skills

You should be familiar with the Expressive Labeling of Objects Program (Chapter 23) because much of the information concerning the teaching of expressive vocal language pertains to teaching visual learners how to express themselves using printed language. In this section of the R&W Program, the student is taught to label an object using the printed word that corresponds to it.

We recommend starting with stimuli the student was exposed to in earlier sections of this program. For illustrative purposes, dinosaur is used as SD1, car is used as SD2, and doll is used as SD3.

▶ **Step 1**

Mass trial SD1–R1 to mastery (the object dinosaur cues the placement of **[dinosaur]**). First,

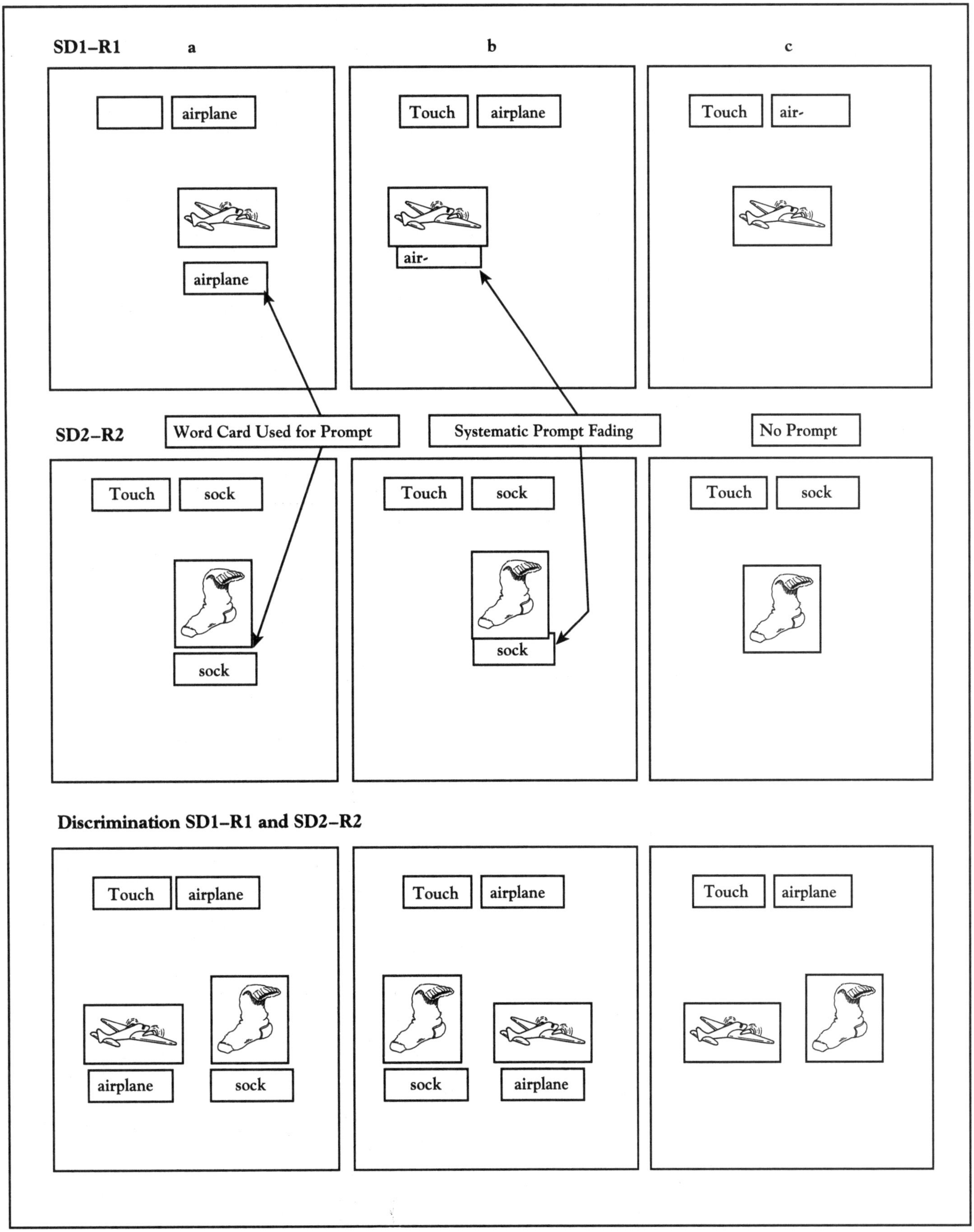

Figure 29.2. Reading: Identifying two-dimensional objects.

place **[What is it?]** on the instruction strip and **[dinosaur]** on the choice strip in a prompted position close to the response strip. Next, center the 3-D dinosaur on the R&W Board about 3 inches above the response strip (i.e., in a prompted position). Point to the printed instruction **[What is it?]**; say, "What is it?"; and then immediately point to the dinosaur. Prompt the student to remove **[dinosaur]** from the choice strip and place it on the response strip directly below the dinosaur. You may have to manually prompt the student's movements. After fading the manual prompt, gradually fade the position prompt by moving the dinosaur away from the response strip and toward the instruction strip. Display the word card **[dinosaur]** in random position on the choice strips. Once the student can correctly retrieve the word card from random positions, gradually move the dinosaur to its final position adjacent to **[What is it?]** on the instruction strip. Place mastery at 5 out of 5 or 9 out of 10 unprompted correct responses.

▶ **Step 2**

Mass trial SD2–R2 to mastery (the object car cues the placement of **[car]**) by following the procedures outlined in the previous step. Again set mastery at 5 out of 5 or 9 out of 10 unprompted correct responses. Once mastery is achieved, go on to Step 3.

▶ **Step 3**

Place the instruction **[What is it?]** and the 3-D dinosaur on the instruction strip and the word cards **[dinosaur]** and **[car]** on the choice strips. Starting with SD1–R1 (the dinosaur cues the placement of **[dinosaur]**), intermix SD1 and SD2 according to discrimination learning procedures. Prompt as necessary. Set mastery at 5 out of 5 or 9 out of 10 unprompted correct responses with the SDs presented in random rotation. Generalize mastery of this discrimination across teachers.

Introduce SD3 and subsequent items by following the procedures employed in Steps 1 through 3. As the student masters new items, gradually increase the number of word cards displayed simultaneously on the choice strips. For example, to label the object presented on the instruction strip, the student will learn to identify the corresponding word from four to five word cards on each choice strip (i.e., a total of 10 to 12 word cards). In other words, the student is taught to scrutinize the environment in order to make increasingly complex discriminations.

After the student masters writing (i.e., labeling) 15 to 20 objects, teach the student to label *pictures* of the mastered 3-D objects (see Figure 29.3). Once the student masters approximately 10 pictures, it is recommended that nonidentical examples of the mastered 3-D and 2-D items are introduced to help ensure generalization. By being able to use both 3-D and 2-D stimuli, the teacher gains flexibility in helping the student acquire the labels of a number of functional items around the house and, later, the labels for colors, shapes, and sizes.

Areas of Difficulty

The presentation of the printed instruction **[What is it?]** together with the object the student is asked to label may cause a problem identical to that which some students in the vocal language program encounter when the teacher asks "What is it?" while presenting of the object the student is asked to verbally label. This problem may be solved by initially withholding the printed instruction **[What is it?]** and then fading it in after the student has learned to write the labels of approximately 15 to 20 objects.

Responding to Printed Instructions

In this section, the student is taught to read and act upon printed instructions. The long-term goal is that the student will read and then follow elaborate chained instructions, such as **[Go to the bathroom, brush your teeth, then come back to Mommy]**. To reach such a complex stage, a foundation of basic skills must first be established. Thus, the initial objective is to teach the student to read and act upon elementary single instructions such as **[drop block]**, **[stomp feet]**, **[wave]**, and **[clap]**. More complex and chained instructions are gradually introduced after this beginning goal is attained.

Note how closely this section parallels the Early Receptive Language Program (Chapter 15). Given the heavy overlap, teaching the skills introduced in this section will be facilitated if you are familiar with the procedures detailed in Chapter 15. If the student mastered the Early Receptive Language Program, you may prompt the correct response when teaching the student to read instructions by verbalizing the instruction (e.g., "Drop block") after saying, "Read." This verbal prompt must be faded.

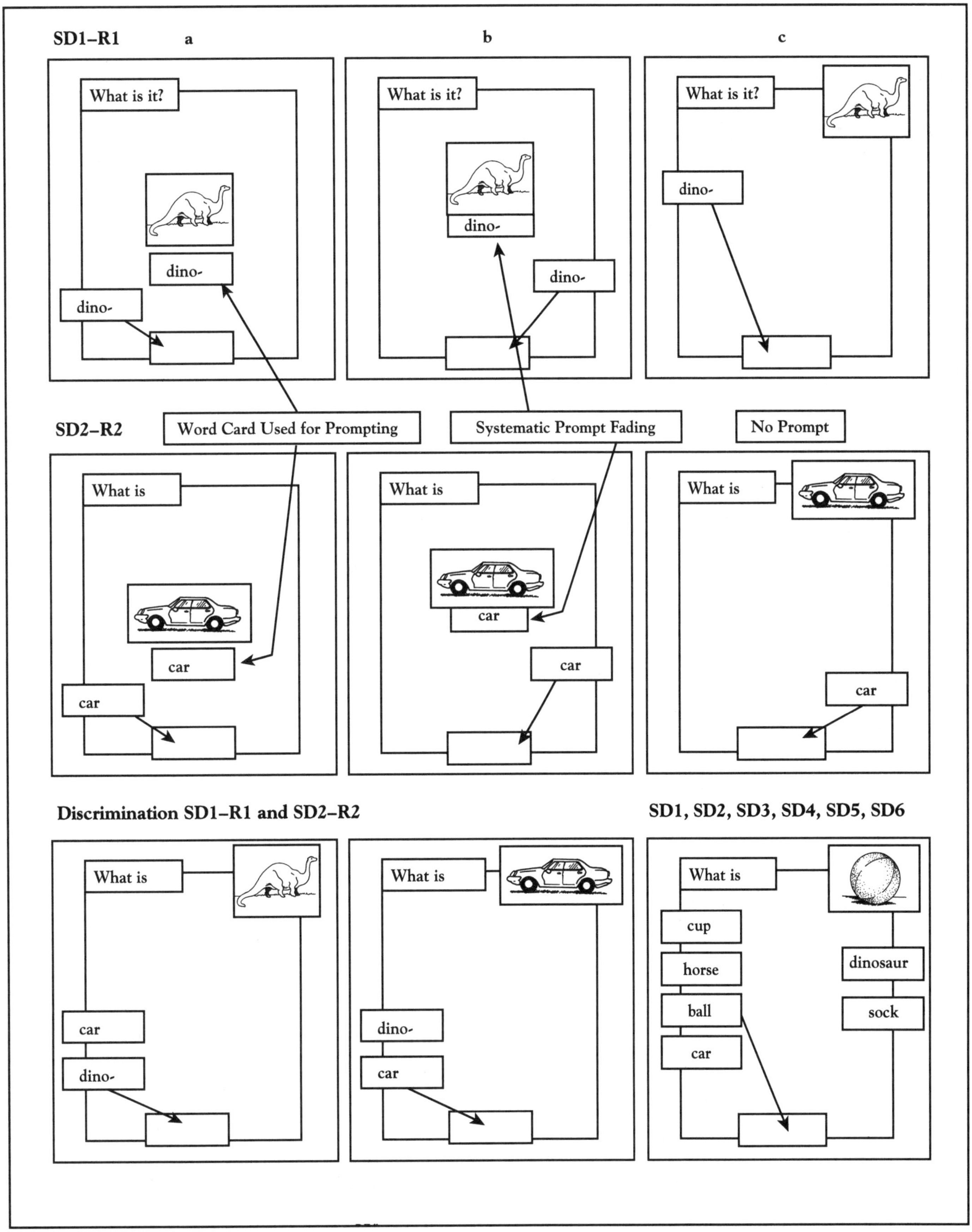

Figure 29.3. Writing: Labeling two-dimensional objects.

The student should possess strong nonverbal imitation skills and word matching skills before being introduced to this reading task. It will also be helpful for the student to have already mastered matching the target printed instructions (e.g., matching **[stomp feet]** to **[stomp feet]**). Through matching, the student shows that she can discriminate among (attend to) the stimuli.

We recommend that the initial instructions require a response that involves object manipulation (objects provide clear-cut visual cues for the student, and the actions are relatively easy to prompt). You may present the printed instructions on the instruction strip on the R&W Board or on some other surface that allows the student a clear view of the instructions (e.g., an easel). At a later stage, instructions may be presented on a computer screen. The instructions **[drop block]**, **[talk on phone]**, and **[stomp feet]** are used to illustrate SD1, SD2, and SD3, respectively, in the steps that follow. (See Figure 29.4.)

▶ **Step 1**

Place a block and a bucket on the table, present the printed instruction **[drop block]** on the instruction strip, then say, "Read" (or "Drop block"), while pointing to the instruction card. It may be necessary to display the instruction card distinctly in front of the student's eyes concurrent with the verbal instruction. Prompt the correct response by modeling the behavior. Place the criterion for mastery at 5 out of 5 or 9 out of 10 unprompted correct responses.

▶ **Step 2**

Mass trial SD2 **[talk on phone]** to mastery by following the procedures described in the previous step. In the current step, a toy phone placed on the table replaces the block and the bucket.

▶ **Step 3**

Position the block and the bucket close together and approximately 4 to 6 inches away from the phone on the table. Intermix SD1 **[drop block]** and SD2 **[talk on phone]** according to discrimination learning procedures, starting with SD1.

▶ **Step 4**

Mass trial SD3 **[stomp feet]** to mastery. Stomping feet is a relatively easy action to prompt and therefore functions as a nice transition to actions that do not require object manipulation. Once SD3 is mastered, intermix it first with SD1, then with SD2, and then with both SD1 and SD2.

Continue to introduce instructions by following the previously outlined procedures. In deciding upon prospective instructions, refer to the list of behaviors provided at the end of Chapter 15. Procedures for chaining two-part instructions are described in the R&W Program manual.

Areas of Difficulty

Some students need prompts beyond those described in the preceding section. One such prompt (a proximity prompt) may be implemented as follows: When introducing SD1 **[drop block]**, first prompt the correct response by placing the instruction card near the block and bucket on the table. Next, hand the student a duplicate instruction card **[drop block]** (i.e., a prompt card) and help her match this card to the instruction card, then immediately manually prompt the student to perform the action of picking up the block and dropping it in the bucket. This position prompt is helpful because it reduces the distance between the instruction and the response (the SD–R relationship occurs closer in time and space). Over trials, first fade the prompt card, then move the instruction card up to the instruction strip. To use a similar proximity prompt when teaching **[stomp feet]**, place the instruction card next to the student's feet, then immediately prompt her to stomp her feet. Gradually move the instruction card up to the instruction strip (see Figure 29.5).

Using Letters to Write Words

Copying Words

As a precursor to teaching the student to identify objects by spelling their labels, the student is taught to copy words. We use the term *copy* at this point because of the common use of this locution in education. Note that, conceptually, copying is analogous to matching.

The meanings of words copied by the student are not taught in this section. The objective here is to teach the student to copy any word presented by the teacher (as a prerequisite to teaching meaning in the next section). Copying, and later spelling, words on the R&W Board are taught as preliminary steps toward teaching the student to type on a computer keyboard.

The materials needed in this section are either (a) lowercase letters (point size 72 bold) pasted on small

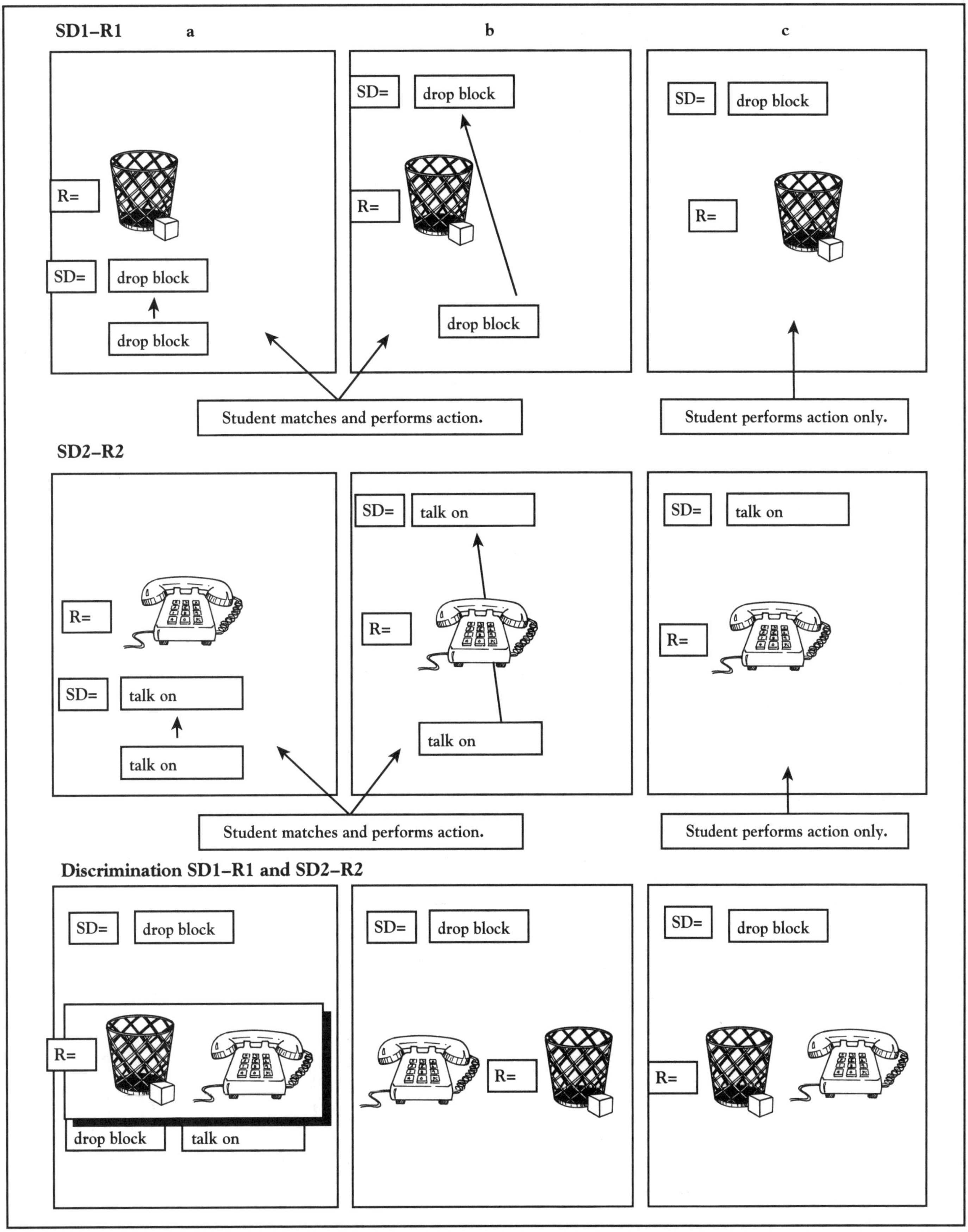

Figure 29.4. Reading: Responding to printed instructions.

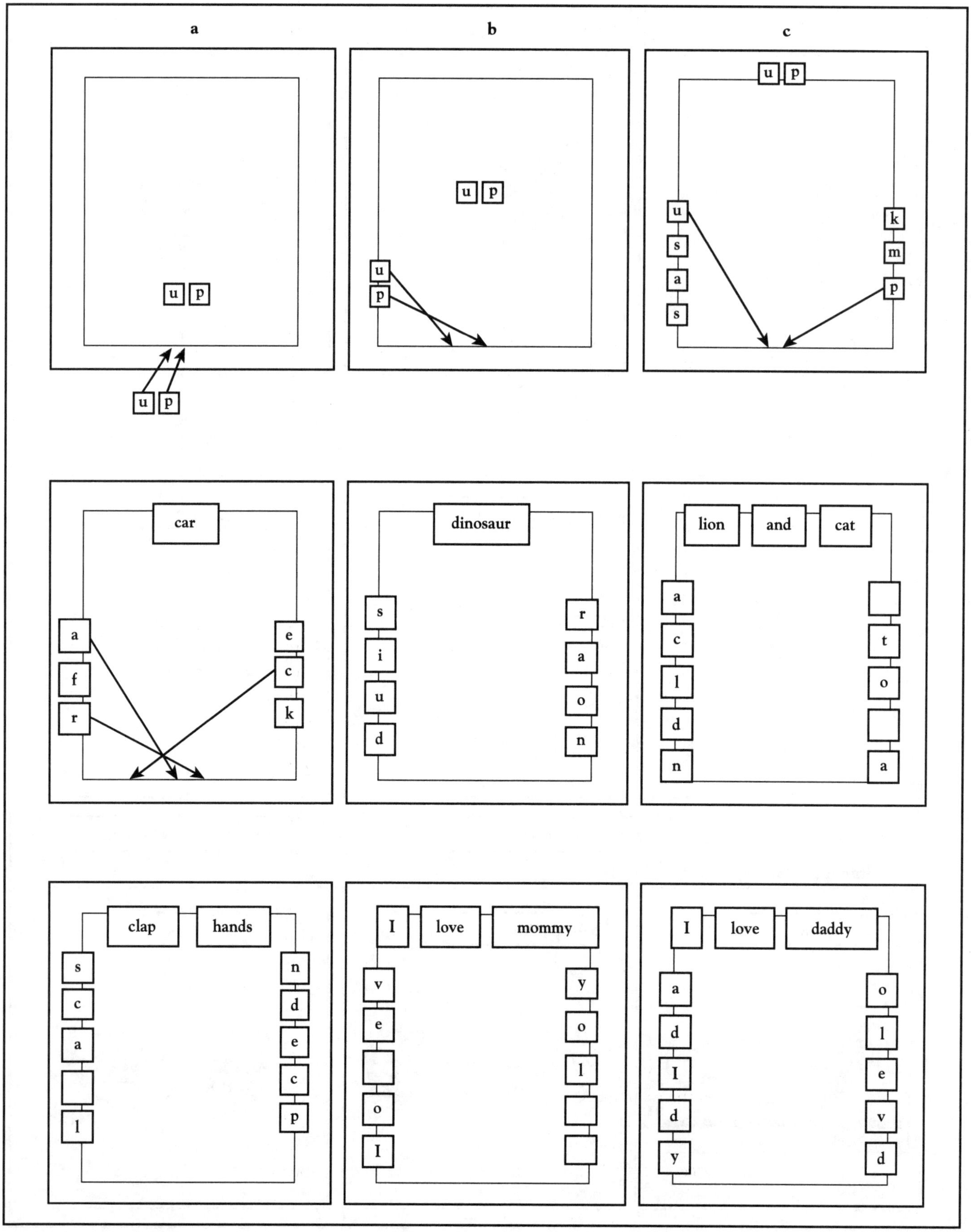

Figure 29.5. Copying words.

squares cut out of white posterboard with a Velcro dot attached to the back of each letter for use on the R&W Board or (b) magnetic tile letters for use on a magnetic board (e.g., "Wonderboard, Fun with Letters" by Dowling Magnets, Sonoma, California, Phone: 800/624-6381; in Europe, Dowling Magnets Europe Limited, Ashley Road, London N179LN, UK). The student is initially taught to copy short words by selecting letters, one at a time, from a group of letters that collectively make up the word to be copied. Later, longer words are presented and distracter letters are added. When this step is reached, the student is taught to select only the letters necessary to copy the particular word displayed.

The following steps illustrate how spelling may be taught on the R&W Board as opposed to a magnetic board. The first SD may be any two-letter combination. In the following steps, SD1 is the combination of the letters "u" and "p" to make the word **[up]**.

▶ **Step 1**

Place the letter combination **[up]** (the sample) in the middle of the board (i.e., in a prompted position). Leave a 1-inch space between the letters in the sample word **[up]** to facilitate the match. Place the letters **[u]** and **[p]** (the matches) on the table directly below the board. Verbally instruct "Match" and immediately prompt the student to move the match letters **[u]** and **[p]** into position on the response strip below the sample (**[u p]**). The letters should be moved one at a time and in order from left to right (i.e., **[u]** first, then **[p]**). The left-to-right order signals the beginning of writing with letters, and it is essential that you follow this rule from the beginning. Reinforce the student after placing the final letter **[p]**. Fade all prompts over subsequent trials.

▶ **Step 2**

Teach the student to copy the same combination of letters used in the previous step (**[up]**) with the match letters placed in a random order on the table. Should the student match **[p]** to **[p]** first (rather than follow the order from left to right), initially avoid consequating the response with an informational "No" because the match in and of itself is correct. Instead, put the match letters back on the table, repeat the SD, and prompt the correct order. Place mastery at 5 out of 5 or 9 out of 10 unprompted correct responses. Once the SD is mastered, copying in an incorrect order may be consequated with an informational "No."

▶ **Step 3**

Move the match letters from the table onto a choice strip, initially placing the first letter of the combination (**[u]**) closest to the response strip. Once mastered, introduce random positioning of the match letters (**[u]** and **[p]**) on the choice strips, and incrementally move the sample combination **[up]** to the instruction strip. Gradually add distracter letters onto the choice strips until a total of 12 letters (10 of them being distracters) are placed on the choice strips in random order. This procedure necessitates that the student scan for the correct letters.

Introduce new letter combinations by following the procedures described above. As the student gains proficiency in copying, present more commonly used words. Gradually increase the number of letters included in the sample words until the student can copy words composed of six to eight letters with distracter letters present the first time the words are introduced.

Eventually teach the student to copy combinations of words. Start with two-word combinations and systematically increase to a maximum of four-word strings. The teacher may need to prompt the student's correct placement of the letters by penciling in prompt boxes on the response strip (one box for each word in the SD).

Writing Object Labels

The student's mastery of copying words and strings of words does not imply that the student understands the meanings of the words he copies. In this section, the student is taught to associate the meanings of the labels he spells with the objects to which they correspond.

Pictures of the objects shoe and duck are used to illustrate the following steps in teaching the student to spell the labels associated with objects.

▶ **Step 1**

Mass trial SD1-R1 to mastery (a picture of a shoe cues the student to spell the word "shoe"). Position the four letters that compose the word "shoe" on a choice strip such that the letter **[s]** is closest to the response strip, **[h]** is the second closest, and **[e]** is the farthest. Present a picture of a shoe on the board about 3 inches above the response strip (i.e., in a prompted position). Place a prompt card **[shoe]** directly below the picture of the shoe. Place the printed instruction **[What is it?]** on the instruction strip; point to it; instruct, "What is it?"; and point to the picture of the shoe. Manually prompt the student to spell the word "shoe" by placing the letters, one by one, ordered from left to right, on the response strip directly below the prompt card **[shoe]**. Over the next several trials, fade the manual prompt, then fade the prompt card **[shoe]** by gradually sliding it under the picture of the shoe until the prompt card is completely hidden. Throughout the prompt fading procedure, occasionally probe unprompted trials. Once manual and visual prompts are faded, begin randomizing the positions of the letters on the choice strips to help prevent inadvertent position cues. Gradually add distracter letters to the choice strips until the student learns to select the letters **[s]**, **[h]**, **[o]**, and **[e]** from a total of 12 to 15 letters. Set mastery at 5 out of 5 or 9 out of 10 unprompted correct responses.

▶ **Step 2**

Mass trial SD2–R2 (a picture of a duck cues the student to spell the word "duck") by following the procedures described in the previous step.

▶ **Step 3**

Place the letters **[s]**, **[h]**, **[o]**, **[e]**, **[d]**, **[u]**, **[c]**, and **[k]** on the choice strip, then intermix SD1 and SD2 according to discrimination learning procedures. Begin by presenting SD1. To respond correctly, the student must learn not to select any of the letters included in the word "duck." If necessary, facilitate this discrimination by adding the letters of the word "duck" to the choice strips one at a time. Once the SD1–SD2 discrimination is mastered, gradually add up to seven distracter letters, giving the student no more than a total of 15 letters to choose from. Continue to teach and intermix new labels according to these same procedures. (See Figure 29.6.)

Although the acquisition of spelling according to the format described in this section is an important achievement, learning to write in a more flexible and efficient manner would benefit any student. Two common methods for efficient writing are longhand and typing. Procedures for teaching the student to write longhand are described in the Arts and Crafts Program (Chapter 20). Procedures for teaching the student to type using a computer are presented in Watthen-Lovaas and Lovaas (2000).

It is difficult to predict whether a student will make more progress writing longhand or typing. It is also difficult to predict whether a student will encounter serious problems with either method. Therefore, it may be best to explore the introduction of both types of writing, and then decide what works best for the individual student. For some students, the Picture Exchange Communication System (see Chapter 30) may be of more value than either method of writing.

Concluding Comments

Working knowledge of the vocal language programs outlined in this manual and the beginning steps of the R&W Program described in this chapter should prepare teachers and parents for making informed decisions regarding whether the R&W Program would be beneficial for the student. If it is deemed appropriate to introduce the R&W Program, an extremely detailed presentation of the program is described in a separate R&W Program manual (Watthen-Lovaas & Lovaas, 2000).

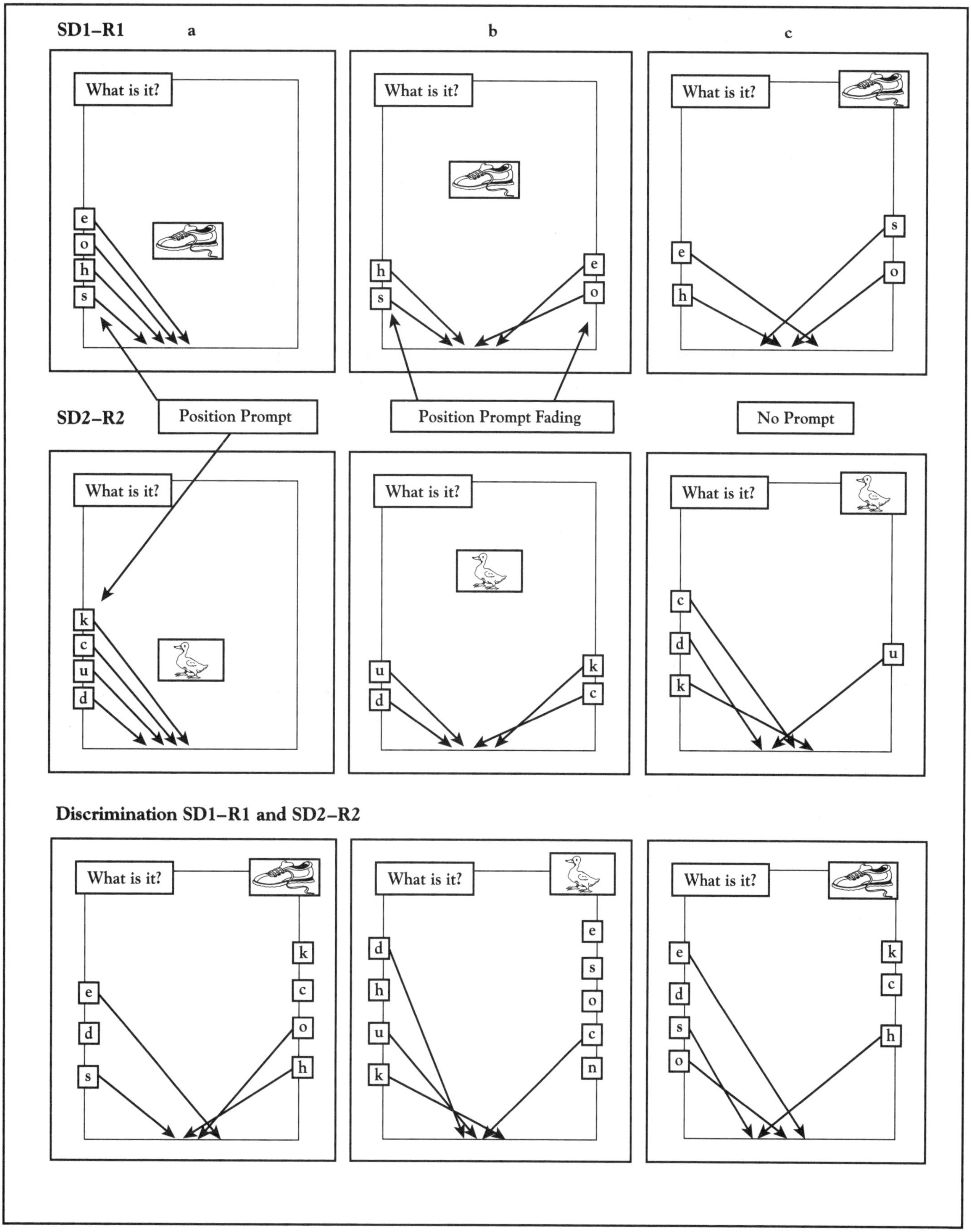

Figure 29.6. Writing: Labeling two-dimensional objects using letters.

Communication Strategies for Visual Learners

CHAPTER 30

Andy Bondy and Lori Frost

One of the most serious problems for individuals with autism is their great difficulty acquiring and using speech. Almost 80% of preschool students entering one public school program had no functional speech (Bondy & Frost, 1994a). Parents and professionals alike want their students to acquire speech as quickly as possible. The earlier chapters in this book describe an approach that is highly successful in helping these students develop speech. However, for reasons that are not currently understood, some students do not rapidly acquire speech or vocal imitation. When students display significant difficulty acquiring speech, it may be appropriate to consider some form of augmentative or alternative communication (AAC) strategy.

In this chapter, we describe an alternative approach to communication training for students who demonstrate difficulty acquiring a strong vocal imitative repertoire—that is, the students who are described in this manual as visual learners. We describe the Picture Exchange Communication System (PECS) and its introduction to individuals with autism and related developmental delays.[1] This system has helped many students learn the basic elements of communication. We also describe the use of pictures and other symbols to help students understand what is expected of them in terms of individual activities and the sequence of activities across a typical day.

What Is Communication?

Before describing several different AAC strategies, it may be helpful to clarify what is meant by *communication*. First, communication must take place between at least two people, one identified as the speaker, and the other identified as the listener. For example, if a teacher asks a student to bring him or her a hammer, then the teacher is the speaker and the student is the listener. On the other hand, if the student says, "I want a cookie," and the teacher brings him one, then the student is the speaker and the teacher is the listener. Communication requires the speaker to behave, or act, directly toward the listener, who in turn rewards the speaker in some manner. Although this description may sound very simple, it is necessary to distinguish communication from other behaviors. For example, a student might go to the refrigerator, open the door, take out a container of milk, and drink some milk. Although this action can be interpreted as indicating that the student wants milk, it will only be confusing to say that the student has communicated his needs. He directs his actions toward the refrigerator and the milk, and not toward any other person. On the other hand, if the student went to someone and said, "I want milk," and that person gave the student some milk, then the student's actions may be described appropriately as communicative.

It also is helpful to point out that communication does *not* require speech; people can learn to communicate without using speech. Individuals who are deaf can learn to use sign language to communicate effectively. Persons who have physical damage to their vocal system (or related physical disabilities) may learn to use various communication devices (some electronic) to type out or select symbols to effectively communicate with others, or they may learn to use a pen to write. In other words, speech is only one modality—although clearly the most common and efficient—through which people can communicate.

One critical element of communication is the reward provided by the listener that supports the communication of the speaker. In the case of teaching students to communicate, it is the teacher who provides the reinforcer for the student's communicative actions. To simplify this

[1] Although this chapter focuses on the use of PECS with young children, PECS has been successfully used with adolescents and adults with a variety of disabilities. The sequence of training is identical for all populations.

analysis, two broad types of reinforcers can be identified as most often involved with communication. One type of reward involves a host of objects, activities, or events that the listener provides to the speaker. For example, when a boy asks for milk, receiving the milk will reinforce asking. In similar fashion, a student may ask for other objects (e.g., toys, magazines, food) or activities (e.g., being tickled, read to, or chased), and receiving these items or activities will promote more communication.

On the other hand, people often communicate for rewards that appear to be purely social in nature. For example, a very young boy may see a dog run by a window and very excitedly say, "Doggie! Doggie!" The boy is likely to persist until his mother or father says, "Yes, it is a dog," or "Yes, I see the dog, too!" In this case, the boy is not asking for the dog itself and therefore does not need to receive the dog to be rewarded for communicating with his parent. Instead, the reinforcer involves the social interaction (attention) with his parent. For typically developing individuals, this type of motivation appears to be as important (and persistent) in forming early language as the direct receipt of objects or activities.

Even speech imitation can occur for these two different reasons. Most often, children learn to imitate what they hear because of the praise they receive when they can clearly say a word, repeat a phrase, or sing part of a song. On the other hand, sometimes parents (or teachers) may say, "If you can say 'cookie,' I'll give you the cookie." In this case, a child may be more likely to imitate because doing so helps to achieve a desired outcome—namely, getting cookies.

When developing AAC strategies for persons with autism, it is helpful to remember that, for many of these individuals, social interactions may not serve as powerful rewards or motivators. In other words, especially early on in training, it is not likely that a student with autism will learn a new skill simply to see his parent or teacher smile. However, during the same period of early training, the student is likely to want a variety of items, activities, or events. If this is the case, then identifying these potential rewards will be important in developing effective communication strategies (see Chapter 7).

What Is Spontaneous Communication?

In addition to understanding the types of rewards that are associated with communication, it is helpful to understand the circumstances (i.e., the stimulus conditions) under which communication occurs. For example, a student may say "cookie" only when someone models the word or someone specifically asks the student, "What do you want?" On the other hand, a student might see a cookie, and without anyone saying something, say, "I want a cookie." In general, we say that speaking in response to someone else's model or question (i.e., a response to a specific SD provided by another person) is not spontaneous, whereas speaking in response to some aspect of the environment (including things happening within the student, such as feeling hunger or pain) is spontaneous.

A similar line of reasoning can be extended beyond requests. If a student names objects only when asked to do so (i.e., "What's this?" "What do you see?") rather than when objects are seen (or heard or felt or tasted), the student's naming of objects would not be described as spontaneous. In general, if a parent's or teacher's model or question is part of what controls the likelihood that the student will respond appropriately, then the student's response is not viewed as being spontaneous. Some students respond only when spoken to; we sometimes refer to these students as being prompt dependent or, to be more technically precise, under narrow stimulus control. (Calling a child prompt dependent misattributes the problem to a supposed characteristic of the child rather than more appropriately noting how the child's behavior was taught to be dependent upon some teacher-arranged prompt.) These students often need to be taught to use their communication skills in a spontaneous manner because their language does not automatically generalize from prompted communication to spontaneous communication.

What Has Been Tried?

Over the past 20 years, various AAC strategies have been tried with young children with autism. For example, researchers have studied the introduction of manual sign language (Carr, 1982; Reichle, York, & Sigafoos, 1991). As with any AAC strategy, there are advantages and disadvantages to this approach. Among the potential advantages is the strong visual support provided within this strategy and the fact that the model (i.e., the stimulus associated with a teacher demonstrating the appropriate sign) of a particular sign can remain part of a child's visual environment far longer than can the sound of a single spoken word. On the other hand, teaching children how to sign has usually involved first teaching them to imitate the appropriate hand motions. For some children, such imitative skills are acquired very slowly. For those children who do acquire these new skills, there is often a lengthy period of time to acquire functional communication skills. Another potential disadvantage is the limited understanding of sign language in the general population. When someone goes into a fast food restaurant, for example, and has only a sign repertoire, an interpreter is needed (which can limit ultimate independence) or the server needs to understand sign language.

Another general approach to AAC involves the use of pictures and related symbols. Until recently, these strategies involved pointing (or similar selection strategies) to pictures or symbols that correspond (or match) various items or events. An advantage of a picture-point system is the fact that there is no need for the student to imitate someone's actions (or words) prior to being taught to use the pictures. Furthermore, some students appear to attend more consistently to visual cues than to auditory cues; such students may then be more attentive to pictures than to spoken words. Pictures also are readily understood by naive communicative partners, such as people in the community.

On the other hand, several potential disadvantages are associated with attempting to teach a picture-point system as a means of teaching functional communication. With these systems, early lessons are led by the teacher[2]; that is, the teacher begins the interaction by holding up an item; asking, "What's this?"; and rewarding the student if she points to the corresponding picture. Some students appear to learn to point to pictures only when asked to do so and do not initiate communication interactions. Other students have been observed to be sitting in a corner, tapping on a picture, and waiting for someone to notice what they are doing. In other words, these students may not have learned to approach someone prior to pointing to the picture, and thus a key element in basic communication has not been acquired. Another difficulty occurs when a student points to a picture but simultaneously looks away. In such cases, it is difficult to interpret the pointing: does the student want what she is pointing to? Does the student want what she is looking at? Does the student simply like the sound of tapping on the picture? Such reasonable questions of interpretation may severely interfere with the development of functional communication skills. Throughout these examples, it is assumed that the point of the lesson is to teach the student to be able to engage in appropriate and self-initiated functional communication rather than to test whether the student can match to sample. That is, although matching to sample is an extremely important skill, it does not necessarily automatically generalize to spontaneous requests or comments.

What Is the Picture Exchange Communication System?

The Picture Exchange Communication System (PECS) was developed within the Delaware Autistic Program during the past decade (Bondy & Frost, 1994b).[3] The primary purpose of introducing PECS to students is to teach them to initiate a communicative interaction within a social context (i.e., approach an adult and deliver a message). From the start of training, the student is taught (without depending on verbal prompts) to approach someone who has something (e.g., a favorite snack or toy) that the student clearly wants. This communication function is taught first because it results in immediate reinforcement for the student and does not rely upon social rewards that may be ineffective at this point in training. The system begins with using single pictures within a request function, then develops symbol selection (i.e., discrimination), then develops sentence structure, and finally addresses additional communicative functions.

Assessing What a Student Likes

Learning about a student's preferences involves doing a reinforcer assessment. Such assessment can be very formal (i.e., highly systematic with very controlled arrangement and data collection); most often, however, we suggest more informal strategies, especially for parents. Most parents already have a very good understanding of what their child likes (and dislikes). Teachers and other professionals should always start the process by discussing this issue with parents. The process may begin by looking for items for which the student readily reaches without direct prompting. If the student reaches for an item, the teacher may try to see how motivating the item is by making access slightly more difficult. For example, the teacher

[2] As in other chapters, the term *teacher* is used to describe the person in a teaching relationship relative to the child, rather than to the profession of teacher. Thus, parents, classroom teachers, instructors, and other professionals or paraprofessionals may all be referred to as teachers.

[3] A detailed training manual is available (Frost & Bondy, 1995), which includes additional problem-solving strategies, data sheets, and suggestions for integrating PECS with other important aspects of behavioral programming.

could grasp an item until the student pries open his fingers, or the teacher could put the item on a low shelf and observe if the student still reaches for the item. This reinforcer assessment should continue until the teacher identifies several items (e.g., 5 to 10 toys or snacks) the student desires.

Various formal and informal strategies are associated with determining what is reinforcing. Among the issues that must be addressed within any strategy are factors that may lead to satiation (i.e., offering a reinforcer so frequently that its potency is seriously, though temporarily, diminished) and the number of potential reinforcers offered (i.e., presenting only one item and observing how hard the student tries to obtain that item vs. offering a choice of reinforcers).

Phase 1: Beginning PECS Training

After the desires of the student have been determined, then PECS training can begin. The first step of PECS is to teach a student the essence of communication, that is, to approach an adult rather than to act directly on an object. (Issues associated with selecting particular messages will be addressed during subsequent lessons.) Therefore, the first element of PECS training involves teaching a student to pick up a picture, extend the picture to the teacher (who functions as the communicative partner for the student), and release the picture into the open hand of that person. Of course, the teacher immediately gives the student what was requested. Although this sequence sounds very simple, this training step requires a special arrangement; that is, the training requires that *two* teachers work with the student. Arranging for one-on-one instruction may seem complicated enough, and planning for two teachers may seem daunting. However, there is need for two teachers for only a short period of time. Attempting to start PECS with only one teacher will likely lead to long-term problems.

Training begins with one teacher—the communicative partner or the "enticer"— sitting in front of the student and displaying something the student wants. One role for this teacher is to entice the student to reach for the offered item. For this example, we will assume that the reinforcer assessment indicated that the student likes cookies. A picture of a cookie is placed between the student and the cookie. The enticer neither asks the student what she wants nor tells the student to pick up the picture. In fact, this teacher should not use any direct verbal cues to help the student learn to *initiate* the interaction. The enticer may put out one hand, palm up, to accentuate his or her role as a receiver. (This gesture will need to be eliminated over time.) The second adult—the physical prompter or the "helper"—sits (or stands) immediately behind the student. This teacher must wait for the student to begin to reach for the cookie. If the helper tries to move the student's hand toward the picture before the student is actively seeking the desired item, then the student may resist the attempt to move her arm. As soon as the student moves toward the cookie (and thus is orienting to the reinforcer), the helper guides the student's hand to pick up the picture, extend it to the open hand of the enticer, and release the picture. As soon as the picture is received, the enticer says, "Cookie! You want the cookie!" in an animated fashion and gives the student the cookie. (An alternative statement by the enticer could be "I want cookie." This phrase immediately models the correct form for the child to eventually imitate. At this time, there is no clear empirical evidence to prefer one type of comment over the other.)

The reason that two teachers are necessary is that there are two separate roles for these teachers from the student's perspective. One teacher—the enticer—has the item that the student wants. The student's initial tendency, as observed during the reinforcer assessment, is to reach for the item and take it. Because the student will be taught to pick up a picture and give it to the enticer, someone must help the student to pick up the picture, extend it to the partner, and release the picture into the enticer's open hand. The teacher helping the student should not be the enticer. If the enticer helps the student, then the student may learn to depend on that help and not learn to *initiate* the exchange.

The role of the helper is very different. His or her first goal is to wait for the student to indicate, by an action, that the object is desired. The most common action to observe is the student reaching for the object. As soon as this action is observed, the helper quickly prompts the student by physically guiding the student's hand to the picture, helping the student (with hand-over-hand assistance) to pick up the picture, extend the picture to the open hand of the enticer, and release the picture into the enticer's open hand. Notice that this second teacher does not say anything to the student before or after the exchange. In fact, the student should show very little awareness of this teacher and instead focus attention on the desired object, the picture, and the enticer's open hand.

It is important to remember that the physical prompter helps the student only after the student starts to reach for the object (or for the picture in later trials). The prompt for the student to pick up the picture should never begin while the student is looking out the window, at her own fingers, and so on. At such times, guiding the student to the picture will have no meaning for the student. If the student seems distracted, the enticer (not the helper) should attempt to attract the student's attention to the potential reward. Once this attention is gained, the enticer can move the object, nibble on the snack, even comment on how good the snack tastes. Even with these enticements, the enticer must still avoid directly telling the student to pick up the picture or asking the student what she wants. The use of such direct prompts may teach the student to wait for the prompt instead of learning to initiate the communicative interaction with someone who has what is desired.

The primary responsibility of the helper is to fade the level of support as rapidly as possible. The most effective way to fade support is to take the view that the student has three steps to learn: (1) picking up the picture, (2) extending the picture toward the enticer, and (3) releasing the picture. Fading should take place through the use of backward chaining (see Chapter 10). To use this strategy as it relates to PECS, support is provided for the first component in the sequence and reduced for the last step. Thus, the helper assists the student in picking up the picture (Step 1) and extending the picture (Step 2), and then fades assistance in releasing the picture (Step 3). Once the student releases the picture without help, the helper guides the student to pick up the picture and begins to fade help in extending the picture toward the enticer. Finally, assistance is reduced for helping the student pick up the picture.

The main point of this first phase of training in PECS is to teach the student to initiate an action toward the picture and proceed to give the picture to the teacher. Many students learn this step within the first session of training (i.e., within the first hour of training). One potential area of difficulty is associated with very low motivation by the student toward the possible reward. To minimize this potential problem, it is helpful to assure that the student continues to reach for freely offered items. If the student does not display much effort in obtaining the reward, she will not display more effort to pick up a picture to exchange for the reward.

It may also be helpful to remember that, although it is preferable to work with the student while seated in a chair, this lesson may need to be arranged in other ways to assure that the student is adequately motivated by what is offered. For example, a lesson can be arranged while the student is playing with blocks or puzzle pieces on the floor. These items are motivating to the student if she is persistent in picking up additional blocks or puzzle pieces. In this situation, the enticer should hold the next puzzle piece and place a picture of a puzzle piece in front of the student. Once the student reaches for the puzzle piece, the helper then assists the student in initiating the exchange as described earlier. Essentially, this lesson should be arranged where the most potent rewards can be controlled by the enticer.

Although the first phase of training may be accomplished with many types of rewards, we have found certain types of rewards easier to use than others. First, we use very small portions of any reward to promote as many rapid trials as possible (and thus reduce satiation). We also prefer to start with rewards that tend to be consumed very quickly. For example, snacks and drinks are swallowed rapidly, bubbles tend to pop quickly, spinning tops tend to stop moving relatively quickly, and radios or tape recorders can be readily turned off. Other types of rewards are often controlled by the student and are difficult to end. For example, looking at a book or playing with a toy may be difficult to stop (i.e., to create another opportunity to request) because the student may get upset when the object is taken by the adult. Although we try to avoid such rewards in the beginning of training, if we need to use these rewards, we simply announce "My turn" and calmly take the object away, rather than trying to begin a "Give me . . ." lesson. If the student is mildly upset by the removal of a favorite object, that is, in our opinion, a good indicator to continue the lesson. We ignore the mild negative reactions and continue to try to guide the student to perform correctly. Of course, if this strategy results in dangerous behaviors (either toward the teacher or self-inflicted), then we suggest using another reinforcer. The goal is to gradually teach the student to request many different types of reinforcers. In our experience, the order in which they are taught to be requested is not critical.

To avoid satiation, it also may be helpful to rotate among different types of rewards, each individually presented with its corresponding picture (see the next section for details). Furthermore, to help maintain motivation over time, keep each of these early lessons relatively brief, 5 to 15 minutes at most. At the same time, disperse this lesson across at least half a dozen opportunities per day. The more the student appears to want specific reinforcers, the more opportunities there are to work on requesting.

During this initial phase of training (and during the next phase, as well), the student is not given a choice of pictures. It is the teacher's responsibility to focus on the importance of the exchange. In our experience, some students appear to look at and manipulate the pictures in a manner that suggests that they know or recognize what the picture represents. On the other hand, some students do not appear to look closely at the contents of the picture. This issue—selection and discrimination of pictures—is addressed in the third phase of training.

Phase 2: Increasing Spontaneity

Once the student successfully completes the first phase of training, he can independently pick up a single picture and give it to the teacher immediately in front of him in exchange for a desired item held (or controlled) by the teacher. (We consider the child to have successfully completed the first phase when he initiates and completes a request without a prompt from the helper on at least 80% of opportunities presented in several situations across the day.) Now the student is ready to learn the steps in the next phase of training. Phase 2 will expand the types of rewards the student can request, increase the distance the student walks to the teacher, increase the distance between the student and the picture, and introduce several different teachers with whom the student can communicate.

To accomplish the goals in Phase 2, each aspect is individually addressed. During this phase, it also is important not to place two (or more) pictures at the same time before the student. Discrimination between pictures will be addressed in the next phase of training. First, how to introduce additional types of rewards within the PECS framework is described.

In general, Phase 1 of training is often accomplished using only one type of reward. It is helpful to avoid associating communication with only one type of reward, such as snacks, so that the student does not come to expect that all pictures bring food. Rather, the goal is to help the student learn that giving pictures is a way to communicate with other people about many different things that the student wants. The second type of reward should be something distinctly different from the first reward. For example, if the first training item involved pretzels, then the next object may involve puzzle pieces or bubbles (depending on the student's preferences) rather than another type of snack food.

It is also important to assure that the student will use the system with many different adults (and ultimately peers). Therefore, very quickly, even during the first training session, the enticer and the helper should switch roles. Then other people, such as other staff and family members, should be included. The key is to be certain that each person with whom the student communicates knows the types of cues to use (e.g., enhancing the potential reward) and the type of prompts to avoid (e.g., direct questions or commands, continued use of an open hand). The continuity in strategy across different teachers will help the student generalize this new skill. We have observed little difficulty in teaching students to use the system with other people because they tend to be focused on obtaining the desired objects and the necessary pictures.

Another aspect of increasing generalization involves having the student learn to move around the room with his picture by gradually increasing the effort needed to complete the exchange. First, the enticer begins to sit straight or even leans back in his or her chair, as opposed to leaning forward, as is usually the case in Phase 1. Then, the enticer gradually moves away from the student, literally inch by inch. Some students show a tendency to remain in their chair; in such cases, the helper, rather than the enticer, should prompt the student with the minimum guidance necessary to start moving toward the partner. Usually, the combined outcome of getting the reward and hearing an enthusiastic reply by the enticer assures subsequent approaches.

Another strategy to further enhance generalization (or independence) involves teaching the student to get his own pictures. This lesson is made easier to teach by placing each picture on a communication booklet with Velcro. Every student using PECS should have his own communication booklet. Three-ring binders have been used with good success. At the earlier phases of PECS, the picture or pictures that the student are currently using are placed on the cover of the binder and other pictures (ones that could be used in other situations) are kept on pages inside the binder. The student learns to pull the picture from its Velcro attachment. This system also helps to minimize losing the pictures. At the start of this phase, the binder is placed immediately in front of the student with only one picture showing. Gradually, the binder is moved away from the student so that the student must move to the binder to retrieve each picture to exchange with the teacher. One helpful option is to maintain the binder in one easy-to-reach location within the home (or group situations), such as attached (via a loop or Velcro) to one particular area on a wall or on a specific chair.

One successful strategy to teach a student to independently retrieve his own communication book involves periodically entering a room eating something that the student likes, such as a bowl filled with popcorn. Start with items that the student has already learned to request in controlled situations. Furthermore, make sure that the corresponding picture is on the front of the student's communication book. If the student simply walks over and reaches for the snack, ignore him and continue to slowly walk around the room while eating the food. If the student does not quickly go over to his communication book, casually wander over to the area where the book is kept. Once the student retrieves his book and offers the appropriate picture, share some popcorn with him. The picture should then casually be returned to the book, and a new trial should begin by walking a little farther from where the book is kept. Over time, students learn to look for their communication book rather than first grab for something that they want. In our opinion, it is helpful to arrange these lessons so that they do not appear to be lessons.

When the student successfully completes this phase of training (by independently initiating in at least 80% of opportunities presented in multiple settings across the day), he can initiate requesting a variety of rewards (individually presented) by retrieving a single picture from his communication binder from anywhere in the teaching area and with a variety of teachers. In general, students typically use from 6 to 12 pictures in three or four different situations with two to four people by the end of this phase.

Phase 3: Discrimination Training

During the initial phases of training, it is possible for a student to select a single picture from the communication board without actually understanding the relationship between the picture and the corresponding item. That is, the student may actually not have learned to "look" at the contents of the picture. This next phase of PECS training focuses on this important issue. As indicated in other chapters of this book, there are several strategies to approaching discrimination training. Rather than reviewing all of these strategies, several will be described that have been helpful with many students. It is also important to note that research on discrimination strategies, including when to begin discrimination training, is ongoing, and therefore much of what follows is best understood as being in accordance with clinical practice, as opposed to derived from specific studies on each topic. (In our opinion, it is possible to begin discrimination training within the PECS format prior to beginning matching-to-sample training. Therefore, we do not recommend waiting to introduce PECS (or its discrimination phase) until a child has successfully completed matching to sample on two-dimensional representations. More research is clearly needed in this important area of training.)

Discrimination training can begin with one teacher and is started within a situation familiar to the student—requesting desired items. The first approach involves presenting the student with two items and two corresponding pictures. One of the items should be something that the student finds very rewarding and the other item should be something that the student simply does not seek to acquire. This pairing creates a situation where there is a big contrast between the items that the student can choose. For example, a favorite food item may be presented along with a sock (assuming the student is familiar with socks but does not seem to want one). Both items are displayed or offered to the student. To be certain that the student is looking at the two choices, training begins after the student clearly has demonstrated a preference for one of the actual objects. The teacher does not need to use any type of verbal prompt at this point (i.e., by asking, "Which one do you want?" or "What do you want?"). Next, the pictures are immediately presented to the student. If the student selects the snack picture, as soon as the student touches the picture of the snack, the teacher says "Oh" in an upbeat fashion. When the student then gives the snack picture to the teacher, the student immediately is given the snack.

If, on the other hand, the student reaches for the picture of the sock, as soon as she touches that picture, the teacher would say something like "Uh-oh" and, upon receiving the picture, give the student the sock. (We suggest that the teacher use a neutral tone and phrase to minimize the possible reinforcing effect that teacher-provided feedback may provide. We have observed situations where the tone of voice used following selection of the "wrong" picture was so reinforcing in itself that subsequent discrimination was very difficult until the tone was modified to reduce its reinforcing association.) At this point, most students look at the sock and then look at the teacher as if the teacher must be crazy. Some students simply get upset, and toss the unwanted item or begin to fuss. If this happens, that is a good sign because the outcome of the interaction with the teacher—getting a sock—does not fit the student's expectation. The situation is quickly repeated, even for a student who is clearly upset about not getting what she expected, by re-presenting both pictures, and the correct picture selection is immediately reinforced. Over time, the location of the pictures relative to each other should be varied to prevent position cues that interfere with attention to the visual contents of the pictures.

It is important to provide some appropriate verbal feedback the moment the student touches a picture (the earliest indication of a selection) rather than wait for the student to give you the picture. (Even if such comments are not initially effective reinforcers, such comments should come to function as conditioned reinforcers over time given their association with the receipt of established reinforcers.) If you wait for the exchange, the feedback comes too late (i.e., it is provided after the picture is given, not after the picture is selected) relative to when the student actually made the choice between pictures. However, if the student is given the sock and simply begins to play with the sock without seeming to be upset that she did not get the snack item, then this strategy may not be very successful. Simply stated, if the student does not seem to care about the outcome of a request, then the student is not very likely to be motivated enough to study the pictures prior to making a choice. Discrimination strategies that yield many errors tend to be less successful than those that can minimize the frequency of errors during acquisition.

If this strategy does not work, you may want to try the following strategies:

1. Spatially align the pictures with their corresponding items. Gradually increase the distance between the pictures and their corresponding items.
2. Put the pictures on clear containers holding desired items; over time, make the containers more and more opaque so that the student must "see" the picture to understand what is in the container.
3. Enhance the visual differences between the pictures by, for example, (a) using a picture of a desired item and a "blank" distracter card (i.e., a card the same size as the picture of the desired item but without a picture on it); (b) initially making the picture of the desired item larger than the picture of the nondesired item, and then gradually making the pictures the same size; (c) initially enhancing the color of the picture of the desired item by coloring the picture or placing a color frame around it, and then gradually reducing the amount of the color enhancement; (d) using product logos, photographs, or other enhanced visual symbols (including the small pictures found on most coupons of favorite foods and drinks) rather than black-and-white line drawings.
4. Use three-dimensional objects instead of pictures. Plastic replicas can be used for many items (often found as refrigerator magnets), or real items can be covered with an acrylic epoxy (found in most art supply stores). Over time, the encased objects can be gradually covered by pictures (Frost & Scholefield, 1996). (See Frost & Bondy, 1994, for more details on these and other discrimination strategies.)

Another important strategy to introduce during this aspect of training is correspondence training. In general, when a student selects a picture of a pretzel from a pair also including a picture of a sock, the teacher would immediately say, "You want the pretzel! Here it is!" and give the student the pretzel. However, if the choice was between a pretzel and a potato chip, the student may not strongly prefer one over the other, as long as she gets something. To determine whether the student is actually making a true selection, after the student gives the teacher a picture (from the pair presented), the teacher should say, "Okay. Go ahead. Take one." Notice that in this case, the teacher would neither say the name of the requested item nor give the item to the student. Instead, the student is simply offered the choice between the items available. If your student reaches for and takes the item requested, say, "Good. Nice paying attention," or something to that effect. However, if the student reaches for the other item (i.e., she gives you the picture of a pretzel but selects a potato chip), then do not permit the student to take the item. Remind the student what she asked for and demonstrate the association between the picture and the item. Set the situation up again (with both pictures), and reward the student for appropriately following up on her picture choice by selecting the corresponding item. (A more comprehensive error-correction sequence that is appropriate in this situation, and for related errors, can be found in Bondy & Frost, 1995.)

After the student masters two-way discrimination between pictures, the number of pictures from which the student can choose is gradually increased. At first, pictures of items the student does not really want are introduced (e.g., one picture of a desired item and two pictures of nondesired items). As the student's performance improves, pictures of things the student may want but that do not fit the current situation are gradually added. For example, while the student is watching TV, the teacher might turn the TV off and present the communication book with a picture of the TV and a picture of a spoon. In this situation, the student is likely to want the TV. At another time, for example, while the student is eating her favorite dessert (e.g., a bowl of ice cream), the same picture choices may be offered. This time, the student is more likely to request the spoon.

The criteria for moving on to the next phase of training involve both the accuracy of the student's performance and the number of pictures in the student's repertoire. Successful discrimination (80%) within an array of at least 5 pictures (arranged as an X) should be demonstrated over a period of at least 3 days. The total repertoire should be at least 10 pictures. At the same time, it is important to foster moving on to the next phase rather than simply expanding the pictures used within this stage (i.e., such as teaching the discrimination of 50 single pictures without developing sentence structure).

Introducing Sentence Structure with PECS

Up to this point in the student's use of PECS, individual pictures have been manipulated. This level of communication development can be compared to that of typically developing individuals who can use only single spoken words. However, typically developing individuals can convey both requesting and labeling functions while using single words by modulating the tone of their voice (or other aspects of their word production). For example, an 18-month-old can voice "doggie" in a manner that conveys that he wants his favorite dog toy or in a manner that implies that he sees a dog running in the yard. Students using PECS will need a comparable mechanism to express whether the picture they are exchanging is used as a request or a comment (label). To accomplish this communicative function, we teach students to develop simple sentences using more than one picture.

To introduce this phase of training, create a removable card (a sentence strip, which is typically about 5 × 2 inches) and an additional card that has "I want" written on it as well as an accompanying symbol (e.g., a pair of open hands). The phrase "I want" is presented as unitary because the student has not yet learned to distinguish "I" from "you" or the names of other people; that step will come later in training. Training begins with the "I want" card already placed on the sentence strip so the lesson that the student first learns is to place the picture of what he wants on the sentence strip and then to give the sentence strip (instead of only the single picture) to the teacher. As in the previous phase, there is no need for verbal prompting by the teacher. Physical prompts are used after the student begins to hand over the single picture to guide his hand toward placing the picture on the sentence strip. When the teacher receives the sentence strip, in addition to giving the student what was asked for, the teacher reads back the sentence strip while pointing to each picture (i.e., "Oh, 'I want' [pausing 2 or 3 seconds] cookie!"). The pause before naming the item requested tends to encourage students to say the name of the item. (The critical word here is encourage. The child is not forced to repeat any of the words in this lesson. The child performs correctly by appropriate manipulation of the pictures and thus deserves a reward for learning to use the sentence strip.) Once the student learns to place the single picture on the sentence strip and give the entire sentence to the teacher, the student is taught to take the "I want" card and place it on the sentence strip (using backward chaining).

Answering Simple Questions

So far, the student has learned to use the PECS Program to spontaneously request a variety of items. In addition to using spontaneous communication, it is important for students to respond to questions. The next step in the PECS sequence introduces the question "What do you want?" Although teachers have been encouraged to avoid that question up to this point in training, the student likely has heard the question. In either case, this step in training usually proceeds relatively quickly. This step also introduces a prompting strategy that is used in subsequent phases.

To begin this phase of training, an item that is reinforcing to the student is placed before the student, along with her communication book. While asking, "What do you want?" the teacher simultaneously points to the "I want" picture on the student's communication book. Most students will pick up the picture to which the teacher points and proceed to make a request with the pictures. Over time, a pause is introduced between the question and pointing to the "I want" picture (this strategy is described as a progressive time-delay prompt procedure). As the delay is gradually increased, the student usually begins to respond to the question before the teacher points to the "I want" picture. Thereafter, the teacher can eliminate the gestural prompt and promote independent answering of the question. Of course, it is still important to arrange for the student to have opportunities to respond spontaneously as well as be able to answer this question.

Teaching Labeling in Response to Simple Questions

At this point in training, the student can request items spontaneously and respond to simple questions. Criteria for moving on to the next step, labeling objects and items in response to simple questions, would be observing the student successfully respond to the question, "What do you want?" in at least 80% of no less than 20 opportunities presented over 3 days. The new labeling skill is taught by relying upon previously learned skills. A new picture is added to the communication board—"I see." This lesson is begun by placing before the student an item that, although somewhat interesting, is not something that the student strongly desires. The teacher asks the student, "Look! What do you see?" while simultaneously pointing to the "I see" picture. This gestural prompt was introduced in the previous phase; therefore, the student is likely to pick up the "I see" picture, place it on the sentence strip, and select the picture corresponding to the item before the student. Upon receiving the sentence strip, the teacher should say, "Oh, I see the ball."

At this point it is very important *not* to give the ball to the student. The appropriate reaction to a student's naming or commenting about something is to agree with the student and provide social reinforcement. Naming an item is not the same as requesting an item. Therefore, to avoid confusing the student, the teacher must react differently to requesting than to naming. The reason that an item that is not highly reinforcing for the student is selected is to lessen the reaction the student may have when he does not receive the item, something the student most likely expects given his prior history with PECS. Over trials, the teacher begins to introduce a pause between asking the question and pointing to the "I see" picture (as done in the previous phase). As the delay is increased, the student gradually comes to respond to the question without any gestural prompt.

During this phase of training, the teacher introduces other simple questions, such as "What do you hear?" "What do you feel?" and "What do you have?" For each question, a corresponding picture is added to the communication book. Of course, it is very important to continue to mix in questions such as "What do you want?" along with providing the opportunity to maintain a reasonable rate of spontaneous requests.

Developing Spontaneous Comments

In addition to naming items when asked to do so, it is important for the student to spontaneously comment about aspects of the environment. For the student to take this step, questions by the teacher must be eliminated as prompts for the student's comments. One strategy for accomplishing this involves fading the length of the teacher's questions by, for example, saying, "Look! What do you . . . ?", then "Look! What . . . ?", then "Look! . . . ," and then using just an expectant look. Comparable phrases can be used with listening (i.e., "I hear . . ."), feeling or touching (i.e., "I feel . . ."), or simply holding other items (i.e., "I have . . ."). In addition, it is helpful to promote spontaneous comments by using surprise or novelty to gain the student's attention. Typically developing individuals tend to comment about aspects of the environment that suddenly change (as when someone walks into a room, something falls or breaks, something does not "fit" into a situation, etc.) rather than static aspects of the environment (e.g., the wall or the floor). Therefore, one helpful strategy is introducing change into the environment by, for example, taking a variety of items out of a bag or playing different sounds on a tape recorder.

Introducing Attributes and Other Complex Aspects of Communication

Another aspect of complex communication involves the description of various attributes associated with objects or events. These attributes can include color, size, shape, type, brand, and so on. These attributes are sometimes first introduced when teaching a student to appropriately respond to teacher requests, such as when asking a student to give the red ball, point to the square, or find the *chocolate* cookie. On the other hand, once a student learns to use PECS to request items with a sentence strip, it is possible to teach the student to use certain attributes within the request prior to using that attribute within a receptive task.

Assume, for example, that a student not only likes M&Ms but prefers red ones (this lesson could be arranged for a student who prefers Oreos over other cookies, Power Rangers over other figurines, etc.). When the student requests an M&M by giving the teacher the sentence strip, the teacher holds up several pieces of candy and asks (or simply gestures), "Which one?" The teacher now guides the student to select a picture signifying "red" and guides the student to place that symbol on the sentence strip (between "I want" and "M&M"). The teacher then clears the sentence strip and guides the student through the new sequence. When the sentence strip including "red" is received, the teacher gives the student the red M&M. No additional reinforcer is needed because the student specified it (although it is always a good idea to add praise or other types of social reward). Another strategy used to assess whether the student truly wants what is indicated on the sentence strip involves having the teacher simply say, "Okay. Take it!" when handed the sentence strip. Rather than immediately giving the student the specified item, the teacher should observe whether the student chooses the item that corresponds to what was requested.

This lesson proceeds to other attributes as long as the teacher can determine how to make the attribute an aspect associated with what the student wants. At times, this approach may be simple, as when teaching a student to ask for the long versus short pretzel or the big versus small cookie, because most students prefer the longer pretzel or the bigger cookie without any specific training. (Although the child selects the long over the short pretzel without training, she needs to learn how to communicate about such choices.) Selecting body parts may be made rewarding by first teaching the student to play a game such as Mr. Potato Head and then teaching the student to request the body part that she wants to place next on the body. In general, an attribute must first be potentially reinforcing to the student before the teacher tries to teach the student to ask for the item using that attribute. For example, if a student never displays any preference along the dimension of color (i.e., the student never chooses favorites by color), then it will be initially difficult to have the student respond to that attribute within a request. In our experience, lessons involving requesting using attributes to which the student already attends are usually more motivating to the student than lessons based on the teacher's selection of attributes and reinforcers.

The Codevelopment of Speech During PECS Use

PECS has been taught to a large number of children and adults with autism and related delays (Bondy & Frost, 1994a). One change that has been reliably observed when using the system with preschool-aged students has been the codevelopment of speech. For some students, speech has been heard within a few months of training; for other students, this development has not been observed for 1 or 2 years; and for another group of students, speech is never reliably displayed. (There are no data yet, however, concerning the codevelopment of speech following the introduction of PECS for children who have previously had extensive, though unsuccessful, training in vocal imitation. The data presented involve children for whom PECS was introduced almost immediately upon their entrance into a school program.) When preschool-aged students with autism develop speech after the introduction of PECS, these students usually go through a period of training when they communicate solely via PECS, followed by a period of time during which they begin to speak while using PECS, and then followed by their complete reliance upon speech as their mode of communication. Although this development has been observed in many (but not all) students, it should be made clear that PECS is taught in order for the student to have a successful means of communicating and not as a method of teaching speech. Several factors seem to be associated with the development of speech.

First, the introduction of PECS to students does not diminish the importance of working on the development of imitation, including vocal imitation. In addition, within the PECS routines, when the student gives the teacher a picture or a sentence strip, the teacher says the appropriate statement back to the student (thus providing a vocal model), including pausing before saying the last word (or phrase). In our experience, many of the students who begin to speak begin to complete the teacher's statement or begin to say the words with the teacher while pointing to each picture. For the students who develop speech, there is a period of time during which they are likely to speak only while using their picture system. These students often use more complex spoken language (i.e., use more words or involve more communicative functions) when they have the opportunity to use PECS (and simultaneously speak) than when they have no pictures to manipulate (Frost, Daily, & Bondy, 1997). During this initial period of vocal acquisition, most students continue to acquire new vocabularies via PECS before they stop using their pictures and rely solely upon spoken language. Although it is tempting to immediately remove all pictures upon hearing the child's first spoken words, the behavior patterns of many students suggests that too early a removal of the pictures can arrest the communication development of some students. Of course, all spoken language will be strongly encouraged and reinforced as it develops.

Not all students who use PECS will develop speech. Research is currently being conducted to help predict which students are likely to learn to speak, but we do not have an accurate early predictor at this time. However, we stress that PECS is taught as a way to provide the student with functional communication and not as the primary way to get a student to speak.

Use of Pictures and Symbols Within Receptive Language Lessons

As noted at the start of this chapter and throughout this book, some students display considerable difficulty acquiring speech. In similar fashion, some students have difficulty understanding the spoken language of others (see Peterson, Bondy, Vincent, & Finnegan, 1995, for an example of this difficulty). For these students, their performance in response to teacher directions (e.g., "Get the spoon") significantly improves when visual cues are added to the spoken instruction.

In some situations, the teacher may use a picture of an item, such as a drawing or photograph of a spoon, while saying, "Get the spoon." In other situations, it may be more effective to present an object associated with a particular activity, such as by giving a student a ball while saying, "Go to the gym." There is no simple test to determine beforehand whether pictures or more concrete objects will be effective with a given student. Some students may need to learn to discriminate between actual objects or 3-D representations before learning how to discriminate between black-and-white line drawings (Frost & Scholefield, 1996). Some students improve not only in their ability to understand what is said to them, but also show a reduction in disruptive reactions during instructional routines, such as fewer tantrums, self-injurious behaviors, or aggressive acts (Peterson et al., 1995).

When such visual cues are added to a teacher's instructions, the teacher should observe whether the student can eventually successfully respond to spoken instructions. Once the student masters successfully responding to the presentation of the visual cues, the teacher begins to reduce the presence of the visual cues. One such strategy can be introduced by gradually reducing the length of time the visual cue is displayed. For example, early in training, the picture is shown to the student during the entire time between the instruction and the student's retrieving the requested item. Over time, the teacher shows the picture for shorter and shorter periods—5 seconds, then 3, then 1, and then just a flash—before removing it entirely. Another strategy is to gradually introduce a pause between saying the instruction "Get the spoon" and showing the picture of the spoon. As this time delay is increased, some students begin to respond to the spoken instruction before the picture cue is introduced. Research associated with this time delay prompting strategy is ongoing (Sulzer-Azaroff & Mayer, 1991).

These strategies can be used when using more concrete objects, especially during transitions from one activity to another or one location to another. Using objects associated with the next activity may help students focus on what the next reinforcer will be (e.g., "Here's your crayon; let's go inside and color") rather than on the current reinforcer they are losing (e.g., "Stop playing and go inside"). Such items can be termed transitional objects (Kanter, 1992) as they may assist the student in understanding what activities are about to begin.

Following a Schedule

Many adults use notes, personal calendars, and other visual aids to remember daily or weekly responsibilities. Many students will be able to move more smoothly through the activities of their day if they are taught to use similar visual cues. When a student is taught to follow certain instructions provided as pictures or other symbols, he is taught to respond to the pictures by retrieving some material and then beginning a particular activity. Schedule following involves teaching students to follow a sequence of pictures. These pictures can be presented in a vertical array (or a left–right sequence as the student gets older) or within a booklet, whereby each page has one picture associated with one activity.

The key to teaching successful schedule following is to minimize the teacher's verbal prompts so that the student comes to rely upon the schedule symbols to get the material, start an activity, complete the activity, put the material away, and return to the schedule array to continue with the sequence (Macduff, Krantz, & McClannahan, 1993). In general, if the student must be told, "Check your schedule," then independence will be harder to achieve than if the teacher uses more physical guidance (which is faded over time).

An advantage of using visual schedule systems with students is that the teacher can review the activities and expectations of the day with the student, potentially reducing surprises the student may find disconcerting. The visual schedule also permits pointing out when the most reinforcing activities will occur. Posted schedules also permit some degree of negotiation with a student. For example, a student may request going to a fast-food restaurant at 9:00 in the morning. Rather than saying, "No," a parent can choose to put the picture of the restaurant on the schedule at a more appropriate time (i.e., lunchtime or dinnertime). In this manner, the student begins to understand that, rather than being totally rejected, he will have to wait to get what is wanted.

Another advantage of using schedule systems is that the teacher can include additional information in the picture. For example, a card on the schedule can indicate that the student will be starting an art project. On the back of the card (or along the bottom edge of the front of the card), the teacher can place pictures associated with each of the materials needed for the project (e.g., paper, crayons, scissors, paste). This system can become very useful for older students who are learning to complete vocational activities that include many items or for students who are learning to follow cooking menus that include many ingredients and utensils.

Pictures and Reinforcement Systems

As has been stressed throughout this book, providing appropriate reinforcement is the backbone of behavioral approaches to teaching. The first part of PECS training relies upon the student learning to request desired reinforcers. In the beginning of such training, it is important to reinforce the request immediately and on a consistent basis. However, it should be understood that a student cannot be given everything that is requested at all times. For a student who has never calmly requested anything, during the first few days of PECS training, when that student repeatedly asks for a piece of pretzel, it is certainly recommended that each request be rewarded. However, as time goes by, no one will want to (or at times be able to) give the student a pretzel every time one is requested. The student needs to continue to be rewarded for making requests; however, teachers and parents want to make it clear that they gradually expect more and more from the student.

One potential solution involves teaching the student to use a visual reinforcement system. The sequence is similar to how all individuals are taught to value money; that is, people learn to appreciate and desire money because they learn that they can exchange money for things that they want. For a student who uses PECS, the process begins when she makes a specific request. For example, when the student requests a pretzel, the teacher places the picture (with Velcro or some similar material) on a special card (about the size of an index card) while saying, "Oh, you want the pretzel." The teacher places on this card a small circle within which is placed (also with Velcro) a type of symbol or token (e.g., a penny, or more age-appropriate trinket or sticker). The teacher immediately asks the student to do a simple task, such as retrieving a pencil on the table or putting a toy in a box. Upon task completion, the teacher gives the student the token, guides her to place it on the card, and immediately takes the token from the card while giving the student what she requested. (The student is not required to give the teacher the picture because she already requested the pretzel and does not need to ask again.)

The student learns the value of the token by trading it in for the desired item. Additional circles are gradually placed on the card until the student needs to earn five tokens before trading them in for the item requested. In this manner, the student has a continuous visual reminder of what she is working for, while at the same time she is gradually taught to accomplish more (i.e., extend the length of time or number of items needed to complete certain lessons or other activities) before being rewarded. As the student completes activities for the teacher and earns tokens, she will see that her card has some circles filled in while others are still empty. This arrangement helps give the student visual cues about how close she is to earning her reward and how much more work is still expected. Of course, it is important to keep in mind a student's age when setting goals for how long the student can be reasonably expected to work.

Putting It All Together

When each of these systems is introduced to a student, there are a number of important things for the teacher to arrange. Most important, a student using PECS must have continuous access to his own communication system. The communication book (or individual pictures) should never be hidden as a way of "silencing" the student. That would be no different from putting tape over the mouth of a typically developing 2-year-old who asks too many questions. Next, a schedule system should be prepared to help the student navigate across the activities of the day. Finally, the student should be given a visual reinforcement system that will help in understanding what he is working for and how much more work is expected. By combining these systems, the student is given a solid basis by which he is better able to communicate with parents, teachers, and people in the community, and he is better able to understand his teachers' and parents' communicative efforts. Further, by stressing the visual aspects of these systems, the student has more continuous access to important information about what he can do and what is expected of him. A complete description of the elements involved in designing effective educational environments that incorporate PECS and other visual systems can be found in *The Pyramid Approach to Education* (Bondy, 1996).

Programmatic Considerations

SECTION 6

Maintaining Treatment Gains

CHAPTER 31

Tristram Smith

Persons who work with individuals with developmental delays are likely to confront the question of whether the gains the individuals make in their programs generated through the classroom or clinic will be maintained after the individuals leave those settings. An intervention is of only limited value if it fails to maintain its effects over time. A study published by Lovaas, Koegel, Simmons, and Long in 1973 illustrates this problem (see Chapter 3 for a more detailed review). In this study, a group of children were treated with intensive behavioral intervention over a period of about 14 months. During this time, the children made substantial progress in speech, toy play, and social interactions while self-stimulatory and tantrumous behaviors decreased. At the end of treatment, about half of the children entered a state institution where they received a great deal of noncontingent care and love and access to special education classes. Several of the remaining children in this study were not discharged to the state institution but rather were returned to their parents who had been trained in the implementation of behavioral treatment. When the institutionalized children were assessed 2 years later, they had all regressed. It was possible, however, to reestablish many of their original gains by introducing the treatment a second time. Unfortunately, these gains were again lost at the time of the second follow-up. The children who had returned home to their parents, however, had not regressed at follow-up. Such results demonstrate that having parents, significant adults, and peers rather than only aides involved in the several facets of treatment is essential for maintaining treatment gains.

A second follow-up study by McEachin, Smith, and Lovaas was published in 1993 and incorporated many of the recommendations we present in this chapter. In brief, the follow-up data generated from the 1993 study are much more encouraging than the results of the earlier study: The 1993 follow-up study showed that 9 of the 19 children who had received the revised intervention maintained the treatment gains 3 to 12 years after the termination of treatment. Ten of the remaining children were placed in special education classes after treatment, many of them regressing over time. The reason the best-outcome group did so well is likely to be based at least partially on the fact that the children composing this group continued to receive treatment in the sense that they were integrated with and learned from typical children.

Whether or not a person maintains the gains made during an intervention is probably a function of a number of variables. Whether a person remembers, recalls, or otherwise maintains what has been learned in the past is a function of changes in that person's environment as well as changes in that person's central nervous system (in the case of individuals with developmental delays, such change is instigated by organic damage). This chapter concerns only the environmental changes contributing to the maintenance of treatment gains.

The means by which the nervous systems of individuals with developmental delays process stimuli resulting in excellent versus poor recall are unknown. What is known, however, is that individuals with autism display superior memory of responses to simple stimuli, such as recalling digits or other visual presentations, when compared to other individuals with delays or typical individuals of the same mental age as the individuals with autism. However, individuals with autism exhibit inferior memory skills when presented with tasks in which the stimulus and response involve different sensory modalities (e.g., auditory and visual). For example, on a task that requires an individual to hear a verbal stimulus and make a visual–motor response (e.g., "Touch nose"), individuals with autism fail to retain the correct response more often than other individuals of the same mental age. Whether this phenomenon is due to the individuals' limited exposure to early educational materials or unique characteristics of the individuals' nervous systems is not known. In any case, it seems reasonable to take advantage of what is known about improving memory and then build upon and incorporate such knowledge into one's intervention program. In this chapter, we consider three basic procedures to enhance the retention of learned material. The first centers on reinforcement control, the second focuses on stimulus control, and the third deals with consistent findings from memory research concerning programming and spacing of trials.

Manipulating Reinforcers

There are two ways in which reinforcers may be manipulated so as to enhance the likelihood that learned behavior will be retained. These are discussed in this section.

▶ **1. Manipulating reinforcement schedules.** Schedules of reinforcement vary in type. One way to deliver reinforcement is to give it contingent on every correct response. This schedule of reinforcement is known as a *continuous schedule*. A second procedure is to provide reinforcement on a more intermittent basis, such as once every eighth correct response or once every 10 minutes. These are called *ratio schedules* of reinforcement and *interval schedules* of reinforcement, respectively, depending on whether a certain number of responses or a certain amount of time elapsed since the last response is used to determine when the reinforcement is delivered.

One can differentiate between high-density and low-density schedules of reinforcement by analyzing the frequency with which reinforcement is provided. One can also differentiate between fixed schedules and variable schedules by observing whether reinforcement is always given after a fixed number of behaviors or amount of time (e.g., reinforcement is always given after every three correct responses or after every 5 minutes) or an irregular number of behaviors or interval of time (e.g., reinforcement is given after a random number of behaviors or random amount of time). For example, in a variable ratio schedule with a density of five, the average number of responses between reinforcements is five, but the number of responses between any two reinforcements may be more or less than five.

It is generally known that continuous reinforcement (i.e., reinforcement for each correct response) is the preferred schedule to use as a behavior is being acquired given that fixed, high-density schedules result in relatively rapid acquisition. However, once the behavior is established, shifting to a thinner variable schedule yields more resistance to extinction; thus, the behavior will be maintained for longer periods of time through this type of schedule. Such a procedure is similar to methods parents often use to raise a typical child. That is, one often provides a dense schedule of reinforcement for a child when the child is very young and is just learning particular skills. As the child grows older, however, one expects that the child will behave appropriately without having to be reinforced so often.

▶ **2. Selection of reinforcers.** Reinforcers that are likely to be present in the student's natural, everyday settings should be used. Note that food reinforcers are not likely to be present with sufficient frequency to maintain learned behaviors once the student enters a new environment. Thus, the student will learn to discriminate between those environments in which she receives food reinforcement and those in which she does not. Consequently, the student's appropriate behaviors will rapidly extinguish in new environments. To avoid such a loss, one must gradually transfer from the use of food reinforcement to reinforcers available in the student's everyday environment. More natural reinforcers are likely to be secondary or acquired reinforcers (reinforcers that are learned, such as praise and recognition) as opposed to primary reinforcers.

Stimulus Control

If a student learns a certain behavior in a particular setting and in the presence of a limited number of persons, such as parents and an aide, it is unlikely that this behavior will maintain itself once the environment is changed. In technical literature, this phenomenon is said to result from narrow stimulus control. To avoid such an occurrence, one must arrange for broad stimulus control over the student's behaviors such that various adults and diverse environments come to cue consistent responding. An example from the everyday lives of typical children may illustrate this problem well. While in the presence of family, one may see a child engage in certain kinds of appropriate and pleasing behaviors. One often hopes that these behaviors learned at home will be transferred to the child's school or peer group. Parents often become quite concerned when they observe their child behave in a radically different manner when he is outside the family; the stimulus control the parents exercise in the home may be nonexistent once the child leaves the home.

There are two strategies for creating common stimuli across settings to help maintain consistency in the student's behaviors. First, one must make certain that the discriminative stimuli present in the teaching environment are also present in the student's everyday environment. For example, students with developmental delays are more likely to generalize the skills they learn in the Receptive Labeling of Objects Program (in Chapter 17) if the labels taught are acquired through the use of three-dimensional objects rather than pictures of objects. Students with developmental delays are also more likely to generalize treatment gains if the persons or situations they encounter outside the instructional setting are similar to those from within the treatment environment.

The second strategy involves teaching the student to respond to numerous exemplars of stimuli. For example, broader stimulus control (greater generalization) will be gained if the student is taught to label not only one dog but several dogs of different sizes, shapes, and colors. In technical literature, such a strategy is referred to as the *method of sufficient examples*, given that it involves teaching enough examples of certain stimuli that the student learns to generalize from these examples to novel examples.

There is a third issue to contend with when strategizing the establishment of stimulus control: When a student enters a new environment, that environment may contain stimuli that distract the student from exhibiting previously learned behaviors or, conceivably, the student may be taught competing behaviors through exposure to certain settings. To compensate for such occurrences, the student should be taught in environments as similar to his everyday settings as possible. In addition, if gains are made in one setting, then an effort should be made to transfer those gains to other settings and other persons. For example, if a student is treated by one professional (e.g., either a speech therapist or a teacher) or if treatment occurs in a single setting (e.g., a single office or classroom), it is likely that whatever gains the student demonstrates with the original person or in the original setting will not be cued by novel persons or settings.

Memory Research

A great deal of research concerning memory facilitation in typical individuals has been carried out and applied to help individuals better remember information they need in order to function in new and different environments. Many of these techniques for improving memory are very involved and too complicated for use in the treatment of students with developmental delays. However, a technique labeled *spacing* or *expanded trials* has proven to be very helpful and particularly appropriate for facilitating recall in students with developmental delays.

Spacing is a technique that consists of gradually increasing the time interval separating trials of a new response after that response is acquired through mass trialing. The exact reason why spacing facilitates memory is largely unknown, but it may be because such a procedure requires the student to *practice* remembering. The more difficult the practice is (i.e., the longer the time interval between trials), the more the student is prepared to remember the correct response after formal teaching is over.

Once a particular behavior is acquired in mass trials, a spacing procedure may be started by expanding the time interval between trials, beginning with short intervals and gradually increasing to longer ones. This may seem contradictory to what was advised in earlier portions of this manual where we recommended that the teacher minimize intertrial intervals. It is important that the teacher discriminate, however, between the acquisition of a behavior and the retention of learned material. In regard to designing treatment, spacing trials relates closely to what we refer to as rehearsing or practicing mastered material placed on a maintenance schedule. That is, when a task is first acquired, it should be rehearsed after relatively short intervals (e.g., 1 hour). As the behavior becomes more established, however, the times at which it is practiced can be spaced over one day, then every third day, then every week, and so on. Note that the speed with which the intervals are increased must be determined by the performance of the student. For example, if at a particular interval the student's performance deteriorates, it is necessary to reestablish the target behavior by shortening the intertrial interval before again expanding the amount of time between trials.

As a common example of the importance of spacing in facilitating recall, we can draw upon several studies (Charlop, Kurtz, & Milstein, 1992; Davis, Smith, & Donahoe, 2002; Dunlap, 1984) that have generated a similar result: In teaching a course, one can either teach the entire course in one day or spread instruction over several days, perhaps even months. If the course is taught in one day, retention of the material is likely to be minimal. In contrast, if the course material is divided up and taught incrementally, one's retention of it will likely exceed that gained in the rapid course.

Involving Parents in Treatment

CHAPTER 32

Eric V. Larsson

Parents have many competing demands for their time. Many have full-time jobs. Many have other children with substantial needs. Many are single parents. For these and other reasons, they may not be involved in the treatment of their child with developmental delays to the extent necessary to fully generalize treatment gains throughout the child's life. When this happens, parents find themselves out of touch with the child's current skills and lacking confidence to follow through with the child. A problem that may arise from this situation is that parents begin to disagree over treatment and interfere with each other's parenting due to lack of knowledge regarding the current state of the child's treatment. Inconsistent treatment then often results, and the child's optimal progress is substantially imperiled.

When this situation exists, one technique that we have found very useful is to change the mastery criterion for each skill. We add a requirement that, before a skill is considered mastered by a child, each parent must be able to obtain the same success level as was obtained by the staff. Initially, parents may find this requirement threatening. However, the following procedure is designed to make this as painless and supportive as possible. In fact, once involved this way, we have found that parents are very satisfied with their participation, feel confident in their knowledge of the treatment, are more likely to volunteer for treatment hours, and generalize their use of skills more readily throughout the day.

Generalization Procedure

First, the senior aide schedules at least one weekly appointment with each parent separately to meet and conduct the generalization assessment. At this appointment, the senior aide has the list of skills mastered during the past week. The aide then presents each skill in turn and assesses generalization to the parent.

For each skill, we use the following procedure. The aide briefly describes the skill and the method being used and answers any questions from the parent. Then the aide models the program as it is typically conducted. During the break, the aide determines whether the child performed appropriately and whether the parent feels ready. Then the parent engages the child in the entire program exactly as modeled by the aide. The aide then gives any necessary feedback to the parent and remodels the program if the child failed to completely generalize to the parent's implementation of the program. The aide and parent then continue to take turns with the program until the child succeeds with the parent at the same level as with the aide.

Key Features

Several features of this procedure are important. First, the parent attempts the program only after the child has mastered it with the aides. This prevents frustration for both the parent and the child. Second, the aide always models the program before requiring the parent to engage. This immediate modeling greatly improves the parent's fidelity to the program. Third, the child then carries behavioral momentum into the parent's turn, which helps overcome any discrimination that the child has learned between parents and aides. Therefore, if the child fails with the aide, the aide must continue the program until the child performs at the mastery level. If necessary, the behavioral momentum may be maximized by having the parent replace the aide in the chair before the aide finishes the program and then conclude the program immediately with the child. Finally, because the programs cannot proceed properly without the parents' involvement, they are very motivated to keep up this participation.

Potential Difficulties

We have encountered two potential difficulties with this procedure. The first is that the special nature of this generalization appointment causes the aide to disregard the importance of effective reinforcement. However, it is doubly important that the parent use effective reinforcers, and that the parent be the one who delivers the reinforcers. The second potential difficulty is that the adults tend to sit and talk too long between programs. This often stimulates the child either to disengage into stereotyped behavior or to engage in attention-getting behavior to compete with the two adults.

Involving Parents in Treatment: The Program of the Week

As emphasized previously, it is imperative that we generalize the skills throughout the day into unstructured activities. During staff sessions, we generally set guidelines for how often a given program should be prompted and reinforced incidentally during unstructured time. The parents, however, have many daily distracters that prevent them from generalizing the programs, and lack of practice with the programs further inhibits their ability to spontaneously prompt a specific skill. Therefore, we have developed the following procedure to facilitate the parents' generalization of programs.

Procedure

At each clinic meeting, we specify a program that will be emphasized that week for incidental training. The program is selected because it has been mastered in a structured setting and has functional utility throughout the day. Then the senior aide schedules an appointment with each parent to practice incidentally prompting the skill. The first step is to go to an unusual part of the house or neighborhood, without standard training materials, and explain and model the program for the parent. The second step is to model how to implement the program in this novel environment. This step is usually the parent's biggest challenge. The aide then prompts the parent to help implement the program in a new setting. The aide takes turns modeling and giving feedback until the parent can independently identify natural materials, SDs, prompts, and reinforcers. Then in the third step, the aide again models the program with the child present until the child successfully responds. Then it is the parent's turn. The aide and parent take turns implementing the program in novel locations until the child makes a successful response to the parent. Finally, the aide gives a treatment assignment to the parent to implement the incidental trial a minimum number of times per day (usually 10 times) and to record the data on a data sheet. Then the aide makes plans to review the progress at the next clinic meeting.

Key Features

Even though there are many skills that need generalization throughout the day, it is overwhelming for the parents to attempt to generalize all of the programs at once. By focusing on only one program per week, parents can then master and probably maintain their performance with that program in future weeks. By so doing, the parents can effectively master about 50 programs per year (approximately one per week). Once that many programs are mastered, it is likely that the parents can generalize to other types of necessary skills. It is very helpful to post the data sheet in an obvious location, such as the refrigerator door, to prompt the parents to initiate the drill. It is also important to plan for all significant times of day, activities, and locations in order to generalize the skill to as many functional activities as possible.

Potential Difficulties

Because it is very difficult for the parents to get used to working as described previously, it is essential that the aide schedule a training time to implement the skill rather than just assign this task and make the parents feel guilty when they do not do it. Further, it is essential to follow up on the program at the next clinic meeting because the parents may not have gotten around to implementing the skill and, with no feedback, will be even less likely to resume this procedure.

Parent Empowerment

In the 1960s we had expected that, upon establishing the basic treatment methods, we could effectively "cure" the child in an institutional setting and then release the child with a warm handshake and a sense of a job well done. However, our first outcome study (Lovaas, Koegel, Simmons, & Long, 1973) informed us of the results that we should have anticipated. The children's skills did not maintain in some subsequent environments. This "failure" was analyzed as a lack of generalization. One response to this analysis was to seek methods of treatment that would generalize more effectively, and we did engage in that course of investigation. However, the more important analysis followed from the basic principle of behavior analysis: that behavior is controlled by its environment, and obviously a child's parents are the most significant feature of the child's environment. Indeed, the 1973 study found that the children who were released to those parents who had received modest training were more likely to maintain and continue their gains than were children released to persons who had received minimal or no training.

In response to this study, we chose to focus our treatment on families of young children for whom we had the opportunity to train parents to use the skills discovered in our research program. As a result, in the 1970s and 1980s, we found that we could successfully train parents so that they could then provide quality treatment to their own child, generalize these skills throughout the day, and even hire and train their own staff. This became the stated goal of our treatment. In fact, we came to realize that parents are best judged truly competent when they demonstrate that they can train others.

Further, the need for 24-hour-a-day, 7-day-a-week follow-through is hugely important. Children are learning all day long, whether or not we are planning their learning. The children we most often treat require consistent follow-through, or they do not reliably learn the skills we teach. Even when we provide 40 hours per week of training, they still have an additional 128 hours per week with the parents. It is imperative that the parents have the skills to follow through appropriately during this great expanse of time.

A word of caution. Some parents and professionals become very uncomfortable when we talk of parent training because it conjures up the psychoanalytic theories, very much alive today as parent blaming. Our emphasis has nothing to do with blaming parents for their children's condition. These children do not become disabled due to the environment their parents provide. For example, most families have typical siblings growing up alongside the child with developmental delays. What we are providing is a professional treatment that has been carefully worked out over many years and at great expense. It is not "normal" parenting—normal parenting does not result in the gains that professional treatment achieves. Normal parenting does not ameliorate the challenging conditions that these children present. However, parents can learn all or most of these professional skills, and they have the motivation and intensity to help their children, even more so than professional persons. Parents have been proving this simple fact over the past 25 years.

Parent Training

To establish a comprehensive behavioral environment that enables the child's therapeutic development, we need to teach all care providers to use the necessary skills. Only then can the child be confronted by pervasive appropriate contingencies for normal behavior and have limited opportunity to practice autistic behaviors. It is a familiar phenomenon to see a child discriminate one adult from another. The children are neither insensitive to environmental contingencies nor incapable of learning; instead, they are hypersensitive to certain immediate contingencies. They appear to quickly adjust their behavior to match the contingencies being provided by different care providers. Therefore, until the child's treatment is complete, all care providers must be taught to follow through consistently. Until this happens, it will not be the child who has trouble learning; it will be the teacher who has trouble teaching.

We have found that we can efficiently teach parents through the same mechanism that we teach staff: in the clinic and home through one-on-one and group supervision (see R. L. Koegel, Glahn, & Nieminen, 1978). However, we have found that some special considerations are important.

The demands of this treatment represent a comprehensive lifestyle change for the parents and child, rather than a part-time job as for staff. The parents must incorporate treatment skills into their 24-hour parenting style in order for their child to make maximum progress. When they reach a certain level of competence, they could, if desired, train and supervise their own staff, thereby delegating some of the treatment to others.

Because of the typical relationship between professionals and parents, the natural tendency of staff and parents alike is to rely on staff to engage the child and complete programs. In human services and education, parents have rarely been genuinely empowered to take a leadership role in meeting their children's needs. Both staff and parents typically expect the staff to fill the "expert" role and place responsibility on the staff to maintain quality control over programming; however, these expectations subvert the therapeutic need to fully involve the parents in intervention. Therefore, supervisors must be vigilant to prevent these tendencies from taking hold. Supervisors should look beyond the staff hours to the family's 24-hour day to analyze where the treatment needs augmentation. In clinic meetings, parents must be given a central role in training and decision making. Parents must meet the competencies necessary to train new staff members in the necessary treatment skills.

Considerations Regarding Family Life

At the start, it is important to recognize that parents and their children with developmental delays have a history of substantial failure communicating with each other, and this legacy affects parents emotionally as they attempt to learn treatment skills in front of the treatment team. It is very supportive of professionals to acknowledge this to parents before requesting parent participation, and also to predict the heightened difficulty parents are likely to face due to their shared history with their children. This will help parents face the adversity with less stress. (Fathers may be even more sensitive to failure in front of a group than may mothers.)

When providing feedback to parents, staff should be sensitive to the impact of negative feedback and be careful to outweigh it with genuine positive reinforcement. Even the natural emotional reactions to the most critical negative feedback can be defused if the feedback is given with a smile, with acknowledgment of the humor in the situation, and with reassurance that the error is common among all aides, even the supervisor.

In providing the first independent assignments for parents, the senior aide should assign fun programs that have a high likelihood of child cooperation and fit into the parents' interests. Skills such as hugging and saying "I love you," reinforcing activities that cause the child to laugh, and play activities that are special interests of the parents and siblings (e.g., sports, reading together) will help support the parents' maintenance of skills.

Tantrumous behavior is a special issue. All parents act instinctively to limit their child's tantrums, and with typical children, these actions usually result in effective child rearing. However, such parenting responses may be counterproductive with children who have with developmental delays. Parents may walk on eggshells to avoid tantrums and placate the child as soon as tantrums arise. Therefore, in both clinic- and workshop-based parent training, parents need to learn to address tantrums directly by purposely using reinforcement contingencies for which the child has been known to tantrum, rather than avoiding using these contingencies out of fear of tantrums.

Further, tantrums on extinction may drive spouses crazy. Two parents are not a monolithic unit. Staff may need to create a community of reinforcement within the family for behavioral treatment—in the face of the parents' natural emotional avoidance of tantrums, for example. Treatment will fail if spouses are in conflict because mom makes the child cry and dad cannot stand it. When one parent is following through, a common reaction is for the second spouse to intervene either to placate the child or chastise the spouse. This normal process must be addressed directly during tantrums in clinic meetings by requesting that both parents reinforce the other for following through with the prescribed treatment for tantrums and acknowledge that this is a sign that the parents are effectively working with the child. The supervisor should follow up on tantrum experiences at later clinic meetings to address the effectiveness of this process.

An ironic issue that may arise is that, when the treatment appears to be effective, the parents' motivation may slacken out of overconfidence. However, the student's attainment of advanced skills is critically important, and requires the parents' active involvement more than ever.

Conflict Resolution

Often conflicts arise within the family or between the family and the aide. The supervisor needs to try to maintain a private, one-to-one relationship with the family to give parents a safe forum for discussing these problems as early as possible so that they can be addressed as proactively as possible.

When conflicts seem intractable, the following skills may help. Staff must address conflicts honestly and directly without passive avoidance. The best strategy is to offer a well-timed, direct solution statement, delivered from the supervisor's honest perspective on the needs of treatment.

Solution statements should be in the form of a request for future appropriate behavior without recrimination for past errors. The statement should offer parents a clearly specified choice and opportunity for negotiation. The statement should be relevant to current treatment goals. It should be realistic. If potential aide action is "threatened," it should refer to a previously agreed upon clinical contract. For a rationale, the aide should summarize patterns rather than specific acts, and state a functional analysis of potential therapeutic consequences of the patterns. To problem-solve the types of solutions to offer, the aide should observe immediate, objective interaction styles rather than infer parents' and staff's roles in unobservable processes. If the clinical staff is the source of the problem, then the supervisor should take responsibility and act accordingly.

If conflict is severe, the solution statement should be well timed. Staff and parents should take a break when real emotions are being acted out. The statement should not be delivered contingent upon an emotional interaction when neither participant will hear it. Instead, it should be offered after a full assessment is made at a later date. It should be offered by a staff person whom the parents like and respect.

The solution statements should embody the best balance of consistency, following through with previously recommended solutions when previous attempts at solutions have failed. Positive reinforcement for objective appropriate behavior should balance any implied criticism. Each issue should be resolved in turn without allowing issues to fester. Each issue should be assertively followed up at later meetings.

Some behaviors commonly seen in conflict resolution can exacerbate conflict or distract from conflict resolution. Mistakes that are made when attempting to resolve conflict include the following: asking for reasons for behavior, using qualifiers, stating that there is only one solution, interrupting, telling the family that they will prefer it the staff's way, labeling a person, mind-reading what a person thinks, taking responsibility for the child away from the parent, and reinforcing dependency on staff.

When parent or staff noncompliance is a difficulty, the following principles are helpful:

- Assign clear, agreed upon homework.
- Directly follow up at an agreed upon time.
- Brainstorm significant impediments.
- Assign a one-on-one session with the appropriate senior staff to work on the skill. Focus first on cooperation within a session while the trainer is present. Second, focus on child progress with accurate use of skills within the session. Third, focus on cooperation with permanent product homework assignments (structured, data-based sessions).

Promoting Generalization and Maintenance of Parents' Skills

Parenting skills should generalize to new child behaviors, other appropriate parenting skills, or other settings, particularly those settings in which the staff are not present. Behaviors that generalize to novel settings may be seen as independent of training stimuli and are, therefore, likely to be maintained after training. When parenting skills do not seem to generalize or maintain beyond clinic meetings, the following techniques can be considered (Stokes & Baer, 1977).

▶ **Program Common Stimuli.** Parent training is best conducted in the home in order to bring the trained parenting responses efficiently under the control of home stimuli. Videotaped modeling and specific written guidelines taken into the home help prompt generalization.

▶ **Program Sufficient Exemplars.** A variety of child behaviors should be presented. More regular contact with parents allows for a greater variety of opportunities to observe successes and difficulties, and therefore more opportunities to instruct. A high rate of appropriate behavior or fluent performance across repeated training situations is a dramatic demonstration of parent competence.

▶ **Instruct Generalization.** Programming generalized skills through written and verbal instructions is frequently employed. Trainers assist parents in planning for community settings and give homework assignments.

▶ **Recruit Natural Communities of Reinforcement.** The development of an ongoing support group through combining isolated parents or including other significant family members can provide for ongoing reinforcement (as well as prompting) of trained skills.

Data Collection

CHAPTER 33

Greg Buch

Data collection plays an extremely important role in behavioral intervention programs. Data on the student's day-to-day performance is often needed to assess (a) whether the student is improving within programs, (b) whether and how programs need to be modified to meet the individual needs of the student, and (c) whether teachers are following the correct procedures. Furthermore, data on the overall effectiveness of intensive early intervention programs, taken before and after treatment, allow parents to make informed decisions regarding the costs and benefits of treatment. Both short- and long-term data are often required to gain or maintain funding from schools or public agencies.

The task of choosing how, where, and what to measure when providing a 40-hour-per-week program can be daunting. As mentioned earlier in this manual, a large amount of information regarding treatment effectiveness can be obtained in weekly meetings where staff and parents observe the student's progress. A well-run program also provides day-to-day supervision of teaching skills by senior aides, who in turn are directed by supervisors or consultants. Much information about treatment effectiveness can also be obtained through viewing videotapes recorded during treatment. Such tapes are often helpful when subtle problems in teaching skills need to be identified, because they allow for repeated viewing and detailed analyses.

In the course of a 2- to 3-year intervention, a student may experience several hundred different programs. Each program presents its own potential difficulties, and the subtlest teaching mistake in a single program has the potential to slow down or stop progress across all of a student's programs. Consequently, the task of assuring treatment fidelity is both critical and extensive. In this chapter, we first review how to take relatively selective data that will allow the team to troubleshoot and document progress without adding substantially to the cost and time burdens of providing treatment. The last part of the chapter describes the Log Book, which provides an efficient way of recording what particular skills within programs have been taught by a team member on any one day. This allows for each team member to instantly be updated as to what the student has been taught and how the student has performed. It also aids in decision making regarding what particular programs should be administered on a given day. Also discussed is the Maintenance Book, which provides information about what particular programs have been mastered and which ones should be rehearsed so as to be maintained.

How To Take Discrete Trial Data

Discrete trial data are primarily useful for analyzing the student's level of performance in a particular program and for troubleshooting problems within programs. Collecting discrete trial data is fairly simple. For each trial of a particular program, the teacher records the instruction given and whether the student's response was correct, incorrect, or prompted. A complete blank data sheet is provided in Appendix 33.A at the end of this chapter.

Figure 33.1 shows some sample data from the Early Receptive Language Program. On Trial 1, the teacher instructed the student to clap, and the student responded correctly, as indicated by the circle around the letter C (for correct). On Trial 2, the teacher instructed the student to wave, and the student responded incorrectly (indicated by the letter I). On Trial 3, the teacher instructed the student to wave again, and then prompted the student

1. SD:	"Clap"	(C)	I	P
2. SD:	"Wave"	C	(I)	P
3. SD:	"Wave"	C	I	(P)
4. SD:	"Wave"	(C)	I	P

Figure 33.1. Sample data from Early Receptive Language Program.

to wave (indicated by the letter P). On Trial 4, the student was instructed to wave a third time, and the student responded correctly.

Note that, in addition to instructions and responses, teachers should also record on the sheet (a) the date that the data were taken; (b) the name of the teacher or aide who did the program; (c) the number of correct, incorrect, and prompted trials; and (d) the percentage of correct responses (see the Discrete Trial Data sheet in Appendix 33.A at the end of this chapter).

If the discrimination training procedure is being used to teach new skills, trials involving a contrasting stimulus should be indicated by a C on the instruction/SD line, as shown in Figure 33.2. However, trials with a contrasting stimulus should not be used to calculate a student's percentage of correct responses.

Teachers working with the same student often inadvertently develop different criteria for what defines a correct, incorrect, or prompted response. When this happens, the value of discrete trial data can be severely compromised. To prevent this, teachers' interrater reliability should be assessed once every 1 to 2 months, or whenever there is suspicion of a problem.

To measure interrater reliability, two teachers should take data concurrently during a session. Their data should then be compared and the percentage of trials on which they agree (on which they both recorded that a student was correct, incorrect, or prompted) is computed. Teachers should be in agreement on at least 90% of their trials. If they are not, they should review the criteria for correct, incorrect, and prompted responses, and practice scoring sessions together until they agree at least 90% of the time.

Weekly meetings are a good time to assess interrater reliability. Teams may also videotape a single teacher's session, and then have all the team members score the tape at their convenience. Using this procedure, a senior team member or parent can determine if the entire team, or only one or two members, are having reliability problems. New teachers should always establish their reliability with an experienced teacher before taking data on their own.

1. SD:	"Clap"	(C)	I	P
2. SD:	C	(C)	I	P
3. SD:	"Clap"	(C)	I	P
4. SD:	C	(C)	I	P
5. SD:	C	(C)	I	P
6. SD:	"Clap"	(C)	I	P

Figure 33.2. Sample data showing use of C for contrasting stimulus.

Tips on Taking Data

We provide the following tips on taking data to help the team members be consistent in their work with students and their recording of data.

1. Teaching and taking data at the same time can be difficult. If teachers work alone, they should do 4 to 5 trials before recording the student's responses (to reduce the length of intertrial intervals). If possible, record responses when the student is occupied with a reinforcer or after the student has been excused for a break.
2. Taking data while teaching is particularly difficult for relatively new teachers. If possible, have a second teacher take data when new teachers are teaching.
3. When totaling percentages of correct responses, make sure that prompted trials are *not* counted as correct responses.
4. Let teachers know that they do not have to complete 20 trials during each program simply because the data sheets go up to 20.

When To Take Discrete Trial Data

Discrete trial data should generally be taken (a) on programs in which the student is showing slow or limited progress and (b) at monthly intervals for all programs to document the student's progress or lack thereof. A common misconception is that one must take discrete trial data on every trial of every program, every day. Taking discrete trial data is time consuming and, consequently, expensive. Therefore, it should be done in response to the specific needs of each student.

If the student is having difficulty in a specific program (progress is slow, the program causes tantrums, etc.), it may be appropriate to have all teachers take discrete trial data on the program for several days. These data may then be analyzed (as described in the next section) by the student's senior aide, parents, or behavioral consultant to see if teachers are making any procedural errors. One to 2 days' worth of data is usually enough to spot most problems. Subsequent to being analyzed, the data gathered may demonstrate that programs need to be modified or placed on hold, or teachers may need to receive additional instruction in how to implement programs.

If the student is having difficulties across several or most programs, or if there is a concern that one or several teachers are making consistent procedural mistakes, it may be necessary to take discrete trial data on all programs for several days. Again, this data should be analyzed as described in the next section.

To document the student's performance in programs that progress smoothly, discrete trial data from the last few days of each month will generally provide an adequate sample. For example, to document the student's progress in the Matching and Sorting Program, you may need to take trial-by-trial data only during the last two to three teaching sessions (approximately 30 to 45 trials) of each month.

Using Discrete Trial Data To Troubleshoot Common Problems

An experienced teacher or parent can spot a wide variety of common teaching mistakes simply by analyzing a student's discrete trial data. Following are some common problems that can be spotted by reviewing such data:

1. Teachers fail to follow prompted trials with unprompted trials. Figure 33.3 shows data from the Early Receptive Language Program. On Trials 2 and 4, the teacher had to prompt the student to occasion a successful response. However, the teacher never followed up these prompted trials with unprompted trials. Consequently, we do not know if the student learned to respond to the teacher's instructions or simply became prompt dependent.

2. Teachers allow the student to be unsuccessful on too many trials. Figure 33.4 shows data from the Early Receptive Language Program. In this sitting, the teacher used massed trials to teach the student to stand up. As can be seen from the data, the teacher prompted the student after 3 unsuccessful trials. After this, the student was again prompted after 3 incorrect responses. In this case, the teacher should have initiated the prompt sooner and then gradually faded the prompt. Overall, the student should be reinforced (and thus successful) in 90% of trials.

1. SD:	"Touch nose"	C	Ⓘ	P
2. SD:	"Touch nose"	C	I	Ⓟ
3. SD:	"Smile"	C	Ⓘ	P
4. SD:	"Smile"	C	I	Ⓟ
5. SD:	"Jump"	Ⓒ	I	P
6. SD:	"Wave"	Ⓒ	I	P

Figure 33.3. Sample data showing teacher's failure to follow prompted trials with unprompted trials.

1. SD:	"Stand up"	C	Ⓘ	P
2. SD:	"Stand up"	C	Ⓘ	P
3. SD:	"Stand up"	C	Ⓘ	P
4. SD:	"Stand up"	C	I	Ⓟ
5. SD:	"Stand up"	C	Ⓘ	P
6. SD:	"Stand up"	C	Ⓘ	P
7. SD:	"Stand up"	C	Ⓘ	P
8. SD:	"Stand up"	C	I	Ⓟ
9. SD:	"Stand up"	Ⓒ	I	P

Figure 33.4. Sample data.

3. Teachers spend too much time on previously mastered responses. The majority of a teacher's time in most sessions should be spent on teaching new skills. However, teachers frequently begin programs by running through all of a student's mastered responses. If a teacher's data show that he or she has spent 15 trials reviewing mastered skills and only 5 trials teaching a new response, he or she should be told to reverse this emphasis.

4. Teachers do too many trials of a program. Enthusiastic teachers may have a student sit for 20 to 30 trials of a program, when only 5 to 15 trials may be appropriate for a single sitting. This is a common cause of tantrums and nonresponsive behavior.

Reviewing data sheets will also reveal whether teachers are using discrimination training procedures correctly, are doing an appropriate number of programs in a given period of time, and are working on the correct target behaviors for a program.

A problem common among both new and experienced teachers is failing to vary reinforcers. It is easy for teachers to use the same food or the same verbal praise as reinforcement, trial after trial, day after day, without realizing they are doing so. Students will generally respond to this situation with tantrums, decreased attention, nonresponsiveness, and incorrect responses. If there is concern that teachers are not varying their reinforcers, it often helps to have them take trial-by-trial data on the exact

1. Reinforcer:	goldfish	C	(I)	P
2. Reinforcer:	tickles	C	I	(P)
3. Reinforcer:	rocked chair	C	(I)	P
4. Reinforcer:	soda	C	I	(P)
5. Reinforcer:	swung upside down	(C)	I	P
6. Reinforcer:	hugged	(C)	I	P

Figure 33.5. Sample data showing reinforcers used.

reinforcers they use. Figure 33.5 presents a sample format for taking reinforcement data. This self-monitoring procedure is generally effective at prompting teachers to use more varied rewards.

Documenting a Student's Progress Over Time

To gain or maintain funding from school districts or other government agencies, concrete evidence of the overall effectiveness of the intensive early intervention program is generally required. Discrete trial data can be used as part of this documentation, but broader measures are also important. Keeping detailed monthly summaries of the student's progress, regularly videotaping programs, and keeping a log of the student's spontaneous language are three tools for providing thorough documentation of the long-term benefits of intensive early intervention programs.

Monthly Summaries

One of the clearest ways to document the student's progress is to keep monthly summaries of her gains in individual programs. These summaries can be brief, but they should focus on objective, concrete facts. The two most important things to include are (1) the number of items the student has mastered within each program and (2) the percentage of time the student performs correctly (this percentage should be derived from the discrete trial data described earlier).

Below is a series of sample monthly summaries for the Expressive Labeling of Objects Program:

- March 1, 2001: Joan is unable to expressively label any objects.
- April 1, 2001: Joan can expressively label 3 objects (car, bubbles, and pizza) with 84% accuracy when the objects are randomly intermixed.
- May 1, 2001: Joan can expressively label 10 intermixed objects with 80% accuracy.
- June 1, 2001: Joan can expressively label 27 intermixed objects with 90% accuracy.
- July 1, 2001: Joan can expressively label 70 intermixed objects and pictures with 81% accuracy. New stimuli are now introduced in the form of pictures *or* objects, and Joan learns pictures as easily as actual objects. Joan also has generalized her labels to exemplars of objects we have not specifically taught her. For example, she can label her mother's shoes even though she was explicitly taught to label only one of her own shoes.
- August 1, 2001: Joan can expressively label 95 intermixed objects and pictures with 90% accuracy. This program has been placed on a maintenance schedule.

For reports given to school districts or used in legal hearings, monthly summary data can easily be collapsed into 3-month, 6-month, or yearly summaries. For example, the monthly summaries just described can be collapsed into the following 6-month summary statement and graph:

> **Expressive Object Labels:** When this program was introduced on March 1, 2001, Joan was unable to expressively label any objects. As of August 1, 2001, Joan was able to expressively label 95 objects and pictures, and had generalized her labels to novel exemplars of 3-D objects and novel exemplars of 2-D representations of objects. A graph of Joan's acquisition of expressive labels is provided (see Figure 33.6).

Video Data

Videotapes of the student's progress over a period of months or years can be one of the most persuasive and easiest ways of documenting the student's gains. The student's first day of one-on-one instruction should be taped from the very beginning. Subsequently, tapes should be made once every 2 to 3 months throughout the student's program. Each taping should include (a) all programs and items within programs mastered since the previous taping; (b) all programs cur-

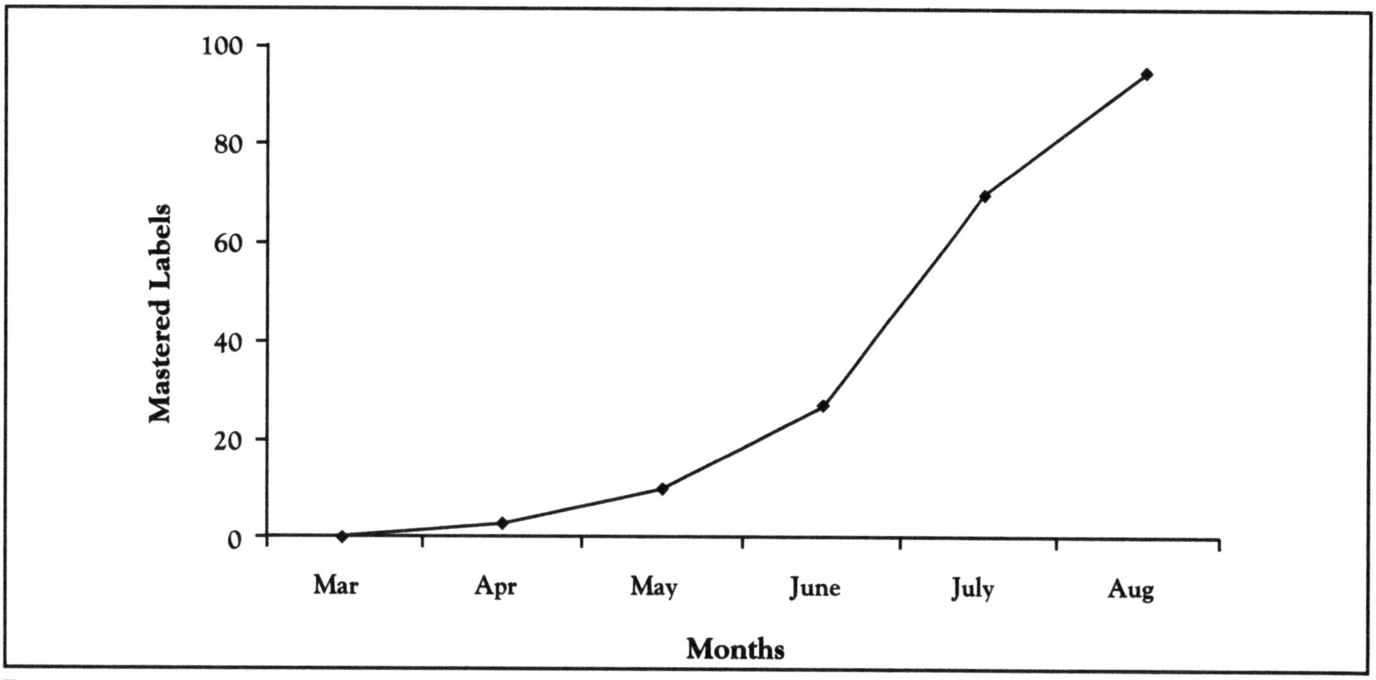

Figure 33.6. Joan's acquisition of expressive objects labels.

rently on acquisition; and (c) baseline performances for several programs that have not yet been introduced.

A common mistake is to record only a student's mastered programs. If this is done, the resulting tape appears to show a very obedient student who does everything she is asked to do, and shows no evidence of growth. By taping programs on acquisition and obtaining baselines on future programs, the ongoing impact of programs is clearly demonstrated.

Recording Spontaneous Language

One of the most important measures of the effectiveness of a program is whether the skills taught in the program generalize to outside the program. Keeping a log of the student's spontaneous language is an effective way to document this generalization. Spontaneous language includes any verbalizations that occur outside the formal teaching environment. These may include the student's responses to questions or instructions (e.g., "Stop it"), or the student's requests (e.g., "I want popcorn") or statements (e.g., "Horse!" or "I see horse!") occurring outside of the formal teaching situation. Choose a consistent 20- to 30-minute time period to take this data. Dinnertime and the time spent getting ready for bed are good examples of situations when spontaneous language may occur. On a monthly basis, record all spontaneous verbalizations the student makes during these periods.

Summary of Basic Steps

- Take discrete trial data on each program for two to three teaching sessions at the end of each month (for a total of approximately 30 to 45 trials).
- Take discrete trial data on every trial of any program the student is having consistent difficulty with. Review data and give teachers feedback within 1 to 2 days.
- Take discrete trial data on all programs if there is a concern that teachers are not following correct teaching procedures. Review data and give teachers feedback within 1 to 2 days.
- Keep monthly summaries of the student's progress in each program. Summaries should include the number of responses mastered and the percentage of correct responses.
- Videotape the first day of the introduction of each new program, and once every 2 to 3 months thereafter. In addition, record all mastered programs, all programs currently on acquisition, and baseline sessions for several programs that have not yet been introduced.
- Keep monthly logs of the student's spontaneous verbalizations.

Log Book

To organize the teaching environment for the student, yourself, and the team, construct a Log Book. When set up, the Log Book provides a continuous overview of the student's current programs and the student's skill level within each individual program. To construct a Log Book, you need a 1½-inch three-ring binder organized with separate and labeled sections for each of the student's current programs. The Log Book's first page should be a sheet listing the names and phone numbers of each teacher. The second sheet should provide the student's weekly schedule. Next in the Log Book comes the summary of each weekly meeting, followed by the student's weekly Program Checklist (See Appendix 33.A). The weekly Program Checklist should list all the student's current programs and the dates and days of the week. (The number of programs in the student's current program schedule should not exceed 20 at any given time.) The boxes under the heading for each day should provide space for team members' initials. When a teacher performs a sitting of a program, the teacher should initial the box corresponding to the day and the program. A quick look at the initials or missing initials will indicate to other teachers on the team whether a program has been performed and how many times during a given day each program has been done.

Each individual program section in the Log Book should have an SD Sheet, which gives the particular discriminative stimulus (SD) and required response (R) for each program, as well as the kind and extent of prompt currently being used. This page must be updated at least once a week. Following the SD Sheet should be a page listing target SDs on acquisition and SDs recently mastered. Provide lined notebook paper behind these two front pages for the team members to write short informational paragraphs about the student's performance. These notes should be precise and short, and provide enough informational data about the student's progress within each program that the next team member knows how and where to start the next session. Each team member should date and initial his or her notes.

Maintenance Book

When the student has mastered approximately 20 responses within a particular program, begin a maintenance schedule for the items mastered early on in teaching. These items should be listed in a separate book, the Maintenance Book. This book should be a 1½-inch three-ring binder, divided into separate sections corresponding to each program on a maintenance schedule. As some of the earliest mastered responses are moved to a maintenance schedule, new SDs should be introduced (one at a time) and their progress should be recorded in the Log Book. With separate binders for items that are current and those on maintenance, you help yourself and the student remember what he has learned, and boredom due to frequent repetition of mastered responses is avoided.

Items on a maintenance schedule should be repeated as often as necessary to ensure that they are not forgotten. The frequency with which these items need to be practiced will vary from student to student. Assign the responsibility of working through the various items on maintenance to a particular but different team member each week to each month (depending on the student). If numerous programs or items within programs are on a maintenance schedule, each team member should be assigned to work through one or several of the programs each week (or more or less often, depending on the student) such that all the programs are practiced. Each team member should initial and date the sheet as the work-through of the programs on maintenance is completed. Each program's items on maintenance may be worked through separately in an informal and generalized format or intermixed with current items.

APPENDIX 33.A
Sample Log Book Sheets

Discrete Trial Data

Program ______________________________

Date __________

Teacher ______________________________

1. SD: ____________________ C I P
2. SD: ____________________ C I P
3. SD: ____________________ C I P
4. SD: ____________________ C I P
5. SD: ____________________ C I P
6. SD: ____________________ C I P
7. SD: ____________________ C I P
8. SD: ____________________ C I P
9. SD: ____________________ C I P
10. SD: ____________________ C I P
11. SD: ____________________ C I P
12. SD: ____________________ C I P
13. SD: ____________________ C I P
14. SD: ____________________ C I P
15. SD: ____________________ C I P
16. SD: ____________________ C I P
17. SD: ____________________ C I P
18. SD: ____________________ C I P
19. SD: ____________________ C I P
20. SD: ____________________ C I P

Correct (C) _____
Incorrect (I) _____
Prompted (P) _____
% Correct _____

Comments ______________________________

Student ______________________________

Date: __________

Teacher ______________________________

1. SD: ____________________ C I P
2. SD: ____________________ C I P
3. SD: ____________________ C I P
4. SD: ____________________ C I P
5. SD: ____________________ C I P
6. SD: ____________________ C I P
7. SD: ____________________ C I P
8. SD: ____________________ C I P
9. SD: ____________________ C I P
10. SD: ____________________ C I P
11. SD: ____________________ C I P
12. SD: ____________________ C I P
13. SD: ____________________ C I P
14. SD: ____________________ C I P
15. SD: ____________________ C I P
16. SD: ____________________ C I P
17. SD: ____________________ C I P
18. SD: ____________________ C I P
19. SD: ____________________ C I P
20. SD: ____________________ C I P

Correct (C) _____
Incorrect (I) _____
Prompted (P) _____
% Correct _____

Comments ______________________________

Program Checklist

Student ______________________

Dates ______________ to __________

Program	Monday	Tuesday	Wednesday	Thursday	Friday	Saturday	Sunday

Current Items Sheet

Program ______________________

Item	Date Introduced	Date Mastered
1. ______________	__________	__________
2. ______________	__________	__________
3. ______________	__________	__________
4. ______________	__________	__________
5. ______________	__________	__________
6. ______________	__________	__________
7. ______________	__________	__________
8. ______________	__________	__________
9. ______________	__________	__________
10. ______________	__________	__________
11. ______________	__________	__________
12. ______________	__________	__________
13. ______________	__________	__________
14. ______________	__________	__________
15. ______________	__________	__________
16. ______________	__________	__________
17. ______________	__________	__________
18. ______________	__________	__________
19. ______________	__________	__________
20. ______________	__________	__________
21. ______________	__________	__________
22. ______________	__________	__________
23. ______________	__________	__________
24. ______________	__________	__________
25. ______________	__________	__________

Considerations in Selecting Consultants for Home-Based Programs

CHAPTER 34

Tristram Smith and Jacqueline Wynn

Recently, comprehensive evaluations of treatment outcomes from several sites have indicated that many children with autism make substantial gains when they receive intensive early intervention based on behavior analytic teaching approaches. Of these sites, the UCLA (University of California, Los Angeles) Young Autism Project may be one of the best known, in part because it has reported long-term follow-up studies in peer-reviewed journals. Such studies, together with increased support from school districts and other agencies for early behavioral intervention, have led to a dramatic increase in the demand for qualified behavioral consultants. Unfortunately, this demand now far exceeds the supply. As a result, parents are often faced with difficult choices when selecting qualified consultants to help their children face a better future.

While the UCLA program is working hard to increase the number of available consultants as quickly as possible, we are also concerned about insufficiently trained consultants. Treatment according to the UCLA model is intensive and directed at establishing very complex skills, such as conversational speech and peer friendships. Given this level of intensity and complexity, consultants must achieve a high level of specialized training and skill. If treatment is done incorrectly, students may experience frustration, boredom, or stress. If it is done right, students may derive considerable benefit. A brief overview of UCLA consultation services and a description of the standards for training and skills developed through the UCLA program follow. To be a UCLA-certified consultant, one must meet or exceed these standards. There are many other behavior analytic programs for individuals with autism that have fine reputations and substantial scientific support. These programs may have different criteria for certifying consultants and should be contacted directly by those wanting additional information.

UCLA Consultation Services

The UCLA program and LIFE (Lovaas Institute for Early Intervention) provide two kinds of services for young children with autism and related developmental delays: clinic based and workshop based. These services differ in terms of the amount of supervision and staff training provided and are likely to yield different treatment outcomes. Clinic-based services provided the basis for both the Lovaas (1987) and the McEachin, Smith, and Lovaas (1993) outcomes. Clinic-based services place major demands on supervision and are personnel intensive; therefore, restrictions are placed on the number of students treated at any one time. Each member of the student's team—staff aides, senior aide, case supervisor, and director of clinical services—must pass quality control. Each student's program is reviewed in weekly clinic meetings of a 1- to 2-hour duration, during which time each team member takes his or her turn treating the student in front of the other team members and one or both of the student's parents. This allows for early detection of treatment mistakes, as well as identification of new and helpful interventions for the student involved.

Each student is assigned four to six staff aides, one senior aide, and one case supervisor. A senior aide may not effectively supervise the treatment of more than three to four students, with each student receiving a total of 40 hours of one-on-one treatment per week. A case supervisor supervises about six students and provides no less than 4 hours of supervision per student per week in cooperation with a student's senior aide. It is our experience that a director of clinical services can provide effective supervision to no more than 14 students at any one time given that 14 students receive 560 hours of treatment per week. Both case supervisors and the director of clinical services assist in staff training, conduct research, and are available to the student's parents to help answer questions about treatment.

Although every student within the clinic is diagnosed as having developmental delays, individual differences are enormous and become manifested in the students' responses to treatment. These differences cannot be predicted or identified by merely observing a student in a school setting, clinic setting, or his everyday environment. Rather, each individual student's response to treatment provides for a more optimal design of that student's treatment and prediction of treatment outcome.

The clinic provides an ideal setting for research, including undergraduate research requirements, master's theses, and doctoral dissertations, as well as research sponsored by funding agencies. The intensity and close supervision of treatment provide opportunities for identifying ineffective interventions and developing and testing effective ones.

In an attempt to meet the large demand for services, the UCLA project and LIFE have developed workshop-based services, or workshop consultation services, with the following characteristics.

1. Consultants certified to supervise treatment receive extensive training. First, they complete course work in learning theory and empirical research on the laws of learning. Second, they fulfill a minimum of 1 year of full-time supervised experience as a staff aide. The practicum experience begins with a 6-month course involving supervised one-on-one treatment with students and lectures on professional ethics, principles of behavior analysis, assessment of behavior change, functional analyses of behavior problems, and review of research and theory in autism. Those who excel in the first 6 months of this practicum are invited to enroll in a more advanced practicum. If they continue to excel, and if they demonstrate skill at teaching incoming student aides and working with parents, educational personnel, and other staff, they may be hired as paid staff aides or senior aides. After at least 1 year of full-time work during which supervision and training occur on an ongoing basis, exceptionally talented senior aides may be promoted to the position of case supervisor/workshop consultant. To qualify for this position, they participate in an additional 40 hours of advanced training seminars. In another format of training, consultants complete an intensive 9-month internship in which extensive coursework, training, and supervision are completed, followed by at least 2 years of follow-up training and supervision. The curriculum covers the skills necessary to supervise treatment programs for students with developmental delays. Once training is complete, the workshop provider must maintain an ongoing relationship with the director of clinical services and the individual who conducted the training so as to help maintain treatment integrity.

To quantify the level of training received, two levels of quality control procedures have been introduced through the UCLA certification project. The two levels of certification—Level I (staff aide) and Level II (supervising aide)—were detailed in Chapter 3. All workshop providers must have passed Level II quality control before conducting workshops. Level II requires mastery of teaching advanced programs such as verbal imitation, conversational speech, time concepts, and interactive play.

2. Before the first workshop, parents receive a packet of information providing a description of the treatment and the most recent follow-up on treatment outcome, along with a consent form for them to sign regarding the nature of the consultation. They are also advised to seek individuals to form a treatment team of aides.

3. The initial workshop typically lasts 3 days, and 1- to 2-day follow-up workshops are scheduled 1 week to 3 months apart for the next 2 to 3 years, the frequency being largely determined by the parents and the family's distance from the clinic facility. Almost all parents have read the *ME Book* (Lovaas, 1981), this manual, and similar manuals prior to the workshop and have encouraged their team members to do the same. During the workshop, the consultant models treatment procedures by working in a one-on-one manner with the student. Parents and aides then take turns working under the consultant's direction. Any technical terms are discussed in connection with such demonstrations. For example, causes of an "extinction burst" are discussed in the context of an increase in the student's tantrums, and an aide's success or difficulty administering discrete trials and discrimination learning procedures allows for discussions of these teaching strategies. Through this course of demonstration, practice, and feedback, mastery and generalization of treatment skills are increased. Parents are advised to videotape the workshop for their own use later on, and they receive detailed reports (usually two to seven pages) after each workshop.

4. Parents are advised to call their workshop leader as needed (from once a week to once a month) for telephone consultations. Almost all parents do so. Each consultation lasts approximately 30 minutes.

5. Given the intensity of services, each full-time consultant from UCLA or LIFE works with a maximum of 10 to 15 families. In addition, each consultant limits services to those families that can be reached within a 3-hour flight from the consultant's home.

6. The director of clinical services at UCLA or LIFE receives confidential ratings and evaluation comments on each consultation from the parents and provides

additional supervision to the consultant based on these ratings. The director of clinical services also conducts weekly meetings, during which senior staff and workshop providers collaboratively review current workshops.

When workshops are conducted as we have described, preliminary data indicate that children with autism who receive workshop consultations substantially outperform similar children who do not receive such consultations. However, it appears that the percentage of children who achieve normal functioning (average levels of intelligence and satisfactory, unassisted performance in a class for typically developing children) is estimated at closer to 10% or 20% rather than the 47% reported for clinic-based treatment at UCLA (Lovaas, 1987). This lower rate may reflect such factors as high staff turnover, less frequent supervision than that which occurs in clinic-based treatment, and the use of aides with less academic background in learning-based theory and research than those provided by UCLA, LIFE, and replication sites. We are currently collecting more data on outcomes obtained from workshops and plan to publish these data in a professional, peer-reviewed journal.

Other Potentially Appropriate Workshop Consultants for the UCLA Program

Former case supervisors and senior aides may be appropriate consultants for the UCLA treatment program. However, there are several issues to consider. First, most aides at UCLA and affiliated sites do not become case supervisors or even senior aides. Therefore, if consultants indicate that they are trained in the UCLA model, we recommend that families question whether they held a supervisory position at a site. Aides who did not hold a supervisory position are likely to be much less qualified to serve as consultants, as discussed in the next section.

Second, in many cases, former case supervisors have chosen to work independently of the UCLA project. This is perfectly appropriate. After all, most professionals move on from the site at which they received their initial training. Nevertheless, when the case supervisor and the UCLA project go their separate ways, the services offered by each may become increasingly different with the passage of time (which may be considerable given that the Young Autism Project has been in existence since 1970 and has had case supervisors throughout this period). We do not know the full extent to which this divergence has happened or what effect such divergence may have had on the overall effectiveness of services. However, we do know that some former supervisors have different policies from ours. For example, some consult on many more cases than we consider optimal to oversee effectively at one time, and some provide less frequent consultations. Some recommend supplemental treatments, such as special diets, sensory integration, speech therapy, and so on, any one of which may interact unfavorably with the UCLA model. Also, some are more likely than we are to recommend less intensive behavioral treatment. If less than 40 hours of one-on-one quality treatment is provided per student, the treatment is not consistent with the UCLA model and it is unlikely that the outcome will be similar. Many consultants offer workshop- or classroom-based services while citing the Lovaas (1987) and McEachin et al. (1993) follow-up reports to support their practice. Because these follow-up studies relied on clinic-based services, misinformation may be provided to parents and other professionals.

Third, having been a senior aide or a case supervisor at UCLA or an affiliated site does not necessarily mean that one can run an independent practice given that there is more to consulting than setting up a behavioral program. Responsibilities include being able to identify and help deal with stress in members of the family other than the individual with autism, interpreting assessments conducted by other professionals, screening and training incoming aides, collaborating with other service providers such as teachers to optimize the student's treatment, keeping up with new research, maintaining familiarity with ethical guidelines, and so forth. Former senior aides and case supervisors not trained as consultants are likely to receive little training from the UCLA project on these topics. Therefore, we recommend that if workshop training is not completed, senior aides and case supervisors who leave the UCLA project work with a licensed psychologist or other doctoral-level mental health professional rather than practicing on their own. Some case supervisors and senior aides from UCLA advertise these positions as their qualifications, but may have served in such a capacity with only one or two clients. Such a short tenure would not constitute a background that is adequate to carry out an independent practice or be representative of the UCLA model. Outcome data from workshop services offered elsewhere provide a sobering note: Investigators in the U.K. report no or minimal gains across a variety of participants and outcome variables following ABA workshop services (Bibby, Eikeseth, Martin, Mudford, & Reeves, 2001).

Other Consultants

Most UCLA-trained aides (including undergraduate students, paid staff members, and parents) become proficient at administering programs with oversight from a case supervisor and a director of clinical services. However, such aides have had little or no formal training in developing programs themselves or in training novice aides. Consequently, we think it quite unlikely that they would be able to serve competently as consultants to families in home-based programs. Therefore, as long these aides are working with us, we do not permit them to conduct workshops, and we recommend that they not do so in the future. Several have become workshop consultants and opened clinics of their own despite our recommendation, and this is a source of great concern to us. Similarly, it is our view that reading the *ME Book* (Lovaas, 1981) or this manual, attending a workshop led by a UCLA-certified consultant, practicing behavioral procedures on several families, or spending a short time at a UCLA-affiliated site does not make a person qualified to consult on the UCLA program.

Professional behavior analysts who have not completed an internship at a UCLA-affiliated clinic site would also not, in our judgment, have appropriate experience to replicate the UCLA program. Applied Behavior Analysis (ABA) has over time evolved subspecialties for dealing with clients diagnosed with attention-deficit/hyperactivity disorder, delinquency, drug addiction, schizophrenia, obesity, sexual dysfunction, marital problems, and so on. Even persons who focus primarily on individuals with autism may have differing areas of expertise. For example, whereas we work primarily in students' homes, other professionals work in schools or group homes. Whereas we work with preschoolers, others work with adolescents or adults and deal with problems that we seldom see, such as severe self-injury. For this reason, we do not think it is possible for anyone to master a comprehensive behavior analytic program such as the one at UCLA unless he or she has extensive, hands-on, supervised experience. Similarly, although we are generally familiar with behavior analytic programs for clients with autism other than the UCLA approach, we would not claim to be proficient at supervising programs such as classroom-based instruction, severe self-injury, job training, and independent living.

A strong background in ABA may help a person provide effective services, particularly if it includes intensive one-on-one instruction with very young students. Such training is not currently offered or required, however, in many behavior analytic programs. In any case, data documenting long-term favorable outcomes are needed to demonstrate that such consultations are effective. Without such data, we risk misinforming both parents and the professional community. For example, it is likely that outcome data from workshop providers who do not comply with the UCLA model show few if any instances of students reaching normal functioning as defined in the Lovaas (1987) report. There is an acute shortage of treatment outcome data from ABA treatment programs, whether clinic based or workshop oriented. Given the large amount of stress experienced by parents of students with autism and other developmental delays, it seems unethical not to provide outcome data to help parents reach informed decisions. If we fail to provide or minimize such assessments, we abandon the defining feature of behavioral approaches to social problems.

It is reasonable, in our judgment, to inquire about data pertaining to the effectiveness of the services offered by a consultant. Maurice (1993), a mother of two students with autism, was one of the first parents to search for follow-up data on which to base decisions about a child's treatment rather than merely accepting the service provider's claims of favorable outcome. In our judgment, treatment outcome data should include objective measures of changes in individual behaviors as well as overall functioning. At a bare minimum, this should consist of standardized tests of intelligence and adaptive behavior (e.g., the *Bayley Scales of Infant Development–Revised* [Bayley, 1993], the *Wechsler Intelligence Scale for Children–Third Edition* [Wechsler, 1991], the *Vineland Adaptive Behavior Scales* [Sparrow, Balla, & Cicchetti, 1984], and tests of educational achievement such as passing grades in typical vs. special education classes) conducted before and after treatment by examiners independent of the service provider. It is desirable, if not essential, that such data be reviewed by peers (e.g., by being published in a professional journal). Data on long-term outcome are especially important because it is entirely possible to obtain short-term gains but fail to bring about long-term benefits, as we discovered in our early research (Lovaas, Koegel, Simmons, & Long, 1973). For example, unless the student achieves normal functioning by the age of 7, it is likely that the student will need lifelong behavioral intervention (although perhaps less intensively than the 40 hours per week given to preschoolers in the UCLA model) to prevent loss of treatment gains and maintain progress.

The qualifications we recommend are comparable to those specified for other programs that represent subspecialties within ABA. For example, Achievement Place, a behavior analytic program for juvenile delinquents developed over the last 30 years by Montrose Wolf and colleagues, requires that prospective supervisors complete an internship and document the quality of their services by having periodic site visits from other supervisors. Without updates and periodic site visits, data show that service providers fail to maintain quality control standards of treatment (Wolf, Kirigin, Fixsen, Blase, & Braukman, 1995). It is unlikely that we or other behavior analysts could replicate Achievement Place without receiving training in that model and periodic updates.

In sum, we believe that consultants must have supervisory experience at UCLA or an affiliated site and appropriate supplementary training, including follow-ups, in order to consult effectively with families on the UCLA treatment model. We are very concerned that individuals without such experience have represented themselves as being qualified UCLA/Lovaas consultants.

Concluding Comments

We are acutely aware of the shortage of qualified service providers and are working hard to remedy this problem. We are also aware of the enormous stress imposed upon parents who seek competent treatment for their students, and we believe that most service providers are motivated by the desire to help and that some help is better than none.

Although there is no easy way to evaluate consultants who claim they can improve the lives of individuals with autism and other pervasive developmental disorders, several issues are important to consider:

- What supervised training has the consultant received in early and intensive one-on-one behavioral intervention? Does this training include data-based procedures for teaching advanced programs (e.g., verbal imitation and conversational speech) and mainstreaming? Has the consultant been trained in developing and assessing programs and training novice therapists? Does this training include other issues such as counseling, diagnosis and assessment, and evaluation of new research findings?
- With whom does the consultant collaborate in order to stay up to date and to receive feedback on service?
- What objective, data-based evidence does the consultant have for the effectiveness of his or her services?
- What assistance does the consultant offer in obtaining services after the completion of early intervention, if such services are needed?

Common Problems in Teaching

CHAPTER 35

One is likely to encounter numerous problems when delivering the kind of intervention detailed in this manual because of both the large number of programs involved in comprehensive intervention and the large individual variability among students in their responses to programs as a whole as well as aspects within particular programs. For example, a student may encounter serious difficulties acquiring receptive language but may proceed rather quickly in acquiring expressive language. At the present time, we have no way of predicting such an occurrence. There is also the question of defining what is meant by "serious difficulties" in learning the skills involved in a particular program or aspect of a program and whether such difficulties are caused by the teacher's mistakes in administrating the treatment or whether they represent unique and idiosyncratic variations of a particular student's nervous system. It would be much less difficult to administer a treatment that was monolithic, as in remedying what some would guess to be a pivotal problem in autism. Unfortunately, no one has been able to identify such a problem, leaving little choice except to address the large range of behavioral excesses and delays shown by individuals with autism and other developmental delays.

Another problem one must face when providing behavioral intervention concerns untrained or poorly trained team members. One must continuously train new persons given that most persons eventually leave one's treatment team, and it is impossible for any one teacher or parent to implement 40 hours of effective one-on-one treatment every week. Seeking adequately trained team members is perhaps the most important factor in facilitating the student's treatment, because persons with good training are able to train others and help identify mistakes early, before treatment mistakes pose significant problems for the student. One may hear of a person who has read a teaching manual, attended one or two workshops on behavioral intervention, gained some background in behavioral literature, and then set out to establish a service that superficially seems to have all the features of integrity, claiming a title of senior aide, case supervisor, and the like. As described in Chapters 3 and 34, there are no data to support that such a person can provide effective treatment.

Identifying and Preventing Common Problems

Because of the likelihood of encountering a variety of difficulties when administering the programs presented in this manual, lists of common problems in a variety of general areas essential to providing effective behavioral treatment are given in this chapter. When problems arise, the teacher may refer to these lists in an attempt to help identify possible teaching mistakes. The areas to monitor closely include (a) how to use instructions, (b) what behaviors to reinforce, (c) how to select and deliver reinforcers, (d) how to prompt, (e) how to pace trials, (f) how to weaken interfering behaviors, and (g) where and when to teach. The lists are followed by examples of various specific problems one may encounter and how these problems may be overcome.

Instructions

1. Avoid talking casually to an individual with developmental delays as if she understands what is being said to her. Perhaps some teachers do this because they draw upon experiences with typical individuals when approaching a student with developmental delays. If the student does not understand what is said to her, if language is experienced merely as noise, then over time the student will learn to adapt to or otherwise ignore the verbal message (e.g., act as if she is deaf). To facilitate the student's attention to instructions, the presentation of instructions must initially include only the most relevant information; instructions must be succinct and distinctive.

In short, do not be verbose when speaking to a student with developmental delays.

2. Present stimuli that are maximally different from each other in both auditory and visual modes. As the student progresses, the stimuli may be made gradually more and more similar, requiring finer and finer discriminations.

3. Once a student can respond correctly to instructions when they are presented alone, be sure to randomly rotate their presentation so as to ensure the student's attention to the instructions, avoiding the adoption of patterns of responding such as a win–stay and lose–shift strategy (see Chapter 16).

4. Make certain that the time elapsed between the instruction and the student's response is as short as possible (i.e., no longer than 3 seconds). If an instruction is given and the student waits for more than 3 seconds and *then* engages in the correct behavior, it is likely that some other stimulus occurring during the time interval will acquire control over the student's behavior. An exception to this rule is when the student develops echolalic speech and gives evidence of repeating the teacher's verbal instructions. The student's repetition of the instructions (rehearsing, storing, or remembering the instructions) may serve to bridge the interval between the teacher's instructions and the student's response.

5. Avoid taking time out between instructions to record the student's response (as correct, incorrect, or a nonresponse). Although spaced trials are important for maintaining treatment gains (see Chapter 31), spaced trials are not likely to provide optimal conditions for acquiring new behaviors. Short intertrial intervals facilitate the student's attention to the task. Ask someone else to record the responses if you cannot recall what occurred in a sitting immediately after it ends.

Selecting Behaviors

A major consideration in selecting behaviors is picking those that lead to the student's success. Maximizing success and minimizing errors establishes a cooperative relationship between the teacher and the student and builds the student's trust and self-confidence. Given the difficulties that students with developmental delays have in understanding what well-meaning adults attempt to teach them, it is likely that the student will respond to teaching with tantrums over the first month of treatment and then periodically thereafter. Should the student show little reduction in tantrums over several weeks into treatment, examine the teaching situation to assess whether tantrums are inadvertently being reinforced. If they are not, consider the following alternatives.

1. For the time being, stop teaching a particular task that gives rise to serious tantrums. Introduce easier tasks, and then return to the more difficult task some weeks or months later.

2. Break down complex behaviors to make them easier for the student to acquire, reinforcing each component and later chaining them together (see Chapter 10).

3. Do not teach eye contact ("look at me") in the early stages of instruction because eye contact is such a subtle response that the student may not be able to associate it with the instruction and the reinforcer.

4. Minimize the length of time the student sits in the chair. It is better to have a student sit in the chair for 1 to 2 minutes in a one-on-one teaching situation and then have 1 minute off to play (*before* the student tantrums) than to have the student sit in the chair for 10 to 20 minutes while tantruming. While tantruming, the student is probably learning very little and the whole teaching situation is likely to acquire aversive properties. To help avoid this situation, short sittings should be performed at the beginning of treatment and gradually lengthened as the student acquires skills conducive to doing so.

5. Examine the teaching situation to ascertain whether two behaviors are accidentally being taught at the same time. For example, the teacher may present one SD such as "Look at me" and almost immediately present another SD such as "Point to the ball." In such a situation, the student may not be able to discriminate what the teacher wants the student to do and may therefore not respond. It is also possible that the student's behavior of looking at the teacher is punished in this situation because it is accompanied by a demand (i.e., being asked to point to the ball is the consequence for looking at the teacher). To solve this problem, the student should be reinforced for looking when the teacher requests this, and then be presented with the second SD, "Point to the ball." For most tasks, it is not even necessary that the student maintain eye contact with the teacher. Eye contact appears to spontaneously increase for most students as they make progress in treatment.

6. Do not assume that the student possesses prior knowledge about a particular task being taught. It is better to assume that the student does not possess such knowledge. Do not assume that a healthy and knowledgeable individual resides inside "an autistic shell" waiting to be let out. The task of teaching–treatment is enormously more complex than that. If the student already knows part or all of the task, this will be evidenced by the speed with which the student acquires the new task.

7. Avoid overwhelming the student. Certain students move along very rapidly, learning difficult concepts such as color, shape, size, and prepositions within the first

3 to 4 months of treatment. Such a student can be very reinforcing for the teacher who, because of the student's tremendous progress, continues to teach more and more difficult tasks at a rapid rate. To everyone's surprise, this student will most likely suddenly and unexpectedly aggress toward the teacher or withdraw into self-stimulation (e.g., gaze off into the distance). The student will likely become overwhelmed by too many demands and have no way of telling the teacher that the rate of introduction of new tasks is too rapid. If this occurs with your student, we recommend dropping most if not all demands for the next few days, replacing lessons with play, and then going back to the beginning, reinforcing the student (e.g., with food) for just coming to you and then leaving without having to work. Reintroduce teaching in a gradual manner. Reestablishing the teaching situation as one associated with success is likely to bring the student around. Do not be concerned that this type of break in treatment will interfere with the student's progress; a student who learns skills quickly will continue acquiring skills when treatment is done in an optimal manner, minimizing the need to be in a hurry.

Selecting Reinforcing Consequences

Teachers will not make any progress in teaching the student unless the teachers select the kinds of reinforcers the student will value and work for. We know now that teachers have available to them a much larger set of reinforcers than the relatively small group postulated some 20 to 30 years ago. We also know that individual differences in preferences for certain reinforcers are enormous. Perhaps novel and idiosyncratic reinforcers emerge in proportion to the individual differences detected among students. If difficulties arise in teaching, consider the following issues related to reinforcement.

1. Avoid relying on a limited set of reinforcers, such as food reinforcement or social reinforcement (e.g., saying, "Good"). Although you may be limited to these types of reinforcers during the first hour or two of teaching when you are still exploring the uniqueness of the student, you should soon be able to identify a much larger range of reinforcers to maximize teaching effectiveness. It may become apparent that saying, "Good," does not even function as a reinforcer in the early stages of treatment considering that social reinforcement in general takes time to learn. A teacher who has access to 10 to 20 reinforcers is clearly much more likely to be effective than someone who has access to only one or two reinforcers. This idea relates closely to the next problem.

2. Avoid having the student become satiated on a particular reinforcer. Often a teacher presents the same consequence such as "Good girl" over and over again. In the early stages of treatment, it is unlikely that the statement "Good girl" has any reinforcing properties at all for most students with developmental delays. Even typical individuals satiate on a reinforcer if it is repeated too often.

One is also likely to promote satiation if food reinforcement is used when the student is given a meal 1 to 2 hours before the teaching session or a relatively large amount of food is given for each correct response. To help prevent satiation, give *small* bites of food when providing food reinforcement, provide *small* sips of liquid, and explore effective reinforcers by following the suggestions presented in Chapter 7. The discovery of new and varied reinforcers motivates the student and allows for a great deal more learning than that which results from limited and monotonous reinforcement.

3. Effectively use primary and secondary reinforcement combinations. Primary reinforcers include items such as food and beverages, physical activities (based on the student's preferences), sensory reinforcers, and escape from unpleasant situations. These reinforcers are likely to be powerful independent of the student's reinforcement history. In contrast, social approval, such as attention and verbal praise, is a secondary (acquired, learned) reinforcer. This means that, to become effective reinforcers, secondary events must be paired with primary reinforcers. Once such associations are established, occasional pairings with primary reinforcers have to occur for the secondary reinforcers to be maintained. For example, repeatedly consequating correct responses by saying, "Good" (or something to that effect), will quickly cease being reinforcing unless the verbal praise is paired and becomes associated with primary reinforcers such as food or a short play break.

4. Consider whether the student likes to be exuberantly reinforced with clapping, laughing, being tossed in the air, and so on. Although many or most students find such enthusiasm reinforcing, a few do not, at least not in the beginning of treatment. Some students are extremely sensitive to sound and may be punished instead of positively reinforced by loud noises. Assess for such sensitivity (e.g., by asking the student's parents) before assuming that ebullience is reinforcing.

5. Do not delay reinforcement. It is not uncommon to see a teacher deliver reinforcement some 4 seconds or longer after the student completes a correct response. By delaying reinforcement, the teacher risks strengthening a behavior other than the target response. For a reinforcer to be effective, it must be given immediately after a correct response (i.e., within 1 second of the completion of a

correct response). Therefore, have reinforcers readily available (e.g., in your hand, under the table) so you do not take undue time retrieving and administering them. The only exception to this rule occurs when a teacher bridges the delay between the response and the desired reinforcer by using some social event, such as smiling and saying, "Good," while reaching for and delivering a primary reinforcer (e.g., food). In such a situation, it is likely that the smile and the teacher's saying, "Good," will acquire secondary reinforcing properties by being paired with the primary reinforcer.

6. Avoid reinforcing the wrong association. As an example, imagine an adult teaching the student expressive labels. To the SD "What is it?" while showing the student a shoe, the student responds, "Ooze." The teacher says, "No," and then prompts the correct response "Shoe." The student responds by saying, "Shoe," and the teacher reinforces the response. In this interaction, the student is not reinforced for labeling the object "ooze," an approximation of the word "shoe." Instead, the student is reinforced for imitating the teacher's prompt, the correct enunciation of "shoe," rather than responding correctly with "shoe" to the sight of the shoe and the teacher's question "What is it?" In this example, the teacher should have provided a consequence for the original response, repeated the SD ("What is it?" while presenting a shoe), prompted the correct response, and then reinforced. As a general rule, do not give several commands at the same time. Rather, follow the guidelines in Chapter 10 that outline discrete trial procedures.

7. Avoid verbally reinforcing a student's behaviors on the assumption that the student understands your comments. This reinforcement is known as behavior-specific praise. For example, the teacher may state, "That is good placing the block in the bucket," after the student places a block in a bucket. Or, while working on verbal imitation, the teacher may reinforce by saying, "That is good saying 'mama' the right way." Typical persons who are 4 years old or older may understand such comments. There is little reason to believe that a student with developmental delays understands the meaning of such statements during the first year of treatment. Nor are there any firm data showing that students with developmental delays learn the meaning of the teacher's remarks from the teacher's incidental comments on the student's behavior. As a general rule, we advise teachers not to talk too much. If the student does not understand what the teacher says, it is likely that the student will learn to tune out the teacher.

8. Do not inadvertently reinforce the student's tantruming by letting the student escape or avoid the teaching situation. In a teaching situation there are two kinds of rewards: positive reinforcement and negative reinforcement. The delivery of something positive, such as food, is considered a positive reinforcer, as is the opportunity to engage in self-stimulatory behavior. Escaping from stress and pain are considered negative reinforcers; these situations reinforce a behavior through the removal of something negative. For example, if the student finds the teaching situation stressful and engages in tantrums, letting the student leave the teaching situation contingent on such behavior (tantruming) negatively reinforces that behavior by the removal of the unpleasant event. In contrast, letting the student leave a stressful teaching situation contingent on correct or appropriate responding strengthens that behavior.

9. Avoid reinforcing errors. Data show that once persons receive information that a student has been labeled autistic or mentally retarded, persons tend to provide encouraging comments (e.g., "Good try") when the student makes mistakes (Eikeseth & Lovaas, 1992). Although such comments may represent sincere attempts at being helpful, by providing them, one runs the risk of reinforcing and thus strengthening errors.

Prompting

1. Avoid unintentional prompts. These prompts include visually attending to the object the student is asked to identify, mouthing the correct response without recognizing that it may be a form of prompting, continually asking the student to identify the item appearing in the center of a display and not recognizing that this could be a position prompt, and so on. If the teacher is unaware of such prompts, they are unlikely to be faded. Thus, it is likely that the student will become prompt dependent by being reinforced for responding to these prompts rather than to the SD. Members of the treatment team should closely monitor each other's teaching to identify inadvertent prompts.

2. Overlap instructions and prompts. That is, avoid delays between the instructions and the presentation of prompts. Prompts serve to facilitate the student's response to the instructions, and any delay between the two is likely to hinder the student's making the association between the instruction and the response.

3. Fade all prompts. Prompts can be faded either abruptly or gradually. Fading a prompt abruptly is called probing. If the student responds correctly on a probe trial, teaching is sped up because the entire prompt fading process does not have to occur. If the probe fails, the least intrusive prompt that is effective should be reintroduced and more gradual fading of the prompt should be

undertaken. Then, at a later stage, a probe should again be attempted.

In selecting prompts, explore the least intrusive prompts first to assess whether or not they are effective. Should the student fail to respond correctly when a prompt is given, repeat the instruction and the prompt on the next trial. If the student still does not respond correctly, pair a more intrusive prompt with the instruction on the next trial. In fading a prompt, the teacher shifts from one prompt to a less intrusive prompt in gradual steps. For example, if a student is physically prompted to perform a task initially, the teacher should gradually lessen the physical assistance over trials and then shift to a subtler prompt, such as pointing to the correct item.

4. In fading prompts, make sure that the student does not pay attention to the decreasing intrusiveness of the prompt, which may block attention to the SD. This problem can be reduced in three ways: (1) Minimize reinforcement for responding on prompted trials while maximizing reinforcement for correct unprompted responses, (2) probe unprompted trials, or (3) switch to another type of prompt.

5. Know how to teach the student to imitate both verbal and nonverbal behaviors. It is easier, more efficient, and more natural to teach most behaviors by modeling them rather than physically prompting them. If the teacher does not know how to teach the student to imitate, it is likely that the student will move slowly in treatment.

Pacing

Pacing refers to the speed with which trials are performed and tasks are intermixed. The following suggestions may be helpful for gaining and maintaining an appropriate pace when teaching.

1. Keep intertrial intervals (i.e., the period between the consequence of one trial and the SD of the next trial) as short as possible, especially in the early stages of skill acquisition. If the intertrial interval is not kept short, the teacher may lose the student's attention. The teacher who takes time out to record whether the student was correct on a particular trial will inadvertently lengthen the time interval between trials. Assign someone else to that task if, immediately after a sitting ends, you cannot remember what occurred during the sitting.

2. Intersperse mastered tasks with new tasks. This strategy is important considering that mastered tasks help the student receive reinforcers, which are likely to increase the student's attention and reduce tantrums. When the student is learning a task, do not let the student experience more than three or four failures in a row before interspersing one or two trials of a mastered task.

3. Prevent the student's attention from drifting when the student is being taught difficult material. Perhaps this drifting is reinforced by the resulting escape from the difficult task. If this wane in attention interferes with the student's learning, introduce attention exercises, in which the teacher presents the student with four or five mastered instructions in quick succession, such as "Stand up," "Sit down," "Turn around," and one or two nonverbal imitation tasks. Quickly reinforce each response and then immediately introduce the difficult material. We call such activities wake-up or attention exercises because they appear to interfere with the student's self-stimulatory behavior and help focus the student's attention.

4. When the student is given time to play between teaching sessions, make sure that these breaks do not involve the kinds of self-stimulatory behavior that lead to the student's being "unavailable" when she returns to the formal teaching situation. For example, some students become completely absorbed in certain Disney cartoons. Some of these cartoons may cue delayed echolalia and other forms of self-stimulation, which may carry over to the teaching situation. Break times should involve play with appropriate toys such as puzzles and engagement in physical activities.

Weakening Interfering Behaviors

1. To weaken behaviors, identify the reinforcers that maintain the behaviors and then withhold these reinforcers (i.e., place these behaviors on extinction). The best way to discover what reinforces and therefore maintains a behavior is by examining what happens *immediately* after the behavior occurs, and then testing for the relevance of that stimulus by withholding it. For example, a student may appear indifferent to the presence of adults unless she is engaged in self-injurious behavior. When the student is engaged in such behavior, one may discover that she visually attends to the teacher's face, observing whether the self-injurious behavior achieves a glance from the teacher. Even a brief glance from the student's teacher or parent can maintain self-injurious behavior, although the same glance may not serve as a reinforcer for any other behavior. Remember that, when extinction is employed, the behavior for which the reinforcement is being withheld will temporarily increase before it subsides, showing an extinction burst. This occurs because the student works harder (e.g., tantrums more intensely) to gain back the reward she is used to receiving for that behavior. Once the student learns that the behavior will

not achieve its customary reward no matter how intensely it is performed, the behavior subsides.

2. When using time-out (e.g., by placing a student in a corner contingent on a tantrum), make certain that this consequence does not serve as negative reinforcement, allowing the student to escape from the teaching situation. Time-out may also allow the student increased access to self-stimulatory behavior, a positive reinforcer. This kind of dual reinforcement may serve to strengthen the very behavior the teacher thinks he or she is weakening.

3. Remember that the rewards inherent in self-stimulatory rituals are most likely sensory or perceptual in nature. Such reinforcers are controlled by the student and cannot readily be removed by the teacher. For that reason, removing social attention is not effective at reducing this form of behavior. This is particularly true of lower level forms of self-stimulatory behavior that involve the body only. The treatment of choice for helping the student overcome lower level forms of self-stimulatory behavior is building higher level and more appropriate forms of self-stimulatory behavior which contain reinforcing stimuli that are external.

Where and When To Teach

1. In the early stages of learning, teach the student in one room and at one table. Once a particular task is mastered, the skill may be transferred to other settings. Avoid abrupt transitions by slowly fading in new environments. For example, generalize mastery first to the doorway connecting the teaching room and the adjoining hallway, then progress to teaching in the hallway, then move slowly into the living room and other parts of the house. If the transfer from the teaching room to other environments is made gradually, the student is likely to make few, if any, errors generalizing skills across environments.

2. Be aware that generalization training occurs when new people join the teaching team. Older and experienced teachers will inevitably leave and have to be replaced by new persons. Make certain that the transition between the old teacher and the new teacher is as gradual as possible so that discontinuity in the student's program is minimized. When a teacher must leave, provide at least a 2-week interval in which the experienced and new teachers work together side by side in an apprenticeship fashion and then take turns teaching. This allows for the new teacher to become familiar with the student and the student's programs and be faded in while the old teacher is slowly faded out.

3. Do not assume that the student, without extensive preparation, will learn new behaviors by being placed in a mainstream class. We are not familiar with any data indicating that merely exposing a student with autism to typical peers helps the student's development. For example, many individuals with autism grow up in the company of typical siblings, and these individuals do not seem to fare better than those without such siblings. We recommend that mainstreaming occur only after the student has mastered most of the programs in this manual.

When placing a student into a mainstream class, use a one-on-one aide experienced in behavioral intervention to help make sure exposure to the typical classroom environment is beneficial to the student. Examine several school programs and select one that has structure and one in which the teacher is willing to be advised about how to handle the student. The teacher should also agree to the presence of an aide from the student's treatment team who is familiar with the student's learning history to help the student participate in the group setting.

Teachers tend to be task-oriented individuals and less likely to be tied up in theoretical systems than other professionals. The great majority of teachers are willing to help. To lessen the burden on the teacher and the student, teach the school activities at home prior to introducing the student to the new classroom environment. Thus, the student initially does not have to learn anything new in school, but rather must transfer learned material from the home to the school environment. Such a practice is not unusual; it is common among typical individuals. A fuller description of how to integrate students into mainstream classes will be provided in an upcoming manual on advanced programs.

4. Be aware that data show that placing a student with mild developmental delays in the company of individuals with severe developmental delays may cause the student to regress (Smith, Lovaas, & Lovaas, in press).

5. Do not expect the student to make optimal progress with less than 40 hours of one-on-one treatment per week. There are no valid long-term outcome data to support that 20 or even 30 hours per week provide adequate treatment intensity.

6. If the student is taught 6 hours per day on a daily basis, reserve most of the difficult tasks, such as verbal imitation, for the morning sessions because the student will likely learn more in the mornings than in the afternoons. Save some portions of the afternoon sessions for working on play skills, arts and crafts, and self-help skills. Some afternoon time may also be used for maintaining mastered tasks and for generalizing treatment gains across teachers and new environments.

Examples of Specific Problems

The first portion of this chapter lists common problems that arise in treatment and ways to avoid them. In the remainder of this chapter, we provide examples of problems that commonly occur to illustrate how problem solving may be carried out in practice.

The following examples are accompanied by potential solutions proposed by a group of experienced teachers. It is possible that the recommendations suggested will not help to overcome the specific difficulties. Rather, by introducing a recommendation in teaching, the teachers can closely examine how the student responds to certain interventions and then, based on the student's behavior, work from there. More often than not, effective solutions for a particular student's difficulties are the result of serendipitous discoveries based on observations of the student's behaviors. Searching for possible causes of problems can be extremely interesting, and answers, when found, are as powerful a reinforcer for a teacher as any reinforcer can be. Herein lies one of the rewards of being able to work with individuals with developmental delays.

Problem 1

A student has mastered several words in the Verbal Imitation Program, such as "bus," "shoe," "juice," and "watch." The student readily learns words and sound blends if they are maximally different, but he experiences considerable difficulty learning the discrimination between similar sounding words such as "bee" and "boo."

Suggestions

1. Teach the discrimination between "dee" and "boo," then go back and teach "bee" and "boo."
2. Maybe the student attends to your facial movements, which blocks the student's response to the auditory input. Cover your face when giving the SD.
3. Perhaps the student is not attending to your face and is not able to use facial expressions as prompts. To help establish facial expressions as prompts to be faded at a later time, teach the student to imitate facial expressions and then return to verbal imitation training, using one distinct facial expression when presenting "bee" and a quite different facial expression when teaching "boo." Then fade the use of facial expressions as prompts. Using facial expressions as prompts for the student's verbal behavior may seem inconsistent with earlier warnings of avoiding such stimuli. The difference lies in *knowing* that prompts are present and using them to facilitate teaching versus inadvertently using prompts and not fading them.
4. Try a reverse chain; that is, instead of teaching the student to imitate "bee" versus "boo," present her with "eeb" versus "oob." If the student learns the discrimination between these SDs, perhaps it may facilitate acquisition of the discrimination in the reverse order. It is possible that consonant–vowel combinations are more difficult than vowel–consonant combinations for the particular student.
5. If the unsuccessful sessions of verbal imitation are conducted in the chair, test whether the student responds better in sessions out of the chair. Try to keep the sessions fun and the student's attention high. In addition, limit each session to just 1 to 2 minutes and provide play breaks between each session. At later stages into the program, when the student has a longer positive reinforcement history in the chair, the student may be returned to the chair or kept in the chair for longer periods of time.
6. Place this discrimination on hold for 2 to 4 weeks, reintroducing it after other discriminations have been mastered.
7. Because the student is confronted with a task that is difficult for her, make sure that easy tasks are intermittently presented so that the student is given the opportunity to receive reinforcement and gain self-confidence. No more than 3 or 4 failed trials should pass without the student being presented with 1 or 2 trials of an already mastered task.

Problem 2

A student has difficulty imitating the teacher jumping when this skill is taught with the teacher and student standing beside the table.

Suggestion

Move away from the table and chairs and have the student imitate jumping on a bed. When this is mastered, move the task back to the table in gradual steps. This is only one example of using objects in the student's environment to help her learn new skills. As another example, one can teach a student to imitate waving bye-bye when she is at the door and provide reinforcement by letting her exit contingent on the imitation. The task can later be brought under instructional control in the chair. Likewise, if the student refuses to play with puzzles while sitting at the table, puzzles may be positioned first on the floor and then gradually moved to the table.

Problem 3

A student encounters major difficulties acquiring the instruction "Touch head." However, the student has learned to imitate the teacher's use of objects (e.g., placing a block in a bucket, moving a toy car back and forth).

Suggestion

Teach the student to touch his head when requested to do so by first having him imitate placing a beanbag on his head following the instruction "Do this." If the student has difficulty with this, the task may be broken down by teaching the student to first imitate placing the beanbag on the table, then on his lap, and then on his shoulder. Next, give the instruction "Touch head," prompting the correct response by having the student imitate you placing the beanbag on your own head. Lastly, gradually fade the beanbag and bring the correct response under the control of the SD "Touch head." In short, use an object or your modeling (visual cues) to facilitate mastery of receptive instruction (auditory cue).

Problem 4

When does a student's aide (i.e., shadow) fade out of the classroom and leave the student with her teacher and classmates? Sometimes parents or teachers want the aide to stay in the classroom for an excessive amount of time, perhaps in an attempt to ensure the student's adjustment. In contrast, some parents and teachers do not want aides to remain in the classroom for very long, and they suggest their dismissal before you feel comfortable leaving the student by herself. Keep in mind that when some teachers are asked how the student functions in the classroom when the aide is not present, they may report that the student acts appropriately, even if this is not the case. This same teacher may, at the end of the term, announce to the child's parents that the child caused so many difficulties that she needs to be transferred to another class. Remember that the teacher must attend to his or her entire class, there are often many problems and many students, and the teacher may not want to take attention away from the other students or favor your student with a disproportionate amount of time.

Suggestion

First and foremost, be certain that the person chosen as the aide is familiar with the student's treatment and programs; if the aide does not have the knowledge acquired through such familiarity, he or she will not be effective at generalizing treatment gains and may very well sabotage the classroom placement. The aide should not leave the class unless data demonstrate that the student can manage on her own. To gather such data, ask a colleague with whom the student is unfamiliar to visit the classroom and observe the student on days when the aide is present and days when the aide is absent, and then report back. Use an unfamiliar observer because the student may not act typically in the presence of a familiar person. Also, for familiar persons to gather data without affecting the outcome, they would have to hide from the student while observing, which is highly impractical. Note also that if a parent or teacher records the data, the report may be very different from the reports provided by someone not personally involved in the student's program. As an additional precaution, ask the colleague who takes data on the student to also take data on other students in the class (e.g., whether the student you work with interacts with the other students, whether the other students in the class act much like the student you work with, etc.). Such information will tell you a great deal about whether the aide should continue his or her involvement.

Problem 5

A student is very distracted by wallpaper or toys in the room where treatment takes place.

Suggestion

Remove the wallpaper or the student's toys from the room, or move the student's treatment into a barren room. Gradually introduce decorations and toys at a later stage in treatment when the student has learned to become more attentive to the teacher.

Problem 6

A student has mastered the expressive labels of 15 or more objects in a 3-D format. When the same objects are presented in a 2-D format, the student fails to make progress. The student appears not to attend to 2-D stimuli.

Suggestion

Rather than placing the pictures flat on the table in front of the student, give the student the pictures, one at a time, to hold in his hand. Another option is to pin or Velcro the pictures to the wall, thus avoiding the angle created by placing the stimuli on a flat table (for some students, stimuli placed at such an angle is difficult to visually attend to). Slowly fade the pictures from the wall onto the table. You may also try using a 3-D object as a prompt by placing the 2-D picture next to or in front of its corresponding 3-D object, then slowly fading out the 3-D object by covering it with its corresponding 2-D picture.

Problem 7

A student does not cry at home except when she enters the treatment room or the teacher enters the student's house.

Suggestion

Crying usually subsides as the student gains success at responding to the teacher's requests or habituates to treatment being a part of her daily routine, provided the student is not somehow reinforced for crying. If you can be certain that crying is not being inadvertently reinforced (e.g., by your delaying the session when the student cries), begin each treatment session with a favorite activity. For example, rather than starting off the session with programs, begin the session by playing with the student. This will not stop the crying right away, but it may do so over time. Another option is to simplify the teaching situation by intermittently calling the student to the table just to receive a favorite reinforcer and allowing the student to leave with no work required. If this suggestion is employed, make sure that such sittings occur *randomly* throughout the session so the student is not able to anticipate when she will receive free reinforcement. Also, make sure that sittings for free reinforcement do not occur contingent on tantruming or other inappropriate behaviors.

Problem 8

In programs requiring verbal responses, a student's enunciation is poor.

Suggestion

Associating visual representations with the student's verbal responses might improve the clarity of the responses. Such associations may be made by introducing a sight reading program, teaching the student to read the words that constitute the correct responses in the verbal programs. These words may be spelled out on flash cards or shown in books.

Problem 9

A student's parents have a newborn baby, and the student handles the baby roughly at times when the parents are out of the baby's room. The parents are concerned that the baby might get hurt. This is a potentially dangerous situation for both the baby and the student. Should the baby be seriously hurt, the parents' feelings about the student may become negative.

Suggestion

Modify the prize board system introduced in Chapter 7 by giving the student a red card for approaching the baby. The student's parents should decide what kind of unpleasant consequence should be paired with the red card to help prevent future occurrences. Reinforce the student for leaving the baby alone until the baby is older and better able to fend for himself, and then teach the student how to interact with the baby in a safe manner.

Problem 10

Whenever one of a student's favorite toys is taken from her, she screams.

Suggestion

Remove the favorite toy and then give it back to the student almost immediately, before the student screams, reinforcing the student for not screaming. (If the student screams and then receives the toy, the student's screaming will be reinforced.) Slowly increase the interval of not screaming from 1 to 2 seconds and gradually up to 10 seconds before returning the toy. Call this exercise in frustration tolerance the "Big Kid Program."

Problem 11

A student has difficulty learning prepositions.

Suggestion

Prompt by keeping the objects used to teach each particular relationship constant while varying these objects across the general concept. For example, use a box as the base when teaching the relationship "on top," use a bucket as the base for teaching "inside," and let the placement of "beside" occur in relation to a book. Once these prepositions are mastered in this format, fade the prompt, replacing the varied objects with a common object.

Problem 12

The student completes the correct action but does so by attending to the teacher's facial expression rather than the auditory instruction. For example, the student is being taught to place a cup on top of a box in contrast to beside the box. The teacher instructs, "On top," and the student begins to move the cup slowly toward the top of the box, then pauses and looks at the teacher. As the student moves the cup toward the top of the box (the correct location), the teacher smiles encouragingly.

Suggestion

As the SD is presented, visually fixate on the student's forehead (or some other neutral place) and do not signal to the student in any way that his movement is toward the correct or incorrect location. Withhold smiling and other reinforcers until the student *completes* the correct response (i.e., the student places the cup on top of the box and then releases the cup).

Problem 13

In workshop-based interventions, there is a considerable amount of turnover; there seems to be an almost continuous outflow of older more experienced staff and influx of new staff who must be trained.

Suggestion

Try to arrange careers for your staff. One way to do this is by joining a local chapter of Families for Early Autism Treatment (FEAT) or a similar parent organization (see Chapter 36). For staff who remain on the job for 9 months or so, consider offering medical insurance or part of a tuition payment needed to complete a bachelor's or master's degree contingent on the person's remaining on the project (per a legal contract between the staff member and the institution or the student's parents). Recruit and train enough student teachers such that the departure of one or two does not seriously jeopardize the student's program.

Problem 14

One often comes across a workshop leader who claims to be qualified to deliver and supervise early and intensive behavioral intervention. This person, however, proposes unreasonable and arbitrary recommendations, such as not beginning expressive labeling prior to the student's mastery of 50 receptive labels. This recommendation is made despite data showing that some children with developmental delays acquire expressive labels before acquiring receptive ones. Rigidity on the part of the service provider may well hide an underlying insecurity about his or her own competence.

Suggestion

Ask for the person's written credentials from outside agencies and for names of parents who have already employed that person, then visit them, phone them, or ask for letters of recommendation. Request the consultant's college or university transcripts. If valid credentials cannot be produced to demonstrate his or her qualifications as a well-trained consultant, replace that person. Remember that attending a 2-day workshop and reading teaching manuals is inadequate preparation. Many parents feel, however, that a little help is better than no help. Although this may be true, parents should be informed that, under the guidance of an inadequately trained consultant, the treatment burden placed on them will likely be larger than if the consultant is well trained. There is also a higher risk of relapse if treatment is terminated.

Problem 15

A student who has mastered the concept of size through the use of blocks then seems to lose the discrimination and begins to perform at chance level (i.e., the student responds correctly approximately half the time).

Suggestion

The student may be bored of using blocks. Change the stimuli, shifting to objects such as large and small cars, cups, animal figurines, and so on.

Problem 16

Rather than appropriately attending to 2-D stimuli, a student uses them to self-stimulate (e.g., eyes them or waves them back and forth).

Suggestion

Velcro the stimuli to the wall, fasten them on cloth, or place them on a slanted surface such as an easel. At the first sign of inappropriate self-stimulatory behavior during the response interval, immediately consequate the incorrect response and then repeat the SD.

Problem 17

A student makes little or no progress in learning receptive identification of objects, letters, numbers, and the like.

Suggestions

1. Write the letters and numbers on a dry-erase board and, as reinforcement, let the student erase stimuli he correctly identifies.

2. To make the program more enjoyable and game-like, remove the stimuli from the table and place them on the floor for the student to retrieve when you name them rather than having the student just point to or touch them.

Problem 18

A student tantrums when she receives an informational "No" as a consequence for incorrect responding.

Suggestion

Replace the informational "No" with "Try again."

Problem 19

A student refuses to urinate in the toilet, urinating only outside on the lawn.

Suggestion

Place a potty chair on the lawn and teach the student to urinate in it. After the student masters this step, gradually move the potty chair into the bathroom, then place it beside the toilet, and then on top of the toilet. Finally, fade the potty chair.

Problem 20

A student refuses to defecate directly into a toilet, but will defecate into a diaper while sitting on a toilet.

Suggestion

Cut a small hole in the rear of the diaper. Gradually increase the size of the hole until only the portion of the diaper around the student's waist remains. Next, replace the diaper with a belt and gradually reduce the width of the belt (e.g., slowly move from a wide belt to a narrow belt, then to a piece of yarn, then string, and so on until no prompt is needed).

Problem 21

A common problem for boys is poor aim when attempting to urinate into a toilet bowl.

Suggestion

Have the student aim for brightly colored disposable items (e.g., Fruit Loops) placed inside the toilet.

Problem 22

Someone other than a student's parents coordinates the treatment, and the student's parents do not make much of an effort to involve themselves in the treatment.

Suggestion

Perhaps the coordinator has taken over much of the treatment from the beginning and has not invited the parents to become actively involved. The student's parents should be involved from the very beginning for several reasons, one being that it will be very difficult for the parents to become effective at teaching the student if they step in 3 to 4 weeks into treatment. At that time, the student may be working on complex programs and the parents may feel incompetent and inadequate if asked to participate (just as any novice person would). Inform the parents that, without their learning some of the basic treatment procedures, their child will be less likely to generalize treatment gains from teachers to parents or from the treatment environment to the outside community, such as shopping centers and restaurants, or to weekends and vacations. More important, their child is likely to regress when the present teachers leave unless the student becomes fully integrated and learns from typical peers. In the long run, it is informed and knowledgeable parents who are able to maintain and expand upon treatment gains as the child grows up.

One way to help parents stay involved is to request that they maintain their own log book, describing their day-to-day interactions with the student in concrete detail and then review their entries with the senior aide or workshop consultant on a weekly basis. Parents, however, should not be given an overabundance of responsibility. For example, if the parents do all of the treatment by themselves, chances are they will burn out, as any person would. Further, by performing all the treatment responsibilities alone, parents will not be able to take advantage of the problem-solving capacity often inherent in the collaboration of a group of people (see Chapter 32 for further help).

Problem 23

Many students with developmental delays are clever at making discriminations among (a) persons who provide treatment versus those who do not and (b) the places and times the treatment is administered versus locations and periods that signal free time.

Suggestion

Start treatment in one room to reduce interfering stimuli, then slowly transfer (generalize) mastered skills to other environments (e.g., to other rooms of the house, then to outside of the house) and persons (e.g., neighbors, family members, people at the grocery store). As the student progresses in treatment, new tasks may be taught in less structured and more varied environments.

Problem 24

A parent reports that he or she is very depressed and anxious, feeling as though he or she is failing the child. In discussing this problem with the student's parents, it appears that the student's grandparents and other relatives are spending a great deal of time in the home and giving a variety of suggestions as to how the parent should improve the treatment (about which they know very little). All these suggestions make the parent feel increasingly confused, anxious, depressed, and incompetent.

Suggestion

Recommend that all relatives refrain from visiting the house for the time being. If the parent is to meet with relatives, suggest that this be done without the child, away from the house, and with an agreement not to discuss the student's treatment.

Problem 25

A parent becomes depressed and anxious and is referred to a professional who is an expert at dealing with depression. The parent, after four or five meetings, feels that he or she is not experiencing any relief.

Suggestion

Refer the parent to a group of parents with similar issues. It is likely that, through participation in such a group, a great deal of support will be provided to the parent. Depression can have a variety of causes, and a particular professional may not have experience helping parents of children with developmental delays (see Chapter 36).

Problem 26

Concurrent with the present treatment, an authority on the treatment of autism recommends other interventions, such as one or more of the following: speech therapy, holistic medicine, Facilitated Communication, Sensory-Motor Training, Auditory Integration, Play Therapy, and various medical interventions to correct for suspected food allergies and intestinal yeast infections.

Suggestion

Although such eclectic combinations may sound promising, be aware that the effectiveness of most or all of these treatments is not supported by scientific data. If other treatments are involved, make certain to communicate closely with these other providers so that one intervention does not sabotage the work of another (e.g., so that a speech therapist does not inadvertently reinforce tantrums). In the case of medical interventions, make certain that medical diagnoses are confirmed by independent physicians and that side-effects of the prescribed medications are thoroughly spelled out. Some medical interventions seem innocuous at first, but may in fact cause serious problems. For example, the medication fenluramine, which was once widely prescribed as a treatment for autism both in the United States and abroad, has since been recalled because it caused heart damage and death for some persons. Be aware that any service provider, even providers with advanced degrees from well-respected institutions, may offer the promise of a miracle treatment.

Problem 27

A teacher gets angry at parents for not following through on treatment recommendations.

Suggestion

The teacher needs some counseling. It is highly inappropriate to express one's feelings in such a manner in a professional environment; if a teacher is concerned for the student's welfare, there are positive and tactful ways of approaching such an issue.

Problem 28

A professional suggests that behavioral treatment is not appropriate for high-functioning persons with autism, or that 20 hours per week of one-on-one intervention is enough for "smart kids."

Suggestion

Although recognized authorities in the field of autism have made such claims, no scientific data support either assertion (see Chapter 40).

Organizational and Legal Issues

SECTION 7

Strategies for Creating an Early Intervention, Parent Support Organization

CHAPTER 36

Ronald Huff

The goal of this chapter is to describe the benefits of, and the steps necessary to establish, a community-based, parent-driven, support organization. This chapter details a cost-effective, in-home, early intervention service delivery model and clarifies the collaborative roles of parents and professionals. Because early intervention programming for children with autism and developmental delays is complex and demanding, it compels parents to work together and share collectively in the resources and support services they create. Hopefully, the ideas presented here will empower you to start a parent organization in your own community.

The Good News

More than ever before, parents of young children diagnosed with autism can feel optimistic about obtaining an early intervention program for their children. A growing body of research shows that behaviorally based early intervention offers significant benefits to young children with autism (Birnbrauer & Leach, 1993; Fenske, Zalenski, Krantz, & McClannahan, 1985; Harris, Handleman, Gordon, Kristoff, & Fuentes, 1991; Lord, Bristol, & Schopler, 1993; Lovaas, 1987; Lovaas & Smith, 1988; McEachin, Smith, & Lovaas, 1993; Perry, Cohen, & DeCarlo, 1995; Sheinkopf & Siegel, 1998; Simeonson, Olley, & Rosenthal, 1987; Strain, Jamieson, & Hoyson, 1986). The behavioral research literature endorses and justifies a parent's efforts to organize early intervention program services (Powers, 1992). A plethora of positive research findings is persuasive evidence in favor of parents organizing community-based, early intervention resources for their own use. Parents with young autistic children are learning to combine their talents and work with dedicated and informed professionals to establish early intervention programs in their communities (Moroz, 1989; Roberts & Magrab, 1991; Wood, 1995).

The Contribution of Parents

It is the task of a parent organization to pull the elements of early intervention programming together, then build its integrity to establish a high-quality service. Quality of application in the in-home program is just as important as the number of one-to-one teaching hours. A quality standard is possible only when professionally trained aides and expert consultations are available. Most communities have access to a university faculty, private professional agencies with behavioral expertise, or public institutions whose mission is to provide developmental services. However, the expertise needed for training competent aides and providing consultation services required by the young child with autism is not readily available. Parent organizations, in most communities, must work with and support local professionals to find the expertise needed to make a community-based project succeed. The parent organization works to secure funding for training professionals to get the necessary expertise. To meet this challenge, the parents of young children with autism must organize themselves to create and administer early intervention projects in their communities.

Parents of children with autism possess an array of talents for creating a stable and self-sustaining community-based organization. Families with autistic children tend to be more functional and proactive and to use their internal resources efficiently. The more active and assertive parents must decide who among themselves is properly motivated and qualified to lead.

Parent-to-parent support and guidance are valuable assets that should be encouraged by the parent organization (Angell, 1993). For the parents of a newly diagnosed child, the opportunity to meet with parents already operating an in-home program is an informative experience. The realities encountered in an early intervention program are openly and candidly discussed during parent-to-parent contact.

Why Start at Home?

Because of the increased opportunities for learning, the best intervention outcome occurs at home.This is true for any child. At home, parents have direct control of the child's learning environment. By the time the in-home program is in operation, parents are typically well informed about the child's treatment program and the qualifications of the persons delivering treatment. Parents can alter the home environment to achieve a focused, intense, and highly individualized learning experience. A comprehensive and uniquely individualized teaching curriculum is compatible with in-home instruction and fulfills the child's right to treatment in the least restrictive environment. As one-to-one teaching produces new abilities, generalization strategies can be more quickly and efficiently implemented in the home and neighborhood. In a home-based approach, structured teaching generates new learning each day, and parents learn effective parenting skills. Enhanced parenting skills promote increased incidental learning outside formal teaching sessions.

Clinic-Based or Workshop-Based Treatment Delivery?

Traditionally, interventionists have delivered treatment for young children with autism in two different ways. One is through a clinic that specializes in research and treatment of children with autism; the other is a series of coordinated training workshops that occur in the home. I will discuss workshop-based treatment here because it is the most common method of treatment delivery. In a Workshop-based approach, the family is responsible for organizing the structural elements of the child's program. Workshop training does not begin until parents learn their responsibilities for coordinating an in-home program, recruit and schedule aides, and prepare a space in the home for teaching. Training consultants come to the home, assess the child's program needs, and model effective teaching while newly initiated aides watch and learn. During the first two to three workshops, beginning aides work directly with the child and receive feedback from the consultant. By the end of the workshop, the consultant develops and explains an individualized treatment program to parents and aides. Aides, using the training received during the workshop, carry out the child's program in the weeks to come. In a workshop-based format, the consultant returns in a few weeks to review the program for 1 day so as to observe, continue training the aides, and suggest recommended changes. The role of the parent in the workshop format is necessarily more demanding and may require direct participation in the child's program.

Whereas quality assurance is the hallmark of a clinic-based approach, exactness in a workshop-based approach is not as great because there is less control over quality treatment. In a clinic-based approach, a higher level of supervision ensures control over the aide's level of competency and assessment of progress in treatment is more routine. Case consultations are more frequent, and solutions to treatment difficulties are likely to occur more quickly. Complex programming (e.g., advanced language training and observational learning) is more likely to be available in a clinic-based approach.

As the UCLA (University of California, Los Angeles) Young Autism Project distributes its early intervention treatment program to other communities, clinic personnel are attempting to ensure that the quality of treatment meets high standards. The UCLA Young Autism Project has developed a system for certifying aides. As discussed in Chapter 3, aide certification occurs at two levels: staff aide and supervising aide. The staff aide must have a minimum of 60 hours of supervised one-to-one treatment experience. He or she must pass a course in behavior modification and show competence at teaching nonverbal learning and language skills sufficient to meet the quality improvement standards. The supervising aide must complete a full-time 9-month internship at UCLA or a replication site, be able to train novice aides, and be familiar with current applied learning theory. In addition, the supervising aide must pass quality control standards for designing programs and one-to-one teaching. At this level of certification, the aide has mastered techniques such as teaching nonverbal imitation, verbal imitation, receptive and expressive language, conversational skills, appropriate play with toys, interactive play with peers, and mainstreaming. The supervising aide recertifies every 2 years. The mark of success for an early intervention parent organization is availability of certified aides.

Preliminary research shows that treatment outcomes in a workshop-based approach are not as favorable as those in of a clinic-based program. In a preliminary study, Buch (1995) examined the effectiveness of parents and untrained college students during the early months of an intensive, in-home, early intervention program. Parents and students received 6 days of workshop-based training distributed over 3 months. Six children received behavioral treatment for 20 hours or more each week. Five of the six children learned receptive commands, and verbal and nonverbal imitation skills. However, they learned more slowly than children treated at the Clinic for the Behavioral Treatment of Children on the UCLA campus. In-home programs hatched from a workshop format receive fewer hours of hands-on supervised training for aides, and turnover among aides is greater. Additionally, fewer expert consultations take place, and program monitoring is not as intense. Reaching 40 hours per week of programming from a workshop-based format is more difficult because parents, along with all their other responsibilities, must recruit, schedule, and supervise aides. Nevertheless, a workshop approach is a desirable and effective early intervention methodology. The purpose of a parent organization is to increase the quality and efficiency of resources used in a workshop-based project. One way to accomplish quality and efficiency is to hire certified clinic-trained workshop leaders and share those leaders among families.

For the unwary parent, the path of the workshop approach can be perilous. The anxious parent is vulnerable to exaggerated claims made by eager aides who want to please the parent. Parents may settle for less experienced, previously unsupervised aides who do not have access to a behaviorally based curriculum. Parents can misjudge which aides are better teachers. With less expert guidance, the young autistic child is at risk for being subjected to programming that can cause behavior problems (i.e., increased self-stimulation and noncompliance). Forms of misapplication include introducing programs before the child achieves readiness and persisting too long with teaching exercises that are beyond the child's developmental ability. The anxious parent may seek to integrate the child into a school program before the child can manage the social and communication demands of the classroom. A quality treatment program involves more than conducting drills. Knowledge of developmental sequence, behavior observational skills, and appreciation for the value of data are critical to ensure an optimal rate of learning.

Collaboration Between Parents and Professionals

A critical moment between parent and professional is in the initial courtship. Unfortunately and all too often, the advice given to most parents along with the diagnosis is, "Go home and try to live with it." In other cases, a well-meaning professional refers a child to the local autism program that may or may not be appropriate for that child and his or her family's needs. An active and well-informed parent group that makes itself available to newcomers is a positive remedy for the disoriented and discouraged parent. Sensitive and caring contact with other parents who know what can be accomplished eases the shock, anxiety, and despair of accepting a diagnosis of autism (Tommasone & Tommasone, 1989).

Collaboration between parents and professionals is the key to a successful parent support organization. Collaboration begins from the first day of the project and continues as the organization continues to provide support. Parents need professionals and professionals need parents. A balanced and forward-looking relationship between parents and professionals guarantees a progressive organization. Parents *actively* participate in the development of the resources they decide are important. By taking a proactive interest in creating and coordinating the resources needed to make an in-home program possible, parents influence the quality and direction of their child's program. By participating in the development of intervention resources and coordinating their child's in-home program, parents retain more control of the variables that determine the outcome. The process of simultaneously sharing responsibilities empowers and motivates the parent and the professional to do a better job.

The community-based approach gives parents the opportunity to contribute actively but in their own way. Parents are actively involved with each other and many different professionals and community agencies, but they focus their efforts on achieving optimal growth for their child. The network of contacts and resources formed by a parent organization is open ended and continually expands and changes as the needs and requirements of the children change. Quality of governance provided by parents, professionals, and business consultants elected to lead determines the direction and ultimately the success or failure of the organization.

Rationale for a Parent Organization

Community-based early intervention projects have shown that the parent-driven organization that solicits collaborative participation from informed dedicated professionals is likely to succeed in developing early intervention program services (Bristol & Schopler, 1993; Huff, 1996; Lovaas, 1993). The successful parent organization works to link with public agencies whose mandate is to help children with developmental disabilities. Representatives of the parent organization can inform themselves and approach the public agency with a clear idea of how that particular agency can contribute. A parent organization, with other agencies, helps in the development of supplemental support services (e.g., counseling, case management, respite, advocacy for school programs, assessment, recreation).

Experience has shown that an organized, well-informed group of parents can accomplish more than a single family working alone. The challenge is to get a working understanding of the benefits, complexities, and limits of early intervention programs. Experienced parents consult with newcomer parents to provide an orientation about the sacrifices demanded by an in-home program. An organization's method of orientation and education should expediently enable parents to decide what is in the best interests of the child and family as a whole. See the discussion by Powell, Hecimovic, and Christensen (1992) for a review of the issues encountered in identifying and meeting the unique needs of the family with an autistic child. Another fundamental task of the parent organization is to work with local agencies to coordinate applications of recent early intervention research.

Promoting public awareness of the need for and benefits of early intervention is another very important part of the organization's outreach and public relations effort. To enhance fund-raising capability, the organization should become known and accepted by potential contributors in the community.

Services provided by the parent-driven organization should enable a family to start a timely and orderly early intervention program. A measure of the organization's success is how quickly and conveniently a family obtains intervention resources. After the organization is running efficiently, starting an in-home program should become routine for new families.

How Do We Get Started?

A parent support organization is initiated when one parent identifies three or four other families and calls for a planning meeting. The planning meeting should include a presentation of the benefits of early intervention. Videotapes that show children in treatment and open discussion of the need for a parent organization dedicated to early intervention should follow. One activity that gives the organization a sense of cohesiveness and purpose is conducting an early intervention demonstration for the benefit of uninformed families. Families that participated in the demonstration project serve as exemplars for other families. Experience gained during the demonstration project smoothes the operation of the organization. Public announcement of the existence of the parent organization should occur near the end of the demonstration project.

After a core group of families has united to create a sense of direction and solidarity, holding public discussions involving other parents and professionals is important. The purpose of the first few public meetings is to assess interest level, identify immediate goals, and recruit organizational leaders. As word spreads about the inauguration of the organization and inquiries about services begin, assigning those families that are willing to commit their time and skills to work groups is appropriate.

Parents should publicize the opportunity for participation in an early intervention project through local media. With professional assistance, the parent organization develops written materials to orient and educate parents about how to coordinate an early intervention program. With the board of director's approval, individuals are selected to form work teams. Work teams secure relations and working agreements with entitlement agencies, raise funds, recruit students, schedule workshops, and plan support meetings. Experienced parent leaders widely recognize that organized public relations events enhance fund-raising, promote community acceptance, and attract volunteers, all of which are necessary for success.

Getting a grant during the first year or two will significantly improve the success of a parent organization. Grant funds enable training of aides and partially offset consulting fees. An immediate goal is to develop a pool of competently trained aides. These aides must be mature enough to understand the importance of receiving training in the basics and value the opportunity to receive more advanced training. The organization should initiate fund-raising activities to support each child's in-home program and, simultaneously, complete and file an application for federal and state nonprofit, tax-exempt status. Preparation for the election of a board of directors and long-range planning should begin. Composition of the board of directors deserves very careful consideration. Achieving a proper balance between parents and professionals is critical, with experienced businesspersons in the majority. Board members with a business background offer expertise in managing budgets and planning. They are well connected to the business community and know where opportunities reside. For example, one parent organization's business consultant solicited the pro bono services of a graphic art firm to design an attractive logo for use in the production of video material, brochures, and fund raising. Another parent group received a year of complimentary lodging, rental cars, and airfare for training consultants who had to travel from another city. Other examples of contributions from businesses that offset the organization's printing and advertisement costs include public announcements on television and radio. Business consultants inspire spirited public relations work and assist with creative requests for sponsorship from local corporations.

Business consultants, like other professionals, must have an abiding interest in developing an early intervention program. The availability of experienced and motivated business consultants may be the most important issue for a parent organization. To survive, the organization needs sound business planning and the objective decision making that is characteristic of successful private businesses. Solid business consulting will set the foundation for unity of purpose and harmony of effort. The result of the business planning process is to have an organization linked to multiple community resources, without total dependence on one institution. Another equally important result is to evolve into an organization that is sustainable for years to come, financially solvent, well organized, and accountable.

FEAT Sacramento—An Illustration

FEAT stands for Families for Early Autism Treatment. FEAT emerged as an organization in Sacramento, California, in 1993 from the individual efforts of parents and professionals who worked collaboratively to create active treatment opportunities for young children with autism. The total absence of early intervention programs designed specifically to meet the unique needs of children with autism forced the creation of FEAT. Parents who were willing and able organized FEAT to take their children's treatment needs into their own hands and aggressively pursue a solution. Published reports that intensive early intervention leads to significantly increased intellectual, communicative, social, and educational development in children with autism initially excited the parents of FEAT. After several families attempted early intervention programming in their own homes and obtained significant and obvious results, they felt that a technically sophisticated and adequately funded effort to develop quality intervention services was not only justified, but necessary.

The following is a summary of some steps that made FEAT a premier community-based, parent support organization. For a more detailed description of how FEAT was founded, see Huff (1996).

Steps That Worked

1. Identified parents with young autistic children who were willing to work cooperatively to create an organization.
2. Conducted a demonstration of in-home treatment programming, including an early intervention workshop.
3. Established ways for reaching out to other families with children with autism.
4. Announced the organization and held public educational lectures for parents and professionals.
5. Procured start-up/demonstration grant funding.
6. Initiated fund-raising activities to start training.
7. Solicited charitable contributions of airfare, rental cars, and lodging for the first year of operation to offset start-up expenses.
8. Publicized the opportunity for volunteers to participate in an early intervention project.
9. Educated parents how to manage an early intervention in-home program.
10. Obtained federal and state nonprofit tax status to simplify corporate and private donations.
11. Quickly elected a board of directors and officers to begin goal setting and planning.
12. Selected work teams to carry out day-to-day activities, such as fund-raising, recruiting, workshop and follow-up consultation scheduling, and parent support meetings.
13. Met with and secured working relationships with entitlement agencies.
14. Conducted board meetings for long-range planning.
15. Involved experienced business consultants to resolve organizational issues.
16. Organized a public relations campaign to enhance fund-raising, gain community acceptance, and attract volunteers.
17. Created and distributed educational materials, such as a video, to educate pediatricians about the importance of early diagnosis.
18. Asked that parents join the boards of local service agencies.
19. Convinced local administrators in school districts and entitlement agencies that the organization was committed to cost savings.
20. Published a bimonthly newsletter.
21. Set up a lending library for teaching materials and information.
22. Got the California State Senate to pass a resolution inaugurating Autism Treatment Awareness Week.

Things That Did Not Work

1. Parents realistically complained they could not run their child's program and be responsible for fund-raising.
2. An intense approach to treatment caught schools off guard; schools did not understand the real benefits of early intervention.

3. The organization was not functioning properly because families were putting their energy into their child's program.
4. Lines of authority within the organization were not clear.
5. Board members were not openly accountable to the organization.
6. New projects were initiated but not finished, creating the impression of many false starts.
7. Methods of recruiting and keeping dependable aides were slow to develop.
8. Starting an in-home program was a confusing process; relevant information was missing.
9. Parents who did not have the resources to conduct an in-home program were frustrated.
10. Borrowing or creating a high volume of teaching materials was stressful.
11. A perceived inequity in distribution of services caused dissent among families.
12. Inconsistency of funding caused anxiety among parents.
13. Families that skipped the orientation or a pretreatment assessment process developed misconceptions about the outcomes of treatment.

Parent as Coordinator of Intervention Activities

Courage and determination are traits typical of the parent who initiates an in-home program. Experience has shown that if an organization backs a family with meaningful support, the child's parents are most often sufficiently competent to maintain the infrastructures of the in-home program. These activities include helping with recruiting aides, scheduling teaching sessions, collecting and organizing teaching materials, participating in weekly treatment team meetings, and interacting with other support agencies to ensure continuity. The parents' keen sensitivity to change in their child is a good reason for parents to be actively involved. Parents who are actively involved with their child's treatment team typically develop awareness for the quality of training received by their child. When problems occur, parents participate as team members regarding changes in the child's program. Informed and aware parents are responsible, along with the consulting aide, for monitoring the effects of change in the child's program or treatment team. Informed professionals do not expect parents to get sufficient knowledge and training to manage a child's program, nor are parents qualified to construct teaching programs beyond an elementary level.

Services Offered by the Organization

Once established, the organization creates time-saving services by networking within the community, establishing work teams, and accumulating and distributing information. The following is a summary of services valuable to families searching for an early intervention program.

1. Outreach and identification of families seeking early intervention services. The organization becomes a focal point for parents to gather, be recognized, and be supported. It produces written materials that describe the mission and services of the organization.
2. Screening, orientation, and education for families deciding if in-home intervention will meet their child's needs
3. Recruitment and training of aides. The organization establishes a readily available recruitment network for locating and recruiting students to be trained as aides.
4. Lending library for teaching materials. A lending library reduces stress on families by making it easier to find materials. After a child masters specific tasks, the materials used to teach those tasks are passed on to another child through the lending library.
5. Monthly support meetings where families discuss topics of mutual interest.
6. Advocacy and support for supplemental services from public agencies. Every parent who successfully transitions a child into an appropriate educational program is potentially a consultant and advocate for other parents. The organization accumulates knowledge and materials that strengthen the parents' efforts to achieve full community and school inclusion.
7. Quick access to parent-to-parent and parent-to-professional communications. A monthly newsletter that supports networking, a handbook that describes services, an Internet chat forum, a phone tree, and periodic meetings with the child's case manager to discuss individual program plans.

Focused Work Teams

Focused work teams composed of parents and professionals create and maintain the services mentioned previously. Parents select the work group that they feel most appropriately matches their talents and skills. To illustrate, parents who feel comfortable as public speakers help families recruit student aides by attending college classrooms to make presentations about the in-home program. Parents who are good planners and are comfortable organizing others assign themselves to the fund-raising work team. If a parent has accounting skills, he or she may agree to manage the organization's financial accounting. Parents who write well draft a grant or produce the monthly newsletter. Parents familiar with educational law may join the Individual Education Program (IEP) work team and assist families in preparing written IEP objectives. Parents who are acquainted with local professionals or who have professional interests in counseling or running groups become involved with organizing and conducting monthly support meetings. The support work team sets the agenda and solicits local professionals to donate pro bono time to address family issues or other topics used for early intervention. The parent familiar with computers provides a time- and money-saving service to other families by serving as scheduler (i.e., coordinating start-up workshops, follow-up consultations, and in-home observation visits). Efficient scheduling reduces costs and optimizes use of limited resources. Parents who have finished an in-home program and have had 1 or 2 years experience managing an intervention team make excellent screening and orientation work group members.

Additional assets accrue to the seasoned parent group. After 1 or 2 years of direct experience operating intensive, in-home programs, a member's insight matures. Success in settling philosophical, administrative, and legal disputes along the way establishes a higher order of thinking. The experienced parent sees the complex problem of treating a child with autism from a more balanced perspective. Enlightened and discerning, parents think objectively when they field complaints from other parents or professionals with less wisdom. Parent leaders use this insight to empower new families and uninitiated professionals to avert conflict. They help defuse problems that are bound to emerge among families in the organization and between families and agencies. By providing informed feedback and objective information, they serve as effective arbitrators in resolving differences between parents and professionals. This saves time, money, and personal stress and assures a smoother operation by reducing the need for fair hearings and lawsuits.

Professional Services Critical to Success

Parents in a community leadership role must be conscious of the need for and value of informed and dedicated professionals. Experienced businesspersons who are willing to work with the organization are invaluable. The organization needs the professional at critical moments of development to consult and advise on key issues. When an organization is just getting started, someone must recognize and evaluate existing resources. Community professionals with knowledge of local resources have an opportunity to be helpful in the initial planning stages of an organization. For example, behavioral psychologists can help by identifying behavior analysts who are motivated and competent to launch an in-home program.

Professionals are essential to grant writing, development of professional and ethical guidelines, progress reports required by grants, evaluation of the child's program, translation of scientific literature, clarifying technical issues, and making referrals for related services. Obtaining a grant may depend on a successful pilot demonstration that will serve as the operating model for the intervention project. Professional say is indispensable for overall project design, evaluation, parent surveys, and determination of training standards. Professionals work intimately with each parent to monitor the child's progress and the treatment program and, when indicated, suggest methods to ensure quality controls for training aides. Business professionals are essential to establishing a functional and productive board of directors; writing bylaws, policies, and procedures; and developing business and expenditure plans. A related and imperative task of each involved professional is to promote and maintain positive parent–professional collaboration (Roberts & Magrab, 1991).

Generally, the more information parents have about their child's strengths and needs, the more comfortable they are deciding to start an in-home program. Children vary in their response to intervention programming. Quality assessment and diagnosis go a long way in preparing parents to understand and appreciate their child's response to early intervention. Appreciation of the heterogeneity between children and the effects those differences have on an intervention outcome is especially important (Lord et al., 1993). The experienced, informed professional is a valuable asset for managing expectations of outcome and authenticating parents' understanding of developmental assessment data.

Parents who affirm the value of offering their child an in-home intervention program may require 4 to 8 hours of orientation before they feel comfortable with the decision to start a program. Use of the interdisciplinary team (IDT) is an effective way to approach the orientation issue. The IDT is composed of all the persons with a stake in the child's treatment outcome. Typically, the IDT meets several times to help the parent appreciate whether or not, and to what degree, a child is benefiting from the program. The IDT must decide how to monitor and measure the child's response to the program. The child's response to treatment demarcates the margins of a child's intervention program. The child's response to treatment determines the need for modifications to the program. Modifications, for example, can involve the number of hours of treatment per week, the number of aides present during treatment, the number of aides on the team, and teaching exercises used. Every child's program requires expert consultation and collaboration between parent, professional, and treatment team members.

A critical point in each child's intervention program arrives when the treatment team, including the parent, objectively determines that a particular teaching technique is not working. Sometimes behavior problems interfere with learning or the child's motivation is low. In these situations, the parent needs a highly trained and experienced behavioral consultant to identify alternatives. Also, the sensitive professional helps families with stress management (e.g., recognizing that it is all right to take a break).

Achieving Cost-Effectiveness and Cost Savings

The success or failure of a support organization likely depends on its ability to achieve cost-efficiency and cost containment. The number of children diagnosed with autism each year in the United States has created an ever-increasing demand for well-trained, highly specialized behavior interventionists. Conducting training within the university setting would greatly contain the cost of developing qualified staff. Establishing university classes taught by existing faculty where students could get practicum credit for learning and using intervention teaching technology would reduce costs. The cost of training a qualified team to carry out an intensive, in-home program can be a formidable barrier, especially at a time when legislatures are redefining entitlement services and funding priorities for developmental services are uncertain. By organizing a self-help initiative, parents position themselves to guarantee optimal savings and maintain cost-effectiveness. The organization that uses verifiable strategies for achieving cost savings can increase its chances of endorsement from funding agencies.

Under the best of circumstances, early intervention programming is expensive. Therefore, a primary function of the organization is to ensure, to the greatest extent possible, that each dollar spent generates a residual benefit. The organization finds ways to avoid duplication of costs across families. Funds expended to benefit one child should translate into benefits for other children. Organizing enables cost savings in small but significant amounts. Intelligent application of volunteers, planned recycling of training resources and teaching materials, and development of efficient fund-raising methods generate cost savings. The two major sources of expense for in-home programs are training aides to a qualified level and reimbursing aides for the daily, hands-on treatment. Training aides is essentially a one-time cost that leads to a durable community resource. Therefore, conserving expenditures for reimbursement of hands-on treatment generates proportionally greater savings over the long term. Using alternative forms of compensation is one way to achieve cost savings. Another is to offer course credit and the opportunity for professionally supervised training in exchange for 4 to 6 hours a week of hands-on teaching from each aide. Maximizing cost savings means reducing large, ongoing expenses, such as office rent, staff salaries, employee taxes, and employee benefits. In the beginning of a community-based effort to organize, as many dollars as possible should go directly to the child's program. This strategy obligates the organization to take advantage of every source of volunteer services and charitable contributions available in the community. The organization's first long-range goal should be to find accessible sources of funding. Having displayed a capacity for stable operation and provision of measurable benefits to children, a well-informed group of parents can effect permanent change in the funding priorities and policies of public institutions. Finally, each child's family must contribute to the organization by donating time and effort and, to its ability, money. Because the cost of an early intervention program is significant and a child's future is at stake, necessity dictates that parents contribute part of the funding.

There remains a broader question about the savings that intensive early intervention programming generates by reducing the risk of institutionalization and increasing functional living and vocational productivity. To date, few comprehensive benefit–cost analyses of programs specific to individuals with autism are available. Wall (1990) estimated the average annual per person placement cost for an autistic group home at $53,509. For individuals with developmental disabilities and challenging behaviors, the cost increases significantly. Knobbe, Carey, Rhodes, and Horner (1995) calculated the average annual cost per person for a community residence at $111,123, compared with $117,277 for institutional care. In an era of deinstitutionalization, placement in a state-operated facility where per diem costs have risen dramatically is less likely. Although group homes are a viable residential living option and a continuing necessity, each out-of-home placement generates a substantial increase in annual costs. Assuming 50 years of protective care for each untreated person with autism, conservative estimates of cost range between $2.7 and $5.6 million per person. The total average cost of an intensive, i.e., 40-hour-per-week, one-to-one early intervention program is around $120,000. This cost is based on $5,000 per month, or $60,000 per year, for an average of 2 years. If preliminary research estimates of a best outcome are accurate (i.e., a best outcome occurs in 20% to 47% of children treated), then the expense of early intervention appears reasonable and warranted. Fujiura, Roccoforte, and Braddock (1994) illuminated this proposition in a study of out-of-pocket costs for family care. Fujiura et al. reported that the marginal costs of supplementing and encouraging family-based care may represent a far more efficient use of limited service resources than purchase of additional out-of-home capacity.

Funding Sources

Funding for operation of the organization, including aide training and expert in-home consultation, must come from multiple sources. Those sources include small grants ($1,000 to $10,000), entitlement funding from public agencies, corporate sponsorship, public donations, solicited donations, parents' contributions, and funding from school districts. In 1986, the U.S. Congress established entitlement to comprehensive programming for children with autism, from birth to age 3, as Part H of the Education of the Handicapped Act Amendments of 1986. In 1990, Congress reauthorized funding and passed the Individuals with Disabilities Education Act. Every participating state has a lead agency, the Interagency Coordinating Council. Federal funding may be available in some states if existing sources of funding do not cover intervention services.

Fund-raising can be conducted quickly. A family member, equipped with descriptive materials, can approach select corporations for cash grants. Included among the ways for families to raise money are the following:

1. Requesting sponsorship from charity groups
2. Holding an annual dinner dance with a silent auction
3. Soliciting a pledge for a percentage of sales from fast-food restaurants
4. Asking the company where parents work for a funding pledge
5. Placing donation cans in restaurants
6. Soliciting donations through television, radio, and newspaper interviews about the project

There exists a strong sentiment to champion the parent organization that helps children with autism. If local corporations and the business community believe the parent organization is genuine, they will be inclined to contribute funding. The business community seems especially inclined to support endeavors that promise to reduce expenditure of state and federal tax dollars. In the political community, the organization can apply different forms of advocacy to carve out sources of funding. Parents should not hesitate to entreat legislative advocates to use their influence to support a grassroots effort. In California, the collaborative efforts of parents and professionals stimulated the state senate to pass a resolution declaring 1 week each year as Early Autism Treatment Awareness Week.

Review of the Steps to Success

As parents of children with autism learn more about the nature of autism and effective treatment options, they must eventually decide whether to carry out an early intervention program. Likewise, professionals must decide whether to become involved with a family in setting up an intervention program. After carefully weighing the options, parents may decide to initiate an in-home program using the teaching technology described in this book. Parents who decide to start an in-home program should consider whether to join with other parents and professionals to create a support organization. A local organization that helps parents with information services, advocacy, emotional support, access to competently trained aides, and funding will greatly improve chances of a successful in-home program.

An established and well-run organization that promotes early intervention services in the community is an indispensable resource for young children with autism and their families. In truth, if parents do not take the initiative to create parent-driven support organizations in their communities, high-quality intervention programs for young children with autism will probably not emerge. Creating a parent organization requires a great deal of hard work, sacrifice, and interpersonal cohesion among the participants. The essence of the successful organization is parent–professional involvement, commitment, and collaboration. Indeed, professionals need parents as much as parents need professionals. Equally important is rock-solid business consulting. Parents and professionals must not forget to run their organization like a business. The organization most likely to succeed will set high standards from the beginning. Its members will take the challenge to create something unique and unfamiliar. Most of all, the organization will maintain a strong belief that its parents have the power to make success happen.

Parents interested in discussing issues related to starting or maintaining a parent support organization or who have questions about autism resources can call FEAT at 916/843-1536. Voice mail messages are monitored weekly, and calls are returned by informed FEAT members. For a faster response, visit the FEAT Web site (www.feat.org). Questions can be e-mailed to FEAT members via the Web site.

Obtaining a Free and Appropriate Public Education for Preschool-Age Children with Autism or Pervasive Developmental Disorders

CHAPTER 37

Kathryn Dobel and Valerie Vanaman

A child who has been diagnosed with autism or pervasive developmental disorder (PDD) qualifies, pursuant to the Individuals with Disabilities Education Act of 1990 (IDEA), (20 U.S.C. § 1400 *et seq.*) and the implementing regulations at 34 Code of Federal Regulations (C.F.R.) 300 *et seq.*, for an Individualized Education Program. The core of the IDEA is a mechanism called the written Individualized Education Program (IEP); it is this document that becomes the critical link between the child with a disability and the special education that the child requires. The IDEA defines special education as "specially designed instruction at no cost to parents or guardians, to meet the unique needs of a disabled child, including classroom instruction, instruction in physical education, home instruction, and instruction in hospitals and institutions" [20 U.S.C. § 1401(25)].

The IEP is also a management tool designed to assure that when a child requires special education, the special education designed for that child is appropriate to his individual education needs, and that the special education designed is actually delivered and monitored. This means that the program must focus on the child's individual needs, and not on an entire class of children.

The IDEA now contains a specific definition in Section 1414(d)(1)(A) describing the components of an IEP as follows:

> a written statement for each child with a disability that is developed, reviewed, and revised in accordance with this section and that includes—
>
> (i) a statement of the child's present levels of educational performance, including—
>
> (I) how the child's disability affects the child's involvement and progress in the general curriculum; or
>
> (II) for preschool children, as appropriate, how the disability affects the child's participation in appropriate activities;
>
> (ii) a statement of measurable annual goals, including benchmarks or short-term objectives, related to—
>
> (I) meeting the child's needs that result from the child's disability to enable the child to be involved in and progress in the general curriculum; and
>
> (II) meeting each of the child's other educational needs that result from the child's disability;
>
> (iii) a statement of the special education and related services and supplementary aids and services to be provided to the child, or on behalf of the child, and a statement of the program modifications or supports for school personnel that will be provided for the child—
>
> (I) to advance appropriately toward attaining the annual goals;
>
> (II) to be involved and advance in the general curriculum in accordance with clause (i) and to participate in extracurricular and other nonacademic activities; and
>
> (III) to be educated and participate with other children with disabilities and nondisabled children in the activities described in this paragraph;
>
> (iv) an explanation of the extent, if any, to which the child will not participate with nondisabled children in the regular class and in the activities described in clause (iii);
>
> (v)(I) a statement of any individual modifications in the administration of state or districtwide assessments of student achievement that are needed in order for the child to participate in such assessment; and
>
> (II) if the IEP team determines that the child will not participate in a particular State or districtwide assessment of student achievement (or part of such an assessment), a statement of—

(aa) why that assessment is not appropriate for the child; and

(bb) how the child will be assessed;

(vi) the projected date for the beginning of the services and modifications described in clause (iii), and the anticipated frequency, location and duration of those services and modifications; . . .

(viii) a statement of—

(I) how the child's progress toward the annual goals described in clause (ii) will be measured; and

(II) how the child's parents will be regularly informed (by such means as periodic report cards), at least as often as parents are informed of their nondisabled children's progress, of—

(aa) their child's progress toward the annual goals described in clause (ii); and

(bb) the extent to which the progress is sufficient to enable the child to achieve the goals by the end of the year.

Section 1414(d)(1)(B) requires that the IEP team include the following individuals:

(i) the parents of a child with a disability;

(ii) at least one regular education teacher of such child (if the child is, or may be, participating in the regular education environment);

(iii) at least one special education teacher, or where appropriate at least one special education provider of such child;

(iv) a representative of the local educational agency who—

(I) is qualified to provide, or supervise the provision of, specially designed instruction to meet the unique needs of children with disabilities;

(II) is knowledgeable about the general curriculum;

(III) is knowledgeable about the availability of resources of the local educational agency;

(v) an individual who can interpret the instructional implications of evaluation results . . . ;

(vi) at the discretion of the parent or the agency, other individuals who have knowledge or special expertise regarding the child, including related services personnel as appropriate; and whenever appropriate, the child with a disability.

Section 1414(d)(3)(A) requires the IEP team to consider the strengths of the child and the concerns of the parents for enhancing the education of their child. Section 1414(d)(3)(B) and (C) require that the IEP team consider, among other things, (a) interventions, strategies, and supports, including behavior management plans, to address behavior for the child whose behavior impedes learning; (b)communication needs for all children; and (c) whether the child needs assistive technology devices and services.

Preparing the IEP

The IEP is the blueprint for determining and receiving a free and appropriate public education (FAPE). Perhaps no other field has as many acronyms and abbreviations as education. The most important abbreviation for the family is the IEP. Parents are entitled to be equal participants in the IEP development. To take an active role, and hopefully one of equal participation, parents must carefully prepare for the IEP meeting. The remainder of this chapter explains to parents how to prepare for an appropriate IEP.

Parents should contact their local educational agency to request an IEP as soon as they are aware of their child's developmental delays. Parents should immediately begin preparation for the IEP meeting as if they are designing a blueprint with an architect when building a house. It is critical to plan and plan carefully. The IEP is the document whereby the child's needs will be identified in terms of goals and objectives or benchmarks. Progress or mastery of these goals will be measured at least annually.

Parents need to carefully read the list of attendees on the written notice for the IEP meeting that they receive prior to the meeting. Parents should invite or ask the school district to invite anyone not on the list whom they deem important to the team making decisions about their child. Also parents need to make sure from the outset that sufficient time is allotted for the meeting; a detailed IEP should take at least 3 hours. If the school staff schedules only 1 hour, additional meetings will likely be needed to complete the IEP. This can make parents weary and wary of school district motivations and expertise.

The following steps help in planning for this important meeting.

► **Step 1**

Assessment [20 U.S.C. § 1414(a)–(c); 34 C.F.R. § 300.532]. In preparation for the IEP meeting, a thorough evaluation must be conducted. First, parents must know what their child's disability is before they can determine the appropriate remedial program. School district evaluations for preschool children with autism or PDD are often limited by time, experience of the evaluator, and scope of the assessment. Rarely do school assessors provide a specific diagnosis. In most instances, prior to intense behavioral intervention, these children are not testable by the average school psychologist or special education teacher using standardized instruments. Thus, the most important data gathered by the school team are from parents' reports. Parents should make sure the written reports they receive later accurately depict what they shared with the school district team during the assessment interview. Parents should also obtain and provide to the school assessment team thorough diagnostic information.

Parents usually know their children best. However, good assessment data from standardized test instruments are critical to planning the IEP, as long as appropriate adaptations, such as the use of assistive technology, have been provided as needed during the assessment. These data will determine the baseline or present levels of performance from which the plan will begin, so that progress can be carefully measured to make sure that the plan is effective for the child.

If the school assessment does not provide the parent with adequate data regarding, among other things, the diagnosis or the present levels of performance, parents have the right to obtain an independent assessment and seek reimbursement from the school district, pursuant to 34 C.F.R. § 300.502. Whether the school district will agree to reimburse without dispute will have to be discussed, but the data from the outside evaluation must be included in the IEP, regardless of who pays for the evaluation. Parents should request copies of the written reports from the school assessment team at least 5 days prior to the IEP meeting, so they will have some idea how the school staff views their child and whether an independent evaluation is warranted.

Although the parent may request that the IEP meeting be postponed until the independent evaluation can be obtained, it may not be a good idea to postpone the meeting, depending on how long the wait will be and whether the child is without any program or services in the meantime. Such a decision would need to be made on a case-by-case basis. However, parents would not want to agree to the ultimate IEP wording until they believe that the plan accurately reflects their child's identified needs. It is best to obtain the evaluation from an expert in autism and PDD, who is experienced in designing programs and monitoring progress over time for this population. Local chapters of Families for Early Autism Treatment (FEAT) and other organizations should have referral lists for professionals who perform thorough evaluations for this population.

▶ Step 2

Present Levels of Performance [20 U.S.C. §1414(d)(1)(A); 34 C.F.R. § 300.346–347]. Before the IEP meeting, parents should create their own detailed written statement of how they see their child in all developmental domains across settings (at home, in the community, and at school or in other group-based programs), including these domains: behavioral, cognitive, social and play, emotional, speech–language and communication, fine and gross motor, preacademic and academic, and self-help. Parents should take this statement to the IEP meeting. If time permits, they can share the statement, as well as any outside evaluations obtained, in advance with the school district IEP team members so the meeting will not be delayed while members read the reports.

The IEP team determines the child's present strengths and weaknesses based on evaluations; observations at home, school, and in the community; and data collection. From the summary of strengths and weaknesses, the team formulates semiannual or annual goals and short-term objectives. Anyone who has attended a business meeting where goals are determined and responsibilities are assigned will readily understand this process, but may not find the IEP meeting as organized, depending on the skill level and expertise of the school staff developing the IEP. A few parents have been heard to say, "If you were on my company's board, you'd all be fired for not doing your job."

▶ Step 3

Goals and Objectives [20 U.S.C. §1414 (d) (1) (A); 34 C.F.R. § 300.347]. The goals and objectives in the IEP must be measurable and based on reasonable expectations of progress given an appropriate program. They are not contractual obligations. On the other hand, if the goals are set too low, the team is not adequately assisting the child in making significant developmental changes. To determine the appropriate goals and objectives in a prioritized manner, the team begins from the baseline information provided in the documentation on the child's present levels of performance and considers the steps necessary to permit the child to make sequential developmental gains.

The following example demonstrates how specific the present level data should be for one behavioral area:

> **Present Level** (Jargoning): Student verbalizes phrases that serve no apparent functional purpose. These phrases are usually dialogue from familiar movies and storybooks. Student exhibits this behavior when a demand is placed on her and while playing alone. In response to a demand during work sessions, student exhibits this behavior on 1 of 10 probed occasions. It occurs when student is not engaged on another 5 of 10 probed occasions.

As the goals and objectives are established, baseline levels and reasonable expectations for growth must be considered carefully. Goals and objectives are not set based on existing program options or what all other students are working on in class. They are set based on the child's individual needs. IEP teams should not hamper the ability to change the child's developmental rate by minimizing the progress that the child can make given appropriate education. The team should not be afraid to write objectives that seem to be a stretch for the child but that will ultimately tap the child's potential. Choosing goal areas, which set forth the desired outcome, is much easier than writing measurable objectives, which are operationally defined in terms of what behaviors the team expects the child to perform, and this section of the IEP meeting is labor intensive. The payoff, however, for the time spent in careful preparation of the goals and objectives, is that the blueprint is almost completed at this point, and the team is ready to start building the foundation.

School district staff usually write a draft of goals and objectives prior to the meeting. Parents should ask the assessment team or the administrator in charge of scheduling the IEP meeting to see that draft also, if available, in advance, so that time at the meeting can be more efficiently used.

Parents are equal participants by law in the IEP process. To participate as equal members of the team, parents should prepare their own draft IEP prior to the meeting. It does not need to be written in exact educational terms. At a minimum, parents should list goal areas they consider important and list what they want their child to be doing in 6 or 12 months. IEPs cannot be written for periods in excess of 12 months, but can be written for shorter time periods. For preschool children with autism, 6 months may be a reasonable measurement period.

Each goal and objective must include the amount of progress required by the child (e.g., 90% or 100% accuracy, or correct responses on 5 out of 5 or 9 of 10 consecutive trials, presented across settings and with a variety of people implementing the goal and objective). The team specifies the data needed to provide evidence of mastery of the goal and objective.

A sample IEP goal and objective in one area of communication (expressive vocabulary) drafted for a preschool student with autism by a parent and the private behavioral therapist prior to the IEP meeting follows. (This statement is not to be used on a general basis for every child.)

Goal: To increase expressive vocabulary.

Objective: Given a variety of group and one-on-one activities, student will increase her functional expressive vocabulary to at least 150 words, including her own name, body parts, action words, peers' names, toys, food, clothing, and animals, to be demonstrated across people and situations on a daily basis over 1 month, with 90% accuracy, or 4 of 5 trials.

The first IEP goal and objective in the same area that the school district team drafted for the same child is as follows:

Goal: To increase expressive vocabulary.

Objective: Student increases her functional expressive vocabulary to 50 words.

It is easy from this example to note the difference in specificity. Specificity is critical to the IEP. How else can the team carefully plan programs and provide accountability for the programs provided for the children? In the parent and behavioral therapist's goal and objective, it is clear what the student will need to learn and how and when she will need to demonstrate that knowledge. In the school district example, the parent and teacher will both be left with many questions about what the student needs to learn and how and when she will demonstrate that knowledge.

To summarize, the team now knows the baseline data, the long-term goals, the short-term objectives, and the percentage of accuracy or performance to expect on each objective.

Now the team must determine how to measure progress or mastery. Data collection on changes in specified behaviors and standardized tests are the best measures of progress. However, a one-time observation is less reliable than multiple observations, and, for students who do not test well, standardized testing by an evaluator inexperienced at testing this population is problematic at best. Systematic daily data collection is the most reliable measure of performance. The team should add daily data collection as a method of measurement for each goal and objective, if not included as a current option on the IEP form.

▶ Step 4

Parameters of Program/Placement Needs [20 U.S.C. § 1400(c); 34 C.F.R. § 300.550–553]. When discussing the parameters of appropriate programs and placements for the preschool child with autism, the team must consider the environment in which the child learns best and the intensity of the program needs in terms of frequency and duration necessary to effect developmental changes. The law is clear that the length of the program, by day, week, month, and year, is not based on a rigid school calendar but rather on the individual needs of the child. If the child needs a program 6 to 8 hours a day, 5 to 7 days a week, 52 weeks a year, then that is what the IEP should provide. Frequency and duration is based on individual need and not school district policy or customary practice.

The team must not consider only traditional speech and language services or school counseling. Often with children with autism who do not develop functional verbal language skills, the team needs to implement a Picture Exchange Communication System (see Chapter 30). Otherwise the children will be penalized for the failure to develop verbal speech. Before dismissing these children summarily as good candidates for early intervention, the team should consider carefully whether it has failed to develop appropriate early intervention programs for them, and not merely that the children have failed to develop sufficient skills to be candidates for such programs.

Further, the intensive behavioral intervention programs are designed to enhance a child's development by first gaining instructional control, while also teaching early developmental skills that typically developing children learn from their environments without the need for specific intervention. These programs are comprehensive and focus on all of the necessary developmental skills. Parent training and participation are essential so that the skills the child learned in the one-on-one setting can be generalized across people and settings. Initially, services will be provided one-on-one at home, in the natural setting where the child is most comfortable. Parents must be ready to respond when they are told at their child's IEP meeting that home is the most restrictive environment, and that a special day class away from home is the least restrictive environment and the only natural setting for their child. In reality, this can be a very artificial setting for the child and the parent. Historically in this country children did not attend school until the age of 6. When they did attend, they had been adequately prepared at home to receive instruction and adjust to a classroom setting. If the team is truly going to effect developmental change, it must include the home as a place to do some significant level of work with the child.

Clearly at some point the goal of early intervention is the generalization of skills into a group setting. The size and type of group depends on the individual needs of the child. The program has not failed if the IEP team is considering a smaller setting than a regular education class, if that is what the child needs. A careful transition must be planned, using behavioral assistants, often called shadow aides, from the home program, who have been specifically trained to work with the child, who know what the child can do in the one-on-one setting, and who can maximize the child's performance and interaction with peers in the classroom.

It is critical for the team to carefully collect data and monitor progress at all stages of the program. If the program is not significantly changing the child's developmental rate, the team needs to return to the drawing board to redesign the intervention for the child. Producing a substantial gain in physical, cognitive, language and speech, psychosocial, and self-help skills development is the goal of early intensive behavioral intervention programs. Because autism is a constellation of behaviors interfering with typical development, the preschool behavioral intervention programs need to be all-encompassing. Without intensive early intervention, children with autism contribute to their own delay in developmental skills, as it is far easier for them to remain isolated in their own world.

Understanding the relationship of autism to the acquisition of developmental skills is essential to planning a program to increase the developmental rate in children with autism. It is frustrating to sit in endless IEP meetings and have team members ask naively whether there are any particular behavior problems. A good response to refocus the team in the right direction is to ask the question, "Do you mean in addition to all the behavioral deviations associated with the autism?"

▶ Step 5

Placement Continuum and Related Services [20 U.S.C. § 1401(22) and (29); 34 C.F.R. §§ 300.346 and 300.551–353]. Now that the team has established the blueprint for developing the program, the team must carefully construct the levels of service and the appropriate placement to implement the program to ensure meaningful progress on the goals and objectives. The IEP team must consider a full continuum of placement options, keeping in mind the least restrictive environment (LRE) mandate in the federal law. Parents must be included as members of any group making placement decisions.

The discussion should begin with the typical setting, either at home or mainstream preschool, with appropriate supports and services. An early intensive behavioral intervention program is often considered by the law to be a related service (or designated instruction and service in California). There is no requirement that the services be attached to a special education classroom setting, as some school districts state to parents. At some point, a school-based component is necessary for the child to generalize skills and develop social interaction with peers. The team should consider adding to the IEP a mainstream preschool component with behavioral assistant support as a gradual transition to a group-based setting. Success should result in gradually increasing expectations placed on the child and gradual fading of the level of support provided.

If the team believes that the child requires placement in a special education classroom, for part or all of the instructional group-based hours, the transition to the group-based setting in a special education classroom with support should be considered and carefully planned, as the team contemplates options on the continuum from least to most restrictive. The continuum should look like this at first:

1. Home-based behavioral intervention with support and services.
2. Home-based behavioral intervention with support and services and mainstream component with support.
3. Home-based behavioral intervention with support and services and special education classroom component and support.

Gradually, the continuum will change to accommodate the child's changing needs to look like this:

1. Mainstream preschool with or without support and home-based behavioral intervention component.
2. Special education classroom with or without support and home-based behavioral intervention component.

During the child's transition from individual instruction to group-based participation, parents and school staff must share and discuss information about the child's performance so that the transition will be successful.

A misperception among some special educators is that the artificial structure of a special day class is less restrictive and a more natural setting than home for a preschool child with autism or PDD. The IEP team should discuss whether there is something about the disability that makes the home an unnatural setting. If the child does not learn skills sufficiently from just growing up in the home setting, like typically developing children do, the team must consider why adding support to the setting so that the child can develop would be considered restrictive or unnatural. Is it restrictive for a blind child to use Braille or a deaf child to use sign language? Must those supports be used only in special education classrooms? If blind and deaf children have otherwise typical abilities, they may never be considered as candidates for special education classrooms. Would professionals then deny them services or supports? It would clearly not be appropriate to do so. Teams' vision of creating appropriate programs, services, and supports for children with autism or PDD must also be broadened.

Unfortunately, there is often nothing special about special education classrooms for preschool children with autism or PDD. If the child requires one-on-one instruction, special education classrooms are generally not set up to provide one-on-one teaching. Special education teachers are stretched to the limit already, given increasingly difficult caseloads and diminishing budgets, and rarely free to work one-on-one with their students, all of whom have special needs. They are not always trained in specific methodologies to work in a direct one-to-one way with children with autism or PDD. The purpose of group-based interaction for a child with autism or PDD who requires one-on-one instruction is to generalize skills learned in the one-on-one setting and to participate socially. If all the peers also have autism or PDD, the team must discuss the efficacy of placement; these children may need to have exposure to typically developing peer models to work on social interaction.

If a child's school district has implemented environmental structures, such as visual schedules and icon-based instruction, to a preschool class for children with autism and PDD, parents need to consider the appropriateness for their child of the visual schedules and icon-based instruction. If the parents' goal at school is social interaction, they should make sure that the environment is conducive to working on those goals.

Parents should make sure that the team considers all of the following in devising a child's IEP:

- Appropriate behavioral intervention specialist services, including structured peer play training and parent training (school districts do not routinely offer these services)
- The benefits of speech and language services by a clinician trained and experienced with this population
- Occupational therapy services by a sensory integration specialist, or other related services beneficial for the child
- One-on-one intervention across settings
- A full 12-month program and the number of hours required each day to provide an intensive program
- The home and community components of any group-based special education class proposed
- Parent training, structured peer play training, and behavioral intervention specialist services across settings

▶ Step 6

Free and Appropriate Public Education [20 U.S.C. § 1401(8); 34 C.F.R. §§ 121–122]. Since 1994, at least in those states located geographically within the Ninth Circuit Court of Appeals where the *Union Elementary School District v. Smith* (1994) case was decided (i.e., California, Oregon, Washington, Arizona, Nevada, Hawaii, and Alaska), a legally sufficient IEP must include a specific written offer of program, placement, and services. Section 1414(d) of the IDEA amendments adopted on June 4, 1997, clearly require the same standard for all states. The IEP cannot merely state a generic "special day class" or "special education classroom." The program, placement, and services for a child must be specifically designed and determined and stated on the IEP document.

What can parents ask for by way of program, placement, and services? How do parents determine whether they have been offered a free and appropriate public education (FAPE)? What does it mean? What does it include? Historically, the meaning of FAPE has been the most litigated issue since the IDEA was enacted in 1975, then called the Education for all Handi-capped Children Act (EHA), as the first all-encompassing federal statute governing the rights of all individuals with disabilities, and the rights and obligations of school districts, county offices of education, special education local plan areas, and state departments of education.

The federal standard of appropriateness was defined in the seminal U.S. Supreme Court case, *Board of Education v. Rowley* (1982), to mean base-level–appropriate education. In other words, the Supreme Court stated that "appropriate" means only appropriate, and not more, unless of course the child lives in a state that has enacted a higher state standard and has declared a statutory intent to provide the best for each child with a disability. FAPE does not mean that school districts have to maximize potential; it means that school districts have to provide access to equal educational opportunities, and school districts have to provide the ability for the student who is disabled to make meaningful growth from year to year, while at the same time school districts have to carefully comply with the procedural protections and safeguards of the IDEA.

The Supreme Court in *Rowley* referred to the IEP as the cornerstone of education. The procedural safeguards of the IDEA are designed to ensure that school districts are going to develop a program that allows the child with a disability to make meaningful progress from year to year. Thus, in determining whether their child has been offered a FAPE, parents should look toward two issues under the holding of *Rowley*: (1), whether the school district or the local educational agency followed the procedural requirements of the IDEA and, if they did not, whether their failure was so significant as to impact the educational progress of the child, and (2) whether the IEP was designed to allow the child to make meaningful progress, according to his or her potential, from year to year.

Rowley was decided in 1982 by the U.S. Supreme Court, in the early years of implementation of the 1975 EHA. Not many children were receiving early intensive behavioral intervention programs in 1982. Neither were many children receiving or requiring massive infusions of assistive technology services and equipment in 1982. Few children with disabilities were included in the mainstream and receiving their educational programs in the least restrictive environment. If we consider the important developments in educational programs, placements, and services available for children with disabilities since *Rowley* was decided, we must now ask what it currently means to make progress from year to year?

The standard set forth in *Rowley* has been impacted by the full inclusion movement in the 1990s, no matter where one stands and by what perspective one considers the issue. The impact has been to talk about progress in a lot of different ways, not merely by asking, "Did your child's score on a standardized assessment battery increase 10 points?" Educators no longer look only at test scores or passing grades; they must consider a whole range of factors when considering meaningful progress, which means that there is a new ballpark open now in terms of redeveloping the standard of FAPE.

Significantly, even under *Rowley*, which involved the appropriate education of a child whom the Court held could pass from grade to grade without the need for a sign language interpreter in her regular education classes, the benefit that must be provided must be *meaningful.*

It is difficult for parents to participate in an IEP meeting, or later sit in a hearing, and listen to a discussion about "some" benefit or the global general benefit that their child has received from attending special education classes, when they know that their child is not toilet trained, is unable to communicate his wants and needs, and is running around in a parking lot when they are trying to go to the grocery store, and when the teacher has to put a gate up at the door of the classroom to keep the child in. We cannot minimize the word *meaningful.* At IEP meetings the team members need to ask themselves and each other, "How meaningful is the progress for the child?"

Even the *Rowley* court, which set a base-level standard of appropriateness, determined that, where there are significant procedural violations in the development and implementation of IEPs, school districts may need to provide compensatory programs and services that they would otherwise not be ordered to provide, based solely on the procedural violations they have caused.

In most cases involving preschool children with autism or PDD that end up in hearing, schools have failed to adequately address the individual needs of the children. School district assessments are by and large not providing good base-level measurements at the beginning of programs; school districts for the most part are not designing intensive programs; and teachers and school psychologists are not collecting and analyzing measurable data during the programs. Thus the schools have been unable to produce outcome data to show the efficacy of their own programs. Special educators often report that they cannot teach with a clipboard in their hands, tallying data.

Additionally, it is difficult to collect useful data unless good preprogram measures were done. Most good early intensive behavioral intervention programs require some good preprogram measures. Thorough evaluations before the commencement of any program are essential. Early intensive behavioral intervention programs are time intensive and costly to run. Parents and school districts alike must insist that the children receive the benefits that the programs are developed to provide, and that the program is efficiently creating changes in the child's developmental rate.

The research and early replication data from the UCLA (University of California, Los Angeles) project are very positive. About 45% of children with autism receiving early intensive behavioral intervention programs are placed in regular education classes by kindergarten or first-grade age, and the other 55%, can be placed in less restrictive settings than ever contemplated for this population before the availability of home-based early intervention programs increased in the 1990s.

Faced with the argument that this type of intensive early intervention is too restrictive and too costly, one must consider the consequences of not providing intervention that is meaningful and beneficial to the autistic population. Historically, children without the benefits of early intensive behavioral intervention, by adolescence if not before, live outside of their homes and communities in costly and restrictive state institutions. Before the provision of intensive behavioral intervention programs, the prognosis for independent living and inclusion in the mainstream of society was not good for this population.

Therefore, the courts redefined FAPE for preschool students with autism during the 1990s. We have already discussed the seminal FAPE case in this country, the *Board of Education v. Rowley*. Every special education case since 1982 has cited *Rowley*; however, the FAPE standard set forth in *Rowley* has been redefined for the preschool students with autism or PDD.

Courts across the country have struggled with a redefinition of FAPE for this population. For the most part, when presented with the raw data, they have decided in the best interests of the children. The decision in *Union Elementary School District v. Smith* changed the definition of FAPE for preschool children with autism in the Ninth Circuit. For the first time the court held that a 40-hour one-on-one behavioral intervention program provided at the Clinic for Behavioral Treatment of Children at the University of California, Los Angeles, now named the Lovaas Institute for Early Intervention, was appropriate for a preschool child with autism who resided in San Jose, California, some 350 miles away. To provide the program for the child, one parent had to reside temporarily in the Los Angeles area with the child.

The school district argued, among other things, that the child's residence had been changed to Los Angeles, that the program was merely "counseling" and was not attached to an educational placement, and, therefore, that the district was not permitted to provide the program as an IEP service. The hearing officer and the court disagreed. The court upheld the hearing officer's ruling that the IEP could provide services only, and that the lodging expenses were reimbursable pursuant to state and federal law. The administrative hearing decision rendered in 1990 is informative for its discussion of FAPE for preschool children in California (*Student v. Union School District*, 1990).

Additionally, the Ninth Circuit included in its decision an important ruling that IEP offers must be specific and must be in writing. *Union* has been cited for this principle in every special education case in California since 1994. The IDEA amendments now require the same standard for all children across the country.

In California, as well as other states, preschool children with disabilities are often afforded elevated rights, even if the school-aged students with disabilities are not. For example, in California the Mission of Preschool Education, California Education Code Section 56441, requires that school districts

> Significantly reduce the potential impact of any handicapping conditions . . .
>
> Produce substantial gains in physical development, cognitive development, language and speech development, psychosocial development, and self-help skills development . . .
>
> Reduce the need for special class placement in special education programs once the children reach school age . . .
>
> Save substantial costs to society and our schools.

The research on early intensive behavioral intervention programs indicates that most have the same purpose, aimed at significantly reducing the potential impact of any handicapping (or disabling) condition. Obviously, if students with disabilities receive a very intensive program before mandatory school age, and 45% can enroll in regular kindergarten or first grade with or without support services, there will be substantial savings to society. It is very expensive to run special education classrooms, a fact often bemoaned by regular educators and reported by newspapers and television news journals.

In an early Applied Behavior Analysis (ABA) case in Pennsylvania, (*Delaware County Intermediate Unit #25 v. Martin and Melinda K. et al.* (1993), the court analyzed the Lovaas-type program that the parents were providing and the TEACCH-type program the school district was offering, and determined that the parent-provided program afforded the intensity required by the child, and that a change in program might cause regression. In a law review article, "The IDEA: A Parent's Perspective and Proposal for Change" (1994) Martin K. discussed a parent's perspective in traversing the IDEA.

Following *Union School District*, hearing officers in California, Washington, and Oregon determined that intensive one-on-one in-home early behavioral intervention programs provide FAPE for preschool children with autism (*Student v. Capistrano U.S.D.*, 1995; *In the Matter of Peninsula School District*, 1995; *C. O. v. Multnomah E.S.D. Columbia Regional Programs, Portland School District, and Oregon Deptartment of Education*, 1996; *Student v. San Diego City U.S.D.*, 1996; *Student v. Old Adobe Union Elementary School District*, 1997; *Student v. Santa Barbara City Schools*, 1998; *Student v. San Bruno Park School District*, 1998). In Nevada, the first intensive one-on-one in-home early behavioral intervention programs provided by the Lovaas Institute for Early Intervention under both Part B and Part C of the IDEA have been found to have provided FAPE (*Student v. State of Nevada*, 2000; *Student v. Clark County School District*, 2000).

Sacramento City Unified School District v. R. H., (1994) set the precedent in the Ninth Circuit for full inclusion with appropriate supplemental aids and services. Following the completion of home-based early intensive behavioral intervention programs, IEP teams must discuss placement in inclusive settings with appropriate support and services as the least restrictive option.

Parents who are unable to reach agreement at the IEP meeting level can request reimbursement through the administrative hearing process for private placements and services that they provide for their children with disabilities. Reimbursement to parents is available for programs they have provided unilaterally for their children in the absence of appropriate offers from the school districts pursuant to *School Committee of the Town of Burlington v. Department of Education*, (1985). Each state has its own statute of limitations on reimbursement, and parents should inquire about the length of time prescribed by the statute in their own states. *Florence County School District Four v. Carter* (1993) permits parents to obtain services that are not certified or approved by the states in which they live, but explains that school districts do not have the same leeway without state permission.

We emphasize the following caution to parents: The 1997 IDEA amendments, effective June 4, 1997, require that parents must specifically inform an IEP team if they are rejecting the district's proposed placement and service offer and inform the district of their alternative request(s) for their child, to the best of their ability. Parents must notify the district of their intent to enroll their child in private school or private services at public expense at the child's most recent IEP meeting or at least 10 business days prior to unilaterally removing a child from public school. If parents do not inform the IEP team or at least provide 10 business days' written notice to the district of this intent, a court or hearing officer may later limit or deny retroactive reimbursement for such private school or private service expenses [20 U.S.C. §1412(a)(10)(C)].

Similarly, a court or hearing officer may limit or deny retroactive reimbursement for the unilateral (i.e., outside of IEP team agreement) placement of a child in private school or private services if, prior to the removal of the child, the district informed the parents of its intent to evaluate the child and the parents did not make the child available for assessment, or if the court or hearing officer makes a finding that the parents acted unreasonably when they unilaterally placed the child in a private placement or services [20 U.S.C. § 1412(a)(10)(C)]. However, pursuant to 20 U.S.C. § 1412(a)(10)(C)(iv), a court or hearing officer may not limit or deny reimbursement to parents if the parents are illiterate and cannot write in English; if complying with the notice provisions would likely result in physical or serious emotional harm to the child; if the district prevented the parents from providing notice; or if the district failed to inform the parents of their obligation to notify the district.

A little used remedy by parents or parent representatives is to seek direct services by the state educational agency if the local educational agency or school district is unable to establish or maintain FAPE [20 U.S.C. §1413(h)].

Each state has an advocacy center that is federally mandated and funded to represent individuals with developmental disabilities. Even where they are unable to provide individual services to clients, they are excellent resources and often have extensive referral lists and inservice programs for IEP preparation. Parent network groups, such as Families for Early Autism Treatment (FEAT), are also great resources for services, as well as great support for new families after receiving the diagnosis of autism or PDD.

Since 1986, private attorneys have been able to be reimbursed for their services when parents obtain a favorable outcome for their children. It remains to be seen whether over time, given the language in the 1997 reauthorization of and amendments to the IDEA, this right will be eroded, and what impact that erosion will have on obtaining quality programs for children with disabilities.

Meanwhile, parties must exhaust administrative remedies prior to bringing an action in court. These cases must be litigated first at hearings known as due process hearings [20 U.S.C. § 1415(f)], which typically are held at the local school district office where the parents reside. Prior to hearing, mediation is a recommended step. In many states, parents do not have the right to mediation until they ask for due process. Mediation is voluntary in every state. In California, according to the statistics released by the Special Education Hearing Office, approximately 95% of the cases filed actually settle in mediation, which is encouraging. If a case does not settle in mediation, it then proceeds to the due process hearing at the local school district. Either side can appeal the case. Generally, a case is appealed to federal court, because the IDEA is a federal statute. The parties do not have the right to a full trial de novo but do have the right to supplement the evidence, according to the statute, and the court must conduct a substantial review of the record [20 U.S.C. § 1415(i)(2)(B)]. Under IDEA, damages are limited to reimbursement for placement, services, and programs already provided unilaterally by parents or requests for compensatory services or programs.

When we began to practice law in this field, we witnessed time after time the placement of students with autism in institutions by the time they reached adolescence, if not before, no matter what their potential was or what type of private or public special class placement had been provided. The problem was that the interventions were not intensive enough, were not provided early enough, and were not designed specifically to significantly change the developmental rate to foster reaching full potential. Only since the 1990s has the meaning of providing FAPE to preschoolers with autism and PDD been redefined to include the provision of early intensive intervention programs, and families all over the country have clamored to obtain programming for their children, thus impacting the future development of an entire population. Educators as well as parents and treating professionals should be proud of the results their collaborative efforts are creating.

Notes from the Front: The Current Wave in ABA Litigation

CHAPTER 38

Gary S. Mayerson

Not too long ago, the battle lines concerning intensive one-on-one Applied Behavior Analysis (ABA) treatment were neatly drawn. The typical due process hearing pitted parents seeking reimbursement for an ABA home-based program against a school district mightily resisting such efforts. Parents prevailed at quite a few of these hearings, where the central issues were the alleged inappropriateness of the school district's program and the demonstrable effectiveness of the parents' data-driven, home-based ABA program.

Under the Individuals with Disabilities Education Act of 1990 (IDEA) (20 U.S.C.§ 1400 et seq.) and its controlling decisional law at 34 Code of Federal Regulations (CFR), it is fundamental that the Individualized Education Program (IEP) be tailored to the individual needs of the child and reasonably designed to provide a meaningful educational benefit. In those situations where school districts had refused to implement *any* ABA, parents had a compelling argument that the school district had evaded the individualization process by improperly failing to consider the full continuum of service and placement options, particularly in light of the available scientific research.

Today, by reason of fiscal, public relations, and other related concerns, relatively few school districts in the nation are willing to run the risk of being perceived as openly anti-ABA. In point of fact, particularly in light of dramatically increased demand for ABA programs, a number of school districts and their attorneys have devised sophisticated defense strategies that are expressly designed to counter any charge that the district is anti-ABA. Indeed, some school districts have developed entire educational programs around legal templates devised by their attorneys, such as a recent one prepared by a powerful law firm in the Midwest brazenly titled "How to Avoid Parents' Demands for Lovaas." Unfortunately, some school districts appear to be concentrating their efforts on building programs that are legally defensible, but that may not be comprehensive and efficacious from an educational perspective.

Reality Versus Virtual Reality

One of the more common alternative defense strategies is for school districts to facially incorporate some components of ABA into the special education program in order to be able to create the *appearance* (i.e., virtual reality) that the school district "does ABA." However, just as decaffeinated coffee may look, smell, and taste like the real article, a district-run autism program may appear to be of the requisite quality and intensity, but may actually be missing one or more of the critical ingredients necessary to wake up a child. Typically, the missing ingredients will be some combination of curriculum, intensity of instruction, staff training, staff experience, staff supervision, staff ratio, and data collection.

Parents facing a "we also do ABA" situation have little choice but to investigate and, in essence, "take data" on the school district's ABA program. Some parents are very effective as educational detectives. However, the investigation process is most effectively done with the assistance of a consultant who knows firsthand from prior experience what components an effective ABA program should have. If due process ensues, it is essential that the person taking data on the school district's program have the ability to persuasively explain and contrast the subtle, yet critical, distinctions which can mean the difference between a program that would be reasonably calculated to work, and one that would be reasonably calculated to fail.

In terms of identifying the salient distinctions that can spell the difference between success and failure, the following criteria should be considered:

1. What is the curriculum, if any? Who is in charge of developing the curriculum and making individual changes?
2. What is the extent of the one-on-one component?

3. What is the training and experience of the staff? Is there appropriate supervision?

4. Are data taken and, if so, how and how often? Are the data reviewed by anyone and, if so, by whom and how often?

5. Is staff sufficiently trained to do a functional analysis?

6. What protocols, if any, are employed to deal with oppositional, self-injurious, or aggressive behaviors? What is the response of staff to displays of stereotypical behavior, self-talk, and other behaviors the child demonstrates?

7. What strategies are employed to keep a child on task? If the child goes off task, how, if at all, does the staff seek to redirect the child?

8. Does the district have an autism consultant or behavior analyst with appropriate expertise and experience who is ready, willing, and able to provide meaningful time and assistance to the program?

9. What is the nature, if any, of parent training? Parent involvement? Parent observations? What communications, if any, go back and forth between home and school?

10. Will the district permit an observation by an independent consultant?

11. Is the intensity level (e.g., hours per week) of intervention sufficient, or is it at a level below the radar screen of demonstrable efficacy?

Least Restrictive Environment Issues

In recent years, school districts and courts have been focusing their attention more carefully on the statutory mandate of least restrictive environment (LRE). The IDEA and its implementing regulations explain that LRE means simply that, to the "maximum extent appropriate," children with disabilities should be educated with their nondisabled (i.e., typically developing) peers [see 20 U.S.C. § 1412(a)(5)(A) and 34 C.F.R. § 300.550(b)(1)].

Some school districts will take the position that a child is not yet ready to be educated with typically developing children in a mainstream setting if the child requires a support aide or other supports to succeed in that kind of environment. The IDEA statute and its implementing regulations make it quite clear, however, that this is a legally erroneous position. C.F.R. §300.550 (b) (2) mandates that a public agency shall ensure not only that LRE must be promoted "to the maximum extent appropriate," but that special classes that involve separate schooling or other removal of children with disabilities from the regular educational environment may occur *only* "if the nature or severity of the disability is such that education in regular classes with the use of supplementary aids and services cannot be achieved satisfactorily."

Just as a person recovering from a stroke might need to rely on a cane to begin to walk again, the IDEA statute and its implementing regulations presuppose and anticipate that mainstreaming is a process that may very well require support aides. To put it another way, if a child with a disability *needs* a support aide or other supplementary services to succeed in a mainstream setting, the child is statutorily *entitled* to have those supports made available.

Although school districts are often quick to condemn home-based ABA programs as unduly restrictive, this is clearly erroneous from a legal perspective, at least with respect to young children who are making good progress in such programs. Significantly, very few, if any, states compel typically developed 3- and 4-year-olds to attend school. Children in that age range typically receive the bulk of their learning at home. Similarly, parents of typically developing boys sometimes elect to defer kindergarten for an additional year and keep the child home.[1]

Parents do not pine for the right to assume the burden of running a home ABA program. Indeed, I have often heard of parents at IEP meetings telling school districts, "We're doing ABA so that we can get *out* of doing ABA!" Ironically, as discussed later, although ABA is the intervention considered by many school districts to be the most restrictive, the reality is that scientific research has proven that ABA actually offers a child diagnosed with an autistic spectrum disorder the best chance for ultimate success in mainstream educational environments with typically developing children. These findings have major implications for school districts that, as

[1] Home schooling, in the technical sense, is an arrangement in which, for religious or other reasons, parents elect to educate their children at home where it is understood and expressly agreed that this will be without cost to the school district. That kind of arrangement is thus different from the situation in which the ABA component happens to be delivered in the child's home.

noted above, are statutorily obligated to promote the requirement of least restrictive environment to the maximum extent appropriate.

The congressional "findings" section of the IDEA speaks volumes as to the legislative intent of Congress. In this prefatory section, Congress explains its policy of "having high expectations for . . . children and ensuring their access in the general curriculum to the maximum extent possible." The same prefatory section of the IDEA speaks of enabling children with disabilities "to be prepared to lead productive, independent, adult lives, to the maximum extent possible." It is significant that, although Congress has established an "appropriate" standard for purposes of measuring the educational component, the education must be delivered so as to promote the child's least restrictive environment, a component that, as noted above, is governed by a "maximum extent" standard.

Today, more than a decade after the publication of Lovaas's seminal 1987 study (in a respected peer-review journal), there is no intervention other than intensive one-on-one ABA that expresses an outcome framed in terms of success in a classic LRE setting (i.e., successful mainstreaming in a typical grade school). In addition to reporting astounding postintervention increases in IQ, the 1987 study reported that, with approximately 2 to 3 years of intervention, nearly half of the experimental group receiving 40 hours per week of one-on-one ABA treatment were able to meaningfully succeed in typical grade school environments and be considered indistinguishable in the sense of appearing asymptomatic.

Even today, Lovaas's 1987 study and its progeny stand alone as reporting an *outcome* for an autism intervention that is consistent with the "maximum" component of LRE and Congress' high expectations. The argument is thus most compelling that, for children diagnosed with autistic spectrum disorders, intensive ABA is the *only* scientifically supported intervention available today that is reasonably calculated to meaningfully promote the congressional mandate of LRE.

Lovaas's 1987 study, however, continues to be criticized for being less than perfect, particularly by persons who have a financial or other stake in different interventions or programs. Ironically, the very persons who regularly voice dismay as to the lack of perfection in the 1987 study do not insist on the same level of perfection in their own professional pursuits. Let it suffice to say that in 1999, the Surgeon General of the United States issued a report that embraced the efficacy of ABA treatment based on "30 years of research" and called Lovaas's 1987 study a well-designed study. The Surgeon General's report followed on the heels of federal decisional law which has recognized the singular efficacy of ABA treatment (e.g., *Malkentzos v. DeBuono*, 1996).

Some school districts will misuse, if not abuse, the concept of LRE. For example, many school districts claim LRE status simply because they make a practice of injecting some typically developing children into the lunch, gym, or assembly environments of the child with autism. A child with a disability is not being educated with typically developing children merely because they are in the same room, breathing the same oxygen. If that were the case, children with autism would get better simply by being in physical proximity with their typically developing siblings.

In those situations where parents have implemented a home ABA program, school districts will argue that even their multiple-handicap class is less restrictive than the home. As noted previously, the mandate of LRE is one that focuses on educating children with disabilities *with* typically developing children, not simply the physical proximity of other children in the classroom who may well be, in fact, the worst possible models. Moreover, many states are following express statutory or regulatory language that makes clear that, at least for preschoolers, the home may well constitute the child's LRE. For children who have additional health issues (e.g., RSV susceptibility, seizures, feeding tubes), the home setting may well be the only effective educational environment.

Today, many families that are doing home-based ABA programs are also regularly incorporating meaningful interactions with typically developing children as soon as their child has acquired sufficient prerequisite skills to benefit from such interactions. For some families, this means that a certain number of intervention hours per week are allocated in a mainstream preschool or kindergarten class. Other families arrange regularly scheduled play dates with typically developing children. Families that document such interactions will find it much easier to counter any charge by their school district that the parents' home program is unduly restrictive in the LRE sense. In this regard, just as a picture is worth a thousand words, a videotape record of these kinds of interactions can offer a compelling window of evidentiary insight.

The Increasing Role of Science

There are many anecdotal reports of "progress" made by children with autism using interventions other than

ABA. These reports, which most often are not published in peer-review journals and normally do not involve scientific studies using controls, typically report mere IQ gains or improvements in certain select social skills. It is difficult, if not impossible, for a court to draw any reliable conclusions from anecdotal reports or other purported "results" that are not based on science.

In the last decade, important federal court decisions have held that a presiding judge in a civil or criminal action has a duty to act as a gatekeeper to keep pseudoscience out of the courtroom. Courts today are insisting upon scientific reliability. This is in recognition of the principle that everyone is entitled to his or her own opinion, but no one is entitled to his or her own facts. This is precisely why properly secured DNA evidence (based on science) normally is admissible, whereas the results of lie detector tests normally are not admissible.

Professional organizations such as the American Medical Association (AMA), whose members often are asked to testify as expert witnesses in court proceedings, have expressed serious concern about the issue of scientific reliability. Just recently, the AMA has proposed significant sanctions for any member who accepts compensation to testify as an expert witness unless there is a good faith foundation, in fact, for such testimony.

Unlike the medical doctor who can be stripped of his or her medical license, or the lawyer who can be disbarred, most expert witnesses who testify at fair hearings, particularly those flown in from distant locales, can testify with relative impunity. For example, although Facilitated Communication has been exposed as a virtual hoax, this does not stop certain people in the field from claiming that they "believe" that Facilitated Communication works. This is a most compelling reason why hearing officers and judges must exercise the gatekeeper function to keep pseudoscience out of the courtroom.

Given the fact that the life and future of a child is normally at issue, and in light of the increasing importance of science to the very courts that will review and adjudicate fair hearing appeals, hearing officers at the fair hearing level should be careful to exercise the gatekeeper function when the parties are battling over different interventions. One thing is all but certain: The science gatekeeper issue is likely to be the source of significant litigation in the next decade.

Documenting Progress

Under the decisional law, it is important to understand that parents and their children can prevail at fair hearings only if it can be shown that the district's program is inappropriate (as proposed or as implemented) and not simply that the parents' program may be incrementally better. For this reason, school districts are spending considerable time at fair hearings trying to establish that the child "mastered" numerous skills in school (i.e., that the school's program must be appropriate because the child has been making such good progress).

Some school districts, however, will report the so-called mastery of skills that the child already mastered in prior time frames. This situation is frustrating for parents, especially for those who have not been collecting and maintaining objective data on their child's progress and functioning. In an abundance of caution, parents should keep progress data as long as possible.

A Word About Settlement

Fortunately for all concerned, most due process cases settle before there is an adjudication on the merits. In the euphoria of settlement, three issues come up frequently that are a point of anxiety to parents and school districts alike.

One such settlement-oriented issue is the school district's insistence on an agreement of confidentiality, which parents often refer to as a gag order. Just as in criminal or civil cases, the concern of a party for confidentiality often is the singular force that can help drive the settlement. Accordingly, provided that the child is getting what he needs, I normally advise parents that if a school district insists on a gag order as a condition of settlement, let the gagging begin. However, I insist on being able to report to third parties that there was a dispute and that the controversy has been settled. In the event of a future dispute, parents also may need to preserve the ability to present historical information to a future hearing officer.

The second issue that often comes up when cases settle is that of providing releases. This is not at all unusual. It is important to recognize, however, that when parents give a "general" release, they are releasing the district from any claims that were asserted or that *could* have been asserted up through the time the release is executed and provided to the school district. Parents should *never* release a school district for matters that will necessarily occur after the settlement is agreed to. For example, if parents are agreeing to a settlement reached in November of 2001, those parents should not agree to release the school district from any claims for the 2001–2002 school year.

The third issue that often comes up in settlements is whether *pendency*, also known as stay put, will attach to the settlement agreement. In the event of a *future* dispute, pendency is what may automatically continue services for a child pending the adjudication of the fair hearing. Normally, pendency attaches to the last agreed upon IEP. Pendency is thus a very valuable right that should not be given away lightly.

The issue of pendency normally comes up in settlements when, as is often the case, the school district asks the parents to waive pendency as a *quid pro quo*. Sometimes, the complexion of the case may be such that it is acceptable, if not advisable, to waive pendency to induce the settlement. In other cases, waiving pendency can present problematic consequences in the event of a future dispute. Before agreeing to waive a pendency right, it is essential that parents and their counsel discuss the attendant risks and rewards.

Conclusion

The landscape of ABA-related litigation is changing very rapidly, particularly with earlier diagnosis and substantially increased demand for efficacious interventions that are based on science. Although intensive one-on-one ABA treatment is now acknowledged by some courts and many professionals in the field as the presumptive, primary intervention for children diagnosed with autistic spectrum disorders, we can expect such litigation to continue, at least for the foreseeable future.

Pyramid Building: Partnership as an Alternative to Litigation

CHAPTER 39

Howard G. Cohen

A pyramid builder feels that knowledge can best be gained by several persons working together, where each piece of information is sought to complement or strengthen other pieces of information, where higher levels are built after lower levels are secured. . . .

(*Lovaas, 1981, p. xii*)

The efficacy of intensive, early childhood, behaviorally based, initially in-home education programs for young children with autistic-spectrum disorders has received increasing empirical support (Dawson & Osterling, 1996; Green, 1996b; Lovaas, 1987; McEachin, Smith, & Lovaas, 1993; Sheinkopf & Siegel, 1998; Smith, 1999). Concurrently, family-friendly publications, such as *The ME Book* (Lovaas, 1981), *Children with Autism: A Parent's Guide* (Powers, 1989), *Let Me Hear Your Voice* (Maurice, 1993), and *Behavior Intervention for Young Children with Autism* (Maurice, Green, & Luce, 1996); the rapid proliferation of Internet Web sites and chat rooms; and rapidly emerging parent grassroots advocacy groups have served both to demystify behavioral treatment methods and to empower parents to advocate for state-of-the-art early education programs on behalf of their children.

As parental demands for early intervention—treatments begun prior to age 5—accelerate, the nation's educational system is reeling. Responses range from skepticism and flat rejection to cautious acceptance and bureaucratic restraints. The need for cost-effective treatment programs and well-trained clinical providers has led to the development of proposed state guidelines for best practices (California Department of Education, 1997; New York State Department of Health, 1999). Parents, frustrated by bureaucratic obstacles and, more often than not, by active resistance from both the education system and professionals, have turned to litigation as a method to compel local school districts to provide state-of-the-art, "appropriate" education for their children (Williamson, 1996). The burden for advocacy often falls on those parents who can muster the courage and financial resolve to challenge and confront an anergic education service delivery system.

The purpose of this chapter is to present a partnership model as an alternative to litigation in order to provide cost-efficient, high-quality clinical treatment–education programs for optimizing the prognosis for children with autistic-spectrum disorders. Although litigation can be successful in obtaining in-home early behavior intervention (California Department of Developmental Services, 1997), it should be reserved as a last resort for a number of reasons. Litigation is

- *Adversarial*—It pits parents against schools.
- *Time intensive*—It can be dragged out for months, even years, delaying service or lessening its effectiveness when it becomes available.
- *Costly*—It is expensive for both sides in terms of money and labor.
- *Emotionally taxing*—It often builds lasting resentments between the parties that go beyond a settlement.
- *Legal oriented*—The focus is not on the child, and typically neither side walks away from the confrontation without feeling a sense of loss and partial vindication of their position.
- *Gains are transitory and individual centered*—The cases, once settled, rarely represent precedents

and therefore do not necessarily help the next child in the same predicament.

Partnership, as an alternative to litigation, is at first a daunting process. If done well, however, it levels the playing field between parents and the agencies mandated to provide services for children with autistic-spectrum disorders (ASD). Collaboration establishes the expectation that diverse groups with differing vested interests and perspectives can work together to actualize common objectives; that is, parent–professional teamwork provides the opportunity for children to reach toward their potential, a goal to which all parties can readily agree. Building coalitions, working through conflicts, and maintaining optimism and trust are arduous, time- and labor-intensive tasks initially. Yet, once working relationships are established, bureaucratic barriers are minimized and education service delivery to the child becomes more efficient and effective. Partnership begins with the following premises:

- *Trust* is earned not given; team members must be willing to suspend and confront preexisting antipathies and suspicions.
- *Cooperation* means a balance between give-and-take, not cooption or exploitation. Team members abide by the principle, "I can live with that decision."
- *Coalition building* signifies willingness to risk transitory feelings of being ganged up on.
- *Shared responsibility* enables team members to cross over and redefine rigid, traditional boundaries separating parents and agencies and apply policy toward problem solving, including but not limited to funding and administrative issues.
- *Common good* as a goal is to develop policy that is precedent setting and that benefits the whole target population rather than selective members, for example, only those who choose to litigate.
- *Team decision making* involves actively seeking each participant to clarify his or her position from the outset and to maintain an active role from start to finish.

This chapter describes a partnership model for the delivery of high-quality, research outcome–guided, early (ages 18 to 60 months), intensive behavioral education of children diagnosed with autistic-spectrum disorder (ASD) that evolved in the northern San Joaquin Central Valley and surrounding foothills in California from 1994 to the present. Geographically, the Central Valley area encompasses five counties with a population of approximately 1 million people. Much of the area is rural, anchored by two mid-sized cities of over 200,000, Stockton and Modesto.

What we learned from that successful collaborative effort will be described using the paradigm of a pyramid construction—that is, as a joint effort whose apex always culminates at the highest point where the best interests of the child are centered. First, the key elements or raw material for such an endeavor will be identified; they form the pyramid's natural base structure. Without good-quality material, the structure, no matter how well intended, will not survive the stresses and strains of time, will decay, and eventually will collapse. Second, the actual construction process will be described; these are the process or engineering components that operationalize early education for children with ASD and make it readily available to families beginning in their homes, without the usual bureaucratic and legal roadblocks. The third section will focus on the corollary benefits of collaboration, one of which is that it can lead to development of other pyramids, thereby expanding education options for children in the region. Navigating a home-based pyramid will be discussed through a case example.

Key Structural Components of a Partnership Pyramid

One of the first major tasks in building a regional, collaborative process is to identify organizations that have a vested, legal, or fiscal interest or a real or perceived responsibility to provide services to children with ASD. Once identified, these agencies become the structure or foundation upon which the partnership pyramid is constructed. In the Central Valley of California, four structure components were identified, Families for Effective Autism Treatment (CV FEAT), Valley Mountain Regional Center (VMRC), Special Education Local Planning Areas (SELPA), and Central Valley Autism Project (CVAP). In other areas of the United States, there may be advocacy agencies or the state may have regional offices that can offer assistance. Across the country, movements are under way to involve health insurance providers (Williamson, 1996) and corporate America (Huff, 1996) as partners in the early education process.

Parent Organization and Leadership

The first of the cornerstone structural components for partnership building is preferably a well-informed, advocacy-focused, high-energy, determined, and committed formal parent organization, or minimally a parent network, which provides the backbone and drive for a collaborative process. Collective voices are much harder to ignore, divert, intimidate, or deny than individual advocacy. However, as a starting place, the courage evidenced and achievements gained by parents threatening or carrying out litigation against funding agencies should never be underestimated.

In 1990, the Central Valley region had no specialized early intervention educational programs for children with ASD. The prevailing attitude among professionals was that most children with autism would be mentally retarded, were better off educated in segregated classes with other children who have severe developmental delays, and would eventually live in group homes or state institutions and spend their daytime hours in activity or sheltered workshops.

Although professional and bureaucratic pessimism is often resistant to attitudinal change, parents' acceptance of this fate for their child is, by its nature, more hopeful. For the Central Valley, one family's, the Pedersons', attendance at a lecture by Lovaas from the University of California, Los Angeles (UCLA), in December 1990 literally set in motion a sequence of events that not only changed prevailing attitudes about treatment in the region, but led to the formation of a parent network.

Within months of Lovaas's talk, the UCLA Young Autism Project (YAP) sent a consultant to the Central Valley to conduct a 3-day behavioral training workshop for three families. The families paid for the consultant's travel and per diem costs, and a regional agency picked up the cost for the workshop itself. The families carried almost the entire financial and programmatic burden for running the intensive, early education programs. They had to recruit, supervise, and train one-on-one tutors to work with their children with a little help from a behavior specialist. The UCLA consultant was not to return for another 6 months, so the parents were left to proceed by their own wits. One child, initially nonverbal with no play skills and daylong self-stimulatory and self-injurious behaviors, began using words within 2 weeks of this parent-initiated and directed 40-hour-per-week program. The mother ended up being hospitalized for exhaustion, and her child eventually was placed in a self-contained special education day class.

Debra Wright, one of the mothers from the original UCLA-trained group, also received little support from outside agencies; her child showed some but not significant developmental progress. Wright persevered, scoured the state for a program that focused on nonverbal communication, found one in the San Francisco Bay Area, and persuaded her local school district to start a private autism program in a public school class, the first, we believe, in the state. Three additional families in the region began litigation against their school district to obtain educational support for enrolling their children in an intensive in-home treatment program at UCLA.

As the number of families with young children with ASD grew in the area, the informal parent network expanded. The first group meeting took place in 1992, and the parents began to gather at members' homes once a month. The Central Valley chapter of FEAT was officially formed in 1994. Currently, over 300 families are affiliated with the organization, meetings are held monthly, and an elected board of directors sets policy for the nonprofit organization.

Under the leadership of Debra Wright, the Central Valley FEAT organization focused on advocacy. The group used the art of negotiation to secure an impressive range of educational options for children with ASD in the region. It is now common for FEAT advocates to accompany parents to meetings about students' Individualized Education Programs (IEPs) and Individualized Family Service Plans (IFSPs) and to sit on various countywide educational and regional planning committees.

FEAT developed a set of guidelines for parents to effectively use during the negotiating process. The following are the basic tenets of *parental advocacy negotiation*:

- *Be prepared*—Know special education federal and state law; know the child's strengths; write out and be prepared to present specific educational goals and objectives.
- *Be confident*—Do not act arrogant, defensive, angry, or hostile.
- *Be assertive*—Listen to all sides; reinforce child-centered statements before presenting your own view.
- *Listen*—Separate out what you may think is in the child's best interests from the parents' wishes and vision for their child. Listen for and support unexpected willingness to compromise from funding agency staff.

- *Be helpful*—Acknowledge agency limitations regarding cost and program resources. Assert that problem solution is the responsibility of the whole team, not one agency.
- *Know your hill to die on*—Be open and willing to compromise, but stop at the point at which the child's right to significantly benefit from an appropriate educational procedure is at risk.

Parental involvement in decision making is now evident in all areas of the Central Valley region. Parents sit on advisory committees in school districts and in the regional center, as well.

Regional Leadership

Like most human service delivery systems, ASD education programs frequently are fragmented and involve multiple agencies that have overlapping responsibilities. Regional leadership is necessary to facilitate communication and coordinate services when cost effectiveness and innovative, research-based treatment options are priorities. There are a number of fundamental elements in establishing regional leadership. First, an agency should have a legal mandate to provide services, not merely advocacy, for young children with developmental disabilities or developmental delays across the geographic area. Local schools may not be the best place to start because several school districts are likely represented in a county or rural region. Second, the agency should be capable of directly expending funds toward treatment management. Third, when possible, program monitoring and diagnostic evaluation should be part of that agency's function within the community.

For the Central Valley, although there are numerous school districts, only one agency has regional responsibility. Valley Mountain Regional Center (VMRC) is one of 21 private, nonprofit, state-funded agencies in California that provide diagnostic, case management, community support, and resource development for individuals, at any age, with significant developmental delays. VMRC played a pivotal role in the collaborative process in that it had preexisting relationships with school districts, parents, and other agencies dealing with early autism intervention and it had limited but discretionary funding capacity.

Collaboration involves actively seeking clarification and continual reassessment of each partner's role in decision making and funding for autism services. Initially, the VMRC argued that its education responsibility was limited either to children enrolled in the early start program (birth to age 3) or after high school graduation/age 22 through adulthood; the school district was considered the legally responsible agency during the span of years between 3 and 22. Parents viewed the VMRC as an ally in their educational advocacy for their children. School districts, on the other hand, were worried about setting precedent and were willing to risk litigation as a check against the potential spiraling costs of funding intensive, early education programs, which they feared could consume their entire special education budget. This created a stalemate for all parties involved and reinforced conflict and confrontation. The school districts and the VMRC could rationalize their respective positions by claiming restricted mandates. Only parents with independent economic resources and the strong will to follow through with fair hearings could be successful. However, alternatively, if through intensive early intervention a substantial number of children diagnosed with ASD could function within the mainstream public education and later become tax-paying citizens, then the California taxpayer, who supports both the regional center and the school budgets, could save millions of dollars in the long run. It is in this context that partnership becomes no longer an option but an economic necessity.

The regional center began to gather research information and to visit innovative treatment providers. There were several meetings between Lovaas and regional center clinical staff that culminated in a UCLA YAP satellite clinic established in September 1994 in the Central Valley region. Moreover, the regional center made a policy decision that it would share the program costs of an early intervention education program with the school, and both agencies agreed to bring the parents in as full partners in the venture.

Education

Federal legislation, particularly the Individuals with Disabilities Education Act (IDEA) of 1990 (amended in 1997) and its predecessor, the Education for All Handicapped Children Act of 1975, form the bedrock for each child's right to appropriate education in the least restrictive environment regardless of type or degree of disability (Herr, 1997). The U.S. Congress' recognition that early educational intervention optimizes the child's future opportunity for inclusion into the mainstream coupled with encouraging behavioral teaching methodology have placed the local school district in the center of a maelstrom revolving around fiscal responsibility and appropriate educational intervention for young children with ASD.

In an all too common scenario, parents walk into IEP and IFSP meetings armed with advocates to support their demands for an aggressive, nontraditional educational intervention strategy for their child. School staff may react by trying to assert control of the meeting and too often fall back on traditional classroom strategies as their only options. Even when the school administrator is sympathetic and concerned about the individual child's right to effective treatment, the financial burden on the local district can be staggering; early, intensive treatment costs can range from \$50,000 to \$80,000 per child per year. Moreover, the classroom-based structure of the school system does not lend itself easily to accommodating a home-centered program. For example, labor and complex liability issues may seem daunting to overcome in putting together an educational treatment team that is based in the child's home. More often than not, the above factors lead to rigid position taking by both sides, parents and school, resulting in mediations and fair hearings.

Meaningful partnership and collaboration must begin far removed from the admixture of heightened emotions and educational planning at the IEP or IFSP meeting itself. Guidelines to assess program appropriateness, a range of early education options, interagency agreements, intraagency policies, and financial or contractual arrangements need to be worked out well in advance of the IEP and IFSP meetings. An IEP or IFSP then becomes centered on the individual child's educational needs and does not become tied to the economics of a particular program.

In California, Special Education Local Planning Area (SELPA) directors, who act as gatekeepers for special education services, represent clusters of school districts. VMRC staff and SELPA directors began to meet and discuss early intervention education treatment for children with ASD. Trust was at the top of the agenda for many of the initial meetings. Despite a long, aggravated history of distrust, miscommunication, and unchecked rumor mongering, once direct, calm, and fruitful discussion started, preconceived ill feelings were readily dispelled and common ground began to materialize. Individual SELPA director leadership began to emerge, and it became clear that two of the SELPA directors would be willing to risk potential censure by their colleagues in the state to move forward with trying a new home-centered education model.

School personnel involvement is an absolutely essential component for regional planning to be successful. As parents and, in our case, VMRC staff began to understand school administrators' fiscal limitations, fears, and staff allocation problems, the group began to problem solve, not to protect each partner's own vested interest, but with a common goal to promulgate each child's opportunity to receive a viable treatment option.

It is not critical that all parents, all school administrators, and all regional agency staff support the partnership process. Collaboration is successful when key decision makers from each of the participating agencies continue to meet and are willing to consider compromises in creating a model. For example, in the Central Valley, not all SELPA directors were either actively involved or willing to take a public position endorsing intensive, early, initially home-based education. However, once the partnership model was solidified, every SELPA in our region, even those not taking part directly in the discussions, agreed to participate in the program at the IEP and IFSP level. Leadership, not unanimity, often moves mountains.

UCLA Young Autism Project (YAP)

The fourth structural component that must be in place is the treatment–educational provider. I recently received a call from a parent in a large metropolitan area who said that the schools and a state insurance provider had agreed to fund a discrete trial program for her child, but she lacked the personnel to actually implement the program. This dilemma is not as uncommon as one might think.

There is still a relative paucity of well-trained providers of in-home intensive treatment for early intervention. The demand for properly trained providers is so high in some geographic areas that a consultant may visit a family once a month to two times a year. This type of technical support may help the child but is certainly not a research-validated approach to optimizing treatment outcome. Reliance on an out-of-area consultant also increases the risk of inappropriate or misguided program objectives and sloppy intervention techniques and, in its extreme, can be so frustrating and confining to the child that it may border on child abuse.

The most efficacious service delivery model is to build a strong local or regional treatment provider team that is linked directly and frequently to a clinical and research treatment expert. The first program developed in the Central Valley involved a consultant from the UCLA YAP who consulted once every 2 months with the local behavior interventionists, parents, and children in the program. The local group relied heavily on the consultant. On the positive side, some of the children made significant progress. Other children, however, languished when they should have been transitioned to other education alternatives, and the potential of still others may have been lost in this inefficient process.

Once the Central Valley's UCLA YAP satellite clinic site was determined in the spring of 1994, Mila Amerine-Dickens, a master's-level behavior specialist, was sent to UCLA for extensive training. This accomplished two things: (1) it provided direct training of and assured a basic competence level for an individual who would return to the Central Valley region as program director and (2) it created a direct link between the regional behavioral treatment–education program directed by Amerine-Dickens and the UCLA YAP. As additional regional staff were identified and accumulated experience, they were then given the opportunity of receiving more information and training by interning at UCLA as well. Thus, a core group of highly trained, well-supervised professional staff began to work in the region.

The initial clinical team treatment structure evolved into the Central Valley Autism Project, Inc. (CVAP), a not-for-profit agency, which, in conjunction with VMRC, continues to serve as a National Institute of Mental Health research and clinical site for the UCLA YAP. Each team member's role and responsibility, including that of the parents, school, and regional center, is clearly defined in a manual developed specifically for the Central Valley satellite clinic.

As other programs began to emerge in our area, including Therapeutic Pathways, Inc., and Applied Behavioral Consultants, this model of direct provider-to-regional staff training with frequent access to doctoral-level clinicians assured that the California's Central Valley would have the highest caliber of treatment providers.

The UCLA YAP instituted a series of training competencies, through videotaped sampling and feedback, that CVAP treatment team providers in the Central Valley satellite must meet in order to continue to practice in our area. Video-conferencing capability between the CVAP satellite clinic and UCLA YAP enables in vivo problem solving of individual treatment issues and enhanced communication among CVAP trainers and supervisors, parents, and UCLA YAP staff to ensure optimal quality and immediate programmatic feedback.

Operationalizing the Pyramid

The present program delivery structure is depicted in Figure 39.1. CVAP, FEAT, VMRC, and SELPA form the basic building blocks for a collaborative process in the Central Valley. Moving upward away from the base of the pyramid, the next task is to create problem-solving structures that require these raw blocks to interact, commingle, and intersect with each other as much as possible in order to produce coalition formations. The operational elements involve establishing a centralized, early diagnostic and treatment planning clinic, creating an ongoing vehicle for communication and discussion among key participants, and obtaining commitments among the participants to develop policy toward a shared responsibility model.

Early Autism Diagnostic Clinic

The following scenario probably repeats itself worldwide for families that suspect that their child has ASD. The parents are referred by their physician or a developmental disability clinic to an expert in autism, who in turn examines the child and makes a diagnosis. If the child is not in school, the parents are told to approach the education system or another appropriate agency for help. Not only are the parents grieving, confused, and likely overwhelmed about what to do next, but they end up going to probably several separate meetings with various agencies that they are told will assist their child. Each agency approached has its own intake process. Time passes, creating increased parental frustration and most likely guilt over not acting quickly enough. Parents begin talking to other parents and are encouraged or sometimes pressured to choose one treatment over the other. The agencies themselves most likely are competitive and territorial, putting the parents right in the middle of a rather unfriendly environment for program planning.

The Early Autism Screening Clinic (EADC) functions to create a centralized, diagnostic starting point for families. The VMRC facilitates the EADC process. Any child between the ages of 1 and 5 residing within the five-county region and suspected of having ASD can be referred to the EADC. Each child is screened using the *Pervasive Developmental Disorder Screening Test–II* (Siegel, 2001), and the Checklist for Autism in Toddlers (Baron-Cohen et al., 1996), and other pertinent medical, developmental, and social family data are gathered. The information is reviewed by a subgroup of clinicians from the EADC, who order or arrange for further diagnostic assessments when warranted.

When the family and child walk into the EADC, they are introduced to team members, including clinical staff from VMRC, personnel from the local school district or SELPA, and a representative from the CV FEAT parent group. Thus, from the outset, this child-centered diagnostic meeting has representatives from all the agencies that will eventually work with this child and her family.

True partnership must begin from the outset. The EADC assists the family in gathering clinical and educa-

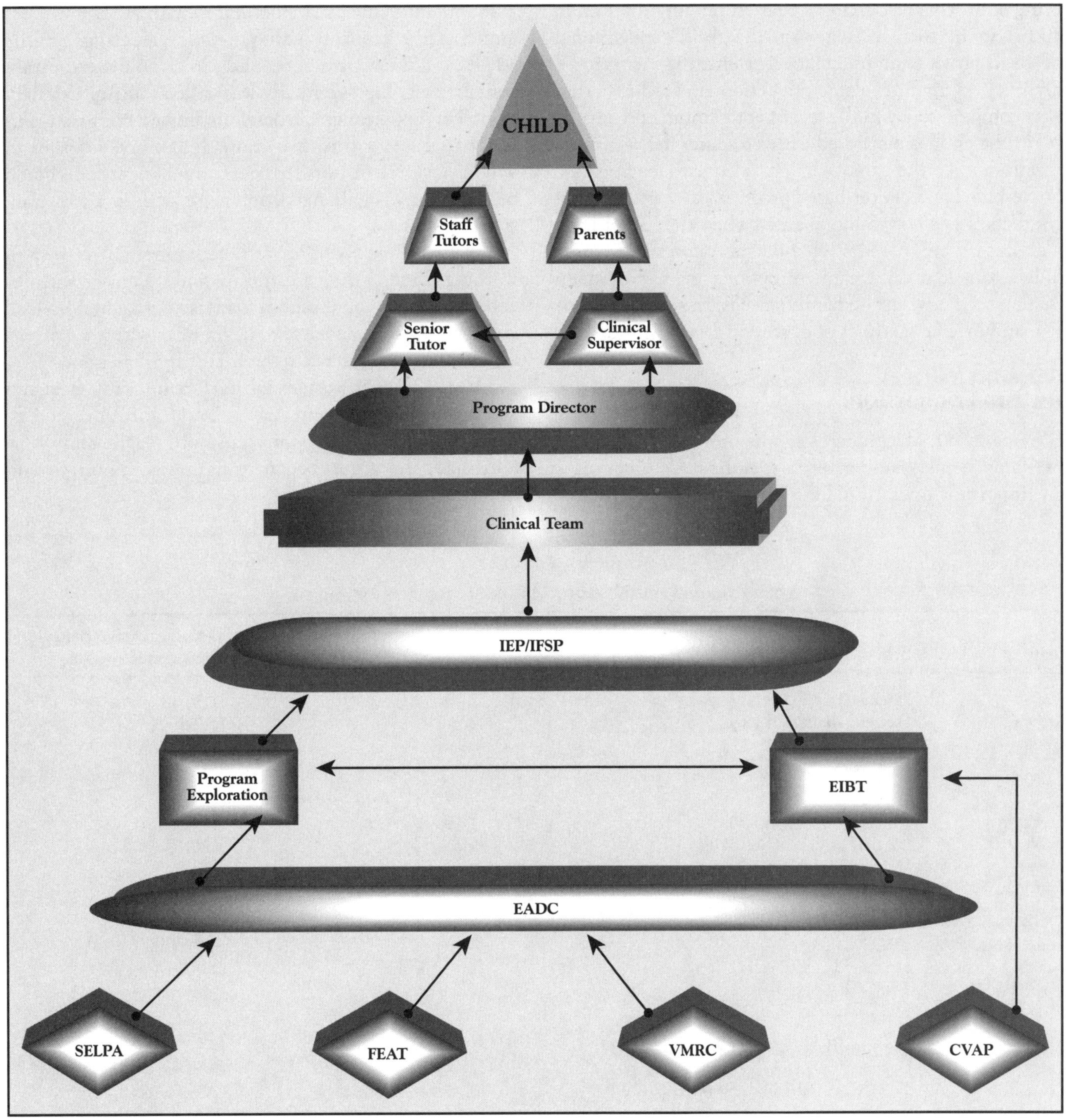

Figure 39.1. Valley Mountain Regional Center Central Valley Autism Project pyramid of service delivery.

tional resources that can be significant in helping their child. Although the EADC cannot alleviate the family's anxiety or grieving process when they first hear the diagnosis of ASD, the clinic helps to focus program planning in an efficient, positive, noncompetitive, and cooperative manner, thus setting a tone for future more formal meetings such as the IEP and IFSP meetings. The clinic lasts from 3 to 4 hours, and the parents are given a blueprint of treatment options to explore once they leave the meeting. If they desire, the parents are linked up with families in their neighborhood who can also act as supports and guides through the program planning process.

Partnership building among parents, agencies, and parent organizations does not mean that parents are forced to choose one path or the other. The key is that, from the outset, families understand that it is possible to bring collective resources to bear on helping their child and that the focus can stay on the child's educational needs. It provides an inoculation against the incursion of divisiveness, rigidity, blame projection, and so forth, that is so common today in the treatment planning process.

If the child is diagnosed with a disorder in the autistic spectrum, then the parents are provided with reading lists, home-based and center-based programs to visit, parental contacts, and so on. Subsequently, when the IEP or IFSP meeting is held, parents have had an opportunity to be fully informed about treatment options and to consider a best match between the family's needs, the child's potential, and specific methods of educational intervention.

Autism Connection

Whereas the EADC focuses on the individual child and her family's needs and priorities, Autism Connection is an important operational structure to discuss the program planning needs of all children with ASD in the region. In the Central Valley, regular meetings among VMRC, SELPA directors, and CV FEAT were established; the group eventually was called Autism Connection. The importance of these ongoing meetings was initially to build a trust coalition. It became a forum in which negative or hostile preexisting assumptions could be questioned, challenged, and dealt with in a constructive manner.

Parents urged VMRC to take a more active role in working through their frustration and stalemate with local schools. Regional school leaders approached VMRC about acting as a mediator to begin talks with the parents away from the pressures of the IEP or IFSP meeting.

VMRC was instrumental in starting joint meetings among the parent group, VMRC, and SELPA directors. As the rigid boundaries of accusatory responsibility diminished, the group began to define common ground from which to operate.

TABLE 39.1
San Joaquin Central Valley Matrix of Programs for Autism

Selpa	School-Based Program Methodology	Location	Early, Intensive Behavioral Treatment Programs
San Joaquin County	Discrete Trial/PECS (Ages 3–6)	Hersh	BEST (Ages 1–3)
	Discrete Trial/PECS (Ages 5–8)	Mcfall	CVAP (Ages 1–5)
		Village Oaks	ABC (Ages 1–5)
	TEACCH (Ages 6–13)	Redwood School	Pathways (Ages 1–5)
		Village Oaks	
Stockton Unified School District	Discrete Trial (Ages 3–6)	Golden Valley	BEST (Ages 1–3)
	Language and Learning Skills	Preschool	ABC (Ages 1–5)
	Discrete Trial (Ages 6–9)		CVAP (Ages 1–5)
	Language and Learning Skills		
	Primary (6–12) Multiple Intervention Strategies	Pulliam	
Lodi Unified School District	TEACCH (Ages 3–5)	Victor	BEST (Ages 1–3)
	Structured SDC Preschool (Ages 3–6)	Leroy Nichols	CVAP (Ages 1–5)
	TEACCH (Ages 3–7)	Bechman	Pathways (Ages 1–5)
	TEACCH (Ages 6–12)		
Modesto City Schools	Discrete Trial; TEACCH, PECS (Ages 3–5)	El Vista	BEST (Ages 1–3)
	Discrete Trial; TEACCH, PECS (Ages 5–11)	Garrison	Pathways (Ages 1–5)
	TEACCH Method Voc Ed (Ages 16–22)	Johannsen/Beyer HS	CVAP (Ages 1–5)
			ABC
Stanislaus County Schools	Diagnostic Preschool (Ages 3–6)	Cloverland School	BEST (Ages 1–3)
	Intensive School (Ages 4–11)	Mildred Perkins	CVAP (Ages 1–5)
	Demonstration (Ages 5–12)	Margaret L. Annear	ABC (Ages 1–5)
	Functional Life Skills (Ages 16–22)	Walter White	Pathways (Ages 1–5)
		JFK	
Tri–County SELPA	Language Based (Amador County)	Jackson (Amador County)	TAC
	Discrete Trial—TEACCH; Full Inclusion (Calaveras County)	San Andreas; Jenny Lind (Calaveras County)	
	TEACCH/PECS (Tuolumne County)	Multiple (Tuolumne County)	

Note. BEST = Behavior Education Strategies and Training; CVAP = Central Valley Autism Project; ABC = Applied Behavior Consultants; Pathways = Therapeutic Pathways; TAC = Teaching Autistic Children.

The most dramatic and affirming work of the Autism Connection was to create the environment for the development of a matrix of programs for ASD in the Central Valley (see Table 39.1). As can be gleaned from perusal of that table, each of the six SELPAs began developing a range of educational options for children in their districts. The most startling fact is that all of these programs have developed in the last several years through the work and support of the Autism Connection and smaller district work groups. *Every* SELPA in the region offers not only a center-based program specifically designed for children with ASD, but also initially home-based 40-hour discrete trial programs.

The Autism Connection also developed a handbook outlining the specific roles and responsibilities of every individual, parent, professional, and student, implementing a UCLA YAP home-based education program. This guideline is cited in Appendix F of the California Department of Education's (1997) "Best Practices for Designing and Delivering Effective Programs for Individuals with Autistic Spectrum Disorders."

In summary, the operational structure of the pyramid is set in motion by creating one focal point to deal with the diagnostic and educational treatment needs of the individual child—via the EADC—and a process of ongoing communication and policy formulation to discuss all children with ASD via the Autism Connection.

Shared Responsibility

The Autism Connection process led to the development of several basic underlying premises for treatment–education services for ASD in the Central Valley as follows:

1. Early identification and treatment of children with ASD is a priority.
2. Early, intensive individualized education treatment using state-of-the-art behavioral-based methodology is empirically and clinically supported by research.
3. Early, intensive education must be cost effective. Single-source financing of intensive education programs places an untenable economic burden on parents, small school districts, and so on.
4. Parents, regional center, and schools have a shared responsibility to support each child's developmental potential throughout his lifetime.

The Autism Connection's endorsement of the shared responsibility tenet led to the development of a contractual agreement among the regional center, school districts, and parents. VMRC and the schools agreed to split the cost of the CVAP's 40-hour-a-week in-home intensive behavioral education program for children identified with ASD between the ages of 3 and 5, contingent on the child's meeting entrance criteria for the program. As the child progresses to an inclusion site (e.g. preschool or regular kindergarten), the school district's financial obligation increases while the regional center continues to underwrite a percentage of the child's reduced number of treatment hours in the home setting.

The Autism Connection group developed an extensive handbook, detailing the roles and responsibilities of the regional center, schools, parents, and treatment team staff, including program director, clinical supervisor, senior tutor, and staff tutor.[1] Under these early intensive education models, parents play a substantial role in the program implementation. The original model involved the parents in the recruitment, hiring, and firing, when necessary, and the administrative supervision and scheduling of the tutors, who are typically students 18 years or older attending local community colleges or universities in the area. In a more recent alternative model, the treatment–education provider is responsible for the administrative and clinical supervision of all staff. Parents are expected to attend the initial 2-day training workshop, maintain and actively participate in a 40-hour-per-week discrete trial program in their home, conduct generalization activities in the home and community for which they receive no compensation, help with supplies and reinforcers, and provide adequate liability insurance. Parents are expected to work collaboratively as an integral member of their child's IEP or IFSP clinical team.

Initially, the regional center became responsible for coordinating and administering the financial components of the program. VMRC funded the parents, senior tutors, and case supervisors and was then reimbursed by the schools for their share of the costs. The school district and regional center contracted separately with the CVAP program director. In a recent modification, CVAP became a nonpublic school agency; a contractual agreement among VMRC, the local school district, and CVAP allows the provider to be paid directly. The advantage of this contractual arrangement between the local school district or SELPA and the regional center effectively reduces technical, bureaucratic roadblocks that schools face

[1] The EIBT Guidelines and Responsibilities Manual is available from Clinical Administrative Assistant, VMRC, P.O. Box 692290, Stockton, CA 95269-2290; Telephone: 209/955-3222.

in supporting home-based programs. The regional center and schools have specific responsibilities for monitoring the child's progress and working directly with parents to sustain an optimal home environment.

In addition to weekly clinical team meetings, the regional center, school staff, parents, and CVAP program director or clinical supervisor meet monthly during the initial phase of the home program to deal with and anticipate "extra-therapy variables that must be quickly identified and corrected, otherwise treatment effort will be sabotaged" (Lovaas, 1996, p. 246). That is, the weekly clinical team meetings focus on monitoring specific intervention objectives and altering teaching strategies when warranted. The monthly parent meetings center on family dynamics, staff–parent interaction, and other home-related issues that may interfere with the smooth implementation of the actual education program. For example, while one of the parents, typically the mother, may be actively participating, the father may be still grieving, which manifests through his social withdrawal or depressive symptoms. He may be irritable with staff and overly critical of his wife or other children in the home. These issues, if left unresolved, can have significant impact on the durability of the family to sustain the intensity of the treatment program. Other siblings often feel left out, and these issues can also be addressed in the context of monthly problem-solving meetings. A more recent innovation, developed by CV FEAT through a California State Department of Developmental Disabilities Wellness Grant, involves the parents of children newly diagnosed with ASD in an 8-hour educational program to assist the family in their transition to an intensive, in-home behavioral treatment program.

Peer play training, a component of intensive behavioral treatment, requires some modification of each participant's role, and this is also addressed in the handbook provided to members of the clinical team. When the child is ready to transition into regular preschool or kindergarten, guidelines for determining appropriateness of the education site for the child are developed and agreed to in the context of Autism Connection meetings. The criteria include, for example, the following:

1. Ratio of teacher-directed activities to student-directed activities should be about 60 : 40.
2. Class size should be no greater than 20 students with one teacher and one aide assistant.
3. Physical arrangement of the school should provide clear demarcations for activities, such as free play, gross motor, preacademic, circle time, art, language, and so on, to meet the developmental needs of each age group and learning style represented.
4. Seventy-five percent or more of peer models in an education setting will speak the primary language of the student with ASD and be able to model appropriate behavior.

The roles and responsibilities of the adult participants are also defined, including the shadow aide. The function of the aide in the classroom, for example, is to assist the teacher and classroom staff, *not* to act as a prompt for the child. The only time the tutor directly prompts the child is when instructional control has not been obtained by the teacher. Although the tutor is assigned to a specific child, he or she should at all appropriate times interact and assist the other children in the classroom so as to give the teacher the mobility to interact more immediately with the child. A skilled tutor blends well in the classroom and does not appear to be with any one child.

In summary, the parents, schools, and regional center form a partnership and share expenses, administrative functions, and program administration. The CVAP treatment–education program director is responsible for quality control and clinical supervision of all clinical team members, including tutors, senior tutors, case supervisors, and parents, when the latter function as tutors.

Putting It All Together: A Case Example

Matthew

Matthew, age 32 months, was referred to the regional center due to developmental delays and suspected ASD. The parents completed the *Pervasive Developmental Disorder Screening Test–II* (PDDST; Siegel, 2001) and additional social, developmental, and medical information was gathered during the intake process. Matthew screened positive for ASD on the PDDST and was referred immediately to UCSF (University of California, San Francisco) PDD clinic for a diagnostic evaluation and to the EADC for diagnostic confirmation and treatment–education planning. Matthew received a diagnosis of autistic disorder and suspected mild mental retardation from Dr. Bryna Siegel from the UCSF evaluation and was seen shortly thereafter at age 35 months at the EADC.

Matthew and his parents were greeted at the EADC clinic by regional center clinical staff, a program specialist and a teacher from the local school district, and a volunteer member of the CV FEAT organization. The UCSF report was reviewed, and the clinic members had an opportunity to interact with Matthew during a structured play observation. During the approximately 3-hour clinic, the parents stated that they had begun reading about autism and had talked to a couple of parents with children who have autistic-spectrum disorders. Matthew's mother anxiously asked the EADC team whether it was too late for Matthew to obtain treatment in that she had been told that there was only a small window of opportunity for children to benefit from a treatment program.

After providing the family with some reassurance, EADC team members provided factual, empirical information about optimal treatment age and educational options. The parents were given a matrix of program options, including both home-based and center-based early intervention programs. The FEAT representative explained that the parent group meets monthly and that, if Matthew's parents would consent, FEAT would assign a parent who lives geographically close to Matthew's family to help them make links with other parents. Regional center and school staff discussed various treatment options on the matrix, and the parents were encouraged to visit as many of these programs as they could manage over the next 2 or 3 weeks.

Because Matthew's parents were interested in looking at home-based programs, referrals were made for them to talk with the program directors of the three available programs in the region. The parents were encouraged not to make a decision too quickly and to consider the needs of their entire family before deciding on a program. They were told that each program has specific entrance criteria and that they could inquire at each site about those criteria. When the parents left the EADC, they emerged with a blueprint for further program follow-up and the understanding that agencies mandated to work with their child have a cooperative relationship with each other and are child centered.

Once the parents are satisfied that they have read sufficiently and observed enough programs to make an informed decision, they are encouraged to contact the assigned agency liaison prior to the IEP or IFSP meeting. In this case, Matthew's parents chose the CVAP program. Program administrators from both the regional center and school met prior to the IEP and agreed on the funding mechanism in principle. At the IEP meeting, specific program objectives were written and the treatment program identified. The family did not have to defend their position or beg or threaten litigation. After the IEP meeting, the program administrators from the participating agencies talked by phone, and contracts were drawn up and signed. In the interim, the family met with the program director of the CVAP clinical and research site to establish the initial workshop and initiation of treatment date. Matthew began treatment at 36 months.

Partnerships in Action: An Overview

Parents, schools, and regional agencies can become partners in bringing high-quality, state-of-the-art, early, intensive education options for young children with ASD. The pyramid construction outlined in this chapter is an apt metaphor for this collaborative process. Partnership requires people in decision-making positions to come together frequently, to suspend preconceived judgments, to actively search for common ground and unifying principles, to bring an openness to new ideas with broad empirical support, to possess the willingness to compromise and risk criticism from those outside the pyramid team, to trust one another, to redraw rigid bureaucratic boundaries, and to invest unflinching commitment that early intervention provides the greatest opportunity for children to optimize their potential.

Pyramid building requires clear vision that the child, regardless of the nature and severity of the disability, remains the pinnacle or focal point of the collaborative effort. Sights of vision in the pyramid always lead to the child.

The knowledge gained from mastering the art of building one pyramid for the CVAP program makes it easier to construct other pyramids that use different teaching methodologies. For example, since 1994, fourteen new school-based programs designed specifically for young children with ASD, as well as five home-based early intervention programs, have become available to children and their parents in the San Joaquin Central Valley region (see Table 39.1). SELPAs in our area have demonstrated their willingness to open their programs to children from another school district whose education needs may not be met by their own districts' current teaching methodology.

The Central Valley region currently represents diverse center-based, early education teaching methodologies including North Carolina–based TEACCH (Lord & Schopler, 1994), Delaware-based *Picture Exchange Communication System* (Bondy & Frost, 1994a), the pragmatic eclecticism of Michael Allasandre, (personal communication) and the California-based STARS program (Sundberg & Partington, 1994). Thus, children entering one type of program, such as an intensive home-based program, may be transitioned into another appropriate program if, for instance, visual learning strategies would be more effective for that particular child.

The bottom line for all this energy by CV FEAT, VMRC, and school districts has translated into the fact that not one mediation, fair hearing, or other form of litigation has been initiated for entry into an early intervention program in the region over the last several years. Currently over 70 children are in home-based, intensive (35 to 40 hours a week), early education programs and over 150 young children in center-based special education programs specifically designed for children with ASD. Although disagreements, skepticism, and some political posturing still exist, the bottom line is that children in our region actually have a choice of treatment options, thus enabling the team not only to select an appropriate treatment–education program for each child but then to continue to provide the child with treatment–education options as the child progresses, stabilizes, and transitions.

This chapter did not deal with the possibility that health insurance companies are also a potential viable funding source for the early intervention programs. Williamson (1996) presents a compelling argument for parents to approach insurance providers. Rather than viewing insurance companies as possible litigants, it may be more prudent and more cost and labor efficient in the long run to invite them to be partners in already established collaborative relationships that are producing positive results. Health insurance companies may respond better when data can be demonstrated to show positive outcomes.

Certification and licensing requirements for behavior specialists, tutors, and aides, as well as labor restrictions, have been impediments to schools' taking greater administrative leadership in the development of early intervention, educational programs for students with ASD. In California, contracting with non–public school agencies (NPA) has gained considerable attention as a possible alternative. Although the NPA approach is currently undergoing challenges and modification through the California Department of Education, other states and county schools may well have the ability to implement such a strategy. No matter which agency ultimately fiscally manages these programs, a shared responsibility model as promoted in this chapter has, perhaps, the greatest chance of controlling and more equitably distributing the potentially high initial costs to taxpayers for these effective early intervention programs.

Clarifying Comments on the UCLA Young Autism Project

CHAPTER 40

Unfortunately, misunderstandings about the UCLA (University of California, Los Angeles) model have been very common, dating as far back as 1967 when Bettelheim accused Lovaas of "stripping the patients of (their) humanity, treating them like Pavlovian dogs" and compared the use of operant conditioning procedures to a lobotomy (pp. 410–411). The spread of erroneous information has continued over time. This is a serious problem because misinformation hinders parents and professionals from making appropriate decisions about services for children with autism. It may also cause funding agencies to set inappropriate priorities for research and treatment and may create an atmosphere of mistrust that inhibits collaborative work on identifying effective therapies.

Reluctantly, therefore, we have concluded that it is necessary to summarize and correct some of the more persistent misunderstandings about the UCLA model. Detailed and peer-reviewed descriptions of the UCLA model of early intervention for children with autism have been presented in a treatment manual and associated videotapes (Lovaas, 1981; Lovaas & Leaf, 1981), as well as in several articles (Lovaas, 1993; Smith & Lovaas, 1998; Smith, Donahoe, & Davis, 2000). We also have reported research on outcomes that children obtain with this intervention (Lovaas, 1987; McEachin, Smith, & Lovaas, 1993; Smith, Eikeseth, Klevstrand, & Lovaas, 1997; Smith, Groen, & Wynn, 2000; Smith, Klevstrand, & Lovaas, 1995). Moreover, in these publications, we have discussed the strengths and weaknesses of the UCLA project and research pertaining to this model.

The following discussion focuses on issues regarding the children who participated in our research, the experimental design of this research, the nature of the treatment the children received, assessments of the effect of this treatment on children and their parents, conclusions drawn from these assessments, cost of intervention, and concerns about testimony in fair hearings. Clarifying comments are made in reply to each distortion expressed about the UCLA project. In addition, an attempt is made to explain why colleagues have distorted the project. The discussion ends with an expression of optimism about future progress in treatment–research.

A. Did Subject Selection Result in a Representative Sample of Children with Autism?

1. All children were independently diagnosed with autism by doctoral-level (MD or PhD) licensed clinicians, and there was high agreement on this diagnosis between the independent examiners (see Lovaas, 1987), providing evidence that subjects met criteria for the diagnosis of autism. Altogether, clinicians assessed 20 pretreatment variables considered to be descriptive of autism, related to outcome, or both. These variables are defined in detail in Lovaas (1987) and include chronological age (CA) at diagnosis; mental age (MA) and CA at beginning of treatment; diagnostic classification by doctoral-level licensed clinicians; and videotaped recordings scored by independent observers in a reliable manner for kind and amount of toy play, self-stimulatory behavior, and recognizable words. From parent interviews, data were obtained on the presence of peer play, aggression toward family and self, suspected sensory deficits, emotional attachment, toilet training, gender, siblings and family composition, socioeconomic status of family, and age of the onset of walking. From medical records, clinicians recorded the presence of denotable neurological signs as determined by electroencephalography, computerized axial tomography, or both.

2. Further evidence for the comparability of Lovaas's (1987) subjects to those diagnosed as having autism in other studies comes from Control Group II, incorporated into the Lovaas (1987) study. Control Group II subjects were evaluated by another research team (the Neuropsychiatric Institute at UCLA). Subjects in this group were selected on the basis of IQ scores similar to the experimental group and Control Group I at intake, according to the same measures of intelligence used

by the UCLA model (see Lovaas, 1987, for a more thorough description of Control Group II). Control Group II showed similar outcome data to those found from Control Group I and to reports of outcome from other investigators (Freeman, Ritvo, Needleman, & Yokota, 1985; Lord & Schopler, 1989; Lotter, 1978; Wing, 1989).

3. Schopler, Short, and Mesibov (1989) wrote that the Lovaas (1987) intake criteria resulted in a restricted and biased sample of high-functioning subjects who had a favorable prognosis regardless of treatment. That is, they argued that the sample of children with autism used in the Lovaas study was not representative of young children with autism. In addition, Schopler and Mesibov (1988) claimed that the Lovaas criteria for selecting subjects would have excluded 57% of their TEACCH (**T**reatment and **E**ducation of **A**utistic and Related **C**ommunication **H**andicapped **CH**ildren) referrals.

A printout of intake data we received from Short shows that Schopler et al.'s (1989) own participants had IQ scores quite comparable to the Lovaas (1987) participants (i.e., mean IQ of 60 in Lovaas, 1987, vs. 57 in Lord & Schopler, 1989). However, the TEACCH sample had a preponderance of children with a chronological age of 40 to 45 months. This distribution is atypical of the general population of children with autism. Also, only 5% of the TEACCH sample spoke in recognizable words, a considerably lower rate than the generally accepted figure of 50% (observed at UCLA and numerous other sites). It appears to us that Schopler and Mesibov (1988) have made errors in their calculations or that the TEACCH sample, not the UCLA sample, is atypical of young children with autism (Smith, 1994). Note also that the higher functioning subjects in the Lord and Schopler (1989) study showed the least improvement over time, rather than the most, the opposite of these authors' hypothesis as it relates to the Lovaas (1987) study. In the only other large-scale investigation of IQ scores in preschool children, Freeman et al. (1985) reported similar results (i.e., higher functioning children with autism showed the least improvement).

B. Did Subject Assignment Result in Equivalent Groups?

1. Assignments to the experimental or control group were made on the basis of therapist availability, which was determined *prior* to family contact with the clinic. That is, if enough therapists were available to provide intensive treatment, then the next family that contacted the clinic would be enrolled in the experimental group. If not enough therapists were available, the family would be assigned to Control Group I. In the project's initial proposal to the National Institute of Mental Health (NIMH), a matched-pair assignment procedure was planned (MH 11440, "Experimental Studies in Childhood Schizophrenia," submitted 8/25/72, p. 21). The use of matched-pair random assignment was presented to parents in Santa Barbara by Robert Koegel, who participated in the early stages of the Young Autism Project. However, parents threatened to stage a protest at the next meeting of the National Society for Autistic Children (the forerunner of the Autism Society of America) in San Diego if this procedure was used. NIMH was contacted about this situation, and Lovaas received approval to assign children to groups based on therapist availability, which is a generally accepted procedure in clinical research (Kazdin, 1980) and one that has been employed in several highly regarded studies on children with autism (e.g., Bartak & Rutter, 1973; Howlin & Rutter, 1987). All subjects remained in the groups to which they were assigned at intake. Only two subjects dropped out, and these subjects were not replaced. Therefore, the original composition of the groups was essentially preserved.

2. The experimental group and Control Group I received the same assessment battery at intake. The groups did not differ on 19 of the 20 pretreatment variables; the differing variable, CA at onset of treatment, was not related to outcome.

3. The number of control group subjects who were predicted to achieve normal functioning had they received intensive treatment was approximately equal to the number of experimental subjects who actually did achieve normal functioning with intensive treatment. This prediction was based on a multiple regression equation combining the 20 pretreatment variables. Thus, the subject assignment procedure yielded groups that were comparable to each other prior to treatment on factors that predicted outcome, supporting the inference that the assignment had produced equivalent groups.

4. Control Group I, which received up to 10 hours per week of one-on-one behavioral treatment, did not differ at posttreatment from Control Group II, which received no treatment from the UCLA model. Both groups achieved substantially less favorable outcomes than the experimental group. Because the three groups (experimental, Control Group I, and Control Group II) were similar to one another at pretreatment, this result confirms that our subjects had problems that responded only to intensive behavioral treatment; these subjects were representative of other children with autism and were not merely noncompliant and masking an underlying, essentially normal level of functioning that would enable them to respond to small-scale interventions.

With regard to the Lovaas (1987) study, Baer (1993) described the subject assignment procedure as "functionally random." It is also important to note that in 1981, NIMH approved of a grant request that formed the basis for the McEachin et al. (1993) follow-up study (MH 11440-15, "Experimental Studies in Childhood Schizophrenia"). This grant was approved after an extensive review and site visit by NIMH pertaining to the experimental design employed in the Lovaas (1987) study. Kazdin (1980), in discussing random assignment in clinical research, states, "The essential feature of random assignment is allocating subjects to groups in such a way that the probability of each subject appearing in any of the experimental groups is equal" (p. 125). He also states, "The usual way to ensure that subjects are assigned randomly is to determine the groups to which subjects will be assigned *prior* to their arrival to the experiment" (p. 125). He then warns that, when used as a "*method* of allocating subjects to groups [matched-pair random assignment] can produce groups that differ on all sorts of measures" (p. 126). Kazdin's warning indicates that a matched-pair random assignment procedure (as initially proposed by the UCLA model) could generate unequal groups, especially when sample size is small and the variables on which subjects are to be matched are not proven to be related to outcome. Kazdin stresses the importance of "reassuring whether there are no differences on measures prior to treatment because this situation partially corroborates the assumption that random assignment has distributed subject characteristics equally across groups" (p. 127). The Lovaas (1987) study appears to satisfy this condition. Further, the U.S. Surgeon General provided a favorable review: "A well-designed study of a psychosocial intervention was carried out by Lovaas and colleagues (Lovaas, 1987; McEachin et al., 1993)" (U.S. Department of Health and Human Services, 1999). In short, there is strong evidence that the superior functioning of the experimental group after treatment was a result of the treatment itself rather than a biased procedure for selecting and assigning subjects to the experimental group.

C. Did Family Characteristics Affect Outcome?

The children's families ranged from high to low socioeconomic status (SES), with SES means in the experimental and control groups almost identical to the national average (Lovaas, 1987). The correlation between SES and treatment outcome was $r(18) = -.13$, indicating an insignificant trend for lower SES families to achieve more favorable outcomes. Number of siblings was not predictive of outcome. Thus, although the Lovaas (1987) treatment required family participation, a diverse group of families was apparently able to meet this requirement.

D. Are Follow-up Data Believable? Are Treatment Effects Durable?

1. In the McEachin et al. (1993) follow-up study, a wide range of measures was administered to avoid overreliance on intelligence tests, which have limitations if used in isolation, such as bias resulting from teaching the test, selecting a test that would yield especially favorable results, failing to assess other aspects of cognitive functioning such as social competence or school performance, and so on (Spitz, 1986; Zigler & Trickett, 1978).

2. The follow-up evaluation used well-normed, standardized tests and double-blind examination procedures (selection of examiners by professionals not associated with the project who were blind to the UCLA clinic as the source of the request, and the use of normal comparison subjects to prevent biases that might occur if examiners tested only subjects with obvious signs of pathology). Such evaluations allowed for an objective, detailed, and quantifiable assessment of treatment effectiveness. A particularly rigorous assessment was given to the best-outcome subjects who demonstrated normal IQ and school placement at age 7. These assessments included the *Wechsler Intelligence Scale for Children–Revised* (WISC–R), the *Personality Inventory for Children*, the *Vineland Adaptive Behavior Scales*, and a structured clinical interview designed to identify subtle signs of autism. These assessments comprised more than 25 subscales, with the scores indicating that the best-outcome group was indistinguishable from normal control subjects. The results of the McEachin et al. (1993) follow-up, which extended several years beyond discharge from treatment for most subjects, are encouraging in that these treatment gains were maintained for an extended period of time.

Five well-known commentators with diverse theoretical orientations unanimously agreed that the Lovaas (1987) study and the McEachin et al. (1993) follow-up presented compelling evidence that the experimental clients improved and that the improvement was due to treatment rather than some extraneous variable (Baer, 1993; Foxx, 1993; Kazdin, 1993; Mesibov, 1993; Mundy, 1993). For this reason, further follow-ups of these subjects appear merited, and the UCLA clinic was recently awarded a grant from NIMH to conduct such a follow-up. This follow-up study is titled "Long-Term Outcome of Early Intervention for Autism" (1 R01 MH51156-01A1; the grant proposal for this study received the highest priority rating NIMH can provide, namely 100). The assessment instruments employed in this follow-up are extensive, reflecting recent advances in detecting residual signs of autism. These assessments include the *Wechsler Adult Intelligence Scale–Revised* (Wechsler, 1981), *Wisconsin*

Card Sorting Test (Grant & Berg, 1984), Absurdities Subtest of the *Stanford–Binet Intelligence Test* (R. L. Thorndike, Hagen, & Sattler, 1986), *Minnesota Multiphasic Personality Inventory–2* (Hathaway & McKinley, 1951), Rorshach (Exner, 1985), Socio-Emotional Functioning (Rutter, 1985), Theory of Mind (Baron-Cohen, Leslie, & Frith, 1985), Narrative Discourse Tasks (Landa, Folstein, & Isaacs, 1991), Social Discourse (Landa et al., 1990), and Abstract Semantics (Ekstrom, French, Harman, & Derman, 1976; E.H. Smith & Palmer, 1979). The importance of such an investigation is also magnified by the paucity of available information on the long-term effects of treatment for clients with autism in any treatment program (see Smith, 1993).

The safeguards discussed provide considerable assurance that the favorable outcome of the experimental subjects can be attributed to the treatment they received rather than to extraneous factors such as improvement that would have occurred regardless of treatment, biased procedures for selecting subjects or assigning them to groups, narrow or inappropriate assessment batteries, biased examiners, and so forth. For more detailed discussions of these concerns, see Lovaas (1987), Lovaas, Smith, and McEachin (1989), and McEachin et al. (1993).

E. Is the Treatment Replicable?

McEachin et al. (1993) emphasized that "the most important void for research at this time is replication by independent investigators" (p. 370), a caution similar to that expressed in Lovaas (1987). Some writers (e.g., Foxx, 1993) have reiterated the need to replicate the Lovaas (1987) study. There are four potential problems pertaining to replication.

1. It has been claimed that the treatment procedures employed in the Lovaas (1987) study were not adequately specified, and thus are not replicable. *Answer*: The following considerations suggest that the treatment procedures are replicable: First, the components of the treatment were published in a large number of peer-reviewed journals, developed by multiple investigators, and often replicated across sites (see Newsom & Rincover, 1989; Schreibman, 1988). Second, a 250-page manual (Lovaas, 1981) and associated videotapes (Lovaas & Leaf, 1981) describe the treatment in extensive detail. Third, the project has shown that it is possible to train therapists to provide high-quality treatment of the kind described in the Lovaas (1987) study. Samples of the one-on-one treatment provided by therapists at replication sites have been scored by project personnel at Washington State University for quality control Level I of treatment involving the appropriate use of instructions, prompts, and reinforcement (using definitions and scoring systems provided by R. L. Koegel, Russo, & Rincover, 1977). The correct use of these procedures ranged from 92% to 100%. Interrater reliability ranged from 94% to 100% (see R01MH48863-01A1, "Multi-Site Young Autism Project"). To reach quality control Level II on high-level programming requires basic coursework in learning theory, applied behavior analysis, or both, followed by a 9-month full-time internship at UCLA or one of the replication sites.

2. Contingent aversives were employed in the Lovaas (1987) study. Many states now prohibit the use of aversives, and many parents object to such treatment. Either of these factors could prevent replication of the Lovaas (1987) study. However, although the UCLA Young Autism Project no longer uses aversives, we have taken advantage of alternatives to aversives developed during and after the time the 1987 study was completed (treatment in the Lovaas, 1987, study took place between 1970 and 1984).

3. It has been argued that most agencies are unable to provide the required amount of treatment. *Answer*: Several sites are involved in the collaboration to provide *intensive* early intervention. These sites include the New Jersey Institute for Early Intervention (Cherry Hill, NJ); Wisconsin Early Autism Project (Madison, WI); Community Services for Autistic Adults and Children (Rockville, MD); Young Autism Project of Pittsburgh, Southwood Community Services, Inc. (Pittsburgh, PA); Iceland Young Autism Project (Kipavogure, Iceland); Early Autism Project, Akershus College (Sandvika, Norway); Central Valley Autism Project (Modesto, CA); Early Autism Project (Edina, MN); Early Autism Project (London, United Kingdom); and Early Autism Project, Ramon Llull University (Barcelona, Spain). All of these sites have been able to secure staff who have met quality control standards so as to deliver the intensive treatment prescribed in the Lovaas (1987) study as well as to test the effectiveness of different levels of treatment intensity.

4. It has been proposed that the Lovaas (1987) study may not be replicated because student therapists were unequally distributed across subjects and some may have developed particularly close relationships with parents, adding unknown variables to the treatment. *Answer*: The 1987 study took steps to ensure that such variables did not come into play. To help reduce these factors, each student therapist worked 6 hours per week for 6 to 9 months, at which point the practicum course was completed. During the 6 to 9 months, student therapists were rotated across families to provide them with a rich exposure to children with autism. In addition, student thera-

pists were instructed to behave as professional persons in a manner consistent with course outlines (no visits to home outside assigned treatment hours, no meals with family, no visits after course completion, no receipt of gifts, etc.). In the Young Autism Project (YAP), student therapists appointed as supervisors after 9 months may stay on the project for upward of 6 years, usually as graduate students, but they are rotated and distributed equally across families.

F. Do Treatment Outcomes from TEACCH and the Neuropsychiatric Institute (UCLA–NPI) or Other Centers Equal the Outcome from the Young Autism Project in the Department of Psychology at UCLA (UCLA YAP)?

Lovaas (1987) compared children in his intensive treatment group with two other groups: (a) a group that received minimal treatment from UCLA Young Autism Project and (b) a group of 21 children seen at UCLA–NPI by Freeman et al. (1985) and never referred to Lovaas (1987). TEACCH also presented data on children of the same age as those in the Lovaas and Freeman studies (Lord & Schopler, 1989). The IQ scores are shown in Table 40.1.

Regarding the UCLA–NPI group, Freeman et al. (1991) noted that 12 of the 53 children in their study showed improvements in their IQ classification (low, medium, or high), whereas 5 showed decreases. They further noted (on p. 481) that "no known special medical, behavioral, or educational interventions" accounted for the changes in status. Regarding TEACCH, Lord and Schopler (1989) noted that most of the improvements occurred with the lowest functioning children (those who were initially nonverbal and had IQs under 50). Lord and Schopler noted that no child with an initial IQ above 50 gained 20 IQ points or more. Overall, then, the intellectual functioning of most children at UCLA–NPI and TEACCH remained stable. This is in contrast to the intellectual functioning of children who received intensive behavioral treatment at UCLA Young Autism Project: Their functioning increased substantially.

TABLE 40.1
IQ Scores of Children Undergoing Various Treatments

Treatment	IQ at Age 2–3	IQ at Age 7
Intensive treatment (UCLA YAP)	63	83
Minimal treatment (UCLA YAP)	57	52
UCLA–NPI (Freeman et al., 1985)	59	58
TEACCH (Lord & Schopler, 1989)	57	64

G. Do Alternate Forms of Treatment Provide Comparable Outcomes?

A prepublication paper presented by Dawson and Osterling at a teleconference to medical personnel in the Northwest and at a conference in Chapel Hill was brought to our attention by parents who questioned the correctness of the data reported. We wrote Dawson on March 19, 1996, to inform her of mistakes in her reporting of the outcome data from the UCLA Project, Project TEACCH, and the Colorado Health Sciences Center. Dawson had reported that 3- and 4-year-old children in the TEACCH program gained an average of 15 to 24 IQ points. We indicated to her that this statistic applied to only 44 of the 142 children in the study (those who attained IQs under 50 and were classified as nonverbal at intake) and was not representative of the sample as a whole. The remaining 98 children showed IQ changes of 0 to −4, and, collectively, the 142 children in the study averaged an IQ change of +5. In a letter dated April 19, 1996, Dawson informed us that she had corrected these errors and promised to send us the final version of her chapter when it became available. However, she continued to describe the TEACCH data as indicating that children typically made large improvements. Because this is not what the TEACCH data show, we wrote to her on May 21, 1996, to request a clarification. We received neither a reply nor the promised final version. However, we did see a preprint of the chapter. In it, Dawson corrected her description of the UCLA data for the most part, though she continued to omit the McEachin, et al., (1993) follow-up data and did not report accurately on the number of intensively treated children with normal IQs, giving us credit for one more child with average IQ at follow-up than we actually reported. Unfortunately, the description of the TEACCH data, while different from the earlier draft, continued to show inaccuracies. To their credit, Lord and Schopler (1989) did not hide the absence of changes in test scores in their original report (e.g., their title refers to the stability of these scores).

Dawson and Osterling also reported on the claim by Rogers and colleagues from the Colorado Health Sciences Center that children in that program made significant increases in their cognitive, language, and other skills. Instead of reporting IQ scores, Rogers and colleagues reported children's developmental ages at follow-up, as well as the developmental ages they would have been expected to have without treatment. However, when data pertaining to cognitive skills are converted to ratio IQ scores, the gains do not support significant increases but rather appear quite small, ranging from 3 to 9 points for the 10 reported pre- and posttreatment comparisons. These increases are apparently lower for the two unreported comparisons. Thus, substantial inaccuracies pervade Dawson and Osterling's review.

Essentials of Dawson and Osterling's paper were subsequently published in the 1996 NIH State-of-the-Science in Autism Conference (Alexander, Cowdry, Hall, & Snow, 1996). The paper was also published in a comprehensive volume on early intervention (Dawson & Osterling, 1996). The widely circulated misleading information in the Dawson and Osterling article risks having an adverse effect on professionals and parents seeking adequate and truthful information to help guide them in their search for effective treatments. For example, Gerald Mesibov cited Dawson and Osterling's data in a fair hearing to argue against parents' requests to use the UCLA program to help their young autistic child (*Sherman v. Pitt County*).

H. Do the Best-Outcome Subjects Show Residual Signs of Autism?

A total of 10 out of the 19 subjects in the experimental group of the Lovaas (1987) study showed obvious signs of autism and mental retardation in the McEachin et al. (1993) follow-up. Some investigators have expressed concern that the 9 best-outcome subjects in the experimental group may evidence residual signs of autism that escaped observation in our previous follow-ups (e.g., Mundy, 1993). (See also Lovaas, 1987, who wrote that "certain residual deficits may remain in the normal functioning group . . . [Answers] will soon be forthcoming in a more comprehensive follow-up.") As described earlier, the McEachin et al. (1993) follow-up study used comprehensive assessment batteries that allowed for multiple opportunities to detect signs of autism. In addition, these batteries were administered by examiners blind to the purpose of the assessment. However, subtle signs of autism may still have escaped attention (or may have become more obvious as subjects grew older). Also, many assessment instruments designed to test for residual signs of autism were not available when NIMH approved funding for the McEachin et al. (1993) study (MH 11440-15, "Experimental Studies in Child Schizophrenia"). The more recently awarded grant (1 R01 MH51156-01A1, "Long-Term Outcome of Early Intervention for Autism") is specifically designed to detect residual signs of autism in the best-outcome group. The assessments involved were referred to previously in Section D.

I. Have the Outcome Data Been Distorted?

1. In addressing the Young Autism Project at an autism conference (Autismus Heute) in Hamburg, Germany, in 1988 attended by more than 1,000 parents and professionals from throughout the world, Edward Ritvo stated that the results of the Lovaas (1987) study were "totally not true," and added, "I regret that a lot of that stuff comes out under the label of UCLA and it is unfortunately disseminated widely and untrue." Ritvo withdrew these remarks, however, when confronted with a UCLA inquiry. Neither Ritvo nor his colleague B. J. Freeman have examined the best-outcome children in the Lovaas (1987) study.

2. The accusations are sometimes directed at others who voice support for the UCLA project. Christopher Gillberg, a well-known psychiatrist from Sweden, resigned from Bernard Rimland's journal (*International Autism Research Review*) after Rimland wrote a positive review of the UCLA program. Gillberg cited in his letter of resignation (October 20, 1987) that "I would not like to be associated with a publication pushing negative reinforcement therapies in autism" and "I certainly don't agree with his (Lovaas') conclusion that autism couldn't be a brain problem since it can be cured with behavior therapy." Note Gillberg's mistaken inference about our supposed use of the term "cure" (see paragraph 4 of this section). In addition, it is regrettable that our position on an organic etiology in autism was not familiar to Gillberg. We have argued that "Autism is almost certainly the result of deficits in . . . neurological structures" and that "intensive and early intervention could compensate for neurological anomalies in such [autistic] children" (McEachin et al., 1993, p. 371). Also note that Gillberg seems unclear on the meaning of negative reinforcement. Negative reinforcement is involved whenever a person (e.g., a parent) helps another person (e.g., a child) overcome stress and fear. Behaviors (e.g., the child going to a parent) are strengthened because an aversive event is removed. All of us use negative reinforcement in our interactions with others, including Gillberg. Hundreds of scientific studies exist on the properties of negative reinforcement. Presumably, what was upsetting Gillberg was not our use of negative reinforcement; what he meant to address was our use of contingent aversives. Our intent was to test the suppressing effect of aversives on severe self-injurious and other deviant behaviors that interfered with the children's opportunities to acquire more adaptive behaviors. Aversives seemed important at the time but became unnecessary because of the development of alternatives. We did not possess this information beforehand; if we had, there would have been no reason

to do the scientific research. The same consideration could (and should) be exercised with Gillberg's test of the drug Fenfluramine in his hope for therapeutic benefits through its administration (Ekman & Miranda-Linne, 1989). We now know that Fenfluramine, a derivative of Phen-Fen, can cause death. The drug has been taken off the market and parents of children who experienced damages can sue.

3. In a conference sponsored by the Bancroft Foundation (Haddonfield, NJ), Eric Schopler, who was then the director of a statewide service agency for children with autism (Project TEACCH) and the editor of the *Journal of Autism and Developmental Disorders*, remarked that he had serious reservations about the Lovaas (1987) study because Dr. R (the real name has been withheld), who was a former student of Lovaas, had sought grant funding and dispensed grant moneys in a fraudulent manner. Lovaas wrote Schopler that Dr. R had been an undergraduate student in his classes at UCLA, one of several thousands of such students over the last 30 years, and that Dr. R had worked much more closely with two colleagues of Schopler's than he had with Lovaas. Schopler did not respond to Lovaas's corrections.

4. An issue that surfaces periodically is the assertion that the UCLA project claims to "cure" autism. Gresham and MacMillan (1997a) report, "We argue in this article that the [UCLA project] is far from providing a cure for autism. With the exception of [studies from UCLA] *none* claim to have a cure [of] autism" (p. 198). They go on to cite Rutter (1996) to back up their accusation that the UCLA project claims a cure. Referring to the Lovaas (1987) and McEachin et al. (1993) studies, Rutter (1996) argues that one of the reasons for being cautious about the acceptance of the "strong claims" of these articles is based on "the claims of cure." Rutter argues that the claims of cure run "counter to both clinical experience and what might be expected on the basis of prevailing theories" (p. 270). *Answer*: The UCLA project has *never* claimed to cure autism. In fact, we have warned that "certain residual deficits may remain in the normal functioning group" (Lovaas, 1987, p. 8). The term *cure* implies removal of the original cause of the problem. Because the cause of autism is unknown, claiming a cure would certainly be unjustified and unethical. It is, however, possible to enable a child with autism to achieve normal functioning without finding a cure for autism, just as it is possible for a physician to help patients *recover* and achieve normal functioning without having found a cure for their illnesses. Hodgkin's disease is a case in point. It can only undermine parents' and professionals' confidence in the UCLA project to imply that we have made unethical claims.

The problem displayed in describing the outcome of the Lovaas (1987) study may stem in part from use of the term "recovered" in Table 3 on page 7 of the publication and the term "normal functioning" which was used and defined in the title of the study ("Behavioral Treatment and Normal Educational and Intellectual Functioning in Young Autistic Children"). We warned that "questions can be asked about whether the children truly recovered from autism" (p. 8) and added "certain residual deficits may remain in the normal functioning group that . . . can only be isolated on closer psychological assessment, particularly as these children grow older" (p. 8). Reference was made to McEachin's (1987) doctoral thesis, which formed the basis for McEachin et al.'s (1993) follow-up. Data from this follow-up were familiar to Lovaas at the time he submitted the 1987 report.

5. Gresham and MacMillan (1997a) liken the UCLA project to Hooked on Phonics which, as they point out, made false claims of treatment gains and was successfully sued by the Federal Trade Commission. They provide no basis for this thinly veiled accusation of fraud.

J. Are the Claims Made of Certain Treatment Aspects Ignored?

1. Some claim that children become dependent on the UCLA Young Autism Project and do not acquire concepts. Parents who have sought consultation about UCLA from TEACCH staff have been warned that "trying to meld the two programs [UCLA and TEACCH] may result in great confusion . . . and considerable anxiety . . . for the autistic child," and that the UCLA program "promotes dependence . . . focusing mainly on compliance training, and does not help the children to understand concepts" (Love & Mesibov, 1995). TEACCH further claims that "operant conditioning programs are very effective with mentally retarded persons, but such procedures are not as effective with autistic persons" (Mesibov, 1993). Greenspan (1992) presented "behavioral schools of thought" as an example of a "common unhelpful approach" that "ignores the delayed child's many needs" and would result in "disorder patterns to become stereotyped and more perseverative as [the children] grow" (p. 5).

There are no data to support these claims. In contrast, there is abundant evidence that behavioral treatment can help children with autism acquire complex behaviors such as language and social interaction (Schreibman, 1988). TEACCH apparently assumes that children diagnosed with autism suffer from a lifelong disability and, accordingly, has designed treatment programs that involve the students' enrollment in special education throughout their educational career. Outcome data from TEACCH are consistent with this pessimistic inference (Lord & Schopler, 1989). However, as mentioned earlier, McEachin et al.'s (1993) follow-up data show major and lasting improvements in the language, emotional, and social behavior of children diagnosed with autism when treated with intensive behavioral intervention.

2. Investigators from UCLA–NPI and TEACCH have suggested that, although intensive behavioral treatment may raise intellectual functioning, it does not foster independence. A direct comparison of independence as assessed by the *Vineland Adaptive Behavior Scales* (Sparrow, Balla & Cicchetti, 1984) exists and can be used to address this claim. The UCLA Young Autism Project data were collected on all intensively treated children at an average age of 13 years (McEachin et al. 1993). The UCLA–NPI data were collected on children originally seen at age 2 to 3 years when these children had reached an average age of 15 (Freeman et al., 1991). The TEACCH data were collected only on high functioning autistic children at an average age of 14 years (Venter, Lord, & Schopler, 1992). The means at UCLA Young Autism Project, UCLA–NPI, and TEACCH, expressed as standard scores, are shown in Table 40.2. As can be seen, intensively treated children from UCLA Young Autism Project appear to function substantially more independently in all areas when compared to children from UCLA–NPI or TEACCH. (Greenspan has yet to publish treatment outcome data in a peer-reviewed journal.)

TABLE 40.2
Mean *Vineland Adaptive Behavior Scale* Standard Scores from Three Programs

Vineland Scale	UCLA YAP	UCLA–NPI	TEACCH
Communication	75.1	56.6	47.6
Daily Living Skills	73.1	54.6	49.1
Socialization	75.5	51.6	38.1
Composite	71.6	50.3	41.6

3. Bristol et al. (1996) appear to make the same mistake as Gresham and MacMillan (1997a, see the following points) when they state that

> flexible behaviors over time are more meaningful than changes in measurements such as IQ. Assignment to regular classes as the criterion for successful outcome is often meaningless because it reflects local political and legal mandates more than individual child need or status. As in other domains of intervention research, studies are needed to determine the long-term effects of all interventions (particularly early intervention). (p. 148)

It is difficult to understand the purpose of making such statements when Bristol et al. were familiar with the McEachin et al. (1993) outcome data from the UCLA project.

4. Gresham and MacMillan (1997a) argue that the intensive treatment group and the control group differed in terms of the amount of attention they received, and that the children could have improved because of therapist characteristics such as warmth and encouragement. There are no data to support that attention and warmth by adults facilitate the improvement of children with autism.

5. Gresham and MacMillan (1997a) further state that the increase in IQ scores "was not due to cognitive gains, but rather due to changes in the child's ability to show what they already know" (p. 190). We know of no data-based research supporting this assertion, but we are familiar with many studies refuting it (reviewed by Rutter, 1983).

6. Gresham and MacMillan (1997a) also claim that "subjects were post-tested with different measures than they received at pretest, . . . thereby making the results of these different testings uninterpretable" (p. 189). Do Gresham and MacMillan suggest that one should give a 3-year-old the same tests as a 13-year-old? They refer to the Bristol et al. (1966) NIH criteria for treatment outcome research to discredit our research and add some concerns of their own as follows:

> a. "The UCLA project is based, in part, on principles of operant learning, however the primary teaching method relies on *discrete trial discrimination learning* and *compliance* with simple commands" (p. 6). *Answer*: Discrete trials and discrimination learning are not separate from operant learning but rather an integral part of such learning. Furthermore, compliance training was *not* a primary element in the UCLA treatment method. These misunderstandings on the part of Gresham and MacMillan reflect their lack of knowledge about the treatment employed.
>
> b. "We do, however, fault him [Lovaas] for failing to randomly assign subjects to treatments" (p. 11). *Answer*: An account of why we refrained from using a matched-pair random assignment was provided earlier (see Section B). Matched-pair random assignment is considered an ideal method for assignment, but with a small number of subjects (i.e., 19 in each group), such an assignment could yield an unequal distribution (Kazdin, 1980).

Evidence for random assignment in the UCLA project is based on similarity between Control Group I and the experimental group at intake (similar scores on 19 of 20 pretreatment variables). Nevertheless, it is possible that some variable not yet identified as predictive of outcome could have been unequally distributed between groups, a problem that all investigators face.

If the parents of a child with autism were informed that their child would be assigned to a control group in which they would receive no treatment, the parents would most likely not participate in the study. Anyone attempting to use matched-pair random assignment in a study of autism today would not be able to do so, including Gresham and MacMillan (when and if they decide to engage in treatment and treatment outcome research). Difficulties encountered by patients in accepting random assignment to either experimental treatment or standard procedures are problems in medical research as well. There are numerous alternatives, such as the use of wait-list controls, multiple-baseline designs, comparison groups, and so on.

c. "We do fault him [Lovaas] for failing to employ measures that tapped more discrete behaviors (more . . . than global IQ and educational placement)" (p. 11). *Answer:* Gresham and MacMillan were aware of the McEachin et al. (1993) follow-up, which assessed the subjects on many dimensions relevant to autism (see Section D). In addition, McEachin's doctoral thesis, which formed the basis for the 1993 publication, was referenced in the 1987 study. Why they chose to ignore data from these publications can perhaps only be answered by Gresham and MacMillan.

d. "Pretest scores" were "optimized" by "reinforcing compliant behavior during testing" and it was "not describe[d] how this compliant behavior was reinforced." By doing so they "violated standardized test administration procedures" (p. 8). *Answer:* We did describe the procedures used during pretesting, which were consistent with those developed by Freeman (1976). The intent of Freeman's procedures is to obtain a more valid assessment of the child's intellectual potential when noncompliance is reduced. In effect, we biased outcome against us by using Freeman's procedures; not using these procedures would likely have resulted in lower intake IQ scores and larger increases in IQ scores at follow-up.

e. "Social class of the children was not measured [which would] restrict the extent to which one can generalize findings" (p. 10). *Answer:* We did measure family characteristics ("number of siblings in the family [1.26 in each group], socioeconomic status of the father [Level 49 vs. Level 54 according to 1950 Bureau of the Census standards], boys to girls [16:3 vs. 11:8"]) (Lovaas, 1987, p. 6). See Section C for a more thorough description of family characteristics and the Lovaas (1987) study.

f. "Control 2 subjects were not treated by [the Young Autism Project] but were receiving some unspecified form of treatment" (p. 6). *Answer:* Control Group II subjects received services that are commonly available to children with autism in the community: special education and speech therapy. The poor outcome in this group is consistent with outcome data from other investigations of such services.

g. "Smith and Lovaas are unwilling to concede any limitations on which the effectiveness of [the Young Autism Project] resides . . . What explains this apparent refusal to admit to a single limitation in these investigations?" (p. 10). *Answer:* We have identified limitations and cautions both in regard to outcome data and treatment integrity. In the Lovaas (1987) report, we warn that "a number of measurement problems remain to be solved" (p. 8) and illustrate this by describing difficulty in measuring play behavior, communicative play, and IQ scores. We also warn that "the term normal functioning raises questions about whether these children truly recovered from autism" (p. 8). In addition, caution is expressed about therapist requirements ("extensive theoretical and supervised practical experience in one-on-one behavioral treatment"; p. 8). We further wrote that "Many treatment variables are left unexplored, such as effect of normal peers" (p. 8). Mention is made of the limitations "on generalization of our data to older autistic children" (p. 8). McEachin et al. (1993) repeat the need for replication: "The most important void for research to fill at this time is replication by independent investigators" (p. 370). This study also repeats the extensive training requirements for therapists. We then go on to describe another void, namely the need to serve the children who did not achieve normal functioning, suggesting that "perhaps such children require new and different interventions that have yet to be discovered" (p. 370). Does this sound like a "refusal to admit to a single limitation" as Gresham and MacMillan have expressed?

h. Greshman and MacMillan cite Schopler et al. (1989) to the effect that our subjects were "clearly not representative of all children with autism" (p. 9). *Answer:* In Section A we provide data indicating how data from Schopler et al.'s (1989) sample were misleading and not representative. We also present data (on diagnosis, child characteristics, etc.) that support our claim that the samples used in the Lovaas (1987) study were in fact representative of children with autism. Gresham and MacMillan fail to indicate the inclusion of Control Group II, which helped ensure representativeness of the Lovaas (1987) sample. Instead, Gresham and MacMillan (1997a) state "it is unclear why this group was included in the design other than because it represented a conveniently available, patched up control group" (p. 187). It is explicitly described in our study that Control Group II helped to guarantee that "the referral process did not favor the project cases." This lack of favoritism was ensured because there were no significant differences between Control Group I and II at intake or follow-up, even though Control Group II subjects were referred to others by the same agency. Furthermore, "the poor outcome in the similarly constituted Control Group I and Control Group II would seem to eliminate spontaneous recovery as a contributing factor to the favorable outcome in the experimental group" (p. 8). Gresham and MacMillan refer to both studies. Why they have chosen to ignore these data can perhaps best be answered by them.

Although it may seem reasonable to specify whether the samples are representative of other clients diagnosed with autism, the value of such an undertaking depends on the usefulness of the diagnosis of autism in research and treatment. There seems to be some consensus building that there are many causes of autism; hence there are likely to be many and different *kinds* of autism, requiring different kinds of treatment and preventive measures. This is analogous to what is happening in cancer research where many types of cancers have been identified with different causes, requiring different treatments and yielding different outcomes. In treatment–research, the definition of different kinds of autism can best be determined by identification of different causes and treatment outcomes based on a functional analysis rather than the traditional identification based on commonality in the appearance of behavioral topographies. This also holds not only for the behavioral grouping termed autism, but also for the separate behaviors involved in that grouping. For example, self-injurious behaviors enjoy three different kinds of determinants: positive, negative, and sensory reinforcement. These determinants vary across clients. The treatment for each is different so that a particular kind of treatment (e.g., contingent social isolation) will decrease one kind of self-injury, increase another, and leave a third kind unaltered. What is required for the effective treatment of self-injurious behaviors is a functional analysis (a cause–effect analysis) of the particular kind of self-injurious behavior confronting the practitioner.

Kanner's (1943) diagnosis of children with autism is based on behaviors of similar physical appearances. Behaviors such as mutism, echolalia, social isolation, emotional aloofness, rituals, self-injury, low scores on IQ tests, and so on, may look similar to the observer. However, as stated previously, similar looking behaviors may have different causes and therefore may not belong together; that is, they may not respond in a similar way to the same intervention. What is often forgotten in traditional autism research is that the diagnosis of autism is a *hypothesis;* the diagnosis is based on the guess that there exists an underlying organizing force tying the behaviors ("symptoms") together. Kanner's diagnosis has shown itself to be a poor hypothesis given that, in the decades since Kanner proposed the diagnosis, no cause or treatment for autism has been found. The most effective treatment addresses the problems of these children on a behavior-by-behavior basis, and there is little evidence of generalization of treatment effects across behaviors. Although searching for the cause of and treatment for autism may seem like a noble effort, Kanner's hypothesis may well be misleading and delaying the discovery of effective treatments for the children affected. The sooner the hypothesis is rejected, the more productive our search for causes and treatments may be. See Hacking's (1999, pp. 112–115) description of autism and schizophrenia as "social constructions" and problems associated with large-scale public acceptance of such constructs.

i. The "precious economic resources for education" (p. 12) are cited as a reason to be concerned about the cost of treatment: "The added benefit of the Lovaas program, given the high cost, should be examined" (p. 12). *Answer*: An approximation of the substantial savings involved in implementing behavioral treatment is provided in Section K of this discussion.

Unfortunately, the battle over trying to obtain treatment funding for children with autism often causes the expenditure of a great deal of money. In *D. B. v. Greenwich*, Frank Gresham testified for 1 day as an expert witness to defend the Greenwich, Connecticut, school district's "10 hour-per-week" ABA program. Ultimately, Gresham admitted under oath that the district's presentation of ABA programs took place with only one quarter the frequency that Gresham considered to be appropriate.

In California, Gresham testified on behalf of another district in an effort to defeat the parents of a child seeking reimbursement for a 40-hour-per-week treatment program. The district lost, and the hearing officer held that a 40-hour-per-week ABA program was precisely what the child needed. To date, Gresham has testified only on behalf of school districts and apparently has never been involved with any district that has prevailed. Expert witnesses such as Gresham are able to charge large fees for their services.

j. We are in full agreement with Gresham and MacMillan's concerns about families receiving services from therapists who have received less than optimal training and little supervision in delivering early and intensive behavioral intervention. Earlier in this chapter (see Section E), we described the training requirements for sites involved in the replication project. We are very concerned that some providers present themselves as competent at providing the UCLA treatment model, often citing the UCLA follow-up studies as support for their treatments. Except for staff at the replication sites, we know of no providers who are recently trained in the UCLA model and receive updated UCLA treatment information. Without regular and frequent updates, treatment quality is likely to suffer (Wolf, Kirigin, Fixsen, Blase, & Braukman, 1995). Also, few, if any, providers supply clinic-based treatment as done in the Lovaas (1987) report, but rather rely on workshop-based treatments in which the family hires staff to be trained in 1 to 3 days of workshops, with supervision 1 to 3 months apart. Hardly any providers supply their own outcome data. We estimate that valid outcome data documenting normal functioning from such services, if completed and made available, would be less than 10%. This does not, however, imply that the children provided with such services will fail to make improvements. Behavioral interventions (e.g., Applied Behavior Analysis) are based on thousands of scientific papers in the field of Learning and Behavior reported in peer-reviewed journals over the last hundred years. There are ample data supporting the effectiveness of behavioral treatments in addressing self-help skills, reduction in self-injury, community functioning, peer play, school adjustment, language development, and so forth, all of which should help the child become both more competent and self-sufficient. The problem is that, for children who fail to reach normal functioning and fail to become integrated and learn from typical peers, services need to continue (e.g., through parents' efforts). If services are not continued, the client will regress, showing little if any benefit from earlier treatment (as was demonstrated by Lovaas, Koegel, Simmons, & Long, 1973).

Another serious concern involves efforts (some of which are supported by federal grants) to compare the UCLA Young Autism Project against alternate forms of treatment, using staff who have not been trained in UCLA procedures and treatment methods that are not controlled for quality. There are many issues related to this concern. One important issue is centered on the failure of alternate treatments to document effectiveness on normed tests in peer-reviewed journals. This includes services such as special education, speech therapy, Sensory Integration, Floor-Time, Options, Holding Therapy, and Gentle Teaching. Parents often win support in fair hearings not because behavioral treatment rectifies all or most problems, but rather because behavioral treatment can demonstrate, in an objective data based manner, that children make improvements through this treatment when other services fail to demonstrate such success. The law is rational; it is data-based. One fortunate consequence of fair hearings is that they may stimulate research in treatment for children with autism and report what treatments and treatment combinations are effective. If treatments are shown not to be effective, the treatment should not be offered or warnings about potential ineffectiveness or harm should be made widely available (as is required in medicine). If this does not occur, parents will continue to be misled.

A major step ahead would be for the field of special education to take advantage of what is known about behavioral treatment. Behaviorists deliver a form of special education, the earliest efforts represented in the work of Itard (1962) some 200 years ago. Itard, considered the father of special education, gave impetus to the work of persons such as Montessori, Sullivan, Kephart, and Fernald. Anyone who reads Itard's descriptions of his treatments will recognize their similarity to behavioral intervention. Unfortunately, Itard's treatments did not survive (except, perhaps, in the case of sensory integration) because Itard did not know how to objectively document treatment outcome. We should not allow the same mistake to occur again.

K. Is the Treatment Cost-Effective?

The price of treatment is often mentioned as a reason for not funding 40 hours per week of one-on-one intervention. The cost is estimated at $60,000 per year, or $120,000 for the average of 2 years required for the child to reach normal functioning, at which point the best-outcome children no longer require special services. This is in contrast to the cost of more than $2 million for lifelong protective care. Seventy-seven percent of the children in the UCLA–NPI study were inpatients at the UCLA neuropsychiatric hospital. The average stay at UCLA–NPI was about a month, and the cost of the stay was approximately $1,000 per day. The children in the UCLA–NPI study then attended special education classes, which have yet to document their effectiveness. The children are expected to need lifelong protective care. At TEACCH, the costs per year are lower (estimated by Lord and Schopler in a 1994 article as $1,200 per year). However, the children continued to be enrolled at the completion of TEACCH's study, and the expectation seems to be that they will be enrolled throughout their lives. For a more detailed analysis of the cost-effectiveness of behavioral intervention, see Jacobson, Mulick, and Green (1998).

L. Are Parents Satisfied with Intensive Behavioral Treatment?

The UCLA Young Autism Project has been accused of being stressful for parents. Our data show otherwise. On a 7-point rating scale (7 being *completely satisfied*), the UCLA project received a mean rating from parents of 6.9 for clients served since 1991. A different survey illustrates data from 140 parents who rated UCLA workshops on a 5-point scale across six dimensions (e.g., "Was therapist polite and sensitive to parent's needs?" "Would you recommend a similar workshop to others?"). Ratings from this survey range from 4.5 to 4.9 (4.5 on the question "How effectively do you think you can now implement behavioral techniques?").

M. Does the UCLA Project Focus on Stimulus Control and Functional Analysis?

A recent grant funded by the Office of Education for the amount of $750,000 to Heartland Area Education Agency (AEA) of Iowa is titled "Development, Testing, and Dissemination of Nonaversive Techniques for Working with Children with Autism: Demonstration of a 'Best Practices' Model for Parents and Teachers." This project is intended to improve upon the UCLA project. The grant proposal, however, is replete with errors similar to those already described in this discussion, and it has serious methodological problems (see Smith & Lovaas, 1997). What is new is the assertion that the UCLA project does not focus on stimulus control and functional analysis of behaviors. In reality, the UCLA project pioneered work in these areas (e.g., Lovaas, Freitag, Gold, & Kassorla, 1965b) and has continuously presented additional empirical data published in peer-reviewed and readily available journals for the last 30 years.

The grant notes that the UCLA project uses "consequent-based techniques" and "ignores the behavior management literature that emphasizes control of antecedents." The misleading nature of these statements can be seen in the many studies from the UCLA project in which discrete trials and so-called consequent techniques are used to enhance verbal and nonverbal imitation (Lovaas, Berberich, Perloff, & Schaeffer, 1966). The child's acquisition of imitation, a product of discrete trial teaching techniques, allows adults and typical children to model behaviors for the child with autism. A model for a behavior is one kind of antecedent stimulus. Another example is conversation, which clearly involves antecedent stimuli (responding appropriately to statements made by others and varying responses depending on these statements). Antecedent stimuli are always present in discrimination learning, which is the major learning-based intervention underlying the UCLA programs. Reinforcement withdrawal instigates frustration, which is a major antecedent of tantrums and self-injury, and has been the subject of research by the UCLA project for a number of years, starting with Lovaas et al. (1965a). Thus, we have devoted extensive research to antecedent stimuli. In order for the child to learn discriminations, however, consequent techniques (reinforcement for correct responses, no reinforcement for incorrect responses) must be used. Without such techniques, children have no way of knowing what skills they are supposed to acquire, and no incentive to find out. It is dismaying that the grant fails to recognize this, yet intends to embark on a project that includes the employment of consequent (i.e., reinforcement) techniques.

It is also stated in the grant that the UCLA project relies "heavily on aversives and negative reinforcement." The combination of concepts such as aversives and negative reinforcement in this sentence is unfortunate. First of all, the UCLA project has not used aversives for years. Second, all therapists, teachers, and parents use negative reinforcement when they reduce a child's stress or discomfort contingent on the child's behaviors. The behavior is reinforced (strengthened) when it results in the removal of an aversive event.

In sum, it is of considerable concern that federal funds are being used to support research projects based on distortions of the UCLA project.

N. Do Discrete Trial Procedures Result in Limited Generalization?

Misleading statements about the use of operant, discrete trials are common. For example, Mesibov (1997) states, "the children following these techniques have been unable to generalize what they have learned" (p. 27), in contrast to the TEACCH curriculum, which facilitates communication "in many situations." On the basis of information reviewed earlier in this discussion (see the *Vineland Adaptive Behavior Scales* data) and Mesibov's familiarity with the McEachin et al. (1993) follow-up study, it appears that Mesibov is providing misleading information to parents and colleagues.

O. Quality Control in Treatment

An article by Sheinkopf and Siegel (1998) introduces a number of misunderstandings about what constitutes replication of the Lovaas (1987) study. The 1987 study was based on clinic-supervised treatment, not on workshop-based consultation services which comprise the focus of the Sheinkopf and Siegel article. Both clinic-based and workshop-based services take place in the home, the difference being the amount of supervision and the quality of staff training. This difference is substantial, and there are no data to suggest that the treatment outcomes would be similar. To illustrate, clinic-based services allow for daily supervision of treatment by senior staff. Through the clinic, only individuals who have shown superior performance in academic and practicum forums and work experience on the project for 6 months to several years are considered for employment. The intensity of the supervision and demands for quality control on treatment have limited the maximum number of clients to 15 per site at any one time. We have warned that "it is unlikely that a therapist or investigator could replicate our treatment program for the experimental [intensive treatment] group without prior extensive theoretical and supervised practical experience in one-to-one behavioral treatment" (Lovaas, 1987, p. 8). Given these considerations, various statements in the Sheinkopf and Siegel article can be dealt with as follows:

1. "Parents reported that their children had received treatment based explicitly on the methods outlined by Lovaas and colleagues" (Sheinkopf & Siegel, 1998 [p. 16], referring to Lovaas, 1981). *Correction:* Reading the teaching manual (Lovaas, 1981), attending a workshop led by UCLA-certified consultants, practicing behavioral treatment on several families, or spending a short time at a UCLA-affiliated site does not make a person qualified to provide UCLA-based treatment. Even professional behavioral analysts who failed to complete an internship at a UCLA-affiliated replication site would not, in our judgment, have appropriate experience to replicate the UCLA program. In the same context, Sheinkopf and Siegel claim that they "were unable to directly observe therapy and as such account for treatment fidelity" (p. 18). It is highly unlikely that either the parents referred to in the Sheinkopf and Siegel study or Sheinkopf and Siegel themselves would be able to ascertain whether children received the UCLA-based treatment because neither group was trained in this treatment.

2. The parents received services from "three behavior therapists in the San Francisco Bay area for guidance in treatment implementation" (p. 18). *Correction:* As far as we can determine, none of the therapists who treated the children mentioned in the Sheinkopf and Siegel article were trained at UCLA, with the possible exception of one who served as a senior therapist on the UCLA program some 15 or more years previous to their article. We find it quite unlikely that this individual would be able to serve competently as a consultant to families in home-based programs. Senior therapists, when they are working with us, are not permitted to conduct workshops, and we recommend to them that they not do so in the future. Several senior therapists have become workshop consultants and have opened clinics on their own despite our recommendation, and this is a source of great concern to us if they claim to provide services based on the UCLA model. Data show that, without updates and regular refresher courses, service providers fail to maintain quality control standards for treatment (Wolf et al., 1995). We expect a less than 10% rate of normal functioning as a result of children receiving workshops of an unspecified nature from such consultants.

3. "It is possible that Lovaas overestimated the minimum number of treatment hours per week needed for therapeutic effect" (p. 21). *Correction:* There are no data to support that an intervention of less than 40 hours per week will result in a 47% rate of normal functioning. If we had evidence that 30 hours or less per week could generate the same outcome, we would be able to serve many more children, a goal of any treatment agency. Furthermore, given the unknown nature of the treatment provided in Sheinkopf and Siegel's article, we are in no position to argue that more or less of that form of treatment would make a difference. Finally, Pomeranz (1998) questions Sheinkopf and Siegel's assertion that children who

received 20 hours per week of treatment gained as much as those who received 30 hours per week. Pomeranz comments that the children who received 20 hours per week received many more months of treatment. It is a major mistake to delete such information. It is also a mistake not to include the children's treatment history (i.e., the treatment the children received prior to the treatment referenced in Sheinkopf and Siegel's study).

When the children in Sheinkopf and Siegel's study are assessed as teenagers, outcome data will in all likelihood show that the children did not maintain their treatment gains and regressed unless workshop services were continued. One can protect children from regressing by helping them develop friendships with typical children and by teaching them to play and talk with typical children, as well as learn in a typical classroom environment. It takes a great amount of skill and numerous hours of treatment to achieve this end, and we have no reason to believe that the workshop-based program by persons described in Sheinkopf and Siegel's article, who did not adhere to the UCLA program, had the ability to do so.

It is difficult to ascertain the full effect of Sheinkopf and Siegel's article on parents and service providers. It is worth noting that Schopler used the Sheinkopf and Siegel article to once more discredit the UCLA project (Schopler, 1998, pp. 3–4).

P. Additional Misunderstandings

1. With the opening of a UCLA replication site (UK Young Autism Project) in London, we are witnessing a flurry of misunderstandings about the UCLA project in newspapers and technical journals in Europe. One such publication by Patricia Howlin (1997) appeared in the prestigious and widely circulated journal *European Child and Adolescent Psychiatry*. The major errors in this article are as follows:

a. "The IQ of the control group children had risen by only 8 points (in the 1987 study)" (p. 60). *Correction:* Both control groups lost IQ points.

b. "McEachin, Smith, & Lovaas . . . reported on the same children" (p. 60). *Correction:* Control Group II children were not made available for assessment in that follow-up study.

c. There was a "lack of random assignment" (p. 61). *Correction:* Pretreatment assessment showed the groups to be equivalent at intake, which is a test of whether random assignment was used and successful.

d. Findings should be questioned because of "the variability of measures used . . . before and after treatment" (p. 61). *Correction:* Few would suggest that 3-year-olds should receive the same assessment as 13-year-olds.

e. There are questions about the "representativeness . . . of groups involved" (p. 61). *Correction:* Control Group II represents children from another agency; data show the children in the UCLA study to be comparable to those in Control Group I.

f. There was a "failure to use independent assessors in the evaluation" (p. 61). *Correction:* The McEachin et al. (1993) follow-up study describes the double-blind assessment involving independent assessors. Howlin should be familiar with this study because she referred to it in her 1997 article.

g. "By far the greatest controversy [involves] . . . the use of terms such as 'cure'" (p. 61). *Correction:* The term *cure* has never been used by the UCLA project. To state that we have claimed cures can only serve to undermine others' confidence in our research.

h. "There are no measures of social interaction, friendships, conceptual abilities, social communication, obsessional and ritualistic behaviors . . ." (p. 61). *Correction:* Howlin references the McEachin et al. (1993) follow-up study and in Table 4 (p. 67) of Howlin's article, the McEachin et al. (1993) study is described as reporting significant improvements in social functioning and decreases in maladaptive behaviors.

i. In Table 4, Howling states that the Rogers and DiLalla (1991) study demonstrated "significant changes in cognition" (p. 66). *Correction:* In fact, when the children's mental age scores are converted to IQ scores, the gain is between 3 and 9 points. This is not a significant gain (see Section G).

2. Following are comments on a circular written in 1995 by Steven R. Love, a clinical assistant professor and the clinical director of the Asheville TEACCH Center, and Gary B. Mesibov, a professor, the director of TEACCH, and the current editor of the *Journal of Autism and Developmental Disorders*. (For a reprint of the circular, please contact the Division of TEACCH Administration and Research, CB# 7180, 310 Medical School, Wing E, The University of North Carolina at Chapel Hill, Chapel Hill, NC 27599-7180.)

On September 5, 1995, Love and Mesibov distributed the circular, providing misleading information about the UCLA Young Autism Project. The September 5, 1995, document is one of several circulars, letters, and publications generated by TEACCH that repeats statements containing misleading information. Although UCLA staff members have brought this issue to the attention of Love and Mesibov, both continue to circulate misleading information. There is also evidence that such information was presented to parents who sought reimbursement (in court) for services from the UCLA Clinic. What follows are our corrections to the misleading information provided in the September 5, 1995, circular.

a. It is argued in the circular that instruction from TEACCH leads to "greater independence and adaptability" because it focuses on "meaningful routines and visual clarity to teach autistic people how to function without constant adult assistance." In contrast, the UCLA program uses "discrete trials" and, with its use of prompts, is "likely to set up dependence on the therapist and result in greater prompt dependence. Children with autism will be less likely to use their skills in vocational and residential programs." *Correction:* Mesibov and Love note that there is empirical evidence that behavioral treatment is effective. However, no such evidence exists for TEACCH. Both UCLA and TEACCH have published data from the same measure of independence, namely the *Vineland Adaptive Behavior Scales*. These data were reviewed earlier in this discussion (see Section J). Obviously, children from the UCLA treatment program perform better than those from TEACCH on well-normed measures of independent living.

b. In the circular, Love and Mesibov claim that "operant paradigms are typically more effective with persons with mental retardation than autistic people." They further argue that "many people with mental retardation show a greater responsiveness to social reinforcement and external motivation and their understanding of contingencies is often more highly developed than those of people with autism." *Correction:* We know of no empirical evidence to support these assumptions. The more we learn about children with autism, the more we become aware of the abundance of external reinforcers that can be used in treatment.

Love and Mesibov also argue that the UCLA project "may not focus as much on what children with autism personally find motivating and interesting." *Correction:* An enormous amount of effort is directed at identifying reinforcers effective for helping children develop motivation to learn. A great deal of emphasis is placed on individual differences as they relate to what a particular child finds reinforcing. Without effective reinforcers, no learning will occur. The UCLA project has amply demonstrated that children with autism can learn.

c. "Another difference between Lovaas and TEACCH is the use of negative consequences of punishment." *Correction:* The UCLA project no longer uses aversive interventions, and it has not done so for several years, relying instead on what has been published in the literature about building behaviors incompatible with self-injurious and self-stimulatory behaviors. TEACCH, on the other hand, endorses the use of aversive interventions if other interventions fail (Schopler, 1986). In fact, TEACCH has recommended the following intervention (Schopler, Lansing, & Waters, 1983): "Each time that Dave spits, put the edge of a washcloth that has been soaked in Tabasco sauce in his mouth for a moment" (p. 227). (Tabasco sauce can cause tissue damage.) Schopler (1994) has also endorsed the use of aversive therapy to help reduce severe self-injurious behavior. A Consensus Development Conference sponsored by the National Institutes of Health issued a preliminary report (NIH, 1990) recommending aversives or "behavior reduction procedures" for short-term use restricted by appropriate peer review and consent.

Love and Mesibov also argue that TEACCH "relies primarily on positive interactions between TEACCH and student." There is a wealth of positive interaction between teachers and students at the UCLA project as well. In addition, parents are involved in administrating treatment at the UCLA project. In contrast to what others have argued, we have not found parents of children with autism to be lacking in the love they show for their children.

d. "One claim from the UCLA project which Drs. Love and Mesibov find particularly troublesome is the suggestion that the intensive Lovaas intervention will lead to a cure (or normal behavioral and intellectual functioning) for almost one half of the children." *Correction:* The UCLA project has never claimed that it cures autism. However, there is ample objective and empirical evidence that almost one half of the intensively treated children obtain scores falling within the normal range of intellectual, social, emotional, educational, and self-help skills on standardized and well-normed psychological tests (McEachin et al., 1993).

e. "There is not good evidence . . . that progress from the UCLA (treatment) is any better than through other individualized, less demanding interventions emphasizing social and communication skills nor that long-term outcomes are any better." *Correction:* There is good evidence that young children who are subjected to the TEACCH program fail to improve on standardized psychological tests (Lord & Schopler, 1989). In contrast, there is an abundance of empirical evidence, published in the American Psychological Association's peer-reviewed journals, that intensive and early behavioral intervention is the treatment of choice for children with autism. Objective long-term outcomes from other treatment facilities (including TEACCH) are simply not available.

f. "The other troubling assumption that the Lovaas group promotes is that more is better." *Correction:* This is not an assumption and it should not be troubling given that there is abundant evidence that more is better. The circular continues: "Forty hours of intensive intervention a week makes it difficult for the parents to meet their child's needs to be a child. Young children with autism are still children and need time for structured play and other less demanding activities." *Correction:* There is no evidence that "structured play" and "less demanding activities" are helpful in improving the functioning of children with autism. No doubt parents of children with autism find time to engage their children in play and less demanding activities, yet their autistic children do not improve despite these efforts. In contrast, there is every reason to believe that, without early and intensive behavioral intervention, development of a child with autism will not be enhanced.

It is important to note that on November 29, 1993, Love circulated a letter to several parents of children with autism. This letter contained most of the same equivocal statements found in the September 5, 1995, circular. Lovaas sent his reply to the November 29, 1993, letter to Love on April 20, 1994. In this letter, Lovaas questioned the factual basis for each one of Love's misleading statements. In his reply to Lovaas on May 3, 1994, Love admitted that he may not have had up-to-date information about the UCLA program and that, in failing to do so, he may have based his statements on personal opinions that could be considered outdated. Love's May 3, 1994, letter left open the door for a dialogue between the UCLA and the TEACCH programs. Such a dialogue may have helped parents gain information from which they could make the most appropriate decisions for their children's future. In that regard it is regrettable that, subsequent to this exchange, in September of 1995, we have a restatement of the same misleading information to parents.

3. The circular titled "Early Intervention for Young Children with Autism and Their Families: Recommended Practices" distributed by the Pennsylvania Department of Education, Bureau of Special Education, Harrisburg, reads, "there is sufficient evidence at this point to suggest a number of guiding principles in the design of individual services for young children with autism and their families" (p. 1). It continues, "the organization and delivery of services to children and families with autism should be based on the most current and credible research. To do otherwise in a field undergoing such profound growth in knowledge generation is to risk denying access to appropriate services" (p. 1). The intent is to "share with parents, on a continuing basis and in a supporting manner, complete and unbiased information" (p.1), to "respect the family's right to accept or reject support and services" (p. 2), to apply "state-of-the-art early intervention and early childhood practices" (p. 2), and to "use evaluative data to improve programs and services outcomes" (p. 2).

The stated intent of the circular, to inform parents in an unbiased manner about what constitutes an adequate data base from which they may make decisions about their child's treatment, represents a major advance toward improving the future of children with autism. However, after having read the circular, we believe that parents and professionals alike are in fact being misinformed and misled. Following are certain major mistakes included in the circular.

It is noted in the circular that "in the largest study conducted to date on early intervention for children with autism, all fifty-one children studied were integrated successfully with typical classmates (Strain, 1994). Significantly, this same study demonstrates long-term outcomes that have not been surpassed by any other service-delivery model" (p. 3). *Correction:* We are respectful of Strain's work. On the other hand, as far as we know, the only study published by Strain pertaining to outcome and published in a peer-reviewed journal is the study by Strain, Hoyson, and Jamieson (1985). This study employed six subjects, reported no firm diagnosis of autism, and did not employ a control group that would allow for a comparison of outcome so as to assess the effectiveness of the treatment provided. With regard to the Strain (1994) reference, "successful mainstreaming" cannot be used as a significant outcome variable without also specifying the extent to which such mainstreaming was accompanied by increased intellectual, educational, adaptive, emotional, and self-help behaviors. This becomes particularly important when one considers the limited gains made by children with autism, as a group, when placed in the company of typical children. (This comment should not be used to encourage placement of children with autism into groups of other children with autism. It simply means that mere exposure to typical children is not sufficient for improving the functioning of children with autism.)

Turning now to the many other studies referred to in the circular in support of relaying unbiased information about appropriate treatment, we call attention to the following:

a. Several of the studies cited do not report socially and educationally meaningful outcome variables submitted to peer review.

b. Many of the reported studies of social skills deal with efforts to generalize skills rather than build new ones. Teaching other skills, such as language, is not described at all, even though language is very important in facilitating socialization.

c. No study advocates replacing discrete trial procedures. Although there have been some efforts to develop a more "natural" intervention, discrete trials remain the standard by which other procedures are judged. In fact, several of the reports make use of the Lovaas (1981) teaching manual or the Lovaas (1977) language book, both of which emphasize discrete trials.

d. It is argued that "for young children with autism we know of no experimental demonstration that has compared two or more levels of intervention intensity" (p. 5). The Lovaas (1987) study, however, which is so frequently cited in the circular, reported that two groups receiving different intensities of intervention were employed and demonstrated that a group that received 10 hours or less of one-on-one treatment did no better than a no-treatment control group.

e. The circular refers to "in-class services ranging from three to six hours, five days per week" as support for what is considered adequate and appropriate treatment (p. 5). We know of no data to support such an inference. Surprisingly, the same paragraph refers to the Lovaas (1987) study as supporting this claim. The Lovaas (1987) study does not support this claim, nor does the UCLA project.

f. In the circular it is stated that "within the range of intensity across effective models there is no evidence that more is better" (p. 6). We must again point out that no data support such a statement.

g. A statement is made that "the identification of children as having autism younger than thirty-six months is still relatively unusual" (p. 6). This statement cannot be supported by data. In fact, the diagnostic instrument that currently employs the best data base is labeled the Autism Diagnostic Interview Revised (ADI–R) by Lord, Rutter, & LeCouteur (1994), and it places the lower cutoff at 12 to 18 months for nonverbal MA. There are other tests also designed specifically for early identification of autism.

We could identify a number of other misleading statements in the circular, but we hope that the information presented is sufficient to allow for consideration of the withdrawal of this publication, and we strongly encourage that this course of action be taken.

Let us return to reemphasize the goal of the circular, namely providing adequate information to parents that would help them choose the most appropriate treatments based on empirical data to date. We strongly endorse such a position.

4. In the following comments regarding the "AUTCOM Memorandum" written in 1995 by the Autism National Committee (Ardmore, PA), the terms "behavioral treatment" and "one-on-one in-home treatment" will be substituted for the term "discrete trial training" (DTT). Discrete trials are used in behavioral treatment, but comprise only a portion of such treatment and are largely used during its beginning phases. Comments pertaining to the several points listed in the memorandum are clarified below in the order in which they appear in the memorandum.

a. It is argued in the memorandum that behavioral treatment teaches a child that she is "damaged goods"; consequently, the child develops a self-image that she is "not good enough." *Correction:* Behavioral approaches emphasize that children with autism have atypical nervous systems and therefore have failed to understand what well-meaning adults have tried to teach them. Such children enter teaching situations with expectations of failure. The treatment program is arranged, however, to maximize success and minimize failure so as to build the child's self-confidence and trust in adults (Lovaas & Smith, 1989). Behavioral psychologists express the most optimism that children with autism can form healthy self-images.

b. The memorandum notes that children need to participate in natural life; it is argued in the memorandum that behavioral treatment precludes this. *Correction:* Behavioral treatment makes every effort to help the child participate in the natural life of family and community and to develop friendships and other social relationships. However, placing the child in a "natural environment" without helping the child develop the skills needed to interact in that environment will in all probability set the child up for failure. There is every reason to believe that children with autism or developmental delays grow up in normal and typical family environments (in contrast to what psychodynamic theories have proposed) and yet fail to develop normally in those environments.

c. The memorandum claims that family members, especially siblings, will suffer when behavioral intervention is implemented. *Correction:* Data show that parents who participate in one-on-one, home-based behavioral intervention do not experience more stress than parents of children with autism who do not participate in such programs (Smith & Lovaas, 1993). There is no reason to believe that siblings of a child who undergoes treatment will fail to develop positive relationships with that child.

d. Child development experts such as Stan Greenspan are said in the memorandum to warn parents that behavioral treatment is likely to increase perseveration and rigidity. *Correction:* This warning has no basis in empirical data because outcome data show that children who receive behavioral treatment are less rigid than a comparable group of autistic children who do not receive such treatment (McEachin et al., 1993).

e. It is noted that Greenspan argues that behavioral programs emphasize simple learning tasks which appeal to the child's "splinter skills" and fail to teach more complex behaviors such as play and social interactions. *Correction:* Numerous studies show that behavioral treatment teaches not only flexible and abstract language but also peer play and toy play (Schreibman, 1988).

f. In the memorandum, it is said that behavioral treatment is used to extinguish echolalia. *Correction:* Behavioral therapists do not extinguish echolalia; they help clients transform echolalia into socially appropriate responding (Carr, Schreibman, & Lovaas, 1974). Data from behavioral treatment show that children who acquire verbal imitative behavior and echolalia during the beginning of treatment are likely to go on to achieve typical language skills (McEachin et al., 1993). In general, it is misleading to state that behavioral therapists extinguish self-stimulatory behavior. Little or no data exist that show that self-stimulatory behavior can be extinguished, but there are data to suggest that self-stimulatory behavior can be changed into socially appropriate forms of behavior through behavioral treatment (Epstein, Taubman, & Lovaas, 1985).

g. Behavioral treatment, it is claimed, does nothing to enhance the child's ability to cope with groups of persons. *Correction:* The one-on-one relationship with adult therapists is employed as a precursor to the development of relationships with other adults and peers. This is similar to what happens in normal development: The child first forms relationships with parents and then subsequently moves on to develop relationships with other adults and peers. Intensive behavioral treatment involves many persons, including parents, relatives, peers, and other persons in the community. A significant part of the UCLA program includes the child's gradual and systematic integration into group settings, such as classrooms and peer play.

h. It is asserted in the memorandum that untrained and minimally trained personnel can implement behavioral treatment. *Correction:* Nine months of apprenticeship training preceded by an academic background in learning processes is required to achieve basic mastery of delivering competent one-on-one behavioral treatment. It takes an additional 4 to 5 years of apprenticeship before a person is competent to direct and supervise such treatment.

It is also an insult to behavioral therapists to describe them as having a "lack of warmth and mutuality in their relationship to the child clients." Contrary to psychodynamic theory, there is no reason to believe that parents of the children, who come to function as therapists, lack warmth and compassion. The many individuals at UCLA and elsewhere who are in practicum courses or volunteer their services also give abundant evidence of warmth, care, and concern toward the children and the children's parents.

i. Although it is correctly stated in the memorandum that one-on-one behavioral treatment no longer uses aversives, it is incorrect and misleading to then go on and argue that "the escalation of therapy to the aversive levels" may now serve as a substitute for aversive procedures.

j. The memorandum notes that the promise of a "cure" for autism is an example of "expansive salesmanship." *Correction:* Behavioral therapists have not claimed that behavioral treatment is a cure for autism or other developmental delays. It is *not* incorrect to use the term "recovered" to describe the best-outcome subjects in the McEachin et al. (1993) study. In fact, behavioral treatment is the only form of treatment that is supported by a body of empirical evidence and that has been described as the treatment of choice for autism (DeMeyer, Hingtgen, & Jackson, 1981).

k. The memorandum asserts that "information about [behavioral treatment] is anecdotal in nature. It is normal and expected to see positive changes in any child's development over lengthy periods of time." *Correction:* Behavioral treatment is supported by a larger range of scientific findings than any other treatment available for children at this time (Schreibman, 1988). The use of control groups in the McEachin et al. (1993) study show that children who did not receive one-on-one treatment did not improve over time. Further, the outcome data reported by Lord and Schopler (1989) and by Freeman et al. (1985) show no improvement in the child's status from pre- to post-treatment assessment.

l. The memorandum affirms that the method of behavioral treatment is hardly new. *Correction:* One-on-one behavioral treatment is continuously evolving and new data-based programs are added at a rapid rate.

m. It is claimed in the memorandum that children with autism show improvements following speech therapy, language therapy, and other therapies. *Correction:* Data, or a lack thereof, show that speech and language therapy, Sensory Integration, special education, and other therapies have failed to demonstrate effectiveness (Smith, 1993).

n. In the memorandum, it is alleged that treatment takes place in a contrived environment. *Correction:* It can hardly be said that treatment conducted in the child's home, and later in preschool and kindergarten classes with typical children, is occurring in "contrived rather than natural" settings. Parents and other adults conduct treatment during the early months of the intervention, and the child is integrated into community settings, such as typical preschools with age-appropriate peers, within the first year of intervention. "An appreciation developed of how and why learning can and should take place in natural environments" was pioneered by behavioral psychologists, contrary to what was implied in the memorandum. For some early data on this development, see Lovaas, Koegel, et al. (1973).

Q. How Valid Are the Testimonies at Fair Hearings?

Many parents who have chosen the UCLA program for their children end up in fair hearings to determine whether educational and other state agencies will agree to pay for services. At such hearings, "expert witnesses" representing the state are called in to testify for or against the parents' requests. The number of misleading statements provided by these expert witnesses is large indeed. One case may be of particular interest, namely that of *Robert P. v. HISD* (1996) in Houston, Texas, in which B. J. Freeman provided testimony.

Freeman began her testimony by claiming that she was familiar with the UCLA project. If nothing else, she was a member of John McEachin's doctoral dissertation committee, and approved of the research that formed the basis for the McEachin et al. (1993) follow-up study. During her testimony, Freeman repeated most or all of the misinformation described earlier in this discussion. Specifically, she claimed that she was concerned about "subject selection bias," referring to Schopler, et al. (1989). She added that "measures of outcome were not adequate," stated that the UCLA project used "untrained graduate students" to examine symptoms of autism, and implied that the UCLA project failed "to follow those children beyond the first grade," withholding her knowledge of the findings of the McEachin et al. (1993) follow-up study. When asked if she personally evaluated subjects from the Lovaas (1987) study, she answered, "Yes, I have." She has *not* evaluated the best-outcome children, although she may have evaluated some of the other children. She also claimed that she had patients who did as well or better than the Lovaas (1987) children, even though her own outcome data (Freeman et al., 1985) demonstrate that the children showed no improvement, consistent with the Lord and Schopler (1989) data. IQ scores do not increase over time with higher functioning children with autism, as Freeman also claimed in her testimony, but in fact such children lose IQ points at follow-up, as is shown in her own data (Freeman et al., 1985). She further claimed that control group children were not matched in the UCLA project, when in fact they were. She stated that she considers it "absurd" that preschool activities are taught first in the home, and asserted that 40 hours per week of one-on-one treatment is "counterproductive for children with autism." She claimed that a few hours of one-on-one intervention and group instruction provide equally favorable results, but she has offered no data to support this assertion. She argued that discrete trial learning results in a "failure to generalize because it hasn't taught a concept." These statements are not only incorrect but also disturbing in view of her knowledge of the McEachin et al. (1993) follow-up.

Sadly, Robert P. was denied funding, and it is our opinion that the inaccuracies in Freeman's testimony contributed to this denial. Note that Freeman's distorted testimony is not unique in fair hearings.

Why All the Distortions?

The reader should not infer that the misunderstandings and distortions reviewed are unique to autism research. Kuhn (1970) provides numerous examples of how, in the physical sciences, scientists often suppress and distort new developments incompatible with "normal science" (i.e., traditional theory and research). He also alludes to the efforts of certain professional educators who attempt to suppress novel approaches as a way of maintaining traditional ones.

In the domain of autism, there is a dire need for treatment outcome research to help curtail the amount of misinformation circulated. Only through empirical and objective research will we identify which treatments are helpful and which ones are ineffective or harmful. No single investigator will finalize the search for the many causes of and treatments for autism. Instead of facilitating a constructive interaction among scientist–practitioners, the many misleading remarks reviewed in this discussion can best be described collectively as an obstruction to inquiry and discovery of effective interventions. The reader may question why the remarks reviewed in this discussion were made. This is difficult to answer, but it may be helpful to propose three possibilities.

First, it seems reasonable to consider that the remarks reflect the evaluators' failure to base their statements on accurate readings of method and data in published papers. Evaluating someone else's research requires training given that most research is complex and demands considerable skill. Most service providers are not trained as researchers; even if they were trained in research at one point, their research is likely not to continue once they enter the service field. The split between clinicians and researchers in the field of psychology is extensive. Education and psychodynamic psychiatry have traditionally not trained their professionals in research; rather, these fields focus on practice. The goal of graduating "scientist–practitioners" is fine in principle but difficult in practice because either field requires the full-time attention of the persons involved.

Second, because practitioners receive pay for their services, they are unlikely to provide data that show their services to be ineffective or harmful. After all, the treatment generates the practitioner's salary, which supports his or her family. Giving up such a practice may be asking too much and seeking a new educational background may be too difficult.

Third, many researchers appear to have narrowed their investigations to a particular theory and acquired the skills to test that theory. Any investigator is likely to become frustrated when confronted with data showing that the anticipated outcome based on one's theory is not realized. Not only does the recognition of treatment failure demand a search for a new approach, but the underlying theory must be rejected. If a theory can be rejected, then a theory can be improved and built upon, a crucial element of all good scientific theories. Freudian and many other theories forming the basis for current treatments in autism are not specified in such a manner as to be rejectable. This allows these treatments to persist even though they may be potentially harmful or at best ineffective. In the field of autism, it appears often to be the parents, rather than the professionals, who help terminate a theory and associated treatments.

Most behavioral psychologists offering treatment today are unlikely to devote a major effort to test a particular theory. Instead, it appears that research has become more data driven and inductive rather than theory driven (the mode of the past). The usefulness of such a shift in research strategy can be illustrated from work on the UCLA project, a project that has given rise to many failed expectations. One of our early outcome studies (Lovaas, Koegel, et al., 1973) illustrates this. When we started our treatment–research, we hoped to discover a pivotal response which, once ameliorated, would produce a beneficial effect on untreated behaviors. For example, psychologists have invested enormous energy in an attempt to facilitate language development in children who are autistic and developmentally delayed, and they have achieved considerable success in this regard. However, reports of generalization of gains from language to other untreated behaviors are still missing; we have yet to discover pivotal responses. We hoped for a transfer of treatment gains across environments, such as from the clinic or school to the child's home and community. Such a transfer did not take place. We entertained high hopes for major and lasting improvements after 40 hours a week of one-on-one treatment (2,000 hours in all). These hopes were not satisfied either. Instead, it was found that most behaviors have to be treated in all environments for most clients' lifetimes in order to avoid regression.

More recently, the failure to offer significant help to those 53% of children who did not reach normal functioning in the Lovaas (1987) study is of major concern. At the same time, it is these children who are the most challenging because we may have exhausted what we know from research in operant learning and need to investigate other forms of learning. We sometimes fail to establish secondary (learned) reinforcers (e.g., when a therapist pairs, over numerous trials, the word "good" and a smile with the delivery of food) (Lovaas, Freitag, et al., 1966). Yet this form of learning (Pavlovian conditioning) is probably a significant basis for child–parent attachment in infancy and early childhood, when signs of autism are said to be detected.

Other leads prompting a shift in strategy come from data showing children diagnosed with autism as forming two relatively distinct groups when exposed to early and intensive behavioral treatment. One group (auditory learners) acquires vocal language (a factor that helps predict best outcome). The remaining children experience significant problems in the vocal language programs. We are currently testing the effectiveness of teaching such children (visual learners) to read and write since they appear to make progress when taught in this modality (Watthen-Lovaas & Lovaas, 2000).

In coming years, we hope to facilitate research that contrasts the brain–behavior relationships of clients who have recovered versus those who have not recovered. We propose to do this through the use of functional magnetic resonance imaging and evoked response potential technology by looking at brain-related patterns that accompany vocal language tasks. Our failure to teach vocal imitation to a subgroup of children is a strong predictor of limited progress in treatment (as it is currently devised) for children in that subgroup. This same subgroup, however, shows the ability to learn to match *visual* stimuli and imitate nonvocal behaviors, such as the gestures and movements of others. It will be an exciting new dimension in learning-based treatments to collaborate with scientifically minded colleagues in neuroscience.

A Case for Optimism

After reading the many distortions and their respective corrections reviewed in this chapter, one can take some confidence in the fact that both the Lovaas (1987) and McEachin et al. (1993) studies were published as lead articles in American Psychological Association journals with rigorous peer review and the highest rejection rates. Furthermore, all research has been funded by NIMH, which also employs a thorough review of research design before allocating funding. As mentioned, the NIMH grant (1 R01 MH51156-01A1, "Long-Term Outcome of Early Intervention for Autism") received a priority score of 100, the highest score NIH offers. See also the Surgeon General's favorable review of the UCLA project (U.S. Department of Health and Human Services, 1999).

In trying to account for and contextualize the misleading information reviewed in this discussion, it may help to remember that, not long ago, children with developmental delays were placed in large institutions, such as state hospitals, in isolation from their families. Persons in charge of the state hospital structure did not have to provide follow-up data. It was an authoritarian system with little or no accountability except for client physical safety and medical health. Few questions were asked, and few were invited. The passing of the Education for All Handicapped Children Act of 1975 helped bring children with developmental delays back into the community to be served by special education and other community-based services. The work of Schopler and staff at TEACCH represents a major step in this direction.

It was not long ago that parents had little or no say in their child's treatment. Now parents have much more control, living with or near their children and assuming responsibility for their treatment and, reasonably enough, demanding accountability and better services now that they can better assess what is happening to their children. The burden on special education to improve services is particularly heavy. For such services to better themselves, it will be necessary to experiment and test new and different ways of teaching; classroom-based instruction may not provide the proper setting for most children with developmental delays. It is likely that progress will be slow and stepwise, requiring the efforts of persons across many disciplines working together in collaboration rather than confrontation.

The young teachers and clinicians who are needed to help to improve the lives of children with developmental delays should not be discouraged by the lag in discovering and implementing effective treatment programs. In all likelihood, the difficulties will be cancelled out by the rewards that emerge from the discoveries and implementation of treatment techniques that help children face a better future. These rewards are large indeed, even when the steps forward are small.

A Typical Day

APPENDIX A

A typical session may run as follows: The student enters the treatment room (e.g., bedroom or playroom), which is set up with "play areas" to occupy the student's free time between programs. In the session, a beginning student will alternate between working directly with the teacher for a few minutes and engaging in free-time activities for a few minutes. Because free time is likely to be reinforcing (both for escaping the teacher's demands and playing with favorite objects), the teacher should provide free time contingent on appropriate behavior and not on tantrums. A student who has been in the program for several weeks should be involved in working directly with the teacher for approximately 75% of the session (with the remaining 25% of the time being designated as free time). In addition, a student who has been in treatment for a number of weeks should receive between 35 and 40 hours of intervention each week. These hours are usually organized in the form of two 3-hour sessions per day: a morning session (e.g., 9:00 A.M. to 12:00 P.M.) and an afternoon session (e.g., 1:00 or 2:00 P.M. to 4:00 or 5:00 P.M.).

During free time, the student is usually allowed to choose a play activity in which to engage. If the student is unable to structure time appropriately (e.g., engages in self-stimulatory behavior or perseverates on specific activities), the teacher should assist the student in structuring the free time such that the student is always appropriately engaged. Free time can also be used as a tool to generalize mastered skills (especially play skills) or simply be spent as time engaging in activities pleasurable for the student. When the student is able to play appropriately without the teacher's direct assistance, the teacher can use this time to record data or plan for the next program.

The student should alternate between working with the teacher and engaging in free time activities for approximately 1 hour. After this time, the student should receive a longer break of 5 to 10 minutes outside of the treatment room. The student and teacher can play in other rooms, play in the yard, or go on a walk. Like free time, break time is meant primarily as a recess, although the student should always be engaged in appropriate behavior. Break time should occur approximately once every hour each session.

When the morning session is complete, the student may have 1 or 2 hours in which to eat lunch, play, or visit with family members until the teacher arrives for the afternoon session. The afternoon session is performed in the same manner as the morning session. After the afternoon session concludes, the student has the remainder of the day in which to eat, play, and spend time with family. It is recommended that the family direct the student, when necessary, so that the student does not engage in inappropriate behaviors during the time in which the student is not in treatment.

For a student just beginning intensive behavioral intervention, the total weekly hours may initially number approximately 20 to 25. The weekly hours should gradually extend so that within a few weeks into treatment, the student receives between 35 and 40 hours of intervention per week. In addition to a decreased number of total hours, it is sometimes preferable to begin with an altered ratio of programs to free time when initially exposing the student to intensive intervention. That is, although the end goal is for approximately 75% of the session to be time spent in programs, this percentage can initially be reduced so that the student is working directly with the teacher for only 50% of the time (with the other 50% consisting of play). Increasing amounts of structure should be introduced so that, within a few weeks, the session follows the typical format. If the student is under the age of 3, a reduced number of hours and a reduced ratio of programs to free time may be continued for an extended period of time.

As a student progresses through treatment, two variations may occur in the structure of therapy sessions. As the student ages and gains the skills to function in group situations, the student may begin to attend school or other group programs. These programs typically begin as a small portion of the overall treatment time and may gradually increase as the benefits of group exposure increase. The student may initially attend a classroom twice a week for approximately 1 hour a day. This hour is usually integrated into the student's morning session for these days. The student's day would therefore be altered so that, in the morning, he or she would have a mixture of school time and one-on-one intervention.

As the student gains skills, the team may also choose to work in the community for generalization purposes. This often takes the form of a Trips Program in which the team works on generalizing mastered skills, increasing language and social skills, teaching community behavior, and possibly the memory of location and events. This would be incorporated into sessions so that 20 to 30 minutes of each daily session may consist of community trips.

Program Timeline

APPENDIX B

The Program Timeline assists the reader in determining when to introduce the programs detailed in this manual. The number of the month directly under a given program name in the figure represents the time at which that program would be introduced to the "average" student. The arrow after a given program in the figure indicates the approximate length of time that program may remain on the Current Schedule (as opposed to the Maintenance Schedule). This figure should be used as a guideline only, as students differ greatly in the rates at which they acquire the skills taught within a particular program (some students move faster than the figure depicts; others move at a slower rate), as well as the order in which they acquire skills taught across programs (e.g., although most students master receptive language first, some students master expressive language before receptive language). Thus, it is of the utmost importance to remain flexible when introducing programs and various phases of programs. The data collected through your student's progress should determine the time at which programs are introduced into the Current Schedule, practiced, and placed on the Maintenance Schedule.

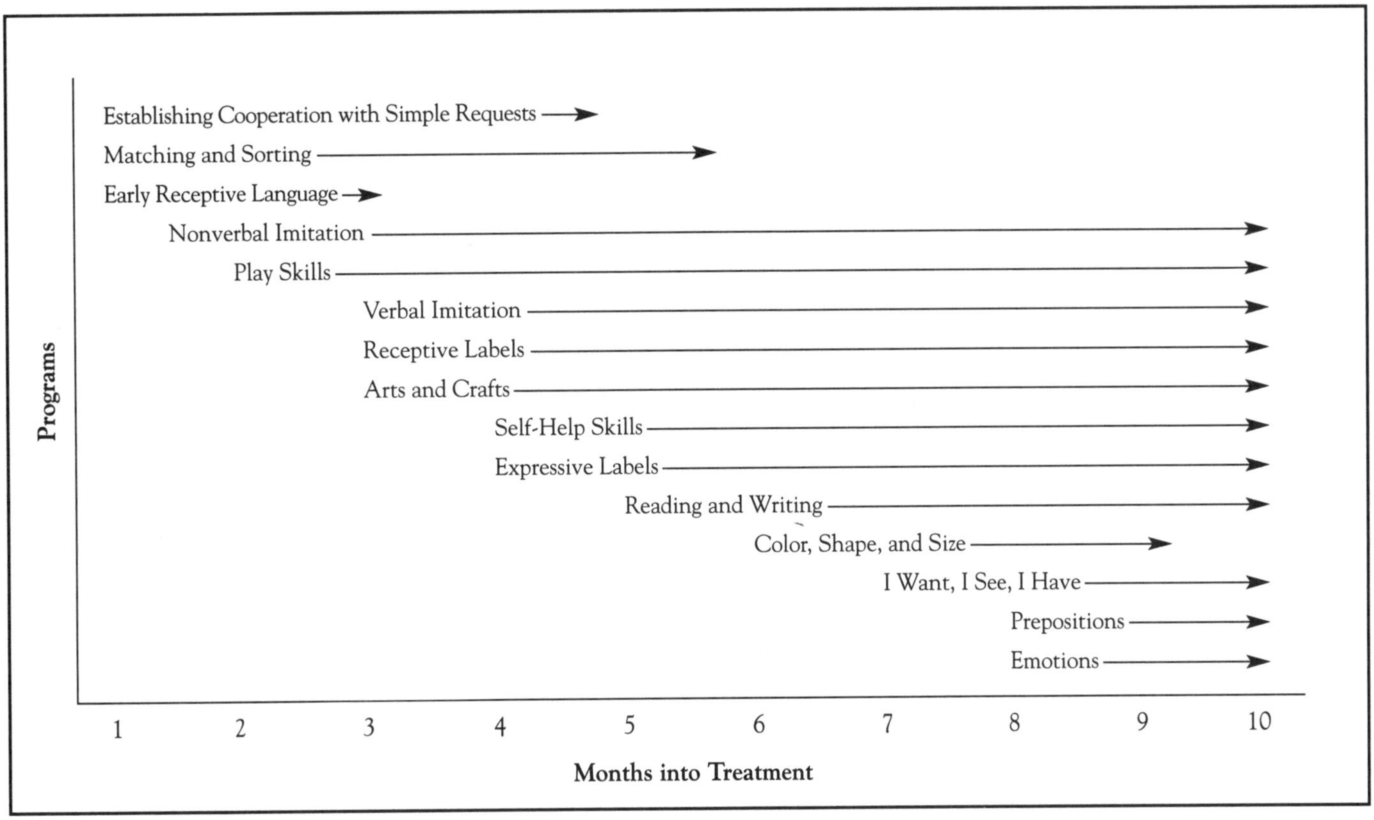

References

Alexander, D., Cowdry, R. W., Hall, Z. W., & Snow, J. B. (1996). The state of the science in autism: A view from the National Institutes of Health. *Journal of Autism and Developmental Disorders*, *26*(2), 117–119.

American Psychiatric Association. (1987). *Diagnostic and statistical manual of mental disorders* (3rd ed., rev.). Washington, DC: Author.

Anderson, S. R., Avery, D. L., Di Pietro, E. K., Edwards, G. L., & Christian, W. P. (1987). Intensive home-based early intervention with autistic children. *Education and Treatment of Children*, *10*, 352–366.

Angell, R. (1993). A parent's perspective in the preschool years. In E. Schopler, M. E. Van Bourgondien, & M. M. Bristol (Eds.), *Preschool issues in autism* (pp. 17–37). New York: Plenum.

Autism National Committee. (1995). *AUTCOM Memorandum: On the exclusive use of discrete trial training for children diagnosed as autistic/PDD*. (Available from the Autism National Committee, 635 Ardmore Avenue, Ardmore, PA 19003.)

Azrin, N. H., & Foxx, R. M. (1971). A rapid method of toilet training the institutionalized retarded. *Journal of Applied Behavior Analysis*, *4*, 89–99.

Baer, D. M. (1993). Quasi-random assignment can be as convincing as random assignment. *American Journal on Mental Retardation*, *97*, 373–375.

Baer, D. M., Guess, D., & Sherman, J. (1972). Adventures in simplistic grammar. In R. L. Shiefelbusch (Ed.), *Language of the mentally retarded* (pp. 93–105). Baltimore: University Park Press.

Baer, D. M., & Sherman, J. A. (1964). Reinforcement control of generalized imitation in young children. *Journal of Experimental Child Psychology*, *1*, 37–49.

Baker, B. L., Brightman, A. J., Blacher, J. B., Heifetz, L. J., Hinshaw, S. P., & Murphy, R. N. (1997). *Steps to independence: Teaching everyday skills to children with special needs*. Baltimore: Brookes.

Ball, T. S. (1971). *Itard, Seguin and Kephart*. Columbus, OH: Charles E. Merrill.

Baron-Cohen, S., Cox, A., Baird, G., Swettenham, J., Nightingale, N., Morgan, K., Drew, A., & Charman, T. (1996). Psychological markers in the detection of autism in infancy in a large population. *British Journal of Psychiatry*, *168*, 158–163.

Baron-Cohen, S., Leslie, A. M., & Frith, U. (1985). Does the autistic child have a "theory of mind"? *Cognition*, *21*, 37–46.

Bartak, L. (1978). Educational approaches. In M. Rutter & E. Shopler (Eds.), *Autism: A reappraisal of concepts and treatment* (pp. 423–438). New York: Plenum Press.

Bartak, L., & Rutter, M. (1973). Special educational treatment of autistic children: A comparative study. I. Design of study and characteristics of units. *Journal of Child Psychology and Psychiatry*, *14*, 161–179.

Bayley, N. (1993). *Bayley Scales of Infant Development–Revised*. San Antonio: Psychological Corporation.

Bernal, M. E., & North, J. A. (1978). A survey of parent training manuals. *Journal of Applied Behavior Analysis*, *11*, 533–544.

Bettelheim, B. (1967). *The empty fortress*. New York: Free Press.

Bibby, P., Eikeseth, S., Martin, N. T., Mudford, O. C., & Reeves, D. (2001). Progress and children with autism receiving parent-managed intensive intervention. *Research in Developmental Disabilities*, *22*, 425–447.

Bilken, D. (1991). Communication unbound: Autism and Praxis. *Harvard Educational Review*, *60*, 291–314.

Bilken, D. (1992, January). Typing to talk: Facilitated communication. *American Journal of Speech and Language Pathology*, pp. 15–17, 21–22.

Bilken, D., Morton, M. W., Gold, D., Berrigan, C., & Swaminanthan, S. (1992). Facilitated communication: Implications for individuals with autism. *Topics in Language Disorders*, *12*, 1–28.

Bilken, D., Morton, M. W., Saha, S. N., Duncan, J., Gold, D., Hardardottir, M., Karna, E., O'Connor, S., & Rao, S. (1991). "I AMN NOT A UTISTIVC OH THJE TYP" (I'm not autistic on the typewriter). *Disability, Handicap & Society*, *6*, 161–180.

Birnbrauer, J. S., & Leach, D. J (1993). The Murdoch Early Intervention Program after two years. *Behaviour Change*, *10*, 63–74.

Board of Education v. Rowley, 458 U.S. 1751 (1982).

Bondy, A. (1996) *The pyramid approach to education*. Cherry Hill, NJ: PECs.

Bondy, A., & Frost, L. (1994a). The Delaware Autistic Program. In S. Harris & J. Handleman (Eds.), *Preschool programs for children with autism* (pp. 37–54). Austin, TX: PRO-ED.

Bondy, A., & Frost, L. (1994b). The Picture-Exchange Communication System. *Focus on Autistic Behavior*, *9*, 1–19.

Bondy, A., & Frost, L. (1995). Educational approaches in preschool: Behavioral techniques in a public school setting. In E. Schopler & G. Mesibov (Eds.), *Learning and cognition in autism* (pp. 311–333). New York: Plenum.

Bristol, M. M., Cohen, D. J., Costello, E. J., Denckla, M., Eckberg, T. J., Kallen, R., Kraemer, H. C., Lord, C., Maurer, R., McIlvane, W. J., Minshew, N., Sigman, M., & Spence, M. A. (1996). State of the science in autism: Report to the National Institutes of Health. *Journal of Autism and Developmental Disorders*, *26*(2), 121–154.

Bristol, M., & Schopler, E. (1993). Introduction to preschool issues in autism. In E. Schopler, M. E. Van Bourgondien, & M. M. Bristol (Eds.), *Preschool issues in autism* (pp. 3–15). New York: Plenum.

Buch, G. A. (1995). *Teaching parents and paraprofessionals how to provide behavioral intensive early intervention for children with autism and pervasive developmental disorder.* Unpublished doctoral dissertation, University of California, Los Angeles.

California Department of Developmental Services. (1997, March). *Office of Administrative Hearing Decisions*. Sacramento: Author.

California Department of Education. (1997, January). *Best practices for designing and delivering effective programs for individuals with autistic spectrum disorders* (Draft). Sacramento: Author.

Carr, E. (1982). Sign language. In R. Koegel, A. Rincover, & A. Egel (Eds.), *Educating and understanding children with autism* (pp. 142–157). San Diego: College-Hill Press.

Carr, E. (1999) *Positive behavior support in people with developmental disabilities: A research synthesis* [Monograph]. Washington, DC: American Association on Mental Retardation.

Carr, E. G., & Durand, V. M. (1985). Reducing behavior problems through functional communication training. *Journal of Applied Behavior Analysis*, *18*, 111–126.

Carr, E. G., Newsom, C. D., & Binkoff, J. A. (1980). Escape as a factor in the aggressive behavior of two retarded children. *Journal of Applied Behavior Analysis*, *13*, 101–117.

Carr, E. G., Schreibman, L., & Lovaas, O. I. (1974). Control of echolalic speech in psychotic children. *Journal of Abnormal Child Psychology*, *3*, 331–351.

Charlop, M. H., Kurtz, P. F., & Milstein, J. P. (1992). Too much reinforcement, too little behavior: Assessing task interspersal procedures in conjunction with different reinforcement schedules with autistic children. *Journal of Applied Behavior Analysis, 25,* 795–808.

Charlop, M. H., & Milstein, J. P. (1989). Teaching autistic children conversational speech using video modeling. *Journal of Applied Behavior Analysis, 22,* 275–285.

Chomsky, N. (1965). *Aspects of the theory of syntax.* Cambridge, MA: MIT Press.

Crossley, R., & Remington-Gurney, J. (1992). Getting the words out: Facilitated communication training. *Topics in Language Disorders, 12,* 29–45.

Davis, B. J., Smith, T., & Donahoe, P. (2002). *Evaluating supervisors in the UCLA Treatment Model for children with autism: Validation of an assessment procedure.* Manuscript submitted for publication.

Dawson, G., & Osterling, J. (1996). Early intervention in autism. In M. J. Guralnick (Ed.), *The effectiveness of early intervention.* Baltimore: Brookes.

Delaware County Intermediate Unit #25 v. Martin and Melinda K. et al., 831 F. Supp. 1206 (E.D. PA 1993).

DeMeyer, M. K., Hingtgen, J. N., & Jackson, R. K. (1981). Infantile autism reviewed: A decade of research. *Schizophrenia Bulletin, 7,* 388–451.

Dube, W. V., McDonald, S. J., McIlvane, W. J., & Mackay, H. A. (1991). Constructed-response matching to sample and spelling instruction. *Journal of Applied Behavior Analysis, 24,* 305–317.

Dunlap, G. (1984). The influence of task variation and maintenance tasks on the learning and affect of autistic children. *Journal of Experimental Psychology, 37,* 41–64.

Eberlin, M., McConnachie, G., Ibel, S., & Volpe, L. (1992, October). *A systematic investigation of "facilitated communication": Is there efficacy or utility with children and adolescents with autism?* Paper presented at the Annual Conference of Northeast Region X of the American Association on Mental Retardation. Albany, NY.

Education for All Handicapped Children Act of 1975, 20 U.S.C. § 1400 *et seq.*

Education of the Handicapped Act Amendments of 1986, 20 U.S.C. § 1400 *et seq.*

Eikeseth, S., & Lovaas, O. I. (1992). The autistic label and its potentially detrimental effect on the child's treatment. *Journal of Behavior Therapy & Experimental Psychiatry, 23*(3), 151–157.

Ekman, G., & Miranda-Linne, F. (with Gillberg, C., Garle, M., & Wetterberg, L.). (1989). Fenfluramine treatment of twenty children with autism. *Journal of Autism and Developmental Disorders, 19*(4), 511–532.

Ekstrom, R. B., French, J. W., Harman, H. H., & Dermen, D. (1976). *Kit of factor-referenced cognitive tests.* Princeton, NJ: Educational Testing Service.

Epstein, L., Taubman, M., & Lovaas, O. I. (1985). Changes in self-stimulatory behaviors with treatment. *Journal of Abnormal Child Psychology, 13,* 281–294.

Exner, J. (1985). *A Rorschach workbook for the comprehensive system* (2nd ed.). Bayville, NY: Rorschach Workshops.

Favell, J. E., McGimsey, J. F., & Schell, R. M. (1982). Treatment of self-injury by providing alternative sensory activities. *Analysis and Intervention in Developmental Disabilities, 2,* 83–104.

Fenske, E. C., Zalenski, S., Krantz, P. J., & McClannahan, L. E. (1985). Age at intervention and treatment outcome for autistic children in a comprehensive intervention program. *Analysis and Intervention in Developmental Disabilities, 5,* 49–58.

Flavell, J. H. (1963). *The developmental psychology of Jean Piaget.* Princeton, NJ: Van Nostrand.

Florence County School District Four v. Carter, 114 S. Ct. 361 (1993).

Foxx, R. M. (1993). Sapid effects awaiting independent replication. *American Journal on Mental Retardation, 97,* 375–376.

Freeman, B. J. (1976). Evaluating autistic children. *Journal of Pediatric Psychology, 1,* 18–21.

Freeman, B. J., Rahbar, B., Ritvo, E., Bice, T. L., Yokota, A., & Ritvo, R. (1991). The stability of cognitive and behavioral parameters in autism: A twelve-year prospective study. *Journal of the American Academy of Child and Adolescent Psychiatry, 30,* 479–482.

Freeman, B. J., Ritvo, E. R., Needleman, R., & Yokota, A. (1985). The stability of cognitive and linguistic parameters in autism: A five-year prospective study. *Journal of the American Academy of Child Psychiatry, 24,* 459–464.

Frost, L., & Bondy, A. (1995). *The Picture Exchange Communication System Training Manual.* Cherry Hill, NJ: PECS.

Frost, L., Daily, M., & Bondy, A. (1997, April). *Speech features with and without access to PECS for children with autism.* Paper presented at Center for Outreach and Services in the Autism Community annual conference, Long Beach, NJ.

Frost, L., & Scholefield, D. (1996, May). *Improving picture symbol discrimination skills within PECS through the use of three-dimensional objects and fading: A case study.* Paper presented at the annual meeting of the Association for Behavior Analysis, San Francisco.

Fujiura, G. T., Roccoforte, J. A., & Braddock, D. (1994). Cost of family care for adults with mental retardation and related developmental disabilities. *American Journal on Mental Retardation,* 99(3), 250–261.

Gaylord-Ross, R. J., Haring, T. G., Breen, C., & Pitts-Conway, V. (1984). The training and generalization of social interaction skills with autistic youth. *Journal of Applied Behavior Analysis, 17,* 229–247.

Grant, D. A., & Berg, E. A. (1984). A behavioral analysis of degree of reinforcement and ease of shifting to new responses in a Weigele-type card sorting problem. *Journal of Experimental Psychology, 32,* 404–411.

Green, G. (1996a). Evaluating claims about treatments for autism. In C. Maurice (Ed.), *Behavioral interventions for young children with autism: A manual for parents and professionals* (pp. 15–28). Austin, TX: PRO-ED.

Green, G. (1996b). Early behavioral intervention for autism: What does research tell us? In C. Maurice (Ed.), *Behavioral interventions for young children with autism: A manual for parents and professionals* (pp. 29–44). Austin, TX: PRO-ED.

Green, W. H. (1988). Pervasive developmental disorders. In C. J. Kestenbaum & D. T. Williams (Eds.), *Handbook of clinical assessment of children and adolescents* (Vol. 1). New York: New York University Press.

Greenspan, S. I. (1992). Reconsidering the diagnosis and treatment of very young children with autistic spectrum or pervasive developmental disorder. *Zero to Three, 13,* 1–9.

Gresham, F. M., & MacMillan, D. L. (1997a). Autistic recovery? An analysis and critique of the empirical evidence on the Early Intervention Project. *Behavioral Disorders, 4,* 185–201.

Gresham, F. M., & MacMillan, D. L. (1997b). Denial and defensiveness in the place of fact and reason: Rejoinder to Smith and Lovaas. *Behavioral Disorders, 4,* 219–230.

Gresham, F. M., & MacMillan, D. L. (1998). Early intervention project: Can its claims be substantiated and its effects replicated? *Journal of Autism and Developmental Disorders,* 28(1), 5–13.

Hacking, I. (1999). *The social construction of what?* Cambridge, MA: Harvard University Press.

Haring, T. G., Roger, B., Lee, M., Breen, C., & Gaylord-Ross, R. (1986). Teaching social language to moderately handicapped students. *Journal of Applied Behavior Analysis, 19,* 159–171.

Harris, S., Handleman, J., Gordon, R., Kristoff, B., & Fuentes, F. (1991). Changes in cognitive and language functioning of preschool children with autism. *Journal of Autism and Developmental Disorders, 21,* 281–290.

Hathaway, S. R., & McKinley, J. C. (1951). *Minnesota Multiphasic Personality Inventory Manual* (rev.). San Antonio: Psychological Corporation.

Herr, S. S. (1997). Reauthorization of the Individuals with Disabilities Education Act. *Mental Retardation, 35,* 131–137.

Hewitt, F. M. (1964, May). Teaching reading to an autistic boy through operant conditioning. *The Reading Teacher.*

Howlin, P. A. (1997). Prognosis in autism: Do specialist treatments affect long-term outcome? *European Child and Adolescent Psychiatry,* 6(2), 55–72.

Howlin, P. A., & Rutter, M. (1987). *Treatment of autistic children*. New York: Wiley.

Hoyson, M., Jamieson, B., & Strain, P. S. (1984). Individualized group instruction of normally developing and autistic-like children: A description and evaluation of the LEAP curriculum model. *Journal of the Division of Early Childhood, 8*, 157–181.

Huff, R. (1996). Community-based early intervention for children with autism. In C. Maurice, G. Green, & S. C. Luce (Eds.), *Behavioral intervention for young children with autism* (pp. 251–266). Austin, TX: PRO-ED.

Hung, D. W. (1977). Generalization of "curiosity" questioning behavior in autistic children. *Journal of Behavior Therapy and Experimental Psychiatry, 8*, 237–245.

Hung, D. W. (1980). Training and generalization of yes and no as mands in two autistic children. *Journal of Autism and Developmental Disorders, 10*, 139–152.

Huttenlocher, P. R. (1984). Synapse elimination and plasticity in developing human cerebral cortex. *American Journal of Mental Deficiency, 88*, 488–496.

The IDEA: A parent's perspective and proposal for change. (1994, Winter). *Michigan Journal of Law Reform, 27*(2).

Individuals with Disabilities Education Act of 1990, 20 U.S.C. § 1400 *et seq*.

Individuals with Disabilities Education Act Reauthorization of 1997, 20 U.S.C. § 1400 *et seq*.

Itard, J. M. G. (1962). *The wild boy of Aveyron*. New York: Appleton-Century-Crofts.

Jacobson, J. W., Mulick, J. A., & Green, G. (1996). *Financial cost and benefits of intensive early intervention for young children with autism: Pennsylvania model achieving cost savings*. (Legislative briefing). Schenectady, NY: Independent Living in the Capital District.

Jacobson, J. W., Mulick, J. A., & Green, G. (1998). Cost–benefit estimates for early intensive behavioral intervention for young children with autism: General models and single state case. *Behavioral Interventions, 13*, 201–226.

James, W. (1981). *The principles of psychology*. Cambridge, MA: Harvard University Press. (Original work published 1890)

Johnson, C., & Crowder, J. (Ed.). (1994). *Autism from tragedy to triumph*. Boston: Branden.

Johnston, J. M. (1988). Strategic and tactical limits of comparison studies. *The Behavior Analyst, 11*, 1–9.

Kanner, L. (1943). Autistic disturbances of affective contact. *The Nervous Child, 2*, 217–250.

Kanter, E. (1992, February). *Transitional objects and their use with students with autism*. Paper presented at Delaware Autistic Program conference, Dover, DE.

Kazdin, A. E. (1980). *Research design in clinical psychology* (pp. 122–159). New York: Harper & Row.

Kazdin, A. E. (1993). Replication and extension of behavioral treatment of autistic disorder. *American Journal on Mental Retardation, 97*, 377–379.

Knobbe, C. A., Carey, S. P., Rhodes, L., & Horner, R. H. (1995). Benefit–cost analysis of community residential versus institutional services for adults with severe mental retardation and challenging behaviors. *American Journal on Mental Retardation, 99*, 533–541.

Koegel, R. L., Glahn, T. J., & Nieminen, G. S. (1978). Generalization of parent-training results. *Journal of Applied Behavior Analysis, 11*, 95–109.

Koegel, R. L., & Koegel, L. K. (1988). Generalized responsivity and pivotal behaviors. In R. H. Horner, G. Dunlap, & R. L. Koegel (Eds.), *Generalization and maintenance: Life-style changes in applied settings* (pp. 41–65). Baltimore: Brookes.

Koegel, R. L., & Koegel, L. K. (1995). *Teaching children with autism: Strategies for initiating positive interactions and improving learning opportunities*. Baltimore: Brookes.

Koegel, R. L., Rincover, A., & Egel, A. L. (Eds.). (1982). *Educating and understanding autistic children*. San Diego: College-Hill Press.

Koegel, R. L., Russo, D. C., & Rincover, A. (1977). Assessing and training teachers in the generalized use of behavior modification with autistic children. *Journal of Applied Behavior Analysis, 10*, 197–205.

Kravitz, H., & Boehm, J. J. (1971). Rythmic habit patterns in infancy: Their sequence, age of onset, and frequency. *Child Development, 42*, 399–413.

Kuhn, T. S. (1970). *The structure of scientific revolutions*. Chicago: University of Chicago Press.

Landa, R., Folstein, S. E., & Isaacs, C. (1991). Spontaneous narrative-discourse performance of parents of autistic individuals. *Journal of Speech & Hearing Research, 34*, 1339–1345.

Landa, R., Piven, J., Wzorek, M. M., Gayle, J. O., Cloud, D., Chase, G. A., & Folstein, S. E. (1990). Social language use in parents of autistic individuals. *Psychological Medicine, 22*, 245–254.

Lane, H. L. (1976). *The wild boy of Aveyron*. New York: Allen and Unwin.

Lindsay, W. R., & Stoffelmayr, B. E. (1982). The concept of generalization in behaviour therapy. *Behavioural Psychotherapy, 10*, 346–355.

Lord, C., Bristol, M. M., & Schopler, E. (1993). Early intervention for children with autism and related developmental disorders. In E. Schopler, M. E. Van Bourgondien, & M. M. Bristol (Eds.), *Preschool issues in autism* (pp. 199–221). New York: Plenum.

Lord, C., Rutter, M., & LeCouteur, A. (1994). Autism Diagnostic Interview Revised: A revised version of a diagnostic interview for caregivers of individuals with possible pervasive developmental disorders. *Journal of Autism and Developmental Disorders, 24*, 659–685.

Lord, C., & Schopler, E. (1988). Intellectual and developmental assessment of autistic children from preschool to school age: Clinical implications of two follow-up studies. In E. Schopler & G. B. Mesibov (Eds.), *Diagnosis and assessment in autism* (pp. 167–181). New York: Plenum.

Lord, C., & Schopler, E. (1989). The role of age at assessment, developmental level, and test in the stability of intelligence scores in young autistic children. *Journal of Autism and Developmental Disorders, 19*, 483–499.

Lord, C., & Schopler, E. (1994). TEACCH services for preschool children. In S. L. Harris & J. S. Handleman (Eds.), *Preschool education programs for children with autism* (pp. 87–106). Austin, TX: PRO-ED.

Lotter, V. (1978). Follow-up studies. In M. Rutter & E. Schopler (Eds.), *Autism: A reappraisal of concepts and treatment* (pp. 475–495). London: Plenum.

Lovaas, O. I. (1970, June). *Strengths and weaknesses of operant conditioning techniques for the treatment of autism*. Paper presented at Second Annual Meeting and Conference of the National Society for Autistic Children, San Francisco.

Lovaas, O. I. (1977). *The autistic child: Language development through behavior modification*. New York: Irvington.

Lovaas, O. I. (1979). Tratamiento de conducta de los niños autistas. Edición a cargo de Francisco Perez y Angel Riviere, *Autismo infantil: Cuestiones actuales actas del I Simposio Internacional de Autismo*. Madrid, Spain: Servicio de Recuperación y Rehabilitación de Minusvalidos Físicos y Psiquicos—Asociación de Padres de Niños Autistas.

Lovaas, O. I. (with Ackerman, A. B., Alexander, D., Firestone, P., Perkins, J., & Young, D.). (1981). *Teaching developmentally disabled children: The ME book*. Austin. TX: PRO-ED.

Lovaas, O. I. (1987). Behavioral treatment and normal educational and intellectual functioning in young autistic children. *Journal of Consulting and Clinical Psychology, 55*, 3–9.

Lovaas, O. I. (1988). *Behavioral Treatment of Young Autistic Children* [45-minute college film]. New York: Focus International.

Lovaas, O. I. (1993). The development of a treatment–research project for developmentally disabled and autistic children. *Journal of Applied Behavior Analysis, 26*, 617–630.

Lovaas, O. I. (1996). The UCLA young autism model of service delivery. In C. Maurice, G. Green, & S. Luce (Eds.), *Behavioral intervention for young children with autism: A manual for parents and professionals* (pp. 241–248). Austin, TX: PRO-ED.

Lovaas, O. I. (in press). Experimental design and cumulative research in early behavioral intervention. In P. Accardo, C. Magnusen, A. Capute, et al. (Eds.), *Autism: Clinical and research issues. John Hopkins 20th Annual Spectrum in Developmental Disabilities.* Timonium, MD: York Press.

Lovaas, O. I., Berberich, J. P., Perloff, B. F., & Schaeffer, B. (1966). Acquisition of imitative speech by schizophrenic children. *Science, 151,* 705–707.

Lovaas, O. I., Freitag, G., Gold, V. J., & Kassorla, I. C., (1965a). Experimental studies in childhood schizophrenia: Analysis of self-destructive behavior. *Journal of Experimental Child Psychology, 2,* 67–84.

Lovaas, O. I., Freitag, G., Gold, V. J., & Kassorla, I. C. (1965b). Recording apparatus and procedure of observation of behaviors of children in free play settings. *Journal of Experimental Child Psychology, 2,* 108–120.

Lovaas, O. I., Freitag, G., Kinder, M. I., Rubenstein, B. D., Schaeffer, B., & Simmons, J. W. (1966). Establishment of social reinforcers in two schizophrenic children on the basis of food. *Journal of Experimental Child Pychology, 4,* 109–125.

Lovaas, O. I., Freitas, L., Nelson, K., & Whalen, C. (1967). The establishment of imitation and its use for the development of complex behavior in schizophrenic children. *Behavior Research and Therapy, 5,* 171–181.

Lovaas, O. I., Koegel, R. L., Simmons, J. Q., & Long, J. S. (1973). Some generalization and follow-up measures on autistic children in behavior therapy. *Journal of Applied Behavior Analysis, 6,* 131–165.

Lovaas, O. I., & Leaf, R. L. (1981). *Five video tapes for teaching developmentally disabled children.* Baltimore: University Park Press.

Lovaas, O. I., & Simmons, J. Q. (1969). Manipulation of self-destruction in three retarded children. *Journal of Applied Behavior Analysis, 2,* 143–157.

Lovaas, O. I., & Smith, T. (1988). Intensive behavioral treatment with young autistic children. In B. B. Lahey & A. E. Kazdin (Eds.), *Advances in Clinical Child Psychology, 11,* 285–324.

Lovaas, O. I., & Smith, T. (1989). A comprehensive behavioral theory of autistic children: Paradigm for research and treatment. *Journal of Behavior Therapy and Experimental Psychiatry, 20,* 17–29.

Lovaas, O. I., Smith, T., & McEachin, J. J. (1989). Clarifying comments on the young autism study: Reply to Schopler, Short, and Mesibov. *Journal of Consulting and Clinical Psychology, 57,* 165–167.

Lovaas, O. I., Varni, J. W., Koegel, R. L., & Lorsch, N. (1977). Some observations of the nonextinguishability of children's speech. *Child Development, 48,* 121–127.

Love, S. R., & Mesibov, G. B. (1995). TEACCH [circular]. (Available from Division of TEACCH Administration and Research, CB# 7180, 310 Medical School, Wing E, The University of North Carolina at Chapel Hill, Chapel Hill, NC 27599-7180)

Macduff, G., Krantz, P., & McClannahan, L. (1993). Teaching children with autism to use photographic activity schedules: Maintenance and generalization of complex response chains. *Journal of Applied Behavior Analysis, 26,* 89–97.

Mackay, H. A. (1985). Stimulus equivalence in rudimentary reading and spelling. *Analysis and Intevention in Developmental Disabilities, 5,* 373–387.

Malkentzos v. DeBuono, 923 F. Supp. 505 (S.D.N.Y. 1996), *rev'd on other grounds,* 102 F.3d 50 (2nd Cir. 1996).

Maurice, C. (1993). *Let me hear your voice: A family's triumph over autism.* New York: Knopf.

Maurice, C., Green, G., & Luce, S. C. (1996). *Behavior intervention for young children with autism: A manual for parents and professionals.* Austin, TX: PRO-ED.

McCartney, P. (1965). Yesterday [recorded by J. Lennon, G. Harrison, P. McCartney, & R. Starr], on *Help!* [LP]. London: Parlophone.

McEachin, J. J. (1987). *Outcome of autistic children receiving intensive behavioral treatment: Residual deficits.* Unpublished doctoral dissertation, University of California, Los Angeles.

McEachin, J. J., Smith, T., & Lovaas, O. I. (1993). Long-term outcome for children with autism who received early intensive behavioral treatment. *American Journal of Mental Retardation, 97,* 359–372.

Mesibov, G. B. (1993). Treatment outcome is encouraging. *American Journal on Mental Retardation, 97,* 379–390.

Mesibov, G. B. (1997). Formal and informal measures on the effectiveness of the TEACCH program. *Autism, 1,* 25–35.

Moroz, K. J. (1989). Parent–professional partnerships in the education of autistic children. *Children & Youth Services Review, 11,* 265–276.

Mundy, P. (1993). Normal versus high functioning status in children with autism. *American Journal on Mental Retardation, 97,* 381–384.

Mundy, P. (1995). Joint attention and social-emotional approach behavior in children with autism. *Development & Psychopathology, 7*(1), 63–82.

Neville, H. J. (1985). Effects of early sensory and language experience on the development of the human brain. In J. Mehler & R. Foxx (Eds.), *Neonate cognition beyond the blooming buzzing confusion.* Hillsdale, NJ: Erlbaum.

New York State Department of Health. (1999). *Clinical practice guideline: Report of the recommendations autism/pervasive developmental disorders assessment and intervention for young children (ages 0–3 years).* Albany: Author.

Newsom, C., & Rincover, A. (1989). Autism. In E. J. Mash & R. A. Barklay (Eds.), *Treatment of childhood disorders* (pp. 286–346). New York: Guilford Press.

Parton, D. A., & Fouts, G. T. (1969). Effects of stimulus–response similarity and dissimilarity on children's matching performance. *Journal of Experimental Child Psychology, 8,* 461–468.

Perry, R., Cohen, I., & DeCarlo, R. (1995). Case study: Deterioration, autism, and recovery in two siblings. *Journal of the American Academy of Child and Adolescent Psychiatry, 34*(2), 232–237.

Peterson, S., Bondy, A., Vincent, Y., & Finnegan, C. (1995). Effects of altering communicative input for students with autism and no speech: Two case studies. *Augmentative and Alternative Communication, 11,* 93–100.

Pomeranz, K. (1998). Letters to the editor. *Autism Research Review International, 12*(3), 7.

Powell, T. H., Hecimovic, A., & Christensen, L. (1992). Meeting the unique needs of families. In D. Berkell (Ed.), *Autism: Identification, education and treatment* (pp. 187–224). Hillsdale, NJ: Erlbaum.

Powers, M. D. (1989). *Children with autism: A parent's guide.* Bethesda, MD: Woodbine House.

Powers, M. D. (1992). Early intervention for children with autism. In D. Berkell (Ed.), *Autism: Identification, education and treatment* (pp. 225–252). Hillsdale, NJ: Erlbaum.

Reed, H. (1955) Only you [Recorded by Platters]. On record. Mercury Records.

Reichle, J., York, J., & Sigafoos, J. (1991). *Implementing augmentative and alternative communication strategies for learners with severe disabilities.* Baltimore: Brookes.

Reynell, J. K., & Gruber, C. P. (1990). *Reynell Developmental Language Scales.* Los Angeles: Western Psychological Association.

Reynold, G. S. (1968). *A primer of operant conditioning.* Glenview, IL: Scott, Foresman.

Rincover, A., Newsom, C. D., & Carr, E. G. (1979). Using sensory extinction procedures in the treatment of compulsive-like behavior of developmentally disabled children. *Journal of Consulting and Clinical Psychology, 47,* 695–701.

Risley, T., Hart, B., & Doke, L. (1972). Operant language development: The outline of a therapeutic technology. In R. L. Schiefelbusch (Ed.), *Language of the mentally retarded* (pp. 107–123). Baltimore: University Park Press.

Risley, T., & Wolf, M. (1967). Establishing functional speech in autistic children. *Behaviour Research and Therapy, 5,* 73–88.

Roberts, R. N., & Magrab, P. R. (1991). Psychologists' role in a family-centered approach to practice, training, and research with young children. *American Psychologist, 46*(2), 144–148.

Rogers, S. J., & DiLalla, D. L. (1991). A comparative study of the effects of a developmentally based instructional model on young children with autism and young children with other disorders of behavior and development. *Topics in Early Childhood Special Education, 11*, 29–47.

Rutter, M. (1978). Diagnosis and definition. In M. Rutter & E. Schopler (Eds.), *Autism: A reappraisal of concepts and treatment* (pp. 1–25). New York: Plenum.

Rutter, M. (1983). Cognitive deficits in the pathogenesis of autism. *Journal of Child Psychology and Psychiatry, 24*, 243–246.

Rutter, M. (1985). The treatment of autistic children. *Journal of Child Psychology & Psychiatry, 43*, 193–214.

Rutter, M. (1996). Autism research: Prospects and priorities. *Journal of Autism and Developmental Disorders, 26*, 257–275.

Rutter, M., & Lockyer, L. (1967). A five to fifteen year follow-up study of infantile psychosis: I. Description of sample. *British Journal of Psychiatry, 113*, 1169–1182.

Rutter, M., & Schopler, E. (1987). Autism and pervasive developmental disorders: Concepts and diagnostic issues. *Journal of Autism and Developmental Disorders, 17*, 159–186.

Sacramento City Unified School District v. R.H., 14 F.3d 1398, cert. denied 1994 (9th Cir., 1994).

School Committee of the Town of Burlington v. Department of Education, 471 U.S. 359, 105 S. Ct. 2003 (1985).

Schopler, E. (1986). Editorial: Treatment abuse and its reduction. *Journal of Autism and Developmental Disorders, 16*, 99–103.

Schopler, E. (1987). Specific and nonspecific factors in the effectiveness of a treatment system. *American Psychologist, 42*, 376–383.

Schopler, E. (1994). Behavioral priorities for autism and related developmental disorders. In E. Schopler & G. B. Mesibov (Eds.), *Behavioral issues in autism* (pp. 61–70). New York: Plenum Press.

Schopler, E. (1998). Preface. *Journal of Autism and Developmental Disorders, 28*(1), 3–4.

Schopler, E., Lansing, M., & Waters, L. (1983). Teaching activities for autistic children. In J. L. Culbertson & D. J. Willis (Eds.), *Individualized assessment and treatment for autistic and developmentally disabled children* (Vol. 3, pp. 319–344). Austin, TX: PRO-ED.

Schopler, E., & Mesibov, G. B. (1988). Introduction to diagnosis and assessment of autism. In E. Schopler & G. B. Mesibov (Eds.), *Diagnosis and assessment in autism* (pp. 3–14). New York: Plenum.

Schopler, E., & Reichler, R. J. (1976). Developmental therapy: A program model for providing individual services in the community. In E. Schopler & R. J. Reichler (Eds.), *Psychopathology and child development: Research and treatment* (pp. 347–372). New York: Plenum.

Schopler, E., Short, A., & Mesibov, G. (1989). Relation of behavioral treatment to "normal functioning": Comment on Lovaas. *Journal of Consulting and Clinical Psychology, 57*, 162–164.

Schreibman, L. (1988). *Autism*. Beverly Hills, CA: Sage.

Sheinkopf, F. J., & Siegel, B. (1998). Home-based behavioral treatment of young autistic children. *Journal of Autism and Developmental Disorders, 28*(1), 15–23.

Sidman, M. (1971). Reading and auditory–visual equivalences. *Journal of Speech and Hearing Research, 14*, 5–13.

Siegel, B. (2001). *Pervasive Developmental Disorder Screening Test–II*. San Francisco: University of California at San Francisco.

Simeonson, R. J., Olley, J. G., & Rosenthal, S. L. (1987). Early intervention for children with autism. In M. J. Guralnick & F. C. Bennett (Eds.), *The effectiveness of early intervention for at-risk and handicapped children* (pp. 275–296). Orlando, FL: Academic Press.

Sirevaag, A. M., & Greenough, W. T. (1988). A multivariate statistical summary of synaptic plasticity measures in rats exposed to complex, social and individual environments. *Brain Research, 441*, 386–392.

Smith, E. H., & Palmer, B. C. (1979). *Smith/Palmer Figurative Language Interpretation Test: Measures for research and evaluation in the English language arts* (Vol. 2). Washington, DC: Committee on Research of the National Council of Teachers of English.

Smith, T. (1993). Autism. In T. Giles (Ed.), *Effective psychotherapies* (pp. 107–133). New York: Plenum.

Smith, T. (1994). Improving memory to promote maintenance of treatment gains in children with autism. *The Psychological Record, 44*, 459–473.

Smith, T. (1996). Are other treatments effective? In C. Maurice (Ed.), *Behavioral intervention for young children with autism* (pp. 45–59). Austin, TX: PRO-ED.

Smith, T. (1999). Outcome of early intervention for children with autism. *Clinical Psychology: Science and Practice, 6*(1), 33–49.

Smith, T., Donahoe, P. A., & Davis, B. J. (2000). The UCLA treatment model. In J. S. Handleman & S. L. Harris (Eds.), *Preschool education programs for children with autism* (2nd ed.). Austin, TX: PRO-ED.

Smith, T., Eikeseth, S., Klevstrand, M., & Lovaas, O. I. (1997). Outcome of early intervention for children with severe mental retardation and pervasive developmental disorders. *American Journal on Mental Retardation, 102*, 238–249.

Smith, T., Groen, A., & Wynn, J. (2000). A randomized trial of intensive early intervention for children. *American Journal on Mental Retardation, 105*(4), 269–285.

Smith, T., Klevstrand, M., & Lovaas, O. I. (1995). Behavioral treatment of Rett's disorder: Ineffectiveness in three cases. *American Journal on Mental Retardation, 100*, 317–322.

Smith, T., & Lovaas, O. I. (1997). The UCLA Young Autism Project: A reply to Gresham and MacMillan. *Behavioral Disorders, 22*(4), 202–218.

Smith, T., & Lovaas, O. I. (1998). Sex and bias: Reply to Boyd. *Journal of Autism and Developmental Disorders, 28*(4), 343–345.

Smith, T., & Lovaas, O. I. (2001). *A scientifically unsound research proposal from Iowa Heartland Area Education Agency 11*. Manuscript in preparation.

Smith, T., Lovaas, N. W., & Watthen-Lovaas, O. I. (2002). *Peer interaction of high-functioning children with autism in integrated and segregated dyads*. Manuscript submitted for publication.

Smith, T., Lovaas, N. W., & Lovaas, I. (in press). Behaviors of children with high-functioning autism when paired with typically developing versus delayed peers. *Behavioral Interventions*.

Sokoloff, L. (1985). *Brain imaging and brain function*. New York: Raven Press.

Spake, A. (1992, May 31). "In Classroom 210 . . ." *Washington Post Magazine*, pp. 17–22, 28–30.

Sparrow, S. S., Balla, D. A., & Cicchetti, D. V. (1984). *Vineland Adaptive Behavior Scales*. Circle Pines, MN: American Guidance Service.

Spitz, H. H. (1986). *The raising of intelligence*. Hillsdale, NJ: Erlbaum.

Stoddard, L. T., & McIlvane, W. J. (1986). Stimulus control research and developmentally disabled individuals. *Analysis & Intervention in Developmental Disabilities, 6*, 155–178.

Stokes, T. F., & Baer, D. M. (1977). An implicit technology of generalization. *Journal of Applied Behavior Analysis, 10*, 349–367.

Strain, P. S. (1983). Generalization of autistic children's social behavior change: Effects of developmentally integrated and segregated settings. *Analysis and Intervention in Developmental Disabilities, 3*, 23–34.

Strain, P. S. (1994). *Peer-mediated treatment of autistic children*. NIMH Competitive renewal. The Early Learning Institute, Pittsburgh, PA.

Strain, P. S., Hoyson, M. H., & Jamieson, B. J. (1985). Normally developing preschoolers as intervention agents for autistic-like children: Effects on class deportment and social interactions. *Journal of the Division for Early Childhood, 9*, 105–115.

Strain, P. S., Jamieson, B., & Hoyson, M. (1986). Learning experiences: An alternative program for preschoolers and parents: A comprehensive service system for the mainstreaming of autistic-like preschoolers. In C. J. Meisel (Ed.), *Mainstreaming handicapped children: Outcomes, controversies and new directions* (pp. 251–269). Hillsdale, NJ: Erlbaum.

Stromer, R., & Mackay, H. A. (1992). Spelling and emergent picture to printed word relations established with delayed identity matching to complex samples. *Journal of Applied Behavior Analysis, 25*, 893–904.

Student v. Union School District, 16 IDELR 978 (SEA CA 1990).

Stutsman, R. (1984a). *Guide for administering the Merrill-Palmer Scale of Mental Tests*. New York: Harcourt, Brace & World.

Stutsman, R. (1984b). *Merrill-Palmer Scale of Mental Tests*. Los Angeles: Western Psychological Services.

Sulzer-Azaroff, B., & Mayer, G. R. (1991). *Behavior analysis for lasting change*. Fort Worth, TX: Holt, Rinehart & Winston.

Sundberg, M. L., & Partington, J. W. (1994, October). *Teaching language to autistic and developmentally disabled children*. Workshop conducted at the Northern California Applied Behavior Analysis Conference, Concord.

Thorndike, E. (1899). Animal intelligence: An experimental study of the associative processes in animals. *Psychological Monographs, 2*(4), 1–109.

Thorndike, R., Hagen, E., & Sattler, J. (1986). *The Stanford–Binet Intelligence Scale* (4th ed.). Chicago: Riverside.

Tinbergen, W., & Tinbergen, E. A. (1983). *Autistic children: New hope for a cure*. London: Allen and Unwin.

Tommasone, L., & Tommasone, J. (1989). Adjusting to your child's diagnosis. In M. D. Powers (Ed.), *Children with autism: A parents' guide* (pp. 31–50). Rockville, MD: Woodbine.

Union Elementary School District v. Smith, 15 F.3d 1519, cert. denied October 31, 1994 (9th Cir. 1994).

U.S. Department of Health and Human Services. (1999). *Mental health: A report of the surgeon general—Executive summary*. Rockville, MD: United States Surgeon General.

Venter, A., Lord, C., & Schopler, E. (1992). A follow-up study of high-functioning autistic children. *Journal of Child Psychology and Psychiatry, 33*, 489–507.

Wall, J. A. (1990). Group homes in North Carolina for children and adults with autism. *Journal of Autism and Developmental Disorders, 20*(3), 353–366.

Watthen-Lovaas, N. W., & Lovaas, E. E. (2000). *The reading and writing program: An alternative form of communication for students with developmental delays*. (Available from the Lovaas Institute for Early Intervention, 11500 West Olympic Boulevard, Suite 460, Los Angeles, CA 90064)

Wechsler, D. (1981). *Manual for the the Wechsler Adult Intelligence Scale–Revised*. San Antonio: Psychological Corporation.

Wechsler, D. (1991). *Wechsler Intelligence Scale for Children–Third Edition*. San Antonio: Psychological Corporation.

Wechsler, D. (1992). *Manual for the Wechsler Individual Achievement Test*. San Antonio: Psychological Corporation.

Welch, M. G. (1987). Toward prevention of developmental disorders. *Pennsylvania Medicine, 90*, 47–52.

Williamson, M. (1996). Funding the behavioral program: Legal strategies for parents. In C. Maurice, G. Green, & S. Luce (Eds.), *Behavioral intervention for young children with autism: A manual for parents and professionals* (pp. 267–293). Austin, TX: PRO-ED.

Wing, L. (1989). Autistic adults. In C. Gillberg (Ed.), *Diagnosis and treatment of autism* (pp. 419–432). New York: Plenum.

Wolf, M. M., Kirigin, K. A., Fixsen, D. L., Blase, K. A., & Braukman, C. J. (1995). The teaching family model: A case study in data-based program development. *Journal of Organizational Behavior Management, 15*, 11–19.

Wood, M. (1995). Parent–professional collaboration and the efficacy of the IEP process. In R. L. Koegel & L. K. Koegel (Eds.), *Teaching children with autism: Strategies for initiating positive interactions and improving learning opportunities* (pp.147–174). Baltimore: Brooks.

Wynn, J. W. (1996). *Generalization between receptive and expressive language in young children with autism*. Unpublished doctoral dissertation, University of California, Los Angeles.

Zigler, E., & Seitz, V. (1980). Early childhood intervention programs: A reanalysis. *School Psychology Review, 9*, 354–368.

Zigler, E., & Trickett, P. K. (1978). IQ, social competence, and evaluation of early-childhood intervention programs. *American Psychologist, 33*, 789–794.

Index

About the Author

O. Ivar Lovaas, PhD, serves as professor of psychology at the University of California, Los Angeles and as director of the Lovaas Institute for Early Intervention (LIFE). Ivar Lovaas and his students have conducted treatment research in autism supported by grants from NIMH since 1962. He has received many honors for his work in the field, including the Edgar Doll Award, a Distinguished Research Contribution Award from the American Psychological Association, the California Senate Award, an Honorary Doctorate, and a Guggenheim Fellowship. He has written many books and articles and directed films on the treatment of autism. He has served on the editorial boards of numerous journals and on the professional advisory boards of several parent and professional organizations.